Pro .NET on Amazon Web Services

Guidance and Best Practices
for Building and Deployment

William Penberthy
Steve Roberts

Apress®

Pro .NET on Amazon Web Services: Guidance and Best Practices for Building and Deployment

William Penberthy
Seattle, WA, USA

Steve Roberts
Seattle, WA, USA

ISBN-13 (pbk): 978-1-4842-8906-8
https://doi.org/10.1007/978-1-4842-8907-5

ISBN-13 (electronic): 978-1-4842-8907-5

Managing Director, Apress Media LLC: Welmoed Spahr
Acquisitions Editor: Jonathan Gennick
Development Editor: Laura Berendson
Coordinating Editor: Jill Balzano

Cover image designed by Freepik (www.freepik.com)

Distributed to the book trade worldwide by Springer Science+Business Media LLC, 1 New York Plaza, Suite 4600, New York, NY 10004. Phone 1-800-SPRINGER, fax (201) 348-4505, e-mail orders-ny@springer-sbm. com, or visit www.springeronline.com. Apress Media, LLC is a California LLC and the sole member (owner) is Springer Science + Business Media Finance Inc (SSBM Finance Inc). SSBM Finance Inc is a **Delaware** corporation.

For information on translations, please e-mail booktranslations@springernature.com; for reprint, paperback, or audio rights, please e-mail bookpermissions@springernature.com.

Apress titles may be purchased in bulk for academic, corporate, or promotional use. eBook versions and licenses are also available for most titles. For more information, reference our Print and eBook Bulk Sales web page at http://www.apress.com/bulk-sales.

Any source code or other supplementary material referenced by the author in this book is available to readers on GitHub. For more detailed information, please visit http://www.apress.com/source-code.

Printed on acid-free paper

This book is dedicated to you, our readers.

Hopefully, we have saved you at least one bout of
"Why isn't this working?"

Table of Contents

About the Authors

William Penberthy has over 25 years' experience in software development (almost 17 of which is .NET) and brings a pragmatic approach to software development. With much of that time spent in consulting, he has worked on many different projects and used many different designs and approaches. In 2021, he joined Unify Consulting where he works with clients in optimizing their software development process and building distributed systems for the cloud.

Steve Roberts is a Senior Developer Advocate for .NET and PowerShell development at AWS. Based in Seattle, Washington, Steve worked for eight years as a Senior Development Engineer on the AWS tools for .NET before switching focus to a developer advocacy role. He was the development lead for the AWS Tools for PowerShell and the AWS Tools for Azure DevOps and contributed to the AWS Toolkits for Visual Studio and Visual Studio Code, and the AWS SDK for .NET. Prior to joining AWS, Steve had over 20 years' experience as a developer focused on IDE tools and integrations.

About the Technical Reviewer

Peter Himschoot works as a lead trainer, architect, and strategist at U2U. He has a wide interest in software development that includes applications for the Web, Windows, Clean Architecture, Domain-Driven Design, and Security. He has trained thousands of developers, is a regular speaker at international conferences, and has been involved in many web and mobile development projects as a software architect. He has been a Microsoft Regional Director (from 2003 to 2019) and cofounded the Belgian Visual Studio User Group (VISUG) in 2006, which is a group of trusted advisors to developer and IT professional audiences and to Microsoft.

Acknowledgments

Kudos to you, the reader, for deciding to learn and try something new. Though, of course, for those of you experienced developers, this is not something new. It's amazing what we, the authors, learned while writing this book – and we thought we were already experts. For those of you that are just starting out your life in software development, know that this is something you will need to continue to do for your entire career as this field changes about as quickly as the water in a river.

We would also like to thank Jonathan Gennick and Jill Balzano from Apress who had the unenviable job of herding the cats. We would also like to mention our appreciation to Brian Beach and Peter Himschoot who had the onerous job of doing our technical review.

Lastly, but certainly not leastly (ha – let's see if we can get it through at least once), is the support for our wives, Jeanine and Deb, who allowed us to spend way too much of our free time working on this project.

Introduction

Cloud computing can be thought of as a way to deliver on-demand computing services. These computing services can be as high level as complete applications, such as Salesforce, or as low level as storage or application processing. Access to these services is generally through the public Internet. The concept of the cloud has taken off, and there is research that says more than one third of all IT spending worldwide is on cloud computing and that number will continue to grow. This book is about a piece of that overall cloud computing pie, the combination of one of the most popular software development frameworks, .NET, and the first and largest cloud computing provider, Amazon Web Services (AWS).

It sounds straightforward when you look at that previous sentence until you really start to think through what that means; it sets the expectation that we will talk about the union of .NET functionality and AWS functionality. That is simply not possible as that union is huge and writing about it would take several volumes and likely be out of date before we even finished the second one. Instead, in this book, we are trying to identify some of the most commonly identified development scenarios, and we will use those to guide our journey.

Before we move into the juicy details of using .NET on AWS, let us first go over some of the fundamental differences between working with a cloud service and working with "your own servers." There are multiple different ways in which companies manage their "own servers." Some lease hardware from an infrastructure or hosting provider and are responsible for everything above the iron, including OS patches, systems drivers, installed applications, and everything in between. If those companies want to run virtual machines, then they have to purchase the management software and maintain that as well. Other companies purchase the server hardware outright and thus add details like network cards or other "pieces of metal" into the areas for which they are responsible. Regardless of the approach that you take, your company will have some system management responsibilities.

That does not necessarily change when you move to the cloud. However, it becomes easier to define the responsibilities that each party has. AWS calls this definition of responsibilities the *Shared Responsibility Model*. This model defines what parts of the overall operational burden will be owned by AWS and what parts of the burden will be owned by the customer. This is important to consider when building your applications as you should be building them in such a way as to help minimize the operational burden that you, as a developer/customer, have when working with AWS services. Not only will this minimize your operational burden, it also, oddly enough, tends to decrease your actual cloud service cost because it allows for a much finer control over the various areas used by your application, such as processing, memory usage, and storage. We promise there will be more on this later when we go into the details of running your .NET application on AWS!

We will be using a sample application through our journey. We called it *TradeYourTools*, and it is a simple tool-sharing application that is designed to help members of a neighborhood group document their available hand and electrical tools and to provide a simple process to reserve a tool and arrange their pickup and return. The application is starting as an ASP.NET MVC v4.6 application that uses ASP.NET Identity for registration. It has a Microsoft SQL Server back end that stores tool data, including pictures, user information, and any uploaded pictures. It works but be warned; it is not pretty – neither one of us claims to be a UX expert!

We will be altering this application through our journey. We are assuming that you are an experienced .NET developer and thus will not be spending any effort talking about the fundamentals of what we are doing. To take full advantage of the sample application, however, requires that you have access to a .NET integrated development environment (IDE). The most used IDE is Microsoft Visual Studio. There are several versions of Visual Studio, each with differing sets of functionality and price points. JetBrains offers a competing IDE, Rider, and there is always the ubiquitous Visual Studio Code, a cross-platform IDE that also supports .NET development. Most of the screenshots will be using Visual Studio unless we are specifically talking about a different IDE.

You will also enhance your experience if you have access to a running SQL Server instance so that you can work with a local, fully running application. The sample application will come with a database creation script that will create all of the necessary tables and relationships as well as load some sample data that will help you understand the application and how all of the pieces go together. While this will be useful, it is by no means required. If you must choose between an IDE and a database, choose the IDE – you will spend more time there!

You can download a trial version of JetBrains Rider at `www.jetbrains.com/rider/`. You can download both Visual Studio and Visual Studio Code at `https://visualstudio.microsoft.com/`. The Community Edition of Visual Studio is free and is our recommended choice if you do not currently have access to a .NET IDE. You can download Microsoft SQL Server Developer 2019, a full-featured free edition of SQL Server that is licensed for use as a development and test database.

PART I

Getting Started

CHAPTER 1

The Core Essentials

Getting started is always the hardest part of new systems, and AWS is no different. Approaching the breadth of services and the functionality available in the AWS cloud can be a daunting prospect! What services should you consider first for hosting your application? How do terms you may be familiar with, such as virtual machines, map to services? How do you, as a developer, authenticate to provision and work with resources? How does your application code authenticate to be able to call AWS services?

In this chapter, we'll look at the essentials – what you really need to know about AWS to get started. We are not going to go particularly deep – that's for later sections of the book – but this chapter will give you an overview of essential services and functionality that will be useful if you've never worked with AWS before. In addition to core services, we will take our first look at the AWS Management Console and use it to set up a "development user" identity as a recommended best practice. You'll use this user identity to work with AWS services, resources, and the tools (outlined in Chapters 2 and 3) during the remainder of the book.

The Essentials of AWS

AWS makes available a portfolio of over 175 services – and the portfolio continues to grow. Let's be honest – you are highly unlikely to make use of all the services in a single application! There's an old maxim – how do you eat an elephant (not that you should of course, elephants are awesome)? The answer is – one piece at a time, and the same applies to getting started on AWS. Once you have an initial understanding of a core set of services and the terms you will routinely encounter working with AWS, you can then pivot to determining how best to map them to the needs of your application.

© William Penberthy and Steve Roberts 2023
W. Penberthy and S. Roberts, *Pro .NET on Amazon Web Services*,
https://doi.org/10.1007/978-1-4842-8907-5_1

Regions and Availability Zones

Let's begin with the layout of AWS' global infrastructure. AWS operates 24 geographic *Regions* around the world (at the time of writing; more are planned). Regions are fully isolated, and each is composed of at least two, usually three, sometimes more, isolated and physically separate *Availability Zones*. Each Availability Zone (or AZ as you'll more commonly see them mentioned) is composed of one or more physically separated data centers. Each data center has redundant power, networking, and high-bandwidth low-latency connectivity. This is different from other cloud providers who may treat a single data center in a geographic area as a region.

Regions are identified both by name, for example, *US East (N. Virginia)*, or *US West (Oregon)*, etc., and by a corresponding code. You'll often make use of this code in your applications. For the two regions just mentioned, US East (N. Virginia) is referred to as *us-east-1*. US West (Oregon) is identified as *us-west-2*.

Availability Zones are identified with a combination of the parent region code and a letter suffix – a, b, c, etc. For example, *us-west-2b* refers to an AZ in the US West (Oregon) region. Your applications and the resources they consume can exist in a single AZ, or be deployed to multiple AZs in a region for high availability. Figure 1-1 shows the logical layout of the US West (Oregon), or us-west-2, region. Also in the figure are illustrations of how one might choose to distribute applications (or not) across Availability Zones.

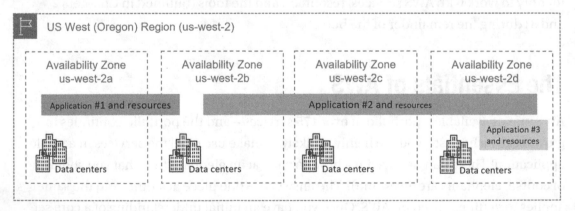

Figure 1-1. *The US West (Oregon) region and zones*

How does this global infrastructure benefit you? Regions and their Availability Zones are designed to provide you the ability to run highly available, fault-tolerant applications nearer to your customer base and to also satisfy data sovereignty laws that you may be subject to. Running applications in a region geographically closer to users helps improve latency, but you can also failover to a different region if needed. Availability Zones provide the basis of fault tolerance and scale for your applications. Assuming you've made use of Availability Zones, by deploying your application to at least two AZs in a region, a failure in a single data center – or even an entire AZ – will be transparent to your application.

This does mean, however, that you usually need to keep this infrastructure layout in mind when working with AWS. With very few exceptions, AWS services are regional, meaning that resources you create in one region are not visible in the AWS Management Console (or the various AWS tools that we'll examine in Chapters 2 and 3) when you are working in a different region. For now, just be aware that when you deploy your application resources to AWS, you'll do so in a region, and optionally across two or more AZs if you want fault tolerance. If not, and a service does not mandate a multi-AZ setup, then go ahead and use a single AZ to keep things simple.

The AWS Free Tier

The AWS Free Tier is a collection of offers spanning 85 products (at the time of writing) to help when gaining experience with AWS services. Some offers in the Free Tier are available for the first year after you create an account (and expire thereafter – so use before you lose!); others are permanently free up to a certain amount of resource usage. Periodically, ad hoc offers may become available during a promotional period, or after a new service is launched. Some examples:

- AWS Lambda serverless compute: Up to 1 million requests, and 400,000 GB-seconds of compute time, per month – always free

- Amazon DynamoDB database: Up to 25GB of storage and 25 provisioned read and 25 provisioned write capacity units per month (this is enough to handle up to 200 million requests per month) – always free

- Amazon EC2 virtual machines: Up to 750 hours of compute on certain instance sizes, for Windows and Linux – free for the first 12 months

- Amazon S3 storage: Up to 5GB of standard storage – free for the first 12 months

Many other examples can be found at the Free Tier home page: *https://aws.amazon.com/free*. Most of the examples in this book can be performed using offers in the Free Tier to reduce or eliminate cost, and we will try to call out those services that may have a charge.

Hosting Your Code – Compute Services

So you have application code to host in the cloud. But where? And using what technology? Virtual machines (VMs)? VMs in Managed Services? Containers? Or maybe you want to adopt a serverless approach and let AWS manage the compute infrastructure in its entirety for you? There's a lot of choice, so let's quickly unpack it. In later chapters, we'll examine each of these areas in more detail.

First, virtual machines. *Amazon Elastic Compute Cloud*, or *EC2* as it's more commonly known, is the virtual machine service on AWS. A virtual machine in EC2 is an *instance*. Each instance is started from an *image*, known as an *Amazon Machine Image*, or *AMI*. EC2 provides multiple "stock" images, for both Windows and multiple Linux distributions, that you can use. These images are generally, but not always, updated monthly to ensure they include the most recent patches and other software updates. There are also 7,000+ images available through the AWS marketplace with each having various software packages pre-installed. Alternatively, you can use your own images – which can be built and snapshotted from an AWS-provided image if you so choose. You might take this route if you have specific installation or configuration requirements and can't perform these actions when launching the "stock" images provided by AWS.

Once an EC2 instance is running, you are in complete control – just as with virtual machines you might run on your own machine. You can pause (suspend), stop, or terminate them. You can also remote into them using SSH or Remote Desktop. Figure 1-2 shows an example of some instances in various states in the AWS Management Console.

	Name ▽	Instance ID	Instance state ▽	Instance type ▽	Status check	Alarm status	Availability Zone ▽	Public IPv4 DNS
☐	WindowsServ...	i-05ada6dcb757ff359	⊘ Running ⊕⊖	t2.micro	⊘ 2/2 checks ...	No alarms ╋	us-west-2c	–
☐	AL2Instance	i-0b33d5055aa9f1a04	⊘ Running ⊕⊖	t2.micro	⊘ 2/2 checks ...	No alarms ╋	us-west-2a	ec2-34-214-163-44
☐	AL2Instance	i-03568c16b0e828e69	⊖ Terminated ⊕⊖	t2.micro	–	No alarms ╋	us-west-2a	–
☐	AL2Instance	i-0e898140e7a70a913	⊘ Running ⊕⊖	t2.micro	⊘ 2/2 checks ...	No alarms ╋	us-west-2a	ec2-34-221-119-13
☐	UbuntuServer	i-05b928c76478469b8	⊖ Stopped ⊕⊖	t2.micro	–	No alarms ╋	us-west-2b	–

Figure 1-2. *EC2 instances in the AWS Management Console*

You are responsible for keeping instances (and custom images) up to date with patches, etc. (AWS also provides additional services that can help you do this). AWS operates a shared responsibility model, which means that AWS protects the physical infrastructure and network but you are responsible for the security on your resources.

How does your application get deployed onto an EC2 instance? As with the virtual machine instance, you have complete control here too. You can write scripts to download the application binaries and other resources and place them onto the instance as it starts, or you can use services such as *AWS CodeDeploy* (among others) to perform the deployment. In the case of CodeDeploy, you simply upload the built application bundle and choose the instance(s) to be involved (by selecting the instance IDs, or some other criteria such as tags or membership in a group), and CodeDeploy does the rest.

If managing running instances sounds like more work than you would like, but you still want to retain some control, then consider services such as *AWS Elastic Beanstalk* or *Amazon Lightsail*. Both build on top of EC2 to offer virtual machines under the hood but abstract away some or most of the management and deployment aspects.

AWS Elastic Beanstalk is a service for deploying and scaling web applications and services and is the fastest and simplest way to get your application up and running on EC2 virtual machines. As a developer, your focus is on building and packaging your application. For .NET Framework applications, you use a Web Deploy package. For .NET Core and .NET 5+, you use `dotnet publish` to build the deployment package. In both cases, you upload the bundle to AWS and instruct Elastic Beanstalk to deploy it to the instance(s) in your application's *environment*. The environment contains the EC2 instance(s) and other resources employed in hosting your application code. Elastic Beanstalk takes care of provisioning and managing your infrastructure resources, and handling deployments, but you can still, if you wish, work with the underlying resources. Should you need to, and network security settings permit, it's possible to remote into the EC2 instances in the environment. Figure 1-3 shows an example of the resources and their chosen configuration in a load-balanced auto-scaled Elastic Beanstalk environment.

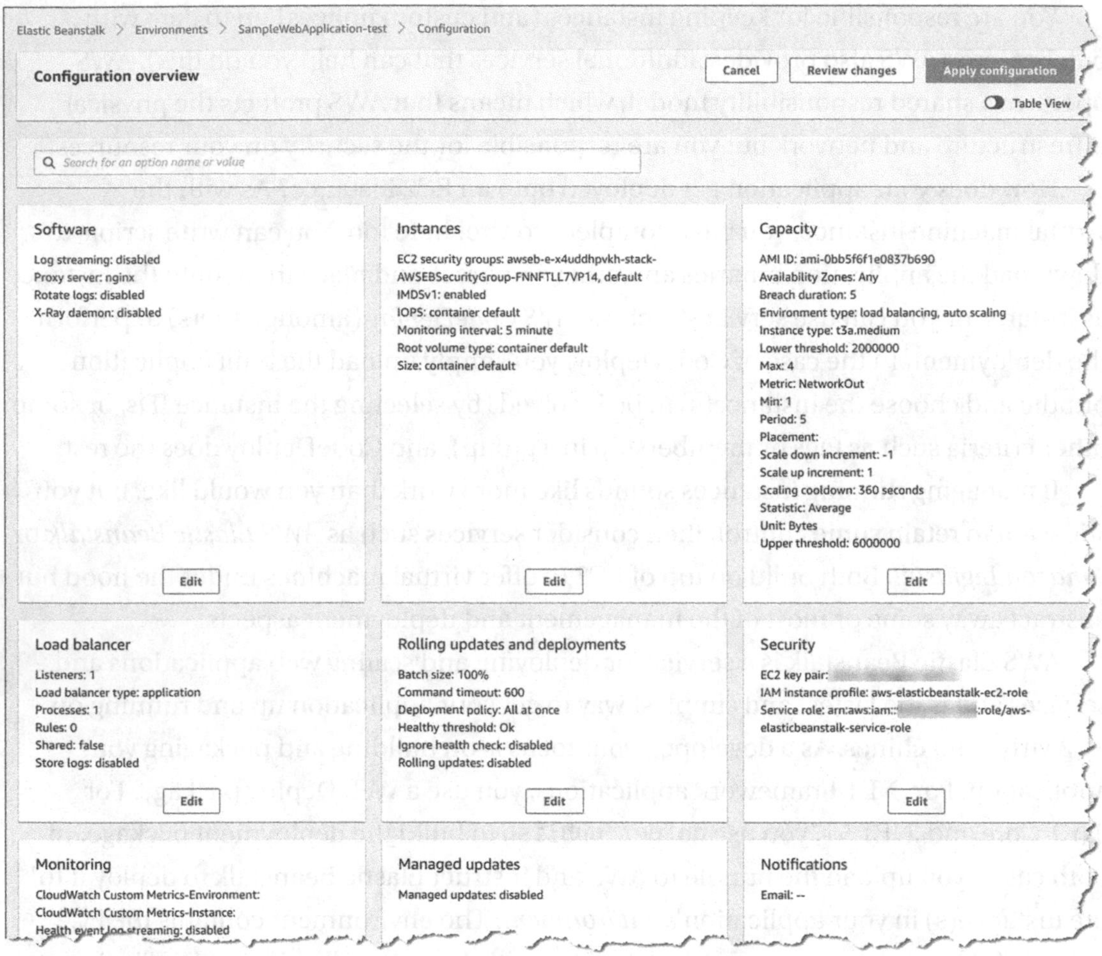

Figure 1-3. *Example Elastic Beanstalk environment and resources*

Amazon Lightsail is another abstraction on top of EC2. Like Elastic Beanstalk, Lightsail takes care of the provisioning of the underlying EC2 resources but takes a more simplified view of managing them. With Elastic Beanstalk, you can tweak and adjust almost all the settings of the underlying resources (even though the service created them for you). With Lightsail, fewer settings are exposed, but you can still remote into the underlying instances if needed. Offering an even more managed experience than Elastic Beanstalk, Lightsail is ideal for simple workloads, or just getting started on AWS, but provides the ability to "grow into" the full EC2 experience later if you need to.

Next, we have the choice of using containers. AWS provides two container services: *Amazon Elastic Container Service* (*ECS*) and *Amazon Elastic Kubernetes Service* (*EKS*). In addition, each has a serverless variant known as *AWS Fargate*, where AWS entirely operates the underlying container infrastructure on your behalf.

ECS runs Docker containers with no changes and supports both Windows and Linux containers. Note, however, that if you choose to use AWS Fargate, then currently only Linux containers are supported, so your application will need to be based on .NET Core or .NET 5+. If your Docker images are hosted in a third-party repository, you can still use ECS. Alternatively, you can upload your images to *Amazon Elastic Container Registry* (*ECR*). As with EC2 virtual machines, you can take advantage of AWS CodeDeploy to minimize downtime when updating applications by using blue/green deployments, with full support for deployment monitoring and rollback.

If you're using Kubernetes, then EKS will be of interest. With EKS, the Kubernetes control plane is run across multiple AZs, and it automatically detects and replaces unhealthy nodes. As with ECS, Windows is supported – first for worker nodes and for scheduling Windows containers. It's also possible to run Windows and Linux worker nodes together in the same cluster. As you might expect, EKS manages the availability and scalability of the control plane nodes for you, freeing you from infrastructure management and allowing you to focus on your application code and deployment topology. We will go deeper into the container offerings in a later chapter.

Finally, AWS offers a serverless compute service known as *AWS Lambda*. Lambda enables you to run your code without provisioning or managing servers – all of that is handled fully by AWS on your behalf. This allows you to focus entirely on your code, which can run in response to events such as an object being created in storage, or a request being received on a web API endpoint, and lots more (your code in Lambda can be triggered from a variety of events across 140 AWS services). You can also configure your code to run on a *cron* schedule, you can call it directly from within your own application code, or you can even invoke functions from the command line. You might find this latter feature useful in automation scripts, for example.

Note   Lambda uses Linux as the underlying operating system host, so your code must target .NET Core 3.1 or .NET 5+; .NET Framework is not supported for writing Lambda functions.

Storage

Now that you have some idea of the range of compute options available to host your application code, let's move on to another common need of applications – storage.

When people think of storage in conjunction with AWS, *Amazon Simple Storage Service*, or *S3* as it's more commonly referred to, is usually what springs to mind. S3 is a service for object storage in the cloud. We use the term "object storage" to distinguish it from "file storage" – it's important to know that S3 is not a file system so it doesn't have a "real" directory structure or well-defined metadata such as the file name and date it was last modified. Obviously, it can store files, but as far as S3 is concerned, objects are just opaque blobs of data of varying lengths. To work effectively with S3, the key elements to understand are buckets, objects, and keys.

Buckets are the top-level organizational unit and are URL addressable – this means that buckets must conform to DNS name rules and, most importantly, they must have a globally unique name. If I have a bucket named `myapplicationbucket` in my account, you cannot have another bucket with the same name in your account.

Objects exist solely within buckets and represent the data you want to store. Objects can be any size up to 5 terabytes currently. You can add metadata tags to objects, as well as various types of access controls. Furthermore, it's possible to add life cycle policies to objects. One example of this would be a policy where older or less frequently accessed objects are automatically moved to different storage classes to take advantage of lower pricing.

A *key* is used to identify the different objects within a bucket. At its core, S3 is a key-value store operating at massive scale. Keys are probably what cause most people to think S3 is a file system when they first encounter it – object keys do in fact look like Linux file system paths. For example, consider the following key: `application.images/frontpage/logo.jpg`. Notice the `/` delimiter in the key – this divides the key into *prefixes* that resemble, but are not, subfolders. S3 keys are a flat structure, and there is no concept of sub-buckets or subfolders. However, using prefixes can help infer a logical structure. In fact, the AWS Management Console and the tools we'll meet in Chapter 2 and beyond use the prefixes to emulate a file system when working with S3. Figure 1-4 shows an example of object keys and prefixes in a bucket (note too that the console uses the term "Folder" for a prefix).

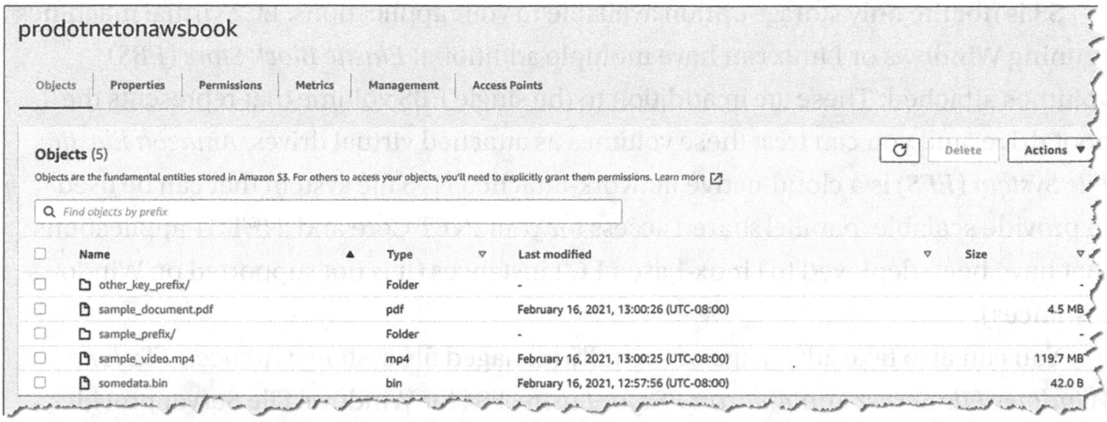

Figure 1-4. *Object keys and prefixes in an S3 bucket*

Listing 1-1 shows the output of a command (from the AWS Tools for PowerShell, which we will introduce in Chapter 2) to list the keys in the bucket. Here, you can see how the prefixes are in fact just parts of keys identifying the objects in storage and are not expressing any form of storage hierarchy.

Listing 1-1. Listing object keys

```
C:\> (Get-S3Object -BucketName prodotnetonawsbook).foreach("Key")

other_key_prefix/
other_key_prefix/image.png
sample_document.pdf
sample_prefix/
sample_prefix/file1.txt
sample_prefix/file2.txt
sample_video.mp4
somedata.bin
```

Even if you don't make use of S3 directly from your application, you'll still find that many AWS services make use of S3 themselves. For example, when you deploy your application to Elastic Beanstalk, the deployment bundle representing your built application must first be uploaded to an S3 bucket. Tooling usually handles this for you, behind the scenes, but it is something to be aware of.

S3 is not the only storage option available to your applications. EC2 virtual machines running Windows or Linux can have multiple additional *Elastic Block Store* (*EBS*) volumes attached. These are in addition to the single EBS volume that represents the boot drive, and you can treat these volumes as attached virtual drives. *Amazon Elastic File System* (*EFS*) is a cloud-native network-attached NFS file system that can be used to provide scalable, parallel shared access for your .NET Core and .NET 5+ applications that have been deployed to Linux-based EC2 instances (it is not supported on Windows instances).

You can also take advantage of two fully managed file systems: *Amazon FSx for Windows File Server* and *Amazon FSx for Lustre.* FSx for Windows File Server provides Windows Server Message Block (SMB)–based file services and is compatible with server applications originally designed for on-premises Windows Server environments. Storage is built on NTFS, and it supports Active Directory integration. FSx for Lustre is designed for high-performance compute workloads. As mentioned, both file systems are fully managed, meaning AWS takes care of the maintenance, backups, and other operational details for you.

Databases

Applications that make use of a traditional relational database are still a popular choice and are equally suited for migration to the cloud. For .NET, this typically means Microsoft SQL Server is being used somewhere in the back end. If this setup sounds familiar to you, know that it's possible to install and run SQL Server on an EC2 instance and manage it 100% yourself – backups, maintenance, you name it – those operational tasks are all yours, just like you used to do when working "on-premises."

Alternatively, perhaps you want AWS to manage all the administrative and operational tasks for you so that you can focus on that which is more relevant to your application: the data in the database. In that case, you'll be interested in *Amazon Relational Database Service,* or *RDS*. With RDS, you can launch several different database engines – PostgreSQL, MySQL, MariaDB, Oracle, and of course Microsoft SQL Server. Different editions and versions are available for each of those database engines. Taking SQL Server as an example, RDS provides access to the 2012, 2014, 2016, 2017, and 2019 editions, including Express, Web, Standard Edition, and Enterprise Edition (although Microsoft ended support for 2012 in July 2022 so 2012 may no longer be available when you read this).

NoSQL, or key-value, databases are also popular for a variety of application workloads. AWS offers *Amazon DynamoDB* for this purpose. DynamoDB is a fully managed database solution that runs at scale and provides single digit millisecond performance. DynamoDB tables are schemaless, meaning you don't need to define the attributes (or columns, in relational terms) and their corresponding data types (string, number, etc.) ahead of time for items (records, or rows) in a table. Different items can also have different sets of attributes.

Naturally, every item in the table must have a unique primary key. Within DynamoDB, you will see that primary key referred to as the *partition key*. You can define an additional *sort key* (also referred to as a "range attribute") to build composite keys. You can also define secondary indexes to enable queries using an alternate key.

An additional optional feature of DynamoDB to be aware of is *DynamoDB Streams*. DynamoDB Streams capture data modification events that occur in DynamoDB tables, such as the creation of a new item, an item update, or an item deletion. You can use streams in conjunction with a serverless function in AWS Lambda. Your function is triggered (run) when the stream captures an event, giving you the ability to run additional workflows in response to an event without having to configure messaging or event queues. During the Amazon Prime Day in 2020 (a "day" that, like international flights with children, lasted 66 hours), DynamoDB processed 16,400,000,000,000 (16.4 trillion) calls from a combination of Alexa, the various Amazon.com sites, and all Amazon fulfillment centers. This traffic flow peaked at 80.1 million requests per second, without affecting any other users of DynamoDB. Now that's scale!

Finally, we come to *Amazon Aurora*. Aurora is a re-imagined relational database for the cloud and offers MySQL and PostgreSQL compatibility. It's fully managed by RDS, so all the time-consuming tasks (hardware provisioning, setup, patching, and backups) are handled for you. As a database, Aurora makes use of a distributed, fault-tolerant, and self-healing storage engine that can scale to 128 terabytes per database instance. Aurora also has a serverless variant that automatically starts up, shuts down, and scales capacity up and down on demand. Unlike traditional databases, you are not charged for Aurora Serverless when the database is stopped. If you have a workload that is burstable with periods of inactivity, this will be an attractive option.

Networking

When you launch resources on AWS, you do so into a *Virtual Private Cloud*, or *VPC*. A VPC is a logically isolated virtual network. You can think of a VPC as your own private section of the AWS cloud. Every account has access to a default VPC in each region, and you can create additional ones if required.

Let's get a bit technical now and briefly dive into how VPCs are architected so that you at least recognize the "lingo" when you see it in the console and tools. A VPC has an IP address range and supports both IPv4 and IPv6 access (most, but not all, AWS resources support both IPv4 and IPv6 addressing). The VPC and its IP address range is then subdivided into one or more *subnets*. Subnets contain your resources. To define an address range for a VPC and for subnets, AWS uses *Classless Inter-Domain Routing* (*CIDR*) notation. CIDR notation uses an IP address, known as the prefix, and a mask suffix. For example, an IPv4 CIDR might be 192.168.50.0/24. 192.168.50.0 is the prefix, and /24 defines the mask, indicating the number of 1 bits in the network mask to apply to the prefix. Using our 192.168.50.0 example, a mask of /24 indicates the leading three bytes of the prefix are selected as the mask evaluates to 255.255.255.0.

For a VPC, we might define the overall IPv4 address range as 10.1.0.0/16. This means all IPv4 addresses assigned to resources inside this VPC will start with 10.1, as a mask of /16 selects all the first two bytes. Moving onto subnets, let's say we decide to partition our VPC into three subnets, with CIDRs of 10.1.0.0/24, 10.1.1.0/24, and 10.1.2.0/24. Depending upon which subnet resources are assigned to, their IPv4 address will start with either 10.1.0, 10.1.1, or 10.1.2.

Besides their CIDR range, subnets in a VPC are divided into *public* and *private* types. A public subnet can receive traffic from the Internet as well as send traffic out. A public subnet is where you would place, say, a load balancer so that it can be reached by Internet traffic. By default, a private subnet cannot receive from, or send traffic to, the Internet; it can only see traffic from within the VPC. Continuing with the example, let's say we have a web application hosted on several EC2 virtual machines and a database, perhaps a SQL Server instance running in RDS. As a best practice, we could put these instances and the database into private subnets and configure routing so that only HTTP traffic that comes into the load balancer, on specific ports, is forwarded to the instances in the private subnet(s). Further, we could configure the RDS database instance to only accept traffic originating from the EC2 instances in the private subnets. This helps keep our web servers and the database secure from malicious traffic as they can't be reached publicly.

How do we turn a subnet into a public subnet? By attaching an *Internet Gateway* resource to it. All subnets that are associated with an Internet gateway are public, and the resources in them can be publicly available on the open Internet (depending on how security firewalls, IP addresses, etc., are configured – we're coming to that).

Private subnets have no association with an Internet gateway – that's what makes them private – but they can be associated with a *NAT Gateway*. Why? Well, we may want to permit outbound traffic to the wider Internet from our web server instances, for example, to permit software updates or contact third-party APIs.

Security groups, *network ACLs*, and *route tables* complete the core essentials you need to be aware of for networking on AWS. Security groups control the access to and from your instances – effectively, they are virtual firewalls. Rules attached to a group define the port or port range, the protocol, and allowable origination points and can be a specific set of addresses, "anywhere," or even another security group. Network ACLs can be used to control the traffic for your subnets if you want an additional security layer. Figure 1-5 illustrates rules in a security group that permits access to everyone on ports 80 and 443, ports 22 and 3389 for a specific IP address, and port 1443 for resources associated with another security group in the VPC.

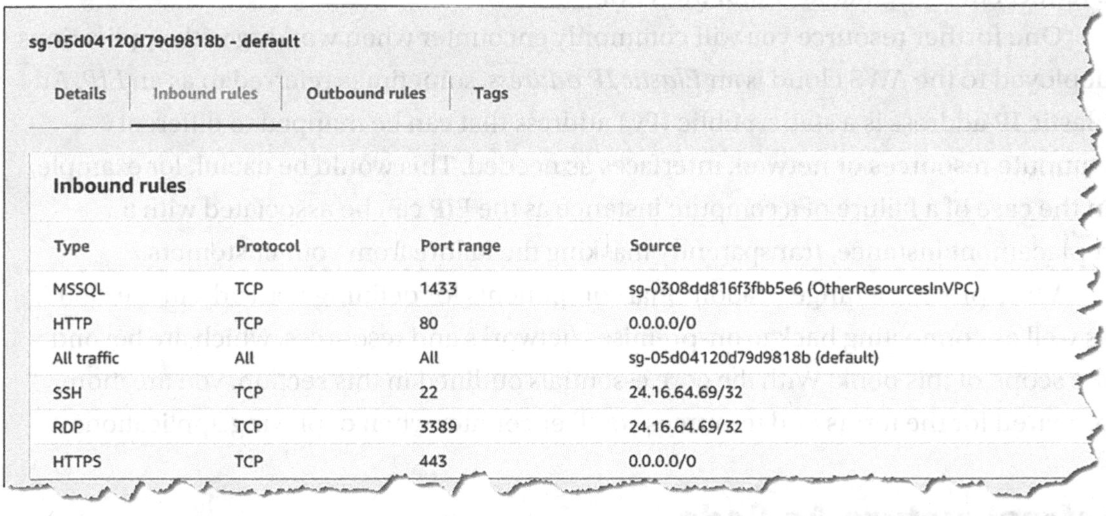

sg-05d04120d79d9818b - default

| Details | Inbound rules | Outbound rules | Tags |

Inbound rules

Type	Protocol	Port range	Source
MSSQL	TCP	1433	sg-0308dd816f3fbb5e6 (OtherResourcesInVPC)
HTTP	TCP	80	0.0.0.0/0
All traffic	All	All	sg-05d04120d79d9818b (default)
SSH	TCP	22	24.16.64.69/32
RDP	TCP	3389	24.16.64.69/32
HTTPS	TCP	443	0.0.0.0/0

Figure 1-5. *Rules in a security group permitting ingress*

Security groups operate at the instance level, and you can assign instances within a subnet to different security groups. Network ACLs operate at the subnet level instead, so changes to a network ACL affect all instances within a subnet. Additionally, security groups rules are used to "allow" traffic – you deny access by simply not adding a rule for that traffic. If, courtesy of a rule, a security group allows inbound traffic, then that traffic is automatically allowed to egress – regardless of any outbound rules. As an example, a web server associated with a security group that has a rule permitting traffic on ports 80 and 443 can respond to those requests without needing an outbound rule to be specified. On the other hand, network ACLs have both allow and deny capability for both inbound and outbound traffic, using a prioritized approach based on numbered lists of rules, with rules being evaluated in order.

Finally, you may encounter route tables when working with VPCs. As the name suggests, route tables are tables of rules that route traffic within the VPC and its subnets. In other words, these route tables determine where traffic from a subnet or gateway is directed. Route tables can be explicitly associated with subnets, or you can rely on an automatic association with a default "main" table. Route tables associated (implicitly or explicitly) with a public subnet contain a rule that routes traffic destined for "anywhere" (i.e., not "local" in the VPC IP address range) to an Internet Gateway instance. For IPv4, *0.0.0.0/0* is used to show "anywhere." Private subnets will be associated with a route table containing a rule that routes outbound traffic to a NAT Gateway instance and, as noted, cannot be reached by traffic inbound from the Internet unless that traffic is a response to a request that originated within the VPC.

One further resource you will commonly encounter when working with applications deployed to the AWS cloud is an *Elastic IP address*, sometimes referred to as an *EIP*. An Elastic IP address is a static, public IPv4 address that can be mapped to different compute resources or network interfaces as needed. This would be useful, for example, in the case of a failure of a compute instance as the EIP can be associated with a replacement instance, transparently masking the failure from your customers.

VPCs provide a range of additional components for defining networks in the cloud, as well as connecting back to on-premises networks and resources, which are beyond the scope of this book. With the core essentials outlined in this section, you are more prepared for the terms and resources you'll encounter when deploying applications.

Infrastructure As Code

In this book, we will make use of the AWS Management Console, a web-based portal into AWS services, and we will be introducing it shortly. However, while a web console that you can use to create and configure resources is great for learning, it's not a scalable approach for production, nor does it promote consistent and repeatable automation. For that, we use *Infrastructure as Code*, or *IaC*, using *AWS CloudFormation*. CloudFormation accepts a template defining your infrastructure requirements, which can be written in JSON or YAML. Using the provided template, CloudFormation then performs all the heavy lifting of creating and configuring your requested resources, as defined by the template, including the ability to wait for resources to stabilize or complete their configuration before proceeding to downstream resources. The resources defined in the template are launched into what is known as a *stack*.

If you're considering adopting a fully serverless approach for deploying your applications, then you may be thinking that IaC, and CloudFormation, is not something you need to pay attention to. But you'd be wrong! Even though your application is running in a serverless environment, there is still a need to define and configure infrastructure resources. Serverless just means that you don't have direct access to those resources. The tools that we will introduce later, and use throughout the remainder of the book, make use of CloudFormation templates (either directly or indirectly) to define resources; therefore, it's worth gaining a basic understanding of CloudFormation as a core skill.

A final note on CloudFormation templates. Although they can be written in JSON or YAML, it is also possible for you to work in the languages you use day to day – C#, Java, TypeScript, Python, etc. – using the *AWS Cloud Development Kit* (*CDK*). As a .NET developer, you can define your infrastructure requirements in C# and use the CDK tools to transform this to the JSON or YAML template that CloudFormation requires for deployment. The CDK tools take care of the deployment of the stack and subsequent updates to add, reconfigure, or remove resources for you. We'll be looking at the CDK from a .NET perspective in a couple more chapters.

Identity and Access Management

No discussion of the core essentials would be complete without mentioning user identity and access permissions. AWS does things slightly differently and employs a deny-by-default, fine-grained permissions model.

When you create a new user identity or other entity within AWS, everything is denied by default. Permissions must be added, not taken away (although you can do that as well, to "fine-tune" if needed).

The fine-grained permissions model means you can control *exactly* what services an entity can access, which APIs (or "actions") the entity can call, on what resources those actions can apply to, and under what conditions those permissions should be scoped.

The core service for working with permissions is *Identity and Access Management*, or *IAM*. We encourage you to get familiar with this service, as it's one you will be using frequently. Remember, AWS operates a shared responsibility model where AWS looks after the physical infrastructure, but you are responsible for the security of the resources you launch and use. You'll do that using IAM.

IAM has the concepts of users, groups, and roles, and policies and permissions. An *IAM User* can map to an actual human, or perhaps an identity related to an external system. You can collate users into *IAM Groups* for convenient management of permissions. Later in this chapter, we'll walk through setting up an IAM user that you will use for your chapter-to-chapter work with AWS. This is not the same as the root user created when you signed up for an AWS account, which, as a best practice, should **not** be used for day-to-day operations. We can't stress this enough.

Note   The AWS root account provides full access to all your resources across all AWS services – including billing information. As such, you cannot reduce the permissions for this user account. For this reason, AWS recommends that you do not create programmatic access keys for this account and rely instead on an account email address and password to sign into the management console. You should also enable multifactor authentication.

An *IAM Role* is a container for policies and permissions governing what something, or someone, can or cannot do. Roles can be attached to users and groups and are also the mechanism by which your deployed application code can get (if it needs them) temporary credentials, allowing the code to call AWS service APIs or to have access to services and their resources. For example, an application that uses an S3 storage bucket will need explicit permissions to access the objects in that bucket – even though the code was deployed using your account. Remember, everything is deny by default.

An *IAM Policy* defines a set of permissions, which can both allow and deny access. There are two types: identity policies and resource policies. Identity policies define what an identity can or cannot do, whereas resource policies define what actions a specified principal – which can be an AWS service – can perform, or not perform, on a resource and under what conditions. Both types of policy consist of a set of permissions and are typically expressed as a JSON document. Listing 1-2 illustrates an example policy, used with an AWS Lambda function that interacts with the Amazon Rekognition service to detect objects in images (Rekognition refers to these as "labels"). The function is invoked when an image file is uploaded to an Amazon S3 bucket, and the function writes the labels representing the found objects back to the image file object as tags, so both it and Rekognition also need permissions to access S3. In the example, the policy is scoped down to only the objects under a specific prefix in a single bucket.

Listing 1-2. Example IAM Policy

```
{
    "Version": "2012-10-17",
    "Statement": [
        {
            "Sid": "ObjectDetectionFunctionPermissions",
            "Effect": "Allow",
            "Action": [
                "rekognition:DetectLabels",
                "rekognition:DetectModerationLabels",
                "logs:*",
                "lambda:*",
                "s3:GetObject*",
                "s3:PutObject*"
            ],
            "Resource": "arn:aws:s3:::mybucketname/images/*"
        }
    ]
}
```

A permission defines one or more actions, resource identifiers, whether the action is allowed or denied, and conditions to further fine-tune the permission. Each policy can define multiple permissions, and you can attach policies to a role, a user, or a group. It's important to note that unless you explicitly allow something, it's denied by default. This equally applies to services – a service cannot access your resources unless you give it permission. Roles that permit services access to your resources are known as *service roles* and *service-linked roles*. Service-linked roles are a unique type of service role and are predefined by the service to include all the permissions the service requires to call other AWS services on your behalf, with no further work on your part.

Identity policies are categorized into *managed policies* and *inline policies*. Managed policies encompass a set of AWS-provided policies that bundle common permissions for working with services, and, of course, you can create your own managed policies. Inline policies are ad hoc policies that you can apply to an individual user, group, or role. One example of usage for inline policies might be to "scope down" permissions included in a managed policy by denying access to some subset of actions.

There's one other aspect of roles to cover, and that's *trust relationships*. Earlier we mentioned that roles can supply temporary credentials to your application code running on an AWS resource, for example, on an EC2 instance. You can do this by attaching a trust relationship to the role containing the name of the AWS service principal. Continuing with our EC2 example, the trust relationship would specify `ec2.amazonaws.com` as the service principal name. When you deploy your application code, you reference the role with the trust relationship. This role should also contain policies defining what actions are permitted; for example, if it calls specific AWS service APIs, it will have permissions for each API action and potentially be further scoped to specific resources. When your application runs, under the scope of this role, the trust relationship that was granted to the service principal (EC2 in this example) permits temporary, time-limited, and automatically rotating credentials to be available to the code. Without these credentials, the code cannot make calls to AWS service APIs.

At this point, you may be asking a common question: Why don't I just deploy my code with credentials, or put credentials into my application's configuration files?

This is not considered a modern best practice (to put it mildly), and if you're doing this already, stop – right now! Credentials embedded into an application are more difficult to update (you need to redeploy), are easy to overlook and forget, and could be discovered when you commit your code into a public source code repository. Trust us, your credentials will likely be discovered by bots and used for nefarious purposes faster than you can even remember that they were there in the first place (oops) and have a chance to take steps to mitigate.

If you take one thing from this chapter, let it be this: by using roles, with appropriate trust relationships and permissions policies, you **never** have to include AWS credentials in your application code and configuration files. For other kinds of credentials, for example, third-party API keys, AWS has services that permit the application to retrieve those dynamically when needed so you do not have to include them in your code and risk potential exposure.

A Short Note for Enterprise Administrators

This book is very much focused on .NET on AWS from the perspective of the individual developer. That developer could be working by themselves or be part of one or more teams in large enterprises. The core essentials outlined previously are to help ground that developer in some of the terminology and services from AWS that they are likely to encounter day to day.

AWS contains many other services and features to help with the management of development teams and accounts at an enterprise scale and which are outside the scope of this book. Enterprise administrators may therefore wish to investigate services such as *AWS Organizations*, for centralized management and governance of resources; *AWS Control Tower*, which simplifies setup and governance of a multi-account AWS environment; and *AWS Single Sign-On*, for centralized management of single sign-on (SSO) across AWS accounts and business applications.

Let's now move on from the core essentials to briefly introduce the AWS Management Console. We will be using it, in conjunction with additional tools to be introduced in Chapters 2 and 3, as we work with AWS resources to host our .NET application code through the remainder of the book.

Introducing the AWS Management Console

The AWS Management Console has been mentioned a couple of times already, but what is it? The console is a web-based portal that you can use to create, configure, and explore resources spanning all AWS services. We will be using it to illustrate working with services as it makes a great resource for learning. However, as we noted earlier, clicking around a web console is not scalable and doesn't provide for an automated, consistent, approach that we will want for production environments. Some companies will restrict or prohibit development teams from working ad hoc with production resources from a console. Generally, we prefer Infrastructure as Code, so we'll be pointing out those approaches alongside the console as we work with services in later chapters.

If you followed the steps in the introduction to create a new AWS account, you will now be signed into the console as the root user. Let's use that user – very briefly – to orient ourselves to what's available and how to find our way around. In the next section, we'll follow best practices and create an IAM user that will be used for the remainder of the book. That will enable us to put our root account user into a box that's not to be opened for normal operations!

Logging into your account will bring you to the AWS Management Console. The AWS Management Console is a collection of per-service home pages, or dashboards, gathered under a single web console application and sign-in experience. Earlier in the chapter, we described how AWS services are available in a regional infrastructure (with very few exceptions, such as IAM, which are considered "global"). Within the console, you need to be aware of the region that hosts the resources you want to work with and ensure you select the right region when inside a service's dashboard. As you're following along in the book and can't find some resource you've launched, it's more than likely you've changed to a different region and not remembered (happens to us all the time!). To switch region at any time, use the Region selector located in the upper right of the console toolbar, as shown in Figure 1-6.

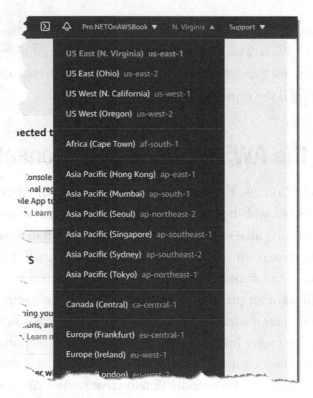

Figure 1-6. *Switching region in the console*

The console home page lists all AWS services, categorized in areas such as Compute, Storage, and Database. It also lists your most recently visited services, as shown in Figure 1-7.

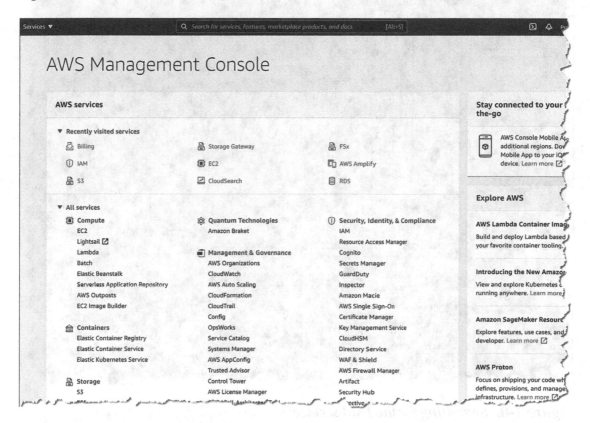

Figure 1-7. *The console home page*

You can also navigate between services without needing to return to the console home page by using the Search functionality. You can find this in the middle of the toolbar; it is the text box that invites you to "Search for services, features, marketplace products, and docs." Typing all or part of a service name into this field will display a list of results. Since we'll be using IAM at the end of this chapter, Figure 1-8 shows the results when you enter "IAM" as the search text (you could also search for "identity").

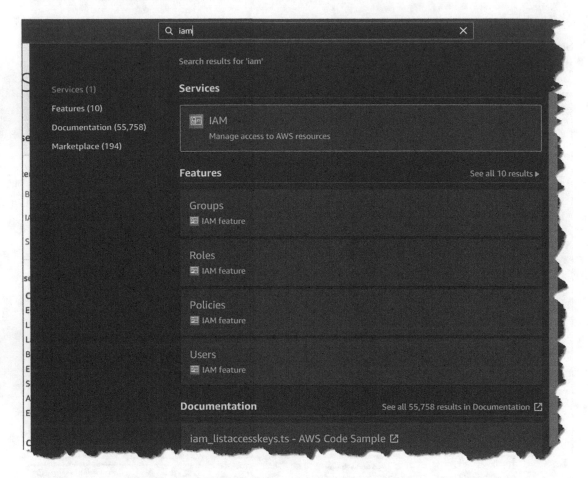

Figure 1-8. *Searching for the IAM service*

Clicking the topmost entry takes you to the IAM home page, shown later in the chapter.

You can also pin favorite services to the Services selector, displayed on the left of the console toolbar. Clicking this displays a panel showing any existing favorites, services you have recently visited, and the categorized collection of all services. Hovering over a service name will cause a star to appear next to the service name – click the star to have the service added to your favorites list, as shown in Figure 1-9.

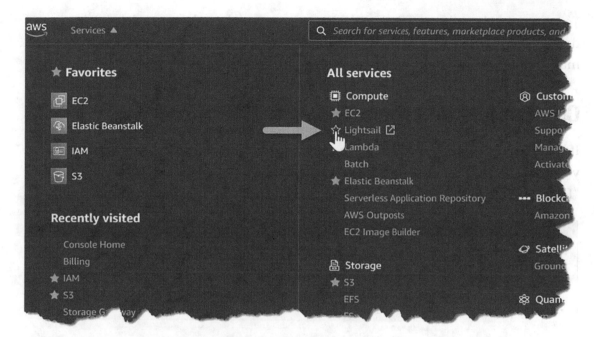

Figure 1-9. *Adding favorite services to the toolbar*

Now that you know how to find your way around the console, let's create a new IAM user that you will use in the remainder of the book when working with AWS from your own machine. We can then "retire" the root account for emergency or billing purposes only.

Creating a User Account for Development

We will be using the IAM user we are going to create in this section for working with AWS from your own machine. This user will have administrator-level privileges and will be used to sign in and work in the console, with the tools we'll be introducing in the next two chapters, and when you deploy applications to the cloud. It will **not** be used for the applications themselves – they will use an IAM Role, with permissions scoped to only the services, APIs, and resources the application needs to run successfully.

How is the IAM user we're creating different from the root user? Firstly, although we are assigning admin permissions, we can reduce the permissions on the IAM user, deny access completely, or even delete it without needing to delete our AWS account.

You cannot reduce the permissions for a root user, and the only way to delete it is to delete your AWS account. Secondly, a root user can get full access to billing and account management, an area where IAM users are more limited.

Creating the IAM User

If you tried the suggested search when exploring the console's Search bar earlier, then you are likely positioned at the IAM home page, as shown in Figure 1-10. If not, enter "IAM" into the Search field and select the Services entry for IAM before proceeding.

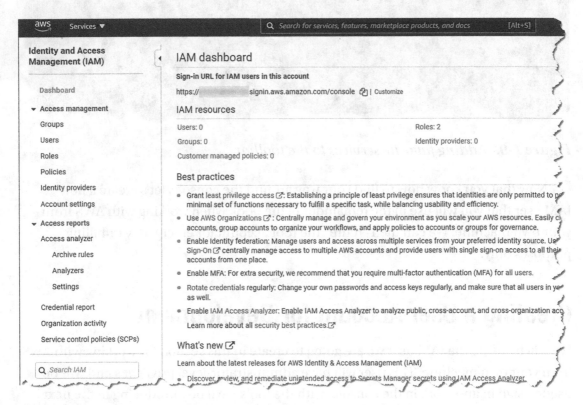

Figure 1-10. *The Identity and Access Management console home page*

Although we can add permissions directly to IAM Users, it's a better practice for future management to create an IAM Group, assign permissions to the group, and then add users to the group.

Begin by selecting **Groups** in the left-hand navigation panel, and then click the **Create New Group** button. Enter a name for the group, for example, ProDotNETonAWSBookUsers, and click **Next Step**. Now we'll attach a policy to the group.

Figure 1-11 shows the Attach Policy screen with the *AdministratorAccess* policy selected. If your screen does not show the policy, enter "Admin" into the Search field to locate and then select the appropriate policy.

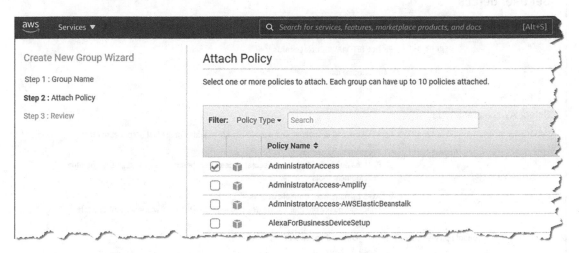

Figure 1-11. *Attaching a policy to the group*

After selecting the policy, click **Next Step** to proceed and review your selections, then click **Create Group** to finish.

Now we'll create a user and add them to the group. Returning to the left-hand navigation panel, as seen in Figure 1-10, click **Users**, and then click the **Add user** button. As shown in Figure 1-12, enter a name for the user and be sure to select both *Programmatic access* and *AWS Management Console access* under **Access Type**. The tools introduced in Chapters 2 and 3 will need the programmatic keys, and as already mentioned, we'll be using this user to work in the management console as well. You can assign a password or leave the defaults. Leaving the default will require you to create a new password the next time you sign into the console.

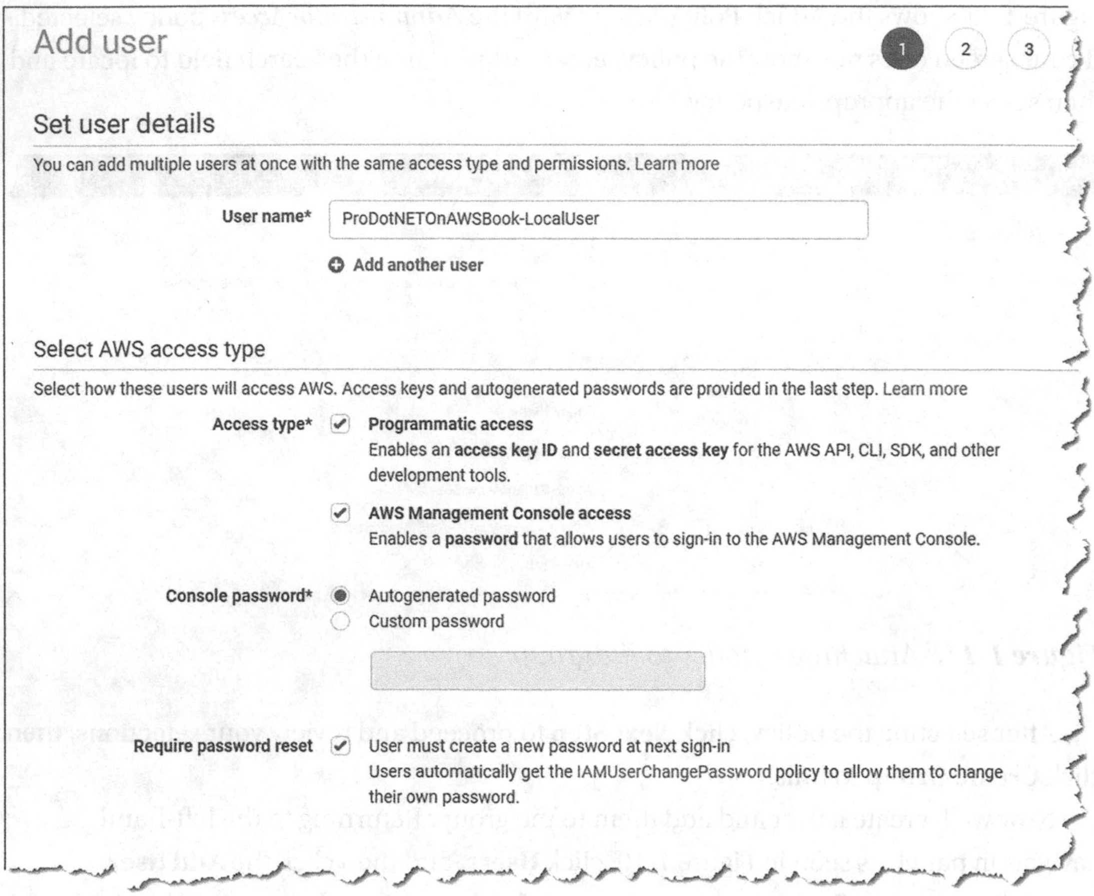

Add user

1   2   3

Set user details

You can add multiple users at once with the same access type and permissions. Learn more

User name*   ProDotNETOnAWSBook-LocalUser

⊕ Add another user

Select AWS access type

Select how these users will access AWS. Access keys and autogenerated passwords are provided in the last step. Learn more

Access type*   ☑ **Programmatic access**
Enables an **access key ID** and **secret access key** for the AWS API, CLI, SDK, and other development tools.

☑ **AWS Management Console access**
Enables a **password** that allows users to sign-in to the AWS Management Console.

Console password*   ⦿ Autogenerated password
◯ Custom password

Require password reset   ☑ User must create a new password at next sign-in
Users automatically get the IAMUserChangePassword policy to allow them to change their own password.

Figure 1-12. *IAM user name and access selections*

Click **Next: Permissions** to proceed and add the user to the group we just created, as shown in Figure 1-13.

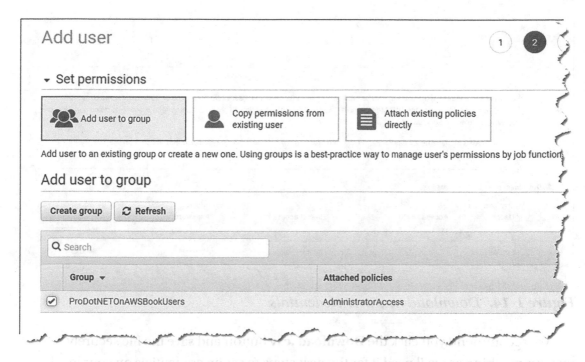

Figure 1-13. *Add the new user to the group*

Click **Next: Tags** to proceed. Adding tags to resources is a recommended best practice for grouping but we don't need it in this case, so continue by clicking **Next: Review**.

Note   If you elected to require the user to create a new password at next sign-in, you'll notice that the user will have an AWS-managed policy attached, named *IAMUserChangePassword*, in addition to their group membership.

Review your selections, and if satisfied, click **Create user** to finish. This will take you to the page shown in Figure 1-14, where you can obtain the programmatic and console sign-in credentials for the new user.

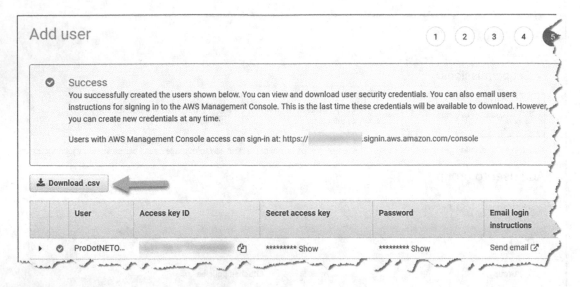

Figure 1-14. *Download new user credentials*

We recommend you click the **Download .csv** button and save the file securely on your machine as we'll need it for the next steps to set up credentials on your local machine. This will get it ready for use in the tools we'll be introducing in the next two chapters. Click **Close** when you have downloaded the credentials. **Take care of this file and don't save or copy it anywhere that other users may be able to access.**

Note   Programmatic credentials consist of an *Access key* and a *Secret access key.* This is the only time you can display or download the Secret access key (although you can always create new keys for a user). Some users rotate their keys periodically by creating new ones and deleting the prior ones, but we won't cover that in this book.

Signing into the AWS Management Console

The credentials file contains the user name, generated programmatic access and secret keys, console password, and a console sign-in URL, like so (this has been altered, so don't waste your time trying to use it):

```
User name,Password,Access key ID,Secret access key,Console login link
ProDotNETonAWSBook-LocalUser,Pa$$w0rd,AKIAIOSFODNN7EXAMPLE,wJalrXUtnF
EMI/K7MDENG/bPxRfiCYEXAMPLEKEY,https://111122223333.signin.aws.amazon.
com/console
```

You'll notice that the console sign-in URL contains your account number. Even though the number is embedded in the URL, you will be asked to enter it into the sign-in form, along with your username and password. We don't find the account numbers all that easy to remember – especially when we are working with multiple accounts – so instead, we prefer to assign an alias and then provide that into the sign-in form.

To assign a more convenient alias, first, exit from the *Add user* page shown in Figure 1-14 by clicking the **Close** button (if you've not already done so), and then select **Dashboard** from the links in the left-hand navigation panel. The dashboard shows the console sign-in URL, and to its right is a **Customize** link – click this to open a pop-up dialog to set an alias, as shown in Figure 1-15. Type in a suitable alias and click **Create alias** to complete the process.

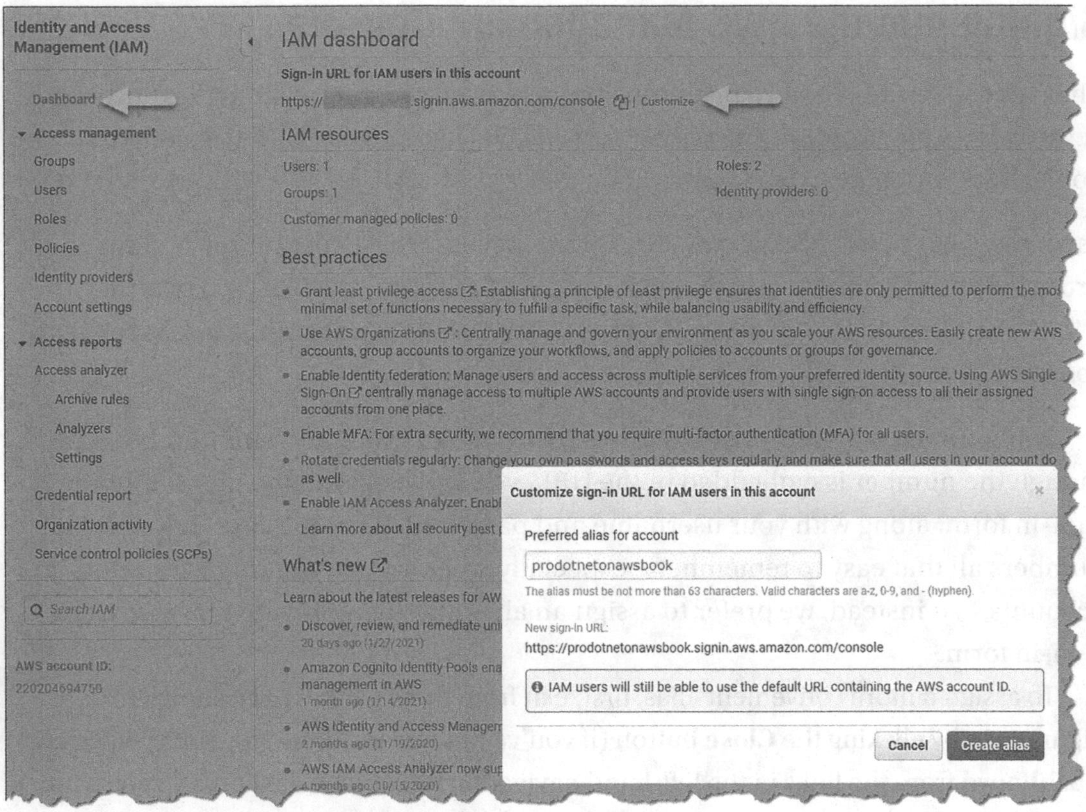

Figure 1-15. *Assigning a convenient alias to the console sign-in URL*

Let's test out signing into the console using our new alias and IAM user. First, copy the new console sign-in URL to the clipboard and then click on your user name in the console toolbar and sign out from your root account. Next, paste the aliased sign-in URL into the browser. The console sign-in page will appear, but this time will be titled **Sign in as IAM user**. In the *Account ID* field, type the alias that you entered (prodotnetonawsbook in the example in Figure 1-15). From the credentials file that you downloaded, copy and paste your user name, then password, and then click **Sign in**.

Note   If you elected to require the user to choose a new password on next sign-in, you'll now be prompted to change the password. Record the new password safely – we suggest back in the credentials file you just downloaded, which you could also update with your new custom sign-in URL.

Congratulations, you are now signed into the AWS Management Console as an IAM user! Next, we'll look at what to do with the programmatic credentials.

Introducing Credential Profiles

In the past, especially for on-premises application development, you may have simply embedded credentials, database passwords, and API keys into the application source code or configuration files. It's an understatement to say that this comes with some risk! For example, let's say you decide to publish the application code to a public source code repository one day. Are you likely to recall that the application files contain your credential keys? This is another reason for making use of IAM users when developing code, and deploying applications to use roles, rather than fixed (and possibly root) credentials in your code.

The AWS tools that we'll be introducing in Chapters 2 and 3 use credential profiles instead. A credential profile is simply a name that references programmatic credentials held in a file on your local machine. Credential profiles can also be role based, but at their simplest, they just hold the access and secret access keys. In the tools and in your application code and configuration files, you simply use the credential profile name, and the actual credentials are obtained when needed. This is much more secure, provided you guard access to the file containing your credential profiles. If you check in and push to a public repository a source or configuration file containing the name of a credential profile, nothing can be inferred from it, and it's certainly not usable by anyone else to create havoc in your account as there are no actual credentials there to use.

Some of the tools that will be covered in Chapters 2 and 3 have mechanisms to help you create credential profiles from the credentials file you downloaded earlier, but to get us started, we'll do it by hand. That way, you'll understand what is going on behind the scenes. You can use any text editor to create and maintain the file containing your credential profiles as it is simply plain text.

First, navigate to your user home location, for example, `C:\Users\`*userid* on Windows. Next, create a folder named `.aws` (note the leading period). Inside this folder, create a text file named `credentials` and open it in a text editor.

The credential profiles file is simply an "ini"-format file. The name of the credential profile – what you use to reference the credentials in the tools and your code – is placed inside square brackets. Following this are the programmatic keys, one per line. From the credentials file that you downloaded, copy and paste the user name, access, and secret access key values into the file so that it looks like the following example:

```
[ProDotNETOnAWSBook-LocalUser]
aws_access_key_id=AKIAIOSFODNN7EXAMPLE
aws_secret_access_key=wJalrXUtnFEMI/K7MDENG/bPxRfiCYEXAMPLEKEY
```

Save the file and close the editor. You now have sign-in capability to the AWS Management Console using an IAM user and programmatic credentials ready to use with the tools and SDKs that we'll describe in the following chapters, all contained safely in a credential profile under your user account location on your machine.

Summary

In this chapter, we outlined the core essentials of AWS – what you really need to know – to get started. Then we took a brief orientation tour of the AWS Management Console and created an IAM user identity that you will use throughout the rest of the book to work with AWS tools and services from your own machine. We also outlined how your deployed applications will use an IAM Role to obtain credentials, saving you from having to embed explicit credentials into your source and configuration files. Finally, we stored the programmatic credentials – access and secret access keys – on your machine in a credential profile that you'll use when working locally on your applications.

In the next chapter, we'll introduce the suite of tools available from AWS, at no cost, for .NET developers. Let's go!

CHAPTER 2

AWS Tools for .NET

With the essentials of AWS now under our belt, and an initial IAM user account and credential profile set up, it's time to look at the tools available from AWS that you can use to work with AWS resources, deploy and manage your applications, and integrate AWS services into your application code.

In this chapter, we will look at the primary collection of tools, all freely available, that are in most cases specific to .NET-based development environments. Chapter 3 will cover additional tools, also all freely available, that round out your toolset.

Integrated Development Environment (IDE) Toolkits

As developers ourselves, we spent significant time working in so-called integrated development environments (IDEs) or source code editors. Many a time we've heard the expression "don't make me leave my IDE" in relation to the need to perform some management task! For those of you with similar feelings, AWS offers integrations, known as "toolkits," for the most popular IDEs and source code editors in use today in the .NET community – Microsoft Visual Studio, JetBrains Rider, and Visual Studio Code.

The toolkits vary in levels of functionality and the areas of development they target. All three, however, share a common ability to make it easy to package up and deploy your application code to a variety of AWS services.

AWS Toolkit for Visual Studio

Ask any longtime developer working with .NET and it's almost certain they will have used Visual Studio. For many .NET developers, it could well be the only IDE they have ever worked with in a professional environment. It's estimated that almost 90% of .NET developers are using Visual Studio for their .NET work, which is why AWS has supported an integration with Visual Studio since Visual Studio 2008. Currently, the AWS toolkit is

© William Penberthy and Steve Roberts 2023
W. Penberthy and S. Roberts, *Pro .NET on Amazon Web Services*,
https://doi.org/10.1007/978-1-4842-8907-5_2

available for the Community, Professional, and Enterprise editions of Visual Studio 2017 and 2019, together, as well as Visual Studio 2022. The toolkit is available on the Visual Studio marketplace.

Note   Developers occasionally ask about AWS support for Visual Studio for Mac. Visual Studio for Mac is a rebranded version of Xamarin Studio and technically is completely different from Visual Studio for Windows, from both a feature and an extension point of view. AWS does not currently offer a toolkit for Visual Studio for Mac. The toolkit for Visual Studio described here is solely for the Windows version of Visual Studio.

The AWS Toolkit for Visual Studio, as the most established of the AWS integrations, is also the most functionally rich and supports working with features of multiple AWS services from within the IDE environment. First, a tool window – **the AWS Explorer** – surfaces credential and region selection, along with a tree of services commonly used by developers as they learn, experiment, and work with AWS. You can open the explorer window using an entry on the IDE's View menu. Figure 2-1 shows a typical view of the explorer, with its tree of services and controls for credential profile and region selection.

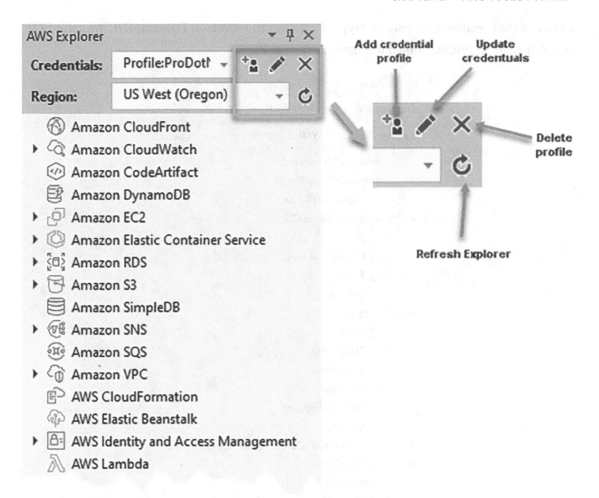

Figure 2-1. *The AWS Explorer*

The combination of selected credential profile and region scopes the tree of services and service resources within the explorer, and resource views opened from the explorer carry that combination of credential and region scoping with them. In other words, if the explorer is bound to (say) US East (N. Virginia) and you open a view onto EC2 instances, that view shows the instances in the US East (N. Virginia) region only, for the user's account. If the selected region or account in the explorer changes, the instances shown in the document view window do not – the instances view remains bound to the original credential and region selection.

Expanding a tree node (service) in the explorer will display a list of resources or resource types, depending on the service. In both cases, double-clicking a resource or resource type node, or using the **Open** command in the node's context menu, will open a view of that resource or resource type. Consider the *Amazon DynamoDB*, *Amazon EC2*, and *Amazon S3* nodes, shown in Figure 2-2.

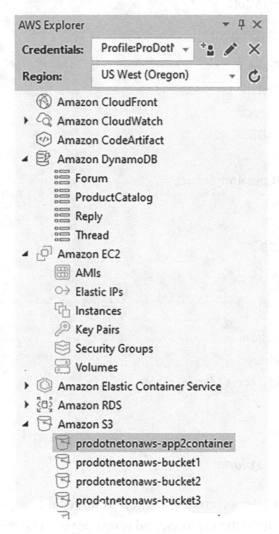

Figure 2-2. *Explorer tree node types*

The *Amazon DynamoDB* node lists your available DynamoDB tables. Opening a view onto a table will display the data in the table. Using the view, you can also edit the table data and construct scan queries to filter the data, as shown in Figure 2-3.

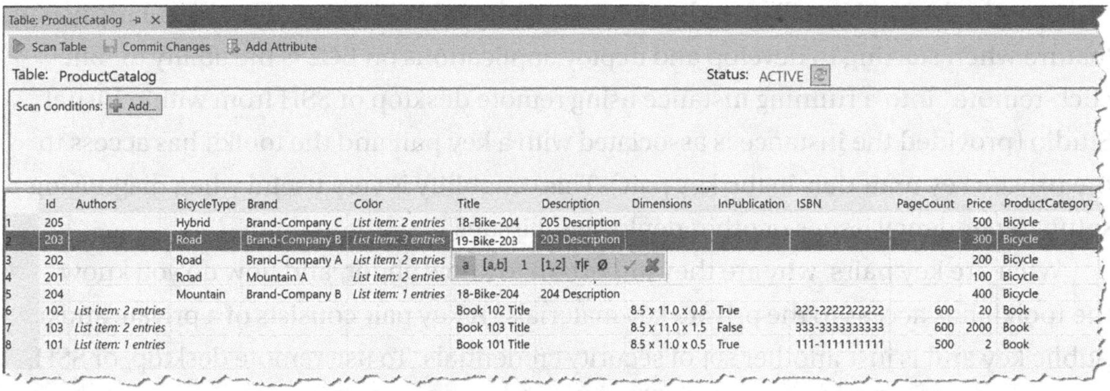

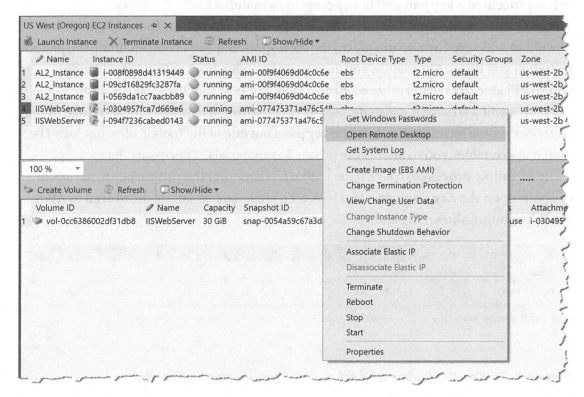

Figure 2-3. *Editing the data of a DynamoDB table*

The *Amazon EC2* node has a different approach in that it shows a collection of resource types, for *images* (AMIs), *Elastic IPs*, *Instances*, *Key Pairs*, *Security Groups*, and *EBS Volumes*. Views opened from these nodes will display the relevant resources, for example, your current EC2 instances, shown in Figure 2-4. Context menus are available on instances enabling you to control their state (stopped, terminated) and other features.

Figure 2-4. *EC2 instances view*

Later in the book, we'll use other features of the EC2 view, but one particularly useful feature when starting to develop and deploy applications on EC2 is the ability to "one-click-remote" into a running instance using remote desktop or SSH from within Visual Studio (provided the instance is associated with a key pair and the toolkit has access to the private key materials in the key pair). This capability is very useful when diagnosing setup dependency issues or other deployment issues.

What are key pairs, why are they important to know about, and how do you know the toolkit has access to the private key materials? A key pair consists of a private and a public key and is just another set of security credentials. To use remote desktop, or SSH, to remote into an EC2 instance, you'll need to decrypt its administrator password – and this is where the key pair comes in.

You can always choose to launch instances without specifying a key pair, but then you can't decrypt the administrator password and so won't be able to remote into them (which may be a security posture you want for production instances). From the AWS Management Console, it is possible to open a browser-based secure command-line shell onto an instance, but to remote into the instance from your own machine, you will need to have specified a key pair and have access to its materials.

You can create key pairs in the AWS Management Console, and you should download and save (in a secure place) the corresponding *.pem* file containing the private key when you do so. Alternately, you can create key pairs from within Visual Studio. You're still able to save the private key materials, but now that the toolkit is aware of the key pair, it will also save those materials, securely, within the toolkit's local storage under your user profile location. If you create key pairs outside of the toolkit, all is not lost. The toolkit also enables you to import the private key materials, if necessary, later.

It's a simple process to check if the toolkit has access to the private key materials of a key pair; open the *Key Pairs* view and look for a green checkmark in the **Stored in AWS Toolkit** column, shown in Figure 2-5.

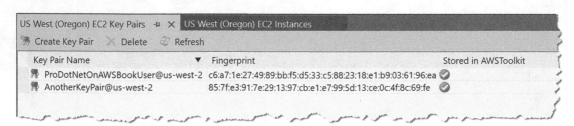

Figure 2-5. *Key Pairs view and a key with stored private materials*

If the view does not show a checkmark for the key pair, right-click on the key pair entry and choose **Import Private Key**, then paste in the key materials from the *.pem* file you downloaded when creating the key into the dialog that's displayed. This situation will occur when you create a key pair in the Management Console, or another tool, and is easy to resolve so long as you have the *.pem* file to hand.

Moving on from EC2, Figure 2-2 showed that the *Amazon S3* node lists your storage buckets. Views opened from these nodes will display the contents of the bucket, using a hierarchical file explorer-style idiom, shown in Figure 2-6, with key prefix components represented as subfolders and a breadcrumb trail of the parent prefix listed at the top of the view. Remember, S3 is not a file system; the AWS tools just make it look like one so it matches the mental picture you developed from working with local storage!

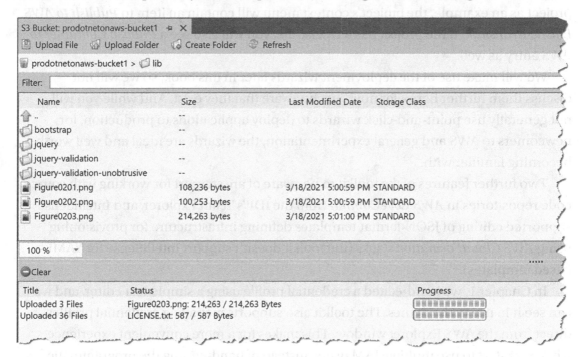

Figure 2-6. *Exploring the contents of an S3 storage bucket*

As an additional convenience, the toolkit supports drag-and-drop upload of files and folders direct from your machine to a bucket, in addition to being able to download content. You can also edit object metadata for objects (files), say, the "Content-Type" metadata attribute for an object.

All nodes in the AWS Explorer, whether they represent actual resources in the cloud or types of resources, support context menus – so we encourage you to "click around" and discover what's available. Using the same three root-level nodes we've just covered, the DynamoDB node has an entry you can use to start a simple wizard to create a new table; the EC2 node has an entry that starts a "launch instance" wizard, and the S3 node has an entry enabling you to create new storage buckets, and so on.

In addition to the AWS Explorer window, the toolkit supports deployment of application code, without leaving the IDE, to AWS Elastic Beanstalk, AWS Lambda, and Amazon Elastic Container Service, container images to Amazon Elastic Container Registry, and infrastructure templates to AWS CloudFormation. All make use of convenient wizard-based workflows.

Access to the various deployment wizards is from the context menus of projects in the Solution Explorer, or the IDE's Project menu. Taking an ASP.NET or ASP.NET Core project as an example, the project's context menu will contain an item to *Publish to AWS Elastic Beanstalk*. If the project has a Dockerfile, you will also see a *Publish Container to AWS* entry as well.

We will make use of the deployment wizards later in this book, so we will not discuss them further here – for now, just be aware that they exist. And while you will not generally use point-and-click wizards to deploy applications to production, for newcomers to AWS and general experimentation, the wizards are ideal and well worth becoming familiar with.

Two further features of the toolkit to be aware of are support for working with source code repositories in *AWS CodeCommit* from the IDE's Team Explorer, and IntelliSense-supported editing of JSON-format templates defining infrastructure for provisioning using *AWS CloudFormation* stacks (the toolkit doesn't support IntelliSense for YAML-based templates).

In Chapter 1, we hand-edited a credential profile using a simple text editor, and we can see it in use in the figures. The toolkit also supports managing credential profiles direct from the AWS Explorer window. This makes for a more convenient experience when you start to use multiple IAM users. Instead of hand-editing the programmatic keys into the credential profiles file, you can use a convenient dialog and even import the csv-format credential file you download for a new user (or new credentials for an existing user), shown in Figure 2-7.

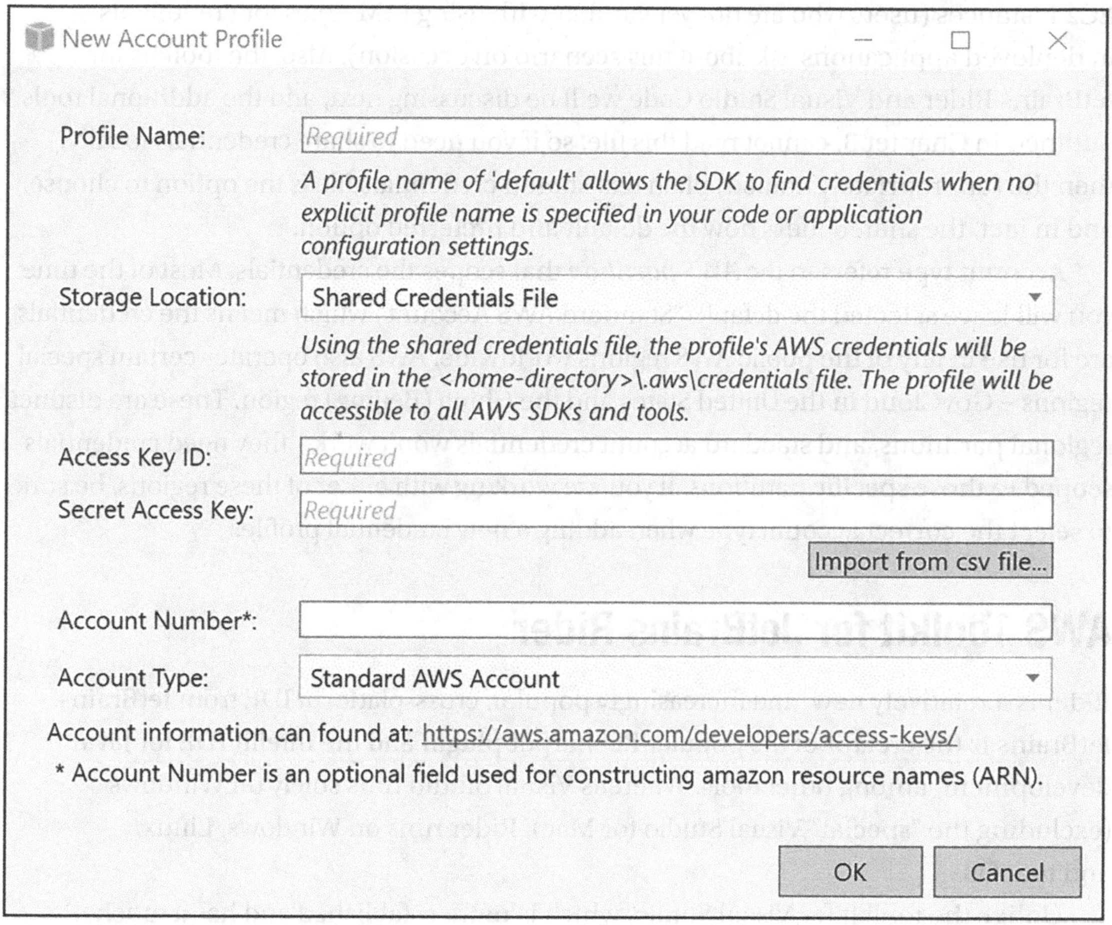

New Account Profile — ☐ ✕

Profile Name: | Required |

A profile name of 'default' allows the SDK to find credentials when no explicit profile name is specified in your code or application configuration settings.

Storage Location: | Shared Credentials File ▼ |

Using the shared credentials file, the profile's AWS credentials will be stored in the <home-directory>\.aws\credentials file. The profile will be accessible to all AWS SDKs and tools.

Access Key ID: | Required |

Secret Access Key: | Required |

Import from csv file...

Account Number*: | |

Account Type: | Standard AWS Account ▼ |

Account information can found at: https://aws.amazon.com/developers/access-keys/

* Account Number is an optional field used for constructing amazon resource names (ARN).

OK   Cancel

***Figure 2-7.** Adding a new credential profile*

Two items stand out in this dialog to be aware of when adding a new credential profile. First is the storage location and second the account type.

The toolkit, in common with the other .NET-specific tools from AWS, supports two storage locations for credentials. We've already used the shared credentials file mechanism in Chapter 1, when we hand-created our first credential profile, in a plain-text file in your %USERPROFILE%\.aws folder location. The .NET tools can also use an encrypted file. If you've chosen to store profiles in it, you will find this file at %USERPROFILE%\AppData\Local\AWSToolkit\RegisteredAccounts.json. This file, encrypted to your user account on your machine, was the first credential profile file supported by the .NET tools from AWS on local machines. You cannot use this file on other machines, including those of your colleagues, or virtual machines such as

EC2 instances (users who are not yet familiar with using IAM Roles for credentials in deployed applications ask about this scenario on occasion). Also, the toolkits for JetBrains Rider and Visual Studio Code we'll be discussing next, and the additional tools outlined in Chapter 3, cannot read this file, so if you need to share credentials locally, then the (appropriately named) plain text shared credentials file is the option to choose, and in fact, the shared file is now the default and preferred option.

Account type refers to the *AWS partition* that scopes the credentials. Most of the time you will leave selected the default, "Standard AWS Account", which means the credentials are for use in any of the public AWS regions worldwide. AWS also operates certain special regions – GovCloud in the United States and the China (Beijing) region. These are distinct regional partitions, and standard account credentials won't work – they need credentials scoped to those specific partitions. If you are working with either of these regions, be sure to select the correct account type when adding a new credential profile.

AWS Toolkit for JetBrains Rider

Rider is a relatively new, and increasingly popular, cross-platform IDE from JetBrains. JetBrains is the creator of the popular ReSharper plugin and the IntelliJ IDE for Java development, among other tools. Whereas Visual Studio runs solely on Windows (excluding the "special" Visual Studio for Mac), Rider runs on Windows, Linux, and macOS.

Unlike the toolkit for Visual Studio, which is more established and has a much broader range of supported services and features, the toolkit for Rider focuses on features to support the development of serverless and container-based modern applications. You can install the toolkit from the JetBrains marketplace by selecting *Plugins* from the *Configure* link in Rider's startup dialog.

Note   The Visual Studio toolkit also, of course, supports the development of serverless and container-based applications. However, it differs in its level of debugging support. The toolkits for Rider and Visual Studio Code (discussed next) both support the debugging of serverless functions in a Lambda-like environment. The Visual Studio toolkit instead relies on the *Mock Lambda Test Tool*, a web-based experience that enables you to run test payloads or actual payloads that failed (if you have attached an *Amazon SQS Dead-Letter Queue* to the function – more on this in Chapter 6).

To complement the toolkit's features, you do need to install a couple of additional dependencies. First, the AWS Serverless Application Model (SAM) CLI. We'll talk more about the SAM CLI in the next chapter; for now, know that the Rider toolkit uses the SAM CLI to build, debug, package, and deploy serverless applications. In turn, SAM CLI needs Docker to be able to provide the Lambda-like debug environment. Of course, if you are already working on container-based applications, you'll likely already have this installed.

With the toolkit and dependencies installed, let's first examine the AWS Explorer window to compare it to the Visual Studio toolkit. Figure 2-8 shows the explorer, with some service nodes expanded.

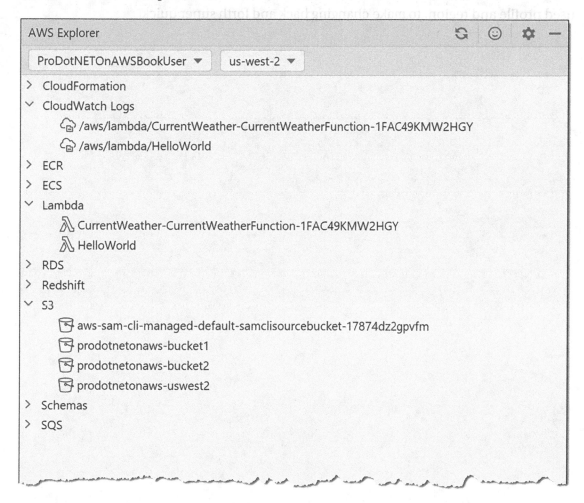

Figure 2-8. *The AWS Explorer in JetBrains Rider*

We can see immediately that the explorer gives access to fewer services than the explorer in Visual Studio; this reflects the Rider toolkit's focus on serverless and container development. However, it follows a familiar pattern of noting your currently active credential profile, and region, in the explorer toolbar.

Controls in the IDE's status bar link to the credential and region fields in the explorer. This enables you to see at a glance which profile and region are active without needing to keep the explorer visible (this isn't possible in Visual Studio, where you need to open the explorer to see the credential and region context). Figure 2-9 shows the status bar control in action to change region. Notice that the toolkit also keeps track of your most recently used profile and region, to make changing back and forth super quick.

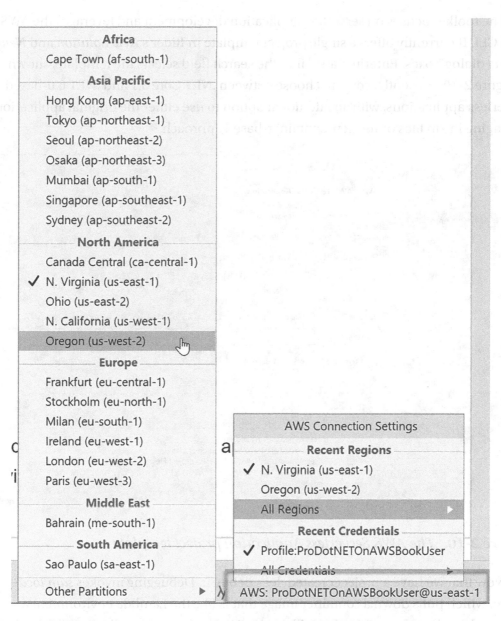

Figure 2-9. *Changing region or credentials using the IDE's status bar*

Note   The toolkit can only read profiles from the text-based shared credential file. It cannot read profiles stored in the encrypted .NET credential file mentioned previously in the discussion on Visual Studio.

The toolkit focuses on serverless application development and leverages the AWS SAM CLI. It currently offers a single project template in Rider's *New Solution* and *New Project* dialog boxes. Entering "aws" into the search field selects the template, shown in Figure 2-10. Presently, you can choose between .NET Core 3.1 and .NET 6.0-based serverless applications, with an additional option to use either the original application packaging in zip files or the new container-based approach.

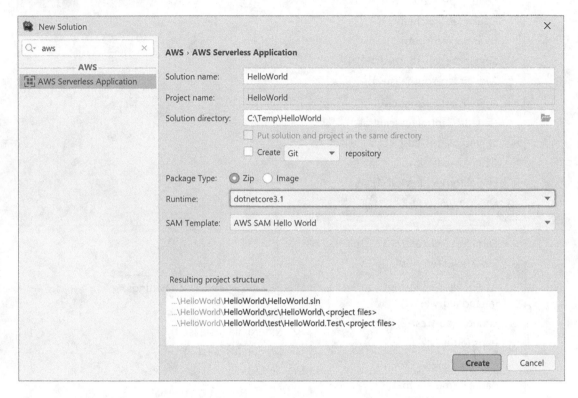

Figure 2-10. *The AWS Serverless Application project template*

Now that we have a project created, let's debug it. Debugging invokes *sam local* mode, which pulls down a container image that is like the Lambda environment a deployed version of your function will run in. So as mentioned earlier, you do need to ensure you have Docker installed first. Rider uses launch configurations to control the startup of debugging sessions. Your new project included an initial launch configuration, and you can add more. Figure 2-11 shows the launch configuration settings, to which we've added some sample input that will be supplied in the body of the request.

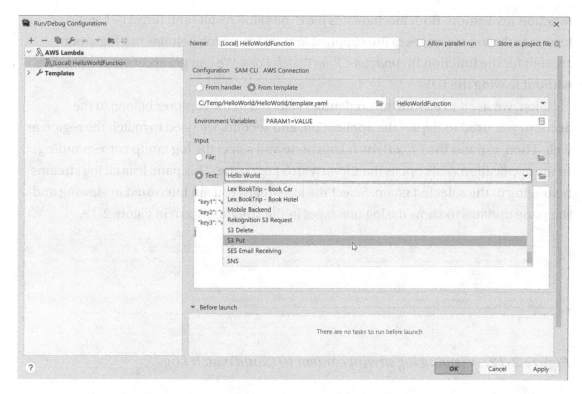

Figure 2-11. Editing the default launch configuration

You can set the input for the function as text or you can accept input from a file.
If you choose text, the toolkit offers several pre-written body text templates that
correspond to real-world events from resources that can trigger your function to run, or
you can enter whatever custom input you need.

Note that you cannot omit some form of input body, even if only an empty
string – which you specify in quotes, for example, "" – when you launch the debugger.
If the input for the selected launch configuration is missing, debugging will pause and
display a dialog (like Figure 2-11). The values entered are then persisted back to the
launch configuration. If you want different inputs, you need to change the default launch
configuration or create multiple configurations.

Debugging functions locally before deployment is obviously useful, but sometimes,
you may need to see what a deployed function has been doing when you weren't
looking, and you can do this by examining its log output. The ability to write log
information is available out of the box to all Lambda functions, and you can log
information by either writing to console (with `Console.WriteLine`) or by using methods
on the logging instance, which you'll find in the context object provided on every

function invocation. Both mechanisms have the same result (and target) – Lambda forwards the log messages to the supplied log stream, which belongs to a log group created for the function in *Amazon CloudWatch Logs*. We can get access to the log data without leaving the IDE.

First, we need to ensure the credentials selected in the explorer belong to the account you used to deploy the application, and second, we need to match the region as well. Then, expand the *CloudWatch Logs* node and select the log group corresponding to the application. This opens the *CloudWatch Logs* pane. This pane lists all log streams belonging to the selected group. Select the log stream you are interested in viewing and the pane updates to show the log messages in the stream, shown in Figure 2-12.

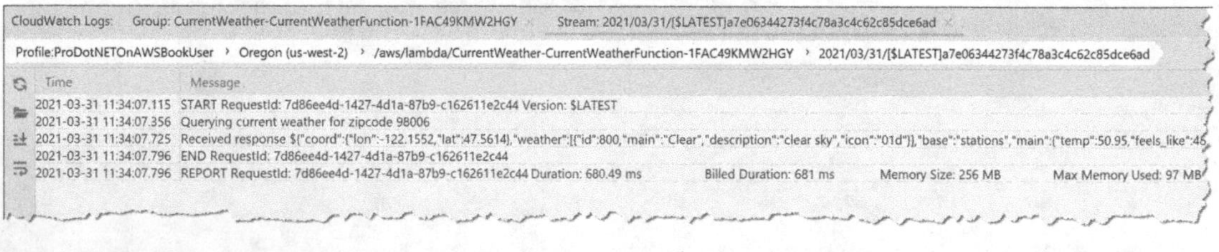

Figure 2-12. *Viewing log stream content in CloudWatch Logs*

In addition to debugging serverless applications locally and deploying them from within the IDE – useful during development or "kicking the tires" scenarios – the Rider toolkit can also debug container applications deployed to Amazon ECS. Now, we must caution strongly – this is **not** something you should attempt with a production application! Attaching a debugger to an application in an ECS cluster **will stop the application** for a period, and it's not a brief period (several minutes upward, in our experience). And you must remember to detach afterward and restore the container back to its original state. If this is your production application, you now have a self-inflicted outage. So we advise you to save this capability for your in-development resources. But it's a useful tool to have in the tool chest. To go along with debugging, the toolkit also enables you to access a terminal into the running container.

We've only scratched the surface of the Rider toolkit in this chapter (and similarly for Visual Studio Code, discussed in the following text). But we'll see more of the features in action in the remainder of this book. For more information, check out the user guide at `https://docs.aws.amazon.com/toolkit-for-jetbrains/latest/userguide/`.

AWS Toolkit for Visual Studio Code

Visual Studio Code (VS Code) is an editor with plugin extensions, rather than a full-fledged IDE in the style of Visual Studio or Rider. However, the sheer range of available extensions makes it a more-than-capable development environment for multiple languages, including C#/.NET development on Windows, Linux, and macOS systems.

Like the toolkit for Rider, the VS Code toolkit focuses on the development of modern serverless and container-based applications. The toolkit offers an explorer pane with the capability to list resources across multiple regions, similar to the single-region explorers available in the Visual Studio and Rider toolkits. The VS Code toolkit also offers local debugging of Lambda functions in a Lambda-like environment. As with Rider, the toolkit uses the AWS SAM CLI to support debugging and deployment of serverless applications, so you do need to install this dependency, and Docker as well, to take advantage of debugging support.

Credentials are, once again, handled using profiles, and the toolkit offers a command palette item that walks you through setting up a new profile if no profiles already exist on your machine. If you have existing profiles, the command simply loads the credential file into the editor, where you can paste the keys to create a new profile.

Note   The toolkit can only read profiles from the text-based shared credential file. It cannot read profiles stored in the encrypted .NET credential store file as mentioned previously in the discussion on Visual Studio.

Figure 2-13 shows some of the available commands for the toolkit in the command palette.

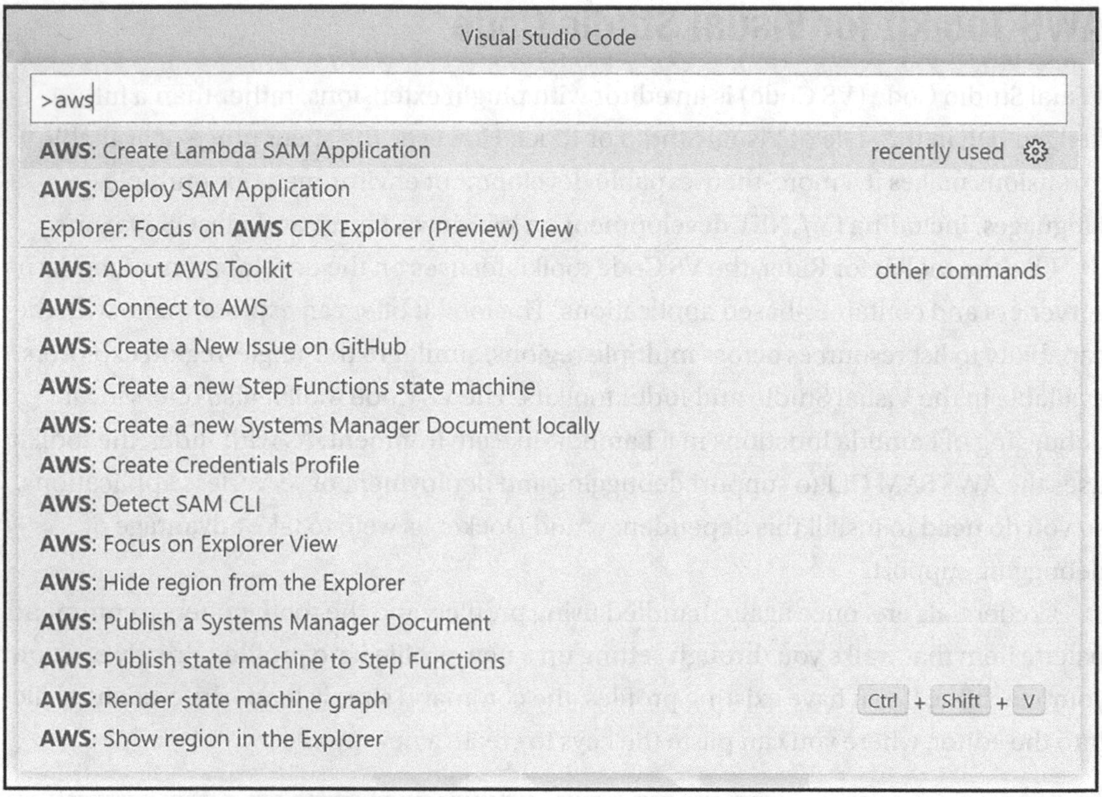

```
                          Visual Studio Code

>aws

AWS: Create Lambda SAM Application                    recently used  ⚙

AWS: Deploy SAM Application

Explorer: Focus on AWS CDK Explorer (Preview) View

AWS: About AWS Toolkit                                other commands

AWS: Connect to AWS

AWS: Create a New Issue on GitHub

AWS: Create a new Step Functions state machine

AWS: Create a new Systems Manager Document locally

AWS: Create Credentials Profile

AWS: Detect SAM CLI

AWS: Focus on Explorer View

AWS: Hide region from the Explorer

AWS: Publish a Systems Manager Document

AWS: Publish state machine to Step Functions

AWS: Render state machine graph                  Ctrl + Shift + V

AWS: Show region in the Explorer
```

Figure 2-13. *Toolkit commands in the command palette*

Figure 2-14 highlights the active credential profile and an explorer bound to multiple regions. Clicking the status bar indicator enables you to change the bound credentials. You show or hide additional regions in the explorer from a command, or using the toolbar in the explorer (click the **...** button).

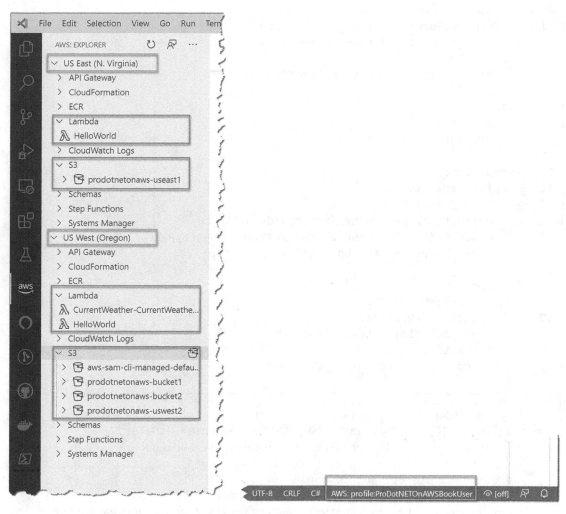

Figure 2-14. *Active profile indicator and multiregion explorer*

Tip   The S3 node in the explorer filters the buckets to list only those created in that region, unlike in Visual Studio.

Just as with JetBrains Rider, debugging in VS Code requires you to set up a launch configuration for the debug session. The toolkit automatically detects the signatures of serverless functions (in your code and template files) and annotates them with an *Add Debug Configuration* link, shown in Figure 2-15. Clicking this link will create a launch configuration entry for the selected function, which you can then edit further, if needed.

```
 1   AWSTemplateFormatVersion: '2010-09-09'
 2   Transform: AWS::Serverless-2016-10-31
 3   Description: >
 4     SAM Template for 'weather' sample
 5
 6   Globals:
 7     Function:
 8       Timeout: 10
 9
10   Parameters:
11     ApiKeyParameterName:
12       Type: 'String'
13       Default: '/openweather/apikeys/default'
14       Description: The name of the Systems Manager Par
                 key value for the OpenWeather service.
15
16   Resources:
       Add Debug Configuration
17     CurrentWeatherFunction:            You, 2 days ago • Add
18       Type: AWS::Serverless::Function
19       Properties:
20         CodeUri: ./src/CurrentWeather/
```

```
0 references | Add Debug Configuration
public async Task<APIGatewayHttpApiV2ProxyResponse> Handler
    (APIGatewayHttpApiV2ProxyRequest request, ILambdaContext context)
{       You, 2 days ago • Added serverless 'current weather' sample
    #region Sample url and response...

    var zipcode = request.QueryStringParameters[ZipCodeQueryParameter];
    if (string.IsNullOrEmpty(zipcode))
```

Figure 2-15. *Adding a launch configuration to locally debug a Lambda function*

You can also deploy serverless applications to AWS from within the editor. Again, the toolkit makes use of the SAM CLI under the covers to perform all the packaging and deployment handling. All you need to do is select the AWS: *Deploy SAM Application* command in the command palette and answer a few simple questions – which template to deploy (you usually only have one), which region to deploy to, the name of the S3 bucket to hold the packaged bundle, and the name to give to the deployed function.

The keen-eyed among you will have noticed the additional services in the explorer shown in Figure 2-14. From within the VS Code environment, you can view Log Groups and their associated *Log Streams* in *CloudWatch Logs* that enables you to view the logging and other console output from your Lambda functions.

There's also integration with *AWS Step Functions*. Step Functions orchestrate serverless functions in state machine workflows, complete with branching, parallel execution, and timeouts. You define your state machine in *Amazon States Language* (ASL), and the tasks in your state machine map to Lambda functions where the output from one function (task) becomes the input to the next function. Using the toolkit, you can create new Step Functions applications, work on the state machine in ASL with IntelliSense support, and deploy the application without leaving VS Code. You can also visualize the state machine inside the editor.

And there's more to the AWS Toolkit for VS Code:

- IntelliSense when editing task-definition files for Amazon ECS.

- Auto-completion of launch config settings for serverless applications.

- Create, edit, and publish *Automation Documents* for use with *AWS Systems Manager*. The toolkit provides getting started templates, code completion, and snippets.

- Search for, view, and generate code for *AWS EventBridge* schemas. EventBridge is a serverless event bus that makes it easier to connect applications (including SaaS applications) using custom and AWS-provided schemas. From those schemas, you can generate code bindings so that in your application code, you work with strongly typed objects rather than blobs of JSON.

- If you have adopted the *AWS Cloud Development Kit* (detailed in Chapter 3) for defining your cloud infrastructure, then the CDK Explorer pane will come in useful. It provides a navigable tree of your CDK application's infrastructure stacks, resources, and policies. The CDK Explorer is currently in preview and is a separate explorer pane.

VS Code and the AWS toolkit are a powerful combination when developing serverless .NET applications on Windows, Linux, and macOS hosts. To learn about all the latest integration features, we recommend you check out the User Guide at https://docs.aws.amazon.com/toolkit-for-vscode/latest/userguide.

Command-Line Tools

As noted earlier, most .NET developers have usually worked with .NET from within the Visual Studio environment, but command-line tools are also available. On Windows, we have had a choice of running commands in *cmd.exe* and PowerShell command-line shells for many years.

AWS has supported PowerShell for many years, both in its Windows-only version and now also in the new cross-platform PowerShell Core version running on Windows, Linux, and macOS, and exposes almost the entire AWS API surface as PowerShell cmdlets.

Beginning with .NET Core 1.0, .NET Core developers gained another command-line interface (CLI) tool, known as the *dotnet CLI*. With the dotnet CLI, developers can scaffold new projects, build, run, and package them for deployment (among other features). The CLI is extensible, with support for adding additional tools and project scaffolding templates, and AWS offers three global tools and a set of templates for Lambda projects.

Let's first look at the AWS extensions for the dotnet CLI, then we'll dive into PowerShell.

Note   The sections on JetBrains Rider and VS Code earlier mentioned a third CLI tool, *AWS SAM CLI*. We'll be looking closer at that tool in Chapter 3.

AWS Extensions for .NET CLI

If you use AWS Lambda, Amazon ECS, or AWS Elastic Beanstalk and need to use (or prefer) a command-line interface, then these tools are ideal for handling the packaging and deployment steps that you would otherwise exercise using a wizard in an IDE. They are also ideal for CI/CD build and deployment tasks

The tools, distributed on NuGet, are installed using a simple command: `dotnet tool install -g` *toolpackage*, where *toolpackage* is one of *Amazon.Lambda.Tools*, *Amazon. ECS.Tools*, or *Amazon.ElasticBeanstalk.Tools* (install all three or just the ones you need).

Once installed, you use the short service name (*lambda*, *eb*, *ecs*) with the dotnet command to view the available options. Figures 2-16, 2-17, and 2-18 show the top-level options for the three tool commands.

```
PS C:\> dotnet lambda
Amazon Lambda Tools for .NET Core applications (5.2.0)
Project Home: https://github.com/aws/aws-extensions-for-dotnet-cli, https://github.com/aws/aws-lambda-dotnet


Commands to deploy and manage AWS Lambda functions:

        deploy-function        Command to deploy the project to AWS Lambda
        invoke-function        Command to invoke a function in Lambda with an optional input
        list-functions         Command to list all your Lambda functions
        delete-function        Command to delete a Lambda function
        get-function-config    Command to get the current runtime configuration for a Lambda function
        update-function-config Command to update the runtime configuration for a Lambda function

Commands to deploy and manage AWS Serverless applications using AWS CloudFormation:

        deploy-serverless      Command to deploy an AWS Serverless application
        list-serverless        Command to list all your AWS Serverless applications
        delete-serverless      Command to delete an AWS Serverless application

Commands to publish and manage AWS Lambda Layers:

        publish-layer          Command to publish a Layer that can be associated with a Lambda function
        list-layers            Command to list Layers
        list-layer-versions    Command to list versions for a Layer
        get-layer-version      Command to get the details of a Layer version
        delete-layer-version   Command to delete a version of a Layer

Other Commands:

        package                Command to package a Lambda project either into a zip file or docker image if --package-type is set to
"image". The output can later be deployed to Lambda with either deploy-function command or with another tool.
        package-ci             Command to use as part of a continuous integration system.
        push-image             Build Lambda Docker image and push the image to Amazon ECR.

To get help on individual commands execute:
        dotnet lambda help <command>

PS C:\>
```

Figure 2-16. *Options for the "dotnet lambda" command*

```
PS C:\> dotnet ecs
Amazon EC2 Container Service Tools for .NET Core applications (3.5.2)
Project Home: https://github.com/aws/aws-extensions-for-dotnet-cli


Commands to deploy to Amazon EC2 Container Service:

        deploy-service         Push the application to ECR and runs the application as a long lived service on the ECS Cluster.
        deploy-task            Push the application to ECR and then runs it as a task on the ECS Cluster.
        deploy-scheduled-task  Push the application to ECR and then sets up CloudWatch Event Schedule rule to run the application.

Commands to manage docker images to Amazon EC2 Container Registry:

        push-image             Build Docker image and push the image to Amazon ECR.

To get help on individual commands execute:
        dotnet ecs help <command>

PS C:\>
```

Figure 2-17. *Options for the "dotnet ecs" command*

```
PS C:\> dotnet eb
Amazon Elastic Beanstalk Tools for .NET Core applications (4.3.2)
Project Home: https://github.com/aws/aws-extensions-for-dotnet-cli


Commands to manage environments:

        deploy-environment      Deploy the application to an AWS Elastic Beanstalk environment.
        list-environments       List the AWS Elastic Beanstalk environments.
        delete-environment      Delete an AWS Elastic Beanstalk environment.

Other Commands:

        package                 Package the application to a zip file to be deployed later to an Elastic Beanstalk environment

To get help on individual commands execute:
        dotnet eb help <command>

PS C:\>
```

Figure 2-18. *Options for the "dotnet eb" command*

To install the project scaffolding templates for AWS Lambda, use the following command: `dotnet new -i "Amazon.Lambda.Templates::*"`. Note the * at the end of the package name – this means install all the available templates in the package. Alternately, you can specify the name of a specific template you want to install.

With the templates installed, run `dotnet new`, or `dotnet new lambda --list`, to view the available project templates, and `dotnet new` *template-name* to scaffold a new project based on the template. Figure 2-19 illustrates the available templates.

```
PS C:\> dotnet new
Template Name                                        Short Name                                     Language      Tags
---------------------------------------------------  -------------------------------------------    ----------    ----------------------
Lambda Empty Function (.NET 6 Container Image)       lambda.image.EmptyFunction                     [C#],F#       AWS/Lambda/Function
Lambda Simple Kinesis Firehose Function              lambda.KinesisFirehose                         [C#]          AWS/Lambda/Function
Lambda Simple Kinesis Function                       lambda.Kinesis                                 [C#],F#       AWS/Lambda/Function
Lambda Simple S3 Function                            lambda.S3                                      [C#],F#       AWS/Lambda/Function
Order Flowers Chatbot Tutorial                       lambda.OrderFlowersChatbot                     [C#]          AWS/Lambda/Function
Lambda Custom Runtime Function (.NET 6)              lambda.CustomRuntimeFunction                   [C#],F#       AWS/Lambda/Function
Lambda Detect Image Labels                           lambda.DetectImageLabels                       [C#],F#       AWS/Lambda/Function
Lambda Simple SNS Function                           lambda.SNS                                     [C#]          AWS/Lambda/Function
Lambda Simple SQS Function                           lambda.SQS                                     [C#]          AWS/Lambda/Function
Lex Book Trip Sample                                 lambda.LexBookTripSample                       [C#]          AWS/Lambda/Function
Lambda Simple Application Load Balancer Function     lambda.SimpleApplicationLoadBalancerFunction   [C#]          AWS/Lambda/Function
Lambda Empty Function                                lambda.EmptyFunction                           [C#],F#       AWS/Lambda/Function
Lambda Simple DynamoDB Function                      lambda.DynamoDB                                [C#],F#       AWS/Lambda/Function
Lambda Annotations Framework (Preview)               serverless.Annotations                         [C#]          AWS/Lambda/Serverless
Lambda ASP.NET Core Web API                          serverless.AspNetCoreWebAPI                    [C#],F#       AWS/Lambda/Serverless
Lambda Empty Serverless                              serverless.EmptyServerless                     [C#],F#       AWS/Lambda/Serverless
Lambda Empty Serverless (.NET 6 Container Image)     serverless.image.EmptyServerless               [C#],F#       AWS/Lambda/Serverless
Serverless Simple S3 Function                        serverless.S3                                  [C#],F#       AWS/Lambda/Serverless
Lambda ASP.NET Core Web API (.NET 6 Container Image) serverless.image.AspNetCoreWebAPI              [C#],F#       AWS/Lambda/Serverless
Lambda Giraffe Web App                               serverless.Giraffe                             F#            AWS/Lambda/Serverless
Lambda ASP.NET Core Minimal API                      serverless.AspNetCoreMinimalAPI                [C#]          AWS/Lambda/Serverless
Step Functions Hello World                           serverless.StepFunctionsHelloWorld             [C#],F#       AWS/Lambda/Serverless
Serverless Detect Image Labels                       serverless.DetectImageLabels                   [C#],F#       AWS/Lambda/Serverless
Lambda ASP.NET Core Web Application with Razor Pages serverless.AspNetCoreWebApp                    [C#]          AWS/Lambda/Serverless
Empty Top-level Function                             lambda.EmptyTopLevelFunction                   [C#]          AWS/Lambda/Serverless
Serverless WebSocket API                             serverless.WebSocketAPI                        [C#]          AWS/Lambda/Serverless
Console Application                                  console                                        [C#],F#,VB    Common/Console
```

Figure 2-19. *Available Lambda project templates*

When specifying the template name for the *dotnet new* command, you can use either the full name (enclosed in quotes) or the short template name. For example, the commands in Listing 2-1 are equivalent.

Listing 2-1. Scaffolding a new AWS Lambda project with the dotnet new command

```
dotnet new "Lambda Detect Image Labels"
dotnet new lambda.DetectImageLabels
```

Note   These same Lambda templates are available if you are working in Visual Studio's New Project wizard. When you select an AWS Lambda or AWS Serverless Application project type, you next select the template, also called a *blueprint*.

As mentioned earlier, the command-line tools are ideal for CI/CD build environments where you can't run graphical wizards. You can perform your development tasks using the convenient wizards in Visual Studio and then transition to a command-line approach when needed, and round-trip between them. The command-line tools and Visual Studio deployment wizards share a common JSON-format settings file. There is one settings file per service, added to your project when you (a) run any of the corresponding deployment wizards in Visual Studio, (b) use the command-line deployment tools for the first time, or (c) create a Lambda project from a template.

When you run one of the deployment wizards in Visual Studio or run a deployment from the command line, the settings you choose are persisted into the appropriate settings file. If the settings file exists when you re-deploy using a wizard, the visible options in the wizard are set according to those persisted values. At the command line, as the settings are already persisted, the command-line deployment tools will deploy without any further prompts. You can also, of course, override any of the persisted settings using command-line switches or wizard controls.

AWS Tools for PowerShell

AWS currently provides three sets of modules under the AWS Tools for PowerShell umbrella. Why three? AWS first released a module for PowerShell in 2013. At that time, PowerShell was a Windows-specific technology, and occasionally, you will hear (or read, if AWS has missed a documentation update!) of the tools with the product name *AWS Tools for Windows PowerShell*. The actual module has the name *AWSPowerShell*. AWS still installs up-to-date copies of this module on all EC2-provided Windows images for backward compatibility.

Roll forward to 2016, when PowerShell became a cross-platform technology with the introduction of PowerShell Core. AWS writes their tools in C#, and at the time it wasn't possible to create a single C#-based module covering both editions of PowerShell. So, instead, AWS released a new variant, *AWSPowerShell.NETCore*. It contained pretty much the same cmdlets as the *AWSPowerShell* module, missing only a couple related to SAML-based authentication that needed to use Windows APIs that were not present in .NET Core at that time.

At the time of the first release of the original *AWSPowerShell* module, it comprised roughly 500 cmdlets covering 20 or so services. Today, the count of modules has grown to over 11,000 cmdlets and 200+ services – and this count is still growing! *AWSPowerShell* and *AWSPowerShell.NETCore* are also now identical in terms of the cmdlets they contain. The difference is the supported platforms. *AWSPowerShell* runs only on Windows PowerShell versions 3 through 5.1 (which is the last version of PowerShell for Windows). *AWSPowerShell.NETCore* requires PowerShell Core version 6 or higher, running on Windows, Linux, or macOS.

While having so much of the AWS API surface exposed in PowerShell modules is tremendously useful from an automation perspective, there is a downside. A single module with so many cmdlets takes a considerable time to load and also cannot take part in a very useful capability that PowerShell users have come to enjoy – tab key expansion of cmdlet names without needing to explicitly load the module (for the curious among you, this is because the PowerShell module manifest cannot handle these many cmdlet names listed in the manifest – this was found out the hard way).

Hence, AWS released a third variant of the tools, known informally as the modularized version. In this version, AWS vends one module per AWS service, and all follow a name pattern of AWS.Tools.*service-name*, for example, *AWS.Tools.EC2*, *AWS. Tools.S3*, *AWS.Tools.Rekognition*, and so on. There's also a shared dependency module, *AWS.Tools.Core*. This variant offers significant installation and load-time advantages over the *AWSPowerShell* and *AWSPowerShell.NETCore* modules. You can now install only the modules you need for the services you use, and because each module now exports only the cmdlets related to the parent service, you again get to enjoy tab expansion of names without having to explicitly import the module. You can use the modular variant with Windows PowerShell version 5.1, or PowerShell Core version 6 or higher on Windows, Linux, and macOS.

So which version should you use? From a cmdlet and service coverage perspective, there's no difference – all the versions contain the same set of cmdlets. The only difference is the packaging. If you value the startup time for your command-line shells on your own machine, then we suggest you adopt the AWS.Tools modular version. However, if you are running scripts on EC2 instances, then you can take advantage of the presence of the "monolithic" versions (on Windows and Linux instances) and continue to use those.

There is one specific use case where we strongly suggest using the modular variant – that of running AWS Lambda functions written in PowerShell. The per-service modules in the modular variant make an impact here, by first reducing the size of your function bundle (since you only reference the modules for services your Lambda function will call). Load time for those modules when your function runs is also faster – thus improving cold start times.

That's a brief history of how AWS came to be actively supporting three different but identical versions of the tools. Now, what can you do with them?

We're not going to use much PowerShell in this book (unless Steve gets his way), so for an in-depth exploration, we will refer you to *Pro PowerShell for Amazon Web Services* by Brian Beach (Apress, ISBN 978-1-4842-4850-8). But we will show you how to find your way around so any PowerShell-based examples later in the book are understandable (we'll assume you have whatever variant of the tools you've chosen to use already installed – you can find all three variants on the PowerShell Gallery).

The cmdlets, with few exceptions, map 1:1 to AWS service APIs, but with almost 9,000 available, how do you know which cmdlet to use for a given operation? PowerShell's built-in Get-Command cmdlet can only take you so far, so AWS provides a cmdlet named Get-AWSCmdletName to help. This cmdlet (implemented in the AWS.Tools.Core module, if you're using the modular variant) enables you to query for cmdlet names based on service, service API name, or AWS CLI command (see Chapter 3 for details on the AWS CLI).

Running Get-AWSCmdletName with no parameters emits the names, and owning service, of all cmdlets contained in the tools. The full listing is too large to include here, but Figure 2-20 shows a snippet of the output.

```
C:\> Get-AWSCmdletName

CmdletName                                   ServiceOperation                        ServiceName                                             ModuleName
----------                                   ----------------                        -----------                                             ----------
Add-IAMAAResourceTag                         TagResource                             AWS IAM Access Analyzer                                 AWS.Tools.AccessAnalyzer
Get-IAMAAAnalyzedResource                    GetAnalyzedResource                     AWS IAM Access Analyzer                                 AWS.Tools.AccessAnalyzer
Get-IAMAAAnalyzedResourceList                ListAnalyzedResources                   AWS IAM Access Analyzer                                 AWS.Tools.AccessAnalyzer
Get-IAMAAAnalyzer                            GetAnalyzer                             AWS IAM Access Analyzer                                 AWS.Tools.AccessAnalyzer
...
Start-IAMAAResourceScan                      StartResourceScan                       AWS IAM Access Analyzer                                 AWS.Tools.AccessAnalyzer
Update-IAMAAArchiveRule                      UpdateArchiveRule                       AWS IAM Access Analyzer                                 AWS.Tools.AccessAnalyzer
Update-IAMAAFinding                          UpdateFindings                          AWS IAM Access Analyzer                                 AWS.Tools.AccessAnalyzer
Add-PCACertificateAuthorityTag               TagCertificateAuthority                 AWS Certificate Manager Private Certificate Authority   AWS.Tools.ACMPCA
Get-PCACertificate                           GetCertificate                          AWS Certificate Manager Private Certificate Authority   AWS.Tools.ACMPCA
Get-PCACertificateAuthority                  DescribeCertificateAuthority            AWS Certificate Manager Private Certificate Authority   AWS.Tools.ACMPCA
...
Get-PCAPolicy                                GetPolicy                               AWS Certificate Manager Private Certificate Authority   AWS.Tools.ACMPCA
Import-PCACertificateAuthorityCertificate    ImportCertificateAuthorityCertificate   AWS Certificate Manager Private Certificate Authority   AWS.Tools.ACMPCA
...
```

Figure 2-20. *Sample output from running Get-AWSCmdletName*

Notice the name format of the cmdlets – for example, `Add-IAMAAResourceTag`, or `Get-PCACertificate`. In the original monolithic modules (AWSPowerShell and AWSPowerShell.NETCore), AWS needed to find a way to distinguish cmdlets for different services that would otherwise have the same name (we'll see why shortly). So AWS decided to prefix the noun portion of the cmdlet with a short prefix that indicated the service. Some prefixes are obvious – EC2, S3, etc. – while others less so.

A quick detour: if you want to see what the service prefixes are, or the AWS.Tools.* module that contains the cmdlets for that service, use the `Get-AWSPowerShellVersion` cmdlet with the `-ListServiceVersionInfo` parameter. This will emit the service name, prefix, implementing AWS.Tools module name, and the underlying assembly version from the AWS SDK for .NET (on which the tools depend). Figure 2-21 shows a small sample of the output.

```
C:\> Get-AWSPowershellVersion -ListServiceVersionInfo

AWS Tools for PowerShell
Version 4.1.8.0
Copyright 2012-2021 Amazon.com, Inc. or its affiliates. All Rights Reserved.

Amazon Web Services SDK for .NET
Core Runtime Version 3.5.2.5
Copyright Amazon.com, Inc. or its affiliates. All Rights Reserved.

Release notes: https://github.com/aws/aws-tools-for-powershell/blob/master/CHANGELOG.md

This software includes third party software subject to the following copyrights:
- Logging from log4net, Apache License
[http://logging.apache.org/log4net/license.html]


Service                                                   Noun Prefix Module Name                  SDK Assembly Version
-------                                                   ----------- -----------                  --------------------
AWS IAM Access Analyzer                                   IAMAA       AWS.Tools.AccessAnalyzer      3.5.2.2
AWS Certificate Manager Private Certificate Authority PCA             AWS.Tools.ACMPCA             3.5.2.5
Alexa For Business                                        ALXB        AWS.Tools.AlexaForBusiness    3.5.0.65
AWS Amplify                                               AMP         AWS.Tools.Amplify             3.5.3.29
Amplify Backend                                           AMPB        AWS.Tools.AmplifyBackend      3.5.0.21
Amazon API Gateway                                        AG          AWS.Tools.APIGateway          3.5.2.31
```

Figure 2-21. *Get-AWSPowerShellVersion output*

Now that we know how to find the noun prefix for a service, and the required AWS. Tools module if needed, let's return to the discussion on finding what cmdlets we need for a given service or service API.

First, to find the cmdlets for a service, and the service API(s) they map to, use `Get-AWSCmdletName -Service <service name or prefix>`, shown in Figure 2-22.

```
C:\> Get-AWSCmdletName -Service ec2

CmdletName                                     ServiceOperation                          ServiceName                          ModuleName
----------                                     ----------------                          -----------                          ----------
Add-EC2CapacityReservation                     CreateCapacityReservation                 Amazon Elastic Compute Cloud (EC2)   AWS.Tools.EC2
Add-EC2ClassicLinkVpc                          AttachClassicLinkVpc                      Amazon Elastic Compute Cloud (EC2)   AWS.Tools.EC2
Add-EC2InternetGateway                         AttachInternetGateway                     Amazon Elastic Compute Cloud (EC2)   AWS.Tools.EC2
Add-EC2NetworkInterface                        AttachNetworkInterface                    Amazon Elastic Compute Cloud (EC2)   AWS.Tools.EC2
Add-EC2SecurityGroupToClientVpnTargetNetwork   ApplySecurityGroupsToClientVpnTargetNetwork  Amazon Elastic Compute Cloud (EC2)   AWS.Tools.EC2
Add-EC2Volume                                  AttachVolume                              Amazon Elastic Compute Cloud (EC2)   AWS.Tools.EC2
Add-EC2VpnGateway                              AttachVpnGateway                          Amazon Elastic Compute Cloud (EC2)   AWS.Tools.EC2
Approve-EC2EndpointConnection                  AcceptVpcEndpointConnections              Amazon Elastic Compute Cloud (EC2)   AWS.Tools.EC2
```

Figure 2-22. *Querying cmdlets for a service*

For the -Service parameter, you can supply either the prefix, or the complete service name, or words from the service. Of course, the prefix or complete name yields the most precise results, whereas ad hoc words from the name may result in the output including cmdlets from other services that so happen to have those same words in their name.

The cmdlet's output shows the underlying service API. What if you know the API name but want to map back to the cmdlet? Use the -ApiOperation parameter instead, shown in Figure 2-23. This is a useful mode if you are reading the API reference material for a service.

```
C:\> Get-AWSCmdletName -ApiOperation describeinstances

CmdletName         ServiceOperation    ServiceName                          ModuleName
----------         ----------------    -----------                          ----------
Get-EC2Instance    DescribeInstances   Amazon Elastic Compute Cloud (EC2)   AWS.Tools.EC2
Get-GMLInstance    DescribeInstances   Amazon GameLift Service              AWS.Tools.GameLift
Get-OPSInstance    DescribeInstances   AWS OpsWorks                         AWS.Tools.OpsWorks
```

Figure 2-23. *Querying cmdlets by API name*

You'll see from Figure 2-23 that AWS can and does re-use the same API name across different services – this is the reason it was necessary to prefix the nouns in cmdlet names in the earlier monolithic modules! While this is no longer a technical requirement in the modular version, however, AWS chose to keep the principal going for backward compatibility reasons (and some users told them they like the approach, so who was AWS to argue?).

When reading AWS documentation and samples, you will also come across examples for the AWS CLI. You can find the corresponding cmdlet to the CLI example using the -AwsCliCommand parameter, shown in Figure 2-24.

```
C:\> Get-AWSCmdletName -AwsCliCommand "ec2 describe-instances"
WARNING: Parameter 'AwsCliCommand' is obsolete. This parameter is deprecated and will be removed in a future version. Use Service and ApiOperation instead.

CmdletName      ServiceOperation  ServiceName                       ModuleName
----------      ----------------  -----------                       ----------
Get-EC2Instance DescribeInstances Amazon Elastic Compute Cloud (EC2) AWS.Tools.EC2
```

Figure 2-24. *Translating AWS CLI command to cmdlet*

Note that this doesn't translate any arguments on the CLI command; it's purely a name translation. It's also marked as deprecated, although hopefully it will remain in the tools for some time. When specifying the AWS CLI command, you can omit the leading "aws" element, as shown, or specify it in full, for example, Get-AWSCmdletName -AwsCliCommand "aws ec2 describe-instances".

Now that you know how to find cmdlets, let's move on to running them, starting with how the cmdlets accept credentials and region data.

All cmdlets accept -AccessKey and -SecretKey parameters, but trust us, you'll soon tire of typing Get-EC2Instance -AccessKey AKIAIOSFODNN7EXAMPLE -SecretKey wJalrXUtnFEMI/K7MDENG/bPxRfiCYEXAMPLEKEY at the command line. Not to mention this is a security risk if you do it in a script and check it into a source code repository! Therefore, the cmdlets also accept a -ProfileName parameter that, as you might guess, takes the name of a credential profile on the local machine – exactly what we set up at the end of Chapter 1. So we could write the preceding example as Get-EC2Instance -ProfileName ProDotNETOnAWSBookUser.

If you use multiple credential profiles, then the -ProfileName parameter is your friend, but if you only have one, it's tedious to add it to every command. To solve this problem, you can either create a default profile, use environment variables, or set a shell or script default using Set-AWSCredential.

A default profile is nothing more than a credential profile with the name *default*. The AWS Tools for PowerShell, the AWS SDK for .NET, and several of the tools outlined in Chapter 3 will all automatically fall back to try and use a credential profile named default if they cannot find any overriding credentials, for example, from a command-line parameter.

If you choose an environment variable approach instead, then you need to create variables with the names AWS_ACCESS_KEY_ID and AWS_SECRET_ACCESS_KEY (there's also an AWS_SESSION_TOKEN variable if you are using temporary credentials).

You can use Set-AWSCredential to both create credential profiles and load credentials from a profile and set them ready for use in your shell or script. This latter ability means you don't need to specify any credentials for the service cmdlets. To create

a credential profile, specify the access and secret key materials and add the -StoreAs parameter, which takes the name of the credential profile to create (or update):
Set-AWSCredential -AccessKey AKIAIOSFODNN7EXAMPLE -SecretKey wJalrXUtnFEMI/
K7MDENG/bPxRfiCYEXAMPLEKEY -StoreAs MyOtherProfile.

To load credentials, for example, into your shell or at the start of a script, use the -ProfileName parameter along with the name of the profile or just the profile name itself. The commands in Listing 2-2 give identical results – the cmdlet reads the keys from the named credential profile and sets them active in the current shell or script.

Listing 2-2. Setting default credentials for a shell or script

```
Set-AWSCredential -ProfileName MyOtherProfile
Set-AWSCredential MyOtherProfile
```

Once run, in your shell or your script, you can run service cmdlets without specifying credentials, for example, Get-EC2Instance instead of Get-EC2Instance -ProfileName -MyOtherProfile.

As we explained in Chapter 1, resources for services belong to a region (IAM is a notable exception), and therefore, when running a command, you need to specify the region it should "run in." In other words, you need to specify which regional endpoint should be used by the command for the service. You do this with the -Region parameter, which takes the region code as its value (the cmdlets support tab expansion for this parameter), as shown in the example in Listing 2-3.

Listing 2-3. Specifying region for a cmdlet

```
Get-EC2Instance -Region us-west-2
```

As with credentials, you can set a default region, this time with the Set-DefaultAWSRegion cmdlet, shown in Listing 2-4.

Listing 2-4. Setting a default region

```
Set-DefaultAWSRegion us-west-2
```

If not supplied with an explicit -Region parameter, or the environment variable AWS_REGION is not set, cmdlets will automatically fall back to using the value set by Set-DefaultAWSRegion.

Finally, a word about running the tools on EC2 instances. Recall that Windows and Linux images provided by EC2 come with the monolithic versions of the tools pre-installed. In Chapter 1, we strongly cautioned against placing your credential files onto instances and instead use IAM Roles to vend credentials to code running on instances. This also works with the AWS Tools for PowerShell cmdlets. When run on an EC2 instance, which itself has a role assigned with a trust relationship, the cmdlets will automatically fetch temporary credentials via the role and can also determine the region in which the instance is running. There's no need to use Set-AWSCredential, or explicit key parameters or environment variables, or even the -Region parameter unless you need to override the credentials in the role – perhaps to make a call under a different account, or access a resource in another region.

Let's end this section with some sample commands (sans credential and region parameters) that we use frequently, shown in Listing 2-5.

Listing 2-5. Some useful commands from the AWS Tools for PowerShell

```
#=========================================================
# Examples for Amazon S3
#=========================================================

## List my buckets
Get-S3Bucket

## Upload a file to a bucket; in the first example, the object
## key is assigned from the file name. In the second, a specific
## key is assigned.
Write-S3Object -BucketName <bucket> -File .\myfile.jpg
Write-S3Object -BucketName <bucket> -File .\otherfile.jpg -Key file2

## Upload all files in a folder hierarchy (omit the -Recurse
## switch to upload just the files in the specified folder)
Write-S3Object -BucketName <bucket> -Folder .\temp -KeyPrefix
tempfiles -Recurse

## Read (download) a file
Read-S3Object -BucketName <bucket> -Key file -File .\otherfile.jpg

## Read (download) an entire 'folder' hierarchy
Read-S3Object -BucketName <bucket> -KeyPrefix tempfiles -Folder .
```

```
#=============================================================
# Examples for Systems Manager
#=============================================================

## Get all latest Windows Server 2019 EC2 image IDs (AMI IDs)
Get-SSMLatestEC2Image -Path ami-windows-latest

## Get latest Windows Server 2019 English EC2 image IDs
Get-SSMLatestEC2Image -Path ami-windows-latest -ImageName
*Windows*2019*English*

## Get specific Amazon Linux image ID in us-west-2 region
Get-SSMLatestEC2Image -Path ami-amazon-linux-latest -ImageName amzn-ami-
hvm-x86_64-ebs -Region us-west-2

# Read Parameter Store value, and details
# (add -WithDecryption $true for SecureString types)
Get-SSMParameter -Name /parameter/key/name

# Create (or update) a parameter value; -Type can be String,
# StringList, or SecureString
Write-SSMParameter -Name keyname -Type String -Value "abc" -Overwrite $true

#=============================================================
# Examples for Amazon EC2
#=============================================================

# Launch a new instance
New-EC2Instance -ImageId ami-1234567890abc -InstanceType m4.2xlarge

# Stop an instance
Stop-EC2Instance -InstanceId i-1234567890abc

# Start a stopped instance
Start-EC2Instance -InstanceId i-1234567890abc

# Terminate an instance
Remove-EC2Instance -InstanceId i-1234567890abc

# Stop all EC2 running instances, without confirmation
```

```
(Get-EC2Instance).Instances |
    Where { $_.State.Name -eq "running" } |
    Foreach { Stop-EC2Instance $_ -Force }
```

AWS SDK for .NET

Finally, we come to the AWS Software Development Kit (SDK) for .NET. AWS provides free SDKs for a variety of languages and tech stacks – Java, .NET, Python, JavaScript, PHP, and Ruby. All the SDKs share the same purpose – to expose the APIs of the various services in a language-idiomatic manner and make integrating AWS services into your application easy and convenient.

What does this mean? Well, instead of (for .NET) creating an HttpClient object, furnishing it with an endpoint URL, adding query parameters, wrangling an XML or JSON payload, and then dispatching it on the wire and subsequently handling the response (or failure), with the *AWS SDK for .NET,* calling an AWS service API is as simple as calling a method on an object.

That object is an instance of a client class provided by the SDK that represents the service. The class implements an interface containing the methods that make up the surface API area of the service. The method you call? It maps to the underlying service API. Data to pass into the call, or received? These are simply additional instances of classes in the SDK, or regular .NET classes (lists, dictionaries, etc.).

Does the service accept a JSON or XML payload (or some new format, awaiting discovery)? Does the service take parameters in a query string, or does it want them embedded in the body of the payload? How do I authenticate my call to the API? What URL endpoint do I need to call for a region? What happens if the call fails, or more data is available than a single call can return? If I encounter API request throttling, how do I handle that? Let's take each of these questions in turn.

- Does the service accept a JSON or XML payload?

    When you use the SDK, you simply don't need to care. You populate an instance of the "request" (and other related) class for the API in question, and the SDK takes care of marshaling that instance in the format the service requires (some AWS services use XML payloads; others take JSON). On receipt of the response, the SDK in turn marshals the data in the response back to .NET objects for your application to work with.

- Does the service take parameters in a query string, or the body?

  Again, you don't need to care. The API definitions for services specify where you must place the parameters into the request on the wire, and the SDKs again take care of handling this for you. So you set the parameter value into the request, or related objects, and the SDK will propagate the value into either the query parameters (properly encoded) or the body on your behalf.

- How do I authenticate my API call?

  We will cover how you specify programmatic credentials for the SDK from your application shortly, but briefly, the SDK uses the credentials to generate an authentication "signature"; the SDK then adds this signature to the request parameters. No need to compute this yourself.

- What URL endpoint do I need to call for a given region?

  As we mentioned in Chapter 1, AWS services for the most part are regional, so when you make an API call from your application to access a resource, you need to know what region the resource exists in. When you construct a service client object, you can specify the region it should be bound to or you can set this in your application configuration. If your application is running on a compute instance, the SDK can also automatically infer the region from metadata associated with the host environment.

- What happens if more data is available than the call yielded?

  AWS refers to this as "pagination." Additional properties in the response objects enable your code to detect whether you can (or need to) make further calls to yield more data, and properties in the request object enable your code to specify where the service should start yielding data from on subsequent calls. The SDK also contains specific *paginator* classes that handle the request and response "markers" for you, making your application code even simpler.

- How do I handle API throttling?

  For the most part, the SDK handles this for you. By this, we mean that the SDK will detect the throttling error returned by the service and automatically enter a "backoff-and-retry" cycle, by waiting for increasing periods of time before retrying the call. There is a limit to the number of times the SDK will do this on your behalf, however, before giving up and finally surfacing the throttling exception to your application – hence why we say "for the most part."

Hopefully, you can now see just how much work the SDKs do on your behalf and how they can greatly simplify calling web service APIs from within your application code. This makes it a snap to integrate using AWS services into your application.

Not convinced? Let's take a closer look with an example call. In this case, we'll construct a call to the DetectLabels API belonging to the *Amazon Rekognition* service. Amazon Rekognition's DetectLabels API performs object detection in image files, returning the found objects as "labels."

AWS distributes the SDK as a set of NuGet packages, one per service with an additional core package containing shared code (this is where all the marshaling, signature generation, and other helpers are located). These NuGet packages all follow a consistent naming pattern, *AWSSDK.servicename*.

First, we need to add a dependency on the AWSSDK.Rekognition package and namespace declarations to our source code file. Within the package, the Amazon.Rekognition namespace is where we will find the service interface and the service client class we will need. The Amazon.Rekognition.Model namespace is where we find the various classes and other types associated with the various API methods. For the top-level request and response types associated with API methods, the SDK uses the naming convention of *apiname*Request and *apiname*Response.

To begin, we construct an instance of the service class, shown in Listing 2-6 (we'll cover how to handle specifying credentials and region later).

Listing 2-6. Instantiating the service client object

```
using Amazon.Rekognition;
using Amazon.Rekognition.Model;
...
var client = new AmazonRekognitionClient();
```

Now that we have a client object, we can start to construct the request object that will convey our parameter settings for the API call.

Tip   You can find the `DetectLabels` API definition at `https://docs.aws.amazon.com/rekognition/latest/dg/API_DetectLabels.html`.

The .NET SDK's documentation for its request class (which corresponds to the API's input parameters) can be found at `https://docs.aws.amazon.com/sdkfornet/v3/apidocs/index.html?page=Rekognition/TDetectLabelsRequest.html&tocid=Amazon_Rekognition_Model_DetectLabelsRequest`, and the response class is documented at `https://docs.aws.amazon.com/sdkfornet/v3/apidocs/index.html?page=Rekognition/TDetectLabelsResponse.html&tocid=Amazon_Rekognition_Model_DetectLabelsResponse`.

From the API definition, we can see that the service expects our code to specify the location of an image file (in an Amazon S3 bucket) to analyze and two additional properties: a confidence level and a maximum number of labels to return. The confidence level sets a minimum confidence level; the service will disregard and not return labels for objects where the service's confidence in the detection is below this minimum.

For this example, let's assume I have already uploaded the image file to analyze to an S3 bucket named "myimagefiles" and that has the name (key) "koala_cuddle.jpg". Further, we want to set a minimum confidence level of 70% (the default is 55%), and we want the service to return only the top five labels.

To do this, we instantiate an object of type `DetectLabelsRequest` and fill in the appropriate members. We specify the location of the image in a subordinate type, also declared in the Model namespace, shown in Listing 2-7.

Listing 2-7. Populating the request parameters

```
var request = new DetectLabelsRequest
{
    Image = new Image
    {
        S3Object = new S3Object
```

```
        {
            Bucket = "myimagefiles",
            Name = "koala_cuddle.jpg"
        }
    },
    MaxLabels = 5,
    MinConfidence = 70
};
```

With the request object populated, we can now call the API and receive the labels, shown in Listing 2-8.

Listing 2-8. Calling the API and processing the returned data

```
var response = await client.DetectLabelsAsync(request);
foreach (var label in response.Labels)
{
    Console.WriteLine($"Found object {label.Name} with confidence {label.
    Confidence}%");
}
```

Listing 2-9 collects together the complete sequence. Figure 2-25 shows the image file and the output results.

Listing 2-9. The complete example code

```
using Amazon.Rekognition;
using Amazon.Rekognition.Model;
...
var client = new AmazonRekognitionClient();
var request = new DetectLabelsRequest
{
    Image = new Image
    {
        S3Object = new S3Object
        {
            Bucket = "myimagefiles",
```

```
        Name = "koala_cuddle.jpg"
    }
  },
  MaxLabels = 5,
  MinConfidence = 70
};
var response = await client.DetectLabelsAsync(request);
foreach (var label in response.Labels)
{
    Console.WriteLine($"Found object {label.Name} with confidence {label.
    Confidence}%");
}
```

Found object Person with confidence 99.154724%
Found object Glasses with confidence 98.0433%
Found object Tree with confidence 94.06231%
Found object Mammal with confidence 91.2783%
Found object Wildlife with confidence 89.92682%

Figure 2-25. *The input image and output results*

In the preceding example, we did not supply any credential or region settings. As the code stands, we could run it on an EC2 compute instance that's been associated with a role that has a trust relationship. That trust relationship makes available temporary credentials to code running on the instance, and the SDK would retrieve those credentials (and determine the region) automatically. But what if we wanted to run the code on our local machine and specify credentials and/or region?

We've already mentioned, possibly several times now, that putting "raw" credential keys into your code and/or configuration files is a bad practice, so although you can do this with the SDK, we're going to take a principled stand and refuse to show you how! Instead, we are going to focus on the named credential profile you set up at the end of

Chapter 1 and show you how you can reference that from your application code and configuration files, for use when running and debugging the code on your own machine. If (or when) you check the code into a public source code repository, you have the satisfaction of a "so what" response, as the name betrays nothing. Contrast this to the panic that (usually) ensues when you realize you just made your secret API keys public, for any provider, not just AWS!

When an application that uses the SDK runs (any AWS SDK, not just the .NET version), the SDK contains code that enables it to reach into the credential store files on the local machine to read actual credentials from the profiles the store file contains. In the case of the AWS SDK for .NET, this means two files: the encrypted .NET-specific store file mentioned earlier in this chapter and the shared text-format store file used with other SDKs and tools. All you need to do as a developer is provide the name of the credential profile to use, and there are a couple of ways to do this. You can specify the name of the credential profile at the point of instantiation of a service client object, or you can set the profile name into the application's configuration files.

Let's address configuration files first, starting with applications that use the .NET Framework. For these applications, one simple method is to add the name of the profile, and region, to the `appSettings` section of the application's `App.config` (or `Web.config`, for ASP.NET) file, shown in Listing 2-10.

Listing 2-10. Specifying profile name, and region, for local debug of .NET Framework applications

```
<configuration>
  <appSettings>
    <add key="AWSProfileName" value="ProDotNETOnAWSBookUser" />
    <add key="AWSRegion" value="us-west-2" />
  </appSettings>
</configuration>
```

AWS, however, recommends a small adjustment to this approach, which will be useful for users wanting to specify further configuration settings for the SDK. This change is to instead add an *aws* settings section to the file and register that section in the `configSections` element. You can see this approach in Listing 2-11. Note the change in the names of the keys used to identify the profile and region and that you specify them on the aws element itself. You can find more information on the section, and possible keys to use, at https://docs.aws.amazon.com/sdk-for-net/v3/developer-guide/net-dg-config-ref.html#net-dg-config-ref-elements-aws.

Listing 2-11. Registering and using an AWS settings section for App.config and Web.config files

```
<configuration>
...
  <configSections>
    <section name="aws" type="Amazon.AWSSection, AWSSDK.Core" />
  </configSections>
  <aws
    profileName="ProDotNETOnAWSBookUser"
    region="us-west-2">
    <!—other AWS-related SDK settings here ➔
  </aws>
...
</configuration>
```

You can use either of the preceding approaches for applications based on the .NET Framework, and for ASP.NET applications, you can take advantage of *Web.config transforms* (https://docs.microsoft.com/en-us/aspnet/web-forms/overview/deployment/visual-studio-web-deployment/web-config-transformations) to remove the section when packing your application for deployment.

.NET Core introduced a new configuration provider mechanism. To read AWS-related settings from this file, you need to add an application dependency on an AWS-provided NuGet package, *AWSSDK.Extensions.NetCore.Setup*, that integrates with the configuration provider mechanism. The package will read the settings data and inject it into the overall application configuration.

For ASP.NET Core applications, the settings file has the name appsettings.*.json. Why the *? This is because ASP.NET Core applications have the notion of a named environment when run (by default blank – meaning "production" and "development" but you can add your own) so we have some flexibility in creating environment-specific

versions of the file. You specify the name of the environment in a variable named
`ASPNETCORE_ENVIRONMENT`. If the variable is not set, the assumption is that the code is
running, or being packaged for, a *Production* environment, causing the `appsettings.`
`json` file to be read (or bundled with the built application code).

Setting the variable's value to *Development* causes the `appsettings.Development.`
`json` file to be bundled – you get the pattern. To debug our ASP.NET Core application
locally, we therefore modify the `appsettings.Development.json` file to contain our
profile name, and region, shown in Listing 2-12.

Listing 2-12. Setting profile, and region, in appsettings.Development.json for an
ASP.NET Core-based application for local development debugging

```
{
    "AWS":
    {
        "Profile": "ProDotNETOnAWSBookUser",
        "Region": "us-west-2"
    }
}
```

Setting a default region in the configuration file works for most applications we write,
as they only access resources in a single region. But for those applications that need to
access resources in regions other than where you deployed the application, or during
local debugging when information from a deployment host won't be available, the SDK
has convenient constructor overloads for service clients to accept a region indicator.
For cases where the application needs to "reach out" to a resource in another region,
construction of a service client targeting that region is simple, shown in Listing 2-13.

Listing 2-13. Creating a service client targeting a specific region

```
var region = Amazon.RegionEndpoint.USWest2;
var client = new AmazonRekognitionClient(region);
```

Before leaving this section, and chapter, it's worth noting that the AWS SDKs also
support a special name, *default*, that you can use for your credential profile. All AWS
SDKs, if they can find no override to the contrary (e.g., an explicit credential name in
an application configuration file, code, or an environment variable), will "fall back"
to probe for a credential profile with the name *default*. If found, the SDKs will load

credentials from this profile automatically, without you needing to set a profile name in configuration files, application code, or environment variables. This can be a convenient approach if you use a single account, and single IAM user, for your local development. We tend to work with multiple accounts and IAM users within each account, so for us, it tends to be more work to keep track of which set of credentials a profile named *default* is referencing at any given time, so we tend not to use it and prefer specifically named profiles.

There's a lot of capability in the SDK for resolving the location of, and loading credentials from profiles, and specifying region information for service client objects. For the full story, we recommend you look at the documentation at `https://docs.aws.amazon.com/sdk-for-net/v3/developer-guide/net-dg-config-creds.html`.

Summary

This concludes an initial outline of the .NET-specific (for the most part) tools that AWS provides. We looked at the IDE integration toolkits for Visual Studio, Visual Studio Code, and JetBrains Rider, and you'll be seeing more of the toolkits later in the book when we start to deploy code.

For developers that prefer command-line tools, or who are working with CI/CD scripting setups, we looked at the "dotnet" CLI extensions for AWS Lambda, AWS Elastic Beanstalk, and Amazon Elastic Container Service, and the AWS Tools for PowerShell. Finally, we examined the AWS SDK for .NET, which enables you to integrate the use of AWS services into your application code and which AWS also uses to write several of its own tools.

All these tools are free to download, install, and use. In the next chapter, we will take a look at some additional tools, also free, that you can use with your .NET applications on AWS.

CHAPTER 3

Additional Tools

Chapter 2 was all about the direct support that AWS offers to .NET developers through IDE toolkits, command-line tools and extensions, and the SDK. As .NET developers, you will likely spend the most time with these tools, as they directly support you in your day-to-day work. However, there are additional tools available that you can use, as needed, each of them giving you additional capability when interacting with AWS services.

In this chapter, we are going to go over a mixed set of tools – a few more CLIs to help you interact directly with AWS services, a few ways to create Infrastructure as Code so that you don't ever have to look at a console again, and lastly a cloud-based IDE that you can use when working with .NET Core. Do you have to know these tools to be able to write .NET applications that run on, or interact with, AWS? Honestly, probably not. Will they make your life easier and help you be productive? Probably, and that is why we are going to go over them here. Please note that we will be using CloudFormation or the Cloud Development Kit (CDK), both introduced in this chapter, as we move through the rest of the book to create and deploy infrastructure.

AWS Command Line Interface (AWS CLI)

The AWS Command Line Interface (AWS CLI) is an open source tool for managing AWS services – you got a preview of the type of work that you can do with command-line tools in the last chapter where we talked about the AWS Tools for PowerShell. There are two different versions of the tool available: AWS CLI version 1 and version 2. Version 2 is the most recent major release of the tool and supports all of the latest features. Version 1 is available for backward compatibility, so we highly recommend version 2 if you are going to install the CLI.

Just as with AWS Tools for PowerShell, the CLI allows you to manage your AWS services without needing to spend time in the console or other GUI. The AWS CLI is different from the PowerShell tools, however, because it is a complete tool and you

© William Penberthy and Steve Roberts 2023
W. Penberthy and S. Roberts, *Pro .NET on Amazon Web Services*,
https://doi.org/10.1007/978-1-4842-8907-5_3

don't have to worry about "modules"; instead, you have a nice, clean, purpose-built command-line tool for managing AWS services. You can get OS-specific instructions for downloading, installing, and verifying your installation of the AWS CLI at `https://aws.amazon.com/cli/`.

Once you have downloaded, installed, and verified your CLI, you will need to configure it. As was briefly mentioned in Chapter 2, the CLI will initially look for a profile section named "default" in your local credentials file. This is the profile that will be used when running the CLI if another profile is not used. If you have completed the steps in the previous chapters, then you should have a credentials file whose content looks something like this:

```
[ProDotNETOnAWSBookUser]
aws_access_key_id = your-access-key-here
aws_secret_access_key = your-secret-access-key-here
```

Since the CLI looks for the "default" profile by default, using a differently named profile means that you will have to pass in that profile name as part of your command. If you don't, the CLI will not be able to authenticate. The following code (ran at a Windows command prompt) shows the output if you (1) do not have a default profile and (2) do not provide a named profile:

```
C:\Source>aws s3 ls

Unable to locate credentials. You can configure credentials by running "aws configure".

C:\Source>
```

Passing in a named profile is done with the *–profile* parameter as follows:

```
aws s3 ls –profile ProDotNETOnAWSBookUser
```

However, this approach will require that you always include a value for the profile that you want to use. To get around that requirement, you can either create a default profile or set your local system so that it uses a different profile than "default" as its expected value. Our recommendation is to set your local AWS profile by running the following commands:

on Windows:

```
setx AWS_PROFILE ProDotNETOnAWSBookUser
```

on Linux or macOS:

```
export AWS_PROFILE=ProDotNETOnAWSBookUser
```

You will then need to exit your command prompt session and restart (if on Windows), as this command does NOT affect any command shell that is already running. After closing and opening a new command prompt, re-running the command to list all S3 buckets, `aws s3 ls`, will return the list of Amazon S3 buckets that you already have running.

Now that we have your local CLI configured with the correct credential, let's take a more detailed look at the commands. You have already seen the command to get a list of the S3 buckets several times, so let us break that command down further. The first part, `aws`, is the program that will be run. The next part is the AWS service with which you wish to interact, which, in the case of this example, is `s3`. The last part is the command that you would like to run on that service, which was `ls` for "list". That means when you think about the commands that you may want to run, they will follow

```
aws service-name command arguments
```

Every service has its own list of commands that it expects; running the `ls` command using `ec2` – `aws ec2 ls` – for example, will fail because it is not a recognized command. You can get a list of the available commands for a service by using the universal command `help`, so to get a list of available commands for running against the S3 service, you would use the command `aws s3 help`. If you want more detail on a particular command, append the command that you would like to know more about with "help": `aws s3 ls help`. Doing this will provide you information about the command as well as a listing of optional values that you can use when working with that command.

Let's end this section with some sample commands that we use frequently, just as we did with the PowerShell tools in Chapter 2, shown in Listing 3-1.

Listing 3-1. Some useful commands from the AWS CLI

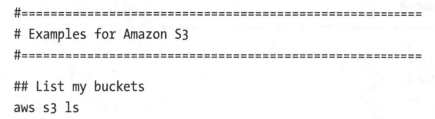

```
#==========================================================
# Examples for Amazon S3
#==========================================================

## List my buckets
aws s3 ls
```

```
## Upload a file to a bucket. The source file name can be a file ## stored
locally or it can be stored in an S3 bucket.
## When interacting with an S3 bucket, use the following format:
## s3://BucketName/FileName
## aws s3 cp sourcefilename destinationname
aws s3 cp example.txt s3://mybucket/example.txt

## Upload all files in a folder hierarchy, the
## sourcedirectoryname to an S3 bucket, destinationbucket
aws s3 cp sourcedirectoryname destinationbucket --recursive

## Downloading a file is done by using the S3 bucket as the
## sourcefilename and the destinationname as your download
## location.
aws s3 cp sourcefilename destinationname

#=========================================================
# Examples for Amazon EC2
#=========================================================

# Get a list of all available AMIs, filtered by owner
aws ec2 describe-images --owners self amazon

# Stop an instance
aws ec2 stop-instances --instance-ids i-1234567890abc

# Start a stopped instance
aws ec2 start-instances --instance-ids i-1234567890abc

# Terminate an instance
aws ec2 terminate-instances --instance-ids i-1234567890abc

#=========================================================
# Examples for DynamoDB
#=========================================================

# Get a list of tables
aws dynamodb list-tables

# Create a new table
```

```
aws dynamodb create-table --table-name DogBreeds --attribute-definitions
AttributeName=BreedName,AttributeType=S --key-schema AttributeName=BreedN
ame,KeyType=HASH --provisioned-throughput ReadCapacityUnits=5,WriteCapac
ityUnits=5

# Add an item to a table - notice how it requires that contained
# quotes are escaped with the "/" character
aws dynamodb put-item --table-name DogBreeds --item "{\"BreedName\":{\"S\":
\"Mutt\"}}" --return-consumed-capacity TOTAL

# Query an item in the table - notice how it requires that
# contained quotes are escaped with the "/" character
aws dynamodb query --table-name DogBreeds --key-conditions "{\"BreedName
\":{\"AttributeValueList\": [{\"S\": \"Mutt\"}],\"ComparisonOperator\":
\"EQ\"}}"
```

AWS CloudFormation

Chapter 1 contained a brief introduction to the concept of Infrastructure as Code (IaC) and mentioned AWS CloudFormation. Let's go a little deeper into that topic now. It may feel a little out of place to be talking about infrastructure in a book aimed at .NET developers, but the ability to easily, quickly, and cheaply configure and start new resources in the cloud has moved some of the responsibility for infrastructure management closer and closer to the developer. At many companies, for example, the responsibility for creating a deployment pipeline has moved into the development team, which means that at some point, you may be the one creating the resources on which your application will run.

One of the biggest reasons that developers have become responsible for their own infrastructure is because it allows the infrastructure to be part of the deployment and testing process along with the code. Think about that for a minute. You test the infrastructure before it goes into production. Do you remember those late-night sessions trying to figure out why your application is behaving differently on your pre-production server than it was on your test server? Deploying your infrastructure helps avoid that problem, and IaC makes it easy for us developers to manage that system. Your infrastructure just becomes code. We like code.

We digress, so let's get back to CloudFormation. CloudFormation is a service that provides developers and businesses an easy way to create a collection of related AWS (and third-party) resources. CloudFormation supports the provisioning and management of those resources in an orderly and predictable fashion. In general, you create a template that describes those resources, and then CloudFormation manages the provisioning and configuring of the resources defined within the template as a single unit, known as a *stack*. These stacks are your basic cluster of resources, with a CloudFormation template representing each stack. You create, update, and delete those resources by creating, updating, or deleting the template.

A JSON CloudFormation template that creates a very simple Amazon S3 bucket is shown as follows:

```
{
    "Resources": {
        "S3Bucket": {
            "Type": "AWS::S3::Bucket",
            "Properties": {
                "BucketName": "prodotnetonawssimplebucket"
            }
        }
    }
}
```

This same template, but in YAML:

```
Resources:
  S3Bucket:
    Type: 'AWS::S3::Bucket'
    Properties:
      BucketName: prodotnetonawssimplebucket
```

Running one of these templates in CloudFormation would create an S3 bucket with the name of "prodotnetonawssimplebucket" (each S3 bucket name must be globally unique across all accounts, so you may have to change it) when processed by CloudFormation. Let's do that now.

Using the Console for Creating CloudFormation Stacks

We will start by creating the stack in the console. To do so, log into the console with the IAM user you created in Chapter 1. Once you are in the console, go to the CloudFormation service. You can find it in the *Management & Governance* section of the services list or you can use the top search bar. From the service home page, select the *Create stack* button as shown in Figure 3-1.

Figure 3-1. *AWS CloudFormation service home page*

This will take you to the *Create Stack* page. This page provides three different options to help you prepare a CloudFormation template: *Template is ready, Use a sample template*, and *Create template in Designer*. Selecting the "Template is ready" option allows you to either upload a template file from your local machine or enter an Amazon S3 URL for when your CloudFormation template is already stored in the cloud. Strangely enough, the "Use a sample template" option allows you to choose from a list of samples. These samples include options such as *LAMP Stack,* which will create a single Linux EC2 instance that is pre-installed with Apache, MySQL, and PHP, and there are many other sample stacks available, such as a *Ruby on Rails stack* and a *WordPress blog stack*. You have the ability to choose each of these samples to be deployed in a single AZ or multiple AZs. You can use these samples as a starting point or just to see some more advanced options for a CloudFormation template. The multi-AZ Lamp Stack, for example, is created by a template that is 515 lines long and provides for the creation of a group of auto-scaling web servers that run post-startup scripts to install the Apache Web Server, MySQL, and PHP as well as create all supporting load balancers and necessary security groups.

The last option is the *Create template in Designer* option. The AWS CloudFormation Designer is a nifty graphic tool that allows you to create, view, and edit CloudFormation templates. The Designer allows you to use a drag-and-drop interface to create the resources where you can then edit the properties of those resources as necessary. You can also work with pre-created templates in this area without having to upload them to S3 or CloudFormation. In our case, since we already have the code for a template, select the *Create template in Designer* option. This will display the "Create template in Designer" section as shown in Figure 3-2.

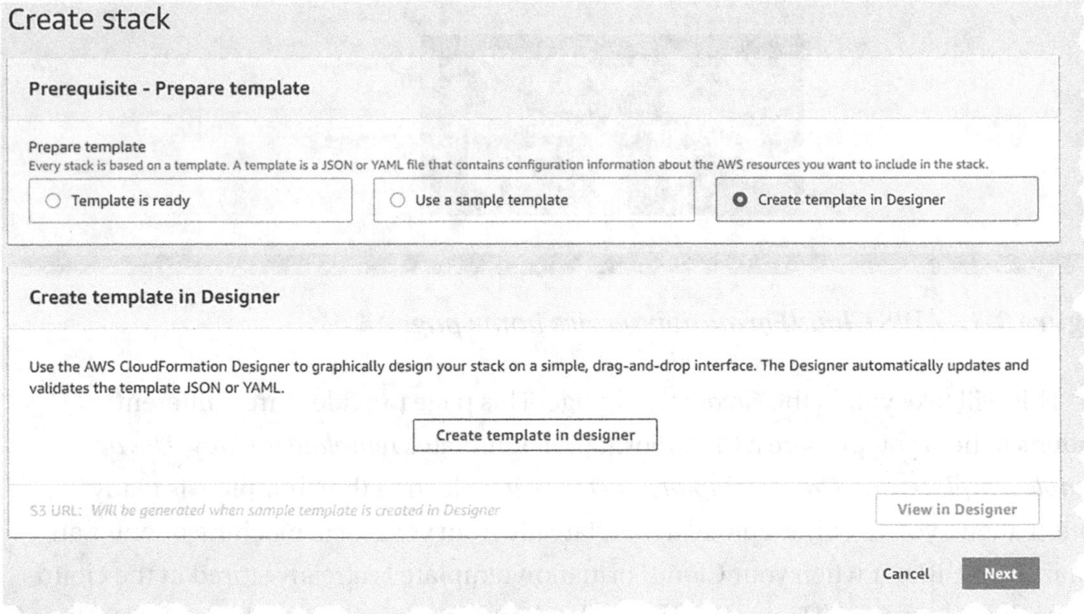

Figure 3-2. *Creating a CloudFormation stack*

Click the *Create template in designer* button. This will bring up the CloudFormation Designer as shown in Figure 3-3.

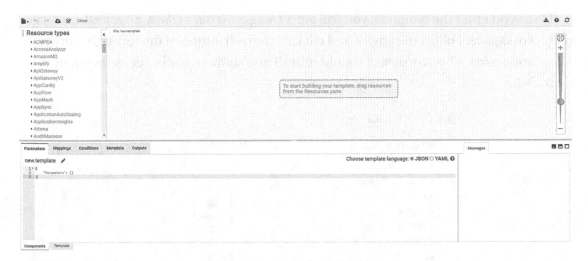

Figure 3-3. *Using the Designer to create a CloudFormation template*

The upper-left area is the list of Resource types that can be drag and dropped onto the template display area. A quick scroll through the list will show that there are a *lot* of different options to choose from, including compute resources, networking resources, machine learning resources, IoT services, and dozens of other options. Using these resources is as simple as expanding a resource type and then selecting one of the resources and dragging them to the workspace.

The lower-left area may be a little confusing at first glance. There are two tabs for looking at resources: *Components* and *Template*. These tabs are on the lower part of the screen. The Components tab displays details, the five tabs that are visible by default, about the selected component. Selecting the Template view hides the Component tabs and allows you to directly enter the template. In this instance, select the Template lower tab and copy in the desired version (JSON or YAML) and ensure that the appropriate template language is selected as shown in Figure 3-4.

Figure 3-4. *Adding template to designer*

Once you enter the template, you will get a *Designer is out of date, hit refresh* message in the workspace. Follow the advice and click the refresh button in the top-right corner of the workspace. This workspace should refresh and show an S3Bucket as shown in Figure 3-5.

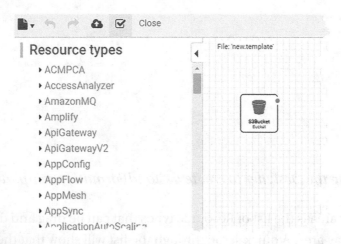

Figure 3-5. *S3 Resource added from a template*

The next step is to create the stack based on the template. Click the *Create stack* icon in the toolbar – it looks like a cloud with an up arrow. This will bring you back to the Create Stack window where you can see that the template was saved into an S3 bucket, and the bucket details are prepopulated as shown in Figure 3-6.

Create stack

Prerequisite - Prepare template

Prepare template
Every stack is based on a template. A template is a JSON or YAML file that contains configuration information about the AWS resources you want to include in the stack.

- ● Template is ready
- ○ Use a sample template
- ○ Create template in Designer

Specify template
A template is a JSON or YAML file that describes your stack's resources and properties.

Template source
Selecting a template generates an Amazon S3 URL where it will be stored.

- ● Amazon S3 URL
- ○ Upload a template file

Amazon S3 URL

https://s3.us-east-2.amazonaws.com/cf-templates-q9xfja8nyfar-us-east-2/2021065yVa-new.templatejmoujlze8in

Amazon S3 template URL

S3 URL: https://s3.us-east-2.amazonaws.com/cf-templates-q9xfja8nyfar-us-east-2/2021065yVa-new.templatejmoujlze8in   **View in Designer**

Cancel   **Next**

***Figure 3-6.** Template available in an S3 bucket*

Click the *Next* button. This will take you to Step 2, where you can specify stack details such as the **Stack name** and **Parameters**. Your stack name can only include letters, numbers, and dashes; no other characters are permitted. The Parameters section lists any parameters that you may have defined in your template and allows you to input custom values when creating or updating a stack. Enter "SimpleS3Bucket" as the stack name and click the *Next* button. This will bring you to Step 3, where you can configure stack options.

Among your options when configuring your stack are tags, permissions, and various advanced options such as rollback configuration, notification options, and stack creation options. Normally, we would, at a minimum, configure the stack's permissions. In this case, however, leave the defaults as they are and click the *Next* button. This will bring you to a review screen where you can review, and edit as needed, the stack details and options. Click the *Create* button to create the CloudFormation stack.

This will bring you to a page that lists all of your stacks on the left, with the stack that you just created selected, and the event list for that selected stack. Unless AWS is feeling especially perky when you are doing this, you will most likely see them in a blue **CREATE_IN_PROGRESS** status as shown in Figure 3-7.

Figure 3-7. *CloudFormation stack being created*

You can click the refresh button on the Events tab to watch the progress. In this case, since we are only creating a single S3 bucket, you will see that it goes pretty quickly. Once the status changes to **CREATE_COMPLETE**, the stack has been saved and the resources created. Figure 3-8 shows the S3 buckets created during this process in the AWS Toolkit for Rider, with the bucket called *prodotnetonawssimplebucket* being the resource that the stack created and the other bucket, prefixed with *cloudformation,* being the S3 bucket created when we loaded and saved the template in the Designer.

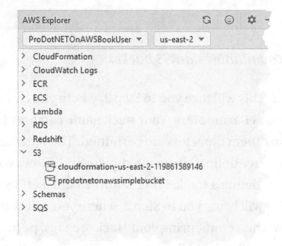

Figure 3-8. *S3 buckets created during stack creation*

While you can create and manage your CloudFormation templates in the console, the different toolkits also allow you a measure of visibility and control over CloudFormation stacks. The AWS Toolkit for Visual Studio Code, for example, permits you to view and delete the stack but does not currently display details about the stack.

The AWS Toolkit for JetBrains Rider allows you to view and delete the stack but also gives you the ability to see the Events, Resources, and Outputs from a CloudFormation stack as shown in Figure 3-9.

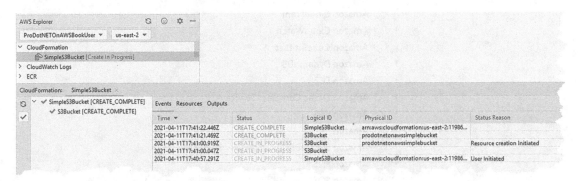

Figure 3-9. *Viewing a CloudFormation stack in JetBrains Rider*

The AWS Toolkit for Visual Studio provides even more support for CloudFormation as it allows you to create stacks by uploading a template and stepping through the creation process. Let's take a quick look at that now.

Using the AWS Toolkit for Visual Studio for Creating CloudFormation Stacks

After you open Visual Studio and the AWS Explorer, expand the *AWS CloudFormation* node, and you should see the CloudFormation template that was just loaded as shown in Figure 3-10.

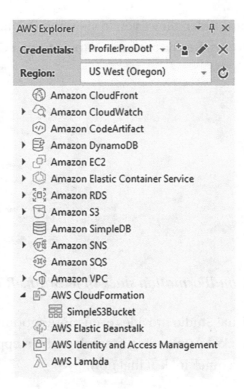

Figure 3-10. *Viewing the created CloudFormation stack in Visual Studio*

If you created the stack earlier but don't see it now, make sure that you are viewing the appropriate region; CloudFormation stacks are on a per-region basis and are not visible outside of their home region.

Note   There is an exception to this per-region basis for CloudFormation templates when you have a stack in a central account that provisions child stacks into another account in two different Regions. You can get more information on these kinds of approaches at `https://aws.amazon.com/blogs/infrastructure-and-automation/multiple-account-multiple-region-aws-cloudformation/`.

Right-clicking on the AWS CloudFormation node will bring up a submenu that allows you to *"Create stack."* Clicking that menu item brings up the Create Stack wizard as shown in Figure 3-11.

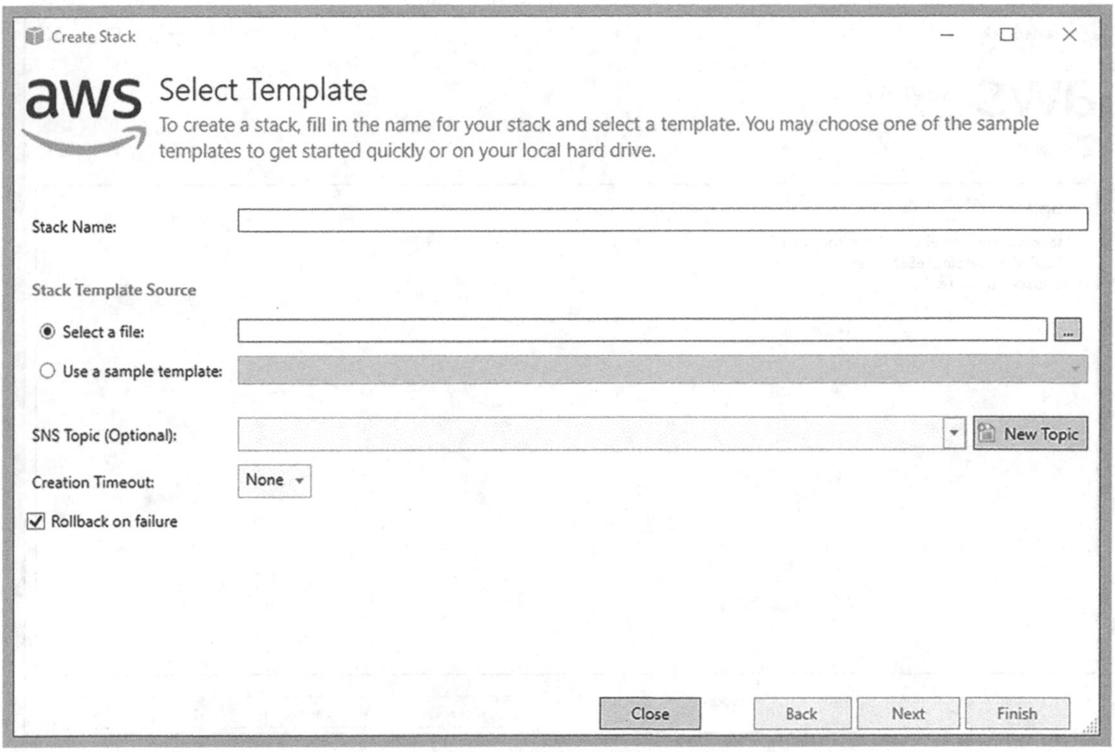

Figure 3-11. *Creating a CloudFormation stack using AWS Toolkit for*
Visual Studio

The wizard allows you to name the stack and either select a template from your local computer or use a sample template. You can also set a timeout for stack creation and choose whether or not you want the process to roll back on a failure. We recommend you keep these values as set by default. Click the *Next* button to proceed once you have entered a stack name; we used "SimpleBucketFromVisualStudio" and selected a template file. This will bring you to the Review screen as shown in Figure 3-12.

Figure 3-12. *Confirming a new CloudFormation stack in AWS Toolkit for Visual Studio*

Once you have confirmed the information, click the *Finish* button. This will bring up the stack details window where you will be able to watch the creation events flow in, as shown in Figure 3-13.

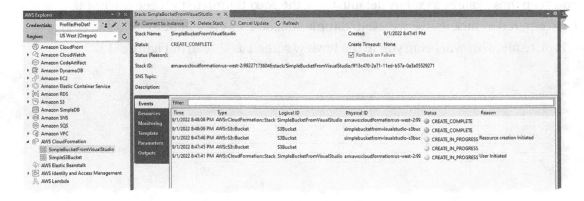

Figure 3-13. *Admiring your newly created CloudFormation stack in AWS Toolkit for Visual Studio*

As you saw, the stack creation process using the AWS Toolkit for Visual Studio is very simple; you do not get the same type of options that you get when working through the console. However, if you already have a template, it is an easy way to load the stack and create the appropriate resources.

AWS CloudFormation Project in Visual Studio

For those times when you do not have a handy CloudFormation template around but are using Visual Studio and have the AWS Toolkit for Visual Studio installed, there is the AWS CloudFormation Project. This project template is not available in Rider or in VS Code.

You create a CloudFormation project the same way that you would any other project in Visual Studio, but the "New Project wizard" is different. Once you have named the project and defined where the files should be stored, the next step is to choose whether you would like to create the project with an empty template, whether you would like to create from an existing AWS CloudFormation stack, or whether you want to define the new project upon a sample template, as shown in Figure 3-14.

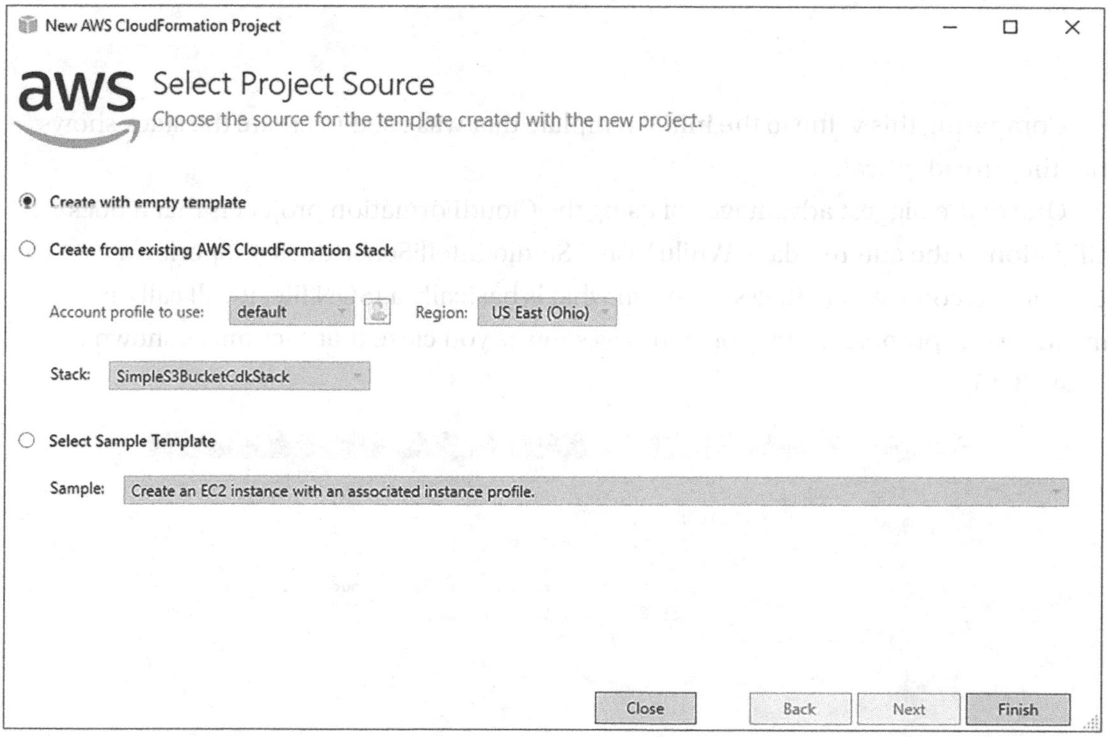

Figure 3-14. *Creating a new project based on the CloudFormation template*

At the time of writing, the set of sample templates available in this process is different from the available sample templates that are available in the console and are obviously much older as they include options such as "SharePoint Foundation 2010 running on Microsoft Windows Server 2008 R2." Thus, we don't recommend using them unless you are a historian! In this case, we will choose the *Create from existing AWS CloudFormation Stack* option and select the **SimpleS3Bucket** stack that we created earlier. This will create a *.template file within the project that contains the CloudFormation template of the stack, which, in this case, looks like the following:

```
{
    "Resources": {
        "S3Bucket": {
            "Type": "AWS::S3::Bucket",
            "Properties": {
                "BucketName": "prodotnetonawssimplebucket"
            }
        }
    }
}
```

Comparing this value to the initial template that was used to create the stack shows that they are identical.

One of the biggest advantages of using the CloudFormation project is that it does validation of the entered data. While Visual Studio IntelliSense does not perform read-ahead context-sensitive support in what is basically a JSON file, it will call out any incorrect property names or values as soon as you close that section, as shown in Figure 3-15.

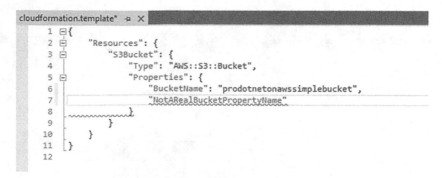

Figure 3-15. *Invalid resource property in a CloudFormation project*

Using a CloudFormation project template will make it easier to create and update stacks when working by hand. However, there are other features that are available when using this project, and you can see this if you right-click on the template file displayed in the Solution Explorer as shown in Figure 3-16.

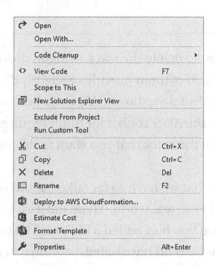

Figure 3-16. *Submenu on *.template file in the Solution Explorer*

The new actions that are available at the time of this writing are *Deploy to AWS CloudFormation,* which deploys the template to the cloud using the same process that we just went over; *Estimate Cost,* which takes you to the Simple Cost Calculator that will help you get some understanding of projected costs for the resources within the template; and *Format Template,* which will neatly rearrange your template to maximize readability. Remember, each template represents a single deployable stack, so you can take all of these actions on any template file, and a CloudFormation project can have any number of files, each representing a single stack.

Deleting CloudFormation Stacks

As mentioned earlier, all of the toolkits for the major .NET IDEs provide you the ability to delete a stack. Obviously, you can also do it through the online console. Deleting a stack will generally also delete the provisioned resources unless the resources, as part of your template, have been configured to be retained when the stack is deleted. We want you to be able to clean up your resources as you go, so none of the resources that you work with in this book will be so configured.

Note   You can configure a stack so that it cannot be easily deleted through the AWS console. You can do this during creation (from the *Advanced options* in the wizard) or when the stack is running by going into the *Stack actions* option of the stack details pane.

The IDE toolkits allow you to delete the stack by right-clicking on the stack and selecting the *Delete* option. Each of them provides a slightly different confirmation routine; the AWS Toolkits for Visual Studio and VS Code both display a yes/no confirmation dialogue, while the AWS Toolkit for Rider requires a confirmation step where you type in the name of the stack that you want to delete before it will process the deletion.

While deleting the stacks that we have so far talked about is painless, you will find that it is not always like that in the real world. There are a lot of different cases when your delete may fail. For example, if you had added a file to the S3 bucket that we created earlier, then deleting that stack would have failed, as shown in Figure 3-17, because the bucket was not empty.

Figure 3-17.   *Deleting CloudFormation stack in console failed because S3 bucket was not empty*

Other resources will have similar requirements in that they must be empty before the resource can be deleted. Other reasons that impact your ability to delete a stack can include the following:

- The user you are using does not have the appropriate IAM permissions needed to delete the resources that are defined in the stack. This is in addition to needing the appropriate IAM permissions to allow for the deletion of the CloudFormation template itself.

- When termination protection is enabled. This will also surface if you have nested stacks and one of the root stacks has termination protection enabled.

You should reach out directly to AWS support – through the Support link in the top-right corner of the console – if you are still unable to delete a template even after checking the cases listed previously.

CloudFormation templates are a very powerful way to manage resources in your AWS account. They allow you the ability to define the characteristics of your resources and group them together into a CloudFormation stack. These stacks can then be managed together, as a group. However, as you saw, the templates themselves can be complex to work with. Imagine trying to build out a virtual private cloud (VPC) with a couple of load-balanced servers, custom security groups, S3 buckets, and a database using either JSON or YAML. Yes, it can be done, but the experience sounds pretty painful, even if you are using a Visual Studio CloudFormation project template and IntelliSense. Thankfully there are CloudFormation extensions to help you.

AWS Cloud Development Kit

The first of these extensions that we will talk about is the AWS Cloud Development Kit (CDK). Let's look at what it is and why it exists. Then we'll look at how it's used.

Understanding the CDK

The CDK brings the "C" part of that phrase even closer to the developer as you can think of the CDK as a language abstraction over CloudFormation with some bells and whistles added. With the CDK, for example, you can write code and run a process that translates that code into a CloudFormation template. You can then deploy that template from the

CDK or use the created CloudFormation template as we did earlier, or within your CI/CD process. The CDK has first-class support for TypeScript, JavaScript, Python, Java, and C#. As .NET developers, we will focus on C#.

Using the CDK

The CDK offers you the ability to write C# code that creates resources. Remember that JSON that defined the S3 bucket we used earlier? That template is one of the simplest ones possible to create. Imagine, instead, needing to use JSON or YAML to configure a much more complex stack? Such as that 515-line-long template that managed the multi-AZ LAMP stack? Yeah, ick – we don't want to do that either. This is what the CDK offers you.

The first step is to install the CDK. While the CDK supports C#, the tool itself was written in Node.js, so you will need to install that first. If you do not already have Node. js available on your machine, you can download and install the latest version at `https://nodejs.org/en/download/`. Once you have confirmed that Node.js is installed and working on your machine, you can use the Node Package Manager, *npm*, to install the CDK:

```
npm install -g aws-cdk
```

Now that you have the CDK installed, let's take our first step by writing the code that will create an S3 bucket just like we worked with in the CloudFormation section of this chapter. The easiest way to create a C# CDK project is to use the CDK command line. Since we recommend that each CDK application be in its own directory, the first step is to open a command-line prompt and move to the directory in which you want to create your first CDK application. In our case, we created a directory called "SimpleS3BucketCdk".

Once in that directory, your next step is to initialize the CDK application using the **cdk init** command. This command creates a C# project and solution using a predefined template that uses the name of the directory in which you are running the command. There are two templates currently available for C# users of the CDK. The first, and the one we use in the following, is *app*. This template is an empty CDK project. The other template, *sample-app*, is an example CDK application containing a few very simple constructs. We haven't talked about any of those constructs yet, which is why we went with the empty one – *app*.

```
cdk init app --language csharp
```

You can open the created solution in your IDE of choice. Figure 3-18 shows the solution opened in Visual Studio. The name of the solution and project show that the preceding command was run in a directory named *SimpleS3BucketCdk*.

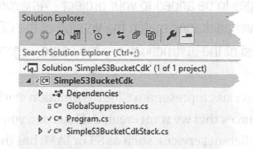

Figure 3-18. *Empty C# project created from the CDK*

There are two main files created: *Program.cs* and *SimpleS3BucketCdkStack.cs*. A brief look into the *Program* class file shows that it is instantiating an **Amazon.CDK.App** class, a *SimpleS3BucketCdkStack* class, and running a command on the instantiated *App*. When creating a simple stack, like what we are going to do, there are no changes to this file. Instead, let's focus on the *SimpleS3BucketCdkStack* class as shown in the following:

```
using Amazon.CDK;

namespace SimpleS3BucketCdk
{
    public class SimpleS3BucketCdkStack : Stack
    {
        internal SimpleS3BucketCdkStack(Construct scope, string id,
        IStackProps props = null) : base(scope, id, props)
        {
            // The code that defines your stack goes here.
        }
    }
}
```

This initial class demonstrates some of the underpinning of the CDK. The generated class inherits from the **Amazon.CDK.Stack** class, which, as you can probably guess, represents a single AWS CloudFormation stack. With this class representing the stack, it would be easy to assume that the code that will build resources belongs in this class – and you would be right. However, let's talk about what's going on here before we jump into the code.

101

Note   The instructions for NuGet packages below refer to working with version 1 of the CDK. For CDK version 2, per-service NuGet packages were retired in favor of needing just 2 packages to be added to your project - *Amazon.CDK.Lib* and *Constructs*. Use whichever packages match the version of the CDK you have installed (don't mix them). The rest of the instructions are the same, regardless of CDK version.

We mentioned that this class represents a CloudFormation stack and will end up being a container for resources that we want created. However, you cannot yet create these resources as each of the different services, such as S3 or IAM, has their own NuGet package that contains the logic to create those resources. Each of these packages follows the same pattern – **Amazon.CDK.AWS.ServiceName**. You can see what this looks when looking at the solution NuGet screen and filtering for *amazon.cdk.aws* as shown in Figure 3-19.

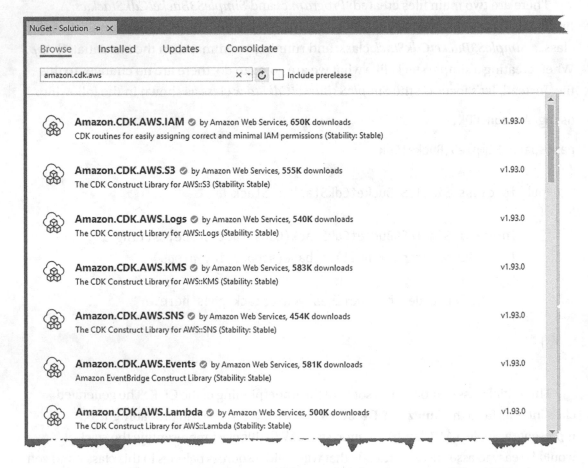

Figure 3-19. *Service-specific NuGet packages for the version 1 of the CDK*

Thus, since we will be creating another simple S3 bucket, we will add the S3 NuGet package, **Amazon.CDK.AWS.S3**, to the project and then go in and add the appropriate statement for that library. Next, simply add a bucket as shown in the following:

```
internal SimpleS3BucketCdkStack(Construct scope, string id, IStackProps
props = null) : base(scope, id, props)
{
    var bucket = new Bucket(this, "ProDotNetOnAws-CDKDemo", new BucketProps
    {
        BucketName = "prodotnetonaws-cdk-demo-bucket"
    });

}
```

At this point, we have created the code that will create a simple S3 bucket with a name of "prodotnetonaws-cdk-demo-bucket", just like what we used in the CloudFormation section.

Let's look further at the Bucket constructor. It is expecting three parameters: the stack, a string id, and a nullable array of properties made up of a bundle of key/value pairs. These properties are used to configure the created resource. All of the CDK construct library classes are instantiated with the same set of parameters, with the only difference being the class used for the property array, which, in the preceding example, is *BucketProps*. We passed in the stack by using the keyword *this*, which refers to the current instance of the class – remember that the current class is based upon a stack. We then gave the bucket a resource id by passing in the string "ProDotNetOnAws-CDKDemo" and then creating a set of bucket properties using the class *BucketProps*. The resource id that we are using here may seem a little odd in that you won't really see it in the resource you are creating; once created, you will be using the BucketName property to access this resource. However, if you need to refer to this resource within some other resource, you will be using the resource id to define that reference rather than using the name of the bucket. Since we are using a defined type, *BucketProps*, IntelliSense will provide guidance on the available properties that can be set. Once you have added your S3 bucket, you can build the application to manually check for errors.

The next step is to "synthesize," or create from code, the AWS CloudFormation template. You do this by returning to the command line where you ran the *init* command and then running *cdk synth*. During this synthesize process, a folder named **cdk.out** is created with several files, including a file with an extension of *template*. If you open this template file, you will see that it is a JSON CloudFormation template that looks somewhat similar to the ones we worked with earlier. However, as you can see in Figure 3-20, there are some differences.

```
SimpleS3BucketCdkStack.template.json  ⊕  ✕
Schema: <No Schema Selected>
 1   ⊟{
 2   ⊟  "Resources": {
 3   ⊟    "ProDotNetOnAwsCDKDemo4442DC2A": {
 4          "Type": "AWS::S3::Bucket",
 5   ⊟      "Properties": {
 6            "BucketName": "prodotnetonaws-cdk-demo-bucket"
 7          },
 8          "UpdateReplacePolicy": "Retain",
 9          "DeletionPolicy": "Retain",
10   ⊟      "Metadata": {
11            "aws:cdk:path": "SimpleS3BucketCdkStack/ProDotNetOnAws-CDKDemo/Resource"
12          }
13        },
14   ⊟    "CDKMetadata": {
15          "Type": "AWS::CDK::Metadata",
16   ⊟      "Properties": {
17            "Analytics": "v2:deflate64:H4sIAAAAAAAACiWMMQ/CIBSEf0t3+igyOZio6NqhGveGPhMkQgMPHQj/XbC54S757k7AXsLQHedv7PViedY+IOQbzdo)
18          },
19   ⊟      "Metadata": {
20            "aws:cdk:path": "SimpleS3BucketCdkStack/CDKMetadata/Default"
21          },
22          "Condition": "CDKMetadataAvailable"
23        }
24      },
25   ⊟  "Conditions": {
26   ⊟    "CDKMetadataAvailable": {
27   ⊟      "Fn::Or": [
28   ⊟        {
29   ⊟          "Fn::Or": [
30   ⊟            {
31                    "n  F
```

Figure 3-20. *CDK-generated CloudFormation template*

The first of these is that there are properties set that you did not set in the *BucketProps*. This happened because the CDK takes an approach where it makes some best guesses about what values should be assigned, on a resource-by-resource basis, to properties that are not set in the code. For example, when looking at this file for a simple S3 resource, you will see that properties for *UpdateReplacePolicy*, *DeletionPolicy*, and *Metadata* were set. The Metadata property, in this example, is used internally by CloudFormation to tie a stack to a CDK run, so it is not something that you would set by hand. However, the other two are values that the CDK will set if your code doesn't. Thus, you will need to set the property yourself if you want a value different than the CDK-default value.

> **Note**   Many AWS CDK stacks that we will write throughout the remaining chapters will include *assets*, or external files that are deployed with the stack, such as Docker Images that are designed to support AWS Lambda functions. The AWS CDK uploads these to an Amazon S3 bucket or other container so they are available to AWS CloudFormation during deployment. Deployment requires that these containers already exist in the account and region you are deploying into. Creating these containers is called bootstrapping. To bootstrap, issue the following command: `cdk bootstrap`.

The other area that we didn't include in the original S3 CloudFormation, nor have we yet gone over it, is the optional **Conditions** section. This section allows you to define statements that define when entities will be created or configured. Let's zoom in on that section in Figure 3-21.

```
14      "CDKMetadata": {
15          "Type": "AWS::CDK::Metadata",
16          "Properties": {
17              "Analytics": "v2:deflate64:H4sIAAAAAAAACiWMMQ/CIBSEf0t3+igyOZio6NqhGveGPhMkQgMPHQ⁺
18          },
19          "Metadata": {
20              "aws:cdk:path": "SimpleS3BucketCdkStack/CDKMetadata/Default"
21          },
22          "Condition": "CDKMetadataAvailable"      1
23      }
24  },
25  "Conditions": {
26      "CDKMetadataAvailable": {      2
27          "Fn::Or": [
28              {
29                  "Fn::Or": [
30                      {
31                          "Fn::Equals": [
32                              {
33                                  "Ref": "AWS::Region"
34                              },
35                              "ap-east-1"
36                          ]
37                      },
3            },
```

Figure 3-21. *Adding conditions to a CloudFormation template*

The area marked as 1 shows how you add a condition onto a resource, while 2 shows the condition that will be added. In this case, this condition dictates that the CDKMetadata resource will be used only when being run within a region that supports the use of the CDKMetadata tag.

Now that you have created the code and synthesized it to get the CloudFormation template, the last step is the deployment. You can either deploy the CloudFormation template like we did earlier or deploy the code that we just wrote through the CDK. The command to do a straightforward deploy to your default region is simply `cdk deploy` as you can see at the top of Figure 3-22.

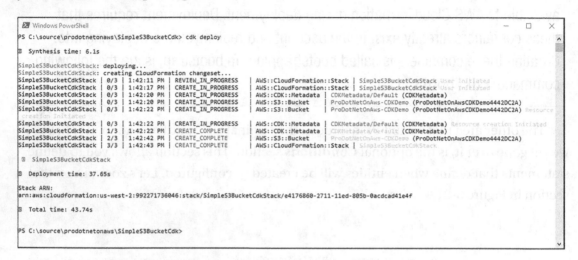

Figure 3-22. *Output when deploying CDK application*

You can verify the deployment through the console or through an IDE toolkit as shown in Figure 3-23.

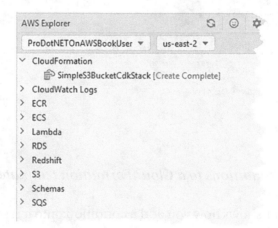

Figure 3-23. *Validating deployment using AWS Toolkit for Rider*

As developers, we know our systems continually evolve. That means that the resources that we define here may evolve as well. The CDK supports this. Many of the commands that you will use when working in the CDK CLI take into account the potential that new code within the CDK application may be different than how the existing system was defined. Let's take a look at how that works.

First thing to do is to change the stack. Let's do that by adding in a second bucket by adding in a new line of code:

```
var newBucket = new Bucket(this, "ProDotNetOnAws-CDKDemo-AddOnBucket", new
BucketProps{});
```

This adds in the second bucket. Note how it is different from the first bucket that we created in that it does not have the *BucketName* property set. Instead, upon deployment, the CDK will create a randomized resource name. As you would expect, there is a command that you can use to see how the CDK will interpret the change to the CDK: cdk diff. The result of running that command – after adding in the unnamed bucket – is

```
C:\Source\prodotnetonaws\SimpleS3BucketCDK>cdk diff
Stack SimpleS3BucketCdkStack
Resources
[+] AWS::S3::Bucket ProDotNetOnAws-CDKDemo-AddOnBucket
ProDotNetOnAwsCDKDemoAddOnBucket5FECB3A8

C:\Source\prodotnetonaws\SimpleS3BucketCDK>
```

The [+] is used to demonstrate that a particular resource is being added. A resource that is being edited will be shown with a [~] and a visual representation of the information that is being changed, and a resource that is being deleted will be marked with a [-]. Removing all of the resources from the stack will result in an empty stack as all of the created resources will be removed; the stack remains but contains no resources.

The best way to delete a stack is to use the CDK command, cdk destroy, in the same way that you did when running the cdk deploy command. The system will request confirmation and then destroy the stack as shown in Figure 3-24.

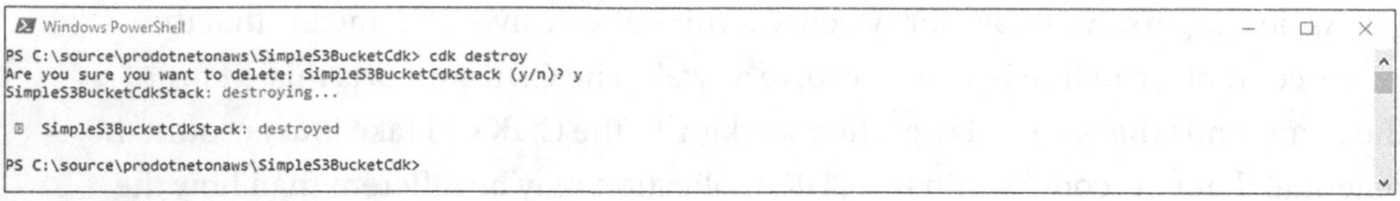

```
Windows PowerShell                                                          —  □  ×
PS C:\source\prodotnetonaws\SimpleS3BucketCdk> cdk destroy
Are you sure you want to delete: SimpleS3BucketCdkStack (y/n)? y
SimpleS3BucketCdkStack: destroying...

 ▣  SimpleS3BucketCdkStack: destroyed

PS C:\source\prodotnetonaws\SimpleS3BucketCdk>
```

Figure 3-24. *Deleting a stack using the CDK CLI*

Running this command will not change any of the code; it will instead simply remove the stack and the resources within the stack (if the resources are not set to be retained).

As you have just seen, the CDK allows the creation of AWS resources through the use of C# code within a .NET project that the CDK will create for you. Adding a resource is as simple as adding the appropriate CDK NuGet package(s) that supports that resource and then adding the desired resource to the stack that is defined within the code. The CDK provides you the ability to create a CloudFormation template from the code as well as support the deployment or deletion of the stack directly from the command line.

AWS Serverless Application Model (SAM) CLI

As briefly mentioned in Chapter 1, *serverless* is an approach that enables you to run your code without provisioning or managing servers, all of which AWS fully handles for you. Even though these resources may be serverless, and you don't have to handle them, it doesn't mean that they are not resources that you can create. And like most other AWS resources, these resources are not ones where you would enjoy the experience of writing the needed CloudFormation template by hand.

That is where the AWS Serverless Application Model (SAM) comes into play. SAM is an extension for CloudFormation that abstracts away much of the repetitive nature of setting up a serverless application. It does this by defining the AWS SAM template specification for serverless applications, providing a simple and clean syntax that you can use to describe the functions, APIs, permissions, configurations, and events that make up a serverless application. You use an AWS SAM template file to manage a single, deployable, versioned entity that is your serverless application. SAM also comes with a CLI that offers additional support for serverless development because it provides capabilities such as validation, packaging, and publishing, as well as provides a local execution environment for stepping through and debugging your code. As mentioned in Chapter 2, this debugging functionality has been incorporated into the AWS Toolkits for

Rider and VS Code. You can get directions on installing the SAM CLI for your preferred operating system at https://aws.amazon.com/serverless/sam/.

Let's take a closer look at how all of this works together. First, you use the SAM specification to define your serverless application. This specification defines SAM templates and how those templates contain resource types, properties, and attributes as well as data types, intrinsic functions, and API Gateway extensions. These templates, as you can likely guess, can be either YAML or JSON and closely follow the CloudFormation template (probably having something to do with how this is an extension of CloudFormation), with a few additions.

The simplest yet most important of these additions is the transform declaration. This is required on every SAM template because it identifies the template as following the SAM definition. This command must be at the top of every template file, else the template will be understood as a regular CloudFormation template rather than a SAM template:

```
Transform: AWS::Serverless-2016-10-31
```

Another section that is added to SAM templates that is not in a standard CloudFormation template is the **Globals** section. This section defines the properties that are common to all of the serverless functions and APIs and is supported by the *AWS::Serverless::Function, AWS::Serverless::Api, AWS::Serverless::HttpApi,* and *AWS::Serverless::SimpleTable* resources. Each of these resources provides a different way to define the resources that will be built from the template:

- **AWS::Serverless::Function** – This resource type creates an AWS Lambda function, an IAM execution role, and the necessary event source mappings to trigger the function.

- **AWS::Serverless::Api** – This resource type is used when creating a collection of API Gateway resources and methods that are designed to be invoked through HTTPS endpoints.

- **AWS::Serverless::HttpApi** – The resource type used to create RESTful APIs. These APIs have a lower latency and cost than using the API resource type.

- **AWS::Serverless::SimpleTable** – This definition creates a DynamoDB table with a single attribute primary key.

There are some changes to several of the base CloudFormation sections as well. The first is that the **Resources** section can now contain a combination of CloudFormation resources and SAM resources (remember, a SAM resource provides abstractions over regular CloudFormation resources). The second template section that is slightly different is the **Parameters** section, which will present additional prompts to the user during the sam deploy step. But before we get to that step, let's instead create a sample SAM application.

Just as with the CDK, the SAM CLI supports the creation of a default project. From the command prompt, and once you are in the directory that you want to use for creating the samples, run sam init. This will step you through the creation. The first option you will get is to select the template source:

```
Which template source would you like to use?
        1 - AWS Quick Start Templates
        2 - Custom Template Location
Choice:
```

Select "1" to use a Quick Start template. The next option is to select an AWS Quick Start application template:

```
Choose an AWS Quick Start application template
        1 - Hello World Example
        2 - Multi-step workflow
        3 - Serverless API
        4 - Scheduled task
        5 - Standalone function
        6 - Data processing
        7 - Infrastructure event management
        8 - Lambda EFS example
        9 - Machine Learning
Template:
```

Select "1" to choose a "Hello World Example". You will then be asked:

```
Use the most popular runtime and package type? (Python and zip) [y/N]:
```

Select "N" because this is a .NET book and not a Python book. This will then present you the choice of runtime to use:

```
Which runtime would you like to use?
        1 - dotnet6
        2 - dotnet5.0
        3 - dotnetcore3.1
        4 - go1.x
        5 - graalvm.java11 (provided.al2)
        6 - graalvm.java17 (provided.al2)
        7 - java11
        8 - java8.al2
        9 - java8
        10 - nodejs16.x
        11 - nodejs14.x
        12 - nodejs12.x
        13 - python3.9
        14 - python3.8
        15 - python3.7
        16 - python3.6
        17 - ruby2.7
        18 - rust (provided.al2)
Runtime:
```

Enter "1" to select .NET 6 or "2" for .NET 5.0, whichever is appropriate for your IDE. Your options are different between the two .NET versions as you move forward, because AWS treats long-term support (LTS) versions differently than non-LTS versions. The .NET 6 version will give you an option to select a package type:

```
What package type would you like to use?
        1 - Zip
        2 - Image
Package type:
```

The .NET 5 version, on the other hand, will automatically be assigned as an Image package and you have no choice.

You then get asked:

```
Would you like to enable X-Ray tracing on the function(s) in your
application?  [y/N]:
```

We selected "N" because we haven't talked about X-Ray tracing yet.

Note   Let's go deeper into the choice that we made between "Zip" and "Image". Using a zip file means that AWS completely controls the operation of the serverless application – you can think of serverless apps deployed in this style as running completely within AWS systems. Using an image, on the other hand, means that you are instead creating a container image that will be used as the system in which your application will be run. This means a bit more work on your part, but it also gives you the ability to make changes to the container image that your system is using. Thus, selecting to use an "Image" package type would have presented you a completely different set of runtime options.

You will then get a prompt to create a project name, with the default value being "sam-app". Enter your desired name. The system will inform you that it is cloning the templates. The SAM CLI will complete the creation of your example application by creating a folder using the name that you entered earlier and copying in several subdirectories and files. If you had used a name of "ProDotNETOnAWS-SAMSample", for example, you would get the following folder and file structure:

```
ProDotNETOnAWS-SAMSample/
    ├── README.md
    ├── omnisharp.json
    ├── events/
    │    └── event.json
    ├── src/
        └── HelloWorld/
                    ├── aws-lambda-tools-defaults.json
    │               ├── Function.cs      #contains the logic
    │               └── HelloWorld.proj
    ├── template.yaml  #Contains the AWS SAM template
    │                      #defining your application's AWS resources.
```

```
└── test/
    └── HelloWorld.Test/
        ├── FunctionTest.cs
        └── HelloWorld.Tests.proj
```

You can examine the various files to get an understanding of what they each represent. The code for the work being done within the serverless function is contained in the **Function.cs** class. The **template.yaml** file contains the SAM template for this project, as shown in Figure 3-25.

```
template.yaml  ⊕  ✕
                                                        ▾  ▪  AWSTemplateFormatVersion
    1   AWSTemplateFormatVersion: '2010-09-09'
    2   Transform: AWS::Serverless-2016-10-31
    3   Description: >
    4     Sample SAM Template for ProDotNETOnAWS-SAMSample
    5
    6     # More info about Globals: https://github.com/awslabs/serverless-application-model/blob/master/docs/globals.rst
    7   Globals:
    8     Function:
    9       Timeout: 10
   10
   11   Resources:
   12     HelloWorldFunction:
   13       Type: AWS::Serverless::Function # More info about Function Resource: https://github.com/awslabs/serverless-application-model/blob/master/versions/201
   14       Properties:
   15         CodeUri: ./src/HelloWorld/
   16         Handler: HelloWorld::HelloWorld.Function::FunctionHandler
   17         Runtime: dotnetcore3.1
   18         MemorySize: 256
   19         Environment: # More info about Env Vars: https://github.com/awslabs/serverless-application-model/blob/master/versions/2016-10-31.md#environment-obj.
   20           Variables:
   21             PARAM1: VALUE
   22         Events:
   23           HelloWorld:
   24             Type: Api # More info about API Event Source: https://github.com/awslabs/serverless-application-model/blob/master/versions/2016-10-31.md#api
   25             Properties:
   26               Path: /hello
   27               Method: get
   28
   29   Outputs:
   30     # ServerlessRestApi is an implicit API created out of Events key under Serverless::Function
   31     # Find out more about other implicit resources you can reference within SAM
   32     # https://github.com/awslabs/serverless-application-model/blob/master/docs/internals/generated_resources.rst#api
   33     HelloWorldApi:
   34       Description: "API Gateway endpoint URL for Prod stage for Hello World function"
   35       Value: !Sub "https://${ServerlessRestApi}.execute-api.${AWS::Region}.amazonaws.com/Prod/hello/"
   36     HelloWorldFunction:
   37       Description: "Hello World Lambda Function ARN"
   38       Value: !GetAtt HelloWorldFunction.Arn
   39     HelloWorldFunctionIamRole:
   40       Description: "Implicit IAM Role created for Hello World function"
   41       Value: !GetAtt HelloWorldFunctionRole.Arn
   42
```

Figure 3-25. *SAM template created as part of the sample project*

A review of Figure 3-25 shows that the code that was created is for a *Function*, as defined in Line 8, and that when this function is executed, it will use the *FunctionHandler* method of the *HelloWorld.Function* class as defined in Line 16.

We won't go into the actual function that the sample application uses, as we will be covering serverless and AWS Lambda in much greater detail in future chapters. Instead, we will simply go ahead and deploy this sample function. Return to your command prompt and change directory into the directory that was just created. Once there, type in the following command:

```
sam deploy --guided
```

This will start walking you through the serverless deployment using a guided process, allowing the SAM CLI to capture the necessary configuration information for your deployment. The first option you will have is *Stack Name*. You can enter any unused value here. You will then be able to enter an *AWS Region*, or simply enter to use the default value that is displayed. You will get the following message once you have entered a region:

```
#Shows you resources changes to be deployed and require a 'Y' to
initiate deploy
Confirm changes before deploy [y/N]:
```

Enter a "y" to get the next prompt to allow SAM CLI to create IAM roles. Enter a "y" here as well, and continue to do so as it works through the next few questions. Once it stops asking "Y/N" questions, accept the default values until it starts the deployment process.

During this deployment process, you will see some text being displayed as the CLI created the CloudFormation template. It will, after several minutes, create a CloudFormation stack changeset that describes the differences between the original definition and the changed definition similar to

```
CloudFormation stack changeset
-------------------------------------------------------------------------
Operation  LogicalResourceId        ResourceType               Replacement
-------------------------------------------------------------------------
+ Add      HelloWorldFunctionHelloWor  AWS::Lambda::Permission   N/A
           ldPermissionProd
+ Add      HelloWorldFunctionRole     AWS::IAM::Role             N/A
+ Add      HelloWorldFunction         AWS::Lambda::Function      N/A
+ Add      ServerlessRestApiDeployment  AWS::ApiGateway::Deployment  N/A
           47fc2d5f9d
+ Add      ServerlessRestApiProdStage  AWS::ApiGateway::Stage    N/A
+ Add      ServerlessRestApi          AWS::ApiGateway::RestApi   N/A
-------------------------------------------------------------------------
```

```
Changeset created successfully. arn:aws:cloudformation:us-
east-2:119861589146:changeSet/samcli-deploy1617587502/
ed59787b-b464-4eac-844b-8c77041198f1
```

```
Previewing CloudFormation changeset before deployment
========================================================
Deploy this changeset? [y/N]:
```

Enter a "y" to deploy the changeset. The CLI will display the resource creation updates until the complete stack is deployed. If you examine the AWS Lambda node of the AWS Explorer, you should see the new function as shown in Figure 3-26.

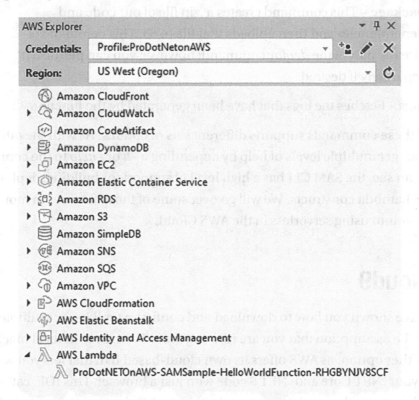

Figure 3-26. *Deployed Lambda function*

There are additional commands available in the SAM CLI along with the *init* and *deploy* commands that we have already gone over. Some of these are listed as follows:

- **validate** – This command verifies whether an AWS SAM template is valid.

- **build** – Builds a serverless application and prepares it for subsequent steps in the workflow, which could be either testing it locally or deploying it to the AWS cloud.

- **local generate-event** – Generates sample payloads from different event sources (such as S3) for sending to your application.

- **local start-api** – Creates a local HTTP server that hosts your functions for local development and testing.

- **package** – This command creates a .zip file of our code and dependencies and then uploads that file to S3. This command is already part of the *deploy* command; however, you can perform it separately if desired.

- **logs** – Fetches the logs that have been generated by the function.

Each of these commands supports different sets of options. As with the other CLI tools, you can get multiple levels of help by appending a *–h* or *–help* to the command.

As you can see, the SAM CLI has a high level of support for building, deploying, and testing AWS Lambda constructs. We will go over some of those features in more detail as we dig deeper into using serverless in the AWS Cloud.

AWS Cloud9

So far, we have shown you how to download and configure toolkits for multiple different IDEs under the assumption that you are running those IDEs on your local machine. You do have another option, as AWS offers its own cloud-based IDE that lets you write, run, and debug your .NET Core and .NET 5 code with just a browser. This IDE, called *AWS Cloud9*, includes an editor, a debugger, and a terminal and comes prepackaged with essential tools for many programming languages.

While Cloud9 feels like a stand-alone service when using it, it is actually a wrapper over a managed Amazon EC2 instance. This EC2 instance is hosting your development environment, and Cloud9 comes with a terminal that includes *sudo* privileges (Cloud9 only runs on top of Linux AMIs) to the instance as well as a pre-authenticated AWS CLI.

Note   We are not going to go over the creation and configuration of an AWS Cloud9 environment here, as it is most likely that you will use local development tools moving forward. However, if you would like to set up a Cloud9 instance, the steps for configuring .NET Core and creating your first sample application are available at `https://docs.aws.amazon.com/cloud9/latest/user-guide/sample-dotnetcore.html`.

Cloud9 does not come ready to run .NET Core applications (or most other languages/frameworks) out of the box, so you will need to take some steps to install the .NET Core SDK and runtimes and to ready the IDE to compile and run .NET Core applications. Once you have Cloud9 configured to run .NET Core applications, you are able to interact with the .NET Core CLI to create new projects and solutions. You can also configure your source code connection and download your source code from there. Cloud9 will then allow you to work within those projects and solutions in a fashion very similar to that of working within VS Code, as shown in Figure 3-27, where you have a project files list (A), a source code file detail (B), a command-line interface (C), and a console output emulator (D).

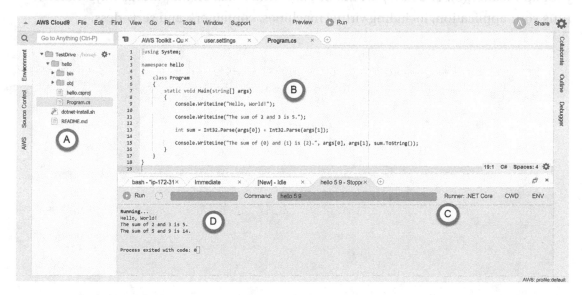

Figure 3-27.   *.NET Core console application in AWS Cloud9*

You will be able to view, create, and edit .NET Framework source code, but since Cloud9 only runs on top of Linux-based EC2 instances, you will not be able to run or debug your .NET Framework applications within the IDE.

Summary

Where Chapter 2 walked you through setting up the most commonly used tools when working with .NET, this chapter introduced other tools and services that you may find useful when working with AWS. The first tool was the AWS CLI, a tool that you can locally install and use for interacting with and managing AWS services. We then went over AWS CloudFormation, which is the base service that supports Infrastructure as Code (IaC) by taking JSON or YAML templates that define a stack of resources and creating the resources as defined within those templates. We went over a couple of approaches that extend CloudFormation, the CDK, and SAM CLI and ended with a cloud-based IDE: Cloud9.

Now that you have everything you need to be able to connect to AWS services through your IDE or within your application, our next step is to show you how to host your application(s). The next part will be going into detail on the various ways that AWS runs your application, including virtual machines, containers, and serverless.

PART II

Hosting Your Applications

CHAPTER 4

Virtual Machines

In the previous chapters, we gained a basic understanding of the essentials of the AWS cloud and awareness of the various tools and IDE extensions and add-ins that AWS makes available to help with the development and deployment of your .NET applications. It's now time to take a deeper look at some of the services and technologies you'll be using, starting with virtual machines in Amazon EC2 – an option for hosting .NET applications on Windows or Linux.

At the end of the chapter, we'll create our first EC2 virtual machine, configure it with additional software at launch time, and connect to it. First, let's get familiar with EC2.

Virtual Machines and EC2

Many developers are probably familiar with virtual machines (VMs), from using tools such as Hyper-V on Windows, VirtualBox, or VMware. A virtual machine virtualizes an entire machine stack – from emulated hardware, through the operating system, and onto the applications hosted on the VM. This machine stack, encapsulated in one or more *image* files, runs in a *hypervisor* (e.g., Hyper-V) yielding a virtual machine instance. The hypervisor acts as an intermediary between the operating system on the VM (known as the *guest*) and the actual real hardware (the *host*), with the hypervisor translating device requests from the OS and applications in the VM to the physical hardware on your machine.

For developers who began their career in the era of containers, and now serverless, virtual machines may no longer seem relevant, but they are a viable and popular approach for many workloads. You can also use VMs as dev/test environments. For example, if we want to try a new preview version of .NET, or Visual Studio, or whatever takes our interest, we can spin up a VM in EC2 in a few minutes, install the necessary software, and explore to our heart's content without affecting our day-to-day machine.

© William Penberthy and Steve Roberts 2023
W. Penberthy and S. Roberts, *Pro .NET on Amazon Web Services*,
https://doi.org/10.1007/978-1-4842-8907-5_4

Note   You can use EC2 virtual machines solely within EC2 itself, or via AWS Elastic Beanstalk, or Amazon Lightsail. The latter two abstract away some of the management aspects of EC2 VMs, saving you effort. This chapter focuses specifically on using VMs within EC2. Later chapters of the book will explore the use of VMs in Elastic Beanstalk.

Before we begin our dive into EC2, let's briefly summarize some of the key items of terminology we'll be using, much of which was first introduced in Chapter 1.

- **Image** – You use images that consist of one or more related files containing the operating system, virtualized hardware drivers, extra attached storage drives, and application software to create virtual machine instances. An image is effectively a template to create a virtual machine. EC2 refers to images as *Amazon Machine Images*, or *AMI*s. EC2 provides you a variety of images, revised periodically, containing various editions and versions of Windows Server, and several distributions of Linux including Amazon's own, Amazon Linux 2, which is based on Red Hat. You can also select AMIs from a marketplace containing third-party custom images, or you can build and curate your own.

- **Instance** – An instance is a running virtual machine, created from an AMI. You can start, stop, restart (reboot), or terminate instances. Instances also have attached storage devices, just like you may have one or more disks attached to your own personal machines.

- **Security group** – Security groups are firewalls controlling access to your instances and contain rules permitting access on given ports or port ranges to specific IP addresses, address ranges, or even security groups controlling access to other resources.

- **Key pair** – A key pair is a set of security credentials you use to decrypt the randomly generated administrative password of instances launched from AMIs provided by EC2. This enables you to use SSH or Remote Desktop Connection to connect into a running instance. The key pair contains the private key data (which you must have access to, usually in the form of a downloaded ".pem" file), and EC2 holds the corresponding public key. You only need a key pair when the instance has a randomly generated password – for custom images you create, you can assign a fixed password, but of course, you are then responsible for the security of that password. In this book, we'll be using key pairs to gain access to our instances.

Tip   It's possible to connect to a running instance using a browser-based shell in the AWS Management Console, known as *EC2 Connect*, even if you launched the instance without specifying a key pair, provided you meet other conditions (see `https://docs.aws.amazon.com/AWSEC2/latest/UserGuide/ec2-instance-connect-set-up.html`). However, if you want to use SSH or Remote Desktop Connection from outside the console, you will need to specify a key pair when launching your instances.

Later in this chapter, we'll walk through how to launch an instance using an Amazon-provided image, configure it with additional software during launch, and connect to it. For now, know that you have multiple ways to launch instances:

- Using the EC2 dashboard in the AWS Management Console

- Using commands in the AWS Tools for PowerShell or the AWS CLI

- Using the EC2 Launch Wizard in the AWS Toolkit for Visual Studio

- Programmatically, by calling EC2's *RunInstances* API, using any of the AWS SDKs

- Automatically by defining an Auto Scaling Group. You can configure an Auto Scaling Group to launch one or more instances based on some metric (e.g., request counts or CPU load) to satisfy increased demand, and to scale down (terminate) instances when that demand drops.

When Should You Consider EC2?

What type of application or workload is best suited to running on an EC2 instance? To be honest, an EC2 instance can serve applications of any purpose. They are just virtual machines to which you have full access and can therefore install any amount of software or dependencies the hosted application(s) or workload requires.

The key thing to bear in mind is that unless you stop an instance, it will run 24×7×365. This differentiates them from, say, serverless approaches that we'll consider in Chapter 6, where the host compute instance is not directly accessible and is transient – it runs to service a request, up to a given maximum period (15 minutes currently). AWS recycles serverless compute hosts when no additional request arrives for a set period, whereas an EC2 instance can sit idle, serving no traffic, until you stop or terminate it (or an Auto Scaling Group determines the instance(s) can terminate, based on metrics you've configured). Therefore, EC2 instances are perhaps better suited to long-running stable workloads such as web or web API applications.

In Chapter 5, we'll look at containers that are also equally suited to many of the tasks that traditionally we've used virtual machines, or EC2 instances, to handle. In many cases, it may well come down to a matter of preference whether to use an EC2 instance or a container to handle your workload.

Key Components of EC2

At the end of this chapter, we will launch, configure, and connect to our first EC2 instance. First, we want to dig a little deeper into some of the key components you'll be working with.

Amazon Machine Images (AMIs)

Since AMIs are at the heart of the instances you will launch in EC2, it makes sense to start there! As already mentioned, you can choose from images provided by Amazon, images available from third parties via the marketplace, or you can craft your own image (which can also be based on those provided by Amazon).

Note   Is it spelled out, letter by letter, like A-M-I or pronounced "army" (or even "amy" or "ahmee")? No one seems to know, and there doesn't appear to be consensus. Both authors have been caught spelling it out, and saying "army," within minutes of each other in meetings, so if we don't know…, go with what makes you comfortable!

It's not possible to capture the full range of images available, even if scoped down to just those provided by Amazon, in a single picture. Figure 4-1 shows just some of the available and commonly used Linux images that you can choose from when you navigate to the EC2 dashboard in the AWS Management Console and start the *Launch instances* wizard.

| 1. Choose AMI | 2. Choose Instance Type | 3. Configure Instance | 4. Add Storage | 5. Add Tags | 6. Configure Security Group | 7. |

Step 1: Choose an Amazon Machine Image (AMI)

An AMI is a template that contains the software configuration (operating system, application server, and applications) required to laun
own AMIs.

🔍 linux

Quick Start (13)

My AMIs (1)

AWS Marketplace (1713)

Community AMIs (80227)

☐ Free tier only ⓘ

🗄 **Amazon Linux**
Free tier eligible

Amazon Linux 2 AMI (HVM), SSD Volume Type - ami-0cf6f5c8a62fa5da6

Amazon Linux 2 comes with five years support. It provides Linux kernel 4.14 tuned f
packages through extras. This AMI is the successor of the Amazon Linux AMI that is

Root device type: ebs   Virtualization type: hvm   ENA Enabled: Yes

---

🔴 **Red Hat**
Free tier eligible

Red Hat Enterprise Linux 8 (HVM), SSD Volume Type - ami-01e78c5619

Red Hat Enterprise Linux version 8 (HVM), EBS General Purpose (SSD) Volume Type

Root device type: ebs   Virtualization type: hvm   ENA Enabled: Yes

---

🦎 **SUSE Linux**
Free tier eligible

SUSE Linux Enterprise Server 15 SP2 (HVM), SSD Volume Type - ami-017

SUSE Linux Enterprise Server 15 Service Pack 2 (HVM), EBS General Purpose (SSD)

Root device type: ebs   Virtualization type: hvm   ENA Enabled: Yes

---

🗄 **Amazon Linux**

Deep Learning AMI (Amazon Linux) Version 44.1 - ami-0cf77af10d63c796

MXNet-1.7.0 & 1.6.0, TensorFlow-2.3.1, 2.1.3 & 1.15.5, PyTorch-1.4.0 & 1.7.1, EI, & other
check: https://aws.amazon.com/sagemaker

Root device type: ebs   Virtualization type: hvm   ENA Enabled: Yes

---

🌀
Free tier eligible

Debian 10 (HVM), SSD Volume Type - ami-0c7ea5497c02abcaf (64-bit x86)

Debian 10 (HVM), EBS General Purpose (SSD) Volume Type. Community developed fr

Root device type: ebs   Virtualization type: hvm   ENA Enabled: Yes

---

🗄 **Amazon Linux**

Deep Learning AMI (Amazon Linux 2) Version 44.0 - ami-03ef2b4a53e06

MXNet-1.8.0 & 1.7.0, TensorFlow-2.4.1, 2.1.3 & 1.15.5, PyTorch-1.4.0 & 1.8.1, Neuron,
experience, check: https://aws.amazon.com/sagemaker

Root device type: ebs   Virtualization type: hvm   ENA Enabled: Yes

---

🗄 **Amazon Linux**

Amazon Linux 2 LTS with SQL Server 2017 Standard - ami-08577794a09

Microsoft SQL Server 2017 Standard edition on Amazon Linux 2 LTS. The AMI also

Root device type: ebs   Virtualization type: hvm   ENA Enabled: Yes

---

🗄 **Amazon Linux**
Free tier eligible

Amazon Linux 2 with .Net Core, PowerShell, Mono, and MATE Desktop E

.NET Core 5.0, Mono 6.12, PowerShell 7.1, and MATE DE pre-installed to run your .NET

Root device type: ebs   Virtualization type: hvm   ENA Enabled: Yes

---

Figure 4-1. *A sampling of Amazon-provided Linux Quick Start images*

Similarly, Figure 4-2 shows a small sample of images running Windows Server.

| 1. Choose AMI | 2. Choose Instance Type | 3. Configure Instance | 4. Add Storage | 5. Add Tags | 6. Configure Security Group |

Step 1: Choose an Amazon Machine Image (AMI)

An AMI is a template that contains the software configuration (operating system, application server, and applications) required to lau
own AMIs.

Q windows|

AWS Launch Wizard for SQL Server offers an easy way to size, configure, and deploy Microsoft SQL Server Always On availabili

Quick Start (19)

My AMIs (0)

AWS Marketplace (914)

Community AMIs (5874)

☐ Free tier only ⓘ

Microsoft Windows Server 2019 Base - ami-0b7ebdd52b84c244d
Windows   Microsoft Windows 2019 Datacenter edition. [English]
Free tier eligible   Root device type: ebs   Virtualization type: hvm   ENA Enabled: Yes

Microsoft Windows Server 2019 Base with Containers - ami-0c342869d
Windows   Microsoft Windows 2019 Datacenter edition with Containers. [English]
Free tier eligible   Root device type: ebs   Virtualization type: hvm   ENA Enabled: Yes

Microsoft Windows Server 2019 with SQL Server 2017 Standard - ami-0
Microsoft Windows 2019 Datacenter edition, Microsoft SQL Server 2017 Standard
Windows   Root device type: ebs   Virtualization type: hvm   ENA Enabled: Yes

Microsoft Windows Server 2019 with SQL Server 2017 Enterprise - ami
Microsoft Windows 2019 Datacenter edition, Microsoft SQL Server 2017 Enterprise.
Windows   Root device type: ebs   Virtualization type: hvm   ENA Enabled: Yes

Microsoft Windows Server 2019 with SQL Server 2019 Standard - ami
Microsoft Windows 2019 Datacenter edition, Microsoft SQL Server 2019 Standard
Windows   Root device type: ebs   Virtualization type: hvm   ENA Enabled: Yes

Microsoft Windows Server 2019 with SQL Server 2019 Enterprise - ami
Microsoft Windows 2019 Datacenter edition, Microsoft SQL Server 2019 Enterprise
Windows   Root device type: ebs   Virtualization type: hvm   ENA Enabled: Yes

Microsoft Windows Server 2004 Core Base - ami-0357bdc4b114c475b
Windows   Microsoft Windows Server 2004 Semi-Annual Channel release [English]
Free tier eligible   Root device type: ebs   Virtualization type: hvm   ENA Enabled: Yes

Microsoft Windows Server 2016 Base - ami-007bf94f3c494b7e3
Windows   Microsoft Windows 2016 Datacenter edition. [English]
Free tier eligible   Root device type: ebs   Virtualization type: hvm   ENA Enabled: Yes

Microsoft Windows Server 2016 Base with Containers - ami-01c5b4d92

Figure 4-2. *A sampling of Amazon-provided Windows Server images*

Figures 4-1 and 4-2 also show you that the mix of images provided by EC2 covers both "bare-bones" operating system images and images that include additional software such as .NET Core, .NET 5+, various editions of SQL Server, PowerShell, and more. Or you could consider looking for an image with the specific combination of pre-installed software in the marketplace and community listings (besides the additional specialized images provided by EC2).

When you create (launch) an instance, you can further customize it with the specific software and dependencies your application needs either during or after launch. Once you've launched, and potentially customized, an instance, you can then create your own custom image from the running instance. Those images will then appear in the *My AMIs* tab in the launch wizard, and you can create an instance from them in the same way as any other. However, do note that you are then responsible for the maintenance of those images such as keeping them up to date with security patches. While EC2 revises its collection of images, usually monthly, it doesn't meddle and apply those patches to your images.

The Launch Wizard in the AWS Management Console isn't the only place you can select images to launch. Figure 4-3 shows the **Launch Wizard** in the AWS Toolkit for Visual Studio. You access this wizard by right-clicking on the **Amazon EC2** node in the **AWS Explorer** window and selecting *Launch instance....*

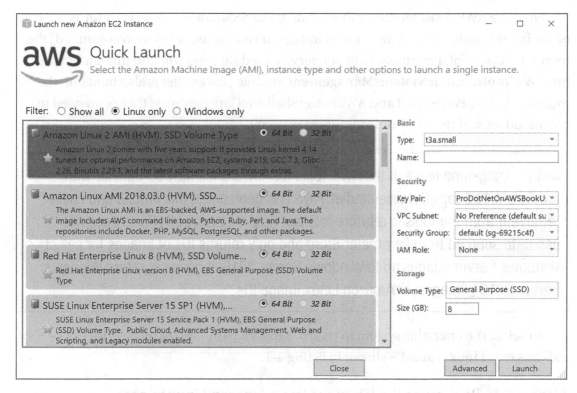

Figure 4-3. *The EC2 Launch Wizard in the AWS Toolkit for Visual Studio*

When launching instances, selecting an image by hand in a wizard is great for learning and exploration, but it's not how you achieve consistency and repeatability in a production use case. In that scenario, you'll probably want to specify your image programmatically. You'll also probably want to find the latest available image.

As noted earlier, EC2 revises its images approximately monthly, and while this doesn't mean older images automatically become unavailable as soon as newer images become available, AWS will eventually remove them.

In Figures 4-1 and 4-2, you can see that each image has an identifier, for example, `ami-0cf6f5c8a62fa5da6`. This is what you'll use, or need to discover, to launch an instance using an image, so let's tackle the problem of finding the latest image ID for a given AMI first.

AWS publishes the latest IDs for all its images to *AWS Systems Manager's Parameter Store* and makes data available to all users (you don't need extra permissions set up to look at it). This means we can programmatically discover, at any time, the ID of an image. There are a couple of ways to do this.

First, the AWS Tools for PowerShell cmdlet, *Get-SSMLatestEC2Image*, returns the IDs of the latest Windows or Amazon Linux images. If you are using (as we recommend) the modular version of these tools, with per-service modules, you will find this cmdlet in the **AWS.Tools.SimpleSystemsManagement** module (the cmdlet is also built into the monolithic AWSPowerShell and AWSPowerShell.NetCore modules; there's no need to download an additional module for these versions).

Note   Long-time users of the AWS Tools for PowerShell may be familiar with the Get-EC2ImageByName cmdlet. AWS has deprecated this cmdlet and could remove it from the tools in a future release. Get-EC2ImageByName does not use data sourced from Parameter Store and only returns IDs of images for select Windows Server images up to Windows Server 2016. It does not return Windows Server 2019+ images, or Amazon Linux image IDs.

To select the operating system to return, supply a path – ami-windows-latest or ami-amazon-linux-latest – shown in listing 4-1.

Listing 4-1. Requesting the IDs of the latest Amazon Linux images

```
C:\> Get-SSMLatestEC2Image -Path ami-amazon-linux-latest

Name                              Value
----                              -----
amzn-ami-hvm-x86_64-ebs           ami-0e7d9fec0da56fa76
amzn-ami-hvm-x86_64-gp2           ami-0c02ff07a6e53e4f5
amzn-ami-hvm-x86_64-s3            ami-0e73dfd8870b02823
amzn-ami-minimal-hvm-x86_64-s3    ami-05c21075f9e2d7503
amzn-ami-minimal-pv-x86_64-s3     ami-0787c7b0790001e55  .
amzn-ami-pv-x86_64-s3             ami-021c09956d096b81b
amzn2-ami-hvm-arm64-gp2           ami-07196cf23edf97d9c
amzn2-ami-hvm-x86_64-ebs          ami-02fb8c9446bd8276d
amzn2-ami-hvm-x86_64-gp2          ami-0cf6f5c8a62fa5da6
amzn2-ami-minimal-hvm-arm64-ebs   ami-08ac6ff108f0c6686
amzn-ami-minimal-hvm-x86_64-ebs   ami-00edd0c226428c793
...
```

It's possible to fine-tune the output even further by asking for an image in the selected path. Listing 4-2 shows a request for the IDs of the latest Windows Server 2019 English images. Notice that you can make use of wildcards in the image name.

Listing 4-2. Requesting specific images with Get-SSMLatestEC2Image

```
C:\> Get-SSMLatestEC2Image -Path ami-windows-latest ↵
-ImageName *Windows*2019*English*Base

Name                                        Value
----                                        -----
Windows_Server-2019-English-Core-Base       ami-0caae78d55db83647
Windows_Server-2019-English-Full-Base       ami-0b7ebdd52b84c244d
...
```

The AWS CLI has no direct equivalent of the Get-SSMLatestEC2Image cmdlet, but you can still query image IDs using Systems Manager commands. To return the full list of all the latest Windows Server images, in this case for the US West (Oregon) region, run the command aws ssm get-parameters-by-path --path /aws/service/ami-windows-latest/ --region us-west-2. Changing the value of the --path parameter to /aws/service/ami-amazon-linux-latest gets you, well, data on the latest Amazon Linux images.

To get the ID of a specific image, use the get-parameters command, shown in listing 4-3.

Listing 4-3. Using the AWS CLI to find the latest, specific image ID

```
C:\> aws ssm get-parameters --names "/aws/service/↵
ami-windows-latest/Windows_Server-2019-English-Full-Base" ↵
--region us-west-2
{
  "Parameters": [
    {
      "Name": "/aws/service/ami-windows-latest/Windows_Server-2019-
      English-Full-Base",
      "Type": "String",
      "Value": "ami-0b9909553e2f757f4",
      "Version": 34,
```

```
      "LastModifiedDate": "2021-05-14T12:47:28.928000-07:00",
      "ARN": "arn:aws:ssm:us-west-2::parameter/aws/service/ami-windows-
      latest/Windows_Server-2019-English-Full-Base",
      "DataType": "text"
    }
  ],
  "InvalidParameters": []
}
```

Now that you know how to find an image to start, to get to a running instance, we need to decide a couple more things. How much, and what type, of storage do you want to attach to the instance? Do you need to set up credentials and permissions for any code you want to run on the instance that calls into other AWS services (or to allow services such as AWS Systems Manager to manage the instance)? Do you want to customize or add to the software on the instance at launch? And finally, how to configure access to the instance?

Storage

Running EC2 instances have one or more storage devices attached, mounted as disks, in the same way your own machines or local virtual machine images have disk drives. And, just like your own machine, the attached storage can be SSD drives or traditional magnetic media.

When you use EC2 instances, you'll primarily work with **Amazon Elastic Block Store (EBS)** and **Amazon EC2 Instance store** to provide disk storage for your instances. Additional services designed for network-attached storage are also available, and while they are out of scope for this book, we will touch on those briefly at the end of this section.

Every instance that you launch has an attached root device volume (e.g., mapped to C: for Windows Servers). This attached device, which supplies the operating system and other files required to boot the instance, uses either an EBS or an Instance Store volume. The question is, which one should you choose?

An EBS volume supplies persistent storage that can exist beyond the running life of an instance. Once attached to an instance, you access data on the volume just as you would a physical hard drive. When you stop the instance, the data on the volume persists until you start the instance again. If, however, you terminate the instance **and** the EBS volume is the root storage device, then you will lose the data stored on it.

You can attach multiple additional EBS volumes to an instance, either at or after launch, and you can detach them at any time. This is the key to having data persist across instance termination – you simply store the data on a non-root volume and then take the volume and attach it to a different instance. You can also take snapshots of EBS volumes and attach those to another instance or simply use them as backups. AWS stores the volume snapshots for you in Amazon S3, although they are not directly accessible within S3 to you. To work with volume snapshots, you use the EC2 console, command-line tools, or APIs.

Instance store volumes still act like physical disk drives but beware – if you stop, hibernate, or terminate the instance, you will lose the data on instance store volumes, even if they are not the root storage volume. You can use instance store volumes for use cases involving temporary storage requirements, such as buffers, caches, and scratch data, as well as other temporary content. Unlike EBS volumes, you can only attach instance store volumes when an instance launches and you cannot detach them. Not all instance types support instance store volumes; for example, Windows server instance types do not, and for those that do, there is some variation in how many instance store volumes a given instance type supports.

Figure 4-4 shows the addition of multiple EBS volumes while working through the EC2 Launch Wizard in the management console. Notice the different types of volumes available, in this case, for a t2.micro instance type, and the options to encrypt and to not delete volumes when the instance terminates.

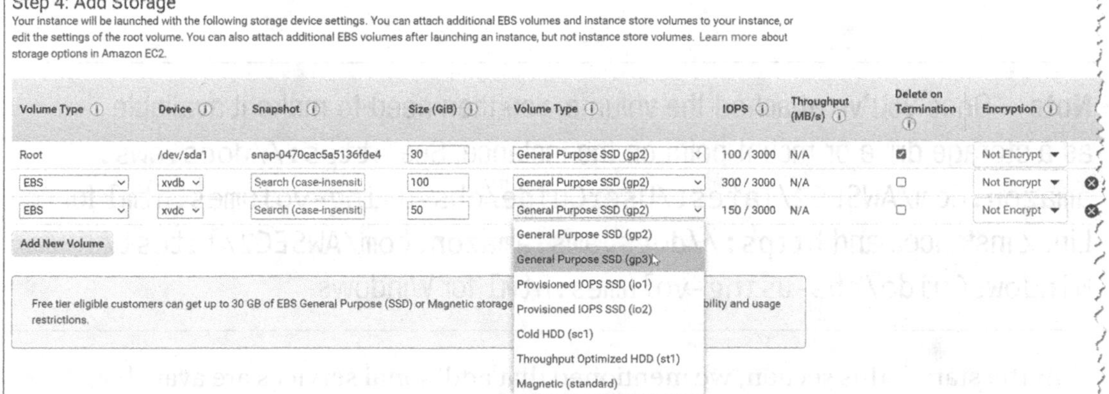

Figure 4-4. *Attaching multiple volumes while creating an instance*

Listing 4-4 illustrates commands from the AWS Tools for PowerShell and the AWS CLI for attaching an existing volume to a running Amazon Linux 2 instance.

Listing 4-4. Attaching a volume to a running instance

```
# AWS Tools for PowerShell
C:\> Add-EC2Volume -InstanceId i-0978c5332b67cdc3e ↵
-VolumeId vol-0d3e1f1254e2aa23d -Device /dev/sdh

AttachTime          : 5/15/2022 11:34:21 AM
DeleteOnTermination : False
Device              : /dev/sdh
InstanceId          : i-0978c5332b67cdc3e
State               : attaching
VolumeId            : vol-0d3e1f1254e2aa23d

# AWS CLI
C:\> aws ec2 attach-volume --instance-id i-0978c5332b67cdc3e ↵
--volume-id vol-0d3e1f1254e2aa23d --device /dev/sdh
{
    "AttachTime": "2022-05-15T18:45:02.017000+00:00",
    "Device": "/dev/sdh",
    "InstanceId": "i-0978c5332b67cdc3e",
    "State": "attaching",
    "VolumeId": "vol-0d3e1f1254e2aa23d"
}
```

Note   Once you've attached the volume, you then need to make it available as a storage drive or mount point on the instance. See `https://docs.aws.amazon.com/AWSEC2/latest/UserGuide/ebs-using-volumes.html` for Linux instances and `https://docs.aws.amazon.com/AWSEC2/latest/WindowsGuide/ebs-using-volumes.html` for Windows.

At the start of this section, we mentioned that additional services are available that provide network-attached storage for your instances. You can attach multiple EBS volumes to a single instance, and you can also attach a volume to multiple Linux instances at the same time, but only in limited regions. Therefore, if you have workloads that require shared storage (both read-only and read-write), you'll need to work with these additional services: **Amazon Elastic File Service**, **Amazon FSx for Lustre**, **Amazon FSx for Windows File Server,** and **Amazon FSx for NetApp ONTAP**.

Note   Full details on these services are beyond the scope of this book, but we wanted to make you aware of them should you have need for shared, scalable, storage across instances, including multi-writer and high-performance workload scenarios.

Amazon Elastic File System, or *EFS*, provides a scalable file system you can attach to Linux-based instances – thousands of them if need be! The file system also grows (and shrinks) dynamically, meaning you don't need to worry about how much storage to provision. And in a typical Amazon fashion, you pay only for the actual storage you use. As with EBS volumes, once you've created the storage, you then need to attach, or mount, it to your instances. By the way, while we're discussing EFS in the context of EC2 here, you can also use EFS storage with Linux-based containers running in Amazon ECS and Amazon EKS. This makes it a good choice if you are considering moving from a VM-based infrastructure to containers in the future and want to reuse existing storage.

Amazon FSx for Lustre is also for Linux instances and, like EFS, is a fully managed file system, with all the provisioning, configuration, maintenance, and backup tasks handled for you. If your workloads involve machine learning, video rendering, or simulations and require fast, low-latency high-throughput access to shared data, then FSx for Lustre could be an ideal choice. You can also link a FSx for Lustre file system to an S3 bucket. This makes the objects in that bucket appear as files in the file system (remember we said S3 is not a file system?). The advantage of this is there is no data transfer cost associated with moving files from S3 into Lustre for processing and of course, as the S3 bucket contents change, the file system updates itself accordingly. Just as with EFS, you can also attach FSx for Lustre storage to Linux-based containers in ECS and EKS.

Amazon FSx for Windows File Server provides scalable and performant storage based on Windows File Server instances running in the cloud. All the administrative features you'd use with traditional on-premise Windows File Server are available such as quotas, end-user file restore, access control lists (ACLs), and integration with Active Directory (this is because it really is Windows File Server running in the cloud!).

And as another fully managed service, you don't need to worry about provisioning, maintenance, and backups. Unlike EFS and FSx for Lustre, you can use FSx for Windows File Server with Windows, Linux, and macOS compute instances – including those running on-premises – and ECS containers due to the use of the industry standard Server Message Block (SMB) protocol for access.

Finally, **Amazon FSx for NetApp ONTAP** provides fully managed shared storage that is built on NetApp's ONTAP file system. Amazon FSx for NetApp ONTAP offers high-performance file storage that is accessible from Linux, Windows, and macOS compute instances through the use of industry standard NFS, SMB, and iSCSI protocols. This storage is fully elastic and virtually unlimited in size and supports compression and deduplication. You can also take advantage of ONTAP's popular data management capabilities, like snapshots, clones, and replication, with the click of a button.

Controlling Access with Security Groups

So far, we've determined which image to run, and what storage to attach, both at launch time and subsequently depending on our workload needs. But what about access to the running instances? How is that controlled?

You may be familiar with firewalls, for example, Windows Firewall, controlling network access to your device. In AWS, Security Groups take on the traditional role of the firewall. Security Groups contain one or more rules that determine which port (or port range), or protocol, is accessible on your running instances, both externally (if instance is reachable from the Internet) and from other resources within the same virtual private cloud (VPC). You read that right – it's possible to restrict access to instances running in the same network. In fact, you need to enable this access by adding rules to the relevant security groups guarding your resources – security groups do not open ports by default. For example, in a given VPC, let's say you have a database running in Amazon RDS. The database instance will be associated with a security group. An EC2 instance (or instances) running in the same VPC will also be associated with one or more separate security groups. Unless you add rules to the database's security group permitting access from either the EC2 instance IPs or the group(s) associated with the instances, your application will not be able to access the database.

Security Groups are the simpler of the choices to protect network access to your instances, but you'll also hear mention of Network ACLs when working with VPCs. Network ACLs are a little more complex but provide even more control. What's the difference? First, Security Groups act at the EC2 instances (or other resources such as Amazon RDS databases) level. Network ACLs act at the network subnet level, that is, controlling ingress into and egress from a subnet. Secondly, Security Groups are stateful. If you configure a rule allowing inbound traffic on a given port, egress traffic in response to that request (e.g., a response to an HTTP request to a web server running on an EC2 instance) is permitted – you do not need to add a corresponding outbound rule.

This is not the case with Network ACLs. For every rule enabling inbound traffic on a given port, you must add a corresponding rule for the outbound response traffic – otherwise, it's blocked by default. Additionally, Network ACL rules have an associated priority, which you determine. Network ACLs evaluate their rules in priority order. A rule disallowing traffic that has a higher priority than a similar rule enabling that traffic will block that traffic, irrespective of the enabling rule. Security Groups don't use priority ordering, which leads to another common question with Security Groups: How to add a rule to disallow traffic for a given port or protocol? The simple answer is that you don't. To disallow traffic on a given port or protocol in a Security Group, just don't add a rule for that traffic. Security Group rules are always permissive, unlike Network ACL rules that can both allow and disallow traffic. We won't cover Network ACLs further in this book, since everything we're going to do to control access to resources is possible with Security Groups, for simplicity.

When you launch an EC2 instance, you can elect to create a new Security Group or associate the instance with an existing group. And you can of course add or delete rules at any time, and the changes take effect instantly. Figure 4-5 shows the creation of a new group during the launch of a Windows-based instance that opens ports 80, 443, and 3389 (Remote Desktop). Notice how ports 80 and 443 are open to all traffic (we're assuming here the instance is intended to be accessible from the Internet). However, access via remote desktop is only permitted when it comes from a specific address, which is specified in CIDR format (explained in Chapter 1).

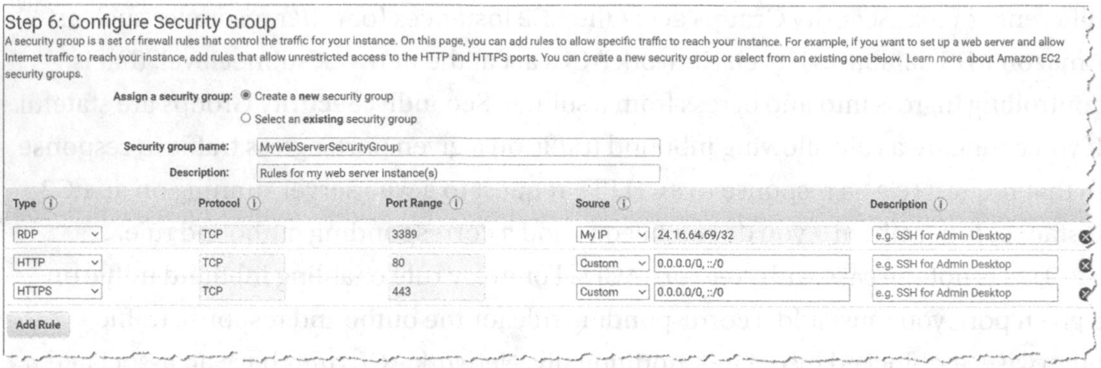

Step 6: Configure Security Group

A security group is a set of firewall rules that control the traffic for your instance. On this page, you can add rules to allow specific traffic to reach your instance. For example, if you want to set up a web server and allow Internet traffic to reach your instance, add rules that allow unrestricted access to the HTTP and HTTPS ports. You can create a new security group or select from an existing one below. Learn more about Amazon EC2 security groups.

Assign a security group: ⦿ Create a **new** security group
                         ○ Select an **existing** security group

Security group name: MyWebServerSecurityGroup

Description: Rules for my web server instance(s)

Type ⓘ	Protocol ⓘ	Port Range ⓘ	Source ⓘ		Description ⓘ	
RDP ⌄	TCP	3389	My IP ⌄	24.16.64.69/32	e.g. SSH for Admin Desktop	✕
HTTP ⌄	TCP	80	Custom ⌄	0.0.0.0/0, ::/0	e.g. SSH for Admin Desktop	✕
HTTPS ⌄	TCP	443	Custom ⌄	0.0.0.0/0, ::/0	e.g. SSH for Admin Desktop	✕

Add Rule

Figure 4-5. *Adding rules to a new Security Group on instance launch*

You can add, modify, and remove rules in a group at any time, although beware if you change an existing rule, perhaps to tighten or widen the address range; then it can cause a temporary access "blip" as EC2 will replace the modified rule with a new rule. In practice though, unless your instances are serving traffic on that rule at a very high rate of knots, you're unlikely to notice.

You can modify rules in a group using the management console, as you'd expect, but you are also able to change them programmatically using the EC2 API, or command-line tools. Listing 4-5 shows commands from the AWS Tools for PowerShell and the AWS CLI to add a new rule to a group to permit access for SSH from a given IP (as mentioned earlier, the traffic source could equally be another security group).

Listing 4-5. Modifying a Security Group from the command line

```
# AWS Tools for PowerShell
C:\> Grant-EC2SecurityGroupIngress -GroupId sg-2482c46b ↵
-IpPermission @{ IpProtocol="tcp"; FromPort="22"; ToPort="22";↵
IpRanges="24.16.64.69/32" }

# AWS CLI
aws ec2 authorize-security-group-ingress --group-id sg-2482c46b ↵
--protocol tcp --port 22 --cidr 24.16.64.69/32 --region us-west-2
```

Customizing an Instance on Creation

While you can create an instance from a "stock" image provided by EC2, customize it with the software dependencies your application needs, and then create a custom image from the instance that you'll use to create identical instances in the future; this approach comes with a maintenance cost. You are responsible for patching the custom image to keep up with security patches, etc.

A better approach (in our opinion) is to customize the stock image on instance creation and treat the instance as disposable. In other words, don't treat the instance as a "pet" you plan to keep for long periods. You can achieve this customization using a user data script, which you optionally specify when you create the instance.

If you create your instance(s) using the Management Console, you can edit or paste the script directly within the console – useful when learning. If you instead create the instance from a command-line tool, you can pass the script to the relevant command (`aws ec2 run-instances` or `New-EC2Instance`). Other instance creation mechanisms, such as using a launch configuration with an Auto Scaling Group, or from a CloudFormation template, or a CDK application, or even by calling EC2's `RunInstances` API from within your application code, also have means by which you can supply the script to run.

So what is a user data script? Put simply, it's either a bash, PowerShell, or even a (Windows) batch script, containing the commands you want to run as the instance is created. By default, user data scripts run only when the instance is first created and not when it's restarted (e.g., after being stopped for a period, or rebooted). You can specify that the script should run on restart by adding a `persist` setting, set to the value `true`, to the script. How you do this depends on how you specify the script.

For bash scripts on Linux instances, the script should start with the `#!` characters followed by the path to the script interpreter. The remaining lines are the commands to run. Listing 4-6 shows a simple script to install the components for a LAMP web server stack on an Amazon Linux 2 (AL2) instance. Note that as the script runs as the administrative user, you don't need to prefix commands with `sudo`.

Listing 4-6. Configuring an AL2 instance on creation with the LAMP stack

```
#!/bin/bash
yum update -y
amazon-linux-extras install -y lamp-mariadb10.2-php7.2 php7.2
yum install -y httpd mariadb-server
systemctl start httpd
systemctl enable httpd
```

On Windows instances, you can use batch or PowerShell for your user data scripts. For traditional Windows batch scripts, enclose the commands in `<script>` tags, shown in Listing 4-7. This script will run on instance creation and on every restart, courtesy of the `<persist>` tag.

Listing 4-7. Using batch commands on Windows

```
<script>
echo Current date and time >> %SystemRoot%\Temp\test.log
echo %DATE% %TIME% >> %SystemRoot%\Temp\test.log
</script>
<persist>true<persist>
```

To use PowerShell, you use a `<powershell>` tag instead, as shown in Listing 4-8. This example installs and configures IIS with additional features, installs WebDeploy, and then the AWS CodeDeploy agent. An instance configured with this script is ready to accept automated deployments (managed by AWS CodeDeploy) of ASP.NET applications, packaged using WebDeploy.

Listing 4-8. Using PowerShell for a user data script

```
<powershell>
Install-WindowsFeature -Name ↵
Web-Server,NET-Framework-45-ASPNET,NET-Framework-45-Core, ↵
NET-Framework-45-Features
Set-ExecutionPolicy Bypass -Scope Process -Force; ↵
iex ((New-Object System.Net.WebClient).DownloadString('https://chocolatey.
org/install.ps1'))
choco install webdeploy -y
```

```
Read-S3Object -BucketName aws-codedeploy-us-west-2 ↵
-Key latest/codedeploy-agent.msi ↵
-File c:/temp/codedeploy-agent.msi
c:/temp/codedeploy-agent.msi /quiet ↵
/l c:/temp/host-agent-install-log.txt
</powershell>
```

In Chapter 2, we mentioned that Windows Server images provided by EC2 come with the AWS Tools for PowerShell pre-installed. This means we can make calls to AWS services as part of our user data script. Listing 4-8 includes the use of the `Read-S3Object` cmdlet to download a file from S3 as part of the instance configuration. Note that for this script to run, the instance will need to be associated with a role that grants credentials via a trust relationship and permissions to the respective APIs and resources, which we'll cover in the next section.

Amazon Linux 2 instances come with the AWS CLI pre-installed, so you can perform similar tasks.

Tip   In a true AWS fashion, these are not the only ways to specify user data scripts; you can always use YAML if that's your thing. See `https://docs.aws.amazon.com/AWSEC2/latest/WindowsGuide/ec2-windows-user-data.html` and `https://docs.aws.amazon.com/AWSEC2/latest/UserGuide/user-data.html` for all the gory details of the different formats.

Instance Role and Permissions

Finally, we come to roles, and the associated credentials and permissions, for your EC2 instances. Do you need a role? Technically, there's nothing stopping you creating an EC2 instance without an associated role. In earlier chapters, we discussed how roles provide both credentials and scope permissions. If the application you are intending to run on an EC2 instance makes no calls to EC2 or other AWS services, then arguably you could proceed without one.

Note   In the EC2 console UI and APIs, you'll see mention of an *instance profile*. An instance profile is the mechanism by which a role gets associated with an instance. The profile contains a reference to the actual role.

Proceeding without a role, however, means you miss out on the management capabilities that AWS provides for instances using services such as Systems Manager. For example, all EC2-provided images come with the Systems Manager agent pre-installed. This agent works with several features of Systems Manager to provide functionality such as running commands, or automation documents, remotely against instances. Taking it to cloud scale, let's say you have a fleet of EC2 instances that number in the thousands. Want to run a script (or single command) against the entire fleet? That's an awful lot of connections to open! Instead, using Systems Manager, you can take that script and have it run on the instances, automatically, just by using the Systems Manager console, APIs, or even from the command line on your local system.

To perform this magic, Systems Manager hands the script off to the agent on each instance. This means Systems Manager needs to be accessible from each instance and the agent on each instance needs permissions to do whatever work the script requires, then communicate back when the script has concluded. These permissions are all wrapped up in a role.

Alternatively, perhaps your instances follow recommended best practices and are not exposed directly to the Internet, since you are running them in private subnets in a VPC. You can't reach these instances from remote desktop or SSH without running what are known as *bastion hosts* – Internet-accessible instances that enable you to hop into the VPC and from there access the "inner" private resources. For this to work, it assumes you have configured the security groups and network ACLs to allow such traffic to reach the private subnets, and that the necessary ports are open in the security groups controlling access to your bastion host. All this is so yesterday!

If, instead, you specify a role that contains the `AmazonSSMManagedInstanceCore` managed policy (which is a policy owned and maintained by AWS) on instance creation, then you can connect remotely and open a command-line shell to the instances, no matter whether they are defined as Internet accessible, from within the EC2 console. All without the need to open the port for RDP (3389) or SSH (22).

Hopefully, you can see that there are benefits to specifying a role when you create instances even if your intended application is not going to make calls to AWS services or resources. So how do you do it, and what does it look like?

While you can create a role as part of the launch wizard in the EC2 console, we recommend you instead create what you need first in the IAM console and then select the created role from the wizard. This keeps things tidy. We maintain several roles in our accounts. We use most with the different sample applications that we deploy as part of talk demos, and these contain a mix of service and API permissions. We use other roles for instances where we don't necessarily want to deploy an application but just use the EC2 instance as a plain VM, perhaps to test software trials or previews, for example, preview releases of .NET. These latter roles also use the managed policy mentioned earlier but contain very few additional permissions since we're not using them with applications that are making calls to AWS.

To create the initial role that we'll use in the next section, first, head to the IAM console and select **Roles** from the navigation panel, then click **Create role** at the top of the page. Remember, roles can have a trust relationship – by which temporary, auto-rotating credentials are provided to the host associated with the role and permissions. The first thing to select is the entity to be referenced in the trust relationship. Since we are about to create an EC2 instance, select **EC2** from the *Common use cases* section, or the service list; shown in Figure 4-6, and then click the **Next: Permissions** button at the foot of the page (you may need to scroll down to find the button).

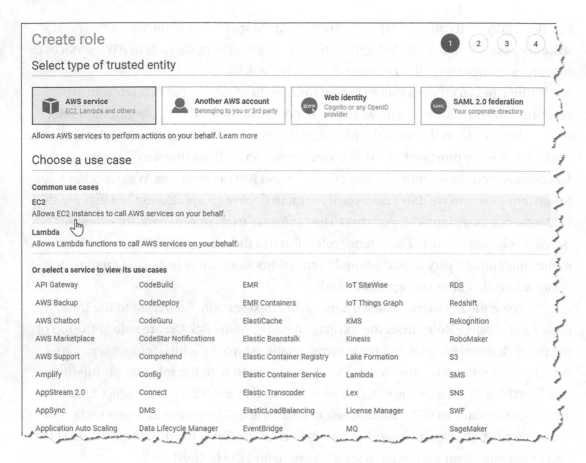

Figure 4-6. *Setting the trusted entity for a role*

Now you'll associate permissions with the role. This will govern access to services, APIs in those services, and other resources for code running on the selected entity (EC2 instance). This is a very fine-grained permissions model, and you'll note that by default, there are no permissions – everything is locked down, requiring you to "open up" the role by adding what you need. This stands in contrast to other approaches where everything is permitted and you "lock down" on deployment, which is, in our opinion, a less secure and more error-prone process to get right.

Let's first add the managed policy we mentioned earlier, `AmazonSSMManagedInstanceCore`. Type *AmazonSSM* into the Search box to see a list of matches and then select the matching policy, shown in Figure 4-7.

Figure 4-7. *Attaching the AmazonSSMManagedInstanceCore policy to the role*

If you want to add more managed policies, or existing policies from your own account, to the role, then you could go ahead and type the names (or partial names) into the search field and select the relevant policies, building up the permissions associated with the role.

Instead, let's create a custom policy for the role that will allow us to make use of some S3 functionality, using PowerShell or AWS CLI commands, when we connect later in the chapter to the instance we're going to create.

Note   There is an *AmazonS3ReadOnly* managed policy you could attach for the same effect, but we want to illustrate how you'd scope to specific API permissions here if needed.

Click the **Create policy** button. A new browser tab will open onto the policy creation wizard. If you're accomplished with roles and policies, you could use the JSON editor at this point to craft your policy, but we'll use the visual editor instead. First, expand **Service**, enter *s3* into the search field, and select **S3** from the results, shown in Figure 4-8.

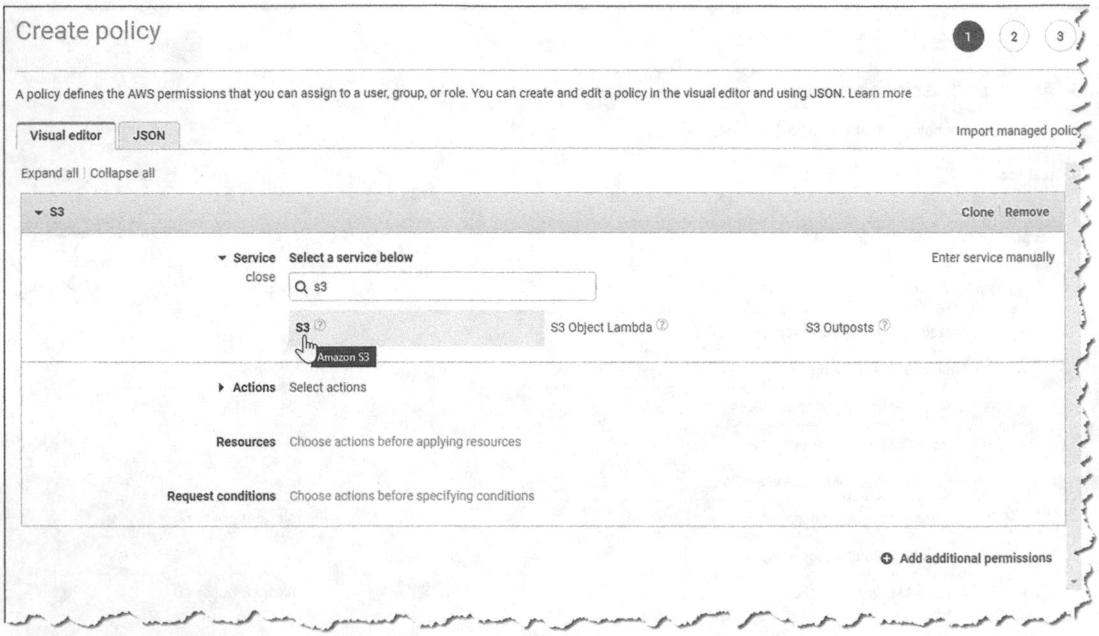

Figure 4-8. *Selecting S3 as the target service for the custom policy*

In the **Actions** panel that's now open, you can see categorized actions (*List, Read,* etc.). We want to be able to list buckets, list the objects in a bucket, and download (read) objects from a bucket. Start by expanding the **List** category and select the ListAllMyBuckets and ListBucket actions. Then, expand the **Read** category and select the GetObject action, shown in Figure 4-9.

▶ Service   S3

▼ Actions   Specify the actions allowed in S3 ⑦   Switch to deny permissions ❶
  close
             🔍 Filter actions

             Manual actions (add actions)
             ☐ All S3 actions (s3:*)

             Access level   Expand all │ Collapse all
               ▼ ☐ List (2 selected)

                 ☑ ListAllMyBuckets ⑦   ☐ ListBucketVersions ⑦   ☐ ListStorageLensConfigurations ⑦
                 ☑ ListBucket ⑦   ☐ ListJobs ⑦
                 ☐ ListBucketMultipartUploads ⑦ ☐ ListMultipartUploadParts ⑦

               ▼ ☐ Read (1 selected)

                 ☐ DescribeJob ⑦   ☐ GetBucketObjectLockConfiguration ⑦ ☐ GetObjectAcl ⑦
                 ☐ GetAccelerateConfiguration ⑦ ☐ GetBucketOwnershipControls ⑦   ☐ GetObjectLegalHold ⑦
                 ☐ GetAccessPoint ⑦   ☐ GetBucketPolicy ⑦   ☐ GetObjectRetention ⑦
                 ☐ GetAccessPointConfigurationForO... ⑦ ☐ GetBucketPolicyStatus ⑦   ☐ GetObjectTagging ⑦
                 ☐ GetAccessPointForObjectLambda ⑦ ☐ GetBucketPublicAccessBlock ⑦   ☐ GetObjectTorrent ⑦
                 ☐ GetAccessPointPolicy ⑦   ☐ GetBucketRequestPayment ⑦   ☐ GetObjectVersion ⑦
                 ☐ GetAccessPointPolicyForObjectLa... ⑦ ☐ GetBucketTagging ⑦   ☐ GetObjectVersionAcl ⑦
                 ☐ GetAccessPointPolicyStatus ⑦ ☐ GetBucketVersioning ⑦   ☐ GetObjectVersionForReplication ⑦
                 ☐ GetAccessPointPolicyStatusForOb... ⑦ ☐ GetBucketWebsite ⑦   ☐ GetObjectVersionTagging ⑦
                 ☐ GetAccountPublicAccessBlock ⑦ ☐ GetEncryptionConfiguration ⑦   ☐ GetObjectVersionTorrent ⑦
                 ☐ GetAnalyticsConfiguration ⑦ ☐ GetIntelligentTieringConfiguration ⑦ ☐ GetReplicationConfiguration ⑦
                 ☐ GetBucketAcl ⑦   ☐ GetInventoryConfiguration ⑦   ☐ GetStorageLensConfiguration ⑦
                 ☐ GetBucketCORS ⑦   ☐ GetJobTagging ⑦   ☐ GetStorageLensConfiguration Tagg... ⑦
                 ☐ GetBucketLocation ⑦   ☐ GetLifecycleConfiguration ⑦   ☐ GetStorageLensDashboard ⑦
                 ☐ GetBucketLogging ⑦   ☐ GetMetricsConfiguration ⑦   ☐ ListAccessPoints ⑦
                 ☐ GetBucketNotification ⑦   ☑ GetObject ⑦   ☐ ListAccessPointsForObjectLambda ⑦

               ▶ ☐ Tagging

Figure 4-9. *Selecting the permitted actions for the policy*

Scroll down to view the Resources section. For a policy intended for real-world production use, we would want to follow best practices and limit the set of resources this policy applies to – to a specific bucket, or set of buckets – needed by our intended application. For this example, let's permit access to any of the buckets in our account. Do this by selecting the *Any* option to the right of the bucket and object resources, shown in Figure 4-10.

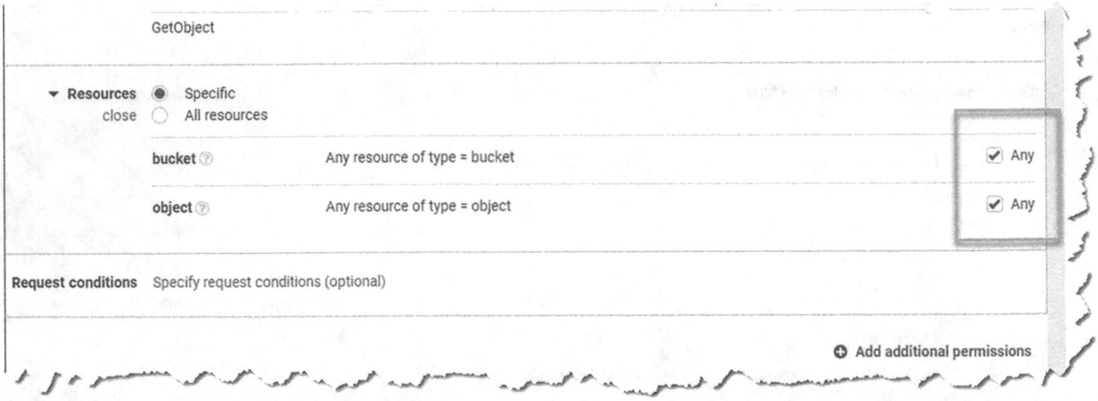

Figure 4-10. *Permitting the policy to access all our buckets and objects*

Click the **Next: Tags** button. Again, in a real-world production use, we may want to apply tags to the policy resource we are creating, but let's skip this step for now and proceed by clicking the **Next: Review** button.

On the **Review** page, shown in Figure 4-11, give the policy a name, and optional description, then click the **Create policy** button (not shown) to complete the process and return to the Policies page.

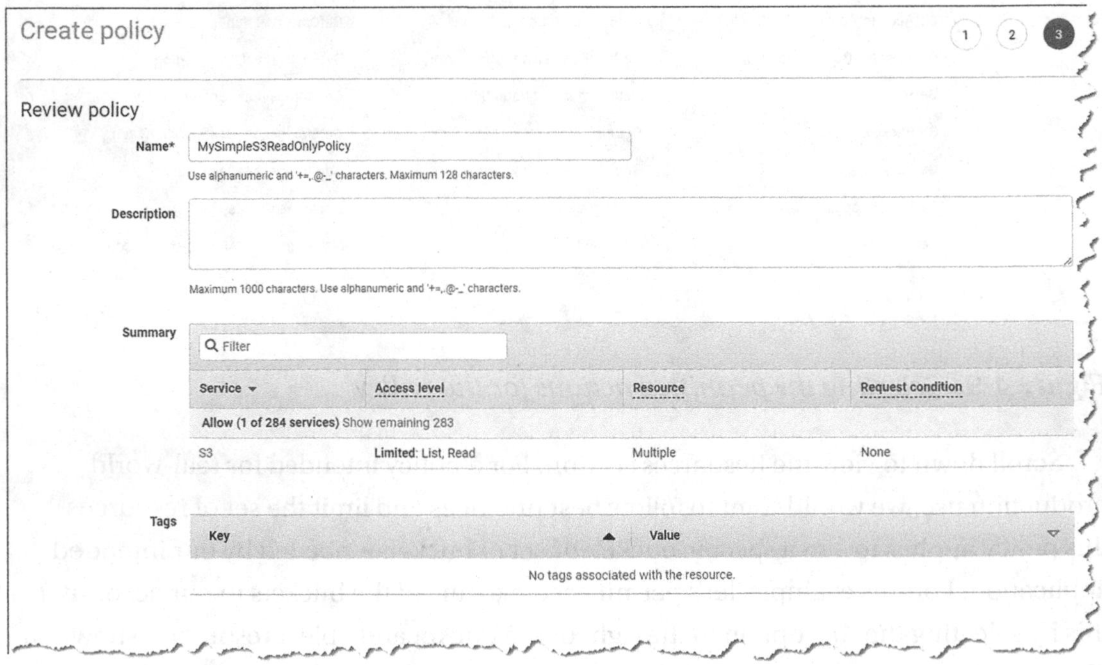

Figure 4-11. *Naming the new policy*

Go back to the browser tab where we left off creating the role. Resume the process by clicking the refresh icon button to the right of the list, then enter *MySimple* (or some of whatever text you chose when you named the policy) to see your new policy listed, like that shown in Figure 4-12. Select the policy, then click the **Next: Tags** button.

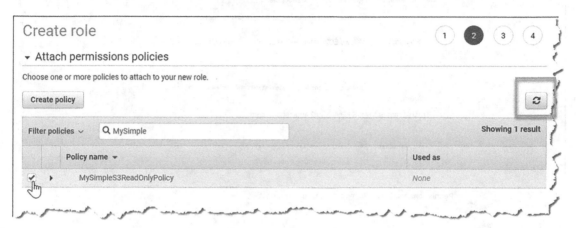

Figure 4-12. *Attaching the new custom policy to the in-progress role*

Once again, skip over tags by clicking the **Next: Review** button. Give the role a name (you can change the description if you wish) and finally click the **Create role** button to complete the process (Figure 4-13).

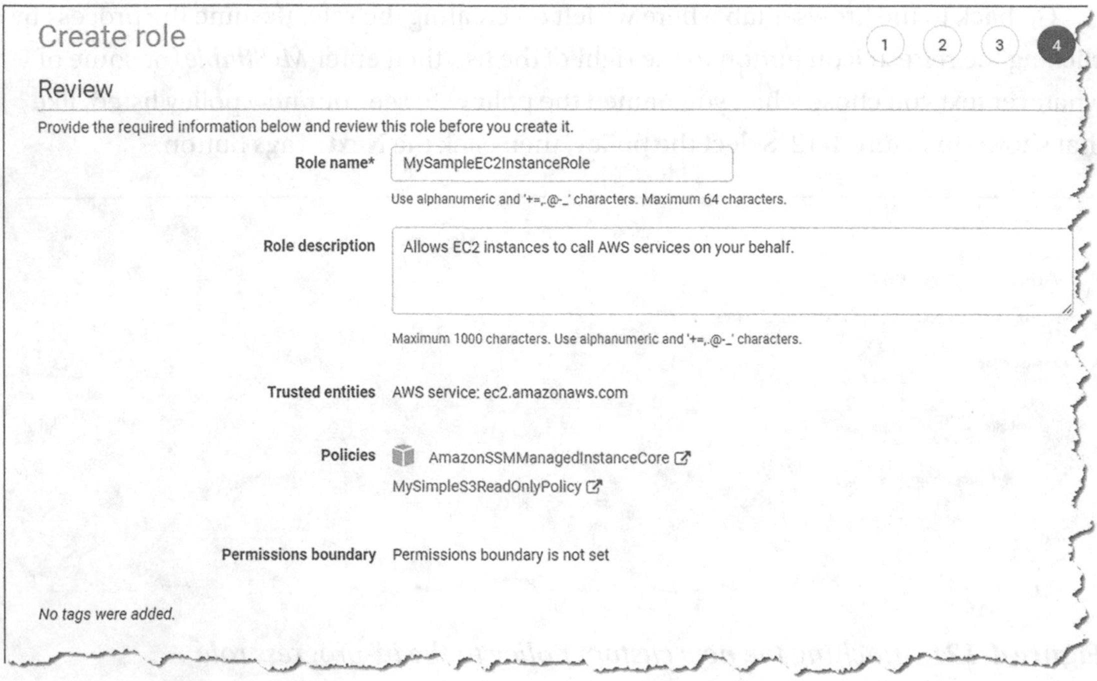

Create role

① ② ③ ④

Review

Provide the required information below and review this role before you create it.

Role name*   MySampleEC2InstanceRole

Use alphanumeric and '+=,.@-_' characters. Maximum 64 characters.

Role description   Allows EC2 instances to call AWS services on your behalf.

Maximum 1000 characters. Use alphanumeric and '+=,.@-_' characters.

Trusted entities   AWS service: ec2.amazonaws.com

Policies   AmazonSSMManagedInstanceCore ☐
MySimpleS3ReadOnlyPolicy ☐

Permissions boundary   Permissions boundary is not set

No tags were added.

Figure 4-13. *Naming the new role*

You'll have now returned to the Roles page for your account, and you should be
able to see your new role listed. You can click the role name to view (and edit) the trust
relationships and permissions if you wish, but at this stage, we have everything we need
to create and configure a new EC2 instance. Let's start!

Creating and Configuring an EC2 Instance

Using everything we've learned, it's now time to create an EC2 instance. For now, we'll
use the AWS Management Console as that's a great way to explore. There's also an
EC2 Launch Wizard built into the AWS Toolkit for Visual Studio, but it doesn't support
everything you can do in the console or via command-line/SDK tools. Later in the book,
we'll use automation or SDKs to launch instances, which is closer to how you'll work
with instances designed for production usage.

For this exercise, we'll be creating an instance based on a stock Amazon Linux 2
image. We'll configure this instance, at creation, with additional software – the .NET
5 runtime – so that the instance can host a simple ASP.NET Core sample application

generated from a template, which we'll connect to from the Internet courtesy of the instance having a public IP address. Then, we'll remote into the instance from both the management console and Visual Studio.

Note   Because this is a simple exercise to allow us to become familiar with the process of launching instances, we'll use Kestrel to expose the sample application to requests from the Internet. This isn't a recommended practice for production, where you would normally place the application behind a reverse proxy such as Nginx (for scenarios where the instance is directly accessible from the Internet) or place the instances into private subnets and use a load balancer in the public subnets to forward traffic to Kestrel.

To begin, navigate to the EC2 dashboard in the management console and click the **Launch instance** button (this button expands to a small menu – select the **Launch instances** option from the menu). You'll arrive at the *Step 1: Choose an Amazon Machine Image (AMI)* page (shown earlier in Figure 4-1). In the Quick Start tab, select the 64-bit (x86) Amazon Linux 2 image and click **Select**.

In Step 2, we select the size of the instance (instance type). Choose the *t2.micro* type, which is part of the AWS Free Tier, and click **Next: Configure Instance Details** to proceed.

There are a few settings we need to set in the *Step 3: Configure Instance Details* page.

- Ensure that the *Auto-assign Public IP* setting shows **Use subnet setting (Enable)**. If it does not, expand the drop-down and select **Enable** (without this, we will not be able to reach the instance from the Internet).

- For IAM role, select the role you created previously in this chapter.

Figure 4-14 shows these settings.

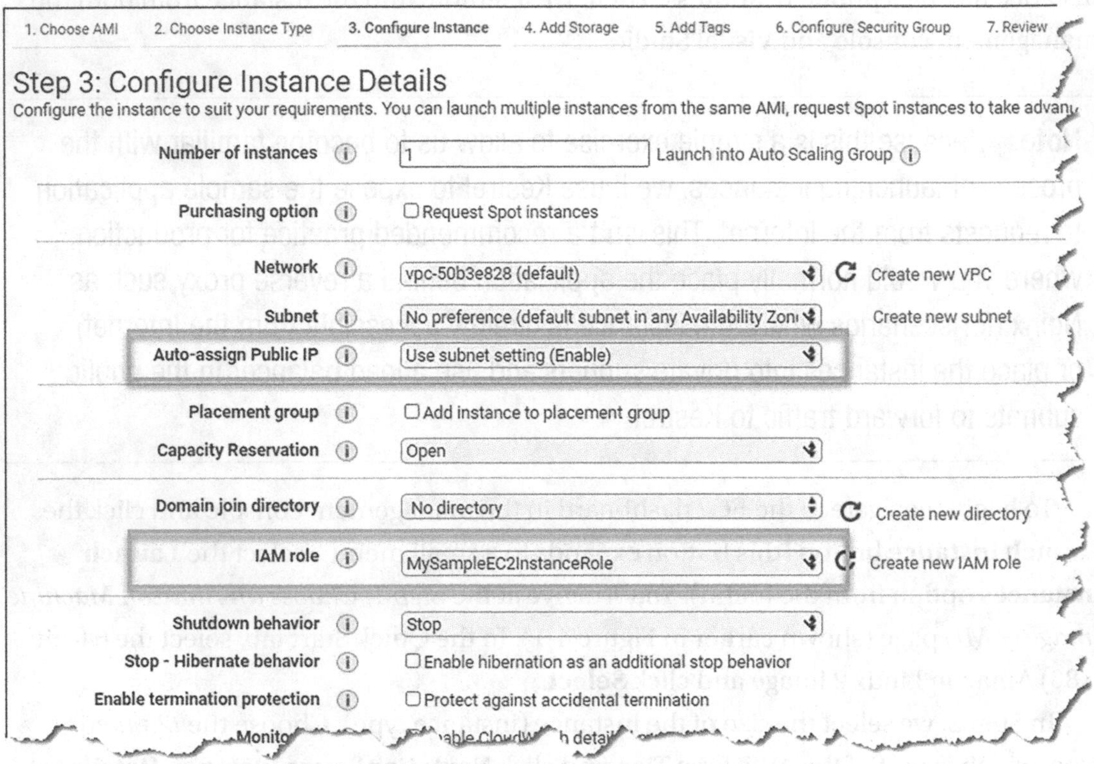

Figure 4-14.   *Requesting a public IP address and setting instance role*

Before moving on, we need to add our user data script to configure our instance during creation with the software we need. Scroll down to the foot of the Step 3 page to find the **User data** field. Ensure the field is set to As text mode, then paste the script from Listing 4-9 into the field. User data scripts run with administrative privileges, so you do not need to prefix the commands with sudo.

Listing 4-9.   The user data script to configure our new instance

```
#!/bin/bash
yum -y update
rpm -Uvh https://packages.microsoft.com/config/centos/7/packages-
microsoft-prod.rpm
yum -y install dotnet-runtime-5.0
yum -y install aspnetcore-runtime-5.0
```

Figure 4-15 shows the completed options for user data.

▼ Advanced Details

Enclave ⓘ	☐ Enable	
Metadata accessible ⓘ	Enabled	⬇
Metadata version ⓘ	V1 and V2 (token optional)	⬇
Metadata token response hop limit ⓘ	1	⬇
User data ⓘ	⦿ As text ○ As file ☐ Input is already base64 encoded	

```
#!/bin/bash
yum -y update
rpm -Uvh https://packages.microsoft.com/config/centos/7/packages-microsoft-
prod.rpm
yum -y install dotnet-runtime-5.0
yum -y install aspnetcore-runtime-5.0
```

Figure 4-15. *User data script to configure additional software on the new instance*

Click **Next: Add Storage** to proceed. The default volume size of 8GB is fine for our purposes, but if you want to increase it, or experiment with adding additional volumes following the material earlier in this chapter, feel free to do so. Click **Next: Add Tags** when you are ready to continue.

For ad hoc and short-lived resources that you create, it's probably not necessary to tag them. For production, it's a best practice. Tags are key-value pairs that can be associated with most resources. For EC2 instances, a useful tag is to apply a name (note – this is different from the instance's hostname). To add a Name tag, click the Add Tag button, and enter *Name* for the key and a value, shown in Figure 4-16.

1. Choose AMI	2. Choose Instance Type	3. Configure Instance	4. Add Storage	**5. Add Tags**	6. Configure Security Group	7. Review

Step 5: Add Tags
A tag consists of a case-sensitive key-value pair. For example, you could define a tag with key = Name and value = Webserver.
A copy of a tag can be applied to volumes, instances or both.
Tags will be applied to all instances and volumes. Learn more about tagging your Amazon EC2 resources.

Key (128 characters maximum)	Value (256 characters maximum)	Instances ⓘ	Volumes ⓘ	Network Interfaces ⓘ	
Name	MyFirstEC2Instance	☑	☑	☑	⊗

Add another tag	(Up to 50 tags maximum)

Figure 4-16. *Adding a Name tag to an instance*

Click **Next: Configure Security Group** to proceed. We want our instance to serve a web application, so we'll need to open port 80. By default, as this is a Linux instance, the group contains a rule to open port 22, but it's open to everyone with a CIDR of 0.0.0.0/0. Let's first change this to allow only from our IP address by clicking the **Source** field and selecting *My IP* (note that the resulting address is a best guess – you may need to find your external address if, for example, you are behind a corporate proxy or firewall). Then, click **Add Rule**. Click the **Type** drop-down and select *HTTP* to fill out defaults for the rest of the rule. In this scenario, a source of anywhere is fine to reach our web application. If you wish, you can add a name and description to the group. Figure 4-17 shows the final security group settings.

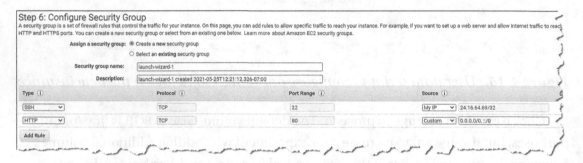

Figure 4-17. Completed Security Group rules

At this point, we've completed the wizard, so click **Review and Launch**. The review page summarizes our selections, and once satisfied they are correct, click **Launch**. You'll immediately get a pop-up dialog asking you to select, or create, a key pair. As you may recall from earlier in the chapter, you use this to decrypt the randomly assigned administrative password for the instance so that you can open remote connections to the instance via SSH or RDP that use the generated password. Select **Create a new key pair** and be sure to then click the **Download Key Pair** button to save the private key data. We'll need this later to connect to the instance. Figure 4-18 shows the completed dialog – do not forget to download the PEM file!

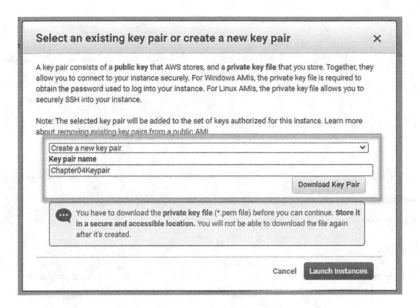

Figure 4-18. *Create a new key pair for the instance*

Finally, click **Launch Instances** to start creating the new instance. EC2 will confirm the launch is underway; then click the **View Instances** button to navigate to a grid view of all your running instances. Select the instance in the grid to populate tabs beneath with details of the instance, shown in Figure 4-19.

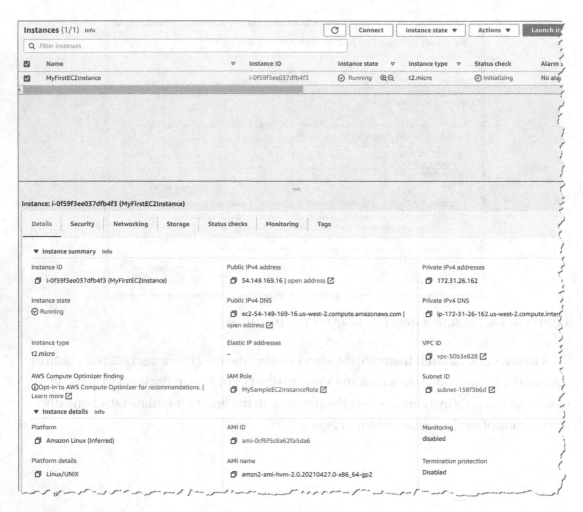

Figure 4-19. *Instance details*

The instance state will transition into *Running*, but this doesn't necessarily mean the instance is fully available. Wait until you see the **Status check** read *2/2 checks passed*; then you're ready to connect (you can also check instance status by accessing the instance's log, which you can find – if you're curious – from the **Actions** drop-down button, under **Monitor and troubleshoot**).

Connecting to the Instance with the Management Console

With the instance running, let's open a remote connection and start a simple web application and then connect to the application from the Internet to test the security group rule we added for port 80.

Earlier, we mentioned that you could use the key pair you created as part of the launch to open an SSH connection at this point. However, because we associated the instance with the role we created, which had the `AmazonSSMManagedInstanceCore` policy attached, we can conveniently connect to it using a browser-based command-line terminal from within the console. This is super useful as it works even if the instance is not publicly accessible from the Internet (e.g., it's running in a private subnet or does not have a public IP address).

To open the terminal, select the instance in the grid (the check box to the left of the Name column) and click **Connect**. On the resulting page, shown in Figure 4-20, select the **Session Manager** tab, and then click **Connect** once more.

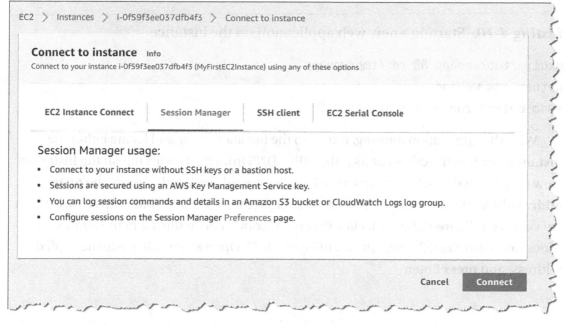

Figure 4-20. Remotely connecting from within the console

We can verify that the .NET 5 and ASP.NET Core 5 runtimes are installed, per the commands we specified in the user data script, as shown in Figure 4-21.

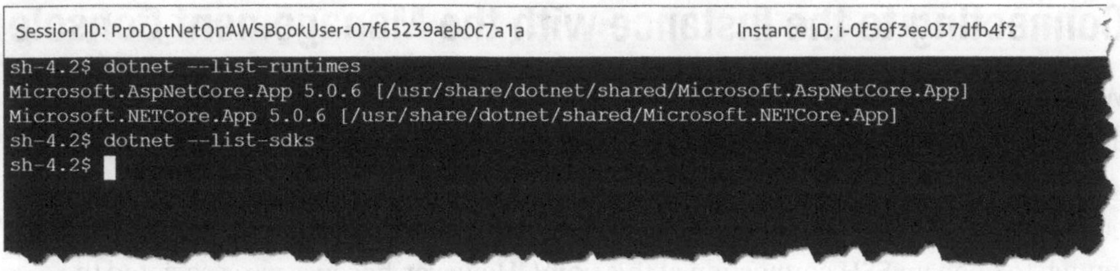

```
Session ID: ProDotNetOnAWSBookUser-07f65239aeb0c7a1a                    Instance ID: i-0f59f3ee037dfb4f3

sh-4.2$ dotnet --list-runtimes
Microsoft.AspNetCore.App 5.0.6 [/usr/share/dotnet/shared/Microsoft.AspNetCore.App]
Microsoft.NETCore.App 5.0.6 [/usr/share/dotnet/shared/Microsoft.NETCore.App]
sh-4.2$ dotnet --list-sdks
sh-4.2$ ▮
```

Figure 4-21. *Verifying runtime installation*

We did not, however, install an SDK, and we need that to be able to run dotnet new to generate our sample application for the purposes of this walkthrough. Run the command sudo yum -y install dotnet-sdk-5.0 (note that this time you must elevate privileges using sudo).

Now generate, and then run, a new web application using the commands in Listing 4-10 (we're using sudo to enable the application to bind to port 80 without additional configuration).

Listing 4-10. Starting a new web application on the instance

```
mkdir /tmp/webapp && cd /tmp/webapp
dotnet new webapp
sudo dotnet run --urls http://*:80
```

With the application running, return to the instances view and locate either the instance's public IP address or its public IPv4 DNS from the Details tab on the Instances view (you'll need to select the instance if it's not already selected). Ignore the **open address** links shown to the right of each address (they open tabs onto https URLs, which we've not configured). Instead, click the small "copy" icon to the left of the addresses (does not matter which one), shown in Figure 4-22. Open a new tab, paste the copied address, and press Enter.

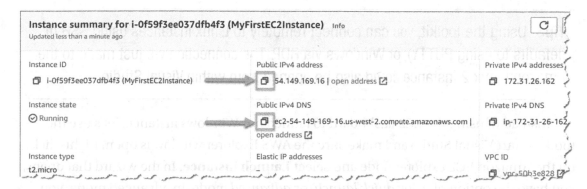

Figure 4-22. *Accessing the web application via public address or DNS*

You should now see the familiar welcome screen of the generated ASP.NET Core 5 sample application, shown in Figure 4-23. Congratulations!

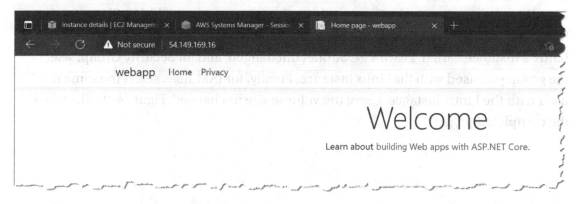

Figure 4-23. *The sample application running on our EC2 instance*

We've finished with the Session Manager–based connection, so feel free to return to the tab hosting the shell and click **Terminate** to close the connection. Of course, using the shell is not how you'll deploy and run applications in production. We'll get to those techniques and best practices later in the book. For now, we've taken our first steps into a much larger world (to coin a movie phrase).

Remote Desktop Connections to Windows Instances

The browser-based terminal provided by EC2 Session Manager works with Windows instances too and uses PowerShell as the shell executable. In Chapter 1, we mentioned the ability to connect remotely to Windows instances using Remote Desktop Protocol (RDP) directly from within Visual Studio if you had the AWS toolkit installed, so let's take a quick look.

Tip   Using the toolkit, you can connect remotely to Linux instances using SSH (it defaults to using PUTTY), or Windows via RDP. The connection we just made to the Amazon Linux 2 instance could also be opened from within Visual Studio.

Instead of using the EC2 dashboard to launch our Windows instance, let's use the toolkit. Start Visual Studio and make sure the AWS Explorer window is open. Right-click on the Amazon EC2 explorer node and select **Launch instance**. In the wizard that opens, you have the option of using *quick launch*, or *advanced* mode. In advanced mode, you walk through several pages of settings related to the new instance – image, instance type, user data, security, etc. – just as in the console. Quick launch uses the single initial page of the wizard, which we'll use for this exercise.

Ensure the wizard is displaying Windows Server images and select *Windows Server 2019 Base*. Select *t2.micro* for **Type**, and give the instance a name (this will map to the Name tag). For **Key Pair**, select the key pair you created when you launched the Amazon Linux 2 instance earlier. Leave VPC Subnet unchanged, and for Security Group, select the group you used with the Linux instance. Finally, for IAM Role, select the same role used with the Linux instance. Leave the volume size unchanged. Figure 4-24 illustrates the completed page.

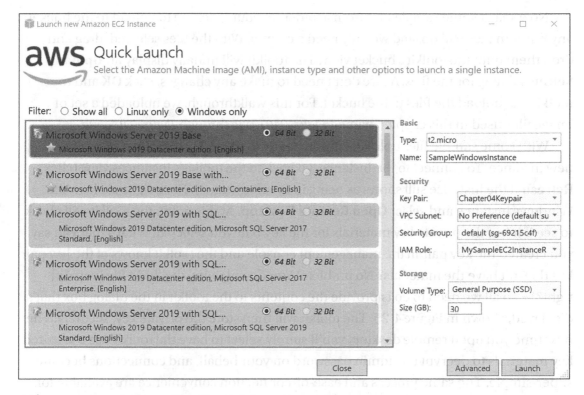

Figure 4-24. *The completed quick launch settings*

Click **Launch**. The toolkit open an Instances view, but if it does not, simply expand
the Amazon EC2 node in the explorer window and double-click Instances.

A Windows Server instance will take a little longer to launch than a Linux instance.
You can right-click the instance in the grid and select **Get System Log** to see how things
are progressing – when you see the text *Windows is ready to use* in the log, you're good
to go (or check the status in the EC2 dashboard you probably still have open in your web
browser). However, rather than waiting for the instance to launch, let's use that time to
set up some test data in S3 for the commands we're going to run on the instance, and
come back to the instance shortly.

In the toolkit's AWS Explorer window, right-click on the Amazon S3 node and
click **Create bucket**. Give the bucket a name (it must be globally unique – we used
prodotnetonaws-chapter04) and click **OK**. The toolkit will expand the S3 explorer node
to show the new bucket. Double-click the bucket name to open a view onto the bucket's
contents (currently empty).

Now select some sample files from a folder on your machine to upload to the bucket; any random files will do, and we only need a couple. With the files selected, drag and drop them onto the toolkit's bucket view. The toolkit will initially display an **Upload Settings** dialog for the files. As we don't need to make any changes, click **OK** and the toolkit will upload the files to the bucket. For this walkthrough, we uploaded a set of image files used in this chapter, named *Figure0401.png* through *Figure0405.png*.

With some sample files uploaded, we're ready to try and access them from our new instance. To connect to the instance, go back to the toolkit's Instances view (click **Refresh** if the instance still shows as being in *Pending* status). Next, right-click on the Windows instance and select **Open Remote Desktop**. At this point, the toolkit will check to see if it has the private key materials for the key pair you selected. What's that you say, you created the key pair in the management console and the toolkit knows of the key pair but doesn't have the materials? No problem! You downloaded the .PEM file (you did, right?) – so all we need to do is provide the contents to the toolkit in the dialog box that's displayed, shown in Figure 4-25. The toolkit will then store the private key, securely. The next time you open remote desktop, you'll simply select to have the toolkit use the stored key materials to decrypt the admin password on your behalf, and connections become super-simple. The same process and ease-of-connection convenience are available for Linux instances too.

Navigate to the stored .PEM file, open it with Notepad (or another text editor), and paste the private key materials into the dialog box, then click **OK**. Figure 4-25 shows the connection dialog when the toolkit is asking for the private key materials – note that we have selected the **Save private key** option, to have the toolkit store the details (securely) so we don't have to enter this data again for this key pair.

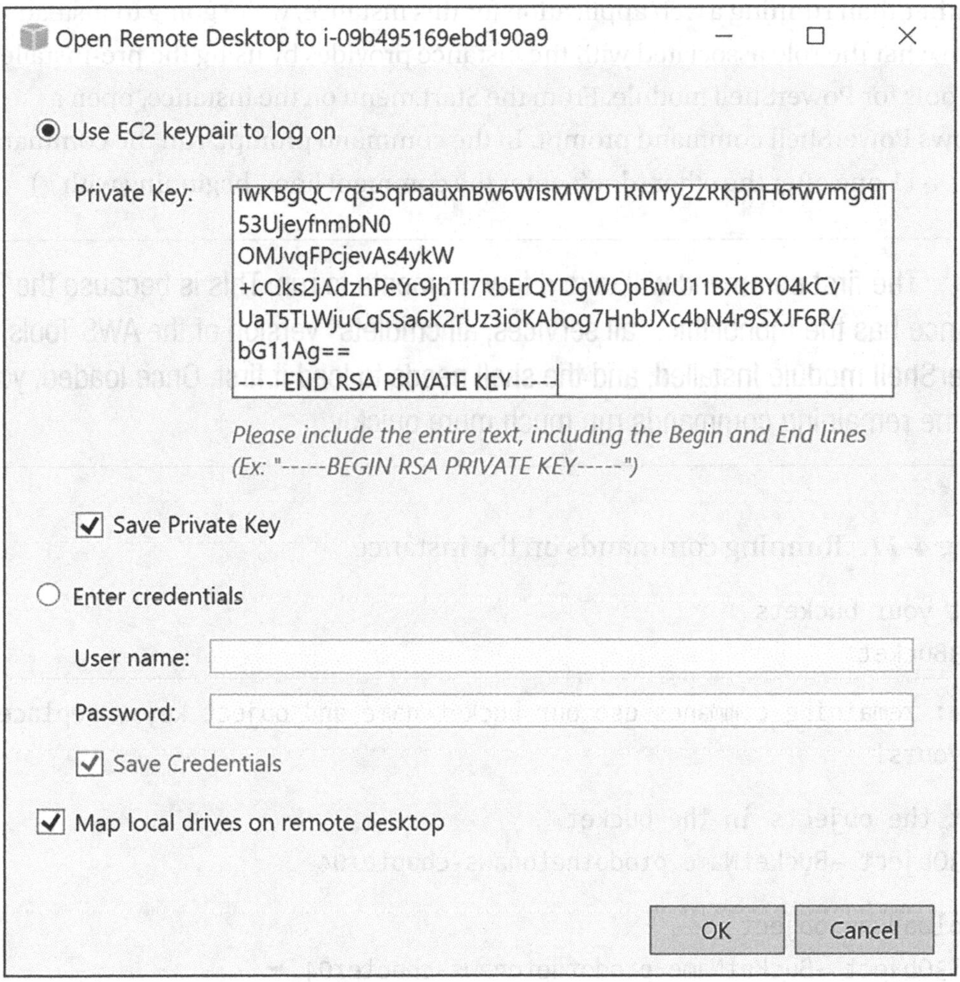

Figure 4-25. *Providing the private key pair materials for use (and storage)*

After you click **OK**, the toolkit will also check to determine if the security group for the instance contains a rule for the port used by remote desktop, 3389. If not, it will ask if you want to add a rule, using your current external IP address – which is a best guess, by the way, so verify it's correct. Confirm the rule dialog, and the toolkit will proceed to open a remote desktop connection. You'll have to confirm some additional Windows security dialogs, but finally, you'll find yourself at the Windows Server desktop for the instance. Future connections to the instance are much quicker because the toolkit has the private materials for the key pair, the security group has a rule for port 3389, and (we assume) you've selected the *Don't ask me again for connections to this computer* option presented in the Windows security dialogs.

Rather than running a web application for this instance, we're going to instead explore what the role associated with the instance provides by using the pre-installed AWS Tools for PowerShell module. From the Start menu on the instance, open a Windows PowerShell command prompt. In the command prompt, run the commands in Listing 4-11 one after the other (don't enter the comment lines, beginning with #).

Note   The first command will take a few moments to run. This is because the EC2 instance has the monolithic, "all services, all cmdlets" version of the AWS Tools for PowerShell module installed, and the shell needs to load it first. Once loaded, you'll find the remaining commands run much more quickly.

Listing 4-11. Running commands on the instance

```
# List your buckets
Get-S3Bucket
```

```
# note: remaining commands use our bucket name and object keys; replace
with yours!
```

```
# list the objects in the bucket
Get-S3Object -BucketName prodotnetonaws-chapter04
```

```
# download an object
Read-S3Object -BucketName prodotnetonaws-chapter04 ↵
-Key Figure0404.png -File .\Figure0404.png
```

```
# try and upload a file - should fail with "access denied"
Write-S3Object -BucketName prodotnetonaws-chapter04 ↵
-Key test.txt -Content "abcdef"
```

Notice what happens – the commands to list your buckets (Get-S3Bucket), and to list the contents of a bucket (Get-S3Object), works fine, as does the command to download an object onto the instance (Read-S3Object). However, the command to upload content to the bucket, Write-S3Object, fails with a permission denied error. Why is this? And how are the commands working at all? We've not placed any credentials onto the instance!

Remember that roles provide (a) temporary credentials via a trust relationship and (b) scope permissions in terms of what services, what service APIs, and what resources those credentials can access. When we created the role associated with the instance, earlier in the chapter, we attached a trust relationship with ec2.amazon.com – so EC2 instances associated with that role are automatically provided with credentials. These credentials expire and rotate without you needing to do anything.

Secondly, we established a custom policy for the role that permitted access to S3's `ListAllMyBuckets`, `ListBucket`, and `GetObject` APIs. That's why those commands (`Get-S3Bucket`, `Get-S3Object`, and `Read-S3Object`, respectively) work. They have access to credentials and permission to invoke those underlying APIs. The command to upload, however, Write-S3Object, fails because we did not permit the relevant S3 APIs it uses in the policy.

We've said it before, we'll say it again (and we'll keep saying it) – *there is no need to place credentials onto EC2 instances*. Use an associated role to provide them, and save yourself the effort and worry of managing credential files in the cloud!

Deleting the Instances

We've finished with these temporary instances, so it's a good practice to delete them. Even though we launched a free tier-compatible instance types, the free tier only covers up to 750 instance hours of usage, and we'd rather keep that for other applications further in the book!

To terminate the instances, head back to the management console and select the instance in the **Instances** view. Click the **Instance state** button and select **Terminate instance**. You will need to confirm, and once you do, EC2 will begin terminating the instance (you can also terminate the instances from within Visual Studio). You can leave the other resources we used – key pair, security group, and the instance role – if you wish as they do not incur any charges.

This brings us to the end of this chapter on using EC2 virtual machines. We've seen how to configure storage, network security, instance permissions, and installed software during launch. By running a temporary web application, we also got a feel for how to work with instances from within the management console and how to connect remotely to both Windows and Linux instances. We'll come back to EC2 later in the book as we dive even deeper, but for now, we're ready to move onto another hosting option – containers. Before we do, we wanted to briefly discuss other services where EC2 virtual machines make an appearance and which of those services you might consider to host your applications.

Summary

In Chapter 1, we mentioned that AWS Elastic Beanstalk also uses EC2 virtual machine instances to serve your deployed applications (as, in fact, does Amazon Lightsail). So why might you choose EC2 directly, over Elastic Beanstalk or Lightsail, to host your application?

In a word, management – how much instance management and maintenance do you want to take on? When you use EC2 directly, you are at the "metal" level (or as close to it as you can get in the cloud). You have near total control of the running instances and can treat them the same as virtual machines in your on-premises or data center infrastructure. With control comes more complexity and responsibility.

Elastic Beanstalk and Lightsail are *managed services,* and they abstract away many of the maintenance and management tasks you would need to take on yourself when using EC2 directly – you trade some control for a simpler management experience. That's not to say that you can't get to the actual EC2 resources if you need to. Just as we did when launching an instance in EC2, you can still connect remotely to managed instances using SSH or remote desktop as needed. And you can configure the instances on creation, although you do this with mechanisms other than user data scripts (in Elastic Beanstalk, for example, you supply an "EB extension" file containing the customization commands).

If you're looking to host a web application (such as ASP.NET or ASP.NET Core), then Elastic Beanstalk is an attractive choice and one you should probably look at first. If you decide you need the additional control that using EC2 directly gives, and you're comfortable taking on the additional responsibilities for the infrastructure hosting your application, then use EC2.

In the next chapter, we'll look at container services in AWS. And, as you might expect, you could equally use these to host your application instead of virtual machine-based services such as EC2, Elastic Beanstalk, or Lightsail. Choice is always welcome!

CHAPTER 5

Containers

We just spent some time going over virtual machines, where a machine stack is virtualized within an image file. This allows you to run multiple virtual machines on a single physical server, with the hypervisor managing the interaction between the guest operating system and the actual hardware, providing a layer of abstraction between the OS and the hardware. However, since each of these VMs must bring their own licensed OS, they are large images, and there tends to be a lot of "wasted space" because, for example, three Windows VMs would be storing three copies of the OS in memory, plus the instance of the OS from the system on which the VMs are running. Containers, on the other hand, are a different approach to system virtualization and permit abstraction above the OS layer instead. This difference in approach results in smaller images that can be loaded much faster than VMs.

In this chapter, we are going to go over containers and how they work and then jump right into the various AWS container offerings. There are several of these container services, as AWS claims at the time this is published, to run 80% of all containers in the cloud. Once we touch on the various container services, we will then deploy an application onto one of these services.

Explaining Containers

One way to think about containers is that they are a bundle of software that includes the application to run as well as all its dependencies. Thus, you can think of a *container image* for .NET applications as a package that contains the application itself, all .NET runtimes necessary for the application, the system libraries that the application may depend on, and all the various application and operating system configurations that ensure that the application runs as expected. Figure 5-1 shows the differences between the two virtualization approaches: VMs and containers.

167

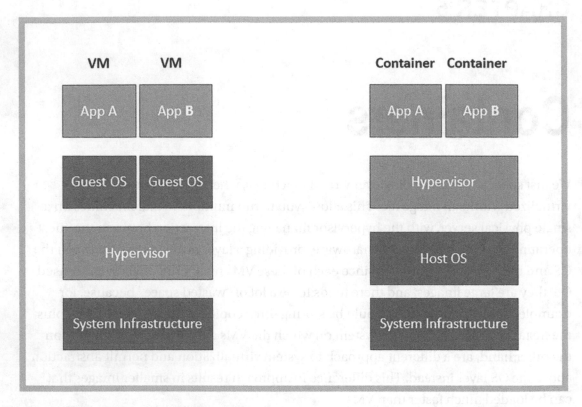

Figure 5-1. *Virtual machines and containers*

As shown in the figure, the primary difference is where the hypervisor sits. It can be "below" the operating system used by the deployed applications, as it is with virtual machines, or it can be "above" the host OS, as it is with containers. This means that each virtual machine can have their own, and possibly different, operating system, while containers all must run on the same OS as the host because they don't carry a copy of an OS.

One of the key components of a container is that containerized software will always run the same, regardless of the infrastructure. If you have been in this business for any amount of time, you have probably run into a case where an application in one environment runs differently than that exact same application in another environment. This could be because of a subtle difference in the software environment, such as if one machine was hot patched for a support library while another was not, or because of some difference in topology, or.... Containers help you eliminate those differences by bundling all of the application components together.

There are a lot of advantages to running containers over virtual machines. Firstly, containers are immutable. This means you can be confident that the same version of everything that was tested in the QA environment will be in the production environment and with the same behavior. More on this in a little bit. The second advantage to containers is that they are lightweight. Since a container image does not have to carry around an operating system, they tend to be much smaller in size and easy to move from environment to environment. Lastly, containers are fast. Because of how lightweight they are, a container starts up much quicker than a virtual machine can, much like how simply opening a program on your computer is much quicker than turning on the computer before starting the application. Because of these advantages, you should get into the habit of thinking of containers as disposable.

Many developers, especially those new to containers, have problems thinking about computing units, such as containers, being "disposable." This leads to some typical missteps that tend to happen when building applications for containers:

- **Local data storage** – Many .NET developers are used to storing files on the server. This can be something as simple as log files to something more complex such as long-term temporary files used during business processing. You cannot do this with containers.

- **Large images** – We mentioned small images as being an important advantage when using containers. However, just like everything else, it is something that can easily be broken. Ensure that you have only the necessary files and libraries for running your application. Many developers have fallen into a trap of doing something like building a common base image that works for all their applications – sure, it may make base image management a bit easier, but it leads to individually bloated images.

- **Multiple processes in a container** – A common .NET deployment approach for virtual machines may have multiple processes running on a single server. This makes sense, especially when those processes may fill similar business needs, or may be small and rarely used. However, do not fall into the trap of putting them into the same container. Doing so means that those applications are now intertwined in an immutable container, so one application being updated, tested, and released means that all other processes in the container need to be redeployed as well.

169

- **Relying on IP addresses** – Since each container will need to have its own IP address and may also be disposable, relying on IP addresses for system discovery becomes problematic.

- **System credentials** – The nature of containers means that each container will likely be used in multiple environments. This means that you should not do anything with login credentials within the container image itself (though you shouldn't be doing that with VMs either) – as these logins would have to be configured the same across many different environments – and who wants the same login in both development and production? Instead, move that information out of the container and manage it through another route.

As we start talking about the specifics of containers, we will continue to point out some of those areas and help you understand how best to take advantage of containers.

Docker

Before we go much deeper into containers, we should probably talk about Docker. Containers have been around for decades. However, their popularity never really took off until Docker, and their open source *Docker Engine* came onto the scene in 2013. Docker Engine is a container runtime that runs on various Linux versions (at least 7 as of this writing) and Windows Server. The growth in popularity of Docker, and their approach to container management, quickly made containers a viable approach for adding virtualization capabilities. Combine the growth of Docker with the growth of cloud providers such as AWS and you can see why we are talking about this!

Docker is especially important to us in this case because it is the container manager that we will be using as we move forward. It is the most popular tool, and in many ways, it has become synonymous with "containers" – just like people interchange "Kleenex" and "facial tissue" – which is why you will hear people saying things like "Docker" or "Docker images" when they are talking about running containers.

Container Image

We have thrown around the term "container image" several times without really explaining it. First, there is a difference between a container image and a container. Think of a container image as a read-only template or snapshot. These snapshots represent an application and its virtual environment at some specific point of time. These templates are used as a base to build a container, as you can think of a container as a running instance of the image. Images can exist without a container, but containers cannot exist without having an image to run.

A container image is a representation of binary data that encapsulates the application and its dependencies. They are executable software bundles that make predefined assumptions about their runtime environment. These bundles are run within the context of the **container runtime**, or container hypervisor. Once you start the container (as defined by a container image) within the container runtime, there is a writable layer on top of the immutable image. This allows for modifications within the container. If that container is stopped, however, then those modifications are lost because those modifications will not be available the next time that container is started – because you will be using the same image that was used previously before the modifications.

A container image is made up of image layers. Think of these layers as sets of files. Layers are important because these various sets of files allow you to standardize your container images and they also allow you to save disk space as well as help reduce the amount of time necessary to build the container image. Each of these layers may represent a common set of files that are available for use across multiple images, much like you will put replicated code into a single method, with the assumption that all these files will be run in the context of the hypervisor above the host operating system. You can have any number of layers but remember the warning to keep the container image, or Dockerfile, as lean as possible!

As part of the process of starting the container, the hypervisor will add a thin read-write layer on top of the image. This layer supports some changes within the container. Figure 5-2 shows what this all would look like.

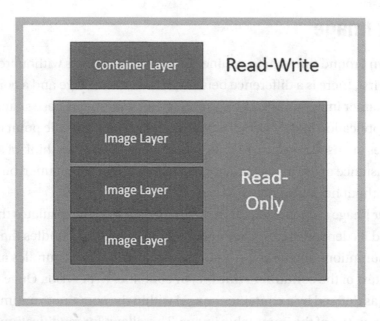

Figure 5-2. *Container image layers*

As mentioned earlier, any changes in the read-write layer of the container will be lost when the container is stopped. However, if there are changes that should be persisted, all container runtime systems provide the ability to take a **snapshot**. This snapshot will add a new image layer on top of the image from which the container was sourced, thus creating a new immutable container image that will have a newly added set of layers.

Note   This is one way to build a container image when moving .NET applications from an existing server or virtual machine to containers – by using a trial-and-error approach. Add known layers, deploy the image, start the container, test, make changes (such as installing another required .NET runtime version or support library), and snapshot the finished container to create a "more correct" container image.

Container Registries

A registry is a service that contains repositories of container images. There are public and private registries. The largest and most well known of these is **Docker Hub**, at https://hub.docker.com. There are (at the time of this writing) 8,196,604 different images available in this registry, each containing various combinations of operating systems and pre-installed software, with some 6,838 of these being various combinations that include the keyword "dotnet" (the use of a "." is not supported), of which over 225 images are from verified publishers.

Public container registries contain images that can be created and provided from any source. When looking at Docker Hub, these sources can be from a *Verified publisher*, where Docker has been able to verify that the image is published and maintained by a commercial entity, and/or can be an *Official image*, a Docker-curated set of open source repositories. Since this is a public registry, anyone can use one of these images as their base image – that is what they are there for.

There are also private registries, which, as you can probably imagine, mean that not everyone has access to the stored images. These would be where you would store your own images, most likely with some of your own libraries already installed. These private registries require authentication to ensure that only authorized users access the image. While not completely necessary for using containers, you may likely find a private repository makes sense as you move into containers.

Regardless of whether they are public or private registries, all registries generally work the same way. Firstly, they are made up of one or more repositories. Secondly, each of the repositories is made up of one or more different images. Thirdly, an image is versioned, so when you are pulling a container image, you can specify a specific version or use "latest". Lastly, any number of hosts can be based on a single image. Figure 5-3 shows the workflow of images in and out of the repository.

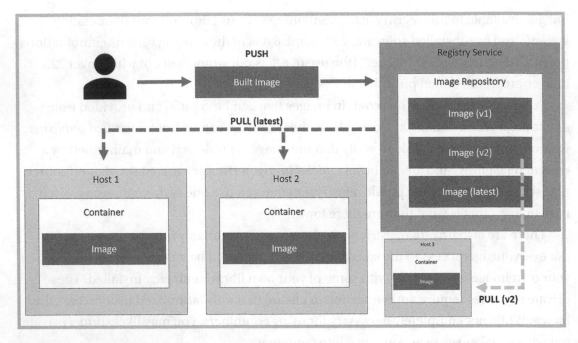

Figure 5-3. *Flow of images in the registry*

Example Container File

Now that we have talked a lot about container images, let us look at a Dockerfile (dockerfile) and work through the various components:

```
# syntax=docker/dockerfile:1
FROM mcr.microsoft.com/dotnet/sdk:6.0 AS build-env
WORKDIR /app

# Copy csproj and restore as distinct layers
COPY *.csproj ./
RUN dotnet restore

# Copy everything else and build
COPY ../engine/examples ./
RUN dotnet publish -c Release -o out

# Build runtime image
FROM mcr.microsoft.com/dotnet/aspnet:6.0
WORKDIR /app
```

```
COPY --from=build-env /app/out .
ENTRYPOINT ["dotnet", "aspnetapp.dll"]
```

This is not the simplest of scripts as it includes both the building of the code to run and creating the runtime to run – thus, a container image file contains the information necessary to build the running container. The **FROM** instruction, of which there are two in the preceding code snippet, defines a new build stage by defining the base image (it is called a base image because there is no parent image specified in the file) that is pulled from a container registry. This instruction is required for a file to be valid.

When you set up your system that will be "running" your container file, part of what you will need to do is to set up the repositories that your system will access when pulling images. That is why the FROM command does not include the repository, which will be configured elsewhere. Also, note the AS instruction, as this gives a name to the image referenced in the FROM command that can be used later in the file. You can see this in the preceding code where the COPY command uses that name.

Once you have defined the base image, the next command you see is **WORKDIR**. The WORKDIR instruction sets the working directory for any different instructions that may follow it in the file. If the directory does not already exist, then it will be created, even if it is never used. The WORKDIR instruction can be used multiple times, and if a relative path is provided, it will be relative to the path of the previous WORKDIR instruction. For example:

```
WORKDIR /init
WORKDIR comp
WORKDIR bin
RUN pwd
```

means that the output of the final *pwd* command in this set of instructions would be */init/comp/bin*.

Now that the initial working directory is set, the next command is COPY *.csproj ./, which uses the **COPY** instruction to move the item (the *.csproj file for the .NET project you are building) to the WORKDIR (working directory) that was just set. This indicates that this file is part of a build-and-deploy process for a .NET application, as shown by the next line RUN dotnet restore, which is the .NET CLI command to restore NuGet packages.

The **RUN** instruction has two different forms. The first, used previously, is the *shell form*, which runs the command listed after the instruction and commits the results. The resulting committed image will be used for any following steps, which in this case means that the restored NuGet files will become part of the image. The second form is the *exec form* and looks like RUN ["executable", "param1", "param2"]. As you can see, this is more akin to running a console application with a set of parameters – but the outcome is the same. The executable will run, and then the outcome will be committed as part of the image.

The next two lines are much the same:

```
COPY ../engine/examples ./
RUN dotnet publish -c Release -o out
```

The source code files are copied, and then the .NET CLI is used to build and publish the application. Once this is completed, the image is committed, and now the image has the base operating system, all the required NuGet packages, and the published application, all put together into a single directory.

Let us look at the last set of instructions – you have seen many of these instructions already:

```
FROM mcr.microsoft.com/dotnet/aspnet:6.0
WORKDIR /app
COPY --from=build-env /app/out .
ENTRYPOINT ["dotnet", "aspnetapp.dll"]
```

First, we get a fresh image for the Docker Hub. Next, set the WORKDIR on that image. The third line, COPY --from=build-env /app/out . uses the COPY instruction to duplicate the content from the initial image onto the new image. That is the purpose of the --from flag; it sets the source location to a previous build stage (created with FROM .. AS <name>) that will be used instead of a build context as set by the user. Once the compiled application is copied onto the new image, the last command is run - ENTRYPOINT ["dotnet", "aspnetapp.dll"].

The **ENTRYPOINT** instruction is used to define the command that gets executed when a container starts and is the instruction used when a container is defined as executable. Starting this container would show that "aspnetapp.dll" is a running process, which means that an HTTP request to this container instance should interact with that application.

Immutability

As mentioned earlier, a container, by both design and intent, is immutable. This means that every time you start a container, it will always start in the same state because, as you saw, that is the way that you have built the container image file. Thus, deploying a new version of the application will require a completely different container image; so a deployment of a containerized application involves building the container image, copying the image to the appropriate place, stopping the container running the previous version, and starting the just copied container with the new image version.

Of course, there are ways to get around the immutability of a container and change the application on the container without recreating and redeploying the entire image. Some companies take this approach in their development environment so that every tiny code change does not require a rebuild and redeployment of an image. It is also possible that you can build a deployment approach that treats virtual machines as immutable, and thus, a redeployment of an application means a creation and deployment of a new virtual machine instance. However, as a rule, containers are treated as immutable so that a new version of an application requires a new container, while virtual machines are treated as mutable so that a new version of an application will replace an already existing application on the same system.

There is one thing that can interfere with containers and immutability: that you can get the "latest" version of a base image. While this makes sense during development, imagine the kind of trouble this could cause in production. Suppose you have a container image in production that is configured to use the latest version of an image and then that container gets updated, say, with a new operating system or version of .NET. This means that you could have a completely different system running in one instance than another instance, even though your intent is that they be identical. This and the typical missteps mentioned earlier in the chapter can all impact your ability to correctly deploy and manage containers.

Amazon Elastic Container Registry (ECR)

Amazon Elastic Container Registry (ECR) is a system designed to support storing and managing Docker and Open Container Initiative (OCI) images and OCI-compatible artifacts. ECR can act as a private container image repository, where you can store your own images, or a public container image repository for managing publicly accessible images and for managing access to other public image repositories. ECR also provides life cycle policies that allow you to manage the life cycles of images within your repository, image scanning, so that you can identify any potential software vulnerabilities, and cross-region and cross-account image replication so that your images can be available wherever you need them.

As with the rest of AWS services, ECR is built on top of other services. For example, Amazon ECR stores container images in Amazon S3 buckets so that server-side encryption is available by default. Or, if needed, you can use server-side encryption with KMS keys stored in AWS Key Management Service (AWS KMS), all of which you can configure as you create the registry. As you can likely guess, IAM manages access rights to the images, supporting everything from strict rules to anonymous access to support the concept of a public repository.

There are several different ways to create a repository. The first is through the ECR console by selecting the *Create repository* button. This will take you to the Create repository page as shown in Figure 5-4.

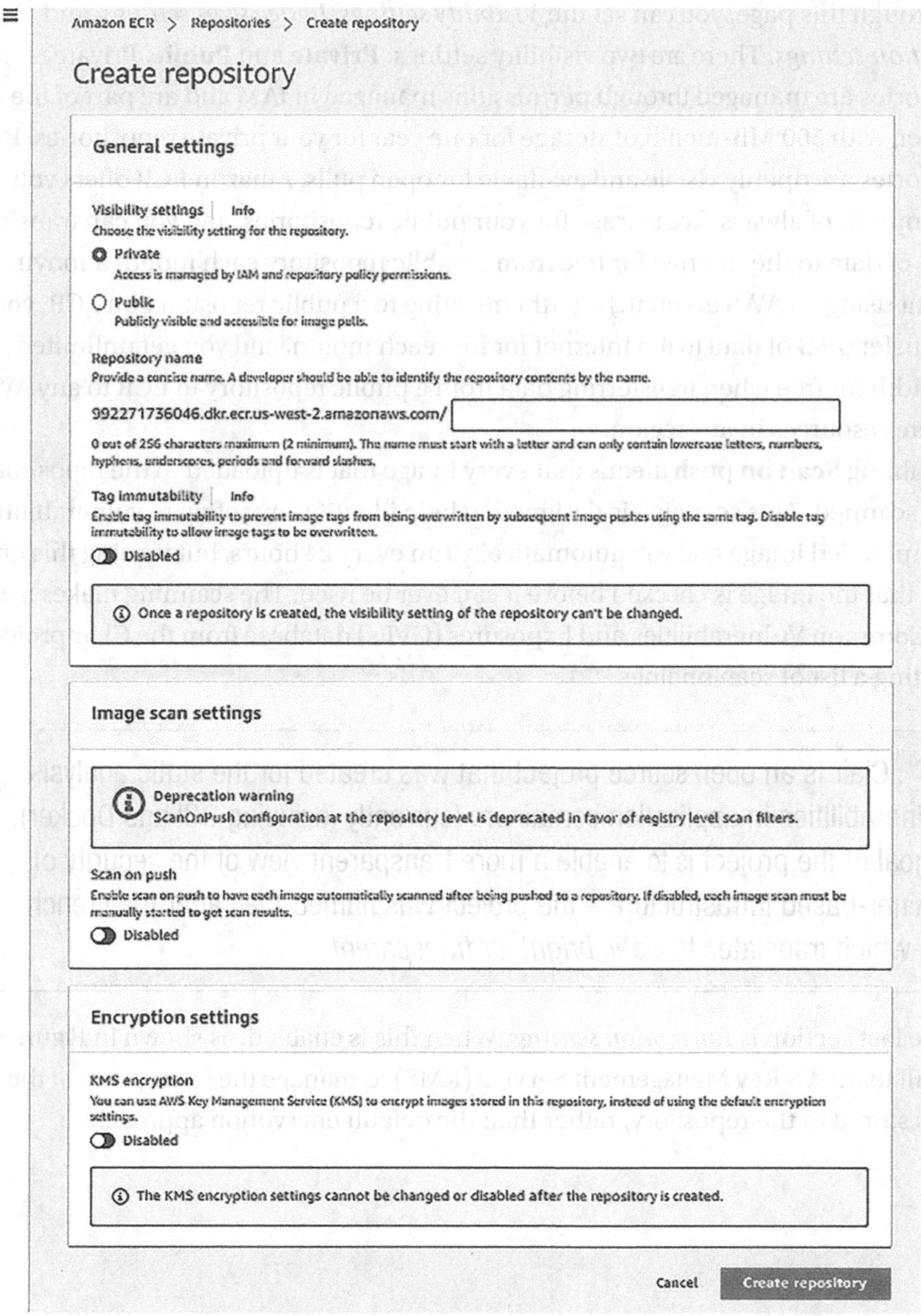

Figure 5-4. *Creating a repository*

Through this page, you can set the *Visibility settings, Image scan settings*, and *Encryption settings*. There are two visibility settings: **Private** and **Public**. Private repositories are managed through permissions managed in IAM and are part of the AWS Free Tier, with 500 MB-month of storage for one year for your private repositories. Public repositories are openly visible and available for open pulls. Amazon ECR offers you 50 GB-month of always-free storage for your public repositories, and you can transfer 500 GB of data to the Internet for free from a public repository each month anonymously (without using an AWS account.) If authenticating to a public repository on ECR, you can transfer 5 TB of data to the Internet for free each month, and you get unlimited bandwidth for free when transferring data from a public repository in ECR to any AWS compute resources in any region.

Enabling **Scan on push** means that every image that is uploaded to the repository will be scanned. This scanning is designed to help identify any software vulnerabilities in the uploaded image and will automatically run every 24 hours, but turning this on will ensure that the image is checked before it can ever be used. The scanning makes use of the Common Vulnerabilities and Exposures (CVEs) database from the Clair project, outputting a list of scan findings.

Note   Clair is an open source project that was created for the static analysis of vulnerabilities in application containers (currently including OCI and Docker). The goal of the project is to enable a more transparent view of the security of container-based infrastructure – the project was named *Clair* after the French term, which translates to *clear, bright, or transparent*.

The last section is *Encryption settings*. When this is enabled, as shown in Figure 5-5, ECR will use AWS Key Management Service (KMS) to manage the encryption of the images stored in the repository, rather than the default encryption approach.

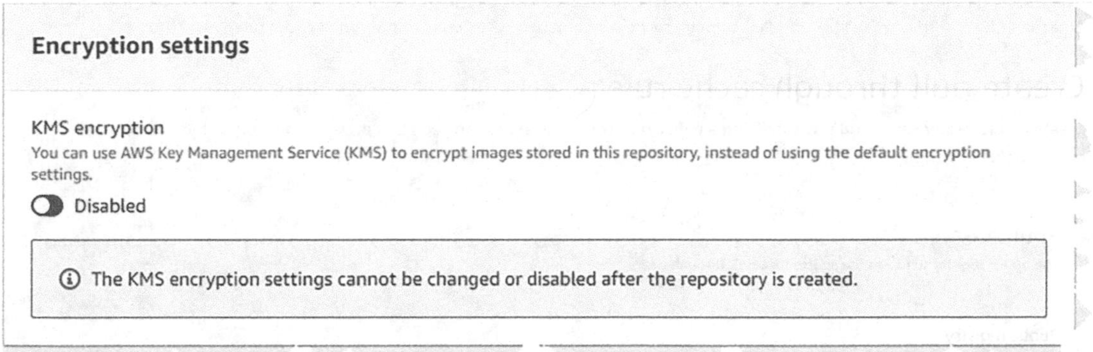

Encryption settings

KMS encryption
You can use AWS Key Management Service (KMS) to encrypt images stored in this repository, instead of using the default encryption settings.

⬤ Disabled

ⓘ The KMS encryption settings cannot be changed or disabled after the repository is created.

Figure 5-5. *Encryption settings*

You can use either the default settings, where ECR creates a default key (with an alias of aws/ecr), or you can *Customize encryption settings* and either select a preexisting key or create a new key that will be used for the encryption.

Pull Through Cache Repositories

Everything we have gone through so far is to upload your own container image into the repository. However, as we will cover in depth a bit later in this chapter, at the heart of virtually all of your container images is a base container image, generally created by a vendor such as Microsoft or Docker. These base images are typically downloaded from a public repository. However, there may be instances where you prefer to source all images from Amazon Elastic Container Registry to take advantage of its high availability and security. If so, the pull through cache repositories may be just what you are looking for as they will pull down referenced images from the source and cache them within ECR.

Note   The pull through cache repository feature was added for re:Invent 2021 so the available public repositories are gradually being added. It is possible that the repository that you may want to pass-through from is not yet available.

Creating a pull through cache repository is a relatively simple process. First, begin by selecting **Private registry** from the left menu, and then click the **Edit** button in the *Pull through cache* panel to change settings. This will bring up the *Pull through cache* configuration page, where you click the **Add rule** button. This will bring up the create window as shown in Figure 5-6.

181

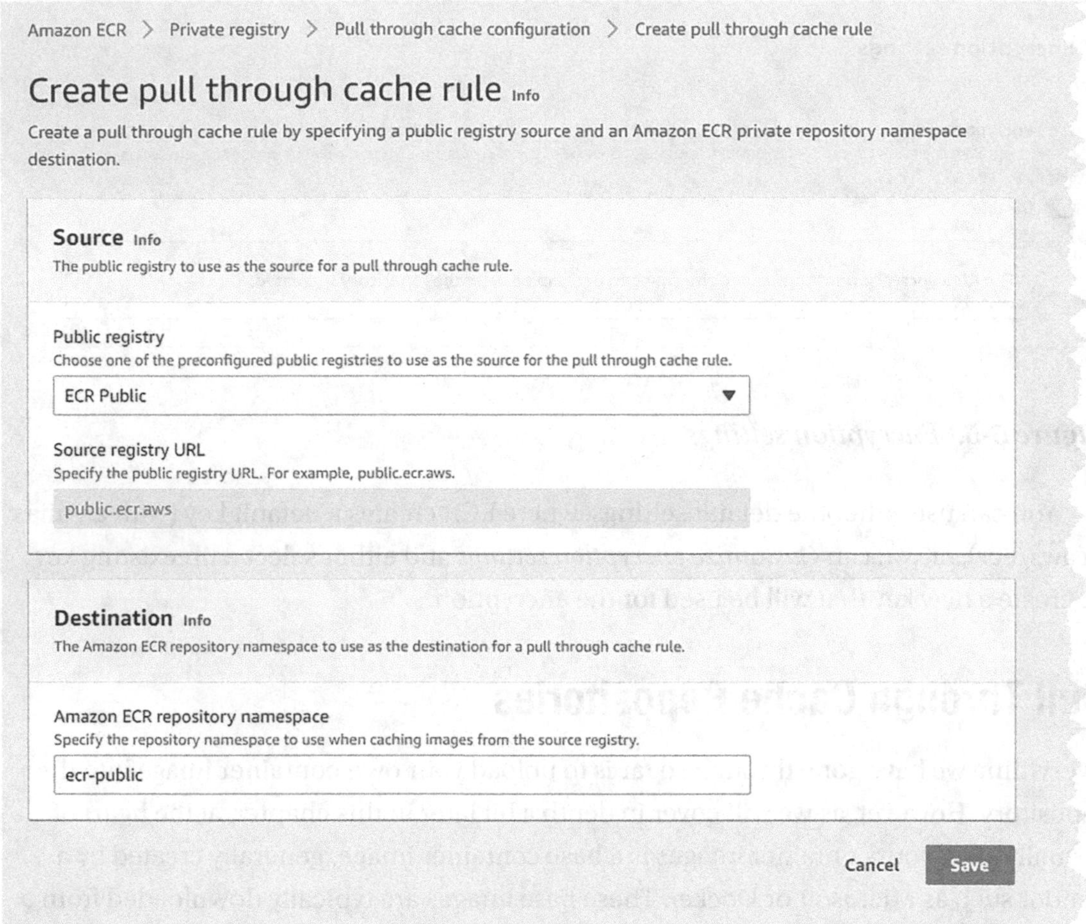

Amazon ECR > Private registry > Pull through cache configuration > Create pull through cache rule

Create pull through cache rule Info

Create a pull through cache rule by specifying a public registry source and an Amazon ECR private repository namespace destination.

Source Info
The public registry to use as the source for a pull through cache rule.

Public registry
Choose one of the preconfigured public registries to use as the source for the pull through cache rule.

ECR Public ▼

Source registry URL
Specify the public registry URL. For example, public.ecr.aws.

public.ecr.aws

Destination Info
The Amazon ECR repository namespace to use as the destination for a pull through cache rule.

Amazon ECR repository namespace
Specify the repository namespace to use when caching images from the source registry.

ecr-public

Cancel   **Save**

Figure 5-6. Creating a pull through cache

The first drop-down, *Public registry*, contains all the preconfigured public registries available; as you can see, we selected *ECR Public*. Clicking the **Save** button will bring you back to the list of pull through cache rules.

Since this is a pass-through, you need to combine both the pass-through URL and the referenced source when using a pull URL using the format of *<accountId>.dkr. ecr.<region>*.amazonaws.com/<namespace>/<sourcerepo>:<tag>. If you look back to the previous example of a container image definition, you may recall the following lines:

```
# Build runtime image
FROM mcr.microsoft.com/dotnet/aspnet:6.0
WORKDIR /app
```

Using the pull through cache means that if you were going to use the ASP.NET Core base image from Bitnami that is available from the ECR Public repository, you would change the FROM command to reference the pull through source, as shown in the following:

```
# Build runtime image
FROM xxxxxxxxx.dkr.ecr.use-east-2.amazonaws.com/ecr-public/bitnami/
aspnet-core:6.0
WORKDIR /app
```

Be aware that this is more than a simple pull through, as the image that you reference will be cached in ECR so that additional calls to that same image will not have to go to the final source repository. This means that the storage used will be charged to your account.

Other Approaches for Creating an ECR Repo

Just as with all the other services that we have talked about so far, there is the UI-driven way to build an ECR like we just went through and then several other approaches to creating a repo.

AWS CLI

You can create an ECR repository in the AWS CLI using the `create-repository` command as part of the ECR service.

```
C:\>aws ecr create-repository ↵
    --repository-name prodotnetonaws ↵
    --image-scanning-configuration scanOnPush=true ↵
    --region us-east-1
```

You can control all of the basic repository settings through the CLI just as you can when creating the repository through the ECR console, including assigning encryption keys and defining the repository URI.

AWS Tools for PowerShell

And, as you probably aren't too surprised to find out, you can also create an ECR repository using AWS Tools for PowerShell:

```
C:\> New-ECRRepository ⏎
-RepositoryName prodotnetonaws ⏎
-ImageScanningConfiguration_ScanOnPush $true
```

Just as with the CLI, you have the ability to fully configure the repository as you create it.

AWS Toolkit for Visual Studio

When using the AWS Toolkit for Visual Studio, you must depend upon the extension's built-in default values because the only thing that you can control through the AWS Explorer is the repository name as shown in Figure 5-7. As you may notice, the AWS Explorer does not have its own node for ECR and instead puts the Repositories subnode under the Amazon Elastic Container Service (ECS) node. This is a legacy from the past, before ECR really became its own service, but it is still an effective way to access and work with repositories in Visual Studio.

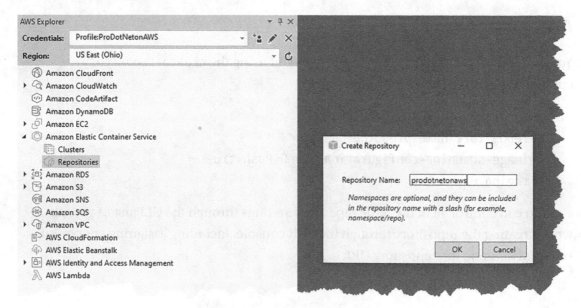

Figure 5-7. *Creating a repository in Visual Studio*

Once you create a repository in Visual Studio, going to the ECR console and reviewing the repository that was created will show you that it used the default settings, so it is a private repository with both "Scan on push" and "KMS encryption" disabled.

At this point, the easiest way to show how this will all work is to create an image and upload it into the repository. We will then be able to use this container image as we go through the various AWS container management services.

Note   You will not be able to complete many of these exercises without Docker installed on your machine. You will find download and installation instructions for Docker Desktop at www.docker.com/products/docker-desktop. Once you have Desktop installed, you will be able to locally build and run container images.

We will start by creating a simple .NET ASP.NET Core sample web application in Visual Studio through *File* ➤ *New Project* and selecting the *ASP.NET Core Web App (C#)* project template. You then name your project and select where to save the source code. Once that is completed, you will get a new screen that asks for additional information. The check box for **Enable Docker** defaults as unchecked, so make sure you check it and then select the Docker OS to use, which in this case is Linux. This will create a simple solution that includes a Dockerfile as shown in Figure 5-8.

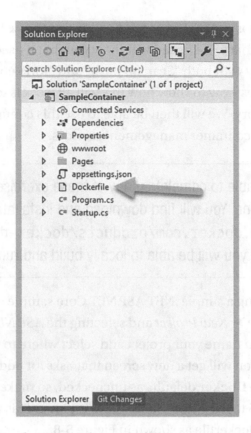

Figure 5-8. *New .NET solution with Dockerfile*

If you look at the contents of the generated Dockerfile, you will see that it is very similar to the Dockerfile that we walked through earlier, containing the instructions to restore and build the application, publish the application, and then copy the published application bits to the final image, setting the ENTRYPOINT.

```
FROM mcr.microsoft.com/dotnet/aspnet:6.0 AS base
WORKDIR /app
EXPOSE 80
EXPOSE 443

FROM mcr.microsoft.com/dotnet/sdk:6.0 AS build
WORKDIR /src
COPY ["SampleContainer/SampleContainer.csproj", "SampleContainer/"]
RUN dotnet restore "SampleContainer/SampleContainer.csproj"
COPY . .
```

```
WORKDIR "/src/SampleContainer"
RUN dotnet build "SampleContainer.csproj" -c Release -o /app/build

FROM build AS publish
RUN dotnet publish "SampleContainer.csproj" -c Release -o /app/publish

FROM base AS final
WORKDIR /app
COPY --from=publish /app/publish .
ENTRYPOINT ["dotnet", "SampleContainer.dll"]
```

If you look at your build options in Visual Studio as shown in Figure 5-9, you will see additional ones available for containers. The Docker choice, for example, will work through the Dockerfile, start the final container image within Docker, and then connect the debugger to that container so that you can debug as usual.

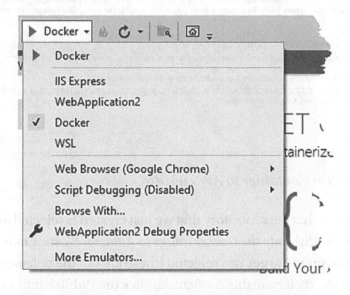

Figure 5-9. *Build options in a containerized application.*

Note   If you want to see what is going on within the container build process, go to the output window, change the Show output from the drop-down to Container Tools, and then debug the application in Docker. You will see Docker commands being processed.

The next step is to create the container image and persist it into the repository. To do so, right-click the project name in the Visual Studio Solution Explorer and select *Publish Container to AWS* to bring up the wizard as shown in Figure 5-10.

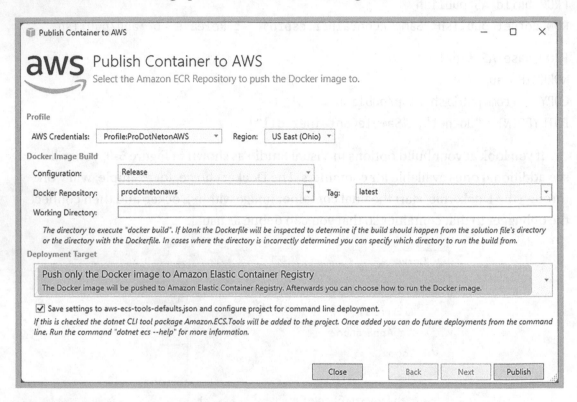

Figure 5-10. *Publish Container to AWS wizard*

Figure 5-10 shows that the repository that we just created is selected as the repository for saving, and the *Publish only the Docker image to Amazon Elastic Container Registry* option in the **Deployment Target** was selected (these are not the default values for each of these options). Once you have this configured, click the **Publish** button. You'll see the window in the wizard grind through a lot of processing, then a console window may pop up to show you the actual upload of the image, and then the wizard will automatically close if successful.

You can see the new repository in Visual Studio, as well as by logging into Amazon ECR and selecting the *prodotnetonaws* repository (the one we uploaded the image into), as shown in Figure 5-11. There should now be an image available within the repository with a *latest* tag, just as configured in the wizard. You can click the icon with the Copy

URI text to get the URL that you will use when working with this image. We recommend that you go ahead and do this at this point and paste it somewhere easy to find as that is the value you will use to access the image.

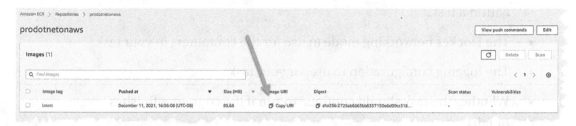

Figure 5-11. Container image stored in Amazon ECR

Now that you have a container image stored in the repository, let's look at how you could use it!

Amazon Elastic Container Service (ECS)

Amazon Elastic Container Service (Amazon ECS) is a fully managed container management service. ECS supports Docker container images (the only container platform currently supported) that are stored in ECR or other repositories and runs these containers on a managed cluster of EC2 instances. Fully managed means it allows you to not worry about installing or managing any container management infrastructure and instead simply provides you the ability to run and manage containers, working by managing containers on customer-controlled EC2 instances or within AWS Fargate (more on this later).

There are two different parts of ECS: **clusters** and **task definitions**. A cluster defines the EC2 instance(s) on which the containers will run. This is where you select the EC2 instance type and AMI, the number of instances of the container to start up, the networking configuration in which the cluster is running, and the container instance IAM role. A task definition defines the container images that run within the cluster. A task definition is a JSON file that describes one or more containers (up to a maximum of ten) on which your application is running. The task definition contains various parameters, including the following:

- The launch type to use, which determines the infrastructure on which your tasks are hosted.

- How much CPU and memory to use with each task or each container within a task.

- The Docker networking mode to use for the containers in your task.

- The logging configuration to use for your tasks.

- Whether the task should continue to run if the container finishes or fails.

- The command the container should run when it is started. This does not override the entry point/run commands in the Dockerfile that built the image.

- Any data volumes that should be used with the containers in the task.

- The IAM role that your tasks should use.

- The Image URI that specifies the image to use when starting a container.

Note   Not all these parameters are valid for every **launch type** that you may choose. There are three different launch types: *Fargate*, *EC2*, and *External*. Fargate is another managed service (more on this later), EC2 is what we will talk about here, and External is a new feature (Amazon ECS Anywhere) that allows you to run your containerized applications on an on-premises server or VM that you have registered to your Amazon ECS cluster and manage remotely.

The task definition contains the reference to the container image. You can see this relationship between these two areas in Figure 5-12, which shows how the container image is contained within the task definition. The cluster, on the other hand, is made up of one or more services, each of which contains a task definition.

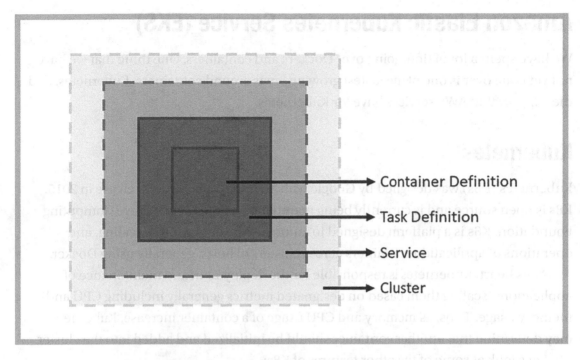

Figure 5-12. *Relationship of task definitions and clusters*

We have already talked about container definitions and even loaded one of those into a repository. We briefly went over clusters and task definitions. The one thing we still have to go over in that diagram is a **Service**. An Amazon ECS service allows you to run and maintain a specified number of instances of a task definition simultaneously in an Amazon ECS cluster. If any of your tasks should fail or stop for any reason, the Amazon ECS service scheduler launches another instance of your task definition to replace it to maintain the desired number of tasks in the service. In other words, the service's role is to ensure that the proper number of task definitions is running.

A full walk-through on ECS would take several chapters all on its own, because there are a lot of different configuration options and they can all lead to significantly different behavior. Let's look at another container management service that is also very configurable but where a lot of the configuration is not within the management service but instead with the container system itself.

Amazon Elastic Kubernetes Service (EKS)

We have spent a lot of time going over Dockers and containers. One thing that we have not yet gone over is one of the fastest growing areas around containers, Kubernetes, and the support that AWS services have for Kubernetes.

Kubernetes

Kubernetes (K8s) was designed by Google with an initial open source release in 2015. K8s is open source and is currently being maintained by the Cloud Native Computing Foundation. K8s is a platform designed to automate the deployment, scaling, and operations of application containers across clusters of hosts, generally using Docker.

At its heart, Kubernetes is responsible for the deployment and maintenance of applications, scaling them based on designated metrics generally including CPU and memory usage. Thus, as memory and CPU usage of a container increase, Kubernetes may determine that another container should be initialized and added into the cluster.

Let's look at some of the other features of K8s:

- **Service discovery** – Kubernetes can expose a container using the DNS name or the container's own IP address.

- **Load balancing** – Kubernetes, because of how it constantly monitors designated metrics, can load balance and distribute network traffic so that the deployment is stable, and the load is balanced as much as possible.

- **Automatic bin packing** – You point K8s at a cluster of nodes that are to be used to run a set of containerized tasks, setting the required amount of CPU and memory that each task needs. Kubernetes will then manage the fitting of those tasks into the various nodes to help ensure that you are getting the best use of your configured resources.

- **Storage orchestration** – Kubernetes supports mounting a storage system of your choice.

- **Automated rollouts and rollbacks** – Kubernetes allows you to define the "desired state" of your deployed containers. K8s will then manage the changing of state (from whatever state it is at before setting) to the desired state at a controlled rate. For example, you can automate

K8s to create new containers for your deployment, remove existing containers, and adopt all the resources from the old containers to the new containers.

- **Self-healing** – K8s will restart containers that fail, replace containers as required, or kill containers that don't respond to your self-defined health check, making sure that the restarted or replaced containers are not available until they are in the desired state.

- **Secret and configuration management** – Kubernetes also lets you store and maintain sensitive information such as passwords, tokens, and keys. You can deploy and update secrets and configurations without rebuilding container images and without exposing any of the secrets within your stack.

Kubernetes is a platform that is made up of various components. The top-level component is the *cluster*. When you deploy Kubernetes, you get a cluster. A cluster is made up of a set of worker machines that run the containerized applications. These worker machines are known as *nodes*. A cluster must have at least one node.

Each of these nodes hosts *pods*, which are components of the application workload with each hosting one or more containers. The pods and the nodes are managed by the *control plane*, with the control plane likely running across multiple computers and a cluster usually running multiple nodes. The control plane has several different components:

- **kube-api-server** – This component is the front end of the control plane and is responsible for performing all of the administrative tasks. Users interact with the control plane by sending commands (in YAML or JSON) to the API Server that processes and executes the commands.

- **etcd** – This is a distributed key-value store that stores the cluster state and configuration details such as subnets and configuration maps.

- **kube-scheduler** – This component is used to schedule the work within each of the nodes. It also manages any new requests coming from the kube-api-server and assigns those requests to healthy nodes.

- **kube-controller-manager** – This component is responsible for getting the desired state from the API Server, comparing the current state to the desire state, and then taking any corrective steps necessary to make the current state match desired state.

There are several different components within the node as well:

- **kubelet** – An agent that runs on the node and communicates with the control plane, listening for tasks such as deploying or destroying a container. The kubelet is also responsible for making sure that the containers running within the pod are always healthy.

- **kube-proxy** – This is used for communicating between the various nodes. It manages network rules on the nodes and is also responsible for ensuring that there are the appropriate rules defined on the node so that the container can communicate.

You can see all these Kubernetes components tied together in Figure 5-13.

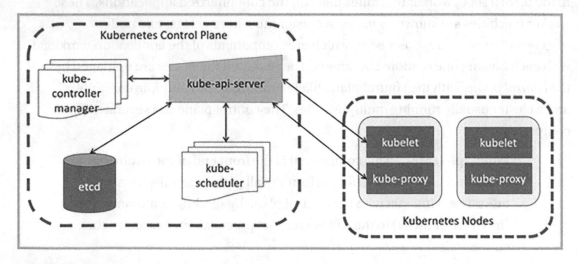

Figure 5-13. *Kubernetes component diagram*

When using K8s, administrators are responsible for configuring every aspect of a Kubernetes system. You need to install and maintain the control plane and its components, install and configure software on the nodes, and then make sure that it is all wired together and communicating correctly. And you must do that for every environment in which you are running K8s. That's a lot going on. However, AWS has a service to take some of that burden off.

Kubernetes with Amazon EKS

Amazon EKS is a managed service for running Kubernetes on AWS, which means that users using EKS can run K8s without needing to install, operate, and maintain their own Kubernetes control plane or nodes (which has got to sound great after the last few pages). EKS will also

- Run and scale the Kubernetes control plane across multiple AWS Availability Zones to ensure high availability

- Automatically scale control plane instances based on load, detect and replace unhealthy control plane instances when necessary, and provide automated version updates as well as any necessary patching.

There are two primary ways to get your containers running in EKS. The first is through the AWS console and AWS CLI, and the other is through the **eksctl**, a simple command-line utility for creating and managing Kubernetes clusters on Amazon EKS. Both approaches require that you have **kubectl**, a command-line tool for working with Kubernetes clusters, installed as well.

Note   The AWS Tools for PowerShell has some support for EKS, but this support is limited compared to that within the AWS CLI and eksctl.

When working with AWS CLI and the console, the high-level process for creation is to first create the appropriate Amazon Virtual Private Cloud (VPC) and then the appropriate cluster role with IAM policy. You can do this through the console or through the AWS CLI, however you prefer. You would next go into the EKS Console and select **Create Cluster** as shown in Figure 5-14.

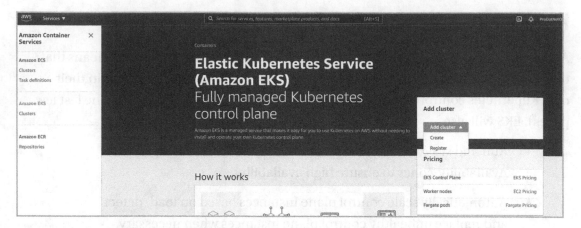

Figure 5-14. *Creating an EKS cluster*

There are four steps to creating a cluster in the console. The first step is to *Configure cluster*. On this page, you name the cluster, assign the cluster role that you created earlier, and then select whether you will be using envelope encryption of Kubernetes secrets using AWS Key Management Services (KMS). It is important to note, however, that once you create the cluster, you are unable to change either the assigned cluster role or whether you will be using KMS to encrypt Kubernetes secrets.

The second step in creating a cluster is to *Specify networking*. Here, you will be able to select the VPC in which the cluster will run as well as determine the cluster endpoint access, or access to the *kube-api-server*. You can select to have the cluster endpoint be accessible from outside the VPC and whether your worker node traffic will leave the VPC to connect to the endpoint. You have three selections: *Public*, where the endpoint is available from outside the VPC and worker node traffic leaves the VPC to connect back into the endpoint; *Public and private,* where the endpoint is available from outside the VPC but all worker node traffic stays within the VPC; and *Private*, where the endpoint is available only from within the VPC and, obviously, all worker node traffic stays within the VPC. You can also use advanced settings to create a list of IP addresses to limit the systems that can access the endpoint.

Step three is where you configure Control Plane Logging, where you can determine whether audit and diagnostics logs are sent from the EKS control plane to CloudWatch. You can configure EKS to send API Server, Audit, Authenticator, Controller manager, and Scheduler logs, with each being individually selected as shown in Figure 5-15.

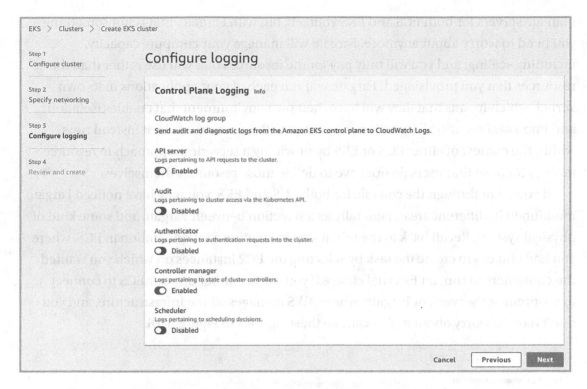

Figure 5-15. *Configuring logging in an EKS cluster*

The last step is to review the cluster settings and create the cluster.

Once the cluster is created, the next step is to configure your local computer so that it can talk to the cluster. The AWS CLI supports this by providing functionality for creating (or adding to the file if it already exists) the *kubeconfig* information for your cluster.

The next step in creating a cluster is creating the nodes. You have two choices for nodes: Fargate – Linux, where your containers will run within the AWS Fargate system, or Managed nodes – Linux, where you run Linux applications on EC2 instances. Selecting Managed nodes will require you to configure the nodes, namely, the IAM policies and the appropriate node role. Once you have your cluster created, you will be able to deploy your applications, or containers, to the configured cluster. This is done using *kubectl* or one of the AWS-specific tooling such as *eksctl*.

AWS Fargate

The easiest way to think about AWS Fargate is that it is a managed service that sits on top of either Amazon ECS or Amazon EKS. As discussed earlier, you need to provision and manage servers for both ECS and EKS yourself, but with Fargate, that is not something you need to worry about anymore. Fargate will manage your compute capacity, including scaling; and you will only pay for the resources that you use rather than the resources that you provisioned. Fargate will run each of your applications in its own kernel, which means that they will have their own environment that enables isolation and improved security. Fargate is not a service with its own console; it instead runs within the context of either ECS or EKS by providing a serverless approach to resource management so that users do not have to define those resources themselves.

If you went through the console for both ECS and EKS, you may have noticed Fargate mentioned in different areas, generally as a selection between Fargate and some kind of physical system. Recall back to the initial step in creating a task definition in ECS, where you had choices to create the task by selecting the EC2 instances on which you wanted the containers to run, an External choice if you wanted to set up your ECS to connect to on-premises servers, or Fargate, where AWS manages all the infrastructure, and you don't have to worry about it. You can see these options in Figure 5-16.

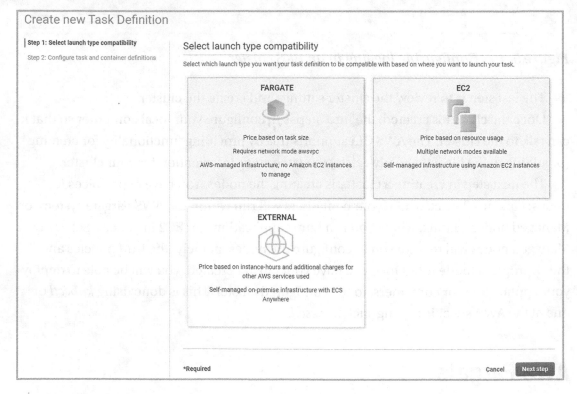

Figure 5-16. *Fargate image*

Selecting the Fargate option will present you a much lighter configuration screen because you do not have to worry about launch types, AMIs, or any of the other system selection options. It also eliminates a lot of the decisions around networking types and other considerations – it just flat out makes it easier to both configure and manage.

This same type of opportunity to lower your management overhead is available when working with Amazon EKS, as EKS integrates Kubernetes and Fargate by using controllers that are built by AWS. These controllers use the upstream, extensible model provided by Kubernetes with the controllers being run as part of the EKS managed Kubernetes control plane and are responsible for scheduling native Kubernetes pods onto Fargate. The Fargate controllers include a new scheduler that runs alongside the default Kubernetes scheduler as well as several mutating and validating admission controllers. When you start a pod that meets the criteria for running on Fargate, the Fargate controllers that are running in the cluster recognize, update, and schedule the pod onto Fargate.

AWS App Runner

The newest entry into AWS container management goes even further in removing the amount of configuration and management that you must use when working with containers. App Runner is a fully managed service that automatically builds and deploys the application as well creates the load balancer. App Runner also manages the scaling up and down based upon traffic. What do you, as a developer, have to do to get your container running in App Runner? Let's take a look.

First, log into AWS and go to the App Runner console home. If you click on the *Services* link, you will find App Runner under the **Compute** section rather than the **Containers** section, even though its purpose is to easily run containers. Click on the **Create an App Runner Service** button to get to the Step 1 page as shown in Figure 5-17.

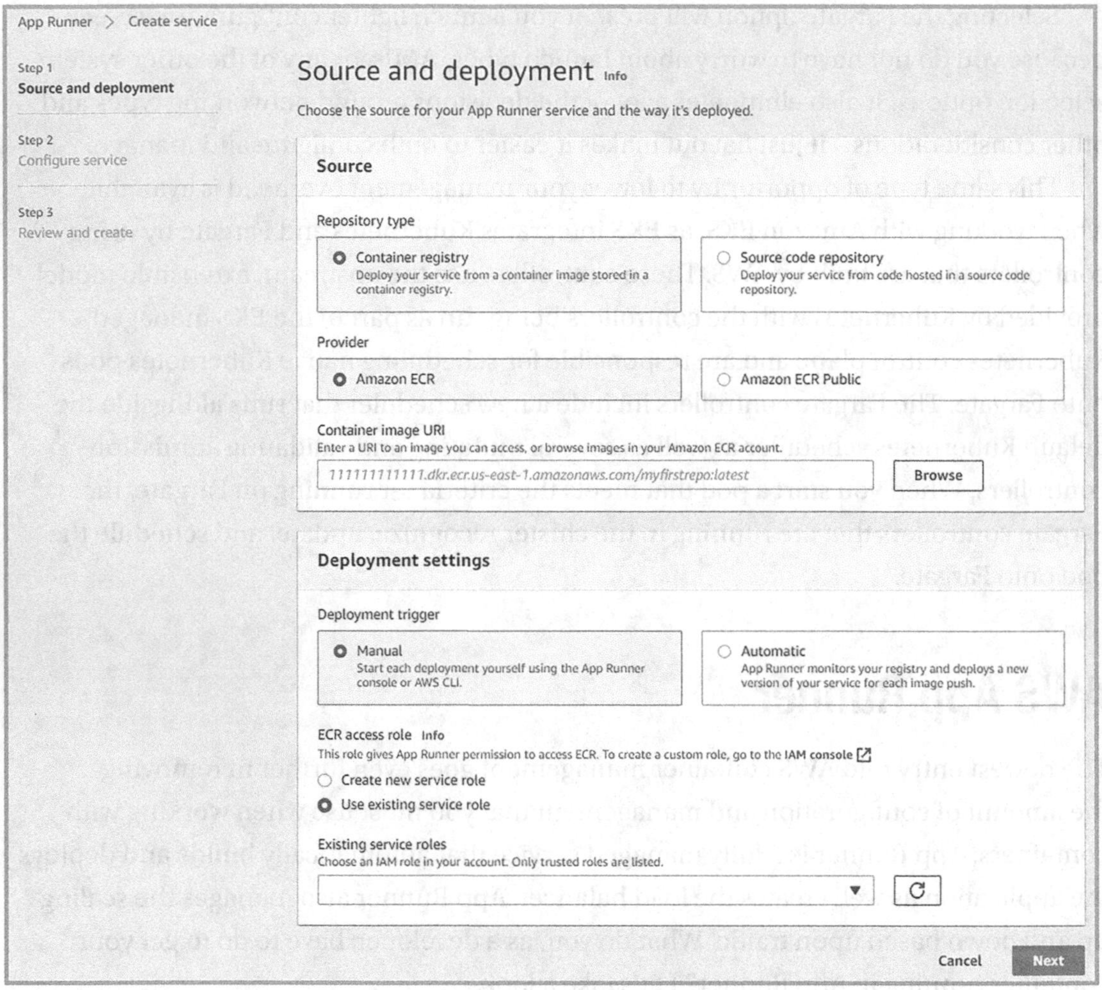

App Runner > Create service

Step 1
Source and deployment

Step 2
Configure service

Step 3
Review and create

Source and deployment Info

Choose the source for your App Runner service and the way it's deployed.

Source

Repository type

- ● Container registry
  Deploy your service from a container image stored in a container registry.

- ○ Source code repository
  Deploy your service from code hosted in a source code repository.

Provider

- ● Amazon ECR

- ○ Amazon ECR Public

Container image URI
Enter a URI to an image you can access, or browse images in your Amazon ECR account.

| 111111111111.dkr.ecr.us-east-1.amazonaws.com/myfirstrepo:latest | Browse |

Deployment settings

Deployment trigger

- ● Manual
  Start each deployment yourself using the App Runner console or AWS CLI.

- ○ Automatic
  App Runner monitors your registry and deploys a new version of your service for each image push.

ECR access role Info
This role gives App Runner permission to access ECR. To create a custom role, go to the IAM **console** ⎘

- ○ Create new service role
- ● Use existing service role

Existing service roles
Choose an IAM role in your account. Only trusted roles are listed.

| ▼ | C |

Cancel   **Next**

Figure 5-17. *Creating an App Runner service*

The first section, **Source**, requires you to identify where the container image that you want to deploy is stored. You currently, at the time of this writing, can choose either a container registry, Amazon ECR, or a source code repository. Since we have already loaded an image in ECR, let us move forward with this option by ensuring *Container registry* and *Amazon ECR* are selected and then clicking the Browse button to bring up the image selection screen as shown in Figure 5-18.

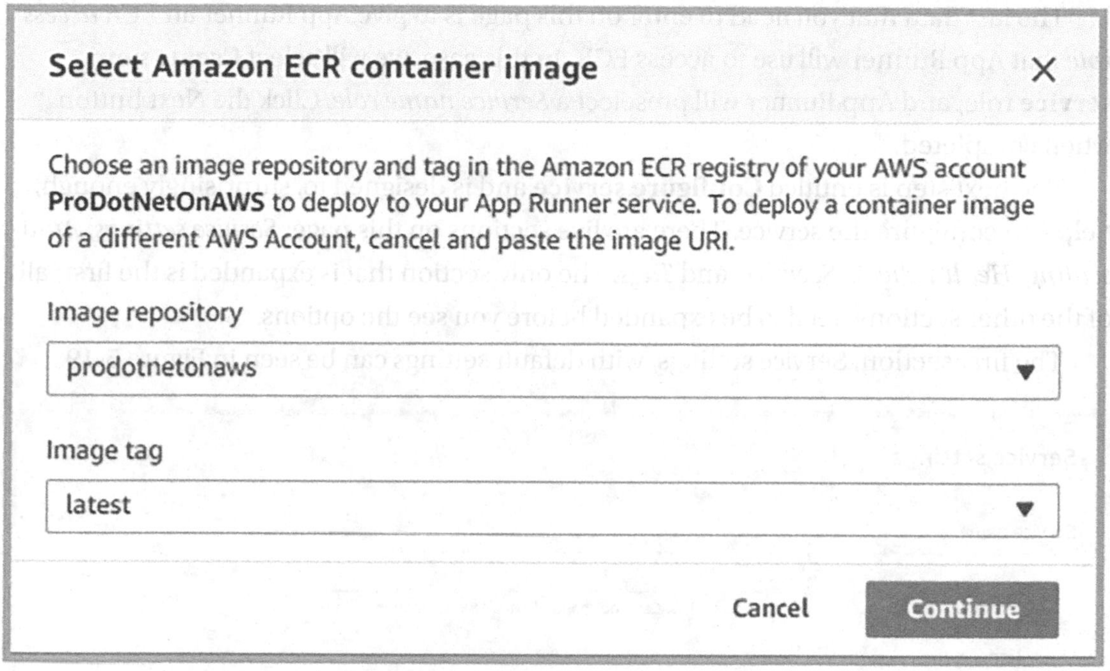

Select Amazon ECR container image   ✕

Choose an image repository and tag in the Amazon ECR registry of your AWS account
ProDotNetOnAWS to deploy to your App Runner service. To deploy a container image
of a different AWS Account, cancel and paste the image URI.

Image repository

| prodotnetonaws   ▼ |

Image tag

| latest   ▼ |

                                              Cancel   **Continue**

Figure 5-18. *Selecting a container image from ECR*

In this screen, we selected the "prodotnetonaws" image repository that we created
earlier in the chapter and the container image with the tag of "latest".

Once you have completed the **Source** section, the next step is to determine the
Deployment settings for your container. Here, your choices are to use the *Deployment
trigger* of **Manual**, which means that you must fire off each deployment yourself using
the App Runner console or the AWS CLI, or **Automatic**, where App Runner watches your
repository, deploying the new version of the container every time the image changes. In
this case, we will choose *Manual* so that we have full control of the deployment.

Warning   When you have your deployment settings set to *Automatic*, every
time the image is updated, App Runner will trigger a deployment. This may be
appropriate in a development or even test environment, but it is unlikely that you
will want to use this in a production setting.

The last data that you need to enter on this page is to give App Runner an *ECR access role* that App Runner will use to access ECR. In this case, we will select **Create new service** role, and App Runner will preselect a *Service name role*. Click the Next button when completed.

The next step is entitled **Configure service** and is designed to, surprisingly enough, help you configure the service. There are five sections on this page: *Service settings*, *Auto scaling*, *Health check*, *Security*, and *Tags*. The only section that is expanded is the first; all of the other sections need to be expanded before you see the options.

The first section, Service settings, with default settings can be seen in Figure 5-19.

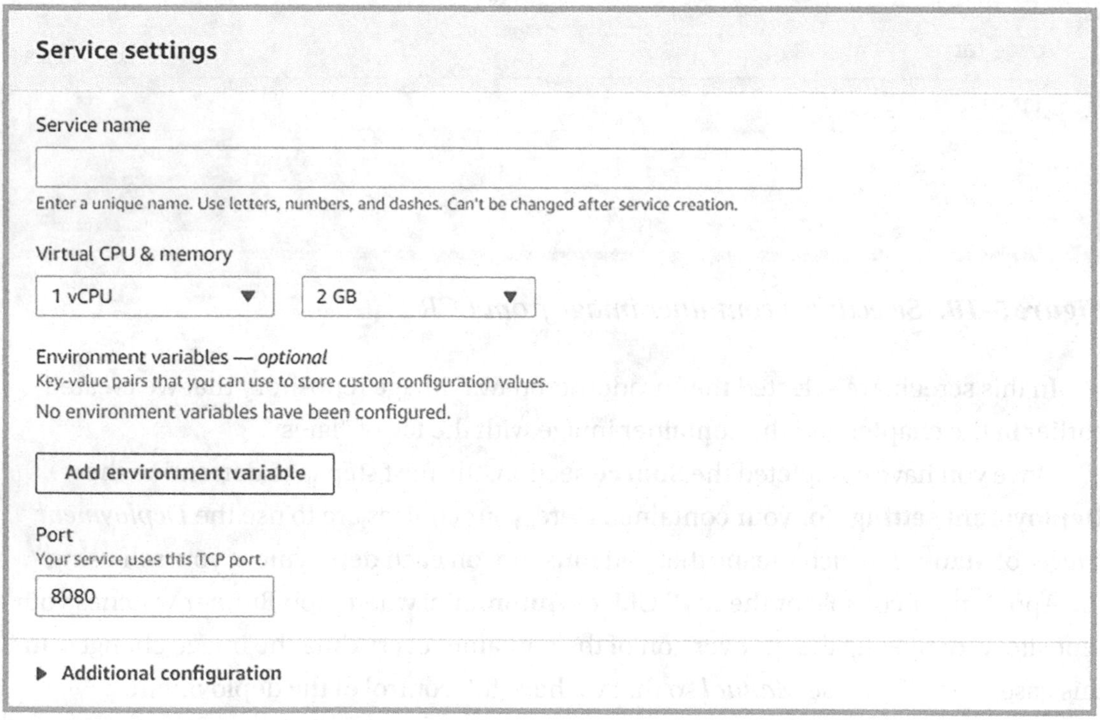

Service settings

Service name

Enter a unique name. Use letters, numbers, and dashes. Can't be changed after service creation.

Virtual CPU & memory

| 1 vCPU ▼ | 2 GB ▼ |

Environment variables — *optional*
Key-value pairs that you can use to store custom configuration values.
No environment variables have been configured.

Add environment variable

Port
Your service uses this TCP port.

8080

▶ Additional configuration

Figure 5-19. *Service settings in App Runner*

Here, you set the *Service name*, select the *Virtual CPU & memory*, configure any optional *Environmental variables* that you may need, and determine the TCP *Port* that your service will use. If you are using the sample application that we loaded into ECR earlier in the chapter, you will need to change the port value from the default 8080 to port 80 so that it will serve the application we configured in the container. You also have the ability, under *Additional configuration*, to add a Start command, which will be run on launch. This is generally left blank if you have configured the entry point within the container image. We gave the service the name "ProDotNetOnAWS-AR" and let all the rest of the settings in this section remain as default.

The next section is *Auto scaling,* and there are two major options, *Default configuration* and *Custom configuration,* each of which provides the ability to set the auto scaling values as shown in Figure 5-20.

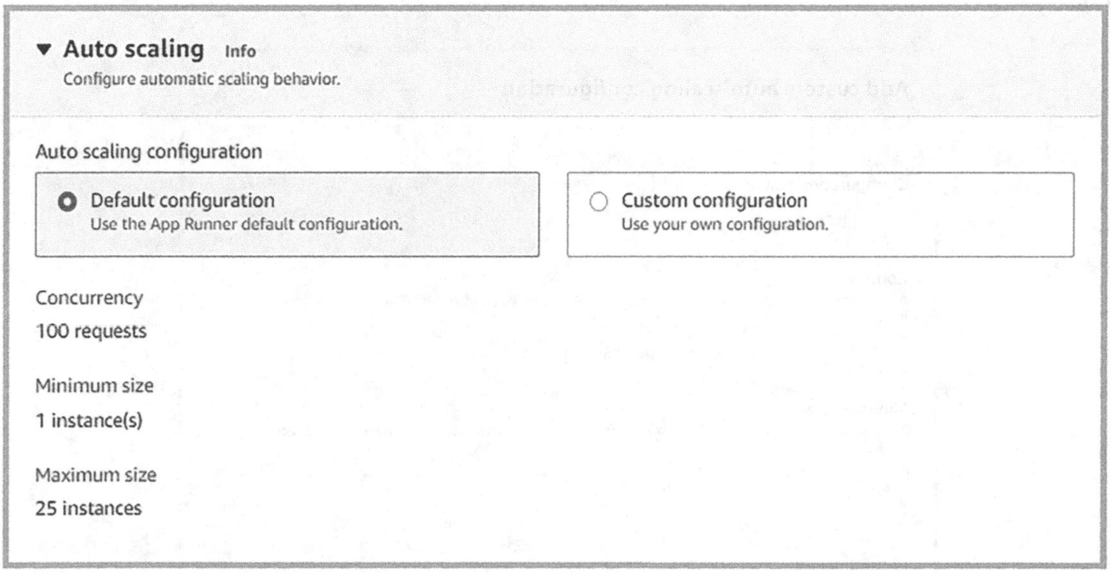

▼ **Auto scaling**   Info
Configure automatic scaling behavior.

Auto scaling configuration

○ **Default configuration**
Use the App Runner default configuration.

○ **Custom configuration**
Use your own configuration.

Concurrency
100 requests

Minimum size
1 instance(s)

Maximum size
25 instances

Figure 5-20.   *Setting the Auto scaling settings in App Runner*

The first of these auto scaling values is *Concurrency.* This value represents the maximum number of concurrent requests that an instance can process before App Runner scales up the service. The default configuration has this set at 100 requests that you can customize if using the *Custom configuration* setting.

The next value is *Minimum size,* or the number of instances that App Runner provisions for your service, regardless of concurrent usage. This means that there may be times where some of these provisioned instances are not being used. You will be charged for the memory usage of all provisioned instances, but only for the CPU of those instances that are actually handling traffic. The default configuration for minimum size is set to one instance.

The last value is *Maximum size.* This value represents the maximum number of instances to which your service will scale; once your service reaches the maximum size, there will be no additional scaling no matter the number of concurrent requests. The default configuration for maximum size is 25 instances.

If any of the default values do not match your need, you will need to create a custom configuration, which will give you control over each of these configuration values. To do this, select *Custom configuration*. This will display a drop-down that contains all of the App Runner configurations you have available (currently, it will only have "DefaultConfiguration" because we have yet to define a different configuration) and an *Add new* button. Clicking this button will bring up the entry screen as shown in Figure 5-21.

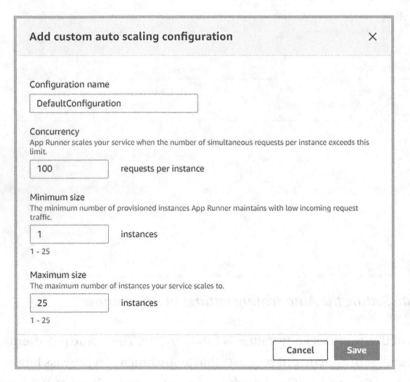

Figure 5-21. *Customizing auto scaling in App Runner*

The next section after you configure auto scaling is *Health check*. The first value you set in this section is the *Timeout*, which describes the amount of time, in seconds, that the load balancer will wait for a health check response. The default timeout is five seconds. You also can set the *Interval*, which is the number of seconds between health checks of each instance and is defaulted to ten seconds. You can also set the *Unhealthy* and *Health* thresholds, where the unhealthy threshold is the number of consecutive health check failures that means that an instance is unhealthy and needs to be recycled and the health threshold is the number of consecutive successful health checks necessary for an instance to be determined to be healthy. The default for these values is five requests for unhealthy and one request for healthy.

You next can assign an IAM role to the instance in the *Security* section. This IAM role will be used by the running application if it needs to communicate to other AWS services, such as S3 or a database server. The last section is *Tags*, where you can enter one or more tags to the App Runner service.

Once you have finished configuring the service, clicking the **Next** button will bring you to the review screen. Clicking the **Create and deploy** button on this screen will give the approval for App Runner to create the service, deploy the container image, and run it so that the application is available. You will be presented with the service details page and a banner that informs you that "Create service is in progress." This process will take several minutes and when completed will take you to the properties page as shown in Figure 5-22.

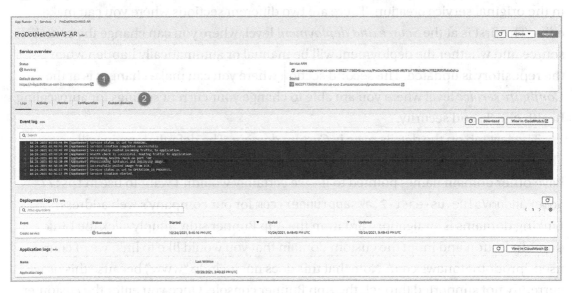

Figure 5-22. *After App Runner is completed*

Once the service is created and the status is displayed as *Running,* you will see a value as indicated by a 1, for a *Default domain,* which represents the external-facing URL. Clicking on it will bring up the home page for your containerized sample application.

The Red 2 highlights the five tabs displayed under the domain: *Logs, Activity, Metrics, Configuration,* and *Custom Domain.* The Logs section displays the *Event, Deployment,* and *Application* logs for this App Runner service. This is where you will be able to look for any problems during deployment or running of the container itself. You should be able, under the *Event log* section, to see the listing of events from the service creation. The *Activity* tab is very similar in that it displays a list of activities taken by your service, such as creation and deployment.

The next tab, *Metrics,* tracks metrics related to the entire App Runner service. This is where you will be able to see information on HTTP connections and requests, as well as to track the changes in the number of used and unused instances. By going into the sample application (at the default domain) and clicking around the site, you should see these values change and a graph become available that provides insight into these various activities.

The *Configuration* tab allows you to view and edit many of the settings that we set in the original service creation. There are two different sections where you can make edits. The first is at the *Source and deployment* level, where you can change the container source and whether the deployment will be manual or automatically happen when the repository is updated. The second section where you can make changes is at the *Configure service* level where you are able to change your current settings for autoscaling, health check, and security.

The last tab on the details page is *Custom domain.* The default domain will always be available for your application; however, it is likely that you will want to have other domain names pointed to it – we certainly wouldn't want to use `https://SomeRandomValue.us-east-2.awsapprunner.com` for our company's web address. Linking domains is straightforward from the App Runner side. Simply click the **Link domain** button and input the custom domain that you would like to link; we of course used "prodotnetonaws.com". Note that this does not include "www", because this usage is currently not supported through the App Runner console. Once you enter the customer domain name, you will be presented the *Configure DNS* page as shown in Figure 5-23.

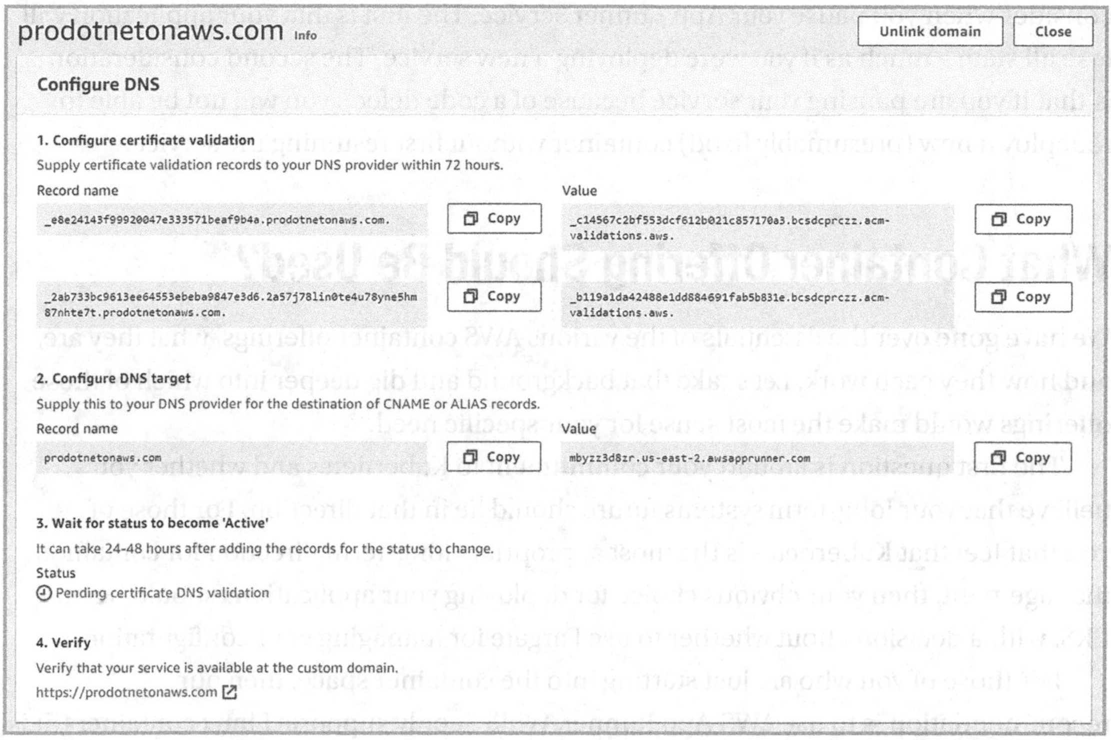

Figure 5-23. *Configuring a custom domain in App Runner*

This page contains a set of certificate validation records that you need to add to your Domain Name System (DNS) so that App Runner can validate that you own or control the domain. You will also need to add CNAME records to your DNS to target the App Runner domain; you will need to add one record for the custom domain and another for the www subdomain if so desired. Once the certificate validation records are added to your DNS, the customer domain status will become *Active,* and traffic will be directed to your App Runner instance. This evaluation can take anywhere from minutes to up to 48 hours, depending upon your DNS provider.

Once your App Runner instance is up and running this first time, there are several actions that you can take on it as shown in the upper-right corner of Figure 5-23. The first is the orange **Deploy** button. This will deploy the container from either the container or source code repository depending upon your configuration. You also can **Delete** the service, which is straightforward, as well as **Pause** the service. There are some things to consider when you pause your App Runner service. The first is that your application will lose all state – much as if you were deploying a new service. The second consideration is that if you are pausing your service because of a code defect, you will not be able to redeploy a new (presumably fixed) container without first resuming the service.

What Container Offering Should Be Used?

We have gone over the essentials of the various AWS container offerings, what they are, and how they each work. Let's take that background and dig deeper into which of those offerings would make the most sense for your specific need.

The first question is around your commitment to Kubernetes and whether you believe that your long-term systems future should lie in that direction. For those of you that feel that Kubernetes is the most appropriate long-term direction for container management, then your obvious choice for deploying your applications should be on EKS, with a decision about whether to use Fargate for managing your configuration.

For those of you who are just starting into the container space, then our recommendation is to use AWS App Runner. While it only supports Linux containers, it is very simple to create and manage, and the App Runner service UI contains all the service and usage metrics that you need to understand how often the system is being hit and how it performs. That being said, if you are committing to running fleets of containers, or if cost is an issue, then consider running your application(s) in Amazon ECS. The price for App Runner is approximately 50% more than ECS with Fargate; for this sample application, you will be paying approximately $.078 per hour in US-East-2, while ECS-Fargate will cost about $.049 per hour.

This chapter described the intermediate level of infrastructure abstraction: containers. In the next chapter, we will take additional steps in abstracting away the hardware on which your applications run as we start talking about AWS Lambda, also known as serverless or sometimes Functions as a Service.

CHAPTER 6

Serverless

In our final look at compute options on AWS, we will be working at an even higher level of abstraction. Since the launch of AWS Lambda in November 2014, the term *serverless* has grown to encompass several domains, and you'll now find it applied by AWS to additional services that all pre-date the introduction of Lambda. Some of these go back to the earliest days of the AWS Cloud itself – presumably, this is because these services don't require you to provision and manage infrastructure. As of late 2021, it's now possible to adopt a serverless approach for

- *Compute*, for example, AWS Lambda, AWS Fargate.

- *Application integration*, for example, Amazon API Gateway, AWS Step Functions, Amazon EventBridge.

- *Databases*, for example, Amazon DynamoDB, Amazon Aurora Serverless.

- *Analytics*, for example, Amazon Redshift Serverless.

- *And others* – see https://aws.amazon.com/serverless/ for a fuller list.

In this chapter, we're going to focus on serverless computing with AWS Lambda. We'll begin our exploration of AWS Lambda using a single stand-alone function deployed and invoked, using tooling that AWS makes available for the dotnet CLI and Visual Studio. Then, we'll expand to place our function behind an API as a *serverless application*, using the Serverless Application Model (SAM) tooling. For both examples, we'll also be looking at the options for debugging your serverless functions.

© William Penberthy and Steve Roberts 2023
W. Penberthy and S. Roberts, *Pro .NET on Amazon Web Services*,
https://doi.org/10.1007/978-1-4842-8907-5_6

Levels of Compute Abstraction

In Chapter 4, we began our look at compute on AWS using virtual machines in Amazon EC2 and briefly touched on their use in AWS Elastic Beanstalk. As we noted, EC2 gives you total control of the VM infrastructure (relative to the fact they're running in the AWS cloud and not in your data center). Elastic Beanstalk is instead a managed service that abstracts away some of the management of the compute infrastructure, enabling you to focus more on your application and less on managing cloud infrastructure.

In Chapter 5, we moved onto containers and added to the mix AWS Fargate (for both Amazon Elastic Container Service and Amazon Elastic Kubernetes Service). Fargate is a serverless approach to running containers. Like Elastic Beanstalk vs. EC2, Fargate vs. ECS/EKS abstracts away the management of the underlying container infrastructure. Again, the benefit to you is the ability to focus more on your application and less on cloud infrastructure management.

What's the purpose of the abstraction levels as you jump from EC2 to Elastic Beanstalk, or from ECS/EKS to Fargate? – *to relieve you, the developer, from much (or even all) of the need to provision and manage cloud resources to host and run your code.* You still have quite a lot of control, if you need it, but for the most part, you don't need to concern yourself with the underlying mechanics unless you really want to. This is the key to serverless. *You focus on your application and its needs – which you know best. AWS focuses on provisioning and managing the cloud infrastructure – which they know best.*

This brings us to AWS Lambda, which runs *functions* on compute infrastructure provisioned and managed by the Lambda service. Your functions run for short durations (no more than 15 minutes), processing any input data provided to them, and then exit, optionally returning some result data. All this happens without you needing to provision any compute infrastructure. You just hand your code to Lambda to take care of running it when needed. You can run your functions manually (by calling a Lambda service API or through tools), or, more commonly, the function runs in response to an event such as the creation or update of an object in an Amazon S3 storage bucket. There are many types of events that you can configure your functions to respond to. And one further benefit – when your functions are not running, you incur no financial costs, unlike leaving a VM or a container running idly 24×7.

Serverless Compute with AWS Lambda

AWS Lambda is an example of *function-as-a-service* compute. It provides zero access to the compute environment your function code is running in. You also have considerably fewer options to configure the environment too. When you configure a function in Lambda, you can choose the virtual CPU (vCPU) and memory and set a custom timeout beyond the default (up to a maximum of 15 minutes). And, of course, you get to specify the runtime – .NET, Java, JavaScript, Python, etc. – appropriate to the language you used to write your function code. You can see the full list of supported runtimes at `https://docs.aws.amazon.com/lambda/latest/dg/lambda-runtimes.html`.

That's all you've got to work with. Lambda really is higher up the abstraction stack, quite literally a "here's my code, run it for me when needed and I care nothing about the details of the rest" approach. We're not sure where abstracted compute levels go from here – maybe the next step is "here's what I want to be done, write and run the code for me on demand"!

So where can you use Lambda in your solutions? Hopefully, microservices have already come to mind. While you could certainly use Lambda to serve a monolithic ASP. NET Core web application (and AWS provides support to do just that), serving full-blown applications is not Lambda's primary use case.

Your Function's Compute Environment

Virtual machines in EC2 and Elastic Beanstalk run your applications 24×7 (unless you stop them). Containers can also run those applications 24×7 (again, until you stop them), or run for single bursts and then stop (e.g., a batch or ETL process).

Lambda runs your short-duration function code, usually in response to an event of some sort, which we'll come to shortly. To run the code, Lambda obtains a compute host, provisioning a new one if needed, from a pool it controls. Lambda downloads your code to the host, initializes and runs the function code, and then takes control back when the function exits, or if your function exceeds the maximum runtime of 15 minutes or the custom timeout you may have configured. The compute host is then available to run the function again, to handle another event if one is ready, or (after an undisclosed time) Lambda will recycle the host back into the pool to run other functions.

The notion of a pool of compute hosts owned and managed by Lambda brings up another difference between it and traditional compute. With EC2 and Elastic Beanstalk, you have access to the underlying compute host. You can connect to it using RDP or

SSH, install additional software and services, debug either remotely or on the virtual machines themselves, and stop and restart the VMs at your leisure. Also, the storage on the instance can exist outside of the VM instances so it can survive a reboot, or you can attach it to a completely different instance.

The same is true for containers. However, Lambda provides the complete compute environment for you, and it's largely fixed in terms of content (operating system, runtimes, etc.). While it is possible to add extra content to the environment (binary dependencies, etc.) using a technique called *Layers* or using container images to hold your functions, storage on a Lambda compute host is ephemeral as far as your function is concerned. This means that once your function has run, you **cannot** depend on the allocated storage being the same the next time your function runs. Lambda may schedule your function to run on a different (maybe even brand new) host. Therefore, you must consider your Lambda function's runtime environment to be stateless so you cannot expect any kind of server-side "memory" of previous requests.

Event-Driven Compute

As developers, we've become used to the concept of event-driven programming since the advent of graphical user interfaces. For example, a mouse click on a button triggers some code in our application to run, and the event notification framework supplies logical details of the "click" event (left, middle, or right button, point coordinates, etc.).

Lambda, at heart, is the same underlying concept except the code runs in the cloud, not in an application on our local device. We can configure our Lambda function to be bound to that event, and then, when the event occurs, Lambda runs our function code in response, passing details of the event as input. A couple of examples:

- You can configure an API endpoint to "front" a Lambda function. When a user, or application code, accesses that endpoint, the Lambda function runs and processes the data passed to it from the endpoint URL, for example, query parameters and the request body data. We'll see this in action later in the chapter.

- A change in the state of a cloud resource, for example, the creation, update, or deletion of an object in an S3 bucket or a DynamoDB database table update.

By the way, you can also invoke Lambda functions directly from within your own application code or scripts, at the command line, or from tooling, as we'll do shortly.

Long-Term Support (LTS) vs. Non-LTS Runtimes

Lambda has the notion of *managed runtimes*. A managed runtime is simply an LTS release, regardless of the individual language. With managed runtimes, Lambda maintains compute environments containing the specific runtime binaries for that LTS pre-installed. This means your function code can be built and packaged as a zip file, without the corresponding runtime binaries, and uploaded to Lambda ready for the function to run. When configuring your function, you simply select the appropriate managed runtime from the set available in Lambda.

Non-LTS versions do not have managed runtimes provided by Lambda, but you can still write functions using a non-LTS runtime. You simply use a different bundling mechanism to make the function code and the corresponding runtime environment needed by the code available to Lambda. We'll look at the two options to do this at the end of the chapter.

LTS vs. non-LTS is the reason you do not see .NET 5 nor will you see .NET 7 as a managed runtime when configuring functions in Lambda. You will see a .NET 6 managed runtime – as it's an LTS release.

Note   When using .NET for your Lambda functions, you must use a .NET Core–based runtime (.NET Core 3.1, .NET 5, .NET 6, and so on into the future). Lambda does not support .NET functions written using the .NET Framework.

You can also use PowerShell to write Lambda functions, but you won't see a PowerShell runtime listed in Lambda. Instead, Lambda functions written in PowerShell use a .NET Core–based runtime. And like .NET Lambda functions, you must use PowerShell Core for your function (so PowerShell 6 or later). Like the .NET Framework, Lambda does not support Windows PowerShell.

> **Note**   AWS provides a PowerShell module to help with writing and deploying PowerShell-based Lambda functions. See `https://github.com/aws/aws-lambda-dotnet/tree/master/PowerShell` for more information. You can install the module, `AWSLambdaPSCore`, from the PowerShell Gallery. See `www.powershellgallery.com/packages/AWSLambdaPSCore/`.

Tooling – dotnet CLI, SAM CLI, Visual Studio, Visual Studio Code, or JetBrains Rider? Oh my…

AWS provides a variety of tooling to work with .NET-based Lambda functions from either the command line or within an IDE, and we're going to look at most of them in this chapter.

There are two command-line experiences available. One integrates with the dotnet CLI and is (as you might expect) specific to .NET. The second, the Serverless Application Model CLI (SAM CLI), works not only with .NET-based Lambda functions but also with functions written in other languages such as Python and TypeScript.

For the dotnet CLI environment, AWS provides the `Amazon.Lambda.Tools` extension package (see `https://github.com/aws/aws-extensions-for-dotnet-cli` and `https://github.com/aws/aws-lambda-dotnet`). You can also install getting-started project scaffolding templates using the `Amazon.Lambda.Templates` package.

If you're a Visual Studio user, then the AWS toolkit for this IDE offers the same getting-started templates as for the dotnet CLI (it calls them blueprints). The toolkit also exposes a *Publish to AWS Lambda* wizard that is functionally identical to the `Amazon.Lambda.Tools` dotnet CLI tool package. In fact, you can round-trip between the IDE and the CLI experiences if you so wish.

Visual Studio Code and JetBrains Rider instead integrate with the SAM CLI command-line tooling. That's not to say you can't use Lambda functions created with the dotnet CLI/Visual Studio toolkit with these two environments – you'll just have to drop to a command line to run deployments or create tasks to invoke the necessary commands. While the SAM CLI offers getting-started templates, there are not as many as offered by the dotnet CLI and Visual Studio toolkit.

One advantage to using the SAM CLI is that it offers convenient debugging of Lambda functions on your machine using a Lambda-like container image. The dotnet

CLI/Visual Studio toolkit environments don't support this approach; instead, you use the Mock Lambda Test Tool (see `https://github.com/aws/aws-lambda-dotnet/tree/master/Tools/LambdaTestTool`). You can use this tool in Visual Studio Code and JetBrains Rider too.

Serverless Functions

Enough theory, let's start writing a Lambda function using .NET. We're going to create, deploy, invoke (run), and debug a serverless function using both the dotnet CLI and Visual Studio tooling (you can choose which you prefer as you follow along, as we'll present instructions for both environments). We'll use the SAM CLI for comparison purposes later in the chapter.

Our serverless function will translate text between languages using the Amazon Translate service. See `https://aws.amazon.com/translate/` for more details on the service, where you'll see one example use case being localizing content for websites and applications. At the time of writing, the free tier enables you to translate up to 2 million characters for free – more than enough for our purposes!

Installing the Tools

If you were following along earlier in the book, then you likely already have the AWS Toolkit for Visual Studio installed. If so, and you're an IDE user, then you're all set as it requires no other components to support deploying serverless functions and applications.

If you're a command-line user, then we need to get the extension tool and templates for the dotnet CLI. These, like other dotnet CLI extensions, are available from NuGet.

First, install the commands for Lambda. These are distributed in a global tools package named `Amazon.Lambda.Tools`. Install using the following command:

```
dotnet tool install -g amazon.lambda.tools
```

Next, add the project templates for the `dotnet new` command:

```
dotnet new -i amazon.lambda.templates::*
```

The * indicates we want all the templates installed. After installation, the complete list of all available templates (for Lambda and otherwise) are displayed. Figure 6-1 shows

the available templates for Lambda functions and serverless applications. These match
the templates available from Visual Studio's New Project wizard when you have the AWS
toolkit installed.

```
Templates                                              Short Name                                      Language       Tags
----------------------------------------------------------------------------------------------------------------------------------
Lambda Simple Kinesis Firehose Function                lambda.KinesisFirehose                          [C#]           AWS/Lambda/Function
Lambda Empty Function (.NET 6 Container Image)          lambda.image.EmptyFunction                      [C#], F#       AWS/Lambda/Function
Order Flowers Chatbot Tutorial                         lambda.OrderFlowersChatbot                      [C#]           AWS/Lambda/Function
Lambda Simple Kinesis Function                         lambda.Kinesis                                  [C#], F#       AWS/Lambda/Function
Lambda Custom Runtime Function (.NET 6)                lambda.CustomRuntimeFunction                    [C#], F#       AWS/Lambda/Function
Lambda Simple S3 Function                              lambda.S3                                       [C#], F#       AWS/Lambda/Function
Lambda Detect Image Labels                             lambda.DetectImageLabels                        [C#], F#       AWS/Lambda/Function
Lambda Simple SNS Function                             lambda.SNS                                      [C#]           AWS/Lambda/Function
Lex Book Trip Sample                                   lambda.LexBookTripSample                        [C#]           AWS/Lambda/Function
Lambda Simple SQS Function                             lambda.SQS                                      [C#]           AWS/Lambda/Function
Lambda Simple Application Load Balancer Function       lambda.SimpleApplicationLoadBalancerFunction    [C#]           AWS/Lambda/Function
Lambda Empty Function                                  lambda.EmptyFunction                            [C#], F#       AWS/Lambda/Function
Lambda Simple DynamoDB Function                        lambda.DynamoDB                                 [C#], F#       AWS/Lambda/Function
Lambda ASP.NET Core Web API                            serverless.AspNetCoreWebAPI                     [C#], F#       AWS/Lambda/Serverless
Lambda Empty Serverless                                serverless.EmptyServerless                      [C#], F#       AWS/Lambda/Serverless
Lambda ASP.NET Core Web API (.NET 6 Container Image)   serverless.image.AspNetCoreWebAPI               [C#], F#       AWS/Lambda/Serverless
Lambda Empty Serverless (.NET 6 Container Image)       serverless.image.EmptyServerless                [C#], F#       AWS/Lambda/Serverless
Serverless Simple S3 Function                          serverless.S3                                   [C#], F#       AWS/Lambda/Serverless
Lambda Giraffe Web App                                 serverless.Giraffe                              F#             AWS/Lambda/Serverless
Serverless Detect Image Labels                         serverless.DetectImageLabels                    [C#], F#       AWS/Lambda/Serverless
Lambda ASP.NET Core Web Application with Razor Pages   serverless.AspNetCoreWebApp                     [C#]           AWS/Lambda/Serverless
Step Functions Hello World                             serverless.StepFunctionsHelloWorld              [C#], F#       AWS/Lambda/Serverless
Lambda DynamoDB Blog API                               serverless.DynamoDBBlogAPI                      [C#]           AWS/Lambda/Serverless
Serverless WebSocket API                               serverless.WebSocketAPI                         [C#]           AWS/Lambda/Serverless
Console Application                                    console                                         [C#], F#, VB   Common/Console
Class library                                          classlib                                        [C#], F#, VB   Common/Library
WPF Application                                         wpf                                             [C#]           Common/WPF
```

Figure 6-1. *New project templates for Lambda*

With the templates and tools installed, we're ready to create our function using
either Visual Studio or the command line.

Creating a Serverless Function

Most of the templates contain pre-written code to illustrate techniques and use packages
from the AWS SDK for .NET to call one or more services. We encourage you to use
some of the templates to "get a feel" for what Lambda functions look like. But for this
chapter, we're going to use the so-called "empty template" to avoid the need to remove
all the pre-written code and dependencies before proceeding with the code for our own
function. We're providing instructions for both command-line and Visual Studio users in
the following text – choose the approach that works best for you.

Using the Command Line

First, create a new folder (we're using "ch06\example1") and set it to be the current location. Then, generate a new serverless function with the following command:

```
dotnet new lambda.EmptyFunction
```

You'll see two new folders created under the example1 folder, *src/* and *test/*, both of which contain an additional folder, *example1* (so *ch06/example1/src/example1* in this case). The src/example1 folder contains a readme file, the Lambda function project file, initial code for the function, and a settings file used during deployment.

The *test/example1* folder contains a unit test – we'll be ignoring this for our purposes. So before proceeding further, set your command-line location to be src/example1. Figure 6-2 shows the structure and generated files.

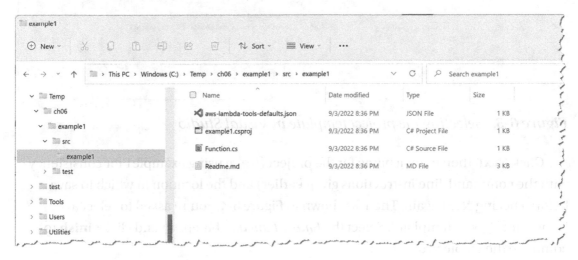

Figure 6-2. *Generated "empty function" project using command-line tools*

Using Visual Studio

In Visual Studio, start the New Project wizard, enter "lambda" into the template search field, and select the AWS Lambda Project (.NET Core – C#) entry shown in Figure 6-3. Note that in Visual Studio, we get the option to create a project without unit tests; you can see the other templates, with tests, listed separately.

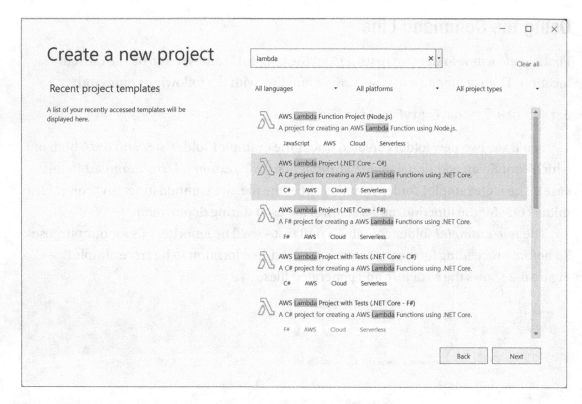

Figure 6-3. *Selecting the project template in Visual Studio*

Click **Next**, then enter a name for the project (we're using example1 for consistency with the command-line instructions given earlier) and the location in which to save, before clicking **Next** again. Then, as shown in Figure 6-4, you're asked to select a "blueprint" (a.k.a. template). Select the *Empty Function* blueprint and click **Finish** to complete the whole process.

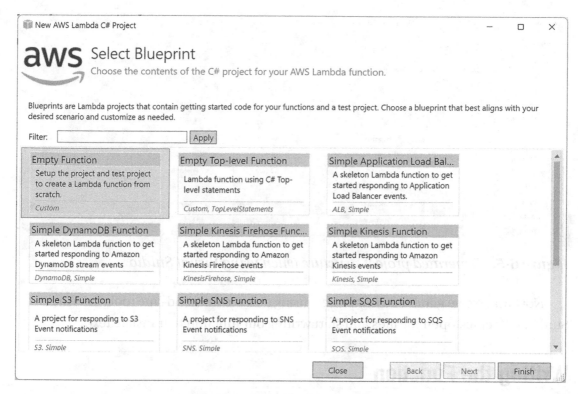

Figure 6-4. *Selecting the empty function blueprint (template)*

While the generated project and code are identical to that created by the command-line approach, there is a slight difference in folder structure when you use Visual Studio as shown in Figure 6-5. Instead of src/ and test/ subfolders, you'll see a subfolder in the chosen location corresponding to the project name and in there, the function code, project file, and settings file. There will also be a *project name.Tests* folder, if you selected the template that included tests. The slight difference in layout is of no concern; we mention it only to avoid surprises when comparing your results with those of others.

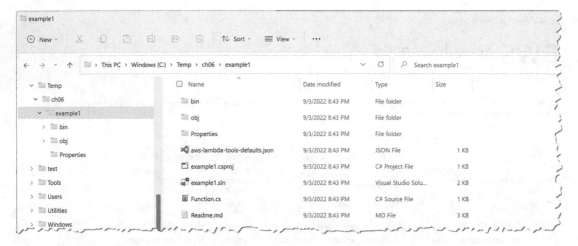

Figure 6-5. *Generated project structure when using Visual Studio*

Now that we've generated our project using either command-line tools or Visual Studio, let's crack open the files and start writing our function to translate text.

Writing the Function

Start by opening the file **Function.cs** in your code editor of choice. Listing 6-1 shows the default code generated by the "empty function" template. You can see we have an assembly-level attribute and a class containing a method, which is our *function handler*. The handler method is the code that Lambda will run when your function runs. You can name this method anything you like, as we'll inform Lambda of the actual handler method name when we deploy the function.

Listing 6-1. The default "empty function" from the template

```
using Amazon.Lambda.Core;

// Assembly attribute to enable the Lambda function's JSON
// input to be converted into a .NET class.
[assembly: LambdaSerializer(typeof(Amazon.Lambda.Serialization.↵
SystemTextJson.DefaultLambdaJsonSerializer))]

namespace example1;
public class Function
{
```

```
/// <summary>
/// A simple function that takes a string and does a
/// ToUpper
/// </summary>
/// <param name="input"></param>
/// <param name="context"></param>
/// <returns></returns>
public string FunctionHandler(string input, ↵
ILambdaContext context)
{
    return input?.ToUpper();
}
}
```

The input and output of Lambda functions are JSON payloads. The [assembly: ...] attribute in the code designates a serializer library, provided by AWS, that takes the JSON payload input to the function and deserializes it into a .NET object that's more convenient to work with. Similarly, the library automatically serializes the output from the function to JSON.

Note   You use assembly attributes, indicated by [assembly: *attribute-name*], to embed global information into an assembly, such as the assembly's identity data, information like company or product information, and manifest data like title and description. You can also write your own assembly attributes, as AWS has done here, to embed – in this case, data noting which JSON serializer should be used on Lambda payloads.

If you inspect the generated project file, you'll notice two dependencies: Amazon. Lambda.Core and Amazon.Lambda.Serialization.SystemTextJson. There's also a custom project attribute, AWSProjectType, with value "Lambda". This project attribute is how, in Visual Studio, the AWS toolkit knows to offer the *Publish to AWS Lambda* action on the project in the Solution Explorer.

Our next step is to update the project file to add a dependency on the AWS SDK for .NET package to enable us to call Amazon Translate. If you're using Visual Studio, use the NuGet package manager to add the dependency or, at the command line, run the following command:

```
dotnet add package AWSSDK.Translate
```

Next, replace the entire contents of the Function.cs file with the contents shown in Listing 6-2. We've added using statements for the SDK package we just took a dependency on and added a class to represent our input data structure. In the revised function handler method, you can see we call Amazon Translate's TranslateText API, which accepts data provided in a TranslateTextRequest object (also part of the SDK). The output from the function is a string containing the translated text.

Note   API calls to AWS services exposed by the AWS SDK are all async and follow the naming convention *serviceapiname*Async. In the handler, we await the async call before extracting from the response object (type TranslateTextResponse) the actual text result.

Listing 6-2. Replacement code for Function.cs

```
using Amazon.Translate;
using Amazon.Translate.Model;

using Amazon.Lambda.Core;

// Assembly attribute to enable the Lambda function's JSON
// input to be converted into a .NET class.
[assembly: LambdaSerializer(↵
typeof(Amazon.Lambda.Serialization.SystemTextJson. ↵
DefaultLambdaJsonSerializer))]

namespace example1;

public class InputData
{
  public string SourceLanguage { get; set; }
  public string TargetLanguage { get; set; }
  public string Text { get; set; }
}
```

```csharp
public class Function
{
  /// <summary>
  /// A simple function that takes text and its source language code,
  /// and translates it into the requested target language
  /// </summary>
  /// <param name="input"></param>
  /// <param name="context"></param>
  /// <returns></returns>
  public async Task<string> FunctionHandler(↵
InputData input, ILambdaContext context)
  {
    var translateClient = new AmazonTranslateClient();

    try
    {
      var request = new TranslateTextRequest
      {
          SourceLanguageCode = input.SourceLanguage,
          TargetLanguageCode = input.TargetLanguage,
          Text = input.Text,
          Settings = new TranslationSettings
          {
              Profanity = Profanity.MASK
          }
      };

      var response
          = await translateClient.TranslateTextAsync(request);
      return response.TranslatedText;
    }
    catch (AmazonTranslateException e)
```

```
    {
        context.Logger.LogLine(e.Message);
        throw;
    }
  }
}
```

Notice the instantiation of the service client type for Amazon Translate:

```
var translateClient = new AmazonTranslateClient();
```

You may be wondering where you will supply credentials and the region in which to call the service. The answer is you don't. An IAM role you'll associate with the function will provide temporary credentials for the code to be able to call Amazon Translate. Additionally, Lambda will provide environment data to the function when it runs, from which the SDK can obtain the region information. All you need to do is use the default parameterless constructor for the service client, and the SDK will take care of the details.

Note   When you need to make an API call to a service endpoint that's in a different region to that in which the Lambda function is running, you can use an override for the service's client type constructor to provide the needed region information.

With the function handler code completed, we're now ready to deploy our function to Lambda (we'll go over testing it locally in a bit).

Deploying the Function

In our example so far, we've used the default name of the function handler. But as we noted earlier, you can change this if you want. If you do decide to change it, then you need to inform Lambda of the name of the method. But how? The answer lies in the `aws-lambda-tools-defaults.json` file generated with your project. This settings file, shared between the dotnet CLI tools and Visual Studio, holds settings related to the configuration and deployment options for your function. Listing 6-3 shows the generated contents of this file.

Listing 6-3. The generated aws-lambda-tools-defaults.json file and handler key

```
{
  "Information": [
    ...documentary info regarding the file...
  ],
  "profile": "",
  "region": "",
  "configuration": "Release",
  "function-runtime": "dotnet6",
  "function-memory-size": 256,
  "function-timeout": 30,
  "function-handler":
    "example1::example1.Function::FunctionHandler"
}
```

The function-handler property specifies the name of the handler method, in the format *assembly-name::namespace.class-name::method-name*. In our example, this maps to *example1* (assembly name), *example1* (namespace), *Function* (class name), and *FunctionHandler* (method name).

To change the handler method name, simply change the method name in the class (and class name, and namespace too, if you like) and then update the settings file key to match. Or when deploying through Visual Studio, you can set the handler details in the wizard, and the toolkit will update the settings file for you. For this chapter, we're going to leave the generated name unchanged.

Note the keys for *profile* and *region*. These relate to the credentials that you use to deploy the function, not run it, and the region in which you want the function deployed. The *function-role* key will eventually hold the Amazon Resource Name (ARN) of the role that we will create to provide credentials and permissions to the function when it runs.

We can deploy our function using either a wizard in Visual Studio or at the command line. Like earlier, we're showing both approaches in the following text, so choose whichever takes your preference and installed tools.

Deploying from the Command Line

In your shell, run the dotnet lambda command shown as follows (if you are using a credential profile named "default", you can omit the --profile option):

```
dotnet lambda deploy-function --persist-config-file true ↵
--profile ProDotNetonAWS
```

Note   The deploy-function subcommand, like all the Lambda subcommands, accepts a variety of switches with which you can supply all the settings for deployment. You can view these subcommands and switches using the command dotnet lambda --help and dotnet lambda *sub-command* –help. The tool will prompt for any required settings not specified using switches, which is the process we'll use in this example.

The deployment tool will ask you to enter the region in which it should deploy the function. Next, you need to supply a name for the function. This is the name you'll use to reference the function in tools and the management console, not the function handler name. Finally, the tool prompts for the name of an IAM role that it will create for you and then associate with the function. In Figure 6-6, which shows the full build and deployment trace, we chose TranslateTextFunctionRole for our role name, and when asked what policy to attach to the role, we chose option 6, AWSLambdaBasicExecutionRole (we'll update this role to add permissions to call Amazon Translate in the next section).

Figure 6-6 shows a screenshot of the deployment, with the input requests marked with arrows.

Note   The screenshots in this chapter show a PowerShell command prompt, however you can also run these tools from shells started with cmd.exe, and Bash, etc., on Linux and macOS systems.

```
PS C:\Temp\ch06\example1\src\example1> dotnet lambda deploy-function --persist-config-file true --profile ProDotNetonAWS
Amazon Lambda Tools for .NET Core applications (5.4.5)
Project Home: https://github.com/aws/aws-extensions-for-dotnet-cli, https://github.com/aws/aws-lambda-dotnet

Enter AWS Region: (The region to connect to AWS services, if not set region will be detected from the environment.)
us-west-2
Executing publish command
Deleted previous publish folder
... invoking 'dotnet publish', working folder 'C:\Temp\ch06\example1\src\example1\bin\Release\net6.0\publish'
... dotnet publish --output "C:\Temp\ch06\example1\src\example1\bin\Release\net6.0\publish" --configuration "Release" --framework "net6.0" /p:Ge
ConfigurationFiles=true --runtime linux-x64 --self-contained false
... publish: MSBuild version 17.3.0+92e077650 for .NET
... publish:   Determining projects to restore...
... publish:   All projects are up-to-date for restore.
... publish:   example1 -> C:\Temp\ch06\example1\src\example1\bin\Release\net6.0\linux-x64\example1.dll
... publish:   example1 -> C:\Temp\ch06\example1\src\example1\bin\Release\net6.0\publish\
Zipping publish folder C:\Temp\ch06\example1\src\example1\bin\Release\net6.0\publish to C:\Temp\ch06\example1\src\example1\bin\Release\net6.0\ex
... zipping: Amazon.Lambda.Core.dll
... zipping: Amazon.Lambda.Serialization.SystemTextJson.dll
... zipping: AWSSDK.Core.dll
... zipping: AWSSDK.Translate.dll
... zipping: example1.deps.json
... zipping: example1.dll
... zipping: example1.pdb
... zipping: example1.runtimeconfig.json
Created publish archive (C:\Temp\ch06\example1\src\example1\bin\Release\net6.0\example1.zip).
Enter Function Name: (AWS Lambda function name)
TranslateText
Creating new Lambda function
Enter name of the new IAM Role:
TranslateTextFunctionRole
Select IAM Policy to attach to the new role and grant permissions
    1) AWSLambdaReplicator (Grants Lambda Replicator necessary permissions to replicate functions ...)
    2) AWSLambdaDynamoDBExecutionRole (Provides list and read access to DynamoDB streams and writ ...)
    3) AWSLambdaExecute (Provides Put, Get access to S3 and full access to CloudWatch Logs.)
    4) AWSLambdaSQSQueueExecutionRole (Provides receive message, delete message, and read attribu ...)
    5) AWSLambdaKinesisExecutionRole (Provides list and read access to Kinesis streams and write  ...)
    6) AWSLambdaBasicExecutionRole (Provides write permissions to CloudWatch Logs.)
    7) AWSLambdaInvocation-DynamoDB (Provides read access to DynamoDB Streams.)
    8) AWSLambdaVPCAccessExecutionRole (Provides minimum permissions for a Lambda function to exe ...)
    9) AWSLambdaRole (Default policy for AWS Lambda service role.)
   10) AWSLambdaENIManagementAccess (Provides minimum permissions for a Lambda function to manage ...)
   11) AWSLambdaMSKExecutionRole (Provides permissions required to access MSK Cluster within a VP ...)
   12) AWSLambda_ReadOnlyAccess (Grants read-only access to AWS Lambda service, AWS Lambda consol ...)
   13) AWSLambda_FullAccess (Grants full access to AWS Lambda service, AWS Lambda console feature ...)
   14) MySimpleS3ReadOnlyPolicy
   15) *** No policy, add permissions later ***
6
Waiting for new IAM Role to propagate to AWS regions
............... Done
New Lambda function created
Config settings saved to C:\Temp\ch06\example1\src\example1\aws-lambda-tools-defaults.json
PS C:\Temp\ch06\example1\src\example1>
```

Figure 6-6. *Command-line deployment of a function using the dotnet CLI*

If you open the aws-lambda-tools-defaults.json file, you'll see that the
deployment updated the profile, region, and function-role keys with the details you
specified, since we provided the --persist-config-file switch with a value of "true"
(short form: -pcfg true). Subsequent deployments will use these values by default,
even if you switch to deploying from Visual Studio. You can always override the settings
file contents using command-line switches by selecting different values in the IDE
wizard or by editing the settings file directly.

Deploying from Visual Studio

In Visual Studio, we use a wizard to deploy to Lambda. Start the wizard by right-clicking the project file for the Lambda function (not the test project, if you generated one) in Solution Explorer and select **Publish to AWS Lambda...** in the context menu that's displayed.

The first page of the wizard asks you to select the credential profile to use to deploy the function (same as the `--profile` switch at the command line) and the region to deploy to. The wizard usually presets the function handler (for projects generated from the supplied templates), but you can also enter it yourself, in the format `assemblyname::namespace.typename::methodname`, shown in Figure 6-7. Also note the option to persist your selections back to the settings file, which corresponds to t he `--persist-config-file` switch at the command line.

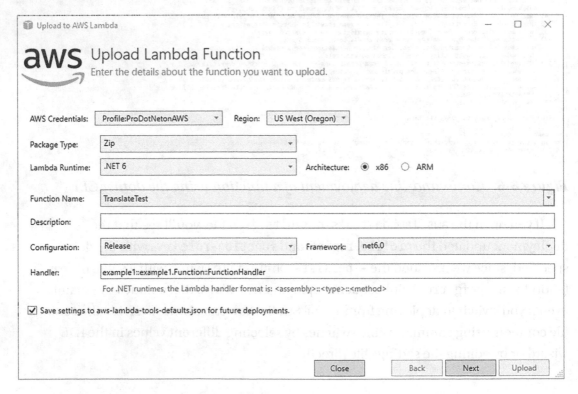

Figure 6-7. *Starting the Visual Studio Lambda publishing wizard*

Click **Next** to access settings related to the role the function should assume when it runs and other configuration settings related to the environment that Lambda should use to run the function, such as memory size, timeout, and environment variables.

For our purposes, we just need to use the Role Name drop-down to elect to have a role created based on the AWSLambdaBasicExecutionRole managed policy, shown in Figure 6-8.

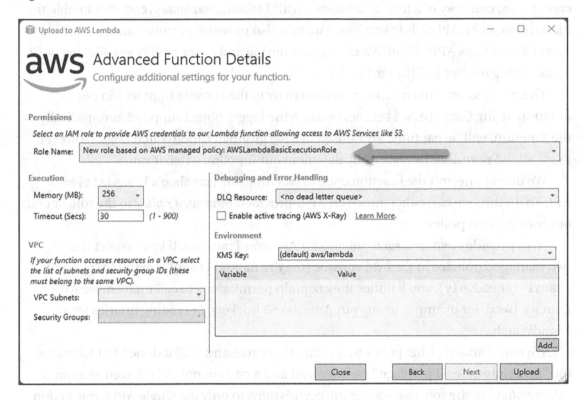

Figure 6-8. *Setting function role and environment settings*

Clicking **Upload** completes the wizard. You'll see notifications listed in the wizard as the toolkit builds, packages, and uploads your function. Unlike the command-line experience where we got to choose the name of the IAM role for the function, Visual Studio automatically assigns a role name in the format lambda_exec_*FunctionName*. For the process we just completed, you'll find it created a role named lambda_exec_ TranslateText.

On closing the wizard after successful deployment, the default Visual Studio behavior is to open a view onto the deployed function that you can use to invoke it with payloads, reconfigure its settings, manage its event sources, and view logs and other data. Put this view aside for now, we'll come back to it later in the chapter. Before we can run the function, we need to update the IAM role to add permissions allowing the code to call Amazon Translate's TranslateText API.

Updating the Function Permissions

Our newly deployed function has a role associated with it that grants temporary AWS credentials, courtesy of a trust relationship with `lambda.amazonaws.com`, that enable the function to make API calls to services. The role also provides permissions to call some CloudWatch Logs APIs. CloudWatch is a monitoring and observability service that we'll be exploring further in Chapter 17.

The permissions mean that any write activity to the console from within our function, using `Console.WriteLine`, or using the logger object supplied automatically to the function, will be captured and stored in a log group in CloudWatch Logs. However, that's all the permissions granted by default to our function when it runs.

We need to permit the function code to call Amazon Translate's `TranslateText` API. To do this, we can either attach an AWS-provided *managed policy* to the role or craft our own custom policy.

AWS provides two managed policies for Amazon Translate. If you inspect the two managed policies in the IAM console (they're named `TranslateFullAccess` and `TranslateReadOnly`), you'll notice they contain permissions to call many more APIs than we need, for example, listing our Amazon S3 buckets, or reading metrics from CloudWatch.

We could attach either policy to our function's role and "call it done," but following the "principle of least privilege," we'll instead add a custom policy (referred to as an *inline policy*) to the role that scopes the permissions to only the single API our function needs to call.

To do this, head to the IAM dashboard in the AWS Management Console and select **Roles** in the left-hand navigation panel. You should find your function role listed. If you followed the aforementioned instructions and used the dotnet CLI to deploy the function, we named the role `TranslateTextFunctionRole` ourselves during deployment. If you deployed using Visual Studio, it automatically named the role `lambda_exec_TranslateText`, since we told it to create a new role for us. Find the role in the list and click its name to open an editor view.

In the editor view, the active tab will be Permissions, which is what we need to update. You'll notice the `AWSLambdaBasicExecutionRole` managed policy we requested during deployment is already attached. At this point, if you wanted to attach the AWS-provided policies noted previously, you would click the **Attach policies** button and select and attach the policies by name. Instead, click the **+ Add inline policy** link positioned on the right-hand side of the display.

You can craft your inline policy using a simple visual editor (the default), or by simply pasting the JSON-format document representing the policy into an editor in the JSON tab.

We'll use the visual editor approach, so first, expand the **Service** option and enter the text `translate` into the *Find a service* text box, then select the result (Translate). Next, you choose the actions (API operations) that the policy will permit access to for the selected service. We need permission to call the `TranslateText` action. Expand the **Read** category beneath **Access level** and select the `TranslateText` option. Expand **Resources** and select **All resources** (don't select the other option, **Specific**, as the only resource type there is *terminology* – which does not work for our example scenario). Our selections are shown in Figure 6-9.

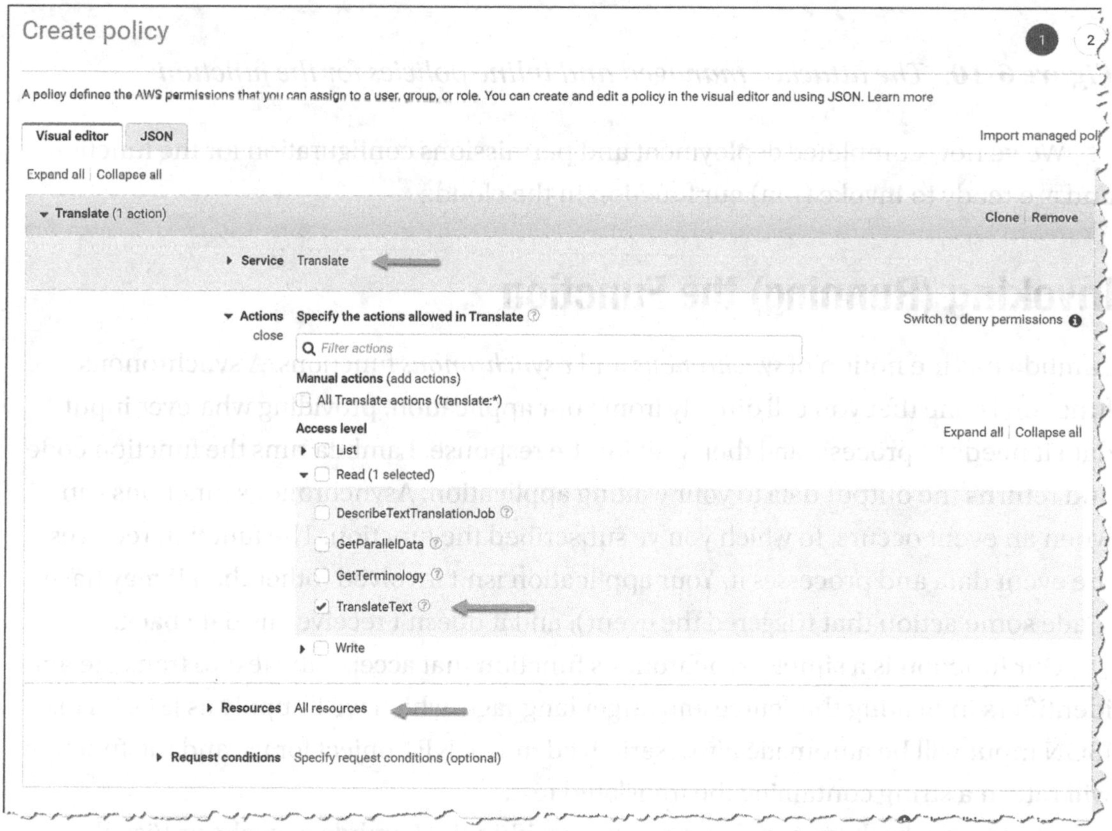

Figure 6-9. *Crafting the policy permissions in the visual editor*

Once you've built the policy, click the **Review policy** button to proceed. Give the policy a name (we used `TranslateTextPolicy`) and click **Create policy** to complete the process. You're then positioned back at the editor view for the role, and you'll see your new inline policy listed, shown in Figure 6-10. This policy provides the permission to call the single API our function needs.

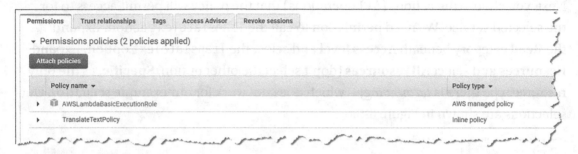

Figure 6-10. *The attached managed and inline policies for the function*

We've now completed deployment and permissions configuration for the function and are ready to invoke (run) our function in the cloud.

Invoking (Running) the Function

Lambda has the notion of *synchronous* and *asynchronous* functions. A synchronous function is one that you call directly from your application, providing whatever input data it needs to process, and then wait for the response. Lambda runs the function code and returns the output data to your waiting application. Asynchronous functions run when an event occurs, to which you've subscribed the function. The function receives the event data and processes it. Your application isn't involved (other than it may have made some action that triggered the event), and it doesn't receive any data back.

Our function is a simple, synchronous function that accepts the text to translate and identifiers indicating the source and target language, which we'll supply as JSON. This JSON input will be automatically deserialized into a .NET object for us, and the function will return a string containing the translated text.

We can run both types of functions from within the Lambda console, or Visual Studio, quite easily. We can also run them using the AWS CLI (`aws lambda invoke ...`) and the AWS Tools for PowerShell (`Invoke-LMFunction ...`) – useful in automation script scenarios – and by invoking the function from our application code. In all cases, all that's needed is to craft the appropriate input payload. Listing 6-4 shows an example of the simple input for our function.

Listing 6-4. Sample data input for our function

```
{
  "SourceLanguage": "en",
  "TargetLanguage": "es",
  "Text": "Hello from Amazon Translate. Pleased to meet you!"
}
```

Invoking the Function from the Console

Open the Lambda dashboard in the AWS console and select your function from the list. Then click the **Test** tab. Enter the sample payload from Listing 6-4, then click the Test button. Figure 6-11 shows the completed test form.

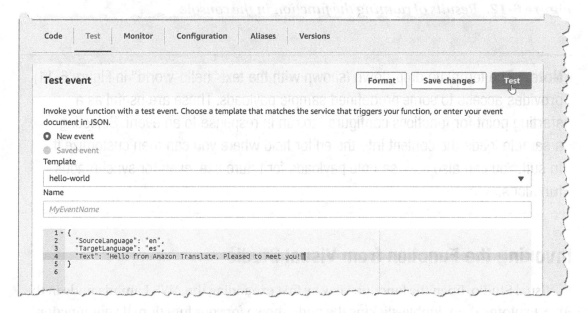

Figure 6-11. *Invoking the function in the Lambda console*

Lambda runs the function and displays the results (success or fail) in the same tab as shown in Figure 6-12. Lambda also shows stats about the invocation, such as the duration (initialization, overall, and billed duration) and memory used.

Figure 6-12. *Results of running the function in the console*

Note   The template drop-down (shown with the text "hello-world" in Figure 6-11) provides access to some predefined sample payloads. These are useful as a starting point for functions configured to run in response to an event. Selecting a sample loads the content into the editor field where you can then customize it to suit. You can also save sample payloads for future use, even for synchronous functions.

Invoking the Function from Visual Studio

In Visual Studio, open the function view by first expanding the AWS Lambda node in the AWS Explorer, then double-clicking the node shown for your function. If your function doesn't appear in the tree, check the credential profile and region shown at the top of the explorer and click the Refresh button, then open the function view. The function view's default tab is like the Test tab in the console, with a test input (and output) panel and a drop-down providing access to some predefined event templates. Other tabs in the view provide access to configuration settings for the function, logs, and event source configuration.

To invoke the function, enter the input payload into the text box beneath the Example Requests drop-down and click the **Invoke** button. Figure 6-13 shows the function view afterward; you can see the output from the function in the Response pane, with invocation stats and other logging data shown in the Log output pane, similar to that shown in the management console.

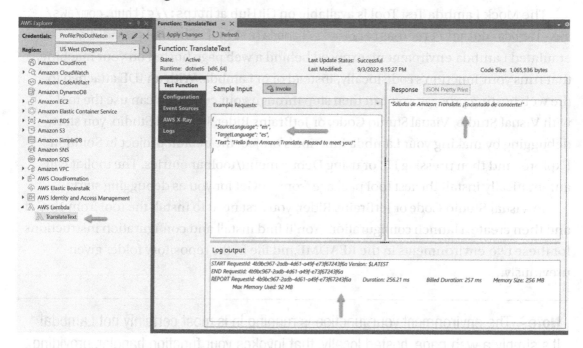

Figure 6-13. Invoking a function from within Visual Studio

Congratulations! You just ran code and deployed to Lambda without needing to provision any infrastructure! You gave Lambda a few basic settings and supplied the code, and Lambda did the rest. You're also not incurring charges unless the code is running. Had you deployed this code to an EC2 virtual machine or a container configured to run 24×7, you'd be incurring charges even when the code wasn't servicing any requests.

Debugging

Whether you used the console or Visual Studio to run the function in the preceding sections, your function ran in the cloud and not locally on your machine. Let's say your function didn't return the result you expected. Or perhaps it threw an exception, or simply timed out, both of which caused Lambda to terminate the function's execution. What now? How do you figure out what happened?

Serverless compute provides zero access to the compute environment, so set aside any expectations of remotely debugging a serverless function! If you're using the dotnet CLI tools or Visual Studio, you can debug your function code using a tool known as the Mock Lambda Test Tool. Debugging is where the dotnet CLI/Visual Studio tooling significantly differs from the SAM CLI tools we'll be looking at in the next section.

The Mock Lambda Test Tool is available on GitHub at `https://github.com/aws/aws-lambda-dotnet/tree/master/Tools/LambdaTestTool`. The tool provides an emulated Lambda environment, exposed behind a web page hosted on your machine, that runs your function's code locally, instead of in Lambda. With an IDE attached to the web hosting process, you can then step through your code. You can use the tool with Visual Studio, Visual Studio Code, or JetBrains Rider. In Visual Studio, you start debugging by making your Lambda function's project the default project in Solution Explorer and then pressing F5, or using Debug menu/toolbar entries. The toolkit will automatically install the test tool package from NuGet for you as debugging starts.

In Visual Studio Code or JetBrains Rider, you first need to install the tool from NuGet and then create a launch configuration. You'll find install and configuration instructions for these two environments in the README.md file in the repository folder given previously.

Note   The environment your function is running in is most certainly not Lambda! It's simply a web page, hosted locally, that invokes your function handler, providing a quick, local debugging experience that requires minimal dependencies.

Figure 6-14 shows the tool, having started debugging in Visual Studio. We've supplied the test payload we used earlier. It should look somewhat familiar in terms of layout to the Lambda console and the function view in Visual Studio we used to run the function in the cloud earlier, but notice that there are no runtime statistics. This is because the function ran locally, within the web app process.

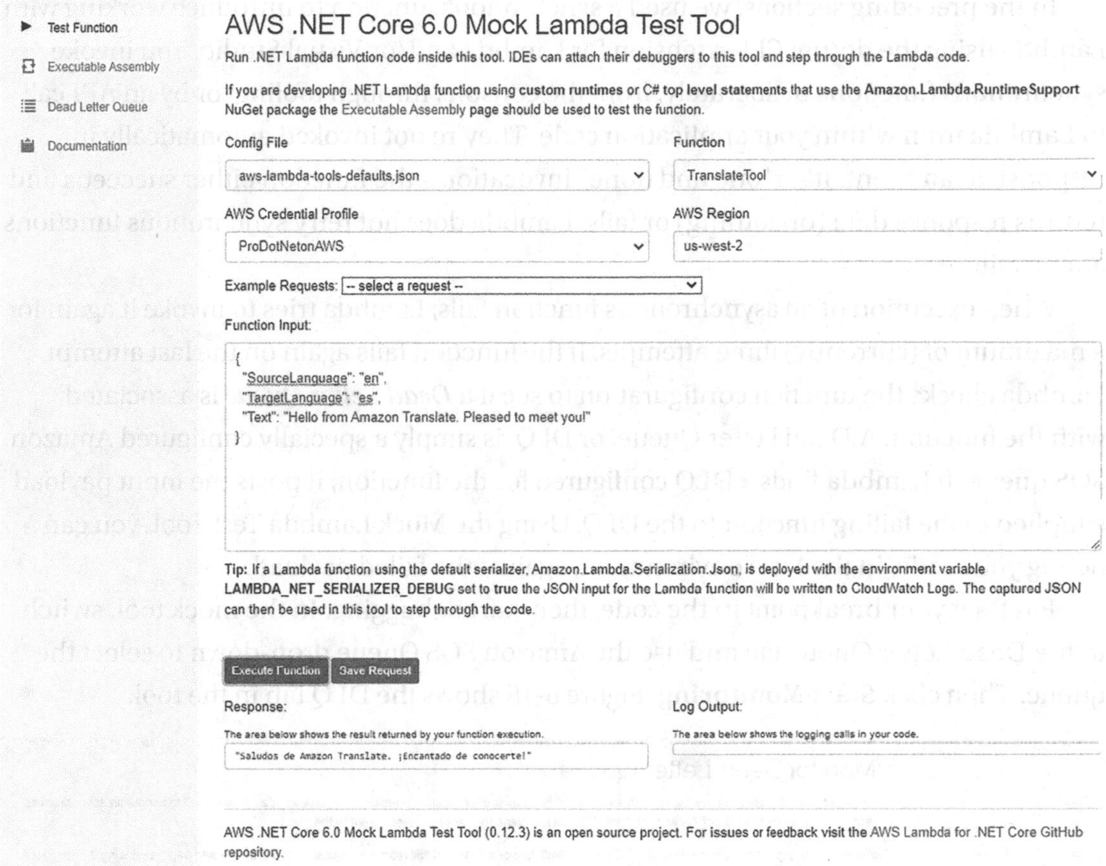

Figure 6-14. *The Mock Lambda Test Tool*

To debug, start the debugger and set a breakpoint at the start of your function handler. Fill out the input field in the mock tool after it launches, or select and edit a sample request, and click **Execute Function**. The debugger will pause execution at your breakpoint, and you can step through your function. Easy!

The Mock Lambda Test Tool and Asynchronous Functions

If you're using an asynchronous function, one that's invoked in response to an event (as we'll be doing in the next section), the Mock Lambda Test Tool contains some functionality we think you'll find useful, which we'll briefly highlight here.

In the preceding sections, we used a synchronous function to introduce working with Lambda using the dotnet CLI extension for Lambda and/or Visual Studio. You invoke synchronous functions deliberately, from the console, through tooling, or by an API call to Lambda from within your application code. They're not invoked automatically in response to an event. It's a "one and done" invocation – the function either succeeds and returns response data (or nothing) or fails. Lambda does not retry synchronous functions after a failure.

When execution of an asynchronous function fails, Lambda tries to invoke it again for a maximum of (currently) three attempts. If the function fails again on the last attempt, Lambda checks the function configuration to see if a *Dead Letter Queue* is associated with the function. A Dead Letter Queue, or DLQ, is simply a specially configured Amazon SQS queue. If Lambda finds a DLQ configured for the function, it posts the input payload supplied to the failing function to the DLQ. Using the Mock Lambda Test Tool, you can debug your code, in the local environment, against the failed payload.

First, set your breakpoint in the code, then start debugging. In the mock tool, switch to the Dead Letter Queue tab and use the Amazon SQS Queue drop-down to select the queue. Then click **Start Monitoring**. Figure 6-15 shows the DLQ tab in the tool.

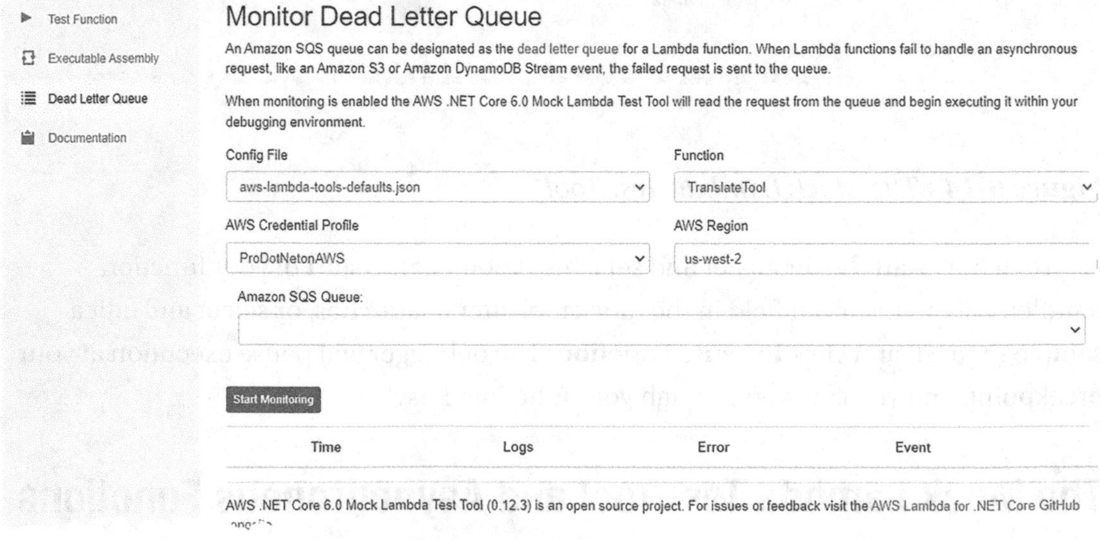

Figure 6-15. Monitoring a Dead Letter Queue in the mock tool

Once you start monitoring, the tool watches the DLQ and will retrieve messages (failed payloads) from it. It then passes the retrieved payload to your function running in the process, thus triggering your breakpoint. You can then step through your code and see where it failed to process the input correctly. This is a useful piece of functionality to keep in mind when working with asynchronous functions to debug failed payloads without needing to come up with your own payloads to try and trigger the failure.

Cleaning Up

A benefit of serverless compute we noted earlier was that unless your code is actively running, there is no charge (well, provided you don't exceed the non-expiring free-tier limits Lambda provides every month to all users). Still, if you're the type that wants to clean up and delete resources as you go, it's an easy process as follows.

At the command line, in the project folder of your Lambda function, you can run the command `dotnet lambda delete-function`. As your settings were persisted into the `aws-lambda-tool-defaults.json` file, the tool knows what function, credential profile, and region to use to delete the resources without needing you to enter them again, although it will ask for confirmation before proceeding.

In Visual Studio, right-click on the function's entry under the AWS Lambda node in the AWS Explorer window and select **Delete** in the context menu. Again, you're asked to confirm.

Neither approach will delete the IAM role and inline policy we created. There's no charge to leave these in place, and indeed, you could use them again in the next section on serverless applications (we won't). Assuming you want to clean up everything, head to the IAM console, select the Role, and delete it there.

Serverless Applications

Now that we've gained experience in using the dotnet CLI and Visual Studio tools to create, deploy, invoke, and debug a single Lambda function, let's turn our attention to using the Serverless Application Model (SAM) tools. In this section, we'll take our serverless function code and repurpose it to sit behind an API resource, deploying it all as a serverless application. Instead of manually invoking our function, we'll instead configure it to run when an end user accesses the API endpoint, although this could equally be code accessing the endpoint (think application code accessing a microservice's URL).

Before we start, what distinguishes a serverless application from a serverless function? Technically, a serverless function is also a serverless application – the actual distinction between the two comes in the definition and deployment.

The function we created in the previous section consisted of just a project file and a class file containing a function handler. The project was built and packaged into a zip file, and the zip file uploaded directly to Lambda using either the `Amazon.Lambda.Tools` dotnet CLI package or the Visual Studio toolkit's Publish to AWS Lambda wizard.

Serverless applications consist of one or more project files, one or more classes that contain your function handlers, *and* an AWS CloudFormation template that defines the functions and other resources. You deploy the template and associated function binaries as a single unit using CloudFormation, instead of uploading directly to Lambda. The tooling makes this difference transparent.

Note Just to be clear, the tools AWS provides for the dotnet CLI and Visual Studio that we used previously can deploy both serverless functions and serverless applications. However, we're switching to SAM CLI in this section so you get an understanding of the other tooling available to you.

Installing the Tools

Unlike the dotnet CLI extension installed from NuGet in the previous section, you need to head to the AWS documentation site to obtain the SAM CLI tools. The page at `https://docs.aws.amazon.com/serverless-application-model/latest/developerguide/serverless-sam-cli-install.html` provides subpages with download links and install instructions for Windows, Linux, and macOS environments. Follow the links and instructions appropriate to your development environment. For Windows, you'll download an .msi file that you need to run (with administrative permissions). For macOS, you use Homebrew; Linux users can choose between a zip file and using Homebrew.

For all environments, you can also optionally install Docker. SAM CLI requires Docker only when you debug locally or choose to deploy your serverless application using Lambda's container option. If you want to follow along with the debugging instructions later in this section, be sure to install Docker before proceeding; otherwise, you can ignore it.

Creating a Serverless Application

With SAM CLI, you create new serverless applications with the `sam init` command from a command-line shell. Like the dotnet CLI extension we saw earlier in the chapter, `sam init` has a collection of starter templates and will prompt you to select one unless you specify it using the `--app-template` parameter. To control the packaging format for your C# serverless application, you specify the `--package-type` option; for example, `--package-type Zip` creates the zip file expected for a managed runtime. Details on the various command-line options can be found at `https://docs.aws.amazon.com/serverless-application-model/latest/developerguide/sam-cli-command-reference-sam-init.html`.

Caution   One catch with `sam init`, at least at the time of this writing, is that although you can set a name for the generated project, using the `--name` parameter, the value is used to name the folder, not the project file!

Instead of having you generate a starter project and then rename files, we've provided the code for you in the GitHub repository that accompanies the book. You'll find it in the ch06/example2 folder. You'll notice a couple of differences between a project generated by `sam init` and those generated by the `dotnet lambda` tool. You won't find an `aws-lambda-tools-defaults.json` file containing initial deployment settings; instead, you'll find an important new file at the folder hierarchy root that we will use to define the resources for the serverless application, template.yaml, shown in Figure 6-16. Your application source code is a couple levels down, beneath the `src` folder.

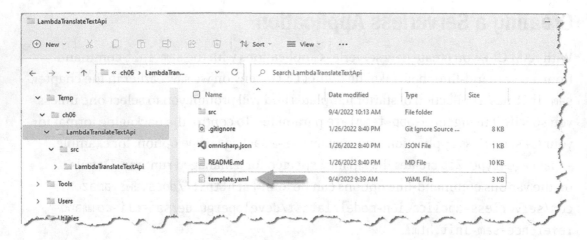

Figure 6-16. *Generated yaml-format resources template*

The generated template is a declarative CloudFormation template. It's declarative in that the template declares the resources and resource settings that we want. CloudFormation then does the work to provision and configure those resources when we deploy.

The template uses additional macros, or extensions, declared in a `transform` section. These transforms enable the use of serverless resource types in the template. Go ahead and examine the generated template contents before we replace them shortly. You'll see the `transform` section, referencing the `AWS::Serverless-2016-10-31` macros, followed by a resource named `helloFromLambdaFunction`, which has the type `AWS::Serverless::Function`. This type comes from the transform reference and defines the settings for the Lambda function whose code you can find in the generated *src/LambdaTextTranslateApi/Function.cs* file.

Writing the Application

Our serverless application will consist of our Lambda function to translate text, but it will be configured to run when someone (or something) accesses an API endpoint. We'll host the API endpoint using Amazon API Gateway.

API Gateway is a fully managed service (which is also serverless) that makes it easy for you to create, publish, and manage APIs. API Gateway will handle all the tasks involved to host an API in front of your application, accepting requests and forwarding them to your application code, and returning the responses. There's no need to stand up a container or EC2 virtual machine to host your web-based API and incur costs to keep the API running even when no one is calling it. Instead, you can use API Gateway and let AWS take care of provisioning and managing the underlying resources – and you only incur charges when something calls your API causing your function to run (assuming you've exceeded the free-tier limits).

Open `template.yaml` in your chosen text editor to view the contents, shown in Listing 6-5. For brevity, we've removed comments from the file that describe each of the sections. Remember, since this is a YAML file, it is important that you retain the indentation if you change it, as that is what the parser uses to understand each value.

Listing 6-5. Application definition in template.yaml

```
AWSTemplateFormatVersion: 2010-09-09
Transform: AWS::Serverless-2016-10-31
Description: >
  LambdaTranslateTextApi

Resources:
  LambdaTranslateTextApiFunction:
    Type: AWS::Serverless::Function
    Properties:
      CodeUri: ./src/LambdaTranslateTextApi/
      Handler: ↵
LambdaTranslateTextApi::LambdaTranslateTextApi.Function::↵
FunctionHandler
      Runtime: dotnet6
      MemorySize: 256
      Timeout: 100
      Policies:
        - AWSLambdaBasicExecutionRole
        - TranslateReadOnly
      Events:
        TranslateText:
          Type: HttpApi
          Properties:
            Path: /
            Method: POST
```

```
Outputs:
  TranslateTextApi:
    Description: "API Gateway endpoint URL for function"
    Value: !Sub "https://${ServerlessHttpApi}.execute-↵
api.${AWS::Region}.amazonaws.com/Prod/"
```

Items of note in the template:

- Events – This entry creates and configures an HttpApi resource in API Gateway to act as our function's event source. HttpApi has a lower latency and costs compared to the full-blown REST Api type we could use instead.

- Policies – We're attaching the AWS-managed TranslateReadOnly policy. We could instead use the more tightly scoped role created earlier in this chapter by removing the Policies section and specifying a Role property, supplying our role's ARN as the value.

- CodeUri – This points to our function's project location.

- Outputs – This will output the URL we need to access the HttpApi resource and call our function.

The project file for the Lambda function is substantially the same as that used earlier in the chapter but contains a new reference, to an Amazon.Lambda.APIGatewayEvents package. This package contains a collection of types related to handling events (for requests and responses) that originate in API Gateway. Once again, the raw JSON passed to the Lambda function is automatically deserialized into a .NET object for convenience, and our output is serialized from .NET to JSON when the function exits. Listing 6-6 shows the project file and NuGet references.

Listing 6-6. Replacement project file for the LambdaTranslateTextApi project

```
<Project Sdk="Microsoft.NET.Sdk">
  <PropertyGroup>
    <TargetFramework>net6.0</TargetFramework>
    <ImplicitUsings>enable</ImplicitUsings>
    <GenerateRuntimeConfigurationFiles>
        True
    </GenerateRuntimeConfigurationFiles>
```

```
    <AWSProjectType>Lambda</AWSProjectType>
    <CopyLocalLockFileAssemblies>
        True
    </CopyLocalLockFileAssemblies>
  </PropertyGroup>
  <ItemGroup>
    <PackageReference
        Include="Amazon.Lambda.Core"
        Version="2.1.0" />
    <PackageReference
        Include="Amazon.Lambda.Serialization.SystemTextJson"
        Version="2.3.0" />
    <PackageReference
        Include="Amazon.Lambda.APIGatewayEvents"
        Version="2.5.0" />
    <PackageReference
        Include="AWSSDK.Translate"
        Version="3.7.5.*" />
  </ItemGroup>

  <ItemGroup>
    <InternalsVisibleTo Include="LambdaTranslateTextApi.Tests" />
  </ItemGroup>
</Project>
```

Listing 6-7 contains the updated code for the Lambda function, which has some differences over the original code earlier in this chapter.

Listing 6-7. Code for the asynchronous Lambda function

```
using Amazon.Lambda.Core;

using Amazon.Lambda.APIGatewayEvents;

using Amazon.Translate;
using Amazon.Translate.Model;
```

```
// Assembly attribute to enable the Lambda function's JSON input to be
converted into a .NET class.
[assembly: LambdaSerializer(typeof(Amazon.Lambda.Serialization.
SystemTextJson.DefaultLambdaJsonSerializer))]

namespace LambdaTranslateTextApi
{
  public class Function
  {
    public async Task<APIGatewayHttpApiV2ProxyResponse>
      FunctionHandler(⏎
          APIGatewayHttpApiV2ProxyRequest apigProxyEvent, ⏎
          ILambdaContext context)
    {
      var translateClient = new AmazonTranslateClient();

      try
      {
        var request = new TranslateTextRequest
        {
          SourceLanguageCode = apigProxyEvent.QueryStringParameters["source
          Language"],
          TargetLanguageCode = apigProxyEvent.QueryStringParameters["target
          Language"],
          Text = apigProxyEvent.Body,
          Settings = new TranslationSettings
          {
            Profanity = Profanity.MASK
          }
        };

        var response
          = await translateClient.TranslateTextAsync(request);

        return new APIGatewayHttpApiV2ProxyResponse
        {
          Body = response.TranslatedText,
```

```
        StatusCode = 200,
        Headers = new Dictionary<string, string>
        {
            { "Content-Type", "text/plain" } }
        };
    }
    catch (AmazonTranslateException e)
    {
        context.Logger.LogLine(e.Message);
        throw;
    }
  }
 }
}
```

The only changes of note in this version of the function, compared to the synchronous version earlier, are as follows:

- We use `APIGatewayHttpApiV2ProxyRequest` as the input type: This object will contain the deserialized input from the API Gateway endpoint as query parameters and body text, instead of the custom POCO (`InputData`) we used in our earlier function.

- We wrap the output from the function in an `APIGatewayHttpApiV2ProxyResponse` object, unlike the simple string we returned earlier. When API Gateway, which stands between the caller of our API and our application code, receives a request on the API endpoint, it forwards the request data to our application code. Subsequently, API Gateway will receive the output data for the request from our code, using this object (automatically serialized to JSON), and will return the data, status code, etc., to the caller of our API endpoint.

Now that we've updated our function code to process input data sent in a request to an API Gateway endpoint that represents our application, we're ready to deploy and test.

Deploying the Application

Before we can deploy the application, we first need to build it and create the deployment bundle. This is different to the experience when using the dotnet CLI tools (or Visual Studio); those tools handle building the deployment bundle during the deployment process itself, whereas we need to build separately when using SAM CLI. This has caught us out a couple times when using SAM CLI to redeploy some changes to our functions and left us wondering for a while why the changes haven't made it to the cloud!

To build the deployment bundle, run the command `sam build` in the folder containing the `template.yaml` file. Figure 6-17 shows an example of the build output. Notice that the build places the deployment artifacts into a subfolder hierarchy named `.aws-sam` and that when building the package, SAM CLI actually downloads and runs the dotnet CLI extension we used earlier in this chapter.

```
PS C:\Temp\ch06\LambdaTranslateTextApi> sam build
Your template contains a resource with logical ID "ServerlessHttpApi", which is a reserved logical ID in AWS SAM. It could result in unexpected beh
ot recommended.
Building codeuri: C:\Temp\ch06\LambdaTranslateTextApi\src\LambdaTranslateTextApi runtime: dotnet6 metadata: {} architecture: x86_64 functions: ['La
xtApiFunction']
Running DotnetCliPackageBuilder:GlobalToolInstall

Tool 'amazon.lambda.tools' was reinstalled with the latest stable version (version '5.4.5').
Running DotnetCliPackageBuilder:RunPackageAction
Amazon Lambda Tools for .NET Core applications (5.4.5)
Project Home: https://github.com/aws/aws-extensions-for-dotnet-cli, https://github.com/aws/aws-lambda-dotnet

Executing publish command
Deleted previous publish folder
... invoking 'dotnet publish', working folder 'C:\Temp\ch06\LambdaTranslateTextApi\src\LambdaTranslateTextApi\bin\Release\net6.0\publish'
... dotnet publish --output "C:\Temp\ch06\LambdaTranslateTextApi\src\LambdaTranslateTextApi\bin\Release\net6.0\publish" --configuration "Release" --
6.0" --runtime linux-x64 /p:GenerateRuntimeConfigurationFiles=true --self-contained false
... publish: MSBuild version 17.3.0+92e077650 for .NET
... publish:    Determining projects to restore ...
... publish:    Restored C:\Temp\ch06\LambdaTranslateTextApi\src\LambdaTranslateTextApi\LambdaTranslateTextApi.csproj (in 507 ms).
... publish:    LambdaTranslateTextApi → C:\Temp\ch06\LambdaTranslateTextApi\src\LambdaTranslateTextApi\bin\Release\net6.0\linux-x64\LambdaTranslat
... publish:    LambdaTranslateTextApi → C:\Temp\ch06\LambdaTranslateTextApi\src\LambdaTranslateTextApi\bin\Release\net6.0\publish\
Zipping publish folder C:\Temp\ch06\LambdaTranslateTextApi\src\LambdaTranslateTextApi\bin\Release\net6.0\publish to C:\Temp\ch06\LambdaTranslateTex
uild\LambdaTranslateTextApiFunction\LambdaTranslateTextApi.zip
Creating directory C:\Temp\ch06\LambdaTranslateTextApi\.aws-sam\build\LambdaTranslateTextApiFunction
... zipping: Amazon.Lambda.APIGatewayEvents.dll
... zipping: Amazon.Lambda.Core.dll
... zipping: Amazon.Lambda.Serialization.SystemTextJson.dll
... zipping: AWSSDK.Core.dll
... zipping: AWSSDK.Translate.dll
... zipping: LambdaTranslateTextApi.deps.json
... zipping: LambdaTranslateTextApi.dll
... zipping: LambdaTranslateTextApi.pdb
... zipping: LambdaTranslateTextApi.runtimeconfig.json
Created publish archive (C:\Temp\ch06\LambdaTranslateTextApi\.aws-sam\build\LambdaTranslateTextApiFunction\LambdaTranslateTextApi.zip).
Lambda project successfully packaged: C:\Temp\ch06\LambdaTranslateTextApi\.aws-sam\build\LambdaTranslateTextApiFunction\LambdaTranslateTextApi.zip

Build Succeeded

Built Artifacts  : .aws-sam\build
Built Template   : .aws-sam\build\template.yaml

Commands you can use next
=========================
[*] Invoke Function: sam local invoke
```

Figure 6-17. *Output from running "sam build"*

Note   The build output contains a warning about a reference to a ServerlessHttpApi resource. We can ignore this; we're using it only to emit the URL to the deployed API.

With the build complete, we deploy the application using the `sam deploy` command. We recommend running this command in "guided" mode the first time you run it, so you can see what's going on, and electing to save your settings when prompted. Then, when redeploying after making changes (and after rerunning `sam build!`), you can simply run `sam deploy` with no parameters. In the example output shown in Figure 6-18, we've enabled guided mode with the `--guided` switch and supplied the credentials to use during deployment (arrowed). We could also have specified the region in which to deploy the application using a `--region` parameter but chose to enter the region when prompted.

```
PS C:\Temp\ch06\LambdaTranslateTextApi> sam deploy --guided --profile ProDotNetonAWS

Configuring SAM deploy
======================

        Looking for config file [samconfig.toml] :  Not found

        Setting default arguments for 'sam deploy'
        =========================================
        Stack Name [sam-app]: LambdaTranslateTextApi  <---
        AWS Region [us-east-1]: us-west-2  <---
        #Shows you resources changes to be deployed and require a 'Y' to initiate deploy
        Confirm changes before deploy [y/N]: y  <---
        #SAM needs permission to be able to create roles to connect to the resources in your template
        Allow SAM CLI IAM role creation [Y/n]:
        #Preserves the state of previously provisioned resources when an operation fails
        Disable rollback [y/N]:
        LambdaTranslateTextApiFunction may not have authorization defined, Is this okay? [y/N]: y  <---
        Save arguments to configuration file [Y/n]:
        SAM configuration file [samconfig.toml]:
        SAM configuration environment [default]:

        Looking for resources needed for deployment:
         Managed S3 bucket: aws-sam-cli-managed-default-samclisourcebucket-████████
         A different default S3 bucket can be set in samconfig.toml

        Saved arguments to config file
        Running 'sam deploy' for future deployments will use the parameters saved above.
        The above parameters can be changed by modifying samconfig.toml
        Learn more about samconfig.toml syntax at
        https://docs.aws.amazon.com/serverless-application-model/latest/developerguide/serverless-sam-cli-config.html

Uploading to LambdaTranslateTextApi/f7e7f417eebeb7018fed56ac63929591  1382707 / 1382707  (100.00%)

        Deploying with following values
        ===============================
        Stack name                   : LambdaTranslateTextApi
        Region                       : us-west-2
        Confirm changeset            : True
        Disable rollback             : False
        Deployment s3 bucket         : aws-sam-cli-managed-default-samclisourcebucket-████████
        Capabilities                 : ["CAPABILITY_IAM"]
        Parameter overrides          : {}
```

Figure 6-18. *Deploying the application with "sam deploy"*

> **Tip** We've chosen to use the SAM CLI directly so that you can see the steps and what's happening. However, you can also build and deploy your serverless application from the AWS toolkits provided for Visual Studio Code and JetBrains Rider. They both provide commands that will guide you through supplying the data we show at the command line in the subsequent figures.

We're not done with questions from the deployment command, however. We deploy serverless applications (those with a template file) using CloudFormation, although you don't need to use CloudFormation directly; the tools abstract it away. Serverless application deployments use something called a *CloudFormation Changeset*, which basically describes a set of changes to apply to a CloudFormation stack. A stack is simply a set of resources instantiated from a template.

As this is the first deployment, the command output notes that CloudFormation will create new resources. However, if this were a redeployment and you'd reconfigured resources in the template, added new ones, or deleted some, then you'd see different changes summarized at the console. The important thing is to remember the prompt to deploy the changeset. This occurs because in the initial set of prompts shown in Figure 6-18, we responded "y" to the question **Confirm changes before deploying**. For CI/CD setups, you obviously wouldn't want this prompt to display and pause your deployment, which is why the default value for this option is "n" to disable the prompt. Run the command `sam deploy --help` to see the full set of options you can use for this and other settings.

Figure 6-19 shows the changes in the changeset and the prompt awaiting confirmation to proceed. Once you respond in the affirmative, the deployment will proceed, and at the end of the process, the URL of the deployed API is output.

```
Previewing CloudFormation changeset before deployment
=============================================================
Deploy this changeset? [y/N]: y

2022-09-04 11:10:07 - Waiting for stack create/update to complete

CloudFormation events from stack operations
-----------------------------------------------------------------------------------------------------------------
ResourceStatus          ResourceType                 LogicalResourceId                        ResourceStatusReason
-----------------------------------------------------------------------------------------------------------------
CREATE_IN_PROGRESS      AWS::IAM::Role               LambdaTranslateTextApiFunctionRole       -
CREATE_IN_PROGRESS      AWS::IAM::Role               LambdaTranslateTextApiFunctionRole       Resource creation Initiated
CREATE_COMPLETE         AWS::IAM::Role               LambdaTranslateTextApiFunctionRole       -
CREATE_IN_PROGRESS      AWS::Lambda::Function        LambdaTranslateTextApiFunction           -
CREATE_IN_PROGRESS      AWS::Lambda::Function        LambdaTranslateTextApiFunction           Resource creation Initiated
CREATE_COMPLETE         AWS::Lambda::Function        LambdaTranslateTextApiFunction           -
CREATE_IN_PROGRESS      AWS::ApiGatewayV2::Api       ServerlessHttpApi                        -
CREATE_COMPLETE         AWS::ApiGatewayV2::Api       ServerlessHttpApi                        -
CREATE_IN_PROGRESS      AWS::ApiGatewayV2::Api       ServerlessHttpApi                        Resource creation Initiated
CREATE_IN_PROGRESS      AWS::Lambda::Permission      LambdaTranslateTextApiFunctionTrans      Resource creation Initiated
                                                     lateTextPermission
CREATE_IN_PROGRESS      AWS::ApiGatewayV2::Stage     ServerlessHttpApiApiGatewayDefaultS      -
                                                     tage
CREATE_IN_PROGRESS      AWS::Lambda::Permission      LambdaTranslateTextApiFunctionTrans      -
                                                     lateTextPermission
CREATE_COMPLETE         AWS::ApiGatewayV2::Stage     ServerlessHttpApiApiGatewayDefaultS      -
                                                     tage
CREATE_IN_PROGRESS      AWS::ApiGatewayV2::Stage     ServerlessHttpApiApiGatewayDefaultS      Resource creation Initiated
                                                     tage
CREATE_COMPLETE         AWS::Lambda::Permission      LambdaTranslateTextApiFunctionTrans      -
                                                     lateTextPermission
CREATE_COMPLETE         AWS::CloudFormation::Stack   LambdaTranslateTextApi                   -
-----------------------------------------------------------------------------------------------------------------

CloudFormation outputs from deployed stack
-----------------------------------------------------------------------------------------------------------------
Outputs
-----------------------------------------------------------------------------------------------------------------
Key             TranslateTextApiEndpoint
Description     API Gateway endpoint URL for default stage for LambdaTranslateTextApi function
Value           https://ongbirwckc.execute-api.us-west-2.amazonaws.com/
-----------------------------------------------------------------------------------------------------------------

Successfully created/updated stack - LambdaTranslateTextApi in us-west-2
```

Figure 6-19. *Confirming deployment of the changeset and URL output*

If you watch the deployment, you'll see the creation start and completion events for the various resources involved and, at the end, the output of the URL of the endpoint we'll use to invoke our function (courtesy of the `TranslateTextApi` output in the template in Listing 6-5). Make a note of this URL; we'll need it shortly.

We're now ready to run our application by invoking the API endpoint URL, which will trigger the event causing our Lambda function to run.

Running the Application

In the application template shown in Listing 6-5, we used an API Gateway `HttpApi` resource as our event source. We could also have used the original `Api` resource type. API Gateway's `HttpApi` resource offers lower latency and costs for REST APIs, but there are some limitations. If we'd used the `Api` resource type, we could test the integration from the API Gateway dashboard, but this isn't supported for `HttpApi` resources.

We configured our endpoint to expect a POST method, so simply accessing the URL in a browser won't work. Instead, for the purposes of this chapter, we'll use Postman, available at `www.postman.com` (you don't need to sign up to complete this exercise).

Having downloaded and installed Postman, start it and open a new request window (click the + button to open a new tabbed window). Configure the method as POST and paste the URL from the deployment output into the request URL field. Then add two keys representing the source and target language identifiers, shown in Figure 6-20 (as before, we're sending a string in English and requesting translation to Spanish). The request URL will update with the query parameters as you enter the keys and values.

Figure 6-20. *Configuring a new request to the API in Postman*

Finally, we need some text to translate. Click **Body** to switch tabs in the request, select the "raw" mode, and enter a string you want translated. Then, click **Send**. You'll see the output from the function appear in the *Response* window, shown in the bottom area of Figure 6-21.

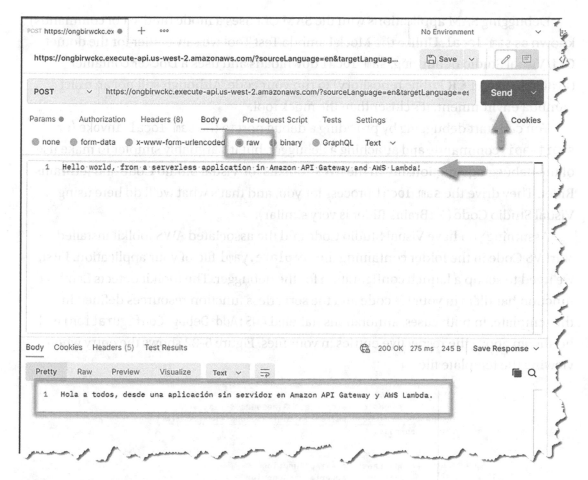

Figure 6-21. *Sending a request to our serverless application endpoint*

Congratulations! You just invoked your serverless application's Lambda function using an event triggered by sending a request to an API endpoint! And just as in the earlier example in this chapter, you ran that code without having to provision any infrastructure yourself, and you're not incurring charges when the code isn't actively servicing a request.

Debugging

Of course, congratulations are only in order if it worked! If it didn't, a little debugging may be required. This is where the SAM CLI tools fundamentally differ from the dotnet CLI/Visual Studio tooling we looked at earlier.

Debugging SAM applications with the SAM CLI uses a mode (and set of commands) known as `sam local`. Unlike the Mock Lambda Test Tool we saw earlier for the dotnet CLI/Visual Studio debugging, `sam local` downloads and uses a Docker container (available in an ECR Public repository) to run your code. Although still not an exact Lambda environment, it's closer than the mock tool.

You can start debugging by providing a debug port to the `sam local invoke` (or `start-api`) commands and attaching a debugger, but it's arguably simpler to make use of the debugging functionality in the AWS Toolkits for Visual Studio Code and JetBrains Rider. They drive the `sam local` process for you, and that's what we'll do here using Visual Studio Code (JetBrains Rider is very similar).

Assuming you have Visual Studio Code and the associated AWS toolkit installed, start VS Code in the folder containing the `template.yaml` file of your application. First, we need to set up a launch configuration for the debugger. The toolkit detects Lambda function handlers in your C# code and the serverless function resources defined in the template. In both cases, annotations (labeled `AWS:Add Debug Configuration`) will be shown above the respective entries in your files. Figure 6-22 shows the entry when viewing the template file.

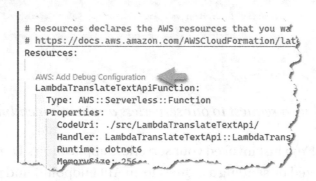

Figure 6-22. *Add Debug Configuration annotation in the template.yaml file*

Click the annotation to add a debug launch configuration to your files, called a *template launch configuration*. If you use the annotation in the C# file, you're asked if you want to add a launch configuration that references the function from the template entry or to execute the function in isolation from the source code entry (known as a *code launch configuration*). Code launches run the function without any regard to other resources specified in the template.

We used an `HttpApi` event source for our function, which at the time of writing isn't supported by the toolkit when automatically creating launch configurations.

The alternate REST resource type, `Api`, is supported and adds an option to set up an API Event configuration. However, all is not lost – we can still debug; we just need to massage the generated launch configuration a little.

Start by clicking the Add Debug Configuration annotation in the template file to get an initial launch configuration to work with, shown in Listing 6-8.

Listing 6-8. Default template launch configuration

```
{
  "configurations": [
    {
      "type": "aws-sam",
      "request": "direct-invoke",
      "name":
        "LambdaTranslateTextApi:LambdaTranslateTextApiFunction",
      "invokeTarget": {
        "target": "template",
        "templatePath": "${workspaceFolder}/template.yaml",
        "logicalId": "LambdaTranslateTextApiFunction"
      },
      "lambda": {
        "payload": {},
        "environmentVariables": {}
      }
    }
  ]
}
```

Next, change the `target` property in the `invokeTarget` settings to have the value **api**. As our function has no environment variables, we can delete the `lambda` settings. Instead, we add a group of settings under an `api` property that specify the URL resource path, method, payload, and query string parameters. Finally, as our function makes a call to an AWS service API, and we'll be running it locally, we need to provide credentials and region information. We do this by adding an `aws` section with `credentials` and `region` properties. The completed launch configuration is shown in Listing 6-9 (once again, we're requesting an English to Spanish conversion).

Note If you're editing this file in VS Code, it will place squiggles for the JSON value for the `payload` property, stating an Object is expected. You can safely ignore this.

Listing 6-9. Launch configuration for a function using an HttpApi resource

```
{
  "configurations": [
    {
      "type": "aws-sam",
      "request": "direct-invoke",
      "name":
        "LambdaTranslateTextApi:LambdaTranslateTextApiFunction",
      "invokeTarget": {
        "target": "api",
        "templatePath": "${workspaceFolder}/template.yaml",
        "logicalId": "LambdaTranslateTextApiFunction"
      },
      "api": {
        "path": "/",
        "httpMethod": "post",
        "payload": {
          "json": "Hello world from the debugger!"
        },
        "querystring": "sourceLanguage=en&targetLanguage=es"
      },
      "aws": {
        "credentials": "profile:ProDotNetOnAWSBook",
        "region": "us-west-2"
      }
    }
  ]
}
```

Open the `Function.cs` file and set a breakpoint at the entry to the function handler, then switch to VS Code's debugger window and start the launch configuration. Watch the output windows and you'll see the download of the container image before the debugger starts up and attaches. Soon after, the debugger will hit your breakpoint, and you can step through your function code, inspect variables, etc., just as you're used to. Also note that VS Code conveniently builds your project before starting debugging – unlike when we deploy where we must remember to run `sam build` before `sam deploy`!

Cleaning Up

A serverless application is, at heart, a CloudFormation stack, so you can simply delete it from the CloudFormation dashboard in the management console. This will clean up and delete all resources created when you deployed the application. Alternatively, you can delete the application using the SAM CLI and the command `sam delete` with the same result.

Choosing Between dotnet CLI Extensions and SAM CLI

Which should you use? Well, it depends! That's not a great answer, we know, but it really does depend on what you want to do. To a large extent, the decision really comes down to your debugging preferences.

If you're not concerned with wanting to debug your Lambda code in a Lambda-like environment, then consider using the dotnet CLI and/or Visual Studio tooling to manage your serverless functions and applications and the Mock Lambda Test Tool to debug test payloads. This keeps you within the "dotnet" ecosystem, where you are installing tools from NuGet and working with a UX you're used to.

On the other hand, if debugging in an environment closer to that in which the real function will run is important, then use the SAM tools. Or you might prefer this route if you've adopted Visual Studio Code or JetBrains Rider, both of which expose convenient integrations with SAM CLI, especially for debugging.

> **Tip**   It is possible to deploy a project generated with the SAM CLI tools using the dotnet CLI tools and get the best of both worlds. To do this, you use the `dotnet lambda deploy-serverless` command and add the `--template` parameter, pointing to the `template.yaml` file, which will be in a different location than the dotnet CLI tools are expecting. Running the command `dotnet lambda deploy-serverless --help` will show you the full set of options.

Using Non-LTS .NET Runtimes

The examples in this chapter used a managed runtime, arguably the easiest way to work with Lambda – certainly when working with the service for the first time. However, this does mean you need to wait until the service and tooling teams build, test, and make available the managed runtime for whatever LTS version of .NET you want to use. Let's be honest, this can sometimes take a little longer than we'd prefer. Like all work, it's subject to available resources and priorities.

For those that like (or need) to live on the "bleeding edge" of .NET releases and want to use a non-LTS version, let's examine how. By the way, you can also use these approaches to use LTS versions that the Lambda team hasn't yet made available as a managed runtime offering, so it's worth knowing about them. You can also use them to experiment with preview versions. In the text that follows, we'll refer to "non-managed" to keep the text simpler, meaning non-LTS versions, preview versions, and LTS versions that Lambda hasn't yet provided a managed runtime for.

To use a non-managed version of .NET, two approaches are available: first, using what Lambda terms a *custom runtime*, and second, using a container image. The custom runtime approach was the first technique supported by Lambda, so we'll cover that first before moving onto the container approach.

Custom Runtimes

Custom runtimes are a feature of Lambda that enables you to implement a runtime in any programming language. A runtime is simply code, in an executable file named *bootstrap*, that runs your function handler when your function is invoked. You bundle your runtime executable and any dependencies with the deployment package containing your function code.

The runtime script or binary you include in your deployment bundle is responsible for several tasks – running your function's setup code, obtaining the name of the handler from an environment variable (set up by Lambda), reading the invocation event data from Lambda (via an API), and passing it onto the function handler. When the function concludes, your runtime gathers the output and hands it back to Lambda.

Your custom runtime code runs in the standard Lambda execution environment (just like your function), which is a version of Amazon Linux. To provide your runtime, you can use a shell script, a script in a language included in Amazon Linux, or even use a binary executable (provided you compiled it on an Amazon Linux environment).

How does this apply to .NET? It's surprisingly easy, as the .NET team at AWS has provided a blueprint, `Lambda Custom Runtime Function`, you can use from the dotnet CLI or Visual Studio to generate the files you need (at the command line, the short name `lambda.CustomRuntimeFunction` is available for convenience). There isn't a blueprint for using custom runtimes with serverless applications, but it's easy to replicate into an application once you see how it's done for a function.

Note   If you're using SAM CLI, you'll need to set up the runtime files by hand. The `sam init` command used to scaffold new serverless functions and applications doesn't support a custom runtime option.

Taking our first example (the synchronous `TranslateText` function that we deployed directly to Lambda), let's examine the changes we need to make to support using a non-managed version, in this case, .NET 5. This was the latest non-LTS version at the time of writing – you can extrapolate this to future versions as needed.

There are no changes to the function handler itself. We just need to ensure that our project build emits an executable named *bootstrap*, as this is what Lambda will look for. Then, we need to add the actual bootstrap code. We can add this to our function's class file by supplying a method with the name `Main` (again, this name is a fixed requirement).

In the project file, set the project's output type to be an *exe* using an `<OutputType>` element, add an `<AssemblyName>bootstrap</AssemblyName>` setting, and set your required target framework in the project properties, shown in Listing 6-10. We're required to change `OutputType` because we need to generate an executable that Lambda can run directly and that in turn calls our function handler, something that can't be done if we were to build a dll.

Listing 6-10. Project file changes to use a custom runtime

```
<Project Sdk="Microsoft.NET.Sdk">
  <PropertyGroup>
    <OutputType>Exe</OutputType>
    <AssemblyName>bootstrap</AssemblyName>
    <TargetFramework>net6.0</TargetFramework>
    ...
  </PropertyGroup>
  ...
</Project>
```

Next, in the function handler class, we add the code that will start when Lambda runs the executable, shown in Listing 6-11. The LambdaBootstrapBuilder type that's used is supplied by the existing dependency on the Amazon.Lambda.RuntimeSupport NuGet package.

Listing 6-11. Bootstrap code in class file

```
...
public class Function
{
  // the bootstrap handler
  private static async Task Main(string[] args)
  {
    Func<string, ILambdaContext, string> handler
          = FunctionHandler;
    await LambdaBootstrapBuilder.Create(handler,
          new DefaultLambdaJsonSerializer()
        )
        .Build()
        .RunAsync();
  }
```

```
// our original function handler, unchanged
public async Task<string>
    FunctionHandler(InputData input,
                    ILambdaContext context)
  ...
}
}
```

If you have an `aws-lambda-tools-defaults.json` file for the project, change the value of the included `function-runtime` setting to `provided.al2` (that's "a-el-2", not "a-one-2") for Amazon Linux 2, or `provided,` to use an Amazon Linux environment. If you don't yet have this file, you can instead specify the `--function-runtime` option when deploying with the dotnet CLI tools. If you're deploying from Visual Studio, the **Lambda Runtime** option on the deployment wizard's first page contains entries enabling you to select a custom runtime using either Amazon Linux or Amazon Linux 2.

Tip   You can use custom runtimes whether you are deploying a serverless function to Lambda or a serverless application that's deployed using CloudFormation. For a serverless application, the process is the same in terms of packaging, but be sure to use the value `provided` (or `provided.al2`) for your function's `Runtime` property in the template.

That's all the changes needed to use a custom .NET runtime! Now you can easily make use of a non-managed release. Let's compare this to the second, newer, approach that uses container images.

Container Images

You might want to consider using container images, even if a managed runtime is available, to gain the ability to easily add further dependencies needed by your functions into the runtime environment that are not there by default. One use case is to install the `libgdiplus` native dependency, enabling the use of the APIs in the `System.Drawing` namespace to process image files in your Lambda functions. Lambda doesn't include this dependency in its managed runtime environments.

At the time of this writing, Lambda publishes a base set of container images for.
NET 5 and .NET 6. Each image comes with the language runtime pre-installed and all
other components needed to run the image on Lambda. If your build targets the x86_64
architecture, you can use either runtime image, but if you're taking advantage of the
ARM64 architecture, perhaps for the performance improvements made starting in
.NET 5, then only the 6.0 LTS runtime is available for that architecture.

Tip   Dockerfiles corresponding to the images are on GitHub at
`https://github.com/aws/aws-lambda-dotnet/tree/master/`
`LambdaRuntimeDockerfiles`.

As with custom runtimes, it's easy to start from the dotnet CLI or Visual Studio using
"new project" blueprints for both function and serverless application project types.
You can also generate a container-based project with SAM CLI's `sam init` command
by specifying the `--package-type image` option and selecting the required base image
for the `--base-image` option. Whichever scaffolding approach you use, your generated
project will contain a Dockerfile that uses your selected base image.

Tip   You can also use a base image for a custom runtime using Amazon Linux
or Amazon Linux 2. This gives you the flexibility to install all your required
dependencies, including a specific .NET runtime, as part of the image build.

As with custom runtimes, there are no changes needed in your function handler
code. Instead, there are a couple of differences in how you specify what to deploy and
how you declare your function handler to Lambda when using container deployments.

Figure 6-23 highlights the differences in the `aws-lambda-tools-defaults.json` file
for a serverless function deployed using a container image.

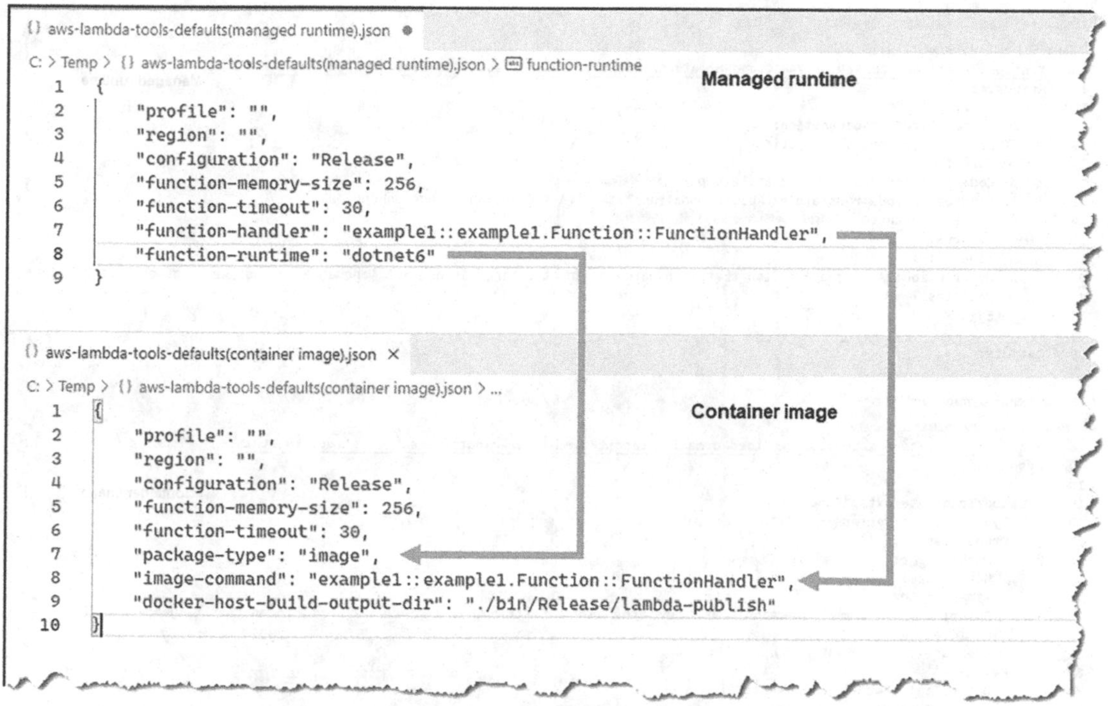

```
{} aws-lambda-tools-defaults(managed runtime).json  ●

C: > Temp > {} aws-lambda-tools-defaults(managed runtime).json > ⊡ function-runtime
   1   {                                                                    Managed runtime
   2       "profile": "",
   3       "region": "",
   4       "configuration": "Release",
   5       "function-memory-size": 256,
   6       "function-timeout": 30,
   7       "function-handler": "example1::example1.Function::FunctionHandler",
   8       "function-runtime": "dotnet6"
   9   }
```

```
{} aws-lambda-tools-defaults(container image).json  ✕

C: > Temp > {} aws-lambda-tools-defaults(container image).json > ...
   1   {                                                                    Container image
   2       "profile": "",
   3       "region": "",
   4       "configuration": "Release",
   5       "function-memory-size": 256,
   6       "function-timeout": 30,
   7       "package-type": "image",
   8       "image-command": "example1::example1.Function::FunctionHandler",
   9       "docker-host-build-output-dir": "./bin/Release/lambda-publish"
  10   }
```

Figure 6-23. *Container image deployment for a serverless function*

For a serverless application, Figure 6-24 highlights the changes to how you specify the code location and deployment package type, and add metadata related to the image to be built, to the serverless template file when using container images.

```
! template(managed runtime).yaml  ×

C: > Temp >  ! template(managed runtime).yaml > ...
 16      # https://docs.aws.amazon.com/AWSCloudFormation/latest/UserGuide/resources-section-structure.html          Managed runtime
 17      Resources:
 18
 19        LambdaTranslateTextApiFunction:
 20          Type: AWS::Serverless::Function
 21          Properties:
 22            CodeUri: ./src/LambdaTranslateTextApi/
 23            Handler: LambdaTranslateTextApi::LambdaTranslateTextApi.Function::FunctionHandler
 24            Runtime: dotnet6
 25            MemorySize: 256
 26            Timeout: 100
 27            Description: A Lambda function that translates an input string, in a given language, to another language, returning th
 28 >          Policies: ···
 32 >          Events: ···
 39
 40 > Outputs: ···
```

```
! template(container_image).yaml  ×

C: > Temp >  ! template(container_image).yaml > ...
 16      # https://docs.aws.amazon.com/AWSCloudFormation/latest/UserGuide/resources-section-structure.html          Container image
 17      Resources:
 18
 19        LambdaTranslateTextApiFunction:
 20          Type: AWS::Serverless::Function
 21          Properties:
 22            PackageType: Image
 23            MemorySize: 256
 24            Timeout: 100
 25            Description: A Lambda function that translates an input string, in a given language, to another language, returning t
 26 >          Policies: ···
 30 >          Events: ···
 37          Metadata:
 38            DockerTag: lambdatranslatetextapi
 39            DockerContext: ./src/LambdaTranslateTextApi
 40            Dockerfile: Dockerfile
 41            DockerBuildArgs:
 42              SAM_BUILD_MODE: run
 43
```

Figure 6-24. *Container image deployment for a serverless application*

Notice in Figure 6-24 that we also removed the function handler. We chose instead to specify it in the Dockerfile using a CMD statement, shown in Listing 6-12.

Listing 6-12. Specifying the function handler in a Dockerfile CMD statement

```
CMD["LambdaTranslateTextApi::LambdaTranslateTextApi.Function::↵
FunctionHandler"]
```

You deploy the container images for Lambda functions to an ECR repository. The dotnet CLI tooling automatically creates a repository for you unless you specify either the `--image-tag` option at the command line or the `image-tag` property in the defaults file. For both, the value is in the format `repository-name:tag`, for example, `example1:latest`. When deploying from Visual Studio, the repository must already exist; you simply select it in the deployment wizard.

If you're using the SAM CLI, you again have the option of having the tooling create the repository for you, or you can elect to specify it using the `--image-repository` command-line option. Although the AWS documentation states you need to supply the repository name, it actually wants the URL of the repository as `<account-number>. dkr.ecr.<region>.amazonaws.com/<repository-name>`. To have the tool automatically create the repo (and delete it when you delete the function), use the switch `--resolve- image-repos` instead. Note that if you deploy in guided mode (`--guided`), the switch is ignored, and you'll be prompted for the behavior you want.

Those are the only file changes needed for serverless functions and applications to deploy as a container image. The dotnet CLI and Visual Studio tools will automatically build the container image as part of deployment. For the SAM CLI, you need to build with an extra flag – `sam build --use-container` – prior to deployment.

Using either custom runtimes or container images, you can deploy your .NET-based Lambda function or serverless application to use any .NET Core–based runtime you like, LTS, non-LTS, or even preview releases. Container images, as noted, also give you the ability to further customize the Lambda environment your functions will run in with additional dependencies that are not part of the base Lambda environment.

Summary

It may be somewhat surprising that a chapter dedicated to introducing how you can simplify your compute operations by choosing serverless approaches, eliminating the need to provision and manage infrastructure yourself, turns out to be one of the longest in the book so far. And we barely scratched the surface! However, it's all down to the extensive collection of tools available to you to choose from when working with Lambda functions and serverless applications.

In the chapter, we compared the available tools for the command line (dotnet CLI extension, SAM CLI), in Visual Studio, and debugging in Visual Studio Code. We simply didn't have space to cover deploying from VS Code, or cover JetBrains Rider (which is very similar to VS Code as it too uses SAM CLI under the covers).

We also covered how to use any version of .NET, LTS or otherwise, using custom runtimes or containers. We didn't have space to cover optimizing cold starts, sharing code with layers, and tracing and observability of serverless applications. And there's also the topic of authorization when working with API endpoints. We'll be covering some of these topics in later chapters as we start to work with the sample application provided with the book.

This brings us to the end of compute; next, we're going to start looking at storage in the cloud, which will lead us onto databases. First, the biggest of them all – object storage with Amazon Simple Storage Service, or S3. In recent years, at AWS' re:Invent conference, the S3 team has usually provided an update on just how many objects S3 handles – the sheer scale of this service is pretty mind-blowing!

PART III

Storing Your Data

## CHAPTER 7

S3 Object Storage

.NET applications running on-premises usually store application data – text and binary files, static website assets, etc. – on local or networked file storage. While cloud-based network storage is still a possibility with services such as Amazon FSx for Windows File Server and others, you'll probably begin using cloud-based object storage with Amazon Simple Storage Service (S3).

In this chapter, we'll take a closer look at S3 from the perspective of an application. We'll start by recapping the organization of objects in S3 and then go on to examine how you store and retrieve those objects from your application code. We'll also look at how you can use Amazon CloudFront, a content delivery network service, in conjunction with S3 to serve assets (e.g., static website content) with ultra-low latency from over 200 Points of Presence (PoP) distributed around the globe.

Object Storage in S3

As we outlined in Chapter 1, the top-level storage resource in S3 is the bucket. Buckets have globally unique names that must conform to DNS naming rules, including the following:

- Between 3 and 63 characters in length, beginning and ending with a letter or a number

- Lowercase letters, numbers, periods (.), and hyphens (-) only

---

Note AWS recommends you do not use periods (or dots, as the S3 documentation calls them) in your bucket names for compatibility reasons unless the bucket hosts a static website. Using periods also means your application cannot take advantage of Transfer Acceleration. For the latest details on naming rules for buckets, see `https://docs.aws.amazon.com/AmazonS3/latest/userguide/bucketnamingrules.html`.

© William Penberthy and Steve Roberts 2023
W. Penberthy and S. Roberts, *Pro .NET on Amazon Web Services*,
https://doi.org/10.1007/978-1-4842-8907-5_7

Buckets, even though they have globally unique names, also belong to a region – this is known as the bucket's location constraint. As we'll see later, when you access data in a bucket, you need to do so either by using the bucket's regional endpoint (e.g., `https://my-bucket-name.s3.us-west-2.amazonaws.com`) or, if using one of the AWS SDKs, an S3 client object constructed with the appropriate region (you'll get a clear and unambiguous error message if you don't!).

Your data exists as objects within a bucket. An object can be a file (text or binary) or a blob of arbitrary bytes that has some meaning within your application. You identify your objects in a bucket using a key, which you can consider like a file name. Using key prefixes, you can also organize objects into what appears to be folder paths. Or you can simply put all your objects into the root of the bucket (i.e., provided the object keys are unique).

Listing 7-1 shows some example object keys and key prefixes. In S3, all the objects in a bucket exist in a flat organization – key prefixes only infer a logical, not physical, hierarchy. As we mentioned in Chapter 1, S3 is not a file system, even if the AWS tools and management console can make it resemble one!

Listing 7-1. Example object keys and key prefixes (Website/)

```
File1.dat
MyReport,pdf
Website/Image1.png
Website/Image2.png
Website/Other/Image1.png
```

Public or Private?

Let's try and answer a common question early: Should buckets, and the objects they contain, be public or private?

In an ideal world, buckets and objects would always be private, and in fact, this is the default setting for buckets that you create. S3 has a feature, *Block Public Access* (`https://docs.aws.amazon.com/AmazonS3/latest/userguide/access-control-block-public-access.html`), that you can make use of to ensure things remain that way. However, there exist scenarios where objects in a bucket need to be publicly readable.

One such scenario is using a bucket to serve assets for use in web applications (e.g., static image, css, and html or script files). For the deployed web application to reach those objects, you need to make them publicly readable (we strongly suggest you don't consider making them writeable!). To reference objects for this scenario, your application uses a URL containing the bucket name and object key. For example, given a bucket named *my-static-assets* in the US West (Oregon) region, you could access an object named *styles.css* (representing a stylesheet needed by your application) from that bucket with a fixed, long-term URL – `https://my-static-asssets.s3.us-west-2.amazonaws.com/styles.css` – provided that object is marked public read-only.

Another scenario involves data sets that you make available to third-party applications using a feature known as *requestor pays*. With requestor pays, you as bucket owner pay the storage costs of the data sets, but third parties who access those data sets pay the transfer charges when downloading them. Again, the objects representing those data sets need to be either publicly readable or shared with a specific AWS account. Again, you share the object using a URL having marked it publicly available.

Tip   A good resource for security considerations for buckets and objects in S3 can be found in the service's user guide, at `https://docs.aws.amazon.com/AmazonS3/latest/userguide/security-best-practices.html`.

Later in this chapter, we'll consider a temporary, time-limited mechanism to share access to objects (for upload or download) known as presigned URLs. You can use presigned URLs to grant access for a period to users, applications, and application components, without needing to open a bucket to public access. You can also use Amazon CloudFront, a service designed to speed up the distribution of web content using a global collection of edge location servers, with S3 buckets. Your application and end users access objects in the bucket via a CloudFront distribution domain URL, rather than a URL to objects in your buckets. You can also, in turn, then force all public access to the bucket to be via CloudFront, enabling you to keep the bucket and objects private. We'll cover CloudFront at the end of the chapter.

The answer to the question "public or private" then is "it depends" (however much we dislike that answer). While as mentioned there are scenarios where objects need to be publicly available for applications to use in general, you should strive to limit this as much as possible. One recommendation to consider is using multiple buckets, keeping one for data sharing with the required objects publicly readable, and put other data into buckets where all public access is blocked. This helps guard against scenarios where you have mixed permissions in a bucket and accidents where data that should be private suddenly becomes public based on a misconfigured setting that applied more broadly than you expected. However, keeping buckets and objects private at all times, and forcing all access to the bucket to go through a CloudFront distribution is our preferred approach, even for read-only data.

Object Versions

"Out of the box," S3 buckets hold a single version of each object you upload and update that single version each time you revise the object. You can, however, turn on object versioning at the bucket level, enabling storage of multiple versions of objects that have the same key. There are a couple of things to be aware of in terms of how versions work, and how object versions behave, when you delete objects.

S3 automatically generates and sets unique version IDs on objects – you have no control over the IDs, and you can't edit them. So you can't upload new content to an object and assign the version ID "version2", for example. Version IDs are opaque UTF-8 strings, which can be up to 1024 bytes in length. You are able to access these IDs when examining the bucket, which is useful because they are not necessarily in any particular order.

When object versioning is set to *off* for a bucket (the default state), all objects will still have a version ID, but the ID will be set to the value *null*. If you subsequently enable versioning for a bucket, all the existing objects don't suddenly gain a non-null version ID. Only new objects, or existing objects you subsequently update while versioning is enabled (you can suspend versioning, or turn it off again), will have a version ID generated and assigned.

When you upload a new object into a versioning-enabled bucket, S3, as we've just said, will generate and assign a version ID. If you then upload content to the same key, S3 doesn't overwrite the existing object. Instead, the original object remains (with its version ID), and S3 generates a new version in the bucket. The subsequent version is now considered "current." The prior versions are still present.

You can "restore" prior versions of an object, effectively making them the current version, by making a copy of a prior version using the same key. S3 will create a new version, with a new unique version ID. For example, let's say you have three versions of an object and copy the object to the same key, specifying the version ID associated with the second version. You'll now have four versions of the object – the original three, plus a fourth (effectively a duplicate of the second version) but with its own unique version ID.

When you delete the current version of object, you might be thinking that the previous version then becomes current. Not so! Instead, S3 inserts a delete marker into the bucket (which has its own unique version ID too). That delete marker is now the current version of the object, and the object won't be displayed when you list the contents of the bucket.

It's possible to "undelete" a deleted current version of an object, and you do this by deleting the delete marker. This makes the version prior to the delete marker "current" and visible in bucket listings. By the way, you can also delete prior versions of an object (by specifying the version ID during deletion). In this scenario, there's no delete marker, and S3 removes the object version – permanently.

The script in Listing 7-2 explores how object versions work using cmdlets for S3 from the AWS Tools for PowerShell.

Listing 7-2. Exploring object versions in S3

```
# Create a new bucket (for brevity, the remaining commands don't
# show the -BucketName parameter name, they treat the first
# unnamed parameter value as the bucket name by default)
C:\> New-S3Bucket -BucketName test

# Create a new object; this object will have a version ID of "null"
C:\> Write-S3Object test -Key file.txt -Content "1st version"

C:\> Get-S3Version test
IsTruncated         : False
KeyMarker           :
VersionIdMarker     :
NextKeyMarker       :
NextVersionIdMarker :
Versions            : {file.txt}
Name                : test
Prefix              :
MaxKeys             : 1000
CommonPrefixes      : {}
Delimiter           :

# Turn on object versioning for the bucket
C:\> Write-S3BucketVersioning test -VersioningConfig_Status Enabled
```

```
# Update the object to create a second version
C:\> Write-S3Object test -Key file.txt -content "2nd version"

# List the versioned objects in the bucket
C:\> Get-S3Version test
IsTruncated         : False
KeyMarker           :
VersionIdMarker     :
NextKeyMarker       :
NextVersionIdMarker :
Versions            : {file.txt, file.txt}
Name                : test
Prefix              :
MaxKeys             : 1000
CommonPrefixes      : {}
Delimiter           :

# Look closer at the versions of the object (columns removed for
# brevity)
C:\> (Get-S3Version test).Versions

BucketName Key      IsLatest VersionId
---------- ---      -------- ---------
test       file.txt True     Al5G8uoE2THZQfN3ThpsrK7w2Bv5kS.W
test       file.txt False    null

# Delete the current version of the object - note the delete
# marker output and its version ID
C:\> Remove-S3Object test -Key file.txt -Force
DeleteMarker VersionId
------------ ---------
true         cSGMx1.nMNIvYV6FunbEm7EVsW2GS5G1

# Inspect the versions - the delete marker is now current
C:\> (Get-S3Version test).Versions

BucketName    Key      IsLatest VersionId
----------    ---      -------- ---------
```

```
test          file.txt True    cSGMx1.nMNIvYV6FunbEm7EVsW2GS5G1
test          file.txt False   Al5G8uoE2THZQfN3ThpsrK7w2Bv5kS.W
test          file.txt False   null

# Try and get the object - there's no output as latest version is
# a delete marker and is "hiding" the prior versions
C:\> Get-S3Object test -Key file.txt

# To undelete deletion of the current version, delete the
# delete marker
C:\> Remove-S3Object test -Key file.txt -VersionId cSGMx1.
nMNIvYV6FunbEm7EVsW2GS5G1

# Verify original 2nd version is now current and visible
C:\> (Get-S3Version test).Versions

BucketName    Key      IsLatest VersionId
----------    ---      -------- ---------
test          file.txt True     Al5G8uoE2THZQfN3ThpsrK7w2Bv5kS.W
test          file.txt False    null

# And verify we can fetch details on the object
C:\> Get-S3Object test -Key file.txt

ETag         : "4ed9407630eb1000c0f6b63842defa7d"
BucketName   : test
Key          : file.txt
LastModified : 6/21/2021 10:15:08 AM
Owner        : Amazon.S3.Model.Owner
Size         : 3
StorageClass : STANDARD

# Clean up and delete bucket and objects (be careful with this
# command in production!)
C:\> Remove-S3Bucket test -DeleteBucketContent
```

Object Metadata

Objects in buckets have metadata associated with them. S3 generates and maintains some of this metadata, for example, the size of the object in bytes (*Content-Length*), object type (*Content-Type*), the date of last modification (*Last-Modified*), version ID (*x-amz-version-id*), and more. Some of this data can also be modified by you or your applications (see `https://docs.aws.amazon.com/AmazonS3/latest/userguide/UsingMetadata.html#SysMetadata`). You can also apply your own metadata to objects in the form of key-value pairs. S3 stores the supplied metadata key in lowercase.

Note   If you change or add metadata after you create an object, S3 creates a copy of the object with the updated metadata applied. If you have enabled versioning for the object's bucket, as discussed earlier, this means you'll have a new object version.

User-defined metadata is distinguished from system metadata by prefixing the metadata key with *x-amz-meta-* (this prefix is required). For example, if you had a user-defined key you wanted to apply to an object (let's say some-custom-metadata), the metadata key you ultimately apply would be *x-amz-meta-some-custom-metadata*. Also, note that there is a limit of 2 KB for user-defined metadata keys and values (i.e., all custom metadata keys, and values, summed together must be less than or equal to 2 KB).

You can update user-defined metadata, and system metadata keys that support end-user modification, using the S3 Management Console, from the command line, or from within Visual Studio. Figure 7-1 shows the Object Properties dialog for an S3 object in Visual Studio, listing the user-editable system metadata keys and the user-defined metadata key prefix for adding custom metadata entries.

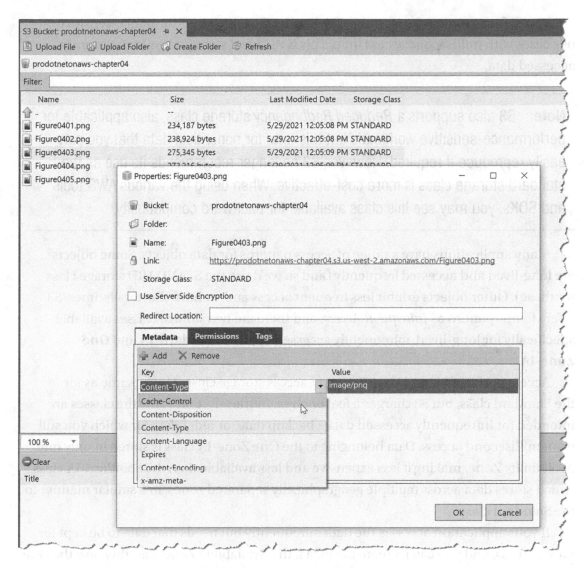

Figure 7-1. *Editing object metadata in Visual Studio*

Storage Classes

Listing 7-2 and Figure 7-1 both show an object detail named **Storage Class** (which in both examples has the value *STANDARD*). Storage classes give you a measure of control over the redundancy, performance access characteristics, and cost you need for your objects (note that changing storage class doesn't change the durability of your data in S3, which is still 11 9's – 99.999999999% durable!).

The default storage class for objects, **Standard**, supports performance-sensitive use cases with millisecond access time. This is the ideal storage class for frequently accessed data.

Note   S3 also supports a *Reduced Redundancy* storage class, also applicable for performance-sensitive workloads but this time for noncritical data that you can easily reproduce if required. However, S3 no longer recommends its use as the standard storage class is more cost-effective. When using the various AWS tools and SDKs, you may see this class available for backward compatibility.

Many applications have a range of access patterns for data objects. Some objects are long-lived and accessed frequently (and so we'd use the STANDARD storage class for these). Other objects exhibit less frequent access and/or have shorter lifetimes. S3 refers to this pattern as *Infrequent Access*, and there are two storage classes available specifically for long-lived, infrequently accessed objects: **Standard-IA** and **One Zone-IA**.

Access performance for the infrequent access storage classes is the same as for the Standard class, but S3 charges a fee for object retrieval – that's why the classes are intended for infrequently accessed data – backup data, or older data for which you still want millisecond access. Data belonging to the One Zone-IA class is stored in only one Availability Zone, making it less expensive and less available than the Standard-IA class, which stores data across multiple geographically separated zones, in a similar manner to the Standard class.

If your application accesses the data infrequently but needs that data to be kept for long periods, and you can recreate the data if the Availability Zone fails, then use the One Zone-IA class. Otherwise, you should consider placing infrequently accessed but long-lived data into the Standard-IA class.

Caution   Both infrequent access storage classes are also only suitable for objects larger than 128 KB that you plan on storing for at least 30 days. Objects smaller than 128 KB are charged the same as for 128 KB, and objects deleted before 30 days are charged for the full 30 days. So these storage classes are not suitable for your temporary application data.

Having control via storage classes is great, but who wants to be constantly analyzing access patterns from applications to determine if objects are in the right storage class? That's where S3 Intelligent Tiering comes in!

The Intelligent-Tiering class lets you optimize storage costs for your applications by handling the access pattern monitoring, and movement of data to more cost-effective storage tiers, for you. It's not free – there is a small monthly fee, but there are no retrieval costs for objects that are moved to an infrequent access tier (unlike where you assign an infrequent access storage class yourself).

On initial upload, S3 stores objects in the standard frequent access tier. If you don't access them for 30 days, S3 moves them automatically to an infrequent access tier. Additionally, S3 moves objects not accessed for 90 days to an Archive Access tier, followed by a Deep Archive Access tier after 180 days of no access. Like the infrequent access tiers, if you delete an object in the Intelligent-Tiering class before 30 days, you're charged for the full 30 days. However, S3 skips over objects smaller than the 128 KB minimum size and keeps them in the frequent access tier.

Storage classes for objects can be set using the S3 console, command-line tools, from within your applications using the SDK, and from Visual Studio too. Figure 7-2 shows changing the storage class for an object from within the IDE.

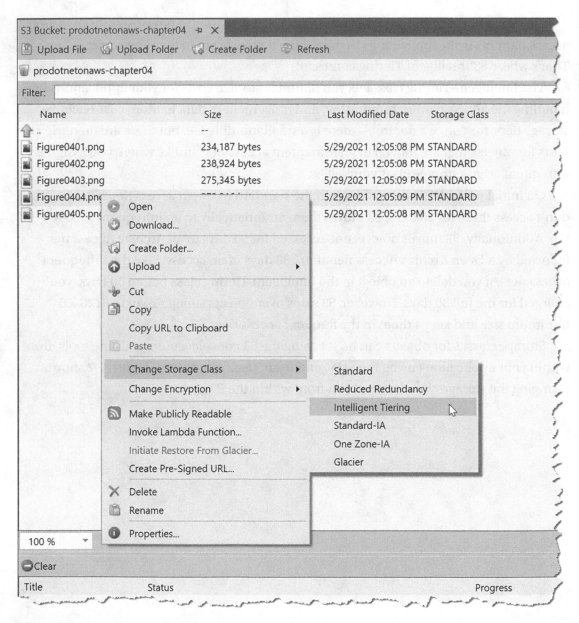

Figure 7-2. *Changing the storage class of objects from within Visual Studio*

Reading and Writing Objects

Next let's look at how we can put (upload) data into a bucket, and download it (get) from within our applications using the AWS SDK for .NET's support for S3's REST-style API. You'll find the SDK's implementation of the API in the AWSSDK.S3 NuGet package, so you'll need to add it to your project anytime you want to work with S3 from your application. In addition to implementing S3's API, the package also includes various helpers and higher-level abstractions that can make your application code simpler, as we'll see shortly.

Get and Put Object

To upload a new object (or update an existing one), S3 provides a PUT API. To download an object, there's a corresponding GET operation. In the SDK, you'll find these implemented as `PutObject` and `GetObject` methods on the SDK's `AmazonS3Client` class. Remember that your code needs to address S3 buckets using their region-specific endpoints, so when you construct an instance of the SDK's S3 client class, you need to either remember to pass the region to the constructor (if you're working with S3 from code running on your own machine) or if the code is running in the cloud on a resource in a different region to the bucket.

If your code is running on EC2 instances, or ECS/EKS container instances, or even Lambda, the SDK can use metadata provided by these host environments to self-determine which region it is running in (as well as credentials). If the S3 resources are in the same region as the compute resource, then you can simply use the parameterless constructor for the client, and the SDK will figure it all out for you. But if you're running on your own machine, or a compute resource in a different region, you need to tell the SDK which region to use. While you could pass this data to the constructor, the simplest approach is to continue using the parameterless constructor and instead place any credential and region data into configuration files (`appsettings.development.json`, etc.). This keeps your code simpler and is the assumed approach for all the examples in the remainder of this chapter. We covered how to supply credentials and region data to the SDK's client classes for services in Chapter 2.

Let's first see how to upload an object to a bucket using the code snippet in Listing 7-3. To keep things simple, we'll just use a simple piece of text for the object content (the SDK will apply automatically a `Content-Type` metadata attribute of *text/plain*).

Listing 7-3. Uploading an object with PutObject

```
// assumes these two namespaces, from the AWSSDK.S3 NuGet
// package, are declared
```

```
// using Amazon.S3;
// using Amazon.S3.Model;

var s3Client = new AmazonS3Client();
var request = new PutObjectRequest
{
    BucketName = "your-bucket-name-here",
    Key = "simple-text-object.txt",
    ContentBody = "Some simple text content"
};
try
{
    var response = await s3Client.PutObjectAsync(request);
    Console.WriteLine("Upload succeeded");
}
catch (AmazonS3Exception e)
{
    Console.WriteLine($"Error in upload, {e.Message}");
}
```

That was simple, but what if we have a file, or even a stream of content, to upload? The PutObjectRequest class contains additional properties enabling our code to specify a file name, or a stream (which the SDK can automatically close after upload). Examples of the request objects for these two scenarios are shown in Listing 7-4.

Listing 7-4. Uploading a file or content from a stream

```
// request properties to upload from a file on disk
var fileRequest = new PutObjectRequest
{
    BucketName = "your-bucket-name-here",
    Key = "your-object-key-here",
    FilePath = System.IO.Path.GetFullPath("filename-here")
};

// request properties to upload from a stream
var rnd = new System.Random();
```

```
byte[] testData = new byte[1024];
for (var i = 0; i < testData.Length; i++)
{
    testData[i] = (byte)rnd.Next(255);
}

var streamRequest = new PutObjectRequest
{
    BucketName = "your-bucket-name-here",
    Key = "your-object-key-here",
    InputStream = new System.IO.MemoryStream(testData),
    // if needed, you can auto reset the stream position before
    // upload (useful for file stream uploads), and auto close
    // the stream after upload. Both settings are true by
    // default.
    AutoResetStreamPosition = true,
    AutoCloseStream = true
};
```

Now that we know how to get data into a bucket, how do we download it? Listing 7-5 shows a sample snippet of code for S3's GET API, implemented as GetObject in the SDK, to access the simple text object uploaded in Listing 7-3 (obviously, echoing the downloaded content to the console isn't that useful but serves our purpose here to show the SDK in action).

Listing 7-5. Downloading an object with GetObject

```
var request = new GetObjectRequest
{
    BucketName = BucketName,
    Key = "simple-text-object.txt",
};

var response = await s3Client.GetObjectAsync(request);

using (var responseStream = response.ResponseStream)
using (var reader = new StreamReader(responseStream))
{
```

```
    var contentType = response.Headers["Content-Type"];
    Console.WriteLine("Content type: {0}", contentType);

    var responseBody = reader.ReadToEnd();

    Console.WriteLine($"Content = '{responseBody}'");
}
```

Note   The object data stream is pulling directly from S3, and the stream will remain open until you read all the data or close the stream. This means your application should read stream in the response as quickly as possible.

It's possible to also download object ranges, and parts, of objects so you don't need to download the whole object content before processing. Look for the ByteRange and PartNumber properties on the GetObjectRequest class.

You may be wondering now what PartNumber is, as we've not yet mentioned anything about parts. PutObject, as it stands, will attempt to upload the supplied content to S3 in one fell swoop, regardless of the size of the content. For the small objects and pieces of data we used in the preceding code snippets, this is likely to work just fine. But what if you have a large, multi-megabyte or multi-gigabyte (or even larger) object? What happens if there's a failure due to network issues during the upload?

The good news is that the SDK will attempt to retry the operation (it retries up to four times by default, and this is configurable – see https://docs.aws.amazon.com/sdk-for-net/v3/developer-guide/retries-timeouts.html). But it will retry from the very start, not from the point where the failure occurred. Let's say the failure occurred during the very last few bytes of a large (MB or GB) object. The SDK retries – all the way from byte 0.

This then brings us to multipart upload, which allows us to upload large objects in several chunks, or parts. Should a failure occur, the SDK (or your application, if the automatic retries also fail) needs to re-process only the affected parts.

Multipart Upload

Multipart upload is a process for uploading that breaks an object into parts, with a minimum size of 5 MB per part (so it's not suitable for objects less than 5 MB in length). The process consists of a set of APIs that you use to

- Inform S3 that you are about to initiate a multipart upload

- Upload each part (5 MB or more per part), in parallel or sequence
  (you can even upload out of order)

- Inform S3 that all parts have been uploaded and S3 should compose
  the final object from the uploaded parts

It's a fairly simple process, but if you want to use multithreading to parallelize the process, then things can get more complicated in your code. The advantage to this process is that if a network glitch interrupts the uploads, your application only needs to retry uploading the parts affected by the glitch.

Listing 7-6 shows the entire process, for a hypothetical file, simplified to ignore any application retries caused by errors, any progress reporting, and sequential uploading of parts.

Listing 7-6. Uploading an object with S3's multipart APIs

```
var filePath = "c:/path/to/some/file.dat";
var bucketName = "your-bucket-name-here";
var objectKey = "your-object-key-here";

// Divide the source file into parts of 5MB each (the
// last part can be less than 5MB)
var fileLen = new FileInfo(filePath).Length;
var partSize = 5 * (int)Math.Pow(2, 20);

// Inform S3 of the upload process. The response data contains
// an ID you must supply on each subsequent call.
var initRequest = new InitiateMultipartUploadRequest
{
    BucketName = bucketName,
    Key = objectKey
};
var initResponse =
        await s3Client.InitiateMultipartUploadAsync(initRequest);

// Create a list to hold the etag for each uploaded part
var partResponses = new List<UploadPartResponse>();
```

```
try
{
    // Loop and upload each part, supplying the part sequence
    // number; retain the etag value returned for each part
    // uploaded
    var filePos = 0;
    for (var partNum = 1; filePos < fileLen; partNum++)
    {
        var partRequest = new UploadPartRequest
        {
            BucketName = bucketName,
            Key = objectKey,
            UploadId = initResponse.UploadId,
            PartNumber = partNum,
            FilePath = filePath,
            FilePosition = filePos
        };

        var partResponse
            = await s3Client.UploadPartAsync(partRequest);

        partResponses.Add(partResponse);

        filePos += partSize;
    }

    // Inform S3 that all parts have been uploaded, passing back
    // the collection of part etags. S3 will compose the final
    // object from the parts, in order
    var completeRequest = new CompleteMultipartUploadRequest
    {
        BucketName = bucketName,
        Key = objectKey,
        UploadId = initResponse.UploadId
    };

    completeRequest.AddPartETags(partResponses);
```

```
    await s3Client.CompleteMultipartUploadAsync(completeRequest);
}
catch (Exception e)
{
    Console.WriteLine($"Error during upload, {e.Message}");
    var abortRequest = new AbortMultipartUploadRequest
    {
        BucketName = bucketName,
        Key = objectKey,
        UploadId = initResponse.UploadId
    };

    await s3Client.AbortMultipartUploadAsync(abortRequest);
}
```

Caution   If you encounter errors with a multipart upload and abandon the process, be sure to call the AbortMultipartUpload API. S3 charges for the storage of parts that have been uploaded successfully until your code calls CompleteMultipartUpload to compose the final object, or you call AbortMultipartUpload to abandon and delete the uploaded parts.

The code in Listing 7-6 is straightforward, but when you add retries for parts the SDK's own retry handlers failed to process automatically, or consider adding threading to parallelize uploads, it can get more complicated. It also begs the question: Do you need to write your application to be aware of the size of objects so that it can select PutObject or multipart upload approaches? Is there an easier approach for those that want it? Enter the transfer utility.

The Transfer Utility

The transfer utility is a higher-level abstraction provided by the SDK (it's not part of S3's native API) that seamlessly handles the switch between PutObject and multipart upload approaches based on object size for you. It also handles threaded part uploads to maximize throughput, which your code can also configure in terms of threads, etc., to employ. You also retain the ability to set storage class, custom headers, part sizes, and more just as if you were using S3's API.

The transfer utility exists in the same NuGet package, AWSSDK.S3, so there's no extra dependency that your code needs to take. Listing 7-7 shows the same approach as Listing 7-6, but using the transfer utility.

Listing 7-7. Uploading a file using the transfer utility

```
// Assumes the following namespace has been declared
// using Amazon.S3.Transfer;
// fileToUpload is the local path of the file to be uploaded

var tu = new TransferUtility(s3Client);

// This example will use the filename object key.
await tu.UploadAsync(filePath, BucketName);

// Same example, but using a stream onto the file
using (var uploadStream
    = new FileStream(filePath, FileMode.Open, FileAccess.Read))
{
    await tu.UploadAsync(fileToUpload, bucketName, "object-key");
}
```

How easy is that?! The advantages don't stop there. The transfer utility can also upload entire folder hierarchies of files and will use the relative subfolder paths too as key prefixes, so the folder structure is mirrored. It can also download single objects or objects that share a key prefix to a folder (and again, the structure is retained). Listing 7-8 contains code snippets illustrating some of the other capabilities of the transfer utility.

Tip   Without realizing it, you've "seen" the transfer utility in action already in this and earlier chapters. Remember the PowerShell cmdlet `Write-S3Object` we've seen in several examples? It uses the transfer utility internally to achieve uploads of files and folders. Its companion, `Read-S3Object`, also uses the transfer utility to download files and folders. The same applies to the S3 support we've shown so far in Visual Studio.

Listing 7-8. Other capabilities of the transfer utility

```
// Assumes the following namespace has been declared
// using Amazon.S3.Transfer;

var s3Client = new AmazonS3Client();

var tu = new TransferUtility(s3Client);

// Recursively upload all files in a given folder hierarchy
// (supply name pattern and SearchOption parameters.
// to upload specific sets of files)
await tu.UploadDirectoryAsync(folderPath,
                                          bucketName);

// Alternate upload of specific files from folder hierarchy,
// additionally placing the files into a parent root prefix.
// Files will be placed under the common root prefix, and
// sub-prefixes, based on their relative location to the
// specified folder root.
var uploadFilesRequest
    = new TransferUtilityUploadDirectoryRequest
    {
        BucketName = bucketName,
        KeyPrefix = "common_root_prefix",
        Directory = folderPath,
        SearchPattern = "*.jpg",
        SearchOption = System.IO.SearchOption.AllDirectories
    };
await tu.UploadDirectoryAsync(uploadFilesRequest);

// Download a single object to 'outputFilePath'
await tu.DownloadAsync(outputFilePath, bucketName, objectKey);

// Download hierarchy to 'folder' output path
await tu.DownloadDirectoryAsync(bucketName, rootPrefix, folder);
```

Note   As with the multipart upload APIs, if an exception is triggered that ultimately causes uploads to fail, you need to signal to S3 that it should discard the parts involved in the failed attempt. However, you don't necessarily know if the SDK used multipart uploads vs. `PutObject` and won't have an upload ID. Instead, to abandon an upload, use the `AbortMultipartUploadsAsync` method on the `TransferUtility` object, passing the `DateTime` of a date *before which* all in-progress multipart uploads should be abandoned.

We recommend that unless you need some advanced feature supplied by the "raw" S3 APIs, you consider using the transfer utility in your application code and taking advantage of the simplicity it offers.

Presigned URLs

There are scenarios where you need to legitimately grant access to users outside of your organization to your buckets, either to read objects that your application has created or to upload some data that your application then makes use of. Presigned URLs are one approach that can be used to provide temporary access to external entities (applications, distributed services, actual people, etc.) to upload to or download from your otherwise private bucket without loosening permissions on your S3 resources by making buckets and objects public.

A presigned URL is a URL to an object in a bucket granting a specific action (GET, PUT, etc.). The URL to the object (which need not exist) contains security token information permitting the recipient of the URL to read or write the object, providing the account that created the URL also has relevant permissions to do the same on the object.

Note   The recipient of the URL can be another application, a component of a distributed application that you want to grant temporary access to, or an external entity such as a user. We frequently use presigned URLs to share files for external users to download.

Presigned URLs expire, so they are ideal for temporary access scenarios. When the security token in the URL expires, the object it referenced and the action granted are no longer available to the recipient. The maximum life span of a URL that you can request depends on the security credentials in use when you (or your application) create the URL.

URLs created under the scope of an IAM Instance Profile (e.g., from an application running on an EC2 instance) expire after six hours. If you obtained the credentials you are using from the Security Token Service (STS), the URL is valid for up to 36 hours. For an IAM user, the URL can be valid for up to a maximum of seven days. An important thing to note – when you generate a URL using credentials involving a temporary token, the URL will expire when the token expires, even if the period of validity you requested for the URL is longer.

You can create presigned URLs from within your application code using the SDK, from the PowerShell tools or the AWS CLI, or from within Visual Studio. Listing 7-9 shows a code snippet to create a presigned URL, valid for four days, to one of the images used in Chapter 4. You'll need to add the NuGet package AWSSDK.S3 (`www.nuget.org/packages/AWSSDK.S3/`) to your project to access this API.

Note   It may look like the code in Listing 7-9 is making a call to S3, but it's not; there is no API to create a presigned URL. The SDK handles all the work to generate the temporary token, etc., that's included in the URL. That's why there is no "Async" version of this method.

Listing 7-9. Creating a presigned URL using the AWS SDK for .NET

```
// code assumes the following namespaces declarations are
// at the top of your code file
// using Amazon;
// using Amazon.S3;
// using Amazon.S3.Model;

var s3Client = new AmazonS3Client(RegionEndpoint.USWest2);
var request = new GetPreSignedUrlRequest
{
    BucketName = "prodotnetonaws-chapter04",
    Key = "Figure0403.png",
    Expires = DateTime.UtcNow.AddDays(4),
```

```
    Verb = HttpVerb.GET // this is the default if not specified
};
```

```
request.ResponseHeaderOverrides.ContentType = "image/png";
request.ResponseHeaderOverrides.CacheControl = "No-cache";
```

```
var url = s3Client.GetPreSignedUrlRequest(request);
```

```
Console.WriteLine($"Presigned URL = {url}");
```

Listing 7-10 shows an example of the URL that this code generates. The entity that receives the URL can use it to download the object (provided they do so within four days of the URL being created, in this example).

Listing 7-10. Example of a presigned URL to an object

```
https://prodotnetonaws-chapter04.s3.us-west-2.amazonaws.com/Figure0403.
png?X-Amz-Expires=345600&response-cache-control=No-cache&response-
content-type=image%2Fpng&X-Amz-Algorithm=AWS4-HMAC-SHA256&X-Amz-
Credential=AKIATGRJY7TPIEXAMPLE/20210624/us-west-2/s3/aws4_request&X-Amz-
Date=20210624T035028Z&X-Amz-SignedHeaders=host&X-Amz-Signature=1aa2bbc8
eaccbfad2a6a48c359b493d6009417749eb66d5b64472c28562cffba
```

You can also generate a presigned URL to enable another entity to upload an object to a bucket in your account (the object does not need to already exist in the bucket). For this scenario, specify HttpVerb.PUT for the Verb property on the GetPresignedUrlRequest object. Then, the recipient of the URL can upload the object using a simple HTTPClient instance, shown in Listing 7-11.

Listing 7-11. Using a presigned URL to upload an object

```
// sample url to upload to object with key
// "object-from-presigned-url.dat" in bucket
// "prodotnetonaws-chapter07"
//
// https://prodotnetonaws-chapter07.s3.us-west-2.amazonaws.com/object-from-
presigned-url.dat?X-Amz-Expires=3600&X-Amz-Algorithm=AWS4-HMAC-SHA256&X-
Amz-Credential=AKIATGRJY7TPIEXAMPLE/20210629/us-west-2/s3/aws4_request&X-
Amz-Date=20210629T213245Z&X-Amz-SignedHeaders=host&X-Amz-Signature=e9f6e404
6e6db6e0011582633b3f2dc75c1b2dc06685a1d867f92bf803c6deee
```

```
// generate some sample data to upload
var rnd = new System.Random();
var testData = new byte[1024];
for (var i = 0; i < testData.Length; i++)
{
    testData[i] = (byte)rnd.Next(255);
}

using (var httpClient = new HttpClient())
{
    var content = new ByteArrayContent(testData);
    await httpClient.PutAsync(presignedUrl, content);
}
```

Now that we have seen how to upload content to use with our applications, either from tools such as Visual Studio or PowerShell, and from within our applications using the SDK to S3, let's finish this chapter with a look at how we can use Amazon CloudFront, a content-delivery network (CDN) service, in conjunction with S3 to serve data from our buckets, such as static website assets, to our application's end users.

CDNs and Amazon CloudFront

At the beginning of this chapter, we briefly touched on whether buckets, and/or the objects they contain, should be public when you need to share the objects across applications or serve static assets needed by applications (e.g., image files, stylesheets, and scripts for web applications).

As we've just seen, you can use presigned URLs to provide temporary access, but because they expire, they are not suitable for long-term sharing. When you're working on a web application and want to use an S3 bucket to hold static assets, the simplest approach is to first make those specific objects publicly readable. Then, in your application code, you reference the assets by URL. For example, to access a stylesheet named styles.css in a bucket in the US West (Oregon) region that has the name *my-static-assets*, your application would use the following URL: https://my-static-asssets.s3.us-west-2.amazonaws.com/styles.css.

While this works, it's not optimal for users who are not local to the US West (Oregon) region. Let's say your application has users in Australia, or in Europe. They will see much higher latencies as the requests from the application for resources route to the US west coast data centers. It's also not optimal from a security perspective. Now you need to remain hyper-vigilant of which objects should be public versus private, or use multiple buckets to separate them. One slip and an object that should be private may become public - possibly without you noticing for some time.

Amazon CloudFront is a service designed to speed up distribution of web content (both static and dynamic) to your application's end users. CloudFront employs a global collection of *edge locations*, or *Point of Presence (PoP)*, servers. These servers receive requests for objects, based on the location that has the lowest latency for the requester. If the edge location has the object cached, then CloudFront serves the object from the edge location, optimizing latency. If the edge location does not currently have the object cached, or the cached object has expired, CloudFront requests the object from the S3 bucket and caches it for the next request, before serving it to the requester. You have control over how long CloudFront keeps the objects in the edge location caches.

Your application accesses the assets it needs via a CloudFront *distribution*, for which the S3 bucket is known as the *origin* (you can also use an HTTP server, in addition to a bucket). Distributions have a CloudFront-generated domain name associated with them, or you can use your own domain. Within your application, you reference the asset using the domain name path, not the S3 bucket name and object key shown earlier (in the example using styles.css). You can also configure the distribution and bucket so that **all** resource requests must come via CloudFront and not via direct URLs to the S3 bucket and objects. This gives you an additional level of security as the objects in the bucket can remain private.

Using S3 and CloudFront with Your Application

To conclude this chapter, let's look at an example of serving static web assets for an ASP. NET Core application from an S3 bucket, fronted by a CloudFront distribution. You'll find these assets in the *wwwroot* folder of a typical ASP.NET Core project.

For this example, we'll keep the assets in the bucket private and configure CloudFront and the bucket so that only requests that come from CloudFront can get access to the objects, using an *origin access identity*. To set up the resources, we'll use the AWS Cloud Development Kit (CDK), although you could also use the management consoles for S3 and CloudFront if you wish.

Listing 7-12 contains the code you can use in a CDK application to create the required resources. To use it, create a new CDK sample application with the command `cdk init app --language csharp` (we named our sample **WebAssets**), then modify the generated class for the stack in the sample (in the file **WebAssetsStack.cs**) with the code in the listing.

Listing 7-12. Resource construction using the CDK's .NET bindings

```
// These namespaces are in the Amazon.CDK package
using Amazon.CDK;
using Amazon.CDK.AWS.IAM;

// Used to represent the desired state
Using Constructs;

// Add the Amazon.CDK.AWS.S3 and Amazon.CDK.AWS.CloudFront
// NuGet packages for these resources
using Amazon.CDK.AWS.S3;
using Amazon.CDK.AWS.CloudFront;

namespace WebAssets
{
  public class WebAssetsStack : Stack
  {
    internal WebAssetsStack(Construct scope,
                            string id,
                            IStackProps props = null)
          : base(scope, id, props)
    {
      var cloudfrontOAI
        = new OriginAccessIdentity(this, "cloudfront-OAI");

      var bucketProps = new BucketProps
      {
          PublicReadAccess = false,
          BlockPublicAccess = BlockPublicAccess.BLOCK_ALL,
          // NOT recommended for production code!
          RemovalPolicy = RemovalPolicy.DESTROY,
```

```
      // NOT recommended for production code!
      AutoDeleteObjects = true
};

var originBucket
  = new Bucket(this, "originBucket", bucketProps);

// Grant access to CloudFront to access the bucket
var policyProps = new PolicyStatementProps
{
  Actions = new [] { "s3:GetObject" },
  Resources = new []
  {
    originBucket.ArnForObjects("*")
  },
  Principals = new []
  {
    new CanonicalUserPrincipal
    (
      cloudfrontOAI.
        CloudFrontOriginAccessIdentityS3CanonicalUserId
    )
  }
});

originBucket.AddToResourcePolicy
(
    new PolicyStatement(policyProps)
);

// CloudFront distribution fronting the bucket.
var distProps = new CloudFrontWebDistributionProps
{
  OriginConfigs = new []
  {
    new SourceConfiguration
    {
```

```
      S3OriginSource = new S3OriginConfig
      {
        S3BucketSource = originBucket,
        OriginAccessIdentity = cloudfrontOAI
      },
      Behaviors = new []
      {
        new Behavior
        {
          IsDefaultBehavior = true,
          Compress = true,
          AllowedMethods
            = CloudFrontAllowedMethods.GET_HEAD_OPTIONS
        }
      }
    }
  },
  // Require HTTPS between viewer and CloudFront;
  // CloudFront to origin will use HTTP but could
  // also be set to require HTTPS
  ViewerProtocolPolicy
    = ViewerProtocolPolicy.REDIRECT_TO_HTTPS
};

var distribution
  = new CloudFrontWebDistribution(this,
                               "SiteDistribution",
                               distProps);

new CfnOutput(this, "Bucket", new CfnOutputProps
{
  Value = originBucket.BucketName
});
new CfnOutput(this, "Domain", new CfnOutputProps
{
  Value = $"http://{distribution.DistributionDomainName}"
```

```
        });
    }
  }
}
```

Next, we deploy the stack that will create the resources. At a command-line prompt, change directory to the folder containing the *cdk.json* file for the sample CDK application and run the command cdk deploy.

Note   Before deployment, update the sample application's Program.cs file to set the region and account where you want the stack to deploy (this is known as the stack's *environment*). For more details on how to do this for CDK applications, see https://docs.aws.amazon.com/cdk/latest/guide/environments.html.

When stack deployment completes, the name of the bucket that should contain the artifacts and the automatically generated domain name for the distribution (we've chosen not to use our own domain name) are output. Make a note of these (Listing 7-13 shows examples) as we'll need them shortly.

Listing 7-13. Example CDK output of bucket and distribution domains

```
C:\> cdk deploy
WebAssetsStack: deploying...

...
Outputs:
WebAssetsStack.Bucket = webassetsstack-originbucket7cdc61a2-...
WebAssetsStack.Domain = https://d2ens40cdbtt0b.cloudfront.net
```

First, we need to upload the assets for our web application. We're using a sample ASP.NET Core application, generated from the *webapp* template (dotnet new webapp). The assets are in the project's *wwwroot* subfolder, and to upload, we'll use the AWS Tools for PowerShell's Write-S3Object cmdlet that we used earlier in this chapter. Listing 7-14 shows the commands (in a real-world setup, build automation would perform this upload).

Listing 7-14. Uploading the web application assets to the bucket

```
C:\> cd wwwroot
C:\> Write-S3Object -BucketName ⏎
webassetsstack-originbucket7cdc61a2-2hzc7vraotz7 ⏎
-Folder . -KeyPrefix / -Recurse
```

We can test the distribution is working by simply attempting to access files we've uploaded using both the distribution's domain URL and an S3 URL in a browser. First, let's try using the distribution URL to serve the application's *site.css* file, shown in Figure 7-3.

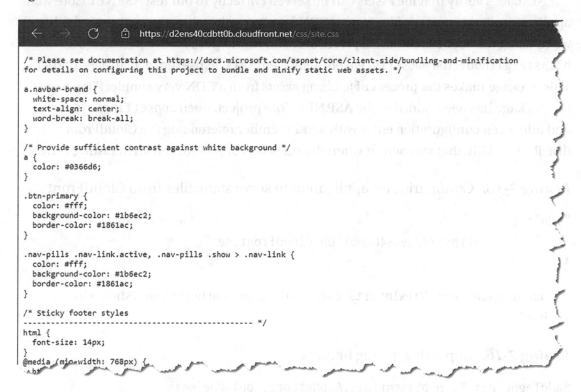

Figure 7-3. *Accessing assets via the distribution URL*

Next, let's try and access the same file via a URL using the bucket name and object key path – this should fail, as we denied public access to the bucket. As Figure 7-4 shows, this is indeed the case.

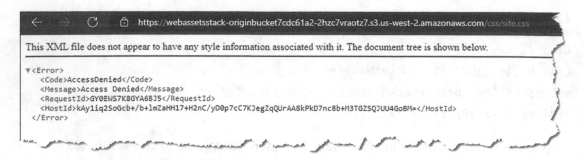

Figure 7-4. *Expected failure accessing assets via S3 URL*

Next, let's verify that the assets can be served correctly to our test ASP.NET Core web application. To serve static files from a CDN location rather than the wwwroot subfolder, we're using the **WebEssentials.AspNetCore.CdnTagHelpers** NuGet package (see https://github.com/madskristensen/WebEssentials.AspNetCore.CdnTagHelpers). This package makes the process of fetching assets from a CDN very simple. First, once the package has been added to the ASP.NET Core project, open appsettings.json and add a cdn configuration entry with a url member referencing the CloudFront distribution URL that was output when the stack was deployed, shown in Listing 7-15.

Listing 7-15. Configuring an application to serve static files from CloudFront

```
"cdn": {
    "url": "https://d2ens40cdbtt0b.cloudfront.net"
}
```

Then, update the _ViewImports.cshtml file to add the tag helpers, shown in Listing 7-16.

Listing 7-16. Importing the tag helpers

```
@addTagHelper *, WebEssentials.AspNetCore.CdnTagHelpers
```

Figure 7-5 shows the application running locally on our machine, pulling assets from the bucket via the CloudFront distribution URL, which you can see in the developer tools window.

Figure 7-5. *Running application with assets served from CloudFront*

The example showed how you can serve web application assets from an S3 bucket, keeping both the bucket and objects private, and at the same time ensure that users who are in more remote locations do not see excessive latency by the use of edge location servers in CloudFront.

Summary

This concludes our look at object storage using Amazon S3. We have gone over several ways in which you can interact with S3 objects as well as how Amazon CloudFront, AWS' content-delivery network, can be used as a way to share these objects in a geographically disbursed manner to increase responsiveness. It's time to look at another aspect of data storage – databases – beginning with Microsoft SQL Server and how you can run it on AWS.

CHAPTER 8

Microsoft SQL Server

You have just spent some time going over object storage and Amazon Simple Storage Service (S3). This may have been a new approach to storage for you, as .NET developers tend to be more familiar with the concept of file-based storage. In this chapter, we are going to return to more "standard" .NET development approaches and talk about one of the most common .NET data persistence approaches around, that of storing data in Microsoft SQL Server.

We will go over the two different ways in which you can run Microsoft SQL Server on AWS. The first, unmanaged, means that AWS will not be managing SQL Server for you. Instead, you have full control over the software just as you would if you were running the software on your own hardware. The managed offering is when AWS manages SQL Server for you; all you need to do is to interact with the database without having to worry about any of the day-to-day tasks. Let's start by taking a look at using an unmanaged SQL Server.

Unmanaged SQL Server on EC2

The title of this section makes it seem like a pretty simple process. I want to manage my own instance so I will simply figure out the appropriately sized EC2 AMI and install SQL Server, and voilà, I have an unmanaged SQL Server instance. I even can use an EC2 AMI with SQL Server already installed. Unfortunately, it is not always that simple. Why? Because of the complicated way in which Microsoft licenses SQL Server.

In the Introduction section, we recommended that you should download and install the full-featured free edition, SQL Server 2019 Developer. This version of SQL Server is licensed for use as a development and test database in a nonproduction environment. Fortunately, you are able to do the same on EC2, and we will go over that in a bit. If, however, you were thinking about running your current versions of SQL Server and using your current set of licenses on EC2, then there are some rules you should know about. If you don't care about SQL Server licenses or are planning on purchasing the licenses with the AMIs that you'll use, then feel free to skip the next section.

303

© William Penberthy and Steve Roberts 2023
W. Penberthy and S. Roberts, *Pro .NET on Amazon Web Services*,
https://doi.org/10.1007/978-1-4842-8907-5_8

Microsoft SQL Server Licensing Limitations on EC2

There are several different variables that affect your SQL Server licensing on EC2. The first of these is whether you own SQL Server licenses that have active Microsoft Software Assurance (SA). If you have SA, then you can bring those licenses to a default (shared) tenant EC2 through the License Mobility benefits. When using License Mobility, SQL Server is licensed by virtual core (vCPU) count, and while there are a limited set of cores and memory combinations, there is the ability to Optimize CPU options when you may need more memory and lower number of cores than are available by default.

Note   You can get complete information on License Mobility including eligibility requirements and how to sign up at *https://aws.amazon.com/windows/resources/licensemobility/*.

You can get more information on how Microsoft licensing works on AWS at *https://aws.amazon.com/windows/resources/licensing/*.

Information on Optimize CPU options, where you can minimize the number of cores used while maximizing memory, can be found at https://docs.aws.amazon.com/AWSEC2/latest/UserGuide/instance-optimize-cpu.html.

For those of you that do not have active SA, you will be able to bring those SQL Server licenses to EC2 dedicated infrastructure if the licenses are purchased prior to 10/1/2019 and are not upgraded to any versions of SQL Server released after 10/1/2019 (SQL Server 2019+). The key part is that you need to use dedicated hosts rather than shared hosts, but AWS recommends that you use dedicated hosts over dedicated instances because a host allows you to manage instance and license placement. This ability helps fulfill another Microsoft licensing requirement – the assignment rules that require a license without SA to remain assigned to the same physical server for at least 90 days. Using dedicated hosts also allows you to license SQL Enterprise at the physical level, which is generally less expensive as well as provides significant virtualization benefits.

We have mentioned *shared* and *dedicated* without having yet provided any context around those phrases. These two terms talk about tenancy – basically what customers are running on a set of given hardware. With the default, shared tenancy, multiple customers will be running on the same actual pieces of hardware, even though they don't interact with one another. In this case, the hypervisor is managing the virtualization of all the different components: memory, CPU, storage, etc. As customers start new EC2 instances, AWS takes that defined slice, figures out where it fits best in the available hardware, and then uses that capacity to run the instance.

Dedicated tenancy, on the other hand, means that your EC2 instances are run on hardware specifically dedicated to your account. Obviously, since this is not the default approach where AWS tries to eke out every possible bit of processing, memory, and storage utilization, there are additional charges for dedicated tenancy. One obvious reason for taking this more expensive approach is for the "bring your own license" (BYOL) licensing mentioned earlier, but there may also be regulatory compliance requirements or business needs where it would make more sense to use dedicated tenancy.

When looking at dedicated tenancy, there are two different options. The first is *dedicated hosts*. In this case, you purchase an entire physical host from AWS, and that host is billed to you on the same basis as your EC2 instances. Once you buy the host, you can spin up as many EC2 instances on the host as desired, at no extra cost. However, there are a few caveats to this approach. The first is that you may not mix EC2 instance families (types) on the same dedicated host. You can use multiple sizes of the same instance, say, by creating 4 x r5.4xlarge and 4 x r5.2xlarge on the same host (instance family is r5), but you cannot, for example, mix r5 and c5 instances on the same host.

The other option for dedicated tenancy is *dedicated instances*. With these, you gain the benefit of having separate hosts, but you don't pay for the entire host all at once. This allows you to not worry about managing the capacity of the hosts, but it does mean that you will be charged a higher rate for the instances.

Note   There is a lot more to dedicated hosts and instances than we are going to talk about here. You can go to `https://docs.amazonaws.cn/en_us/AWSEC2/latest/UserGuide/dedicated-hosts-overview.html` for more information on dedicated hosts or get more information about dedicated instances at `https://docs.amazonaws.cn/en_us/AWSEC2/latest/UserGuide/dedicated-instance.html`.

Using SQL Server on EC2

Using license-included SQL Server, where AWS charges you for the SQL Server license, can be as simple as creating an EC2 instance based upon an AMI that comes with a pre-installed version of SQL Server. Figure 8-1 shows some of these AMIs after performing a search for "SQL Server."

Figure 8-1. *Some of the EC2 AMIs with SQL Server*

As the image shows, there are (at the time of this writing) 15 "Quick Start" AMIs available where SQL Server has been pre-installed in the AMI. A closer examination of those AMIs, however, shows that there are only two different types of SQL Server available from AWS: *Standard* and *Enterprise*. This means that Developer, Web, and Express editions are not available as part of an AWS AMI.

Thankfully, however, there are other AMI sources. The main one of these alternative sources is the AWS Marketplace where you will find an additional 270+ AMIs that can be used that includes both Web and Express editions of SQL Server. A search for AMIs using "sql server express" will return more than 30 AMIs in the Marketplace and more than 100 in the Community AMIs group.

You are probably wondering how there could be >30 AMIs for SQL Server Express. This is because there are different creators as well as different combinations of operating systems, such as Amazon Linux 2, Ubuntu Server 20, Windows Server 2012, 2016, and 2019 as well as different versions of SQL Server Express such as SQL Server 2016, 2017, and 2019. Other search results may include additional software, such as the ESRI ArcGIS shown in Figure 8-2. All these different AMIs indicate examples of EC2 instances that you can use for creating your own running instances.

Figure 8-2. Additional packages in AWS Marketplace with SQL Server Express

Creating a SQL Server AMI is a similar process that you used for the EC2 instance that you created in Chapter 4. In this case, we will use the marketplace-provided AMI entitled "Microsoft SQL Server 2019 Express on Windows Server 2019." To do so requires that you find that particular AMI by either searching or scrolling through and select the **Select** button. This will bring up a pop-up screen that will provide some information about pricing, and clicking through that will bring you to the "Choose an instance type" screen.

Note   At the time of this writing, there are no instances in the *Free Tier* that have SQL Server installed, so following this process may lead to charges on the account that you are using when working through the book.

You will see that there are some choices that are not available; select one of the available types and proceed to create your EC2 instance as shown in Chapter 4 up through *Step 6: Configure Security Instance* where you will need to add a new rule that will allow for external connections to SQL Server. You do this by clicking the **Add Rule** button to add a row and then selecting **MS SQL** from the drop-down in the *Type* column. This will populate values in the rest of the row as shown in Figure 8-3, which also shows that all rows have had the *Source* set to use **My IP** to ensure that only connections from this machine are able to connect to both the Windows and SQL Server. Of course, you would not normally allow this as you would secure your database from the Internet, but that would make it more difficult for us to run through the following steps.

Figure 8-3. *Configuring a SQL Server instance*

Continue to go through the rest of the setup until you get the launch status screen as shown in Figure 8-4.

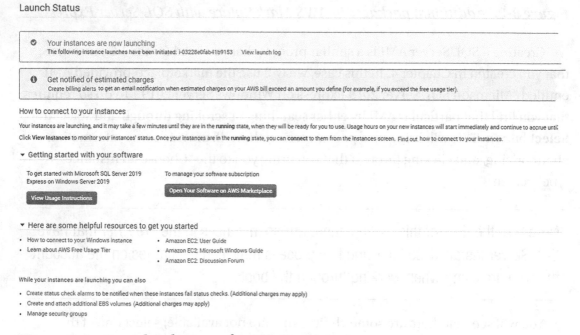

Figure 8-4. *Completed set up of a SQL Server instance*

Once your EC2 instance is running, remote desktop into the instance (refer to Chapter 4 as necessary for instructions). Once you have remotely accessed the server, your next step will be to go into SQL Server Management Studio (SSMS) and make some configuration changes. These changes are necessary because you do not have any access to the installation process for SQL Server, so steps that you would normally configure during installation will instead have to be done post installation.

Once SSMS is open, connect to the local database. The connect value should already be filled out for you, and you will be connecting to the server using Windows authentication. Currently, these AMIs install SQL Server so that they allow Windows Authentication as the only way to log in. Our first step will be changing that so that SQL Server logins can also authenticate. This is important so that we don't have to worry about setting up Windows domains or managing Windows-based authentication – that is a completely different book!

Since SQL Server was installed supporting only Windows authentication (one of those things you could change during installation), you will need to make a change to the SQL Server instance itself. To do this, ensure that you are connected to the local SQL Server, right-click on the instance name, and select the *Properties* menu item. Select **Security** under the *Select a page* section and select the *SQL Server and Windows Authentication mode* option as shown in Figure 8-5.

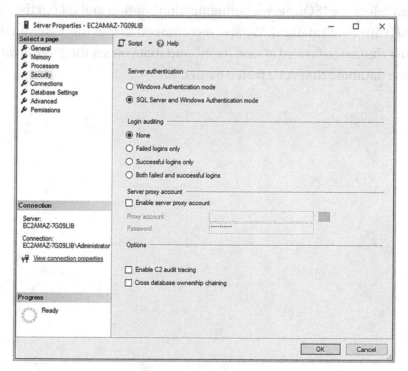

Figure 8-5. *Turning on SQL Server Authentication*

Clicking the **OK** button will save all your changes. You will also get a pop-up message telling you that "Some of your configuration changes will not take effect until SQL Server is restarted." We will take that action after we create our initial database and then configure the user that we will use to access that designated database in SQL Server.

As mentioned, we will first create the database that we will use when interacting with this SQL Server instance. While not completely necessary, by doing so, we will ensure that only a single database running on the server can be accessed, a much better security arrangement than just giving full access to a machine outside of the network, even if access from other machines is limited by the Security Group that we configured earlier when creating the EC2 instance. Since all we are looking to do is to create the database itself, right-click on **Databases** in the SSMS Object Explorer and select the *New Database...* option. When the New Database window opens, you can add a *Database name* (we used ProDotNetOnAWS), accept all other default options, and click the **OK** button to create the empty database.

While still in SSMS, right-click on the **Security** – **Logins** folder in Object Explorer and select *New Login*. This will bring up the Create login screen, shown in Figure 8-6, where you can select the "SQL Server authentication" option and fill out the *Login name* and *Password* (with confirmation). We also recommend that in this case you unselect the "User must change password at next login" and that you set the *Default database* selection to the database that you created earlier.

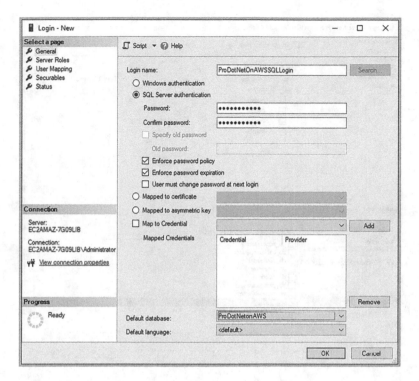

Figure 8-6. *Creating a new SQL Server login*

Next, click on the **User Mapping** link. You should see a list of databases, including master, model, msdb, tempdb, and the database that you just created. Click the check box next to the new database and ensure that the db_owner check box is checked, as shown in Figure 8-7, and then click the **OK** button.

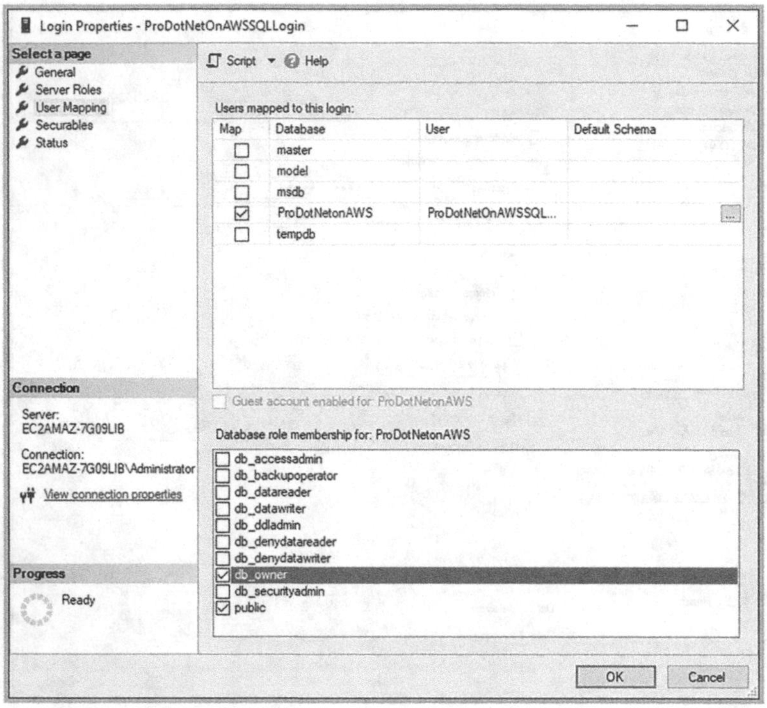

Figure 8-7. *Setting up SQL Server user*

So far you have created the EC2 instance with SQL Server, updated SQL Server to allow for access via SQL Authentication, created the initial database, and then created the initial user. The last step before testing it from an external system is to restart the SQL Server service – remember, we need to do this because we performed that SQL Server reconfiguration.

The easiest way to restart the database is to open a Windows PowerShell window on the server and run the following commands:

```
PS C:\Users\Administrator> net stop mssqlserver
The SQL Server (MSSQLSERVER) service is stopping..
The SQL Server (MSSQLSERVER) service was stopped successfully.

PS C:\Users\Administrator> net start mssqlserver
The SQL Server (MSSQLSERVER) service is starting...
The SQL Server (MSSQLSERVER) service was started successfully.

PS C:\Users\Administrator>
```

Now that the service has restarted, you can try and access it from your local machine using your local SQL Server Management Studio. Refer back to the instructions in the Introduction if you do not have SSMS installed.

To connect from your local machine, first, start SSMS and select **Connect ➤ Database Engine**. This will bring up the *Connect to Server* dialogue box. The first value you must provide is the **Server name**, which is available from the AWS console under the EC2 service. Once you go into the EC2 instance details, you will see the instance summary much like Figure 8-8 where the value shown in the *Public IPv4 DNS* field is the value that you should use when connecting to the SQL Server. Remember, you can click the boxes icon on the left of the value to copy to your clipboard.

Figure 8-8. *Getting the server name from the EC2 console*

Once you have the server name, paste it into your Server name field. This will make sure that SSMS will call the correct machine. We now must make sure that we are calling the correct port number. To do this, append ", 1433" after the server name you already pasted so that your entire entry looks similar to `ec2-somevaluehere.us-east-2.compute.amazonaws.com, 1433`.

Next, ensure that you have configured the connection to use SQL Server Authentication, and then enter the username and password that you just created on the server as shown in Figure 8-9 and click **Connect**. After several seconds, your instance should appear in the SSMS Object Explorer pane.

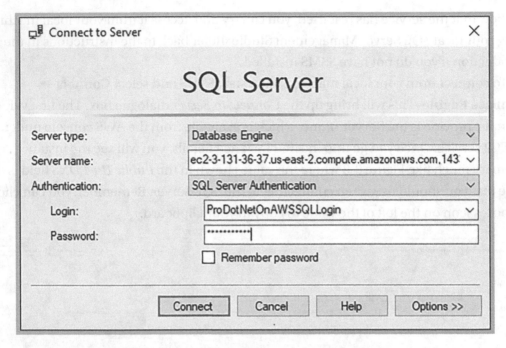

Figure 8-9. *Connecting to the EC2 database from local machine*

Missing any of the steps listed previously will ensure that you are not able to reach the SQL Server from your local machine. There are two main reasons for failure:

1. **Unable to reach the SQL Server** – If you get an error message that suggests that you are unable to reach the SQL Server, then there are several different possibilities. The first is that you did not correctly enter the server name and port number in the Server name field of the login screen. Double-check these against the EC2 console. For example, stopping and starting the EC2 instance will generally lead to a new DNS name being assigned to the EC2 instance – which would mean saved connections may not be correct. The second possibility is that there is something in your instance configuration that is disallowing access. Check security groups and other areas that may limit access. It is also possible that your IP address is different than what it was when you configured your security group during setup.

2. **Unable to log in to SQL Server** – These errors occur when the login that you are using is incorrect, invalid, or may have a data problem. Validate that the user is set up, active, and has access to at least one database with an appropriate database role.

The most common problem will be an inability to access the SQL Server. Make sure to review the preceding steps if you are still unable to access SQL Server.

Now that you have gone through all of the work to set up your own custom SQL Server, we will show you a much easier to way to manage a SQL Server database.

Managed Services, SQL Server on Amazon RDS

SQL Server running on EC2 allows you complete control over the database installation and configuration. That may be invaluable for some people, but for others, it will require too much administration, maintenance, and operational support. This is where Amazon Relational Database Service (RDS) comes in. With RDS, you can set up, operate, and scale a relational database in the cloud without having to worry about provisioning the instance, or setting up/installing the database server, or patching the operating system or database, or even setting up backups. All of that is done for you. There are six different relational database engines that you can use as part of Amazon RDS, with the one that we care about right now being Microsoft SQL Server. We will go over the remaining RDS database engines in Chapter 9.

There are many advantages of RDS over the "roll-your-own" approach. We already mentioned that there are much less installation, configuration, and maintenance. RDS also comes with software license included, so there is no need to worry about SQL Server license management. Another advantage to using RDS includes your ability to scale up or down your database's access to compute or storage resources with a few clicks of the mouse without any downtime. You can also provision a multi-Availability Zone database instance, which means that RDS will manage the synchronous replication of data to a standby instance in a different Availability Zone. The final benefit is that in many instances, it may be less expensive than running your own server because you only pay for the resources that you use rather than an entire EC2 instance.

At this point, the easiest way to go over RDS SQL Server will be to create one in the console. The first step is to log in and go to the *Amazon RDS* service by searching or by selecting it from the services drop-down. This should bring you to the landing page as shown in Figure 8-10.

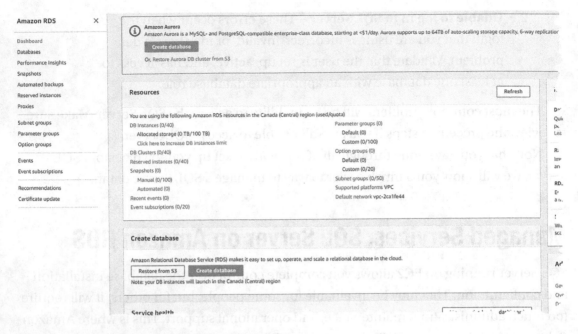

Figure 8-10. *Amazon RDS landing page*

Clicking one of the **Create database** buttons starts the wizard. The first section of the wizard is the Choose a database creation method option as shown in Figure 8-11.

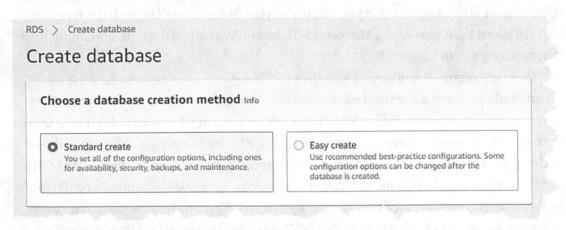

Figure 8-11. *Selecting the database creation method when creating an RDS database*

There are two different database creation methods that you can use when using the console: *Standard create* and *Easy create*. The standard approach allows you to set all the configuration options, including availability, security, backup, and maintenance. The easy approach takes all those decisions out of your hands and provides configurations based upon AWS' best practices. In this case, so we can see all the different options, select to perform a *Standard create*.

The next section, under the creation method, is the Engine Options. This is where you choose the RDS database engine that you wish to work with as shown in Figure 8-12.

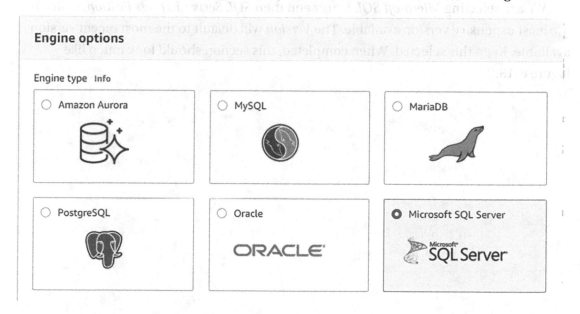

Figure 8-12. *RDS database engine options*

Selecting Microsoft SQL Server will give you *a Database management type* selection, update the list of editions that you can choose, as well as provide you a drop-down list that you can use to select the version.

There are two options for the management type: *Amazon RDS,* where the service supplies the Amazon Machine Image (AMI) and database software, and *RDS Custom*, where you are responsible for uploading your own installation files and patches to Amazon S3. We will stay with the default selection: Amazon RDS.

You have four editions of SQL Server from which you can select:

- **SQL Server Express Edition** – Free of licensing fees, this edition is affordable and supports databases up to 10GB.

- **SQL Server Web Edition** – This edition can only be used to support public and Internet-accessible systems and services.

- **SQL Server Standard Edition** – An edition of SQL Server that can be used to support any kind of system.

- **SQL Server Enterprise Edition** – Ideal choice for those companies that need high-end capabilities.

We are selecting *Microsoft SQL Server* and then *SQL Server Express Edition*, which is the least expensive version available. The *Version* will default to the most recent version available. Keep this selected. When completed, this section should look much like Figure 8-13.

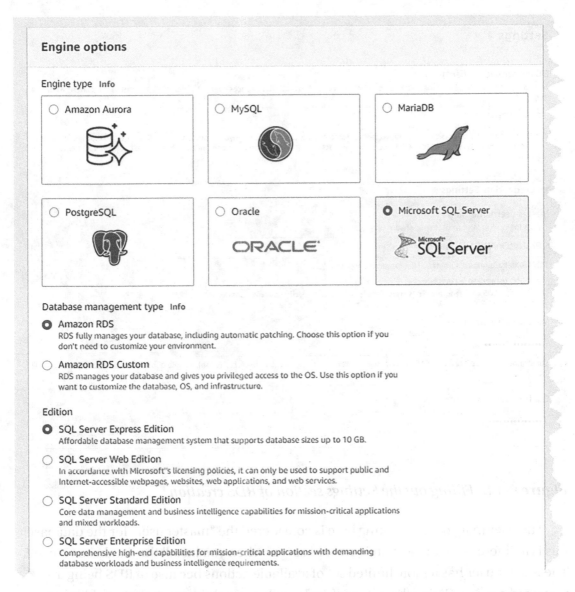

Figure 8-13. *RDS selection screen*

The next section asks you to provide the *settings*. The first of these settings is the **DB instance identifier** where you define a name for the instance, as well as **Credentials settings** for the master user of the database as shown in Figure 8-14.

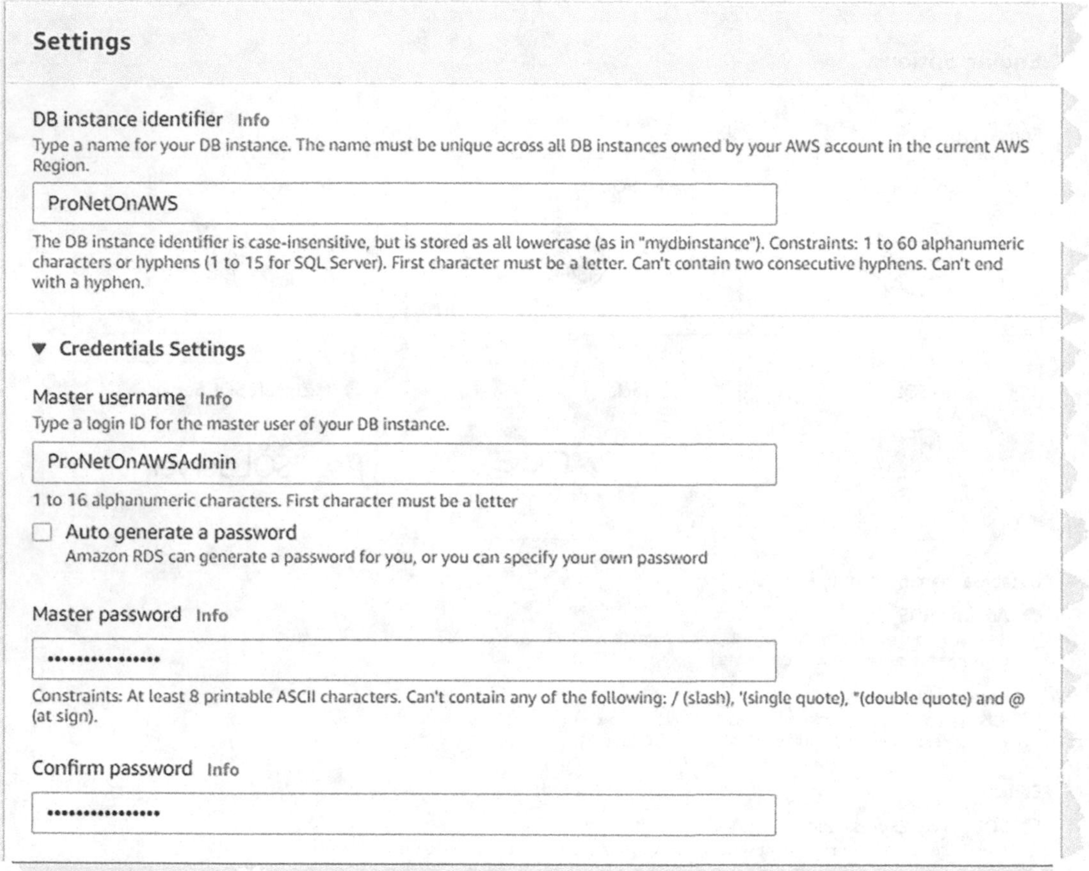

Settings

DB instance identifier   Info

Type a name for your DB instance. The name must be unique across all DB instances owned by your AWS account in the current AWS Region.

```
ProNetOnAWS
```

The DB instance identifier is case-insensitive, but is stored as all lowercase (as in "mydbinstance"). Constraints: 1 to 60 alphanumeric characters or hyphens (1 to 15 for SQL Server). First character must be a letter. Can't contain two consecutive hyphens. Can't end with a hyphen.

▼ **Credentials Settings**

Master username   Info

Type a login ID for the master user of your DB instance.

```
ProNetOnAWSAdmin
```

1 to 16 alphanumeric characters. First character must be a letter

☐ Auto generate a password
    Amazon RDS can generate a password for you, or you can specify your own password

Master password   Info

```
••••••••••••••••
```

Constraints: At least 8 printable ASCII characters. Can't contain any of the following: / (slash), '(single quote), "(double quote) and @ (at sign).

Confirm password   Info

```
••••••••••••••••
```

Figure 8-14. *Filling out the Settings section of RDS creation*

The user that you are creating here is considered the "master user" for the database; this is a different user type than is created as "sa" when you install the database yourself. The master user has a more limited set of available actions because of RDS being a managed service. Giving the full set of "sa" privileges to the master user would mean that AWS is giving up the control that it needs for ensuring the validity and correctness of the service that it is managing. You need to enter the **Master username** and a **Master Password** (with confirmation). You also have the option to have AWS auto-generate a secure password for you; if you take this option, you will be presented with your generated password once the database instance has completed setup. You will only be able to access that password that one time!

The next section is the *DB instance class*. This is where you select the type of system on which the database instance will be run, including the number of virtual CPUs as well as the available RAM. The available choices will change based upon the database edition that you choose. Using the Express edition in the us-east-2 region, for example, means that you will have only **db.t3** instances available for selection, as shown in Figure 8-15.

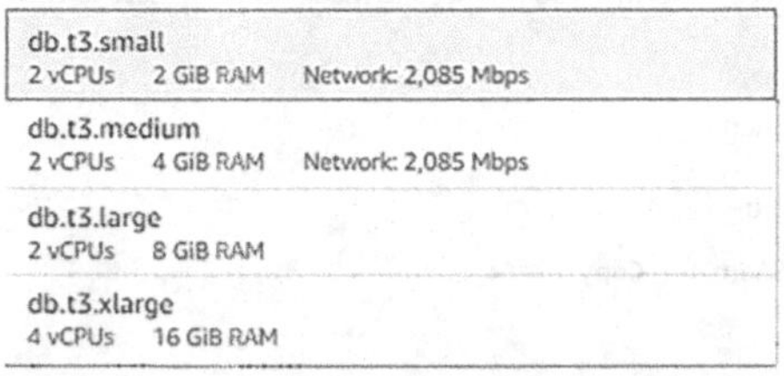

Figure 8-15. *Database instance class drop-down for SQL Server Express Edition*

As you go down the database creation screen, you will see additional sections, such as **Storage**, where you identify the type and size of allocated on-disk storage, **Connectivity**, where you determine the VPC in which the database will run, VPC security groups, or Availability Zone, and whether you wish to enable **Microsoft SQL Server Windows Authentication**. There are also an **Additional configuration** section that has been minimized and an **Estimated monthly costs** section that provides insight on how much your current configuration would cost per month. We recommend that at this point you accept the defaults of all of the remaining configurations and click the *Create database* button at the bottom of the page.

After the entries on the page are validated and submitted, you will be taken back to the database list screen where you will see the database that you just created in a "Creating" status. At the top of the list, as shown in Figure 8-16, is a blue area that contains a "Creating database" message on the left and a *View credential details* button on the right.

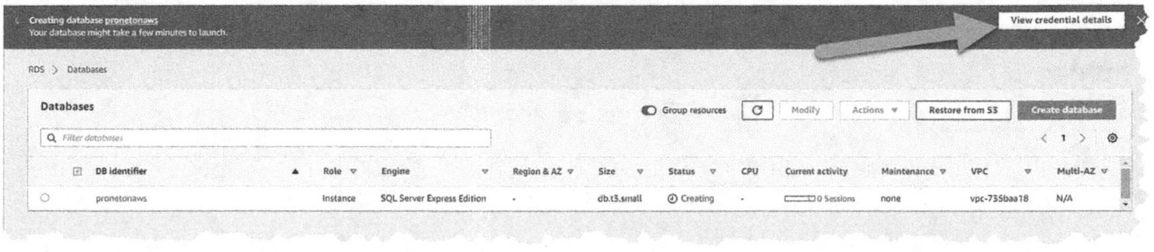

Figure 8-16. *Creating database banner with button*

Clicking the button in the banner will pop up a window with the username and password in plain text as shown in Figure 8-17.

Password for your database pronetonaws	✕
This is the only time you will be able to view this password. Copy and save the password for your reference, otherwise you will need to modify the database to change it.	
Master username	
ProNetOnAWSAdmin	
Master password	
ProNetOnAWSAdmin Copy	
	Close

Figure 8-17. *Display of Master username and password*

As is mentioned in the top section of the popup, this is the only time that you will be able to view the password for your master user. This may not be a big deal if you created the password yourself, but if you allowed AWS to auto-generate your password, then this is a bigger deal because this is the **only** time you will be able to see that password. Click the *copy* button to copy the password to your clipboard. Refreshing the Databases list page will remove the blue banner and the button and will result in you no longer having access to the password, so be careful!

Once your database has become *Available,* you can click on the *DB identifier* to go to the details. The database details page has a **Summary** section at the top and a series of tabs, including *Connectivity & security, Monitoring, Logs & events, Configuration, Maintenance & backups,* and *Tags.* Let us first take a look at the *Connectivity & security* tab.

This tab has four subsections. The first subsection is also called Connectivity & security and is shown in Figure 8-18.

Figure 8-18. *Connectivity & security section*

There are four major areas of data. The first, marked in Figure 8-18 as **1**, is the endpoint and port. These values provide the information necessary to be able to reach the database – what you would put in your connection string or into SQL Server Management Studio so you can access the database. The *Networking* section, marked as **2**, provides details around the VPC, Subnet group, and Subnets. The last section, *Security* (marked as **3**), provides information about the VPC security groups and the certificate. There is one other section, marked as **4**, that shows whether the instance is publicly accessible. Your instance will currently (because it is the initial setting) be marked as NOT publicly accessible, which means that there is no IP address assigned to the database instance so EC2 instances or other devices outside of the VPC will not be able to connect.

The next subsection within this tab is the **Security group rules**, of which there may be some created based upon the rules within your default VPC. Security groups are used to control the access that traffic has in and out of the RDS instance. There are two major types of security groups:

- **VPC security groups** – Controls access to a DB instance inside a VPC. Only resources within the VPC can be assigned a VPC security group.

- **DB security groups** – These are used with DB instances that are not within a VPC. Each security group allows a source to access that DB instance. These groups are part of an RDS instance. This type of security group is used much less than are VPC security groups.

The last two sections on this screen are your **Replication** settings, where you can view any SQL Server replication rules that may be configured, and **IAM roles** that have been assigned to this server. These IAM roles are especially useful when other AWS services will be accessing the instance.

Making an RDS SQL Server Instance Accessible from Outside the VPC

By default, network access is disabled for an RDS DB instance. Those looking to access this data from outside the instance's VPC will need to configure several additional areas to allow connection requests from outside VPC. The first of these changes is to set the database to be publicly accessible. To do this, go into the RDS console, select the RDS instance you would like to access, and click the **Modify** button so that you can edit these default settings.

Note   You will find that different AWS services have different behaviors when you try to change or modify their settings. Some will let you modify and save new configurations at any time, regardless of whether the service is currently running. Others, like RDS, will not allow you to modify any settings unless the service is running.

Scroll down until you see the **Additional configuration** expander. Click that arrow. You should now see a *Public access* set of radio buttons as well as a *Database port* field. Select the *Publicly available* option and make sure that the port is set to the default port value, 1433. This will ensure that your instance is publicly accessible and that it is listening on the expected port.

The next step is to configure the security group rules. Remember, these rules act as a way to manage traffic to and from the RDS instance. At this point, because this was set up through the default approach, the created security groups do not have the appropriate rules. Instead, delete the current security group that is assigned to the RDS instance and add the security group that we used earlier when setting up the EC2 SQL Server instance. We are taking this approach instead of editing the current group because we are trying to limit the amount of security groups in your account that do the same thing – it defeats the purpose of a group if every resource "has their own." When completed, your configuration should look like that shown in Figure 8-19.

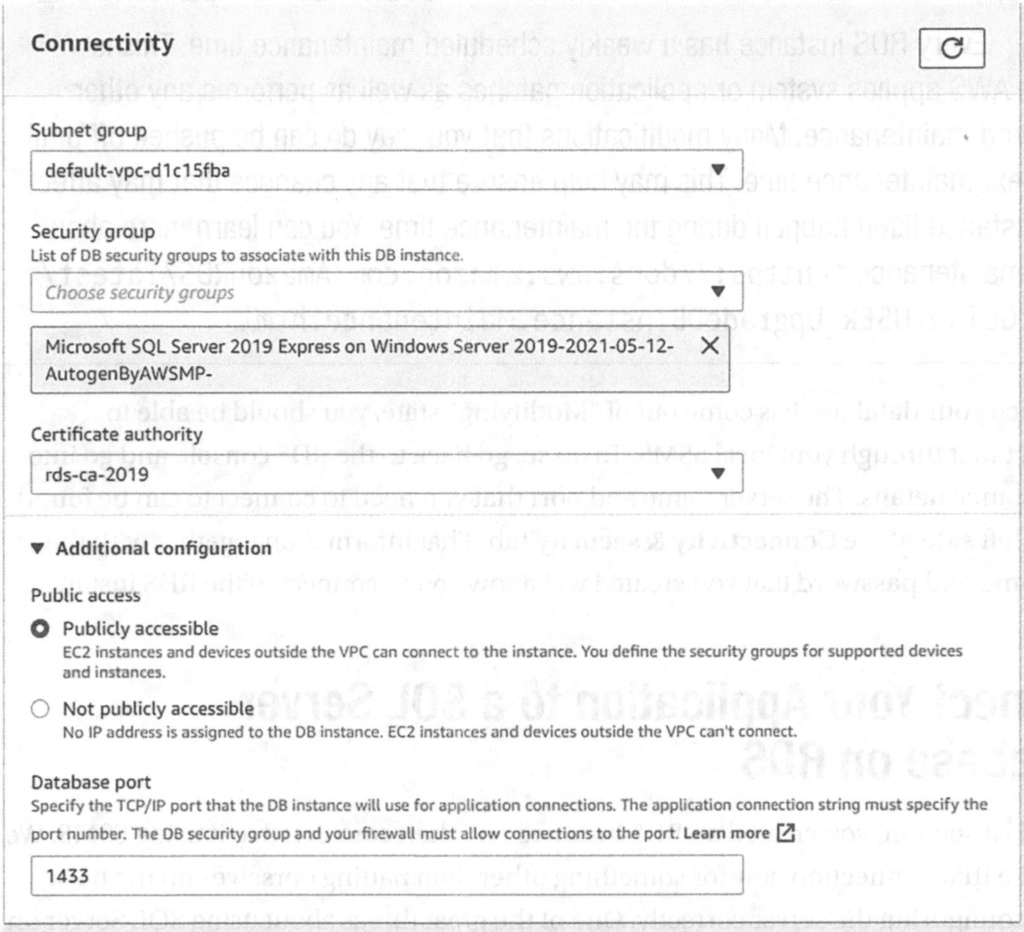

Connectivity

Subnet group

default-vpc-d1c15fba

Security group
List of DB security groups to associate with this DB instance.

Choose security groups

Microsoft SQL Server 2019 Express on Windows Server 2019-2021-05-12-   ✕
AutogenByAWSMP-

Certificate authority

rds-ca-2019

▼ Additional configuration

Public access

◉ Publicly accessible
EC2 instances and devices outside the VPC can connect to the instance. You define the security groups for supported devices
and instances.

○ Not publicly accessible
No IP address is assigned to the DB instance. EC2 instances and devices outside the VPC can't connect.

Database port
Specify the TCP/IP port that the DB instance will use for application connections. The application connection string must specify the
port number. The DB security group and your firewall must allow connections to the port. **Learn more** ☑

1433

Figure 8-19. *Updating the RDS settings for access*

When you have finished your updates, select the **Continue** button to save your
changes. This will bring you to a page that has a section called *Summary of DB
modifications,* which lists the changes that you made, and a section called *Scheduling of
modifications,* which has two different options for when the change should take place:
Apply during the next scheduled maintenance window or *Apply immediately*. Select the
Apply immediately option and then click the **Modify DB Instance** button to complete
the process. The modification may take several minutes, during which you will not be
able to perform any more modifications.

Note   Every RDS instance has a weekly scheduled maintenance time. This is when AWS applies system or application patches as well as performs any other required maintenance. Many modifications that you may do can be pushed off until the next maintenance time. This may help ensure that any changes that may affect the instance itself happen during the maintenance time. You can learn more about RDS maintenance at `https://docs.aws.amazon.com/AmazonRDS/latest/UserGuide/USER_UpgradeDBInstance.Maintenance.html`.

Once your database has come out of "Modifying" state, you should be able to connect to it through your local SSMS. To do so, go back to the RDS console and go into the instance details. The server name and port that you need to connect to can be found on the left side of the **Connectivity & security** tab. That information together with the username and password that you created will allow you to connect to the RDS instance.

Connect Your Application to a SQL Server Database on RDS

In the last section, you created an RDS instance and then connected to it using SSMS. We shall use that connection now for something other than patting ourselves on the back about configuring the server correctly. One of the great things about using SQL Server on RDS is that there are no changes that you have to make to your application if it is already using SQL Server for data persistence; you simply need to change the connection string as long as you have your database set up and the data loaded. Let's do that part now.

Firstly, let's create the database structure.

1. Connect to your RDS instance with SQL Server Management Studio (SSMS). For the *Server name,* use the value shown in Figure 8-18 at "1", making sure that you have selected **SQL Server Authentication** for *Authentication* and inputting the *Login* and *Password* that you used when creating the instance. Your connection screen should be like Figure 8-20. You need to make sure that at the end of the server name, you add a comma and the port number so that it looks something like this: `pronetoaws.somevalue.com,1433`.

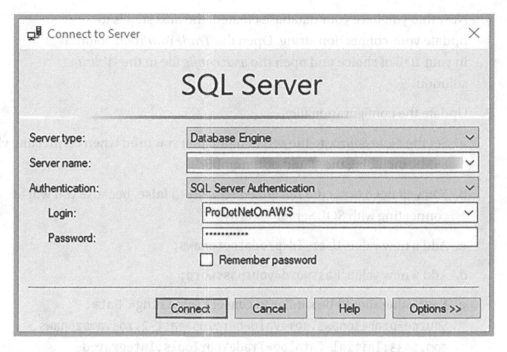

Figure 8-20. *Connecting to RDS*

2.   The next thing you need to do is create the database. To do so,
     open your database in the SSMS Object Explorer, right-click on the
     Databases folder, and select **New Database**. This will bring up the
     New Database screen.

3.   Enter the value "TradeYourTools" as the *Database name* (the
     scripts supplied with the sample application expect this name; if
     you use a different one, then you will need to change the scripts).
     You can keep all the rest of the settings as default and then click
     the *OK* button.

4.   In SSMS, open the *CreateStructure.sql* that is within the **SQL-
     Scripts** folder in the source code.

5.   Click the **Execute** button or press your **F5** key to execute the
     script. You should get a "Commands completed successfully"
     message.

6. Now that you have your database created, the next step is to update your connection string. Open the *TradeYourTools* solution in your IDE of choice and open the *web.config* file in the *Website* solution.

7. Update the configuration file:

    a. Set the *Data Source* to the server name that you used when connecting via SSMS, including the "," and port number.

    b. You will need to set the *Integrated Security* to **false**, because you will be connecting with SQL Server security.

    c. Add a new value, `User Id=prodotnetonaws;`

    d. Add a new value, `Password=yourpassword;`

    e. Your value should be similar to `connectionString="Data Source=pronetonaws.somevaluehere.us-east-2.rds.amazonaws.com,1433;Initial Catalog=TradeYourTools;Integrated Security=false;User Id=prodotnetonaws;Password=yourpassword`

8. Run your application and see that your sample application is running, now against the RDS database.

More About Using SQL Server on AWS

We have gone over initializing SQL Server on EC2 as well as using SQL Server on Amazon RDS. We have connected to our RDS database from our local machine by using configuration in RDS that allows for external access. However, you obviously will only want to take that approach when you are accessing your database instance from outside of AWS.

When running your RDS-accessing applications completely within the AWS infrastructure, however, you will most likely not want to use the connection string approach that we used. Instead, more secure approaches such as AWS Secrets Manager would be more appropriate. You will see this approach later after we start moving the entirety of the application processing onto AWS rather than this hybrid approach with the application running outside of AWS on your local machine and connecting to the database.

Also, there is always the option to create and maintain Amazon RDS databases using IaC with CloudFormation and the CDK. There are advantages to this approach, especially when trying to test your environment the same way that you test your application. Other advantages include the fact that using the CDK to create your RDS instance and configuring to use AWS Secrets Manager will also configure the actual secret as part of the process, as well as other, similar ways in which configuration can be simplified.

As you saw when we created the SQL Server instance in RDS, there are many other different products supported by RDS, from open source databases such as PostgreSQL, MySQL, and MariaDB to other proprietary systems like Oracle database and Amazon's own proprietary RDBMS system, Amazon Aurora. In the next chapter, we will go deeper into those different options and go over their potential use in your .NET applications.

CHAPTER 9

Other RDS Databases

For .NET developers, SQL Server is likely the most well-known of the database engines available in RDS. However, it is certainly not the only one! There are five other different relational databases where AWS offers a managed version: MySQL, MariaDB, PostgreSQL, Amazon Aurora, and Oracle. There are several reasons that you may choose to use one of these other databases, whether it is because of other existing systems that use the database, such as the plethora of applications built on top of the Oracle database, or simply because the cost around the open source databases such as PostgreSQL, MySQL, and MariaDB is much less than what you would pay for an instance of SQL Server as shown in Figure 9-1.

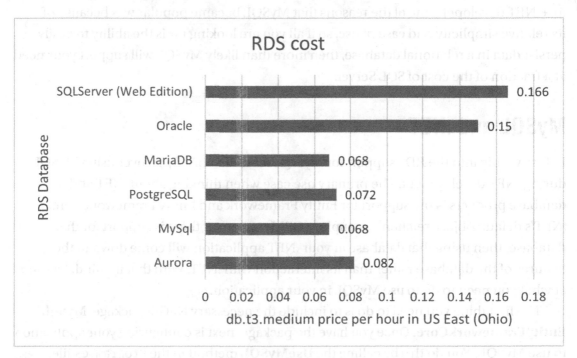

Figure 9-1. *RDS cost per database engine*

© William Penberthy and Steve Roberts 2023
W. Penberthy and S. Roberts, *Pro .NET on Amazon Web Services*,
https://doi.org/10.1007/978-1-4842-8907-5_9

In this chapter, we will go through these different databases and then look at their use within a .NET application. We will also walk through configuring an instance of each so that you get an understanding of the options that you have and the effect they may have when running your .NET applications.

MySQL

Let's start with one of the oldest open source relational databases out there: MySQL. Originally released in 1995, MySQL has gone through a series of "owners" since then, with it currently being primarily developed by Oracle. As mentioned, MySQL is free and open-sourced under the terms of the GNU General Public License (GPL). That AWS does not have to pay any licensing fee is one of the primary reasons that the cost for MySQL on Amazon RDS is the lowest in the chart; you are only paying for hardware and management rather than hardware, licensing, and management.

MySQL may not be as fully featured or high powered as some of the commercial systems such as SQL Server and Oracle; however, that does not mean that it is not of use to a .NET developer. One of the reasons that MySQL became popular was because of its relative simplicity and ease of use, so if all you are looking for is the ability to easily persist data in a relational database, then more than likely MySQL will support your need at a fraction of the cost of SQL Server.

MySQL and .NET

Before we dig into the RDS support for MySQL, let us first briefly go over using MySQL during .NET development. The primary use case when thinking about .NET and database products is the support for Entity Framework and Entity Framework Core, .NET's default object-relational mapping (ORM) system. If there is support for that database, then using that database in your .NET application will come down to the features of the database rather than its interaction with .NET. With that in mind, let's look at what you need to do to use MySQL in your application.

The first thing you need to do is to include the necessary NuGet package, **MySql. EntityFrameworkCore**. Once you have the package, next is configuring your application to use MySQL. You do this by calling the **UseMySQL** method in the `Program.cs` file:

```
var connectionString = builder.Configuration.GetConnectionString("Default
Connection");
builder.Services.AddDbContext<ApplicationDbContext>(options =>
{
    options.UseMySql(connectionString, ServerVersion.
    AutoDetect(connectionString));
});
```

A connection string for MySQL has four required fields:

- **server** – Server with which to connect

- **uid** – Username

- **pwd** - Password

- **database** – Database with which to connect

Let's now go create a MySQL database.

Setting Up a MySQL Database on Amazon RDS

Now that we know how to set up our .NET application to access MySQL, let's go look at setting up MySQL. Log into the console, go to the RDS console, and select *Create database*. On the *Create database* screen, select *Standard create* and then *MySQL*. Doing this will show you that there is only one *Edition* that you can select: **MySQL Community**. You then have a lot of different release versions that you can select from; however, the NuGet packages that we used in our earlier example require a reasonably modern version of MySQL, so unless you have any specific reason to use an older version, you should always use the default, most updated version.

Once you have defined the version of MySQL that you will use, your next option is to select the *Template* that you would like to use. You have three different templates to choose from:

- **Production** – Defaults are set to support high availability and fast, consistent performance.

- **Dev/Test** – Defaults are set in the middle of the range.

- **Free tier** – Defaults are set to the minimal, free version.

We are going to select the Free tier version to limit our costs for this walkthrough! This will create many of the default system values that you will see during the server configuration, more on these later.

The next section is Settings. Here, you will create the **DB instance identifier** and the **Master username** and **Master password**, the login credentials as shown in Figure 9-2. Note that the DB instance identifier needs to be unique across all the account's DB instances in this region, not just MySQL database instances. We used "prodotnetonaws" as both the instance identifier and the Master username. If you choose to *Auto generate a password*, you will get an opportunity to access that password immediately after the database is created.

Settings

DB instance identifier Info
Type a name for your DB instance. The name must be unique across all DB instances owned by your AWS account in the current AWS Region.

```
prodotnetonaws
```

The DB instance identifier is case-insensitive, but is stored as all lowercase (as in "mydbinstance"). Constraints: 1 to 60 alphanumeric characters or hyphens. First character must be a letter. Can't contain two consecutive hyphens. Can't end with a hyphen.

▼ Credentials Settings

Master username Info
Type a login ID for the master user of your DB instance.

```
prodotnetonaws
```

1 to 16 alphanumeric characters. First character must be a letter.

☐ Auto generate a password
  Amazon RDS can generate a password for you, or you can specify your own password.

Master password Info

```
••••••••••••
```

Constraints: At least 8 printable ASCII characters. Can't contain any of the following: / (slash), '(single quote), "(double quote) and @ (at sign).

Confirm password Info

```
••••••••••••
```

Figure 9-2. *Naming the DM instance and creating the master user*

Scrolling down to the next section, **DB instance class**, will show that the instance class being used is the *db.t2.micro* (or comparable, depending upon when you are reading this), which is the free tier–compatible instance type. The next section down the page, **Storage**, is also filled out with the free version of storage, defaulting to 20 GiB of *Allocated storage*. Do not change either of these values to stay within the "free" level.

There are four additional sections. The first of these is **Availability & durability**, where you can create a replica in a different Availability Zone. Amazon RDS will automatically fail over to the standby in the case of a planned or unplanned outage of the primary. If you selected the "Free" template, then this whole section will be grayed out, and you will not be able to create a *multi-AZ deployment*. The second section is **Connectivity**. This is where you assign your *Virtual private cloud* (VPC) and *Subnet group*, determine whether your RDS instance has *Public access*, and assign a *VPC security group*. You can also select an *Availability Zone* if desired. We left all these values at their default.

The third section is **Database authentication**. You have three options in this section, with the first being *Password authentication* (the default value) where you manage your database user credentials through MySQL's native password authentication features. The second option in this section is *Password and IAM database authentication* where you use both MySQL's password authentication features and IAM users and roles, and the last is Password and Kerberos authentication, where you use both MySQL's password authentication features and an AWS Managed Microsoft Active Directory (AD) created with AWS Directory Service.

The last section when creating an RDS database is **Additional configuration**. This allows you to add any *Database options*, configure *Backup*, add *Monitoring*, and configure *Logging* and *Maintenance*, and to turn on *Deletion protection*. When deletion protection is enabled, you are not able to delete the database without first editing the database to turn off that setting. Select the *Create database* button when completed. This will bring you back to the Databases screen where you will likely see a notice that the database is being created as shown in Figure 9-3.

Figure 9-3. *Notice that an RDS database is being created*

If you had selected to auto-generate a password, the button shown in Figure 9-3 also shows the *View credential details* button that you would need to click to see the generated value. Once the database is *Available*, you can interact with it like any other database using endpoint and port values that are shown in the **Connectivity & security** tab in the database details, as shown in Figure 9-4, for the connection string in your .NET application.

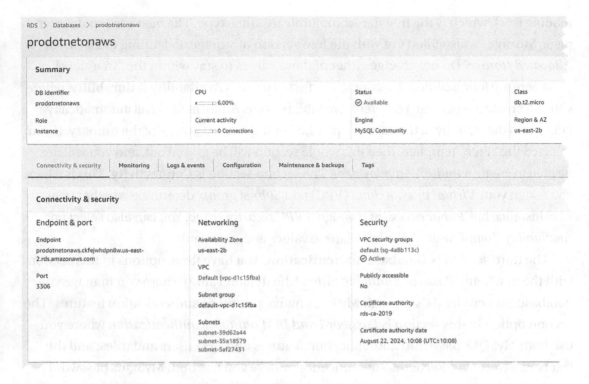

Figure 9-4. *MySQL database details screen showing endpoint and port*

MySQL is the most used open source relational database in the world. However, as mentioned earlier, Oracle took control of the project in 2010, and this created some angst among MySQL users. This led to a forking of the source code by some of the original MySQL developers and a creation of a new open source relational database based upon the MySQL code: MariaDB. Let's look at that next.

MariaDB

MariaDB is a community-developed, commercially supported fork of MySQL that is intended to remain free and open source software under the GNU General Public License (the same license that MySQL started under). As just mentioned, it was forked because of MySQL's acquisition by Oracle where many of the initial MySQL developers were afraid that because of how MySQL competed against the Oracle database, progress would be slowed or stopped on MySQL. MariaDB's API and protocol are compatible with those used by MySQL, plus some features to support native nonblocking operations and progress reporting. This means that all connectors, libraries, and applications that work with MySQL should also work on MariaDB. However, for recent MySQL features, MariaDB either has no equivalent yet, such as geography, or deliberately chose not to be 100% compatible. This list of incompatibilities will likely continue to grow with each version and can be seen at `https://mariadb.com/kb/en/compatibility-differences/`.

MariaDB and .NET

Using .NET with MariaDB is easy to configure because of how similar the APIs are for MariaDB and for MySQL. To be honest, they are so identical that the easiest way to consume MariaDB in a .NET application is to use the same MySQL NuGet package and connection approach as we went over in the MySQL section. The MariaDB team does not really spend any time building connectors and instead works to ensure that the connectors that are out there, such as those built by the MySQL team, are compatible.

Setting Up a MariaDB Database on Amazon RDS

Now that we know how to set up our .NET application to access MariaDB, let's go look at setting up MariaDB in Amazon RDS. Log into the console, go to RDS, and select *Create database*. On the *Create Database* screen, select *Standard create* and then *MariaDB*. You will have a list of versions, starting with version 10.2 at the time of this writing up through the most recent release.

The rest of the setup screen, surprisingly enough, will look eerily familiar if you just went through the MySQL setup steps, mainly because they are identical! You will have the same three options for the *Template* that you would like to use (*Production, Dev/Test,* and *Free tier*) as well as all of the configuration sections that follow.

Since we took the Free tier route with MySQL, let's mix it up a little bit and go with the Dev/Test version for MariaDB, and we can talk about some of the areas that we glossed over when creating the MySQL database.

The first of these is after you create the database instance identifier and have provided the master user information and is entitled **DB instance class**. There are three options available for instances:

- **Standard classes** (includes m classes) – Provides a balance of compute, memory, and network resources and is the best all-around choice for many different database workloads.

- **Memory-optimized classes** (includes r and x classes) – Has large memory allocations to support those database workloads that process large data sets in memory.

- **Burstable classes** (includes t classes) – Is the only option available for the free tier and is designed to provide a baseline CPU performance with the ability to burst above this baseline as needed.

Selecting one of these options changes the instances that are available in the instance drop-down from which you make your selection. Selecting the *standard classes* as shown in Figure 9-5 will present a drop-down of the *m*-class instances.

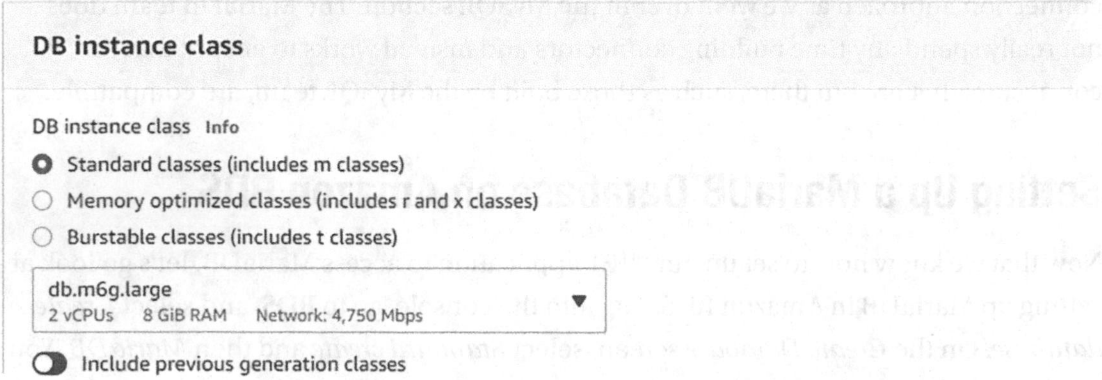

DB instance class

DB instance class   Info

◉ Standard classes (includes m classes)

○ Memory optimized classes (includes r and x classes)

○ Burstable classes (includes t classes)

| db.m6g.large | ▼ |
| 2 vCPUs   8 GiB RAM   Network: 4,750 Mbps | |

🔘 Include previous generation classes

Figure 9-5. *DB instance class selection for MariaDB (and MySQL)*

Selecting one of the other options will filter the list in the drop-down to the applicable classes.

Caution   The lowest m instance class, db.m5.large, with 2 vCPUs, 8 GB RAM, and 4,750 Mbps network connectivity will run you $124.83 a month in the US East (Ohio) region, us-east-2, so even a momentary creation has the chance to cost you! The t instance classes are the ones that include the free tier versions.

The next section in the setup is the storage section, with the same options that you had when going through the MySQL steps, though the default values may be different based upon the instance class that you selected. After the storage section is the second "grayed-out" area that we saw when we walked through setting up MySQL: **Availability & durability**.

One of the best features of RDS is how it makes the installation and configuration of a new RDBMS painless when you think about what you would have to do to manage the configuration and maintenance of a standby instance on your own. For those instances where your data needs to be as available as possible, the ability to create (and forget about) a standby instance by checking a radio button can't be overlooked. Creating a replica will configure a synchronous standby replica in a different Availability Zone than the primary DB instance. In the case of a planned or unplanned outage of the main instance, RDS will automatically fail over to the standby. When using a multi-AZ deployment, however, you will be paying approximately twice as much for the duplicated instances as shown in Figure 9-6.

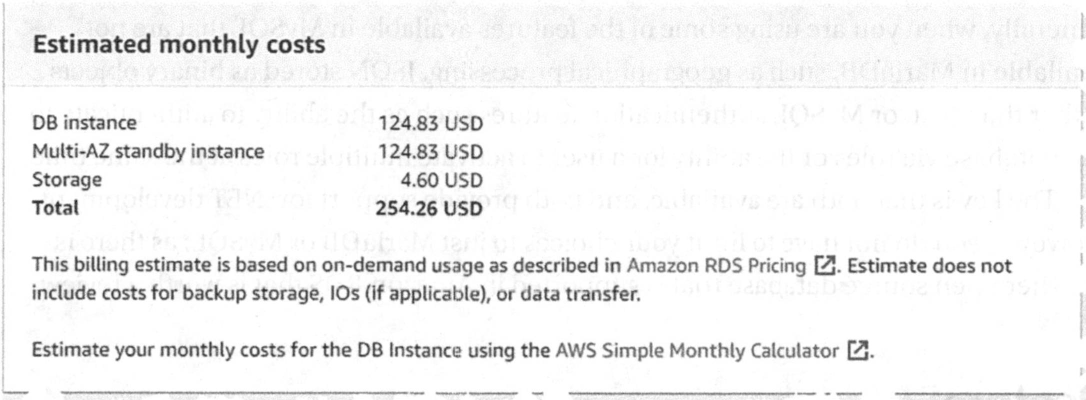

Estimated monthly costs

DB instance	124.83 USD
Multi-AZ standby instance	124.83 USD
Storage	4.60 USD
Total	**254.26 USD**

This billing estimate is based on on-demand usage as described in Amazon RDS Pricing ☑. Estimate does not include costs for backup storage, IOs (if applicable), or data transfer.

Estimate your monthly costs for the DB Instance using the AWS Simple Monthly Calculator ☑.

Figure 9-6. *Estimated monthly costs with standby enabled*

Once you have selected the appropriate availability option, in this case, we chose to enable a standby instance, the rest of your experience will be the same as it was for MySQL, setting up Database authentication and Additional configuration. You can keep the defaults in these sections and go ahead and create your database or change the values as desired to get a better understanding of each area.

With identical pricing between MySQL and MariaDB, and similar APIs and other interactions, you may be wondering what the differences are between the two.

Selecting Between MySQL and MariaDB

Our recommendation when you are trying to select between MySQL and MariaDB? All other things being equal, go with MariaDB. Why? Primarily because of the advanced capability that MariaDB offers such as its optimization for performance and its ability to work with large data sets. MariaDB has also spent a lot of effort adding query optimizations for queries that use joins, subqueries, or derived tables; so its overall performance is better than you will find with MySQL. Lastly, MariaDB provides better monitoring through the introduction of microsecond precision and extended user statistics.

However, there are occasions when MySQL makes more sense than does MariaDB, generally, when you are using some of the features available in MySQL that are not available in MariaDB, such as geographical processing, JSON stored as binary objects rather than text, or MySQL authentication features such as the ability to authenticate to the database via roles or the ability for a user to activate multiple roles at the same time.

The key is that both are available, and both provide support for .NET development. However, you do not have to limit your choices to just MariaDB or MySQL, as there is another open source database that is supported in Amazon RDS that is worth a review.

PostgreSQL

The next database we are going to talk about that is available in Amazon RDS is PostgreSQL. PostgreSQL is a free, open source database that emphasizes extensibility and SQL compliance and was first released in 1996. A true competitor to commercial databases such as SQL Server and Oracle, PostgreSQL supports both online transaction processing (OLTP) and online analytical processing (OLAP) and has one of the most advanced performance features available: multi-version concurrency control (MVCC). MVCC supports the simultaneous processing of multiple transactions with almost no deadlock, so transaction-heavy applications and systems will most likely benefit from using PostgreSQL over SQL Server, and there are companies that use PostgreSQL to manage petabytes of data.

Another feature that makes PostgreSQL attractive is that not only does it support your traditional relational database approach, but it also fully supports a JSON/JSONB key/value storage approach that makes it a valid alternative to your more traditional NoSQL databases; so you can now use a single product to support the two most common data access approaches. Because of its enterprise level of features and the amount of work it takes to manage and maintain those, even though it is also open source and free software like MySQL and MariaDB, it is slightly more expensive to run PostgreSQL on Amazon RDS than those other open source products.

PostgreSQL and .NET

As with any database products that you will access from your .NET application, its level of support for .NET is important. Fortunately for us, there is a large community involved in helping ensure that PostgreSQL is relevant to .NET users.

Let's look at what you need to do to get .NET and PostgreSQL working together. The first thing you need to do is to include the necessary NuGet packages, **Npgsql** and **Npgsql.EntityFrameworkCore.PostgreSQL**, as shown in Figure 9-7.

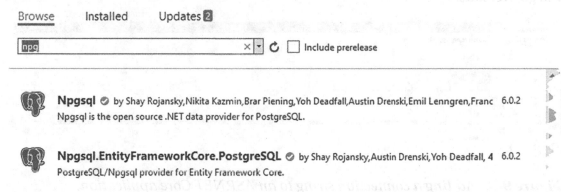

Figure 9-7. *NuGet packages required to connect to PostgreSQL*

Once you have the packages, the next thing that you need to do is to configure your application to use PostgreSQL. You do this by using the **UseNpgsql** method in the Program.cs file as shown in the following:

```
var connectionString = builder.Configuration.GetConnectionString("Default
Connection");
builder.Services.AddDbContext<ApplicationDbContext>(options =>
{
    options. UseNpgsql(connectionString);
});
```

A connection string for PostgreSQL has six required fields:

- **server** – Server with which to connect

- **port** – Port number on which PostgreSQL is listening

- **user id** – Username

- **password** - Password

- **database** – Database with which to connect

- **pooling** – Whether to use connection pooling (true or false)

When working in an ASP.NET Core application, the connection string is added to the *appsettings.json* file as shown in Figure 9-8 where you can give it the appropriate value during your build process. You can also store this information in Secrets Manager as we will go over later.

```
appsettings.json  ⊣ ×
Schema: https://json.schemastore.org/appsettings.json
 1    ⊟{
 2    ⊟   "Logging": {
 3    ⊟     "LogLevel": {
 4          "Default": "Information",
 5          "Microsoft": "Warning",
 6          "Microsoft.Hosting.Lifetime": "Information"
 7        }
 8      },
 9    ⊟   "ConnectionStrings": {
10        "DefaultConnection": "Server=RDSServer;port=5432;user id=ProDotNetOnAWS;password=passwordhere;database=TradeYourTools;pooling=true"
11      },
12      "AllowedHosts": "*"
13    }
14    |
```

Figure 9-8. *Adding a connection string to an ASP.NET Core application*

Let's now go create a PostgreSQL database.

Setting Up a PostgreSQL Database on Amazon RDS

Now that we know how to set up our .NET application to access PostgreSQL, let's go look at setting up a PostgreSQL instance. First, log into the console, go to *RDS*, and select *Create database*. On the Create Database screen, select *Standard create* and then *PostgreSQL*. You then have a lot of different versions that you can select from; however, the NuGet packages that we used in our earlier example require a reasonably modern version of PostgreSQL, so unless you have any specific reason to use an older version, you should always use the default, most updated version.

Once you have defined the version of PostgreSQL that you will use, your next option is to select the **Template** that you would like to use. Note that you only have two different templates to choose from:

- **Production** – Defaults are set to support high availability and fast, consistent performance.

- **Dev/Test** – Defaults are set in the middle of the range.

Note   Both MySQL and MariaDB had a third template, *Free tier*, that is not available when creating a PostgreSQL database. That does not mean that you must automatically pay, however, as the AWS Free Tier for Amazon RDS offer provides free use of Single-AZ Micro DB instances running PostgreSQL. It is important to consider that the free usage tier is capped at 750 instance hours per month across all your RDS databases.

Selecting the template sets defaults across the rest of the setup screen, and we will call those values out as we go through those items.

Once you select a template, your next setup area is **Availability and durability**. There are three options to choose from:

- **Multi-AZ DB cluster** – As of the time of writing, this option is in preview. Selecting this option creates a DB cluster with a primary DB instance and two readable standby instances, with each instance in a different Availability Zone (AZ). Provides high availability and data redundancy and increases capacity to serve read workloads.

- **Multi-AZ DB instance** – This option creates a primary DB instance and a standby DB instance in a different AZ. Provides high availability and data redundancy, but the standby instance doesn't support connections for read workloads. This is the default value if you chose the Production template.

- **Single DB instance** – This option creates a single DB instance with no standby instances. This is the default value if you chose the Dev/Test template.

The next section, **Settings**, is where you provide the *DB instance identifier*, or database name, and your *Master username* and *Master password*. Your database identifier value must be unique across all the database instances you have in the current region, regardless of engine option. You also have the option of having AWS auto-generate a password for you.

The next section allows you to select the **DB instance class**. You have the same three filters that you had before of *Standard classes*, *Memory optimized classes*, and *Burstable classes*. Selecting one of the filters changes the values in the instance drop-down box. You need to select Burstable classes and then one of the instances with micro in the title, such as a *db.t3.micro,* as shown in Figure 9-9.

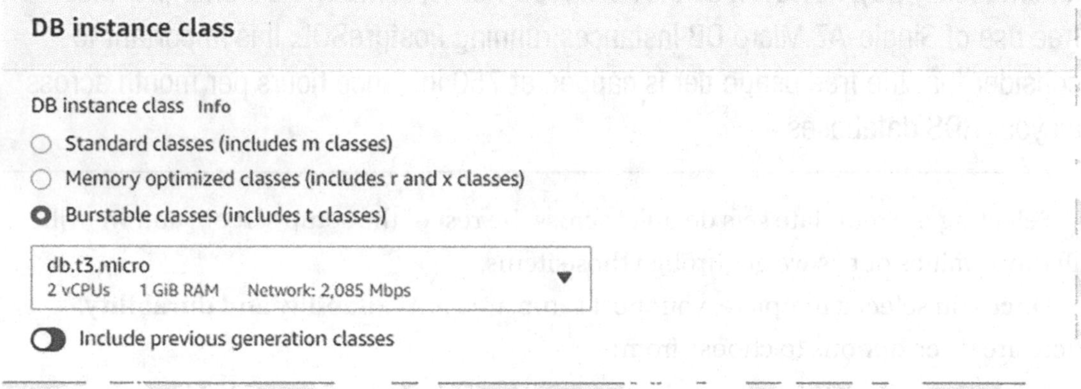

Figure 9-9. *Selecting a free tier–compatible DB instance*

The next section in the setup is the **Storage section**, with the same options that you had available when going through the MySQL and MariaDB setups, though the default values may be different based upon the instance class that you selected. After the Storage section are the **Connectivity** and **Database authentication** sections that we walked through earlier, so we will not go through them again now – they are standard across all RDS engine options. Selecting the *Create database* button will take you back to the RDS Databases screen where you will get a notification that the database is being created as well as a button that you can click to access the connection details. Make sure you get the password if you selected for AWS to create your administrative password. You will only be able to access the password this one time.

The pricing for PostgreSQL is slightly higher than MariaDB or MySQL when looking at compatible configurations, about 6% higher.

Selecting Between PostgreSQL and MySQL/MariaDB

There are some significant differences between PostgreSQL and MySQL/MariaDB that can become meaningful when building your .NET application. Some of the more important differences are listed as follows. There are quite a few management and configuration differences, but those are not mentioned since RDS manages all of those for you!

- **Multi-version concurrency control** – PostgreSQL was the first DBMS to roll out multi-version concurrency control (MVCC), which means reading data never blocks writing data, and vice versa. If your database is heavily used for both reading and writing, then this may be a significant influencer.

- **More types supported** – PostgreSQL natively supports NoSQL as well as a rich set of data types including Numeric Types, Boolean, Network Address, Bit String Types, and Arrays. It also supports JSON, hstore (a list of comma-separated key/value pairs), and XML, and users can even add new types.

- **Sequence support** – PostgreSQL supports multiple tables taking their IDs from the same sequence while MySQL/MariaDB does not.

- **Index flexibility** – PostgreSQL can use functions and conditional indexes, which makes PostgreSQL database tuning very flexible, such as not having a problem if primary key values aren't inserted sequentially.

- **Spatial capability** – PostgreSQL has much richer support for spatial data management, quantity measurement, and geometric topology analysis.

While PostgreSQL is considered one of the most advanced databases around, that doesn't mean that it should automatically be your choice. Many of the advantages listed previously can be considered advanced functionality that you may not need. If you simply need a place to store rarely changing data, then MySQL/MariaDB may still be a better choice. Why? Because it is less expensive and performs better than PostgreSQL when performing simple reads with simple join. As always, keep your use cases in mind when selecting your database.

> **Note**   AWS contributes to an open source project called Babelfish for PostgreSQL, which is designed to provide the capability for PostgreSQL to understand queries from applications written for Microsoft SQL Server. Babelfish understands the SQL Server wire-protocol and T-SQL. This understanding means that you can use SQL Server drivers for .NET to talk to PostgreSQL databases. As of this writing, this functionality is not yet available in the PostgreSQL version of RDS. It is, however, available for Aurora PostgreSQL. We will go over this in more detail later in the chapter. The project can be seen at `www.babelfishpg.org`.

MariaDB, MySQL, and PostgreSQL are all open source databases that have existed for years and that you can use anywhere, including that old server under your desk. The next database is only available in the cloud and within RDS: Amazon Aurora.

Amazon Aurora

Amazon Aurora is a MySQL and PostgreSQL-compatible relational database designed for the cloud. AWS claims that with some workloads, Aurora can deliver up to 5× the throughput of MySQL and up to 3× the throughput of PostgreSQL without requiring any application changes. Aurora can do this because its storage subsystem was specifically designed to run on AWS' fast distributed storage; in other words, Aurora was designed with cloud resources in mind, while those other "non-cloud only" databases are simply running on cloud resources. This design approach allows for automatic storage growth as needed, up to a cluster volume maximum size of 128 tebibytes (TiB), and offers 99.99% availability by replicating six copies of your data across three Availability Zones and backing up your data continuously to Amazon S3. It transparently recovers from physical storage failures; instance failover typically takes less than 30 seconds.

> **Note**   A tebibyte (TiB) is a unit of measure used to describe computing capacity. The prefix *tebi* comes from the power-of-2 (binary) system for measuring data capacity. That system is based on powers of two. A terabyte (the unit normally seen on disk drives and RAM) is a power-of-10 multiplier, a "simpler" way of looking at the value. Thus, one terabyte = 10^{12} bytes, or 1,000,000,000,000 bytes, as opposed to one tebibyte, which equals 2^{40} bytes, or 1,099,511,627,776 bytes.

Also, because of this customized design, Aurora can automate and standardize database replication and clustering. The last, unique Aurora feature is the ability to use push-button migration tools to convert any already-existing RDS for MySQL and RDS for PostgreSQL applications to use RDS for Aurora instead. The argument for this ease in migration, and for Amazon Aurora in general, is that even though Aurora may be 20% more expensive than MySQL, Amazon claims that Aurora is 5× faster than MySQL, has 3× the throughput of standard PostgreSQL, and is able to scale to much larger data sets.

Creating an Amazon Aurora Database in RDS

Let's next look at creating a new Aurora database. First, log into the console, go to *RDS*, and select *Create database*. On the Create Database screen, select *Standard* create and then *Aurora*. This should bring up some Aurora-specific sections as shown in Figure 9-10.

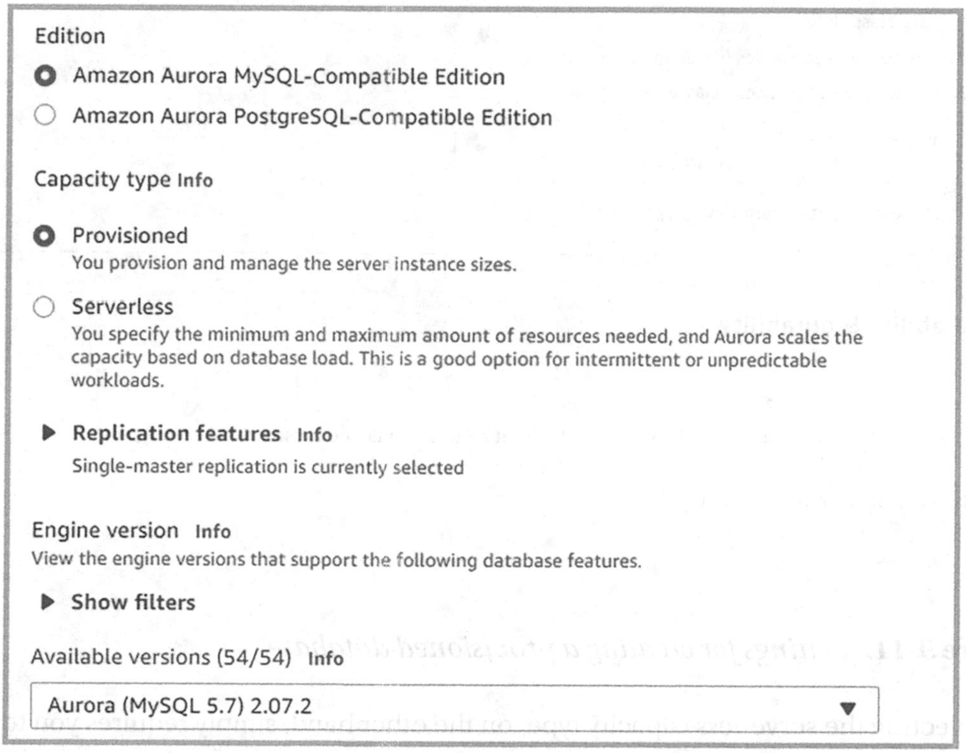

Figure 9-10. *Selecting edition and capacity type when building an Aurora database*

The first selection, **Edition**, asks you to determine whether you wish a *MySQL* or *PostgreSQL*-compatible edition.

MySQL-Compatible Edition

The default selection when creating an Aurora database is **MySQL**, as shown in Figure 9-10. By making this choice, values will be optimized for MySQL, and default filters will be so set for the options within the *Available versions* drop-down. The next area, **Capacity type**, provides two choices: *Provisioned* and *Serverless*. Selecting a provisioned capacity type will require you to select the number and instance classes that you will need to manage your workload as well as determine your preferred **Availability & durability** settings as shown in Figure 9-11.

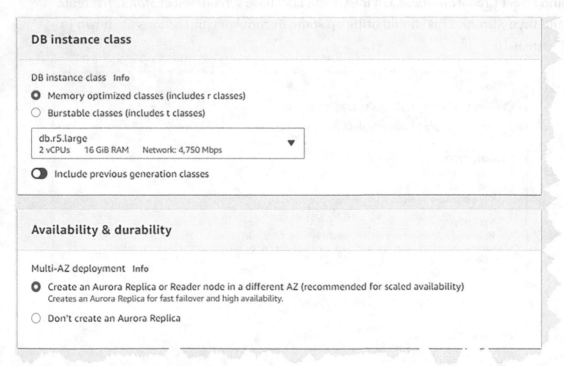

Figure 9-11. *Settings for creating a provisioned database*

Selecting the serverless capacity type, on the other hand, simply requires you to select a minimum and maximum value for capacity units as shown in Figure 9-12. A capacity unit is comparable to a specific compute and memory configuration. Based on the minimum capacity unit setting, Aurora creates scaling rules for thresholds for

CPU utilization, connections, and available memory. Aurora then reduces the resources for the DB cluster when its workload is below these thresholds, all the way down to the minimum capacity unit.

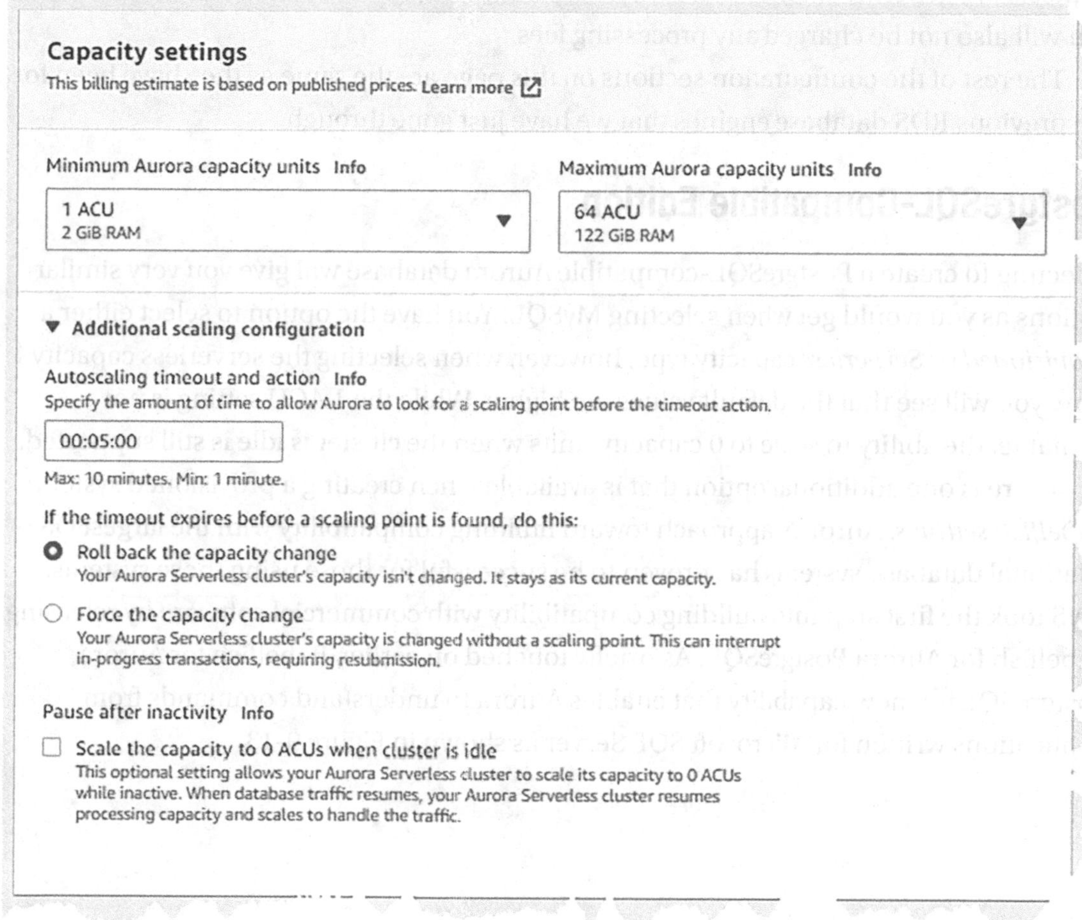

Capacity settings

This billing estimate is based on published prices. Learn more

Minimum Aurora capacity units Info

| 1 ACU |
| 2 GiB RAM |

Maximum Aurora capacity units Info

| 64 ACU |
| 122 GiB RAM |

▼ Additional scaling configuration

Autoscaling timeout and action Info

Specify the amount of time to allow Aurora to look for a scaling point before the timeout action.

| 00:05:00 |

Max: 10 minutes. Min: 1 minute.

If the timeout expires before a scaling point is found, do this:

● Roll back the capacity change
Your Aurora Serverless cluster's capacity isn't changed. It stays as its current capacity.

○ Force the capacity change
Your Aurora Serverless cluster's capacity is changed without a scaling point. This can interrupt in-progress transactions, requiring resubmission.

Pause after inactivity Info

☐ Scale the capacity to 0 ACUs when cluster is idle
This optional setting allows your Aurora Serverless cluster to scale its capacity to 0 ACUs while inactive. When database traffic resumes, your Aurora Serverless cluster resumes processing capacity and scales to handle the traffic.

Figure 9-12. *Capacity settings when creating a serverless database*

You also have the ability to configure additional aspects around scaling using the **Additional scaling configuration** options. The first value is *Autoscaling timeout and action*. Aurora looks for a scaling point before changing capacity during the autoscaling process. A scaling point is a point in time when no transactions or long-running queries are in process. By default, if Aurora can't find a scaling point within the specified timeout period, it will stop looking and keep the current capacity. You will need to choose the *Force the capacity change option* to make the change even without a scaling point. Choosing this option can affect any in-process transactions and queries. The last selection is whether you want the database to *Scale the capacity to 0 ACUs when cluster is idle*. The name of the option pretty much tells the story; when that item is selected, then your database will basically shut off when not being used. It will then scale back up as requests are generated. There will be a performance impact on that first call; however, you will also not be charged any processing fees.

The rest of the configuration sections on this page are the same as they have been for the previous RDS database engines that we have just gone through.

PostgreSQL-Compatible Edition

Selecting to create a PostgreSQL-compatible Aurora database will give you very similar options as you would get when selecting MySQL. You have the option to select either a *Provisioned* or *Serverless* capacity type; however, when selecting the serverless capacity type, you will see that the default values are higher. While the 1 ACU setting is not available, the ability to scale to 0 capacity units when the cluster is idle is still supported.

There is one additional option that is available when creating a provisioned system: *Babelfish settings*. Aurora's approach toward building compatibility with the largest OSS relational database systems has proven to be successful for those using those systems. AWS took the first step into building compatibility with commercial software by releasing Babelfish for Aurora PostgreSQL. As briefly touched on earlier, Babelfish for Aurora PostgreSQL is a new capability that enables Aurora to understand commands from applications written for Microsoft SQL Server as shown in Figure 9-13.

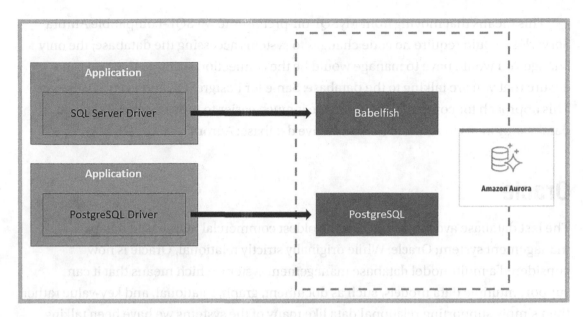

Figure 9-13. *Accessing Amazon Aurora through Babelfish*

With Babelfish, Aurora PostgreSQL now "understands" T-SQL and supports the SQL Server communications protocol, so your .NET apps that were originally written for SQL Server will work with Aurora – hopefully with minimal code changes. Babelfish is a built-in capability of Amazon Aurora and has no additional cost, although it does require that you be using a version greater than PostgreSQL 13.4, which at the time of this writing was not available on Serverless and is why this option is unable to be selected from that mode.

Amazon Aurora and .NET

As briefly touched on earlier, the primary outcome of your making a choice between PostgreSQL and MySQL is that the choice determines how you will interact with the database. This means that using the MySQL-compatible version of Aurora requires the use of the **MySql.EntityFrameworkCore** NuGet packages, while connecting to the PostgreSQL-compatible edition requires the **Npgsql** and **Npgsql. EntityFrameworkCore.PostgreSQL** packages, just like they were used earlier in those sections of this chapter. If you are considering using Babelfish with the PostgreSQL compatible, then you would use the standard SQL Server NuGet packages like we worked with last chapter.

This means that moving from MySQL on-premises to MySQL-compatible Aurora Serverless would require no code changes to systems accessing the database; the only change you would have to manage would be the connection string so that you can ensure that you are talking to the database. Same for PostgreSQL and even SQL Server. This approach for compatibility has made it much easier to move from well-known database systems to Amazon's cloud-native database: Aurora.

Oracle

The last database available in RDS is the oldest commercial SQL-based database management system: Oracle. While originally strictly relational, Oracle is now considered a multimodel database management system, which means that it can support multiple data models, such as document, graph, relational, and key-value rather than simply supporting relational data like many of the systems we have been talking about up until now. It is also the database of choice for many different packaged software systems and is generally believed to have the largest RDBMS market share (based on revenue) – which means that it would not be surprising to be a .NET developer and yet be working with Oracle. And Amazon RDS makes it easy to do that in the cloud.

Oracle and .NET

Let's first talk about using Oracle as a .NET developer. Since Oracle is a commercial database system, which is different from the rest of the systems we have talked about in this chapter, it has a lot of additional tools that are designed to help .NET developers interact with Oracle products. The first of these is the Oracle Developer Tools for Visual Studio.

Oracle Developer Tools for Visual Studio

There are a lot of .NET applications based upon Oracle, which means that it is to Oracle's advantage to make that interaction as easy as possible. One of the ways that they did this was to create the Oracle Developer Tools for Visual Studio (ODT for VS). This tool runs within Visual Studio 2017 or 2019 (2022 was not supported at the time of this writing) and brings in features designed to provide insight and improve the developer experience. Examples of the features within this tool include the following:

- **Database browsing** – Use Server Explorer to browse your Oracle database schemas and to launch the appropriate designers and wizards to create and alter schema objects.

- **Schema comparison** – View differences between two different schemas and generate a script that can modify the target schema to match the source schema. You can do this by connecting to live databases or by using scripts within an Oracle Database project.

- **Entity Framework support** – Use Visual Studio's Entity Designer for Database First and Model First object-relational mapping ("Code First" is also supported).

- **Automatic code generation** – You can use various windows, designers, and wizards to drag and drop and automatically generate .NET code.

- **PL/SQL *editor and debugger*** – Allows you to take advantage of Visual Studio's debugging features from within PL/SQL code, including seamlessly stepping from .NET code into your PL/SQL code and back out again.

You need to have a free Oracle account before you can download the tools from www.oracle.com/database/technologies/net-downloads.html. Please note that installing these tools will also install functionality to interact with Oracle Cloud, but those details are for a different book! Once the tools are downloaded and installed, you will see a new section in your **Tools** menu as shown in Figure 9-14.

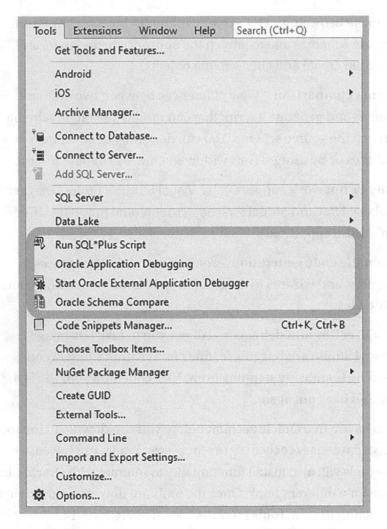

Figure 9-14. *New features added to Tools menu by ODT for VS*

You will also find four new project templates added to the **Create a new project** wizard:

- **Visual C# Oracle CLR project** – Creates a C#-based project for creating classes to use in Oracle database.

- **Visual Basic Oracle CLR project** – Creates a Visual Basic project for creating classes to use in Oracle database.

- **Oracle Database project** – Creates a project for maintaining a set of scripts that can be generated using Server Explorer menus. This project type does NOT support schema comparison.

- **Oracle Database project *version 2*** – Creates a project for maintaining a standardized set of SQL scripts that represent your Oracle database schema. This project type supports schema comparison.

There are additional features to these tools, so suffice to say that Oracle provides various ways to help .NET developers interact with their Oracle databases. A lot of ways. Many more than you will find for any of the other databases we have looked at in this chapter. And it should not surprise you to find that they also support connecting to Oracle databases from within your .NET application.

Oracle Data Provider for .NET (ODP.NET)

Where the ODT for VS is designed to help improve a developer's productivity when interacting with Oracle databases, ODP.NET instead manages the interconnectivity between .NET applications and Oracle databases. ODP.NET does that by providing several NuGet packages, **Oracle.ManagedDataAccess.Core** and **Oracle.EntityFrameworkCore**, that support .NET 5 and more recent versions and several NuGet packages supporting .NET versions prior to 5.0, **Oracle.ManagedDataAccess** and **Oracle.ManagedDataAccess.EntityFramework**. Once you have the packages, the next thing that you need to do is to configure your application to use Oracle. You do this by using the **UseOracle** method when editing the Program.cs file as shown in the following:

```
var connectionString = builder.Configuration.GetConnectionString("Default
Connection");
builder.Services.AddDbContext<ApplicationDbContext>(options =>
{
    options. UseOracle(connectionString);
});
```

A connection string for Oracle has three required fields:

- **User Id** – Username for use with the connection

- **Password** – Password

- **Data Source** – The Transparent Network Substrate (TNS) name is the name of the entry in **tnsnames.ora** file for the database server. This file can be found in the *$ORACLE_HOME/network/admin* directory.

This makes it seem like this should be an easy task to manage a connection string. However, of course, there is a caveat – you must be willing to deploy a file that has to be in a very specific place on the server and contain a reference to the server to which you need to connect. If you are okay with that approach, then this is a simple connection string – `"user id=prodotnetonaws;password=password123;data source=OracleDB"`. However, since a lot of the flexibility inherent in the cloud will go away if you start making this a requirement (you are no longer simply deploying just your application), then you will have to build a much uglier connection string using a Connect Descriptor:

```
"user id=prodotnetonaws;password=password123;data source="(DESCRIPTI
ON=(ADDRESS=(PROTOCOL=tcp)(HOST=servernamehere)(PORT=1521))(CONNECT_
DATA=(SID=databasename)))"
```

This means that we will need to build our connection string with additional values:

- **Host** – The address of the server to which the application will connect
- **SID** – The database, on the host server, to which the application is connecting

Let's now set up our Oracle database and see where you get those values from.

Setting Up an Oracle Database on Amazon RDS

Now that we know how to set up our .NET application to access an Oracle database, let's go look at setting up an Oracle instance. First, log into the console, go to *RDS*, and select *Create database*. On the Create Database screen, select *Standard* create and then *Oracle*. This will bring up the remainder of that section as shown in Figure 9-15.

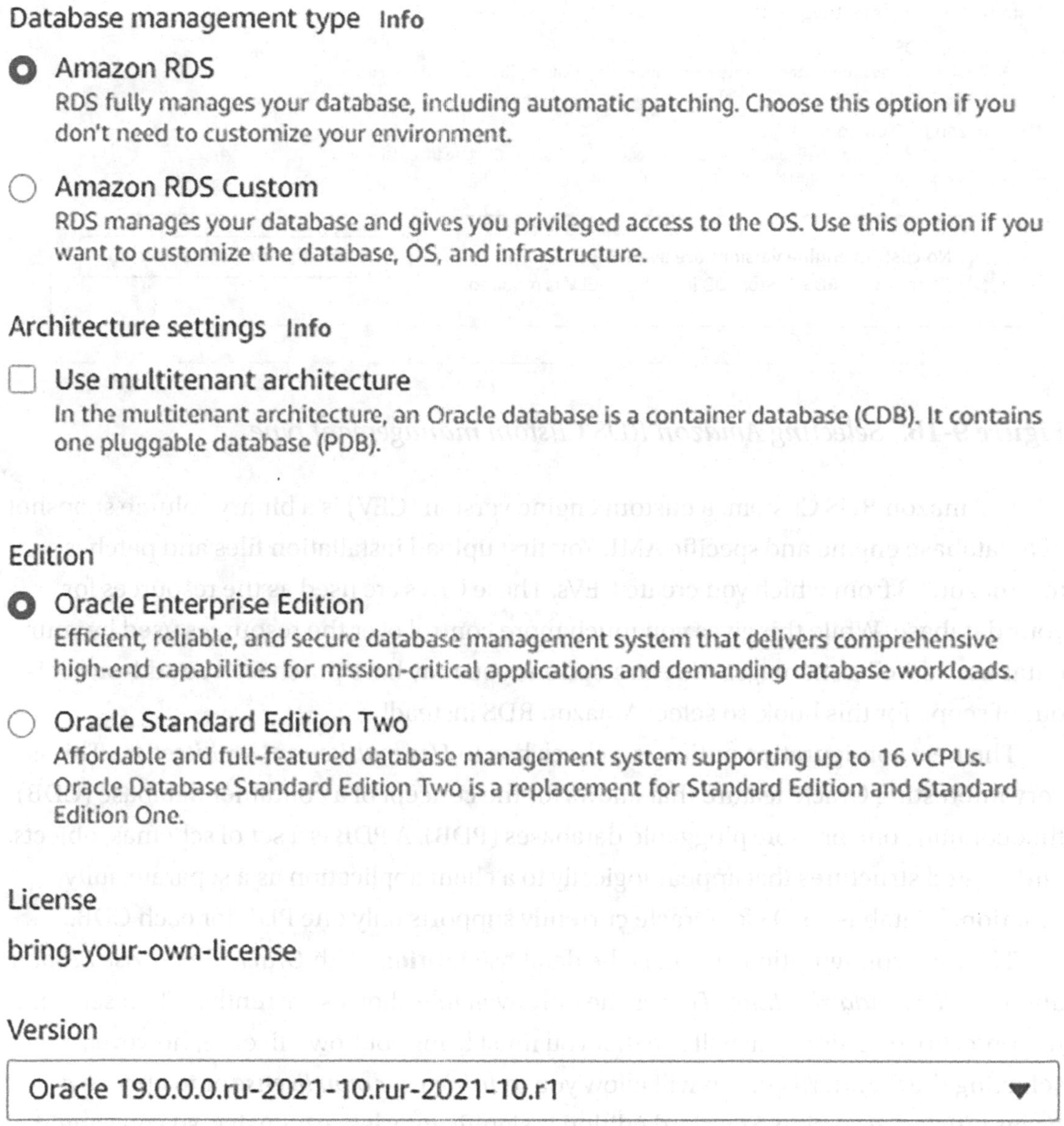

Database management type Info

● Amazon RDS
RDS fully manages your database, including automatic patching. Choose this option if you
don't need to customize your environment.

○ Amazon RDS Custom
RDS manages your database and gives you privileged access to the OS. Use this option if you
want to customize the database, OS, and infrastructure.

Architecture settings Info

☐ Use multitenant architecture
In the multitenant architecture, an Oracle database is a container database (CDB). It contains
one pluggable database (PDB).

Edition

● Oracle Enterprise Edition
Efficient, reliable, and secure database management system that delivers comprehensive
high-end capabilities for mission-critical applications and demanding database workloads.

○ Oracle Standard Edition Two
Affordable and full-featured database management system supporting up to 16 vCPUs.
Oracle Database Standard Edition Two is a replacement for Standard Edition and Standard
Edition One.

License

bring-your-own-license

Version

Oracle 19.0.0.0.ru-2021-10.rur-2021-10.r1	▼

Figure 9-15. *Options after selecting Oracle when creating a new RDS Database*

As you can see, your next option is to select the *Database management type*, for
which there are two options: the default *Amazon RDS* and *Amazon RDS Custom*. The
Amazon RDS Custom management type requires you to upload your own installation
files and patches to Amazon S3. Selecting that management type will change the UI as
shown in Figure 9-16.

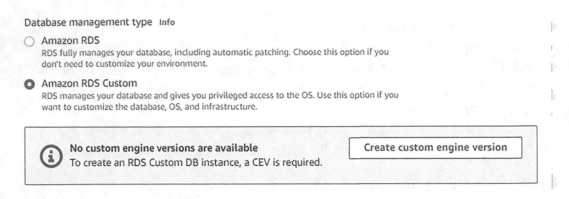

Figure 9-16. *Selecting Amazon RDS Custom management type*

In Amazon RDS Custom, a custom engine version (CEV) is a binary volume snapshot of a database engine and specific AMI. You first upload installation files and patches to Amazon S3 from which you create CEVs. These CEVs are used as the resources for your database. While this gives you much more control over the resources used by your database as well as manages the extra options you may have purchased as add-ons, it is out of scope for this book, so select Amazon RDS instead!

The next configuration option is a check box to *Use multitenant architecture*. This is a very interesting Oracle feature that allows for the concept of a container database (CDB) that contains one or more pluggable databases (PDB). A PDB is a set of schemas, objects, and related structures that appear logically to a client application as a separate, fully functional database. RDS for Oracle currently supports only one PDB for each CDB.

The next configuration option is the database **Edition**, with *Oracle Enterprise Edition* and *Oracle Standard Edition Two* as the only available choices currently. When selecting the Enterprise edition, you will see that you must bring your own license; however, selecting the Standard edition will allow you to *bring your own license* or to choose *a license-included* version. Standard edition is significantly less expensive, so you should consider that approach unless you need the full enterprise functionality. We chose the Standard edition, license-included, most-recent version.

Once you have gone through those, all the remaining sections are ones that you have seen before as they are the same as are available on MySQL, MariaDB, and PostgreSQL (there is no serverless instance approach like was available with Amazon Aurora). However, this will not enable us to be able to automatically connect with our .NET application.

If we look back at our Oracle connection string:

```
"user id=prodotnetonaws;password=password123;data source="(DESCRIPTI
ON=(ADDRESS=(PROTOCOL=tcp)(HOST=servernamehere)(PORT=1521))(CONNECT_
DATA=(SID=databasename)))"
```

there are two values that are needed: the *servername* and the *databasename*. We know that once the server has been created, there will be a servername, or host, but there is not yet a database with which to connect. Remember, this work you are doing right now is not to create the Oracle database; it is instead around getting the Oracle server set up and available. You can create an initial database by expanding the **Additional Configuration** section and filling out the *Initial database name field* in the *Database options* section as shown in Figure 9-17.

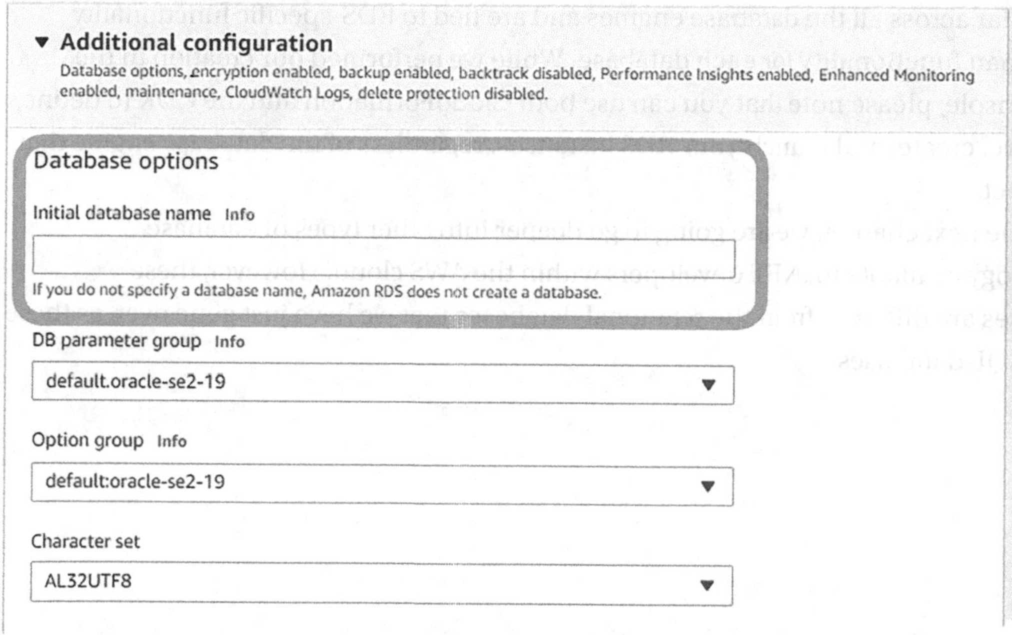

▼ **Additional configuration**
Database options, encryption enabled, backup enabled, backtrack disabled, Performance Insights enabled, Enhanced Monitoring enabled, maintenance, CloudWatch Logs, delete protection disabled.

Database options

Initial database name Info

If you do not specify a database name, Amazon RDS does not create a database.

DB parameter group Info
default.oracle-se2-19

Option group Info
default:oracle-se2-19

Character set
AL32UTF8

Figure 9-17. Creating an initial database during setup

Add in an initial database name and complete the setup. Once you click the *Create* button, then the process will start. However, since Oracle is a much more complicated server than any of the others, this initial creation and setup process will be considerably longer than it was with the other databases.

Once your database is available, clicking on the *DB identifier* will bring up the database details. This is where you will be able to see the endpoint of the server. Using that value plus the database name that you created during the setup process will finish the process for updating your application to use Oracle as its primary database.

Summary

In this chapter, we walked through the non-SQL Server databases that are available in Amazon RDS: MySQL, MariaDB, PostgreSQL, Amazon Aurora, and Oracle. We also showed the code changes necessary to be able to connect to those databases and use them as the repository accessed by Entity Framework Core. We then walked through each of their setups from within the console and showed how many of the setup steps are similar across all the database engines and are tied to RDS-specific functionality rather than functionality for each database. While we performed our creation in the AWS console, please note that you can use both CloudFormation and the CDK to define, configure, create, and launch your RDS instances, regardless of the database engine that you select.

In the next chapter, we are going to go deeper into other types of database technology available to .NET developers within the AWS cloud. However, these databases are different from the relational databases that we have just gone over, as these are NoSQL databases.

CHAPTER 10

NoSQL Databases and AWS

We have just spent a few chapters talking about relational databases – those databases that have a table-based data structure and require a strict, predefined schema. NoSQL databases, called that because of how querying the data does not require the use of SQL, offer a different approach as to how they manage data. Where relational databases specialize in supporting structured data, NoSQL databases specialize in supporting semi-structured, and even unstructured, data instead.

In this chapter, we are going to focus on explaining NoSQL databases and then go into how you can use semi-structured data in your .NET applications. We will then do an even deeper dive into AWS' flagship NoSQL services: DynamoDB and DocumentDB.

Explaining NoSQL Databases

Relational databases and NoSQL databases tend to differ in their promises to their users. Generally, relational databases support Atomicity, Consistency, Isolation, and Durability (ACID) guarantees, where *atomicity* guarantees that either all the transaction succeeds or none of it does, *consistency* guarantees that the data will be valid, *isolation* guarantees that no transaction will be affected by any other transaction, and *durability* guarantees that once a transaction is committed, it will remain in the database. This differs from NoSQL databases, as those generally don't provide ACID guarantees (although some do).

© William Penberthy and Steve Roberts 2023
W. Penberthy and S. Roberts, *Pro .NET on Amazon Web Services*,
https://doi.org/10.1007/978-1-4842-8907-5_10

CAP Theorem

Another way to look at the differences between these two types of databases is to use the CAP theorem. This theorem defines a set of principles applied to distributed systems that store data and states that distributed data systems (think clustered databases here) will offer a trade-off between consistency, availability, and partition tolerance and that any database will only be able to guarantee two of the three properties:

- **Consistency** – Every node in the cluster responds with the most recent data, even if the system must block the request until all replicas update. Querying a "consistent system" for an item that is currently updating will result in a wait until all replicas are successfully updated. When that is complete, you'll receive the most current data.

- **Availability** – Every node returns an immediate response, even if that response isn't the most recent data. Querying an "available system" for an item that is currently updating will result in an immediate response with the best possible answer the service can provide at that moment.

- **Partition tolerance** – Guarantees the system continues to operate even if a replicated data node fails or loses connectivity with other replicated data nodes.

Relational databases typically provide consistency and availability, but not partition tolerance, as they are typically provisioned to a single server. NoSQL databases, on the other hand, typically support high availability and partition tolerance. Figure 10-1 shows the three properties of the CAP theorem.

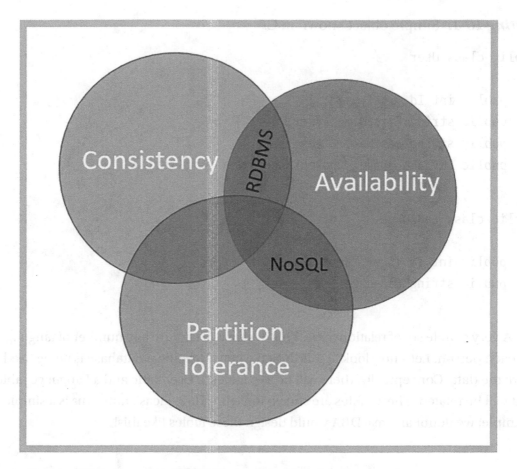

Figure 10-1. *CAP theorem, RDBMS, and NoSQL databases*

One item of note, however, is that the CAP theorem is slowly becoming irrelevant for databases built for the cloud. Consider Amazon Aurora, for example, which is a cloud-native relational database that bakes in partition tolerance – so it would be better displayed in the three-way intersection in the center of Figure 10-1 rather than in one of the two-way intersections. However, if non-cloud-native databases continue to exist, then the CAP theorem will still be an interesting approach for evaluating the trade-offs.

Data Storage Design

The last, and perhaps clearest, way to look at the differences is to visualize the differences in how data is modeled when being stored. Let's first look at a simple object, say, a person and their spoken languages. The C# representation of this is shown in Listing 10-1.

Listing 10-1. Simple object shown in C#

```csharp
public class User
{
    public int Id { get; set; }
    public string FirstName { get; set; }
    public string LastName { get; set; }
    public List<Language> SpokenLanguages { get; set; }
}

public class Language
{
    public int Id { get; set; }
    public string Language { get; set; }
}
```

A very simple set of relationships. This design will capture any number of languages for each person. Let's now look at this design when a relational database is being used to store the data. Conceptually, there will be two tables, a User table and a Language table, that will be related. These tables are shown in Figure 10-2. Please note, this is a simple example; we doubt any real DBA would design these tables like this!

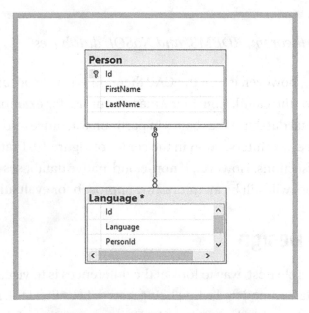

Figure 10-2. *Relational database interpretation of object*

As shown in Figure 10-2, the tables are related through a foreign key, a column labeled *PersonId* in the Language table that has the foreign key relationship to the Id column of the Person table and defines the Person to which that language is related. That ability to relate different tables together is what defines a relational database.

A NoSQL database, on the other hand, will store this data very differently. Rather than breaking this data into multiple, related tables, a NoSQL database will instead store the data in a much "simpler" format as shown in Figure 10-3.

```
{
    "Id": 105,
    "FirstName": "Bill",
    "LastName": "Penberthy",
    "SpokenLanguages": ["English-American", "Pirate"]
}
```

Figure 10-3. *NoSQL database interpretation of object*

Thus, retrieving the Person becomes one database call without requiring any joins. This means that this call will most likely be more performant than would the same call into a relational database, at the cost of extra data being stored.

Also, think about what happens when you add a new property onto your Person, say, their Middle Name. Making that change in a system that uses a relational database for persistence means that you will have to change the database design itself, which brings its own set of risks and complications. In a NoSQL environment, you do not have to make any change to the database, so the impact of that change is limited to the code rather than to both the code and the database.

Different Types of NoSQL Databases

So far, we have talked about NoSQL databases as if they are a single way of "doing business." However, there are multiple types of NoSQL databases, each with its specializations and ways in which they approach persisting and accessing information. The main flavors of NoSQL databases are document databases, key-value stores, column-oriented databases, and graph databases.

Document Databases

A document database stores data in JSON as shown in Figure 10-3, BSON, or XML.

Note   BSON stands for "Binary JSON." BSON's binary structure allows for the encoding of type and length information. This encoding tends to allow the data to be parsed much more quickly, and it helps support indexing and querying into the properties of the document being stored.

Documents are typically stored in a format that is much closer to the data model being worked with in the application. The examples used previously show this clearly. Additional functionality supported by document databases tends to be around ways of indexing and/or querying data within the document. The Id will generally be the key used for primary access, but imagine cases like where you want to search the data for all instances of a Person with a FirstName of "Steve". In SQL, that is easy because that data is segregated into its own column. It is more complex in a NoSQL database because that query must now go rummaging around the data within the document, which, as you can probably imagine, will be slow without a lot of work around query optimization. Common examples of document databases include MongoDB, Amazon DocumentDB, and Microsoft Azure Cosmos DB.

Key-Value Stores

A key-value store is the simplest of the NoSQL databases. In these types of databases, every element in the database is stored as a simple key-value pair made up of an attribute, or key, and the value, which can be anything. Literally, anything. It can be a simple string, a JSON document like is stored in a document database, or even something very unstructured like an image or some other blob of binary data.

The difference between Document databases and Key-Value databases is generally their focus. Document databases focus on ways of parsing the document so that users can do things like making decisions about data within that document. Key-Value databases are very different. They do not care what the value is, so they tend to focus more on storing and accessing the value as quickly as possible and making sure that they can easily scale to store *a lot* of different values. Examples of Key-Value databases include Amazon DynamoDB, Berkeley DB, Memcached, and Redis. Those of you familiar with the concept of caching, where you create a high-speed data storage layer that stores a subset of data so that accessing that data is more responsive than calling directly into the database, will see two products that are commonly used for caching: Memcached and Redis. These are excellent examples of the speed vs. document analysis trade-off between these two types of databases.

Column-Oriented Databases

Yes, the name of these types of NoSQL databases may initially be confusing because you may think about how the data in relational databases are broken down into columns. However, the data is accessed and managed differently. In a relational database, an item is best thought of as a row, with each column containing an aspect or value referring to a specific part of that item. A column-oriented database instead stores data tables by column rather than row.

Let's take a closer look at that since that sounds pretty crazy. Figure 10-4 shows a snippet of a data table like you are used to seeing in a relational database system, where the *RowId* is an internal value used to refer to the data (only within the system) while the *Id* is the external value used to refer to the data.

RowId	Id	FirstName	LastName
1	100	Steve	Roberts
2	101	Bill	Penberthy

Figure 10-4. *Data within a relational database table, stored as a row*

Since row-oriented systems are designed to efficiently return data for a row, this data could be saved to disk as

```
1:100,Steve,Roberts;
2:101,Bill,Penberthy;
```

In a column-oriented database, however, this data would instead be saved as

```
100:1,101:2;
Steve:1,Bill:2;
Roberts:1,Penberthy:2
```

Why would they take that kind of approach? Mainly, speed of access when pulling a subset of values for an "item". Let's look at an index for a row-based system. An index

367

is a structure that is associated with a database table to speed the retrieval of rows from that table. Typically, the index sorts the list of values so that it is easier to find a specific value. If you consider the data in Figure 10-4 and know that it is very common to query based on a specific LastName, then creating a database index on the LastName field means that a query looking for "Roberts" would not have to scan every row in the table to find the data, as that price was paid when building the index. Thus, an index on the LastName field would look something like the following snippet, where all LastNames have been alphabetized and stored independently:

```
Penberthy:2;
Roberts:1;
```

If you look at this definition of an index and look back at the column-oriented data, you will see a very similar approach. What that means is that when accessing a limited subset of data or the data is only sparsely populated, a column-oriented database will most likely be much faster than accessing a row-based database. If, on the other hand, you tend to use a broader set of data, then storing that information in a row would likely be much more performant. Examples of column-oriented systems include Apache Kudu, Amazon Redshift, and Snowflake.

Graph Databases

The last major type of NoSQL databases is graph databases. A graph database focuses on storing nodes and relationships. A node is an entity; is generally stored with a label, such as Person; and contains a set of key-value pairs, or properties. That means you can think of a node as being very similar to the document as stored in a database. However, a graph database takes this much further as it also stores information about relationships.

A relationship is a directed and named connection between two different nodes, such as Person *Knows* Person. A relationship always has a direction, a starting node, an ending node, and a type of relationship. A relationship also can have a set of properties, just like a node. Nodes can have any number or type of relationships, and there is no effect on performance when querying those relationships or nodes. Lastly, while relationships are directed, they can be navigated efficiently in either direction.

Let's take a closer look at this. From the preceding example, there are two people, Bill and Steve, that *are friends*. Both Bill and Steve *wrote* the book "Pro .NET on AWS". This means there are three nodes, with four known relationships:

- Bill is friends with Steve.

- Steve is friends with Bill.

- Bill wrote "Pro .NET on AWS."

- Steve wrote "Pro .NET on AWS."

Figure 10-5 shows how this is visualized in a graph model.

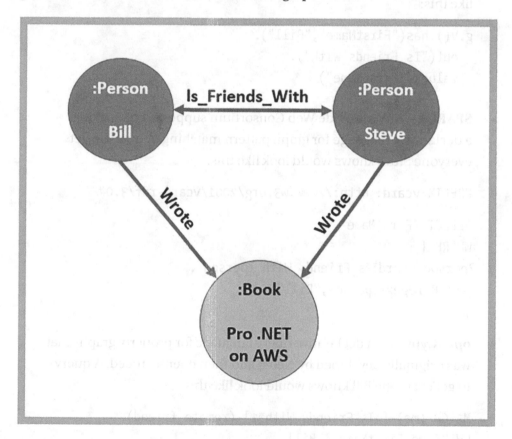

Figure 10-5. *Graph model representation with relationships*

Since both nodes and relationships can contain additional information, we can include more information in each node, such as LastName for the Persons or a Publish date for the Book, and we can add additional information to a relationship, such as a StartDate for writing the book or a Date for when they become friends.

Graph databases tend to have their own way of querying data because you can be pulling data based upon both nodes and relationships. There are three common query approaches:

- **Gremlin** – Part of an Apache project is used for creating and querying property graphs. A query to get everyone Bill knows would look like this:

```
g.V().has("FirstName","Bill").
  out("Is_Friends_With").
  values("FirstName")
```

- **SPARQL** – A World Wide Web Consortium supported project for a declarative language for graph pattern matching. A query to get everyone Steve knows would look like this:

```
PREFIX vcard: http://www.w3.org/2001/vcard-rdf/3.0#

SELECT ?FirstName
WHERE {
?person vcard:Is_Friends_With ?person .
FILTER regex(?person,"Bill")
}
```

- **openCypher** – A declarative query language for property graphs that was originally developed by Neo4j and then open-sourced. A query to get everyone Bill knows would look like this:

```
MATCH (me)-[:Is_Friends_With*1]-(remote_friend)
WHERE me.FirstName = Bill
RETURN remote_friend.FirstName
```

The most common graph databases are Neo4j, ArangoDB, and Amazon Neptune.

Deciding Between Relational and NoSQL

All that background and miscellaneous information gives you an understanding of the differences between the two different high-level approaches; however, it doesn't necessarily make it easier for you to understand which approach suits your needs the best. Let's look at Table 10-1, which shows some common use cases, and see which approach suits that use case the best.

Table 10-1. *Use cases and the recommendation on data storage*

Use Case	Recommendation
Requires the use of complex queries across multiple aspects of the data	Relational, as you get much more performance when requiring more granular filtering
Data Consistency is not an issue, such as a product review that must be available eventually, not at the same time for every user	NoSQL, which traded the ability to scale for consistency
High transaction system where the same data is frequently accessed and manipulated	Relational, as integrity across transactions is one of its primary considerations
Constantly adding new features that require changes in data structures	NoSQL, as these changes can be managed in code with no changes to the database schema

There are additional decision points that you can go into about the type of NoSQL database that is the best fit for your project, but the most important one to consider is generally around how structured is your data. To get a better understanding of this, we will now look at the two biggest NoSQL databases at AWS: DocumentDB and DynamoDB.

Amazon DocumentDB

Amazon DocumentDB is a fully managed, scalable, and highly available document database service that uses a distributed, fault-tolerant, self-healing storage system that auto-scales up to 64 TB per cluster. Amazon DocumentDB reduces database I/O by only persisting write-ahead logs and does not need to write full buffer page syncs, avoiding slow, inefficient, and expensive data replication across network links.

This design allows for the separation of compute and storage. This means that you can scale each of those areas independently. DocumentDB is designed for 99.99% availability and replicates six copies of your data across three Availability Zones. It also continually monitors cluster instance health and automatically fails over to a read replica in the event of a failure – typically in less than 30 seconds. You can start with a single instance that delivers high durability and then, as you grow, can add a second instance for high availability and easily increase the number of instances you use for read-only. You can scale read capacity to millions of requests per second by scaling out to 15 low-latency read replicas that can be scattered across three Availability Zones.

One of the interesting characteristics is that DocumentDB was built with MongoDB compatibility. Why is that important?

MongoDB

MongoDB is a source-available cross-platform document database that was first released in 2009 and is, by far, the most popular document database available. Since it was both the first and available open-sourced, it tended to be adopted early by companies running on-premises and experimenting with the concept of document stores so there is a huge number of on-premises software systems that rely completely on, or in part on, MongoDB. This means that any movement of systems to the cloud would have to come up with a way to support the software written around MongoDB; otherwise, this would be a massive impediment in migrating to the cloud.

AWS realized this and released DocumentDB to include compatibility with the MongoDB APIs that were available at the time. At the time of this writing (and at release), DocumentDB implements the MongoDB 3.6 and 4.0 API responses. However, MongoDB released version 5.0 in July 2021, so there is no feature parity. Also, since there were annual releases for 4.2, 4.4, 4.4.5, and 4.4.6 that AWS did not support, it appears that there will not be additional support moving forward.

While current compatibility with MongoDB is not supported, the design of DocumentDB, together with optimizations like advanced query processing, connection pooling, and optimized recovery and rebuild, provides a very performant system. AWS claims that DocumentDB achieves twice the throughput of currently available MongoDB managed services.

Setting Up a DocumentDB Database

Now that we have a bit of understanding about DocumentDB, let's go set one up. Log into the console, and either search for DocumentDB or find it using Services ➤ Database ➤ Amazon DocumentDB. Select the **Create Cluster** button on the dashboard to bring up the *Create cluster* page as shown in Figure 10-6.

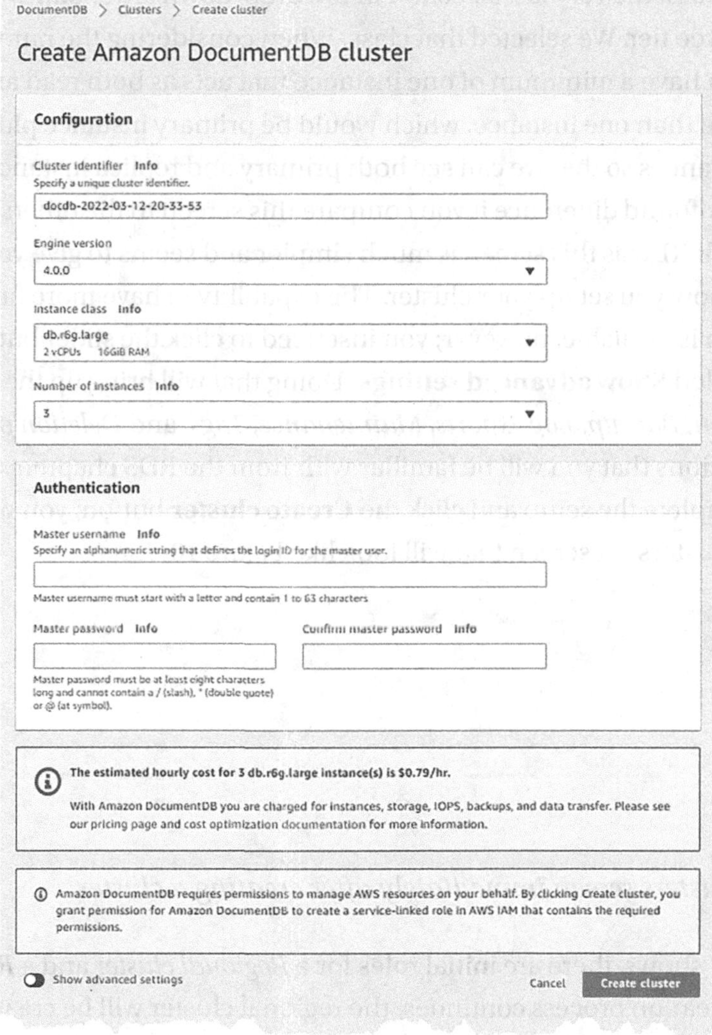

Figure 10-6. Create Amazon DocumentDB cluster screen

First, fill out the Configuration section by adding in a *Cluster identifier*.
This identifier must be unique to DocumentDB clusters within this region. Next, you'll

see a drop-down for the *Engine version*. This controls the MongoDB API that you will want to use for the connection. This becomes important when selecting and configuring the database drivers that you will be using in your .NET application. We recommend that you use 4.0 as this gives you the ability to support transactions. The next two fields are *Instance class* and *Number of instances*. This is where you define the compute and memory capacity of the instance as well as the number of instances that you will have. For the Instance class, the very last selection in the drop-down is *db.t3.medium*, which is eligible for the free tier. We selected that class. When considering the number of instances, you can have a minimum of one instance that acts as both read and write, or you can have more than one instance, which would be primary instance plus replicas. We chose two instances so that we can see both primary and replica instances.

You'll see a profound difference if you compare this screen to the others that we saw when working with RDS as this screen is much simpler and seems to give you much less control over how you set up your cluster. The capability to have more fine control over configuration is available, however; you just need to click the slider button at the lower left labeled **Show advanced settings**. Doing that will bring up the *Network settings, Encryption, Backup, Log exports, Maintenance, Tags*, and *Deletion protection* configuration sections that you will be familiar with from the RDS chapters.

Once you complete the setup and click the **Create cluster** button, you will be returned to the Clusters list screen that will look like Figure 10-7.

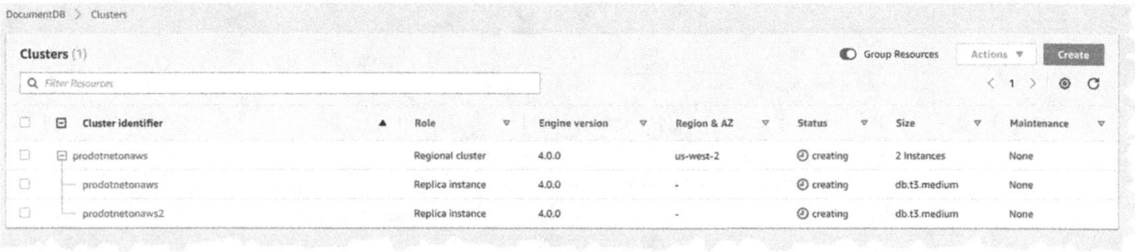

Cluster identifier		Role	Engine version	Region & AZ	Status	Size	Maintenance
prodotnetonaws		Regional cluster	4.0.0	us-west-2	creating	2 Instances	None
prodotnetonaws		Replica instance	4.0.0	-	creating	db.t3.medium	None
prodotnetonaws2		Replica instance	4.0.0	-	creating	db.t3.medium	None

Figure 10-7. *Clusters screen immediately after creating a cluster*

As Figure 10-7 shows, there are initial roles for a *Regional cluster* and a *Replica instance*. As the creation process continues, the regional cluster will be created first, and then the first instance in line will change role to become a *Primary instance*. When creation is completed, there will be one regional cluster, one primary instance, and any number of replica instances. Since we chose two instances when creating the cluster, we show one replica instance being created. When the cluster is fully available, you will also have access to the regions in which the clusters are available. At this point, you will have a cluster on which to run your database, but you will not yet have a database to which you can connect. But as you will see in the following text when we start using DocumentDB in our code, that's ok.

DocumentDB and .NET

When looking at using this service within your .NET application, you need to consider that like Amazon Aurora, DocumentDB emulates the APIs of other products. This means that you will not be accessing the data through AWS drivers but instead will be using MongoDB database drivers within your application. It is important to remember, however, that your database is not built using the most recent version of the MongoDB API, so you must ensure that the drivers that you do use are compatible with the version that you selected during the creation of the cluster, in our case, MongoDB 4.0. Luckily, however, MongoDB provides a compatibility matrix at `https://docs.mongodb.com/drivers/csharp/`.

The necessary NuGet package is called **MongoDB.Driver**. Installing this package will bring several other packages with it including *MongoDB.Driver.Core, MongoDB.Driver. BSON*, and *MongoDB.Libmongocrypt*. One of the first things that you may notice is there is not an "Entity Framework" kind of package that we got used to when working with Amazon RDS. And that makes sense because Entity Framework is basically an Object-Relational Mapper (ORM) that helps manage the relationships between different tables – which is exactly what we do not need when working with NoSQL systems. Instead, your table is simply a collection of things. However, using the MongoDB drivers allows you to still use well-defined classes when mapping results to objects. It is, however, more of a deserialization process than an ORM process.

When working with DocumentDB, you need to build your connection string using the following format: `mongodb://[user]:[password]@[hostname]/[database]?[options]`

This means you have five components to the connection string:

- **user** – Username

- **password** – Password

- **hostname** – URL to connect to

- **database** – Optional parameter – database with which to connect

- **options** – A set of configuration options

It is easy to get the connection string for DocumentDB, however. In the DocumentDB console, clicking on the identifier for the regional cluster will bring you to a summary page. Lower on that page is a *Connectivity & security tab* that contains examples of approaches for connecting to the cluster. The last one, *Connect to this cluster with an application,* contains the cluster connection string as shown in Figure 10-8.

Figure 10-8. *Getting DocumentDB connection string*

You should note that the table name is not present in the connection string. You can either add it to the connection string or use a different variable as we do in the following example.

Once you have connected to the database and identified the collection that you want to access, you are able to access it using lambdas (the anonymous functions, not AWS' serverless offering!). Let's look at how that works. First, we define the model that we want to use for the deserialization process.

```
public class Person
{
    [BsonId]
    [BsonRepresentation(BsonType.ObjectId)]

    public string Id { get; set; }
```

```
    [BsonElement("First")]
    public string FirstName { get; set; }

    [BsonElement("Last")]
    public string LastName { get; set; }
}
```

What you'll notice right away is that we are not able to use a plain old class object (POCO) but instead must provide some MongoDB BSON attributes. Getting access to these will require the following libraries to be added to the using statements:

```
using MongoDB.Bson;
using MongoDB.Bson.Serialization.Attributes;
```

There are many different annotations that you can set, of which we are using three:

- **BsonId** – This attribute defines the document's primary key. This means it will become the easiest and fastest field on which to retrieve a document.

- **BsonRepresentation** – This attribute is primarily to support ease of use. It allows the developer to pass the parameter as type `string` instead of having to use an `ObjectId` structure as this attribute handles the conversion from `string` to `ObjectId`.

- **BsonElement** – This attribute maps the property name "Last" from the collection to the object property "LastName" and the property name "First" to the object property "FirstName".

That means that the following JSON shows a record that would be saved as a Person type:

```
{
  "Id": "{29A25F7D-C2C1-4D82-9996-03C647646428}",
  "First": "Bill",
  "Last": "Penberthy"
}
```

We mentioned earlier that accessing the items within DocumentDB becomes straightforward when using lambdas. Thus, a high-level CRUD service could look similar to the code in Listing 10-2.

Listing 10-2. CRUD service to interact with Amazon DocumentDB

```
using MongoDB.Driver;
public class PersonService
{
    private readonly IMongoCollection<Person> persons;

    public PersonService ()
    {
        var client = new MongoClient("connection string here");
        var database = client.GetDatabase("Production");
        persons = database.GetCollection<Person>("Persons");
    }

    public async Task<List<Person>> GetAsync() =>
        await persons.Find(_ => true).ToListAsync();

    public async Task<Person?> GetByIdAsync(string id) =>
        await persons.Find(x => x.Id == id).FirstOrDefaultAsync();

    public async Task<Person?> GetByLastNameAsync(string name) =>
        await persons.Find(x => x.LastName == name).FirstOrDefaultAsync();

    public async Task CreateAsync(Person person) =>
        await persons.InsertOneAsync(person);

    public async Task UpdateAsync(string id, Person person) =>
        await persons.ReplaceOneAsync(x => x.Id == id, person);

    public async Task RemoveAsync(string id) =>
        await persons.DeleteOneAsync(x => x.Id == id);
}
```

One of the conveniences with working with DocumentDB (and MongoDB for that matter) is that creating the database and the collection is automatic when the first item (or document) is saved. Thus, creating the database and book collection is just as simple as saving your first book. Of course, that means you have to make sure that you define your database and collection correctly, but it also means that you don't have to worry about your application not connecting if you mistype the database name – you'll just have a new database!

Amazon DynamoDB

Where DocumentDB is a document store that is built around the MongoDB API, DynamoDB is a fully managed, serverless, NoSQL, key-value database. While originally built as a key-value database, DynamoDB also supports document data models, which allows you to get the speed of key-value databases along with the ability to do searches within the document that was stored as a value. It uses built-in horizontal scaling to scale to more than 10 trillion requests per day with peaks greater than 20 million requests per second over petabytes of storage. In other words, DynamoDB scales really well!

There are two different capacity modes in which you can configure each DynamoDB database: *On-demand* and *Provisioned*. If these terms sound familiar, that should not be a surprise as these are the same options you get with Amazon Aurora, the serverless relational database offering we went over in the last chapter. With on-demand capacity, you pay per request for data reads and writes into your database. You do not have to specify how many reads or writes there will be as DynamoDB scales itself to support your needs as that number increases or decreases. With provisioned capacity, you specify the number of reads and writes per second. You can use auto-scaling to adjust capacity based on the utilization for when the usage of your system may grow. Provisioned capacity is less expensive, but you may end up overprovisioning your server and paying more than you need.

Setting Up a DynamoDB Database

The easiest way to get a feel for DynamoDB is to use one, so let's set one up. Log into the console, and either search for DynamoDB or find it using Services ➤ Database ➤ DynamoDB. Select the **Create table** button on the dashboard to bring up the *Create table* page. The first setup section is Table details and is shown in Figure 10-9.

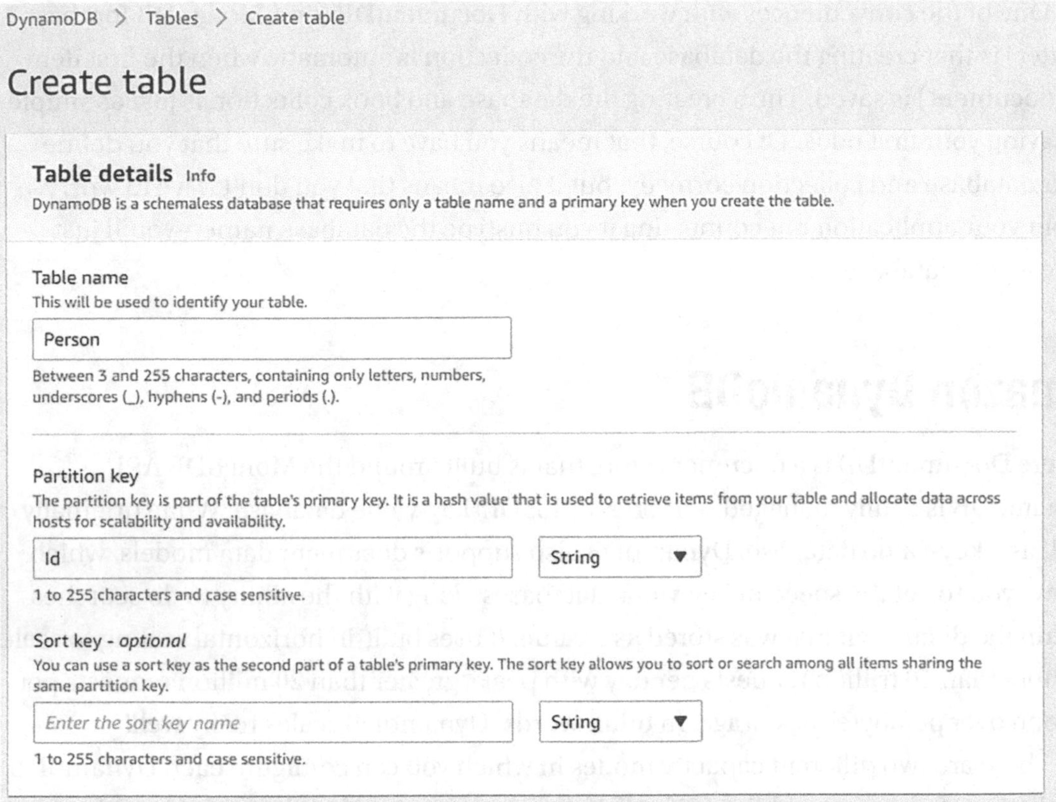

DynamoDB > Tables > Create table

Create table

Table details   Info

DynamoDB is a schemaless database that requires only a table name and a primary key when you create the table.

Table name

This will be used to identify your table.

Person

Between 3 and 255 characters, containing only letters, numbers, underscores (_), hyphens (-), and periods (.).

Partition key

The partition key is part of the table's primary key. It is a hash value that is used to retrieve items from your table and allocate data across hosts for scalability and availability.

Id		String ▼

1 to 255 characters and case sensitive.

Sort key - _optional_

You can use a sort key as the second part of a table's primary key. The sort key allows you to sort or search among all items sharing the same partition key.

Enter the sort key name		String ▼

1 to 255 characters and case sensitive.

Figure 10-9. Creating a DynamoDB table

There are three different values that you can enter. The first, *Table name*, is straightforward and needs to be unique by region. We used "Person" to identify the type of data that we are going to be storing in the table. The second value is the *Partition key,* and the third value is an optional *Sort key*. A simple primary key is made up only of the partition key, and no two items in the table can share the same partition key. A composite primary key, on the other hand, is made up of both a partition key and a sort key. All items with the same partition key are stored together, sorted by the sort value. If using a composite primary key, you can have multiple instances of a partition key; however, the combination of partition key and sort key must be unique.

Note   One instance where we have seen a composite key used to great effect is when different versions are being kept. As a new version is created, it gets the same partition key but a new sort key, in that case, a version number.

The keys can have different types: *Binary, Number,* and *String.* In our case, as you can see in Figure 10-9, we created a string partition key of "Id" without a sort key.

The next configuration section on the page is Settings, where you can select either the *Default settings* or *Customize settings.* Going with the default settings takes all the fun out of the rest of the configuration section of this chapter, so select to customize settings.

The next section is *Table class,* where you have two options: *DynamoDB Standard* and *DynamoDB Standard-1A.* The determination between these two is based upon the frequency with which data will be accessed. The less frequently your table will have reads and writes performed against it, the more likely that the 1A version will be appropriate.

Next comes the *Capacity calculator* section. This is an interesting tool that helps you translate your typical (or predicted) usage into the generic Read and Write units that are used for configuration, pricing, and billing. You will need to expand the section before it becomes fully available, but when you do, you will get a series of fields as shown in Figure 10-10.

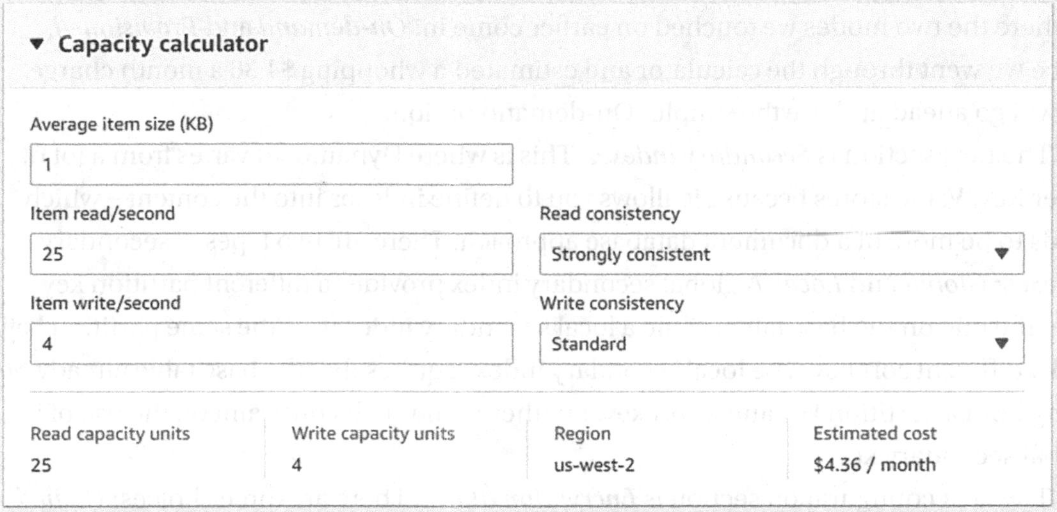

▼ Capacity calculator

Average item size (KB)

1

Item read/second		Read consistency	
25		Strongly consistent	▼

Item write/second		Write consistency	
4		Standard	▼

Read capacity units	Write capacity units	Region	Estimated cost
25	4	us-west-2	$4.36 / month

Figure 10-10. *DynamoDB Capacity calculator*

The questions that it asks are straightforward: how big your average payload is, how many reads per second will you have, how many saves per second, and what your business requirements are for those reads and writes. Let's look at those options in a bit more detail. *Average item size (kb)* is an integer field capturing your average payload rounded to the nearest kilobyte. This can be frustrating, because many times your payloads may be considerably smaller than a kilobyte – but go ahead and choose 1 if your payloads are relatively small. The *Item read/second* and *Item write/second* are also straightforward integer fields, and we used 25 items read per second and 4 items written per second.

The *Read consistency* and *Write consistency* fields are a little different as they are drop-downs. Read offers *Eventually consistent*, where it is possible that a read may not have the most recent version of the data (because it is coming from a read-only copy of the data); *Strongly consistent*, where all reads will have the most recent version of the data (because it is coming from the primary table); and *Transactional*, where multiple actions are submitted as a single all-or-nothing operation. Write consistency offers two approaches: *Standard*, where the data is inserted into the primary, and *Transactional*, which is the same as for Read consistency. In our example, we selected Strongly consistent for reads and Standard for writes. The calculator then estimated our costs at $4.36 a month in US-West-2. As you can see, it's a pretty inexpensive option.

The next section in the table creation screen is the *Read/write capacity settings*. This is where the two modes we touched on earlier come in: *On-demand* and *Provisioned*. Since we went through the calculator and estimated a whopping $4.36 a month charge, we will go ahead and use the simpler On-demand option.

The next section is *Secondary indexes*. This is where DynamoDB varies from a lot of other Key/Value stores because it allows you to define indexes into the content – which tends to be more of a document database approach. There are two types of secondary indexes: *Global* and *Local*. A global secondary index provides a different partition key than the one on the base table, while a local secondary index uses the same partition key and a different sort key. The local secondary index requires that the base table already be using both a partition key and a sort key, but there is no such constraint on the use of a global secondary key.

The next configuration section is *Encryption at rest*. There are three choices: *Owned by Amazon DynamoDB,* where the application manages encryption using AWS keys; *AWS managed key,* where AWS creates keys and then manages those keys within your AWS Key Management Service (KMS); and *Customer managed key*, where you can create and manage the KMS key yourself. We selected the AWS-owned key.

The last configuration section is *Tags*. Once your table is configured, select the **Create table** button at the bottom. This will bring up the Tables listing with your table in a "Creating" status as shown in Figure 10-11. Once the creation is complete, the status will change to "Active".

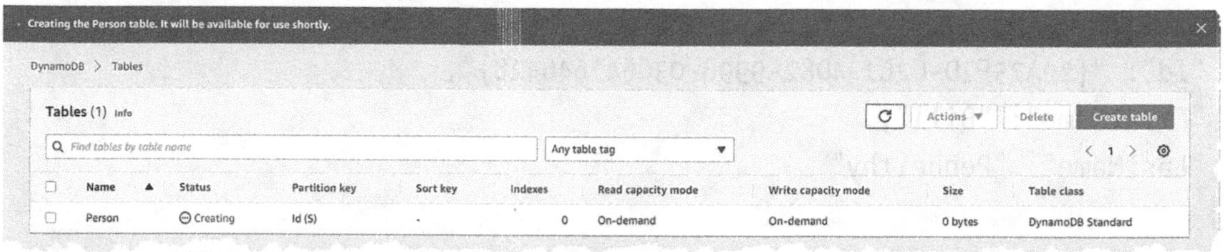

Figure 10-11. *Tables listing after creating a table*

Unlike Amazon DocumentDB, DynamoDB gives you the ability to work directly with the data within the table. Once the table has been created, click on the table name to go into the table detail screen. This page gives you a lot of information, including metrics on table usage. We won't go into that into much detail, simply because this could use its own book, so instead click on the button at the top, **Explore table items**. This will bring you to a page where you can interact with the items within the table. There is also a **Create item** button at the top. We used this button to create two simple items in the table, with the first shown in Figure 10-12.

Figure 10-12. *Creating an item in Amazon DynamoDB*

If this format seems a little unusual, it is because this is the DynamoDB JSON, which is different from "traditional" JSON in that it stores the items as their own key/value pairs. If you turn off the View DynamoDB JSON selector at the top, then you will see the more standard JSON:

```
{
  "Id": "{29A25F7D-C2C1-4D82-9996-03C647646428}",
  "FirstName": "Bill",
  "LastName": "Penberthy"
}
```

DynamoDB and AWS Toolkit for Visual Studio

Unlike DocumentDB, which has no support in any of the IDE toolkits, you have the ability to access DynamoDB from the Toolkit for Visual Studio. Using the toolkit, you can both view the table and look at items within the table as shown in Figure 10-13.

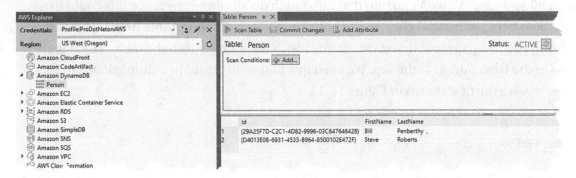

Figure 10-13. *Using the Toolkit for Visual Studio to view DynamoDB items*

You can even use the toolkit to filter returns by selecting the **Add button** within the top box. This will add a line with a drop-down that includes all of the field names (Id, FirstName, and LastName) and allow you to enter a filter value. Selecting "FirstName" "Equal" "Steve" and then clicking the **Scan Table** button will result in only one result remaining in the list as shown in Figure 10-14.

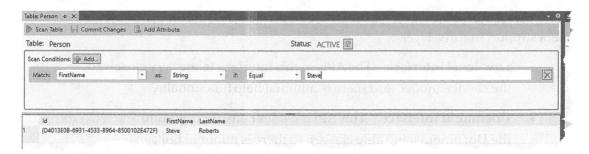

Figure 10-14. *Filtering DynamoDB items in Visual Studio*

The toolkit will also allow you to add, edit, and delete items simply by double-clicking on the item in the result list. Since you are working with the items in a list form, you can even use the **Add Attribute** button to add a new "column" where you can capture new information. Once you add a value to that new column and **Commit Changes**, those items (where you added the value) will be updated.

As you can imagine, the ability to interact with the data directly in Visual Studio makes working with the service much easier, as you can look directly into the data to understand what you should get when parts of your code are run in Debug or when running integration tests. Unfortunately, however, this functionality is only supported in the AWS Toolkit for Visual Studio and is not available in either Rider or Visual Studio Code toolkits.

DynamoDB and .NET

The last step is to take a look at using DynamoDB within your .NET application. As mentioned earlier, using DynamoDB means that you will not be using Entity Framework as you did with the relational databases earlier. Instead, we will be using a DynamoDB context, cunningly named DynamoDBContext, which provides very similar support as does the DBContext in Entity Framework.

Note   One of the interesting features of using DynamoDB within your development process is the availability of a downloadable version of DynamoDB. Yes, you read that correctly, you can download and locally install a version of the DynamoDB as either a Java application, an Apache Maven dependency, or as a Docker image. Details on this can be found at https://docs.aws.amazon.com/amazondynamodb/latest/developerguide/DynamoDBLocal.html.

In many ways, the .NET SDK for DynamoDB is one of the more advanced SDKs as it offers support in three layers:

- **Low-level interface** – The APIs in this interface relate very closely to the service model, and there is minimal help functionality.

- **Document interface** – This API includes constructs around the Document and Table classes, so there is minimal built-in functionality to help do things like converting to business objects.

- **High-level interface** – This is where AWS provides support around converting Documents to .NET classes and other helpful interactions.

Your code can interact with any of the interfaces based upon your business need. We will be relying on the high-level interface as we move into the code examples.

First, you need to add the appropriate NuGet package: **AWSSDK.DynamoDBv2**. Once you have that added, the next thing that you need to do is to configure your connection to the database. Listing 10-3 shows a constructor method to do this.

Listing 10-3. Configuring a DynamoDB connection to the database

```
private AmazonDynamoDBClient client;
private DynamoDBContext context;

public DataClient()
{
    client = new AmazonDynamoDBClient();
    context = new DynamoDBContext(client);
}
```

There are two objects introduced in this snippet. The first class introduced is the `Amazon.DynamoDBv2.AmazonDynamoDBClient`. This class provides the default implementation for accessing the service. The constructor used in the example will default to credentials stored in the application's default configuration. Running this on your local machine means that the application will use your "default" profile to connect. There are other constructors that you can use, ranging from passing in your Access Key ID and Secret Key to using Credentials stored in AWS Key Manager. For this example, however, we will stick with the default constructor. The second object introduced is the `Amazon.DynamoDBv2.DataModel.DynamoDBContext`. The **DataModel** part of the namespace indicates that this is a high-level interface based upon the low-level interface offered by the *AmazonDynamoDBClient* class.

Now that we have defined the context, let's look at how you would use it. The following is a method to save an object into the table:

```
public async Task SaveAsync<T>(T item)
{
    await context.SaveAsync<T>(item);
}
```

This is where you start to see the power offered by the high-level interface. Let's step out of this class and look at how this is used.

```
public class Person
{
    public string Id { get; set; }
    public string FirstName { get; set; }
    public string LastName { get; set; }
}
public async Task<string> Add(string firstName, string lastName)
{
    var client = new DataClient();

    Person itemToAdd = new Person {
        Id = Guid.NewGuid().ToString("B").ToUpper(),
        FirstName = firstName,
        LastName = lastName
    };

    await client.SaveAsync<Person>(itemToAdd);
    return itemToAdd.Id;
}
```

This **Add** method is taking in a first name and a last name, creates a Person object, persists the information to DynamoDB, and then returns the *Id* to the calling method. And that is what the high-level interface offers. You could do the same work yourself using the Document interface, but you would have to manage all of the serialization and deserialization necessary to convert from the business objects to the JSON that is stored in the table.

One other feature of the high-level interface is much less obvious. Think about when we created the DynamoDB table earlier and the name that we used – "Person". By default, the high-level interface expects the class name of the item being persisted to be the same as the table name, as it is in our case.

We just went over adding an item to the table through the high-level interface. Let's now look at an example of retrieving an item.

```
public async Task<T> FindByIdAsync<T>(string id)
{
    var condition = new List<ScanCondition> {
                    new ScanCondition("Id", ScanOperator.Equal, id) };
    AsyncSearch<T> search = context.ScanAsync<T>(condition);
    var list = await search.GetRemainingAsync();
    return list.FirstOrDefault();
}
```

You can see that this gets a little more complicated. Because this code is doing a scan of the data, it is going to always return a List<T>, even though we set the *Id* as the primary key on the table. This happens because the high-level interface does not know anything about the definition of the table itself and thus generalizes the result set.

This scanning approach should not feel new, however. Think back to how the filtering was set in the AWS Toolkit for Visual Studio (Figure 10-14) and you will see that this is the same approach. This approach is used because of those enhancements into DynamoDB that make it more document database-like; it allows you to scan through the data looking for a specific condition, in this case, the Id equal to the value passed into the FindByIdAsync method. And, just as shown in the toolkit, you can use multiple conditions.

```
public async Task<List<T>> FindByValueAsync<T>(Dictionary<string,object>
searchDict)
{
    var conditions = new List<ScanCondition>();
    foreach(string key in searchDict.Keys)
    {
```

```
    conditions.Add(
      new ScanCondition(key,
              ScanOperator.Equal,
              searchDict[key]));
  }
  AsyncSearch<T> search = context.ScanAsync<T>(conditions);
  return await search.GetRemainingAsync();
}
```

In this instance, we are simply accepting a `Dictionary<string, string>` where we are assuming the key value will be the field name, such as *LastName*, and the dictionary value will be the value to use when filtering. An empty dictionary means that no filters will be set, which, as you can imagine, would be somewhat terrifying if you consider a massive table with petabytes of data. That's where the return class from the `ScanAsync` method comes into play: the `AsyncSearch<T>` class.

`AsyncSearch` is an intermediate class that provides several ways of interacting with the service. In the preceding code example, the method used on that object was `GetRemainingAsync()`. The `GetRemainingAsync` method is used to get all the remaining items that match the filter condition and bring them back as a single unit. However, there is another method on `AsyncSearch`, `GetNextSetAsync`, which manages a finite set of items – up to 1 MB of items. You can examine a property on the `AsyncSearch` object, `IsDone`, which tells you whether the current result set is the final one and gives you the ability to manage the pagination yourself.

We have spent time going through the high-level interface provided by the SDK. We have not even touched on the powerful Document interface and how that provides more specific control over the values stored in DynamoDB. There are many examples of development teams using the document-level interfaces and writing their own high-level interfaces where they can incorporate their specific requirements rather than using the SDK's more generic approach. That approach is not wrong, as no one understands your needs as well as you do – but having the high-level interface allows you to easily get a large majority of requirements fulfilled, and then you can customize using the Document interface as you see fit.

There is a lot more that we can go into about using DynamoDB with .NET, like an entire book, so we won't do that here. Let it suffice to say, yes, you can use DynamoDB with .NET.

Summary

In this chapter, we went over the barest of definitions of NoSQL and talked at a high level about several of the most common types of NoSQL databases, including document, key/value, column-oriented, and graph databases. We then went into more detail about Amazon DocumentDB, the AWS version of a document database, and how it was designed to emulate MongoDB, the most common document database. We also walked through creating a DocumentDB cluster in the AWS console and connecting and using that cluster in a .NET application by using the MongoDB drivers. We then looked at Amazon DynamoDB, creating a database and then using that database in our .NET application using the DynamoDB SDK high-level interface.

In the next chapter, we will finish up our storage section by looking at other "purpose-built" databases provided by AWS that may help you solve one or more of your specific business needs. While we have briefly touched on one of these purposes, graph database, there are several other unique offerings that may be of interest.

CHAPTER 11

Purpose-Built Databases

So far, we have talked a lot about relational databases and some about NoSQL databases, especially document and key/value databases. Those are different types of purpose-built databases, or databases designed to fulfill a set of use cases. These purpose-built databases tend to be designed around diverse data models as their primary use case, just like how a relational data model is different from a document database data model, which is different from the key/value data model.

In this chapter, we will round out the list of purpose-built databases offered by AWS. We will go through the use cases driving each one of them and then talk about interacting with the database using .NET, though generally not at the level that we have so far.

Why Purpose-Built Databases Exist

As we have already discussed, the "default database" for many years was a relational database. A relational database is a collection of different data items that have predefined relationships (hence the name). Through this ability to set up relationships, the amount of data stored was able to be minimized through the concept of *normalization* where common data needs to be only stored once and objects needing that data would need to understand those relationships. This makes data management much easier, as common data stored in multiple locations will easily get out of sync.

However, the times, they are a changing. First, the amount of data being managed is growing. A lot. And as the amount of data increases, so does the velocity of data creation. Imagine an Internet-of-Things (IoT) sensor that is sending a piece of data every second. That doesn't seem bad until you realize a factory may have several hundred thousands of those sensors sending data in every second.

© William Penberthy and Steve Roberts 2023
W. Penberthy and S. Roberts, *Pro .NET on Amazon Web Services*,
https://doi.org/10.1007/978-1-4842-8907-5_11

As the amount and velocity change, so do the variety and complexity of the data being managed. Think about data contained within a video, a genomic analysis, or the onboard analyzed surroundings from a driverless vehicle – all of which are very complex and unique data sets that represent a use case that may be helped by a purpose-built database.

Now, AWS does not currently offer purpose-built databases for all those use cases. But there are types of purpose-built database engines that AWS does support: relational, document, key/value, in-memory, time series, ledger, and graph databases. We have already talked about the first three (relational, document, and key/value), so let's now go over the remaining types.

In-Memory Databases

In-memory databases are typically used for applications that require "real-time access" to data. In-memory databases do this by storing data directly, wait for it, *in memory*. In-memory databases attempt to deliver microsecond latency to applications for whom millisecond latency is not enough, hence why it is called real-time access.

In-memory databases are faster than traditional databases because they store data in Random-Access Memory (RAM) and can rely on a storage manager that requires far fewer CPU instructions as there is no need for disk I/O. They are able to use internal optimization algorithms in the query processor that are simpler and faster than those in traditional databases that need to worry about reading various blocks of data rather than using the direct pointers available to in-memory databases. Figure 11-1 shows how all these pieces interact.

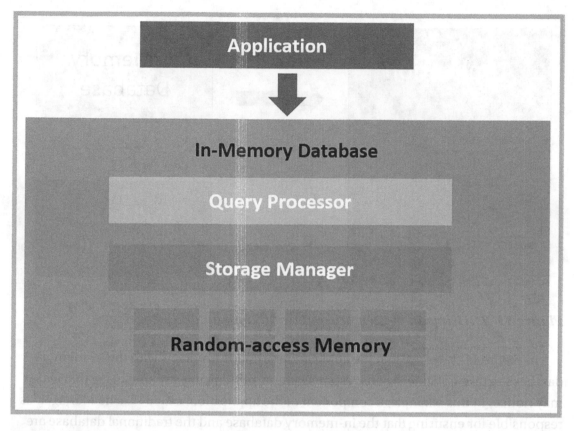

Figure 11-1. *Internals of an in-memory database*

Of course, this reliance on RAM also means that in-memory databases are more volatile than traditional databases because data is lost when there is a loss of power or the memory crashes or gets corrupted. This lack of durability (the "D" in ACID) has been the primary stopper of more common usage with the expense of memory being a close second. However, memory has gotten cheaper, and system architectures have evolved around the use of in-memory databases in a way where the lack of durability is no longer a showstopper, mainly as caches or as a "front end" to a more traditional database. This allows the best of both worlds, real-time persistence with an in-memory database and durability from the traditional database. Figure 11-2 shows an example of how this could work.

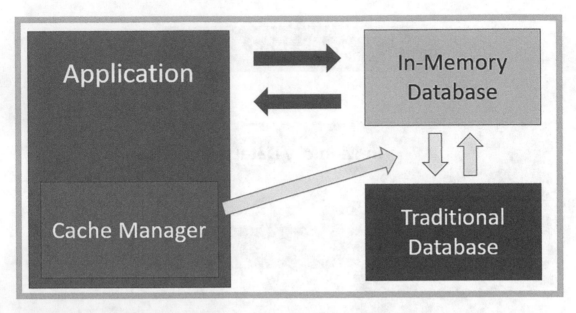

Figure 11-2. *Using an in-memory and traditional database together*

In Figure 11-2, we see that the application primarily interacts with the in-memory database to take advantage of its responsiveness, minimizing any kind of lag that a user may notice. In this example, a component of the application, called "Cache Manager," is responsible for ensuring that the in-memory database and the traditional database are in sync. This component will be responsible for populating the cache upon cache startup and then ensuring all changes to the in-memory database are replicated through to the traditional database.

Obviously, the more complex the systems, the more difficult this cache management may become – say there is another application that may be changing the traditional database in the same way. This could be problematic because the cache manager in your first application may not know that there is a change, and thus, data in the in-memory database will become stale because of the changes from the other application. However, ensuring the same approach to a shared in-memory database can help eliminate this issue as shown in Figure 11-3.

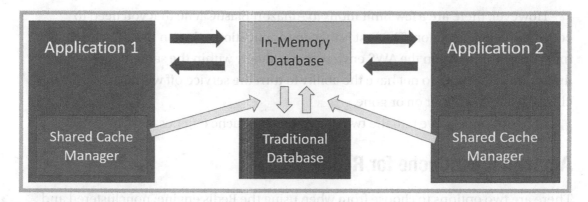

Figure 11-3. *Two applications managing their changes to a shared cache*

More and more systems are relying on in-memory databases, which is why AWS has two different services: Amazon ElastiCache and Amazon MemoryDB for Redis. Before we dig too far into these services, let's add some context by doing a quick dive into the history of in-memory databases as this can help you understand the approach that AWS took when creating their products.

Memcached, an open source general-purpose distributed memory caching system, was released in 2003. It is still maintained, and since it was one of the first in-memory databases available, it is heavily used in various systems including YouTube, Twitter, and Wikipedia. *Redis* is another open source in-memory database that was released in 2009. It quickly became popular as both a store and a cache and is likely the most used in-memory database in the world. The importance of these two databases will become obvious shortly.

Amazon ElastiCache

Amazon ElastiCache is marketed as a fully managed in-memory caching service. There are two ElastiCache engines that are supported: Redis and Memcached (see, we told you that these would come up again). Since it is fully managed, ElastiCache eliminates a lot of the work necessary in hardware provisioning, software patching, setup, configuration, monitoring, failure recovery, and backups than you would have if you were to run your own instance of either Redis or Memcached. Using ElastiCache also adds support for event notifications, monitoring, and metrics without you having to do anything other than enabling them in the console.

However, there are a few limitations to Amazon ElastiCache that you need to consider before adoption. The first is that any application using an ElastiCache cluster must be running within the AWS environment, ideally within the same VPC. Another limitation is that you do not have the ability to turn the service off without deleting the cluster itself; it is either on or gone.

Let's do a quick dive into the two different ElastiCache engines.

Amazon ElastiCache for Redis

There are two options to choose from when using the Redis engine: nonclustered and clustered. The primary difference between the two approaches is the number of write instances supported. In nonclustered mode, you can have a single shard (write instance) with up to five read replica nodes. This means you have one instance to which you write and the ability to read from multiple instances. In a clustered mode, however, you can have up to 500 shards (write instances) with one to five read instances for each.

When using nonclustered Redis, you scale by adding additional read nodes so that access to stored data is not impacted. However, this does leave the possibility of write access being bottlenecked. Clustered Redis takes care of that by creating multiple sets of these read/write combinations so that you can scale out both read, by adding additional read nodes per shard (like nonclustering), and write, by adding additional shards with their own read nodes. As you can probably guess, a clustered Redis is going to be more expensive than a nonclustered Redis.

As a developer, the key thing to remember is that since ElastiCache for Redis is a managed service offering on top of Redis, using it in your .NET application means that you will use the open source .NET drivers for Redis: **StackExchange.Redis**. This provides you the ability to interact with objects stored within the database. Listing 11-1 shows a very simple cache manager for inserting and getting items in and out of Redis.

Listing 11-1. Saving and retrieving information from Redis

```
using StackExchange.Redis;
using Newtonsoft.Json;

namespace Redis_Demo
{
    public interface ICacheable
    {
```

```csharp
    public string Id { get; set; }
}

public class CacheManager
{
    private IDatabase database;

    public CacheManager()
    {
        var connection = ConnectionMultiplexer.Connect("connection
        string");
        database = connection.GetDatabase();
    }

    public void Insert<T>(T item) where T : ICacheable
    {
        database.StringSet(item.Id, Serialize(item));
    }

    public T Get<T>(string id) where T : ICacheable
    {
        var value = database.StringGet(id);
        return Deserialize<T>(value);
    }

    private string Serialize(object obj)
    {
        return JsonConvert.SerializeObject(obj);
    }

    private T Deserialize<T>(string obj)
    {
        return JsonConvert.DeserializeObject<T>(obj);
    }
}
```

The preceding code assumes that all items being cached will implement the
ICacheable interface, which means that there will be an Id property with a type of string.

Since we are using this as our key into the database, we can assume this Id value will likely be a GUID or other guaranteed unique value – otherwise, we may get some strange behavior.

Note   There is another very common Redis library that you may see referenced in online samples: **ServiceStack.Redis**. The main difference is that ServiceStack is a commercially supported product that has quotas on the number of requests per hour. Going over that quota will require paying for a commercial license.

Now that we have looked at the Redis engine, let's take a quick look at the Memcached engine.

Amazon ElastiCache for Memcached

Just as with Amazon ElastiCache for Redis, applications using Memcached can use ElastiCache for Memcached with minimal modifications as you simply need information about the hostnames and port numbers of the various ElastiCache nodes that have been deployed.

The smallest building block of a Memcached deployment is a node. A node is a fixed-size chunk of secure, network-attached RAM that runs an instance of Memcached. A node can exist in isolation or in a relationship with other nodes – a cluster. Each node within a cluster must be the same instance type and run the same cache engine. One of the key features of Memcached is that it supports *Auto Discovery*.

Auto Discovery is the ability for client applications to identify all of the nodes within a cluster and initiate and maintain connections to those nodes. This means applications don't have to worry about connecting to individual nodes; instead, you simply connect to a configuration endpoint.

Using ElastiCache for Memcached in a .NET application requires you to use the Memcached drivers: **EnyimMemcached** for older .NET versions or **EnyimMemcachedCore** when working with .NET Core–based applications. Using Memcached in a .NET application is different from many of the other client libraries that you see because it is designed to be used through dependency injection (DI) rather than "newing" up a client like we did for Redis. Ideally, you would be using DI there as well, but we did not take that approach to keep the sample code simpler. We don't have that option in this case.

The first thing you need to do is register the Memcached client with the dependency injection (DI) container management system. If working with ASP.NET Core, you would do this in the Program.cs file, which would look like Listing 11-2.

Listing 11-2. Adding the Memcached client

```
using Enyim.Caching.Configuration;

public static void Main(string[] args)
{
    var builder = WebApplication.CreateBuilder(args);
    builder.Services.AddEnyimMemcached(o =>
        o.Servers = new List<Server> {
            new Server {Address = "end point", Port = 11211}
        });
    ...
}
```

Using another container management system would require the same approach, with the key being the **AddEnyimMemcached** method to ensure that a *Memcached* client is registered. This means that the Memcached version of the CacheManager class that we used with Redis would instead look like Listing 11-3.

Listing 11-3. Saving and retrieving information from Memcached

```
using Enyim.Caching;

namespace Memcached_Demo
{
    public class CacheManager
    {
        private IMemcachedClient client;
        private int cacheLength = 900;

        public CacheManager(IMemcachedClient memclient)
        {
            client = memclient;
        }
```

```
        public void Insert<T>(T item) where T : ICacheable
        {
            client.Add(item.Id, item, cacheLength);
        }

        public T Get<T>(string id) where T : ICacheable
        {
            T value;
            if (client.TryGet<T>(id, out value))
            {
                return value;
            }
            return default(T);
        }
    }
}
```

The main difference that you will see is that every item being persisted in the cache has a cache length, which is the number of seconds that something will stay in the cache. Memcached uses a lazy caching mechanism, which means that values will only be deleted when requested or when a new entry is saved, and the cache is full. You can turn this off by using 0 as the input value. However, Memcached retains the ability to delete items before their expiration time when memory is not available for a save.

Choosing Between Redis and Memcached

The different ElastiCache engines can solve different needs. Redis, with its support for both clustered and nonclustered implementations, and Memcached provide different levels of support. Table 11-1 shows some of the different considerations when evaluating the highest version of the product.

Table 11-1. *Considerations when choosing between Memcached and Redis*

	Memcached	**Redis (nonclustered)**	**Redis (clustered)**
Data types	Simple	Complex	Complex
Data partitioning	Yes	No	Yes
Modifiable clusters	Yes	Yes	Limited
Online resharding	No	No	Yes
Encryption	No	Yes	Yes
Data tiering	No	Yes	Yes
Multithreaded	Yes	No	No
Pub/sub capabilities	No	Yes	Yes
Sorted sets	No	Yes	Yes
Backup and restore	No	Yes	Yes
Geospatial indexing	No	Yes	Yes

An easy way to look at it is if you use simple models and have a concern for running large nodes with multiple cores and threads, then Memcached is probably your best choice. If you have complex models and want some support in the database for failover, pub/sub, and backup, then you should choose Redis.

Amazon MemoryDB for Redis

Where Amazon ElastiCache is a managed services wrapper around an open source in-memory database, Amazon MemoryDB for Redis is a Redis-compatible database service, which means that it is not Redis but is instead a service that accepts many of the same Redis commands as would a Redis database itself. This is very similar to Amazon Aurora, which supports several different interaction approaches: MySQL and PostgreSQL. As of the time of this writing, MemoryDB supported the most recent version of Redis: 6.2.

Because MemoryDB is a fully managed service, creating the instance is straightforward. You create your cluster by determining how many shards you would like to support as well as the number of read replicas per shard. If you remember the ElastiCache for Redis discussion earlier, this implies that the setup defaults to Redis with clustering enabled.

When looking at pricing, at the time of this writing, MemoryDB costs approximately 50% more than the comparable ElastiCache for Redis pricing. What this extra cost buys you is data durability. MemoryDB stores your entire data set in memory and uses a distributed multi-AZ transactional log to provide that data durability, a feature that is unavailable in ElastiCache for Redis. MemoryDB also handles failover to a read replica much better, with failover typically happening in under ten seconds. However, other than the pricing difference, there is a performance impact to using MemoryDB over ElastiCache because the use of distributed logs has an impact on latency, so reads and writes will take several milliseconds longer for MemoryDB than would the same save in ElastiCache for Redis.

As you can guess, since the Redis APIs are replicated, a developer will work with MemoryDB in the same way as they would ElastiCache for Redis, using the **StackExchange.Redis** NuGet package.

In-memory databases, whether ElastiCache or MemoryDB, offer extremely fast reads and writes because they cut out a lot of the complexity added by performing I/O to disks and optimize their processing to take advantage of the speed inherent in RAM. However, working with them is very similar to working with "regular" document and key/value databases. Our next purpose-built database takes a different approach to the data that it manages.

Time-Series Databases

Where the databases that we have talked about so far are optimized around working with key/value-based data, a time-series database is a database optimized for time-stamped or time-series data. Typical examples of this kind of data are application performance monitoring logs, network data, clicks in an online application, stock market trading, IoT sensor data, and other use cases where the time of the data is important. So far, it seems like something that any of the databases we have talked about can manage, right? Well, the difference comes around the way the data will be accessed.

All the NoSQL and relational databases we have talked about depend upon the existence of a key, generally some kind of string (NoSQL) or integer (SQL). In a time-series database, however, the timestamp is the most important piece of information. This means that applications that look at data within a time range, and it is the time range that is crucial, would be well served by a time-series database because that data will be stored together (much like how relational databases store data in order by primary key), so getting a range of data based on a time range will be faster than getting data stored with a different type of key. Figure 11-4 shows how this works.

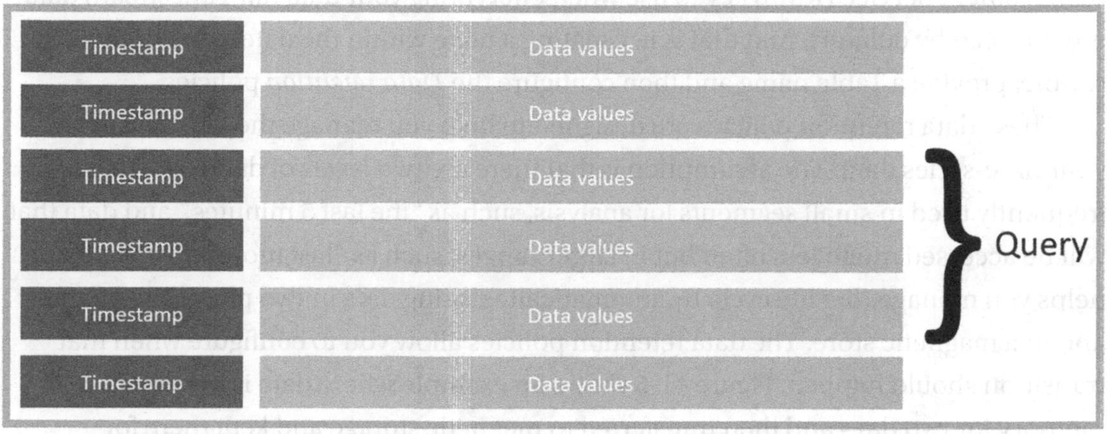

Figure 11-4. *Time-series data stored by timestamp*

A typical characteristic of time-series data is that when data arrives, it is generally recorded as a new entry. Updating that data is more of an exception than a rule. Another characteristic is that the data typically arrives in timestamp order, so key scanning is minimized, and the data-write can be very performant. A third characteristic is that the non-timestamp data is stored as a value and is rarely included as part of the filtering in a query. Scaling is also especially important in time-series databases because there tends to be a lot of frequently created data that ends up being stored in this type of database. The last characteristic, as already mentioned, is that time is the primary axis. Time-series databases tend to include specialized functions around dealing with time series, including aggregation, analysis, and time calculations.

Amazon Timestream

Now that we have briefly defined the concept behind a time-series database, let us look at the AWS entry into the field: Amazon Timestream. Timestream is a serverless, automatically scaling, database service that can manage trillions of requests per day and is exponentially faster than a relational database at a fraction of the cost. Timestream uses a purpose-built query engine that lets you access and analyze recent and historical data together within a single query as well as support built-in time-series analytics functions.

Creating an Amazon Timestream database is one of the simplest processes that you will find in AWS. All you need to do is to provide a *Database name* and decide on the Key Management Service (KMS) key to use when encrypting your data (all Timestream data is encrypted by default). And that is it. Creating a table within the database is almost as simple; provide a Table name and then configure the *Data retention* policies.

These data retention policies are designed to help you manage the life cycle of your time-series data. The assumption is that there are two levels of data: data that is frequently used in small segments for analysis, such as "the last 5 minutes," and data that will be accessed much less often but in larger ranges, such as "last month." Timestream helps you manage that life cycle by automatically storing data in two places: in-memory and in a magnetic store. The data retention policies allow you to configure when that transition should happen. Figure 11-5 shows an example where data is persisted in memory for two days and then transferred to magnetic storage and kept there for one year.

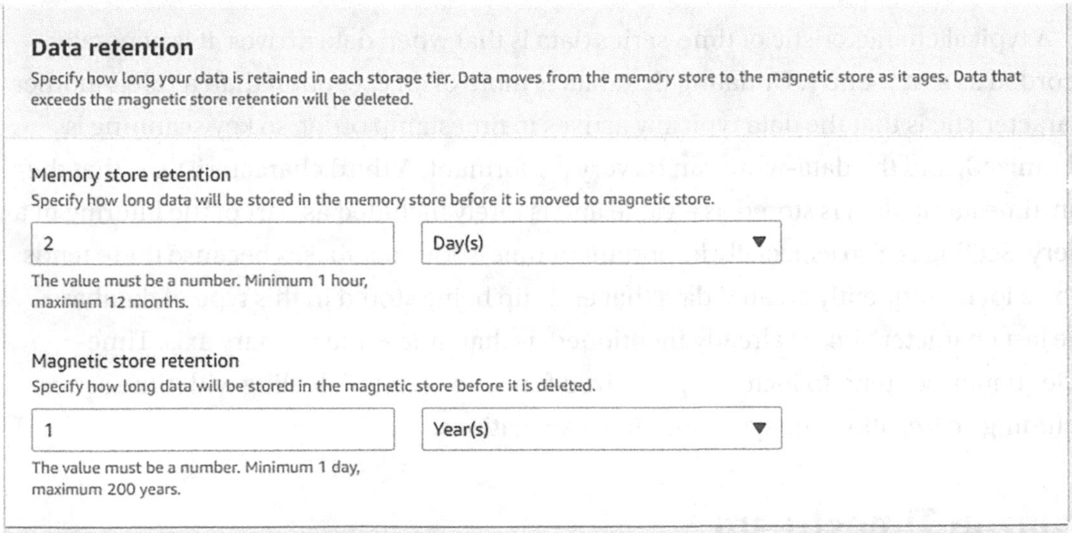

Data retention

Specify how long your data is retained in each storage tier. Data moves from the memory store to the magnetic store as it ages. Data that exceeds the magnetic store retention will be deleted.

Memory store retention

Specify how long data will be stored in the memory store before it is moved to magnetic store.

2		Day(s) ▼

The value must be a number. Minimum 1 hour, maximum 12 months.

Magnetic store retention

Specify how long data will be stored in the magnetic store before it is deleted.

1		Year(s) ▼

The value must be a number. Minimum 1 day, maximum 200 years.

Figure 11-5. *Configuring the Data Retention policies for a Timestream table*

Now that we have looked at creating a Timestream database and table, the next step is to look at how the data is managed within the database as this will help you understand some of the behavior you will see when using the database programmatically. The following are key concepts in Timestream:

- **Dimension** – Describes metadata as key/value pairs and can be 0 to many within a record. An example could be the location and type of a sensor.

- **Measure** – The actual value being measured, as a key/value pair.

Now that we have briefly discussed Timestream databases, our next step is to look at using it in a .NET application.

.NET and Amazon Timestream

We have spent some time accessing database services on AWS that are designed to emulate some other product, such as Redis. Timestream does not take that approach. Instead, you need to use the AWS SDK for .NET to write data to and read data from Timestream. The interesting thing about this is that AWS made the decision to break this data access process down by providing two discrete .NET clients for Timestream: the *Write SDK client* that persists data to the table and the *Query SDK client* that returns data from the table.

Let's start our journey into Timestream by looking at a method in Listing 11-4 that saves an item, in this case, a *Measurement*.

Listing 11-4. Saving data in Amazon Timestream

```
1   using System;
2   using System.Collections.Generic;
3   using System.Threading.Tasks;
4   using Amazon.TimestreamWrite;
5   using Amazon.TimestreamWrite.Model;
6
7   public class Measurement
8   {
9       public Dictionary<string, double> KeyValues { get; set; }
10      public string Source { get; set; }
11      public string Location { get; set; }
12      public DateTime Time { get; set; }
13  }
14
```

```
15 public async Task Insert(Measurement item)
16 {
17     var queryClient = new AmazonTimestreamQueryClient();
18
19     var dimensions = new List<Dimension>
20     {
21         new Dimension
           {
               Name = "location",
               Value = item.Location
           }
22     };
23
24     var commonAttributes = new Record
25     {
26         Dimensions = dimensions,
27         MeasureValueType = MeasureValueType.DOUBLE,
28         Time = ConvertToTimeString(item.Time)
29     };
30
31     var records = new List<Record>();
32
33     foreach (var key in item.KeyValues.Keys)
34     {
35         var record = new Record
36         {
37             MeasureName = key,
38             MeasureValue = item.KeyValues[key].ToString()
39         };
40         records.Add(record);
41     }
42
43     var request = new WriteRecordsRequest
44     {
45         DatabaseName = databaseName,
```

```
46          TableName = tableName,
47          CommonAttributes = commonAttributes,
48          Records = records
49      };
50
51      var response
            = await writeClient.WriteRecordsAsync(request);
52      // do something with result, such as evaluate HTTP status
53  }
```

When persisting data into Timestream, you will use a **WriteRecordsRequest**, as shown on Line 43 in Listing 11-4. This object contains information about the table and database to use as well as **CommonAttributes** and **Records**. The CommonAttributes property expects a **Record**, or a set of fields that are common to all the items contained in the Records property; think of it as a way to minimize the data sent over the wire as well as act as initial value grouping. In this case, our common attributes contain the Dimensions (as discussed earlier) as well as the MeasureValueType, which defines the type of data being submitted (although it will be converted to a string for the submission), and Time. This leaves only the list of measurement values that will be put into the Records property. The response from the WriteRecordsAsync method is an HTTP Status code that indicates success or failure.

Pulling data out is quite different, mainly because the process of fetching data is done by passing a SQL-like query string to the **AmazonTimestreamQueryClient**. This means that a simple query to retrieve some information could look like this:

```
SELECT location, measure_name, time, measure_value::double
FROM {databaseName}.{tableName}
WHERE measure_name='type of measurement you are looking for'
ORDER BY time DESC
LIMIT 10
```

All of which will be recognizable if you have experience with SQL.

This is all well and good, but the power of this type of database really shines when you start to do time-specific queries. Consider the following query that finds the average measurement value, aggregated together over 30-second intervals (binned), for a specific location (one of the dimensions saved with each submission) over the past two hours.

```
SELECT BIN(time, 30s) AS binned_timestamp,
    ROUND(AVG(measure_value::double), 2) AS avg_measurementValue,
    location
FROM {databaseName}.{tableName}
WHERE measure_name = 'type of measurement you are looking for'
    AND location = '{LOCATION}'
    AND time > ago(2h)
GROUP BY location, BIN(time, 30s)
ORDER BY binned_timestamp ASC"
```

As you can probably imagine, there are many more complicated functions that are available for use in Timestream.

Note   These time-series functions include functions that will help fill in missing data, interpolations, functions that look at the rate of change for a metric, derivatives, volumes of requests received, integrals, and correlation functions for comparing two different time series. You can find all the time-series functions at `https://docs.aws.amazon.com/timestream/latest/developerguide/timeseries-specific-constructs.functions.html`.

Once you have built the query, running the query is pretty simple, as shown in the following:

```
public async Task<QueryResponse> RunQueryAsync(string queryString)
{
    try
    {
        var queryRequest = new QueryRequest();
        queryRequest.QueryString = queryString;
        var queryResponse =
                await queryClient.QueryAsync(queryRequest);
        return queryResponse;
    }
```

```
    catch (Exception e)
    {
        return null;
    }
}
```

However, the complication comes from trying to interpret the results – the **QueryResponse** object that is returned by the service. This is because you are simply passing in a query string that could be doing any kind of work, so the response needs to be able to manage that. Figure 11-6 shows the properties on the QueryResponse object.

```
[C#] AWSSDK.TimestreamQuery                                    ▾ | ⚙ Amazon.TimestreamQuery.Model.QueryResponse
  1   ⊞ Assembly AWSSDK.TimestreamQuery, Version=3.3.0.0, Culture=neutral, PublicKeyToken=885c28607f98e604
  4
  5   ⊞ using  …
  8
  9   ⊟ namespace Amazon.TimestreamQuery.Model
 10     {
 11   ⊞      … public class QueryResponse : AmazonWebServiceResponse
 15        {
 16          public QueryResponse();
 17
 18   ⊞      … public List<ColumnInfo> ColumnInfo { get; set; }
 24   ⊞      … public string NextToken { get; set; }
 32   ⊞      … public string QueryId { get; set; }
 38   ⊞      … public QueryStatus QueryStatus { get; set; }
 43   ⊞      … public List<Row> Rows { get; set; }
 49        }
 50     }
```

Figure 11-6. *Object definition of the QueryResponse object*

There are five properties in the QueryResponse type. The QueryStatus returns information about the status of the query, including progress and bytes scanned. The QueryId and NextToken properties are used together to support pagination when the result set is larger than the default number of items returned per request, ColumnInfo provides details on the column data types of the returned result set, and Rows contains the results set.

You can see a simple request/result as captured in Telerik Fiddler Classic in Figure 11-7.

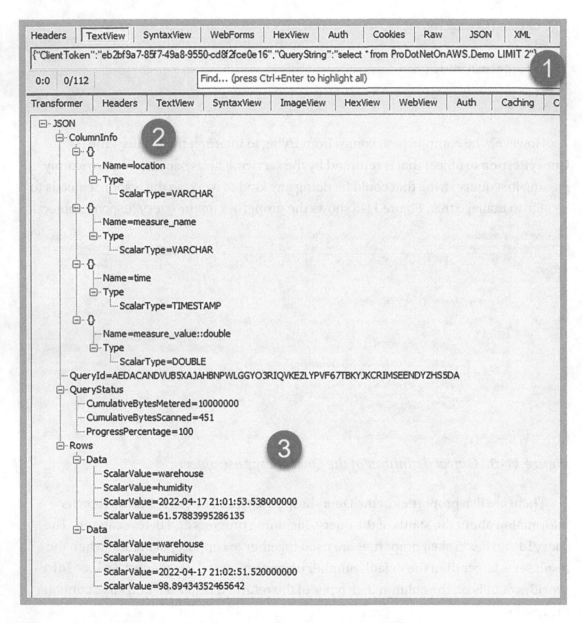

Figure 11-7. *Amazon Timestream query response in JSON*

There are three areas called out. Area 1 is the query that was sent, as you can see it is a simple "SELECT ALL" query with a request to limit the results to two rows. Area 2 shows the ColumnInfo property in JSON, with each item in the array corresponding to each of the ScalarValues found in the array of Data that makes up the Rows property.

Looking at this, you can probably see ways in which you can transform the data into JSON that will deserialize nicely into a C# class. Unfortunately, however, AWS did not provide this functionality for you as part of their SDK. The next purpose-built database that we are going to look at suffers from the same problem; however, like time-series databases, the nature of the functionality supported by the database adds additional complications.

Ledger Databases

A ledger database is a NoSQL database that provides an immutable, transparent, and cryptographically verifiable transaction log that is owned by a central authority. The key here is that you never actually change the data in the table. What we generally consider an update, which replaces the old content with the new content, is not applicable when working with a ledger database. Instead, an update adds a new version of the record. All previous versions still exist, so your update never overwrites existing data. The cryptographically verified part comes into place because this ensures that the record is immutable.

Ledger databases are generally used to record economic and financial activity within an organization, such as tracking credits and debits within an account. Other common use cases are generally around workflows, such as tracking the various steps taken on an insurance claim or tracing the movement of an item through a supply-chain network. For those of you that ever needed to implement audit tables in a relational database, you can start to see how managing that automatically will be of benefit.

Note   A ledger database may seem very similar to Blockchain. However, there is one significant difference, which is that the ledger database is generally a centralized ledger whereas Blockchain is a distributed ledger. There will be times when the organization, such as a bank or financial organization, is not comfortable with a distributed ledger and instead prefers a simpler architecture with the same guarantee of immutable and verifiable data to manage compliance requirements.

Now that we have discussed, at a high level, the features of a ledger database, let's take a look at AWS' version: Amazon QLDB.

Amazon QLDB

In traditional, relational database architecture, the approach is to write data into tables as part of a transaction. This transaction is generally stored in a transaction log and includes all the database modifications that were made during the transaction. This allows you to replay the log and those transactions in the event of a system failure or for data replication. However, generally, those logs are not immutable and generally aren't designed to allow easy access to users.

This approach is different with QLDB, as the journal is the central feature of the database. In a practical sense, the journal is structurally similar to the transaction log; however, it takes a write-only approach to storing application data with all writes, inserts, updates, and deletes, being committed to the journal first. QLDB then uses this journal to interpret the current set of your data. It does this by materializing that data in queryable, user-defined tables. These tables also provide access into the history of the data within that table, including revisions and metadata.

While a lot of the functionality seems similar, some of the terminology is different. Table 11-2 shows the mapping between these terms.

Table 11-2. *Terminology map between RDBMS and QLDB*

Relational Term	QLDB Term
Database	Ledger
Table	Table
Index	Index
Table row	Amazon Ion Document
Column	Document Attribute
SQL	PartiQL
Audit Logs	Journal

The key difference is around the difference between the table row and column from a relational database that was replaced with an Amazon Ion Document. Amazon Ion is a richly typed, self-describing, hierarchical data serialization format that offers interchangeable binary and text representations. The text format is a superset of JSON and is easy to read and work with, while the binary representation is efficient for storage and transmission. Ion's rich type system enables unambiguous semantics for data (e.g., a timestamp value can be encoded using the timestamp type). This support for rich types allows an Ion document to be able to conceptually replace a database row.

Note   The Ion Document format provides a lot of the support lacking in the Amazon Timestream SDK where columns and values are defined separately. This seems to be an unfortunate example of how various service teams seem to never talk to one another nor follow a single standard.

Creating an Amazon QLDB ledger is very simple. In the AWS console, navigate to Amazon QLDB. Here, you will be given the ability to **Create ledger**. Creating a ledger only requires the following:

1. **Ledger name** – The name of your ledger, needs to be unique by region.

2. **Ledger permissions mode** – There are two choices here: *Standard* and *Allow all*. The "Standard" permissions mode is the default, and it enables control over the ledger and its tables using IAM. The "Allow all" mode allows any user with access to the ledger to manage all tables, indexes, and data.

3. **Encrypt data at rest** – Where you choose the key and key management approach to use when encrypting data. There is no ability to opt out – all data will be encrypted at rest.

4. **Tags** – Additional label describing your resource.

You can also create a table at this time; however, there is no way through the UI for you to be able to add an Index. So, instead, let's look at how you can do that in .NET as well as add data to your newly created table.

.NET and Amazon QLDB

The first thing you will need to do to work with Amazon QLDB is to add the appropriate NuGet packages. The first one we add is **Newtonsoft.Json**, which we will use in our examples to manage serialization and deserialization. The next ones to add are specific to QLDB: **AWSSDK.QLDBSession, Amazon.IonObjectMapper, Amazon.QLDB.Driver,** and **Amazon.QLDB.Driver.Serialization**. If you install the Driver.Serialization package, NuGet will install all the other required QLDB packages as dependencies.

The next step is to build an **Amazon.QLDB.Driver.IQldbDriver**. You do that with a Builder as shown in the following:

```
private IQldbDriver qldbDriver;

var amazonQldbSessionConfig = new AmazonQLDBSessionConfig();

qldbDriver = QldbDriver.Builder()
    .WithQLDBSessionConfig(amazonQldbSessionConfig)
    .WithLedger(ledgerName)
    .Build();
```

Note how you cannot just "new" up a driver and instead must use dot notation based upon the **Builder()** method of the QldbDriver. Next, you need to ensure that the table and applicable indexes are set up. See Listing 11-5 that contains a constructor that sets up the client and calls the validation code.

Listing 11-5. Validating table and index creation

```
private IQldbDriver qldbDriver;
private IValueFactory valueFactory;

private string ledgerName = "ProdDotNetOnAWSLedger";
private string tableName = "Account";

public DataManager()
{
    valueFactory = new ValueFactory();

    var amazonQldbSessionConfig = new AmazonQLDBSessionConfig();

    qldbDriver = QldbDriver.Builder()
        .WithQLDBSessionConfig(amazonQldbSessionConfig)
        .WithLedger(ledgerName)
        .Build();

    ValidateTableSetup(tableName);
    ValidateIndexSetup(tableName, "AccountNumber");
}
```

As you can see in the following, checking for the existence of the table is simple as the driver has a **ListTableNames** method that you can use to determine the presence of your table. If it doesn't exist, then process the query to create it.

Let's pull that method out and examine it, because this is how you will do all your interactions with QLDB, by executing queries.

```
private void ValidateTableSetup(string tableName)
{
    if (!qldbDriver.ListTableNames().Any(x => x == tableName))
    {
        qldbDriver.Execute(y => { y.Execute($"CREATE TABLE {tableName}"); });
    }
}
```

The Execute method accepts a function; in this case, we used a lambda function that executes a "CREATE TABLE" command. The code takes a similar approach to creating the index; however, you have to go through more steps to be able to determine whether the index has already been created as you have to query a schema table first and then parse through the list of indexes on that table. That code is shown in Listing 11-6.

Listing 11-6. Validating indexes in Amazon QLDB

```
private void ValidateIndexSetup(string tableName, string indexField)
{
    var result = qldbDriver.Execute(x =>
    {
        IIonValue ionTableName = this.valueFactory.NewString(tableName);
        return x.Execute($"SELECT * FROM information_schema.user_tables
        WHERE name = ?", ionTableName);
    });

    var resultList = result.ToList();
    bool isListed = false;

    if (resultList.Any())
    {
        IIonList indexes = resultList.First().GetField("indexes");
        foreach (IIonValue index in indexes)
```

```
            {
                string expr = index.GetField("expr").StringValue;
                if (expr.Contains(indexField))
                {
                    isListed = true;
                    break;
                }
            }
        }
    }
    if (!isListed)
    {
        qldbDriver.Execute(y => y.Execute($"CREATE INDEX ON {tableName}
        ({indexField})"));
    }
}
```

As mentioned earlier, the save is basically a query that is executed. A simple save method is shown in Listing 11-7.

Listing 11-7. Save query for Amazon QLDB

```
public void Save(object item)
{
    qldbDriver.Execute(x =>
        {
            x.Execute($"INSERT INTO {tableName} ?", ToIonValue(item));
        }
    );
}

private IIonValue ToIonValue(object obj)
{
    return IonLoader.Default.Load(JsonConvert.SerializeObject(obj));
}
```

This example and the one before this where we did a check to see whether an index exists both have some dependence on Ion. Remember, Ion is based upon richly typed JSON, so it expects values to be similarly represented – which is why there are two different approaches for converting an item to an `IonValue`, even something as simple as the tableName, for comparison. The first of these is through the **Amazon. IonDotnet.Tree.ValueFactory** object as shown in the index validation snippet, while the other is through the **Amazon.IonDotnet.Builders.IonLoader** as shown in the `ToIonValue` method.

Once you have the ledger, table, and any indexes you may want set up, the next step is to save some data into the table. This is done by executing a SQL-like command as shown in the following:

```
public void Save(object item)
{
    qldbDriver.Execute(x =>
        {
            x.Execute($"INSERT INTO {tableName} ?",
                        ToIonValue(item));
        }
    );
}
```

Getting it out of the database is a little bit trickier as you want it to be cast into the appropriate data model. The approach for retrieving an item from the database and converting it into a plain old class object (POCO) is shown in the following:

```
public List<T> Get<T>(string accountNumber)
{
    IIonValue ionKey = valueFactory.NewString(accountNumber);

    return qldbDriver.Execute(x =>
    {
        IQuery<T> query = x.Query<T>(
            $"SELECT * FROM {tableName} as d
              WHERE d.AccountNumber = ?", ionKey);
        var results = x.Execute(query);
        return results.ToList();
    });
}
```

You can see that this is a two-step process. First, you create a generic query that is defined with the SELECT text and the appropriate model for the return set. You then Execute that query. This brings you back an `Amazon.QLDB.Driver.Generic.IResult<T>` object that can be converted to return a list of the requested items matching the *AccountNumber* that was passed into the function.

That's a quick review of the general functionality of QLDB. Let's look at one more specific case, the history of an item – one of the prime drivers of using a ledger database. You do this by using the history function, a PartiQL extension that returns revisions from the system-defined view of your table. The syntax for using the history function is

```
SELECT * FROM history(table,`start-time`,`end-time` ] ] ) AS h
[ WHERE h.metadata.id = 'id' ]
```

The start time and end time values are optional. Using a start time will select any versions that are active when the start time occurs and any subsequent versions up until the end time. If no start time is provided, then all versions of the document are retrieved, and the current time is used in the query if the end time value is not explicitly defined. However, as you can see, the optional WHERE clause is using a `metadata.id` value – which we have not yet discussed. This metadata.id value is used by QLDB to uniquely identify each document and can be accessed through the metadata of the document. One way to get this information is shown in the following:

```
public string GetMetadataId(Account item)
{
    IIonValue ionKey =
                valueFactory.NewString(item.AccountNumber);
    var result = new List<IIonValue>();

    qldbDriver.Execute(x =>
    {
        result = x.Execute($"SELECT d.metadata.id as id
                FROM _ql_committed_{tableName} as d
                WHERE d.data.AccountNumber = ?", ionKey);
    });
```

```
IIonValue working = result.First();
return working.GetField("id").StringValue;
}
```

This code snippet accesses the "committed" view, one of the different views provided by QLDB that provides access to information about your data. Taking the result from that query and plugging it into the previous snippet where we queried using the history function will get you the history of that document for the time period defined in the query. Thus, you can access the current version as well as have access to all the history, all by executing SQL-like commands.

There is a lot more we can go into about using Amazon QLDB and .NET together, probably a whole other book! To recap, however, Amazon QLDB is a ledger database, which means it provides an immutable, transparent, and cryptographically verifiable transaction log that you can access and evaluate independently from the active version.

The final type of database that we are going to go over, a graph database, serves a completely different purpose. As discussed in some detail in the previous chapter, a graph database focuses on storing nodes and relationships. A node is an entity, generally stored with a label, such as Person, and contains a set of key-value pairs, or properties. Let's take a closer look at that now.

Graph Databases

A graph database is a database that depends on graph structures to define relationships between various items. Graph structures are based upon the mathematics field of graph theory – or mathematical structures used to model pairwise relations between objects. These items are generally defined as *nodes* or *edges* and contain properties that store data. The graph relates the data stored in the database into a collection containing these nodes and edges where edges represent the relationship between the nodes. These edges, or relationships, are prioritized within the data structure because they are expected to be a primary reason for storing and/or accessing data.

You may remember this picture from Chapter 10, here shown in Figure 11-8.

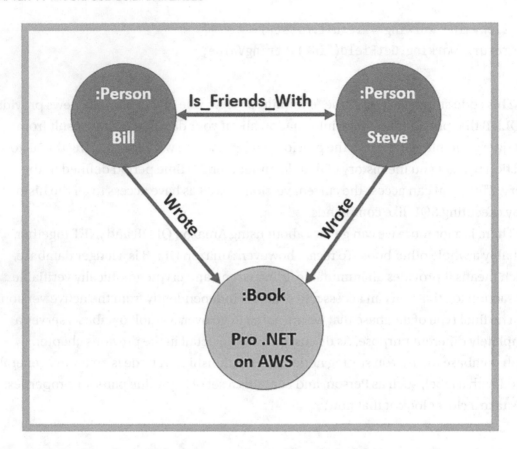

Figure 11-8. *Graph model representation with relationships*

The circles represent the nodes, and the arrows (also known as *links* or *lines*) represent the edges. Each of these items is persisted in the database as discrete items, which makes queries against them highly performant. Let's look at how all this works in real life using Amazon Neptune, AWS' version of a graph database.

Amazon Neptune

Amazon Neptune is a fast, scalable, fully managed graph database service that offers greater than 99.99% availability. It replicates six copies of your data across three Availability Zones, and instance failover typically takes less than 30 seconds. You can create an instance with up to 64 TB of auto-scaling storage, six-way replication across Availability Zones, and support for up to 15 read replicas, and you pay only for the resources that you use. AWS claims that Neptune is optimized for storing billions of relationships and querying the graph with milliseconds latency. Neptune supports the popular graph query languages, *Apache TinkerPop Gremlin*, the *W3C's SPARQL*, and *Neo4j's openCypher*, enabling you to build queries that efficiently navigate highly connected data sets.

Note   If you are still unsure as to when it would make the most sense to take advantage of the special features of a graph database, then take a look at a set of AWS reference architectures around graph data. You can find these at `https://github.com/aws-samples/aws-dbs-refarch-graph`.

Let's now build a database that we can use as an example for our study. Log into the AWS console and select Amazon Neptune by searching or under the Database set of services. Next, select the **Launch Amazon Neptune** button. This will bring you to the *Create database* screen.

The first setup item on this page is the *Engine options* where you select the *Version* of the database engine that you would like to use. At the time of this writing, Neptune 1.1.0.0.R1 is the default version, but the drop-down list allows you to select the more recently released version, 1.1.1.0.R1. We are staying with the default version. The next option is to enter the *DB cluster identifier*, which needs to be unique across all DB clusters for this account in this region. After this is the Templates section with two choices as shown in Figure 11-9.

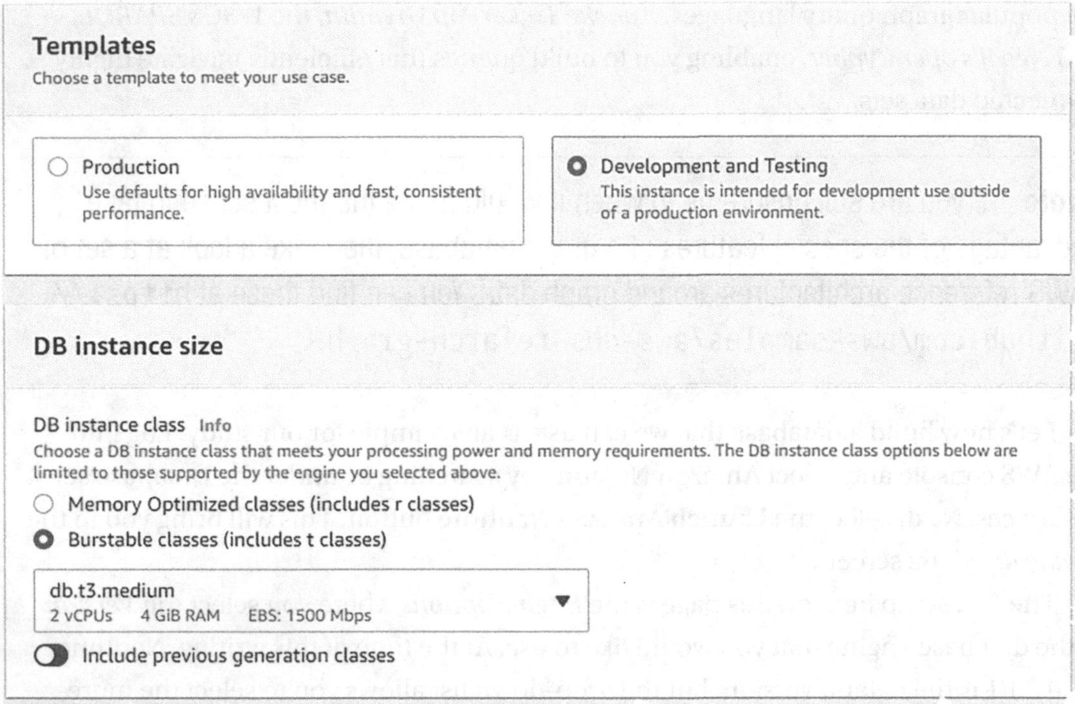

Templates

Choose a template to meet your use case.

○ **Production**
Use defaults for high availability and fast, consistent performance.

◉ **Development and Testing**
This instance is intended for development use outside of a production environment.

DB instance size

DB instance class   Info

Choose a DB instance class that meets your processing power and memory requirements. The DB instance class options below are limited to those supported by the engine you selected above.

○ Memory Optimized classes (includes r classes)

◉ Burstable classes (includes t classes)

db.t3.medium
2 vCPUs   4 GiB RAM   EBS: 1500 Mbps   ▼

◯ Include previous generation classes

Figure 11-9. *Selecting template and DB instance size when creating a Neptune cluster*

Just as with many of the RDS databases, selecting one of the templates changes the available selections and default value of the *DB instance size*. As shown in Figure 11-9, we selected the **Development and Testing** template and then selected the smallest available instance size because, as you will note, there is no free version based upon instance size as we have seen in some of the other database services. So don't forget to clean it up when you are done!

The next two sections are *Availability & durability* and *Connectivity*. We stayed with the default versions in both of those cases. The next configuration item is going to be something we haven't seen before: *Notebook configuration*. When selected, a Jupyter notebook will be created and configured to query your Neptune database. This notebook is hosted and billed through SageMaker, AWS' flagship machine learning service, and allows you to visualize the data within your graph database. We recommend you uncheck it to avoid charges, but if this is not a problem, then keep it checked! Keep the default values for the rest of the configuration items and then complete the creation of your database. You will be returned to your databases page, which will look like Figure 11-10.

Figure 11-10. *Databases page after creating a Neptune database*

Now that we have created a database, let's look at what we need to do to use it in our .NET application.

.NET and Amazon Neptune

There are some choices that you need to make when you are looking at tying your .NET application to Neptune, and that is mainly around the language that you want to use for accessing information. As discussed earlier, there are three main approaches: SPARQL, Gremlin, and openCypher. SPARQL is a query language with SELECT and WHERE clauses, while Gremlin is a graph traversal language. openCypher is like Gremlin in that they are both property-graph languages. Whereas Gremlin is imperative, openCypher has a more declarative syntax that may be more familiar for people experienced with SQL or SPARQL. We will use Gremlin in the following examples because its approach to graph transversal should give you a better idea of how graph databases work.

Warning   Interacting with Neptune is not as easy as working with some of the other purpose-built databases for other reasons as well, mainly that you cannot easily connect to a Neptune database directly from your local machine as they are only reachable from within the VPC in which they are set up.

Adding Gremlin support is as simple as adding the **Gremlin.Net** NuGet package from Apache TinkerPop. You next need to configure the connection. You do this by first creating a server, then attaching a client to that server, and then using that client to create the connection as shown in the following. This connection is finalized as a GraphTraversalSource object.

```
private GraphTraversalSource source;
public DataManager()
{
    var endpoint = "endpoint from cluster";
    var gremlinServer = new GremlinServer(endpoint, 8182,
                                   enableSsl: true);
    var gremlinClient = new GremlinClient(gremlinServer);
    var remoteConnection = new
         DriverRemoteConnection(gremlinClient, "source");
    source = Traversal().WithRemote(remoteConnection);
}
```

Once you have a traversal source available, you can start working with the data. Adding a node, or vertex, is straightforward:

```
public class Person
{
    public string Id { get; set; }

    public string Name { get; set; }
}

public void Add(Person item)
{
    source.AddV("person")
          .Property(T.Id, item.Id)
          .Property("Name", item.Name)
          .Iterate();
}
```

This example has you adding the vertex with AddV and then setting two properties on that vertex, one of which is identified as the primary ID (by the use of T.Id) and the other property is the Name. The command is processed when the Iterate method is run. This last command, Iterate, is one of several terminal commands used in Gremlin. There are several terminal commands that you can use, each of which has different behavior. The most common of these are as follows:

- **Iterate** – Processes the command without returning anything

- **Next** – Processes the command and returns the next result

- **ToList** – Returns all results in a list

- **ToSet** – Returns all results in a set, thus removing any duplicates

The earlier example used Iterate because the Add method in the code did not return a value. If the expectation was to return a value, then the appropriate terminal step would have been Next.

Getting a node back out of the database is very similar, although there is some extra work to do when projecting the return values into a C# type. Listing 11-8 shows what this looks like.

Listing 11-8. Projecting Amazon Neptune return values to C#

```csharp
public Person Get(string id)
{
    var result = source.V()
                    .HasId(id)
                    .HasLabel("person")
                    .Project<Person>("Id", "Name")
                    .By(T.Id)
                    .By("Name")
                    .ToList();
    if (result == null || result.Count == 0 || result.Count > 1)
    {
        return default(Person);
    }
    return result.First().Values.First();
}
```

This code has us requesting a vertex from the source using the V method and then using HasId to define the Id that is requested and using HasLabel to define the label. If you think back to the graph model representation in Figure 11-8, there were two types of vertices there: a "person" and a "book". You can think of each of those as a label as it defines the thing that is represented by that vertex. Once it defines the desired item(s), the code then uses Project to define a type and the properties in that type that need to be mapped. These are then mapped using the By methods, with the whole execution terminated by the ToList method to ensure that all values matching that set of criteria are returned. The last part that is being performed in the code is ensuring that there is only one appropriate Person returned, so cases where there are zero or multiple values are discarded.

The vertices are easy to work through, but we are still missing a critical piece, the edges that define the relationship between two vertices – the whole point of using a graph database. Doing this requires that you identify the two vertices between which there is going to be a relationship and then add the relationship using the cleverly named AddE method. The following code snippet shows how this is done:

```
public void AddRelationship(string fromId, string toId,
                            string relationship)
{
    source.V()
            .HasId(fromId)
            .HasLabel("person")
            .As("from")
        .V()
            .HasId(toId)
            .HasLabel("person")
            .As("to")
        .AddE(relationship)
            .From("from")
            .To("to")
        .Iterate();
}
```

The As method allows you to use aliasing to identify a specific vertex. This is necessary because you can use that aliasing to define the direction of the relationship, which is managed by the From and To methods after the edge has been added. This code also uses the Iterate terminator.

Using dot notation together with the graph traversal approach from Gremlin allows you to string any number of commands and vertices together. You can use multiple AddE and/or AddV in the same command chain as well as provide filters on information being returned from the server. There are many different things that you can do as you work deeper into the language and methodology, including iterating through a graph as well as moving in different directions. Suffice it to say that Gremlin and Amazon Neptune, together, provide you the ability to persist and then examine all aspects of your vertices and their relationships.

Summary

In this chapter, we went over four types of purpose-built databases: in-memory, time series, ledger, and graph. We also touched on using those various databases within a .NET application. Each of these databases is designed to support a specific set of use cases, and if your application requirements include those use cases, then it would be appropriate to consider their use. However, as we saw, using these databases in your .NET application is not as simple as using a relational database with Entity Framework.

Our next section is around moving existing applications to AWS. This usually means moving the system from an on-premises data center to the public cloud. We will first go over the traditional "lift and shift" where applications get redeployed onto VMs, and then we will talk about containerizing your applications, migrating your data, and re-platforming your older .NET applications to work on Linux.

PART IV

Moving Existing Apps to AWS

CHAPTER 12

Moving to Virtual Machines

The past few chapters have concentrated on the options for making data available to applications in the cloud, using either object storage in Amazon S3 or in one of the varieties of traditional relational databases and other purpose-built databases. It's now time for the "rubber to meet the road," so to speak, and look at hosting the code for our applications in the cloud.

We first looked at running code in the cloud in Chapter 6 when we examined serverless options with AWS Lambda. In this chapter and the next, we'll look at two other approaches. In this chapter, we'll examine hosting applications in virtual machines. These still have a role to play despite all the noise around containers! In the following chapter, we'll look at deploying code to containers. Once you've completed Chapter 6, this one, and Chapter 13, you'll have a good understanding of what compute option best suits your comfort level and the needs of your application.

Virtual Machine Services on AWS

In Chapter 4, we introduced Amazon EC2, the virtual machine service that powers many other compute services on AWS. See, we told you VMs still had a role to play! In this chapter, we'll cover deploying .NET and .NET Framework applications to EC2. First, though, we're going to look at using virtual machines with AWS Elastic Beanstalk. A managed service, Elastic Beanstalk takes care of the work involved in provisioning and managing EC2 virtual machines and deploying your code onto them. This makes it an attractive approach to becoming familiar with deploying applications such as ASP.NET web apps into the cloud or getting started with moving your on-premises applications (so-called "lift-and-shift" migrations) onto AWS.

© William Penberthy and Steve Roberts 2023
W. Penberthy and S. Roberts, *Pro .NET on Amazon Web Services*,
https://doi.org/10.1007/978-1-4842-8907-5_12

Introducing AWS Elastic Beanstalk

Elastic Beanstalk is described on the service's product page as "...the fastest and simplest way to get your application onto AWS," and to a large extent, this is true. You simply build and package your application code and upload it, and Elastic Beanstalk provisions the necessary infrastructure before deploying the code to the instance(s) it has provisioned. No need to mess around launching and configuring EC2 instances, or load balancers, or autoscaling. Beanstalk also manages updates to the underlying VMs. It's all managed for you, leaving you free to focus on your code. That's not to say you have no control – there are plenty of knobs and dials available to tweak the infrastructure to your needs, without needing to get too involved.

Elastic Beanstalk has the concept of *Applications* and *Environments*. Applications in Beanstalk are a logical container for different versions of your application. Each time you upload and deploy a new version of your application, a new version is registered in the Beanstalk application associated with it from the very first deployment. Earlier versions can be redeployed if needed, for example, to roll back an update that's causing issues.

An environment, on the other hand, is much more interesting. Environments represent the infrastructure hosting, scaling, and controlling access to your application. A given Beanstalk application can be associated with multiple environments. For example, you might choose to have separate environments for your "dev", "test", and "prod" deployments for a single application. Figure 12-1 illustrates how Beanstalk applications and environments work together.

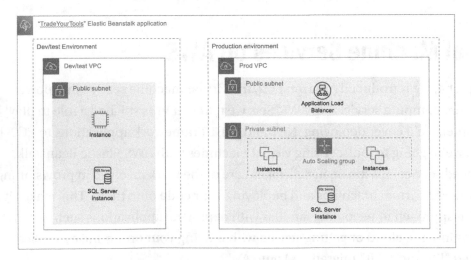

Figure 12-1. *Application and environments in Elastic Beanstalk (simplified!)*

Elastic Beanstalk and .NET

Elastic Beanstalk supports the deployment of web applications written with both .NET Framework and .NET. As you might expect, .NET Framework applications are restricted to using Windows Server VMs, whereas .NET applications can be deployed to either Windows Server or Linux. We recommend using Linux if you can, as the VMs start faster. Depending on your application's needs, that might be an important consideration when scaling up under load.

The different operating systems and their supporting software (IIS, Tomcat, nginx, etc.) are called *platforms*, which are versioned. At the time of this writing, the operating system platforms available that have relevance for .NET are as follows:

- Windows Server Core 2019 (IIS 10.0)

- Windows Server 2016 (IIS 10.0)

- Windows Server Core 2016 (IIS 10.0)

- Windows Server 2012 R2 (IIS 8.5)

- Windows Server 2012 R2 Core (IIS 8.5)

- Amazon Linux 2 (nginx 1.20.0 and .NET Core 3.1, .NET 5, and .NET 6 pre-installed)

Tip   The service team maintains a documentation page listing all platforms and software versions. See `https://docs.aws.amazon.com/ elasticbeanstalk/latest/platforms/platforms-supported. html#platforms-supported.net` for the latest information.

Knowing the platforms is useful, but you, however, don't work directly with platform and platform versions when deploying applications. Instead, you refer to the required platform version using a *Solution Stack Name*. For example, the platform version *Windows Server Core 2019 with IIS 10.0 Version 2.10.2* is used by selecting the solution stack named *64bit Windows Server Core 2019 v2.10.2 running IIS 10.0*. The solution stack name is what you'll see offered in the management console, Visual Studio, and other tools when you deploy an application for the first time.

When using Windows Server solution stacks, IIS is always the web server your application will be deployed into, which probably isn't a surprise. For .NET applications deployed to Linux solution stacks, nginx is pre-installed, ready to act as a proxy server to Kestrel (Microsoft recommends placing Kestrel behind a reverse proxy). However, if the instances hosting your application are behind a load balancer, we've not found the additional reverse proxy to be necessary.

In addition to Beanstalk managing the infrastructure, it also manages downloading your application's deployment bundle and installing it onto the VMs during deployment. Let's now take a quick look at the different deployment bundles for .NET and .NET Framework applications.

Packaging Applications for Deployment

ASP.NET applications using the .NET Framework must be packaged for deployment as *web deploy archives*. These archives, in zip files, contain the application binaries and any additional resources such as CSS files and static images that you don't want to serve via a CDN, and installation scripts that register the application with IIS. Microsoft supplies a command-line tool called *msdeploy* that you can use to create, and deploy, these archives. Alternatively, you can create a web deploy archive for your ASP.NET applications using the *package* msbuild target (`msbuild /t:package`), or use a Publish profile within Visual Studio.

Tip   You can learn more about web deploy at `https://docs.microsoft.com/ en-us/iis/publish/using-web-deploy/introduction-to-web-deploy`. The components required are pre-installed on Beanstalk's Windows images, ready to unpack your deployment bundles.

ASP.NET Core applications instead use the newer "dotnet" publishing format, regardless of whether they are deployed to Windows or Linux platforms. This is built using the `dotnet publish` command. It builds the applications and places the binaries and dependencies into a folder hierarchy, which can then be zipped and uploaded for deployment.

Regardless of the package format (web deploy or dotnet publish), the archive zip file representing the build application needs to be uploaded to a bucket in Amazon S3. If you're working with the service directly, for example, in the Management Console or via custom scripting, then the creation and upload of the archive are your responsibility. If, however, you're using the .NET tooling provided by AWS, that tooling handles the build, packaging, and upload for you.

On the Elastic Beanstalk side of things, it takes on the responsibility of downloading the archive from the bucket onto the instance(s), unpacking it, and performing whatever other work is needed to register the application to make it available to serve traffic.

Deploying ASP.NET Applications

If you're looking to deploy ASP.NET applications, written with the .NET Framework, to Elastic Beanstalk using tools available from AWS, then you have two choices: the AWS Toolkit for Visual Studio or the AWS Tools for Azure DevOps. We'll look at Visual Studio here and then cover the Azure DevOps option later in the chapter.

Deployment of ASP.NET applications to Beanstalk from within Visual Studio uses a wizard. Before anyone queries this approach, let's be clear – AWS does not expect you to deploy to production from inside Visual Studio. No one does that, right? Instead, the wizard is intended to support the develop/deploy iterative cycle of day-to-day development, to dev/test staging environments, without needing developers to leave the comfort of the IDE. With that in mind, let's look at the process.

Start the wizard by opening the context menu for your ASP.NET application's project file in Solution Explorer and selecting the **Publish to AWS Elastic Beanstalk** menu item. The wizard has five major pages for you to complete. Not all pages are displayed, depending on whether you're performing a new deployment vs. a redeployment:

- Credentials, region, and deployment vs. redeployment selection

- Application, environment, and CNAME

- Infrastructure settings, such as VPC options, single vs. multi-instance (with load balancer), instance size, and more

- IAM role selections for the deployed application and to provide Beanstalk access to resources needed in your account

- Final review

The first page of the wizard is where you select the credentials you'll use to deploy the application and the region in which it will be deployed. It's important to distinguish the credentials used to deploy from those used by the application when it's running on the instances (if any). You specify runtime credentials later in the wizard by specifying an IAM role for the application to use.

The first page of the wizard is also where you select to create a new deployment or to redeploy. The first time you run the wizard, you likely have no existing Beanstalk environments, so the page won't be that interesting. However, should you have existing environments, they'll be listed as potential **Deployment Targets**. To redeploy, select the relevant environment listed in the targets before proceeding in the wizard.

The second page of the wizard, shown in Figure 12-2, is equally simple and is only shown for new deployments. It asks for the name of the application (defaulting to the project name), the name of the associated environment, and a CNAME that will be used to form the URL to the deployed application. Recall that a single Beanstalk application can have multiple environments, each with a different infrastructure. The wizard pre-populates the **Environment** drop-down with three potential names, based on the **Application** field value – one for a dev stage, one for a test stage, and one for a production stage. Feel free to select a pre-canned value or enter one of your own. This value then feeds into the next option: the **URL** field.

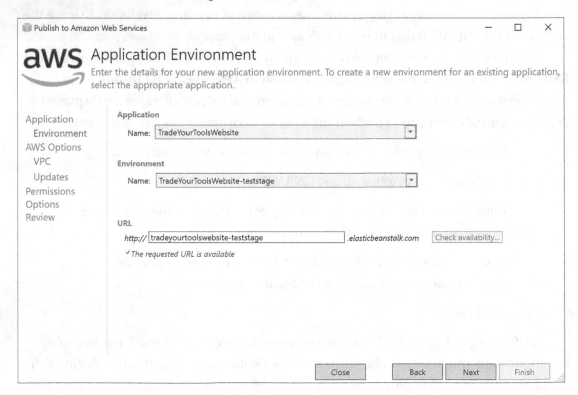

Figure 12-2. *Checking that the CNAME is available*

Every deployment environment has a Beanstalk-provided URL used to access the deployed application. You have some control over the front part of the URL (the so-called CNAME). However, just like S3 bucket names have to be globally unique, so too does the Elastic Beanstalk-suffixed URL. Curiously, someone, somewhere in the world, has captured the URLs `http://webapplication-dev.elasticbeanstalk.com` and `http://webapplication-test.elasticbeanstalk.com` for, quite literally, years (the URLs, for whatever reason, do not resolve, however).

To check that the URL is available, type in the name, or use the suggested default based on what you've entered previously on the page, and choose the **Check availability** button. If needed, edit the text (it doesn't need to match the application and environment names) and repeat until the URL is available, then move on in the wizard.

The next page of the wizard is where things start to get interesting as shown in Figure 12-3.

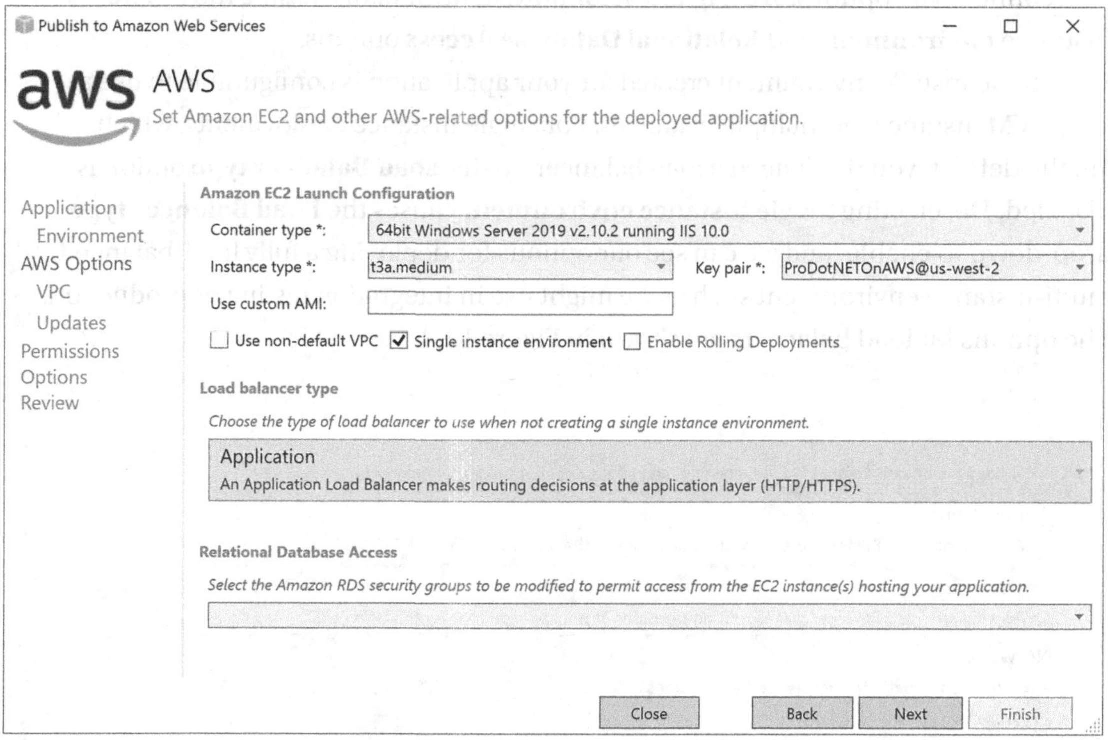

Figure 12-3. *Defining the required infrastructure*

437

Container type is a little confusing – we're not deploying to containers here, but virtual machines. This field actually maps to *Solution Stack Name,* which we mentioned earlier. As the TradeYourTools sample is a .NET Framework application, only Windows Server solution stacks are available here for us to choose from. Both Windows Server and Linux solution stacks would be available for .NET applications.

Instance type is the size of the virtual machine (refer back to Chapter 4, where we discussed EC2 images and instances), and **Key pair** is only needed if you intend to remote into the running VM from within Visual Studio or other tools on your local machine.

When first starting out with AWS, your first deployments will probably be to your default Virtual Private Cloud (VPC) network, so you can likely ignore the **Use non-default VPC** option for now. You might need to select it, however, if your deployed application will use resources created in another VPC, and that VPC isn't connected to the one the application is being deployed to (using VPC Peering or some other interconnectivity option). We'll ignore it for now, in favor of discussing the **Single instance environment** and **Relational Database Access** options.

The Beanstalk environment created for your application is configurable to use a single VM instance, or multiple instances. For single instance deployments, which are the default, you don't need a load balancer, so the **Load Balancer type** option is disabled. Deselecting **Single instance environment** causes the **Load Balancer type** drop-down to enable, and we can see our options for deploying a fully load-balanced, multi-instance environment such as we might use in integration testing or production. The options for load balancers are shown in Figure 12-4.

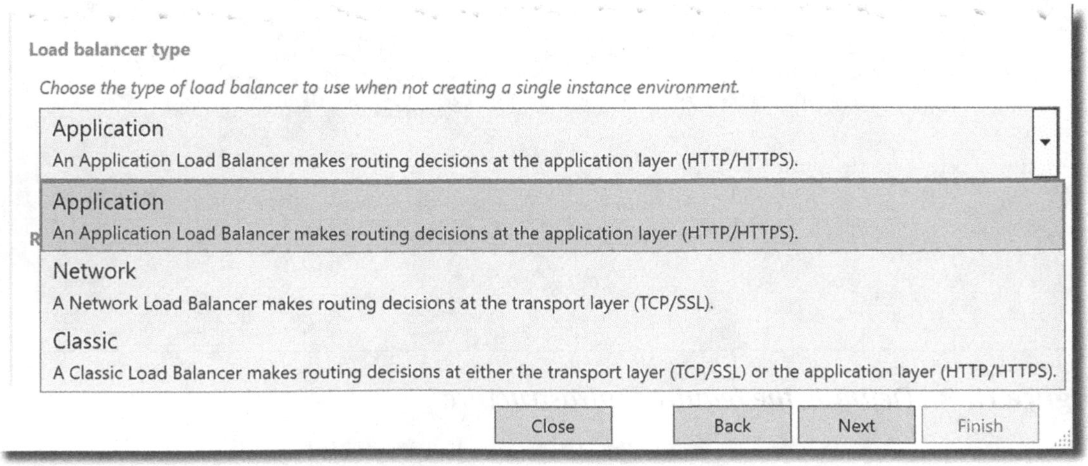

Figure 12-4. *Available load-balancing options for multi-instance deployments*

The newer *Application* load balancer type is the default, which we recommend you stay with as it's simpler to configure. Note, however, that adding any load balancer resources adds cost, so unless you know you need a multi-instance, load-balanced environment, we recommend reselecting **Single instance environment** before proceeding. Keep load-balanced environments for integration testing and production environments.

This now brings us to **Relational Database Access**, a very useful feature in the wizard. The TradeYourTools application uses a SQL Server database in Amazon RDS, which, as things stand, is not accessible by the deployed application – even with credentials specified in the connection string. This might surprise you, after all both sets of resources are in the same account and the same VPC. However, it comes down to the out-of-the-box "deny" security posture of AWS – resource A usually can't access resource B unless you proactively take action to allow it.

The TradeYourTools database is guarded by a security group containing one or more rules that permit access to the database instance by other resources. The deployed application will also have a security group, created by Beanstalk, with a rule permitting traffic from the Internet on port 80 (HTTP). So our application is reachable by end users, but that's as far as it goes. In order for the deployed application to then access the database, the security group guarding the database will need a rule permitting access from the instance(s) hosting the application.

We could create these connections manually using the Management Console or a CLI command; however, it's much more convenient to let the toolkit do it, and that's the reason why this option in the wizard is so useful. Drop down the list in the field and select the relevant database entry. The toolkit will then wire up the security groups for you during deployment, saving time and effort. Figure 12-5 shows the drop-down more closely. Note we've selected the database that the application needs to access.

Relational Database Access

Select the Amazon RDS security groups to be modified to permit access from the EC2 instance(s) hosting your application.

	Security Group	Database Instances	
☐	sg-025c49a3cb548363...	contosodb (port 1433)	
☐	sg-0bff8edb16353d7f...	mysqltest (port 3306)	
☑	sg-067706cb7ae8da8...	tradeyourtoolsdb (port 1433)	

Figure 12-5. *Connecting the deployed application to its database*

With the infrastructure options selected, moving on in the wizard brings us to permissions. The text on the page is fairly self-explanatory; the **Deployed Application Permissions** field is where you select an IAM role that grants permissions to call AWS services. Any credentials needed to make those calls, through the AWS SDK for .NET, will be provided by a trust relationship configured on the role. The trust relationship needs to specify a service principal, ec2.amazonaws.com, since that's where the VMs are running. The TradeYourTools sample doesn't make any calls, so the default role selected by the wizard, `aws-elasticbeanstalk-ec2-role`, is appropriate here (the role will be created if required).

The second role, *Service Permissions*, enables Elastic Beanstalk to access your resources and monitor the VMs on your behalf. The default selection, `aws-elasticbeanstalk-service-role`, is usually appropriate here (and will also be created as required).

One final page (not counting the traditional "review" page) remains, **Options**, shown in Figure 12-6.

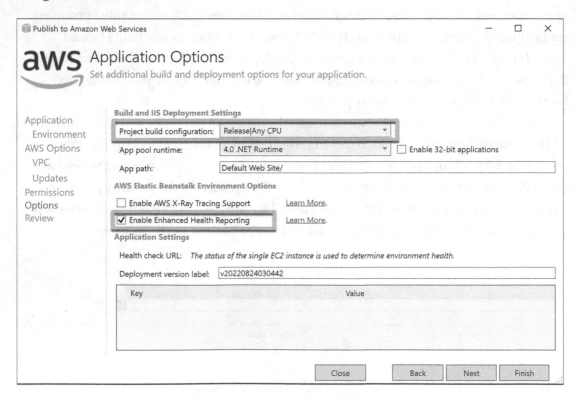

Figure 12-6. *Additional options for the deployment*

Project build configuration defaults to the current build configuration in the IDE but can be changed. Here, we've selected the *Release* configuration. We've also enabled **Enhanced health reporting**. This uses an on-instance agent, installed by Beanstalk, to provide more comprehensive monitoring insight and status information on the health of the underlying instance.

AWS X-Ray is a tracing service that enables you to follow traces of requests made to an application as they transition to different services. We'll have more to say on AWS X-Ray and how to use it from .NET applications (Core and Framework) in Chapter 17. The sample application doesn't make calls to AWS services, so we've left this option unchecked.

At this point, we can click **Finish** to move to the Review screen, check our settings, and start the deployment by clicking the suitably named **Deploy** button. The toolkit will then build the application and create the web deploy archive zip file, upload it to Amazon S3 (it uses a bucket provided by Elastic Beanstalk in your account), and start the build-out of the infrastructure to match your selected settings. A document window will open, and you can follow along with the provisioning and deployment events. The URL to the deployed application is also displayed, which, when clicked (wait for the READY status!), opens a browser to your deployed application running on one or more VM instances on EC2 but managed by Elastic Beanstalk.

Figure 12-7 shows the document window, event trace, and URL to the deployed application. From this window, you can also manage the environment, including restarting instances or terminating it altogether. You can also remote into a VM instance right from within the IDE if you chose a key pair in the wizard.

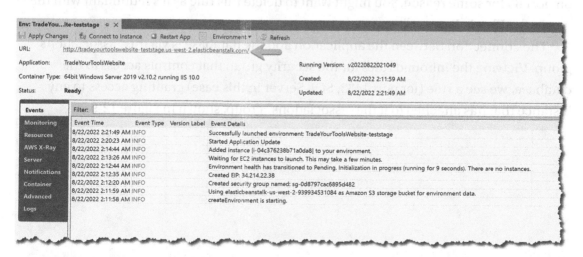

Figure 12-7. *Deployment events and the application URL*

Earlier, we mentioned the useful feature in the wizard that handles setting up the connection between your deployed application and an Amazon RDS database (if it uses one, of course). For reference, let's review what actually happened behind the scenes. In the Management Console and looking at the EC2 instance hosting the application, we can see it has two security groups attached, as shown in Figure 12-8.

Figure 12-8. *Security groups attached to the EC2 instance*

One security group was created by Elastic Beanstalk (sg-0d8797… in Figure 12-8), which opens ports 80 and 22 to the world (CIDR 0.0.0.0/0). The other, however, was created by the toolkit during deployment. It has a group name suffixed with …*rds-associations*. Inspecting it, we see one rule – for port 80. If your application isn't listening on port 80 for some reason, you might want to delete this rule as it's redundant with the one in the Elastic Beanstalk–created group.

The connection between the application and the database is via this "associations" group. Viewing the inbound rules for the security group that controls access to the database, we see a rule (for port 1433, SQL Server in this case) granting access to any instance that has attached to it the "associations" group, shown in Figure 12-9.

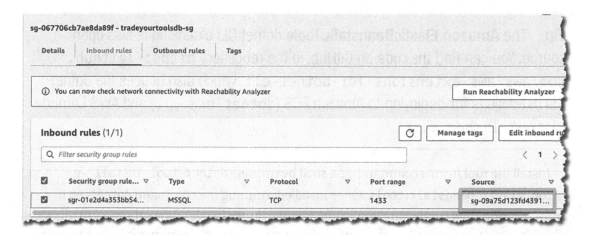

Figure 12-9. *Database security group rule permitting access from the application*

As we mentioned earlier, you could equally manage this setup yourself; however, having the toolkit manage it saves some time and effort when you're new to working with security groups.

Tip   If you set up the rules yourself, you don't need to create an additional "associations" group. The extra group is created by the toolkit to avoid meddling with the Beanstalk-created group and to avoid the need to "watch" for the Beanstalk group to be created to add the rule at the right time. You can simply directly connect the Beanstalk-created group to the database group.

Deploying ASP.NET Core Applications

The Publish to AWS Elastic Beanstalk wizard we just showed can also deploy ASP.NET Core applications to either Windows Server or Linux solution stacks. Apart from the wider set of solution stacks, and that the deployment mechanism will use dotnet publish to package up the application bundle, there's very little difference from deploying ASP. NET applications, so we'll not show it here.

One additional piece of functionality available for ASP.NET Core deployments to Beanstalk is the option to install and use a dotnet CLI extension instead of the wizard in Visual Studio. The tool, named *Amazon.ElasticBeanstalk.Tools*, is available on NuGet at www.nuget.org/packages/Amazon.ElasticBeanstalk.Tools.

Tip   The **Amazon.ElasticBeanstalk.Tools** dotnet CLI extension is also open source. You can find the code on GitHub, in the repository `https://github.com/aws/aws-extensions-for-dotnet-cli`, which also houses the dotnet CLI extensions for deploying to Amazon ECS (`dotnet ecs ...`) and AWS Lambda (`dotnet lambda ...`).

Install the tool from a command-line shell by running `dotnet tool install -g amazon.elasticbeanstalk.tools`. Once installed, running the command `dotnet eb` in a command-line shell (make sure you're inside your project folder) shows the view of top-level options for deploying and managing Beanstalk deployments for ASP.NET Core applications. For example, the command `dotnet eb deploy-environment` will start a deployment.

The command-line extension and Visual Studio can share a settings file, enabling round-tripping between the two experiences, or share the settings with a development team working from different platforms. The command-line option is useful if you don't have access to Visual Studio or want to script deployments for a CI/CD pipeline, for example, one based on AWS' own Code* services.

However, there's a new kid on the block. You will notice, if you use the wizard, that the context menu item has the suffix *(legacy)*. There's also a banner on the front page of the wizard guiding you to consider using a new deployment mechanism, *Publish to AWS*. Publish to AWS is opinionated tooling that guides you to the best hosting service for a wider choice of applications than the older wizards, based on inspection of your application code. The older wizards relied on you knowing the service you wanted to use; this newer approach figures out and lists all your options. It supports the deployment of .NET applications to virtual machines in Elastic Beanstalk, or containers in Amazon ECS with AWS Fargate, or AWS App Runner. In short, it's a lot more flexible and doesn't require much up-front knowledge of AWS (even though you are almost experts now!), so let's take a look.

Using Publish to AWS to Deploy to Elastic Beanstalk

The new Publish to AWS deployment tooling is available in two forms: firstly, as an extension to the dotnet CLI, and secondly, within Visual Studio. Both forms have dependencies on the AWS Cloud Development Kit (CDK), which in turn depends on Node.js, so you'll need to install both before using the new deployment tooling.

Note   The AWS Cloud Development Kit is a tool that enables defining Infrastructure as Code (IaC) – quite literally. Using the CDK, you can define your infrastructure requirements using the languages you use day to day, including C#. Find out more about the CDK in Chapter 3.

Publish to AWS is included with the AWS Toolkit for Visual Studio, so no further installs are needed if that's your environment of choice. If you're using the command line (perhaps on macOS, or Linux, or even Windows), or installing it for CI/CD pipelines, then you need to install the extension **AWS.Deploy.Tools** (NuGet: `www.nuget.org/packages/AWS.Deploy.Tools`). To install, run the command `dotnet tool install -g aws.deploy.tools` in a command-line shell. Check installation by running `dotnet aws.` The output, the set of top-level commands, is shown in Figure 12-10.

```
PS C:\Samples\ContosoUniversity> dotnet aws
AWS .NET deployment tool for deploying .NET Core applications to AWS.
Project Home: https://github.com/aws/aws-dotnet-deploy

dotnet-aws:
  The AWS .NET deployment tool for deploying .NET applications on AWS.

Usage:
  dotnet-aws [options] [command]

Options:
  --version          Show version information
  -?, -h, --help     Show help and usage information

Commands:
  deploy                                 Inspect, build, and deploy the .NET project to AWS using the recommended AWS
                                         service.
  list-deployments                       List existing deployments.
  delete-deployment <deployment-name>    Delete an existing deployment.
  deployment-project                     Save the deployment project inside a user provided directory path.
  server-mode                            Launches the tool in a server mode for IDEs like Visual Studio to integrate
                                         with.
```

Figure 12-10.   *Top-level commands for the "dotnet aws" command*

We're going to focus on the Visual Studio experience in this chapter, and the great news is that it doesn't matter whether you use the IDE or the command line! AWS deliberately created the command-line tool first and then added the Visual Studio experience to ensure the graphical tooling didn't "lock" users into functionality that couldn't be used elsewhere. This is the opposite to the approach used with the wizards. Out of the gate, the command-line version is easily usable from CI/CD and supports all of the deployment options you'll see in the IDE. Running the command `dotnet aws deploy` inside your application project folder is the same as starting **Publish to AWS** from the project's context menu in the IDE. All that differs is how you choose the deployment target and edit settings for the deployment. At the command line, numbered menus and prompts are used (unless you use the --silent option, which of course is used with CI/CD pipelines).

Back in the IDE, starting the tool from the context menu results in your application project being analyzed and a set of suitable *recipes* shown for you to choose from for deployment. The application we're using in this section is an ASP.NET Core version of Contoso University, which has not been configured with a Dockerfile, so the tool suggests deployment to Linux virtual machines in Elastic Beanstalk, shown in Figure 12-11. If the project had a Dockerfile, a container-hosting solution would have been proposed as the preferred recipe.

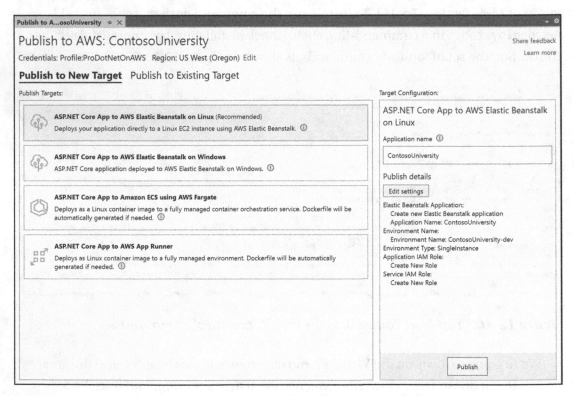

Figure 12-11. Suggested deployment recipes for the application

---

Note Just because a virtual machine recipe has been chosen, it doesn't stop you choosing to switch to containers – even if the project doesn't have a Dockerfile. The tool (including the command-line version) will create a Dockerfile for you if you switch to a container recipe.

Look at the settings on the right-hand side of Figure 12-11. They should seem familiar by now – it's the same settings, albeit a shorter list, that we saw in the wizard previously in the chapter. Why shorter? It's because the tool is abstracting away all but the essential settings, as part of its aim to help developers new to the cloud and AWS not get overwhelmed by settings. In fact, with the sample application we're using here, we could click the Publish button right now. Compare that – two clicks – to the five pages of wizard, and settings on each page, we had to use previously. However, if you want to delve into all those settings, it's easy to do. Just click the **Edit settings** button in the right pane and you'll be presented with a scrollable list of all available options, grouped into categories. Figure 12-12 shows a small sampling of the options.

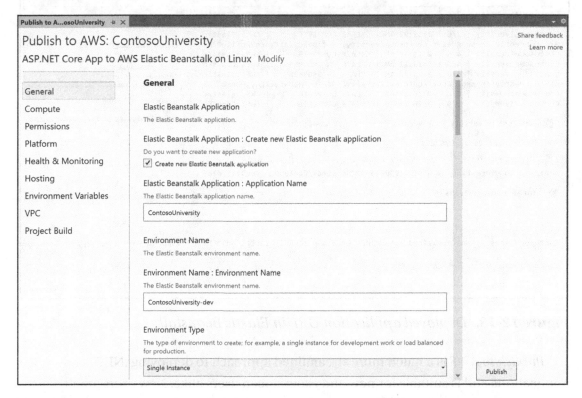

Figure 12-12. *Editing the settings for an Elastic Beanstalk deployment recipe*

If your application needs to customize settings (maybe it needs custom IAM roles to be specified, or you want a specific instance type), scroll down and make the necessary adjustments and then click **Publish** to start. As with the wizard we saw earlier, the toolkit will switch the display to a rolling stream of events from the build and deployment process, helpfully categorized.

First comes the build and packaging of the application, which we've already covered. Then, the tool checks that the CDK is configured and creates a temporary CDK project to control the deployment infrastructure before finally starting the deployment of the CDK project (which in turn creates a CloudFormation stack, which itself creates the Elastic Beanstalk resources). At the end of the deployment, the window updates with the deployed application URL, shown in Figure 12-13.

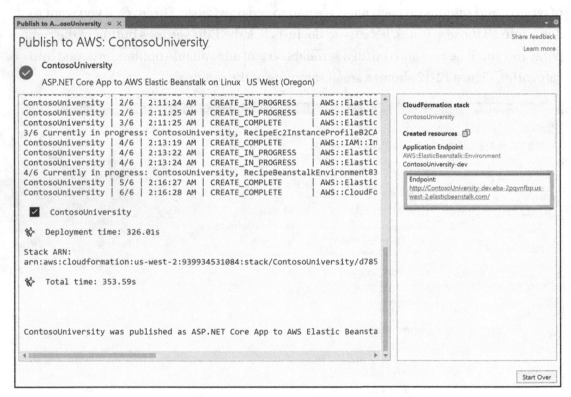

Figure 12-13. *Deployed application URL in Elastic Beanstalk*

Publish to AWS is a much more streamlined approach to deploying .NET applications and is suitable for new and experienced users alike. New users aren't immediately overwhelmed by having to choose the "right" service and settings, and experienced users get a simpler, single page to configure every deployment setting relevant to the chosen recipe. Unfortunately, though, it's not for everyone – .NET Framework applications are not supported.

For CI/CD pipelines, deployment is performed by running `dotnet aws deploy --silent --apply config-file.json` in a command-line shell. The `--silent` switch suppresses prompts for any required values, something that would stop your pipeline dead while it waits for someone to respond to an invisible prompt! The `--apply` switch is used to pass the name of a JSON-format configuration file containing the settings (required and optional) for the deployment. The configuration file can be checked into source control and shared across your development team and CI/CD builds.

Publish to AWS has one additional trick up its sleeve – the ability to create custom deployment projects based off the supplied AWS recipes. These surface as additional recipes in the tooling. At the time of this writing, the ability to create custom deployment projects is reserved to the command-line tool. However, the recipe associated with the custom project is accessible from both command-line and Visual Studio versions of *Publish to AWS*.

Custom deployment projects are useful for scenarios where you want to add custom settings, or even new infrastructure resources for a deployment, or to remove settings from the UX in favor of hard-wired values, so team members can't change them accidentally. With the old wizards, you were locked into the settings AWS provided. No longer! We're not going to cover deployment projects further here since we're focused on deployment to virtual machines with Elastic Beanstalk and EC2, but we encourage you to check them out.

Tip   To learn more about the configuration file format and custom deployment projects, check the documentation at `https://aws.github.io/aws-dotnet-deploy/`. The command-line tool, *AWS.Deploy.Tools*, is also open source and can be found at `https://github.com/aws/aws-dotnet-deploy`.

Customizing the Virtual Machines

Customizing the images used in deployment is an approach you might need to consider if you need a particular software or other dependencies to be pre-installed. However, we would remind you that ideally, compute instances running our applications in the cloud should be replaceable at a moment's notice – don't get attached to them!

In Chapter 4, when discussing launching EC2 instances, we showed using *UserData* scripts (for bash or PowerShell) to customize the launch of an instance by installing the latest version of .NET. Neither the wizard we showed earlier, for ASP.NET, nor *Publish to AWS* just now, allows you to specify custom scripts. Instead, you have two options to customize the virtual machine environments – using scripts, called *.ebextensions*, to perform customization as instances launch or creating your own custom launch image based on the Beanstalk source (a.k.a. "stock") images. Let's briefly examine the two approaches.

Using .ebextension Scripts

.ebextensions are textual configuration files for customizing the runtime environment on the virtual machine instances at launch time. They're named after the folder that you add to your application deployment bundle, which contains the scripts. Individual configuration files, which use JSON or YAML, have the file extension **.config**. It doesn't matter whether you choose JSON or YAML as the same configuration tasks can be expressed in either format, although you should probably standardize on one format for sanity's sake. YAML might be the best format in that it supports comments, multiple quote types, and easier multi-line command expressions, which outweigh persnickety white-space indenting requirements.

A single .ebextension configuration file can contain several optional sections, or *keys*, and each key can be used at most once per file. A best practice is to use different files for different logical customizations, rather than wedging everything into one file. The keys available are listed as follows and should give you a good idea of the level of customization of the environment that's available to you.

- **commands** – Exactly what you'd expect, this is a collection of one or more commands to run on the instance. Each individual command is identified by a name, which is used to run the commands in alphabetical order. We recommend using a prefix on the name, 01_, 02_, and so on, to make the order obvious. Commands are run on the instance before the application version is extracted and the web server configured.

- **container_commands** – These commands run prior to the deployment of the application into the web server. When they run, the deployment bundle has been unpacked (but not yet installed) and the web server set up. In the case of Windows platforms, this is the time immediately prior to the unpacked application archive contents being copied to beneath *inetpub/wwwroot*. The commands run in the context of the folder containing the extracted application archive.

You can configure the commands to only run the first time an instance is provisioned, vs. running on provisioning and every update, or to run on only a single instance (known as a leader) during initial provisioning only. For dev/test environments, the latter option could be useful for seeding databases using EF migrations without worrying about race conditions during a multi-instance launch. Of course, you wouldn't use this approach for production deployments – or, at least, we don't know of anyone who does!

- **files** – Using this key, you can create files on the instance at launch time. The content for the file can be downloaded using a URL or specified inline in the configuration file. Unlike the packages and sources keys described shortly, this key can download content from private S3 URLs provided you set up authorization using an instance profile using the **resources** key.

- **groups** – For Linux environments only, creates Linux/UNIX groups and assigns group IDs. The group ID is optional and will cause group creation to fail if a group with the same ID already exists.

- **option_settings** – Modifies the Elastic Beanstalk configuration settings, which are arranged into namespaces. You can also use this key to set environment variables for the application to consume.

- **packages** – On Windows, specifies installer (.msi) packages that Elastic Beanstalk should download and install from a publicly available URL (including S3 URLs). Linux environments support a wider range of package sources, such as *yum* and *rpm*, among others. Note that installation order, for both operating system platforms, is not guaranteed.

- **resources** – This key enables the creation and configuration of additional AWS resources in the environment. Under the covers, Elastic Beanstalk takes the settings defined under the resources key and uses them to extend the AWS CloudFormation template the service is using to launch the environment. Therefore, at least in theory (we've not tested it), there's no limit to the additional resources you can add to your environment – queues, alarms, caching clusters, and whatever else CloudFormation supports.

- **services** – Enables starting, and stopping, services when an instance is started. You can also specify additional packages, sources, files, or commands that should trigger a service restart if changed (or run, in the case of a command).

- **sources** – Similar to packages, except here you point to an archive file using a publicly available URL. Elastic Beanstalk downloads the archive and extracts the contents to a specified location on the instance. For Windows, only zip files are supported.

- **users** – Again a Linux-only option, used to create local users on the EC2 instance.

Hopefully, this list of keys has sparked ideas on the extent to which you can customize the stock Elastic Beanstalk environments at launch time, by simply defining what you need in a series of one or more configuration files and adding them, beneath a folder named *.ebextensions*, to the root of the folder containing your built application assets (the folder name must begin with a period). They will then be included in the deployment archive that's uploaded.

Tip   The Elastic Beanstalk team maintains a GitHub repo of commonly used extensions, some from AWS and others from the community. You can find the repository at `https://github.com/awsdocs/elastic-beanstalk-samples`.

Figure 12-14 shows an .ebextension script added to the TradeYourTools project. The file sns-topic.config (taken from the samples repository) is being used to create an Amazon SNS topic (more on these in Chapter 16) using the **resources** key. Our use case is to create a topic that can broadcast notifications to subscribers that a user has uploaded details of a new tool. We'll need the ARN of this topic in the application code to be able to send the notification, so we use the *option settings* key to export the ARN into an environment variable on the instance.

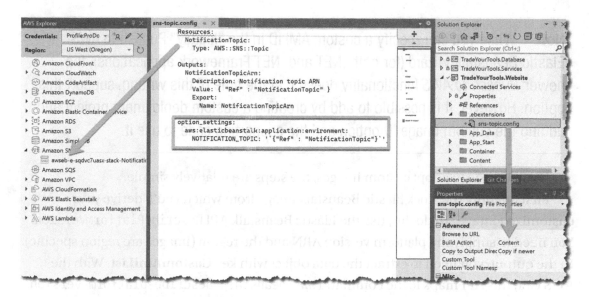

Figure 12-14. *Configuring .ebextensions in Visual Studio*

Using a Custom Launch Image

The sharp-eyed may have noticed in Figure 12-3, when we were deploying an ASP.
NET application, the field **Use custom AMI**. You can create your own custom Amazon
Machine Image (AMI), derived from those curated by Elastic Beanstalk, and specify your
own image ID during deployment.

Configuring the default Elastic Beanstalk images via .ebextension scripts during
launch might add significantly to the overall launch time if a lot of time-consuming
customization is required, such as downloading and running installers, or adding further
packages. In these situations, creating a custom image, pre-loaded with all the software
and configuration settings you need, avoids this delay.

Conversely, once you create custom images, it's your responsibility to keep
them up to date with patches, or re-baseline them periodically as Elastic Beanstalk
updates its own images. If you elected to use Elastic Beanstalk because, as a managed
service, it takes care of things such as image maintenance, then this might not be an
attractive option.

Note   While you can specify a custom AMI ID in the "legacy" Publish to AWS
Elastic Beanstalk wizard (for both .NET and .NET Framework applications), the
newer *Publish to AWS* functionality doesn't, at the time of this writing, support this
option. However, it is possible to add by creating a custom deployment project and
adding the custom image ID option and the supporting code to use it.

If you decide to adopt custom images, the steps are relatively simple.

First, identity the stock Elastic Beanstalk image from which you'll derive your
customized image. To do this, use the Elastic Beanstalk API `DescribePlatformVersion`.
You need to supply the platform version ARN and the region (images are region specific).
In the output, you need to extract the data object with key **CustomAmiList**. With the
AWS CLI, this API maps to the command aws `beanstalk describe-platform-version`.
With the AWS Tools for PowerShell, use `Get-EBPlatformVersionDetail`. Listing 12-1
shows an example command using the AWS CLI.

Listing 12-1. AWS CLI query for stock image ID

```
C:\> aws elasticbeanstalk describe-platform-version ↩
    --platform-arn ↩
'arn:aws:elasticbeanstalk:us-west-2::platform/IIS 10.0 running ↩
on 64bit Windows Server Core 2019/2.5.8' ↩
-query PlatformDescription.CustomAmiList

[
    {
        "VirtualizationType": "pv",
        "ImageId": "ami-091c68903faee8fbc"
    },
    {
        "VirtualizationType": "hvm",
        "ImageId": "ami-0bf6afd6329b5023e"
    }
]
```

Listing 12-2 shows the equivalent PowerShell query.

Listing 12-2. AWS Tools for PowerShell query for stock image ID

```
C:\> (Get-EBPlatformVersionDetail -PlatformArn ⏎
'arn:aws:elasticbeanstalk:us-west-2::platform/IIS 10.0 running ⏎
on 64bit Windows Server Core 2019/2.5.8' ⏎
-region us-west-2).CustomAmiList

ImageId                  VirtualizationType
-------                  -------------------
ami-091c68903faee8fbc pv
ami-091c68903faee8fbc hvm
```

Using the image ID, launch an instance being sure to specify a key pair to which you have access. When the instance has launched, connect to it using SSH or RDP. Once connected, make whatever configuration changes, and install whatever additional software and/or files, your application needs. When your changes are complete, if the instance is running Windows Server, run EC2Config's *SysPrep* tool (pre-installed on the instance) and ensure that *SysPrep* is configured to generate a random password.

Back in the Management Console, stop the EC2 instance. Then, from the **Instance Actions** menu, find and select the **Create Image (EBS AMI)** command. Terminate the original instance once the new image has been created.

You're now ready to make use of the custom image during launch. Assuming you created a custom Windows Server image and are launching with the wizard shown earlier, simply supply the new image ID when you reach the *AWS Options* page (shown in Figure 12-3).

Deploying to Elastic Beanstalk from Azure DevOps

Before moving on from this section of the chapter focused on Elastic Beanstalk, there's one more option for deployment that we want to bring to your notice. It involves one toolkit we've not mentioned so far in this book – the *AWS Tools for Azure DevOps*. This toolkit contains a free collection of build tasks from AWS you can use with Azure DevOps, or Azure DevOps Server to deploy from Azure DevOps pipelines to AWS, including Elastic Beanstalk. While we're not going to cover them in any depth here, if your development team is working with AWS but maintaining source repos and CI/CD pipelines in Azure DevOps, as a lot of .NET shops may well do, then this toolkit might be of interest to save you from some custom scripting.

> **Tip** The toolkit is available on the Azure DevOps marketplace at `https://marketplace.visualstudio.com/items?itemName=AmazonWebServices.aws-vsts-tools`. It's also maintained as an open source project on GitHub at `https://github.com/aws/aws-toolkit-azure-devops`.

The tools contain two build tasks related to Elastic Beanstalk: **AWS Elastic Beanstalk Create Version** and **AWS Elastic Beanstalk Deploy Application**.

The **AWS Elastic Beanstalk Create Version** task builds and packages your ASP.NET or ASP.NET Core application and uploads it to Amazon S3 where it's then registered as a new application version ready for deployment. It can also accept an existing deployment bundle already uploaded to S3 and register the version using it instead.

AWS Elastic Beanstalk Deploy Application similarly builds and packages ASP.NET or ASP.NET Core applications but adds the additional step of deploying the build bundle to an environment. Note that for both tasks, the application and target environments must already exist – they don't get created for you by these tasks.

Figure 12-15 shows a partial setup for an instance of the *AWS Elastic Beanstalk Deploy Application* task. You can see the options to build the correct deployment package based on your .NET application type, or to use preexisting deployment bundles you've built and uploaded in other tasks, or an application version registered with the *AWS Elastic Beanstalk Create Version* task providing a lot of flexibility in how you craft your build and deployment pipelines.

Figure 12-15. *Setting up deployment to Elastic Beanstalk from Azure DevOps*

A (Short) Word About HTTPS and Elastic Beanstalk

Newcomers to Elastic Beanstalk, especially those who've used similar services on other cloud providers, are sometimes surprised that out of the box Elastic Beanstalk does not provide an HTTPS endpoint to the deployed application.

For multiple-instance environments, with a load balancer, the approach expected by the service team is to terminate SSL at the load balancer. This is relatively easy to do by assigning a certificate to the load balancer in the environment. Requests transiting the load balancer then proceed to the instances (which are not publicly accessible) using simple HTTP.

However, what if you must terminate SSL at the instance level in a multi-instance environment? Or you're using a single instance environment with no load balancer, either because you don't need one or want to avoid the additional cost? Things get a little more complicated here, but it is possible. To help, the service team provides documentation and .ebextension scripts to set up HTTPS on the instances in the environment. Rather than reiterating the documentation, here are the links you'll need:

- For applications running on Windows Server instances, an .ebextension script that uses PowerShell to download a certificate and install onto the instance is provided at `https://docs.aws.amazon.com/elasticbeanstalk/latest/dg/SSLNET.SingleInstance.html`. The script takes advantage of the AWS Tools for PowerShell being pre-installed on the instances to download the certificate from an S3 bucket in your account.

- For .NET applications targeting Linux instances, see the corresponding extension and documentation at `https://docs.aws.amazon.com/elasticbeanstalk/latest/dg/https-singleinstance-dotnet-linux.html`.

In both cases, don't forget you'll also need to open port 443 in the security group for the instances.

Deploying to Amazon EC2 Instances

Now that we're familiar with using virtual machine instances provided by EC2 via Elastic Beanstalk, let's drop down the stack to examine deploying directly to EC2 instances.

Back in Chapter 4, we showed how to make use of *UserData* scripts to configure EC2 instances at launch time. You could use these scripts to install an application to an instance as it configures. If you're of a mindset to treat instances as discardable infrastructure (rather than feeding and caring for instances, like pets), this seems to make for a simple setup. Deploying a new revision? Launch a new set of instances, which self-configure and deploy the revision from a *UserData* launch script, then register the new instances with a load balancer and deregister the original instances, removing the older revisions from service.

While it sounds a simple and workable approach, there's actually some complexity involved in doing this yourself:

- Identifying when a new instance is ready to be put into use and a corresponding older instance removed from use.

- Keeping a certain percentage of older instances serving traffic while switching in the replacement instances. They can't all be deregistered at once; otherwise, your application stops serving traffic to customers.

- Rolling back failed deployments.

A better approach is to use a service to handle this complexity for you. You write the necessary install scripts for your application, bundle them into the deployment archive, upload the archive, and have the service take it from there. In AWS, the service that handles all this for you is AWS CodeDeploy.

Introducing AWS CodeDeploy

AWS CodeDeploy is a relatively simple, but powerful, service that's used to automate deployments to EC2 instances, as well as on-premise machines. It's also able to deploy updates to services in Amazon Elastic Container Service and serverless functions in AWS Lambda.

The deployment archive containing the code and other assets you want to deploy can be uploaded to Amazon S3, or you can connect GitHub or Bitbucket repositories.

Like any AWS service, there are some terms to become familiar with before starting to work with CodeDeploy:

- **Application** – Similar to Elastic Beanstalk, an application in CodeDeploy is a container for deployment revisions. It's also linked with deployment configuration and deployment group resources, which define the "how" and the "where" of the deployment process.

- **Deployment configuration** – This specifies how the deployment should be handled in terms of keeping a minimum percentage of the target fleet running and serving traffic while the deployment proceeds.

- **Deployment group** – This identifies the instances (EC2 and on-premise machines) that will be deployed to. Instances can be identified using tags, or as part of an Auto Scaling group, or a combination of the two.

- **AppSpec file** – The application specification file, which must be placed at the root of the deployment archive, references the application files and supporting scripts in the archive that install and configure the application on the instance. For EC2 and on-premise deployments, the AppSpec file must be authored in YAML, and be named *appspec.yml*.

- **Lifecycle hooks** – These are stages that the deployment of a new revision on an instance proceeds through. Each hook (*ApplicationStop*, *BeforeInstall*, *AfterInstall*, *ApplicationStart*, and more) is associated with one or more scripts in the archive using the lifecycle hook name. As deployment reaches each stage, CodeDeploy checks if the associated hook has been referenced in the AppSpec file, and if so, it runs the indicated scripts at that time.

- **CodeDeploy agent** – An agent takes care of downloading the archive, unpacking it, and running the commands and scripts referenced by the AppSpec file. The agent can be run on EC2 instances and on-premises machines (and VMs). CodeDeploy makes the agent available as a publicly accessible file in a set of service-owned S3 buckets, one for each region. You can download and install the agent from a *UserData* script, or you can use AWS Systems Manager to install, and optionally update, the agent when required.

CodeDeploy supports two types of deployments: *in-place* and *blue/green*.

Note   Blue/green deployments are supported for EC2 instances only.

For in-place deployments, on each instance in the deployment group, CodeDeploy downloads the latest revision to be deployed, stops the currently running version of the application, installs and verifies the update, and then restarts the application. If the instances are behind a load balancer, each instance can be deregistered from the load balancer during the process before being re-registered and able to serve traffic running the new revision.

For blue/green deployments, CodeDeploy provisions a replacement set of instances matching the number in the deployment group, installs the new revision, optionally waits ("bake" time) allowing for testing and verification, and then switches the new instances into the load balancer, deregistering the older instances.

For both types of deployment, if an error occurs during install, or testing during bake time indicates issues (e.g., CloudWatch alarms that you've configured against metrics start to fire), automated rollback can be triggered. All without user intervention. As you can see, what looks like a simple process of downloading and installing updates, while keeping your application serving traffic and rolling back on errors, is actually quite complex. So, it makes sense to have someone else do all the work, letting you focus on the application!

Tip   The Amazon Builders Library contains an excellent paper on safely automating hands-off deployments at scale. Even if you're not deploying software updates on an "Amazon" scale and frequency, it's worthwhile reading. Find it, and other excellent articles written by principal engineers at Amazon, at `https://aws.amazon.com/builders-library/automating-safe-hands-off-deployments`.

Working with CodeDeploy

Let's work through an example of using CodeDeploy to deploy the TradeYourTools sample application to a fleet of EC2 instances. To make things a little more "real world," our fleet of instances is managed by an Auto Scaling group that's behind an Application Load Balancer. This will enable us to perform blue/green deployments so that the application will continue to serve traffic during a deployment – our store does not go down for an update!

However, as this is a book about .NET on AWS and not on building Auto Scaling groups, load balancers, and networking configurations, we've taken the "cooking show" route and won't subject you to wading through all those screens (this is where Infrastructure as Code really shines, by the way!). Figure 12-16 shows the general infrastructure setup for the application, representing our "production" fleet and the deployment resources that we're going to discuss.

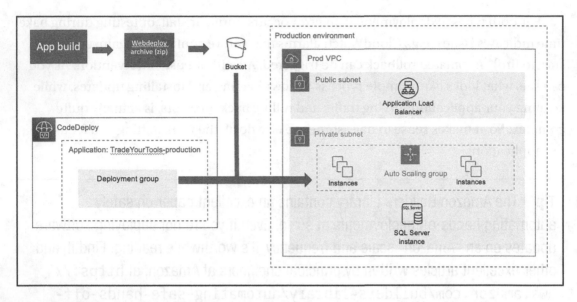

Figure 12-16. *"Production" TradeYourTools infrastructure (simplified)*

Since TradeYourTools is a .NET Framework application, for convenience, we'll use a WebDeploy deployment package for the application binaries. This enables us to use generated scripts within the package to perform the actual install into IIS. All we need to do is call those scripts from within our appspec.yml file in the appropriate lifecycle hook. However, this means we need to install WebDeploy onto each instance and enable IIS.

To achieve this, we've used the *UserData* script shown in Listing 12-3. As noted in the script, WebDeploy archives contain quite long file paths. On the instances, CodeDeploy will unpack the archive to a temporary path beneath C:\ProgramData\Amazon\ CodeDeploy*guid**deployment-id*. This exacerbates the problem, leading on occasion to deployment errors stating that a file cannot be found (even when it's present). To fix this, we set a registry key to allow paths to exceed 260 characters (who'd have thought that path lengths would still be an issue...).

Listing 12-3. UserData script to configure EC2 instances during launch

```powershell
<powershell>

# Install IIS
Install-WindowsFeature -Name Web-Server,
    NET-Framework-45-ASPNET,
    NET-Framework-45-Core,
    NET-Framework-45-Features,
```

```
   NET-Framework-Core -IncludeManagementTools
# Use Chocolately to conveniently obtain webdeploy
Set-ExecutionPolicy Bypass -Scope Process -Force
iex ((New-Object System.Net.WebClient).DownloadString( ↵
      'https://chocolatey.org/install.ps1'))
choco install webdeploy -y

# Download and install the CodeDeploy agent from the regional
# bucket location
$region = (Get-EC2InstanceMetadata -Category Region).SystemName
Read-S3Object -BucketName aws-codedeploy-$region ↵
-Key latest/codedeploy-agent.msi ↵
-File c:\temp\codedeploy-agent.msi

c:\temp\codedeploy-agent.msi /quiet ↵
/l c:\temp\host-agent-install-log.txt

# webdeploy archives contain long paths, which worsen when
# unpacked by CodeDeploy into an even longer path!
Set-ItemProperty 'HKLM:\System\CurrentControlSet\Control\FileSystem' ↵
-Name 'LongPathsEnabled' -Value 1

</powershell>
```

With our production fleet running (we'll pretend it's already serving application traffic courtesy of a previous update), let's move on to deploy an updated version of the application with CodeDeploy.

Setting Up CodeDeploy Resources

Before we can start performing deployments using CodeDeploy, we need to set up, at a minimum, the application and deployment group resources. For this example, we'll skip creating a deployment configuration and use a built-in configuration that will deploy to one instance at a time.

Head to the CodeDeploy dashboard in the management console and click **Getting started**, followed by **Create application** on the Getting started page. To create an application, all we need is a name and to set the **Compute platform** to *EC2/On-premises*, shown in Figure 12-17.

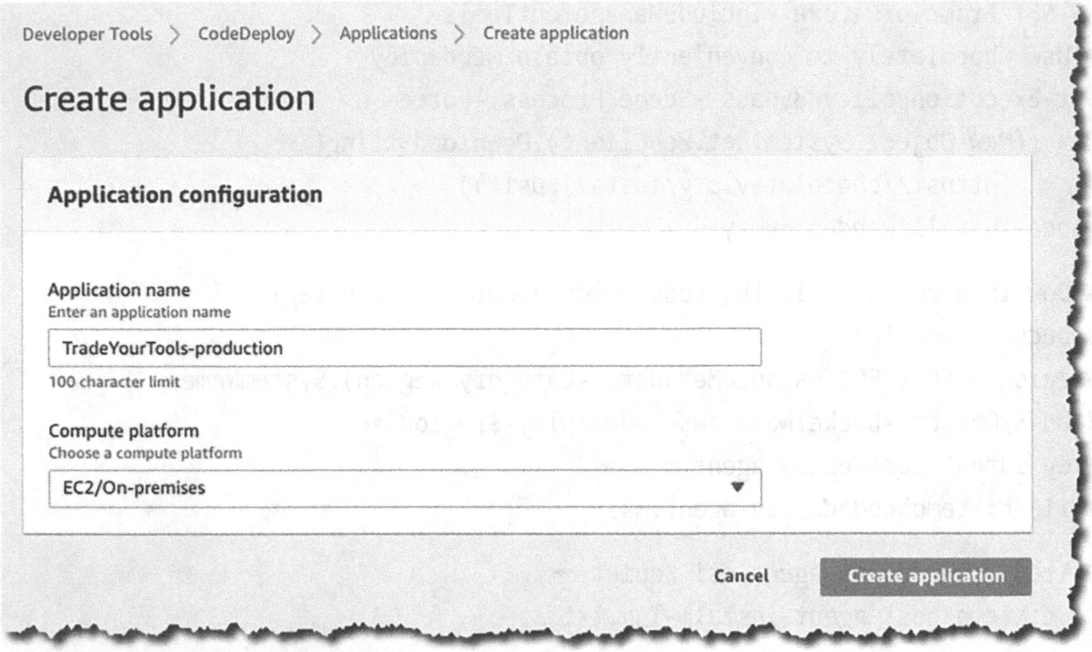

Figure 12-17. Creating the CodeDeploy application

Clicking Create application will take you to an Application details view. Here, click the **Create deployment group** button. Note that you can have multiple deployment groups for a CodeDeploy application, if you want, targeting different combinations of instances based on their Auto Scaling group and/or tags.

Figure 12-18 shows the initial deployment group settings:

- A name for the group (**TradeYourTools-prod-deployment**).

- The service role that provides permissions for CodeDeploy to access our resources (Auto Scaling group, instances, and load balancer). The role must already exist; there's no provision to link out to the IAM console to create a new role. See `https://docs.aws.amazon.com/codedeploy/latest/userguide/getting-started-create-service-role.html` for details on creating a suitable role.

- The deployment type (in-place or **blue/green**).

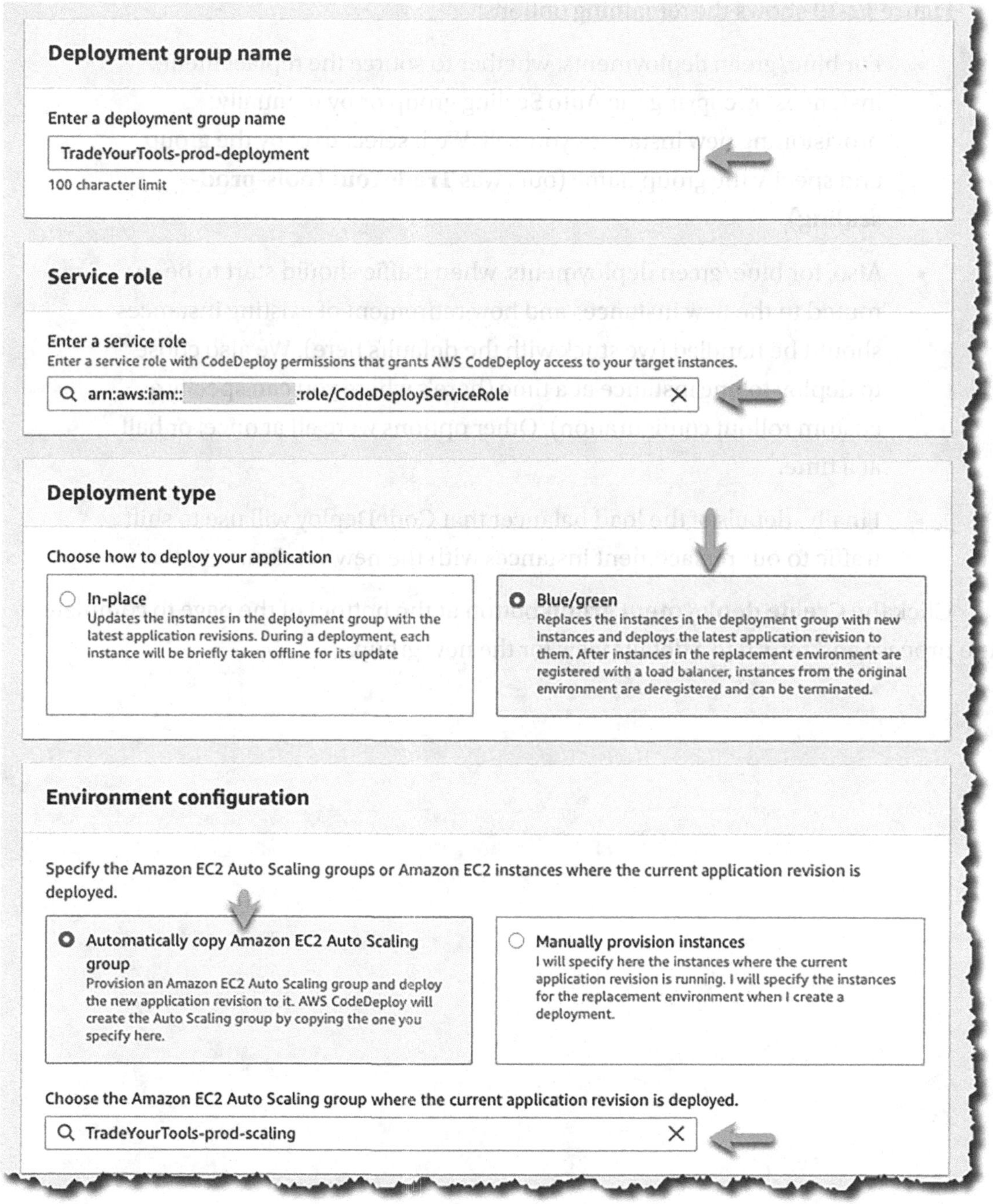

Deployment group name

Enter a deployment group name

TradeYourTools-prod-deployment

100 character limit

Service role

Enter a service role
Enter a service role with CodeDeploy permissions that grants AWS CodeDeploy access to your target instances.

🔍 arn:aws:iam::   :role/CodeDeployServiceRole   ✕

Deployment type

Choose how to deploy your application

○ **In-place**
Updates the instances in the deployment group with the latest application revisions. During a deployment, each instance will be briefly taken offline for its update

● **Blue/green**
Replaces the instances in the deployment group with new instances and deploys the latest application revision to them. After instances in the replacement environment are registered with a load balancer, instances from the original environment are deregistered and can be terminated.

Environment configuration

Specify the Amazon EC2 Auto Scaling groups or Amazon EC2 instances where the current application revision is deployed.

● **Automatically copy Amazon EC2 Auto Scaling group**
Provision an Amazon EC2 Auto Scaling group and deploy the new application revision to it. AWS CodeDeploy will create the Auto Scaling group by copying the one you specify here.

○ **Manually provision instances**
I will specify here the instances where the current application revision is running. I will specify the instances for the replacement environment when I create a deployment.

Choose the Amazon EC2 Auto Scaling group where the current application revision is deployed.

🔍 TradeYourTools-prod-scaling   ✕

Figure 12-18. *Name, service role, and deployment type*

465

Figure 12-19 shows the remaining options:

- For blue/green deployments, whether to source the replacement instances by copying the Auto Scaling group or by manually provisioning new instances yourself. We'll select to copy the group and specify the group name (ours was **TradeYourTools-prod-scaling**).

- Also, for blue/green deployments, when traffic should start to be routed to the new instances and how retirement of existing instances should be handled (we stuck with the defaults here). We also chose to deploy to one instance at a time (here's where you can specify a custom rollout configuration). Other options were all at once, or half at a time.

- Finally, details of the load balancer that CodeDeploy will use to shift traffic to our replacement instances with the new version.

Click the **Create deployment group** button at the bottom of the page to complete the process and return to a details view for the new group.

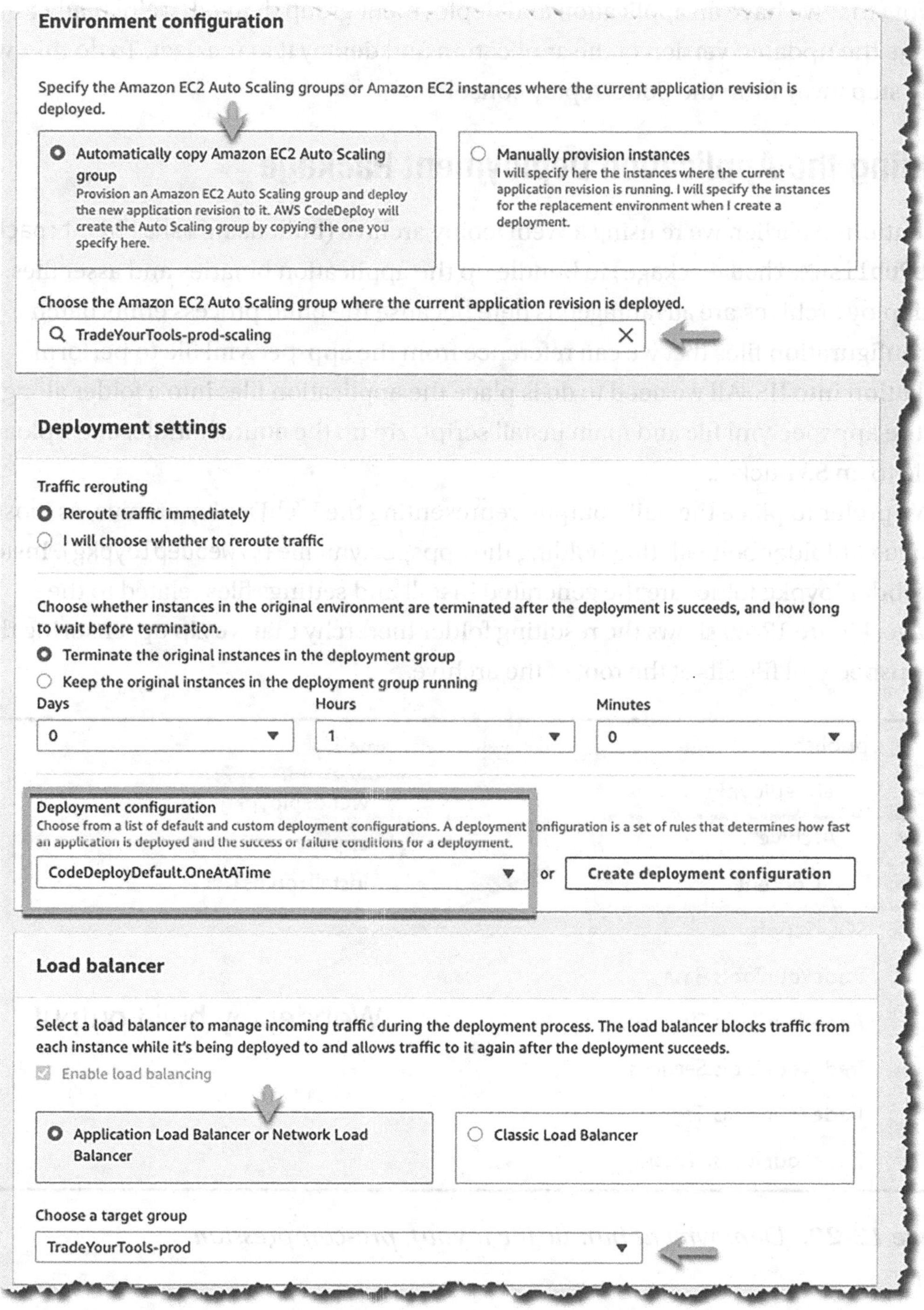

Environment configuration

Specify the Amazon EC2 Auto Scaling groups or Amazon EC2 instances where the current application revision is deployed.

○ **Automatically copy Amazon EC2 Auto Scaling group**
Provision an Amazon EC2 Auto Scaling group and deploy the new application revision to it. AWS CodeDeploy will create the Auto Scaling group by copying the one you specify here.

○ **Manually provision instances**
I will specify here the instances where the current application revision is running. I will specify the instances for the replacement environment when I create a deployment.

Choose the Amazon EC2 Auto Scaling group where the current application revision is deployed.

Q TradeYourTools-prod-scaling   ✕

Deployment settings

Traffic rerouting
○ Reroute traffic immediately
○ I will choose whether to reroute traffic

Choose whether instances in the original environment are terminated after the deployment is succeeds, and how long to wait before termination.
○ Terminate the original instances in the deployment group
○ Keep the original instances in the deployment group running

Days	Hours	Minutes
0 ▼	1 ▼	0 ▼

Deployment configuration
Choose from a list of default and custom deployment configurations. A deployment configuration is a set of rules that determines how fast an application is deployed and the success or failure conditions for a deployment.

CodeDeployDefault.OneAtATime   ▼   or   **Create deployment configuration**

Load balancer

Select a load balancer to manage incoming traffic during the deployment process. The load balancer blocks traffic from each instance while it's being deployed to and allows traffic to it again after the deployment succeeds.

☑ Enable load balancing

○ **Application Load Balancer or Network Load Balancer**

○ Classic Load Balancer

Choose a target group

TradeYourTools-prod   ▼

Figure 12-19. Remaining options for the deployment group

Now that we have an application and deployment group defined, we're ready to package the updated version of the application and deploy it to the fleet. To do this, we'll briefly step away from the CodeDeploy console.

Building the Application Deployment Package

As mentioned earlier, we're using a WebDeploy archive (built using `msbuild /t:package p:WebPublishMethod=Package`) to bundle up the application binaries and asset files. Webdeploy archives are advantageous here because the build process emits batch and configuration files that we can reference from the appspec.yml file to perform installation into IIS. All we need to do is place the application files into a folder along with the appspec.yml file and main install script, zip up the entire bundle, and upload the file to an S3 bucket.

We prefer to place the build output, representing the WebDeploy archive, as loose files in a subfolder beneath that holding the appspec.yml file (`./webdeploypkg`). Inside the webdeploypkg folder are the generated install and settings files related to the package. Figure 12-20 shows the resulting folder hierarchy that we zip up, ensuring that the appspec.yml file sits at the root of the archive.

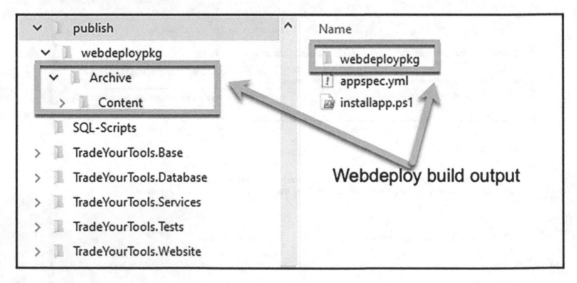

Figure 12-20. *Deployment bundle file layout, pre-compression*

> **Tip**   To build a WebDeploy archive as loose files, use the
> `/p:PackageAsSingleFile=false` build option. You can equally have the
> webdeploy output packaged as a zip file if you prefer.

Let's now look at the *appspec.yml* and custom install script files. The `installapp.ps1` script is simply a helpful one-liner that invokes the generated installation batch file. We don't need to pass or customize any parameters here but certainly could do. Listing 12-4 shows our "one-liner" install. `Archive.deploy.cmd` was generated during the package build; your file name may be different.

Listing 12-4. The installapp.ps1 script that runs the generated installation script

```
& "$PSScriptRoot\webdeploypkg\Archive.deploy.cmd" /Y
```

So far, so simple. Earlier, we noted that a deployment onto an instance goes through a series of lifecycle hooks, or stages, which we can reference inside the *appspec.yml* file to run scripts at each stage. This file can also contain additional keys to control which files need to be placed onto an instance, permissions (for Linux instances), and more. Full details on the hooks and their use in the appspec.yml file for EC2/on-premises deployments can be found in the documentation at `https://docs.aws.amazon.com/codedeploy/latest/userguide/reference-appspec-file-structure-hooks.html#appspec-hooks-server`.

Our particular appspec.yml file, shown in Listing 12-5, couldn't be much simpler.

Listing 12-5. The appspec.yml file to drive the install

```
version: 0.0
os: windows

hooks:
  AfterInstall:
    - location: .\installapp.ps1
```

We're using the `AfterInstall` hook here because we don't need CodeDeploy to copy the application assets to the *C:\inetpub\wwwroot* folder for IIS – the generated script will do that for us. Lest you feel cheated, Listing 12-6 is the appspec.yml file from a .NET 6 application that we can deploy to Linux instances for comparison. It makes use of more lifecycle hooks and custom scripts and a files section to move the application binaries into place on the instance.

Listing 12-6. Comparison appspec.yml file for a .NET 6 install onto Linux

```
version: 0.0
os: linux
files:
  - source: appbin
    destination: /var/www
  - source: scripts/webapp.service
    destination: /etc/systemd/system
hooks:
  ApplicationStop:
    - location: scripts/application_stop.sh
      timeout: 10
  BeforeInstall:
    - location: scripts/before_install.sh
      timeout: 10
  ApplicationStart:
    - location: scripts/application_start.sh
      timeout: 10
  ValidateService:
    - location: scripts/validate_app.sh
      timeout: 300
```

Deploying the New Version

We're finally ready to trigger a blue/green deployment! Start by zipping up the folder contents (the appspec.yml file **must** be at the archive root) and upload the zip file to an S3 bucket (we could also upload to GitHub).

Note   The instances we're deploying to must have an instance profile (role) attached to them granting permissions to access the S3 bucket containing the deployment archive. See `https://docs.aws.amazon.com/codedeploy/latest/ userguide/getting-started-create-iam-instance-profile.html`.

Back in the management console, from the details view of the deployment group we created earlier, click **Create deployment**. Select S3 as the revision type and provide the S3 URI to the uploaded zip file, then click **Create deployment**. Figure 12-21 shows our selections.

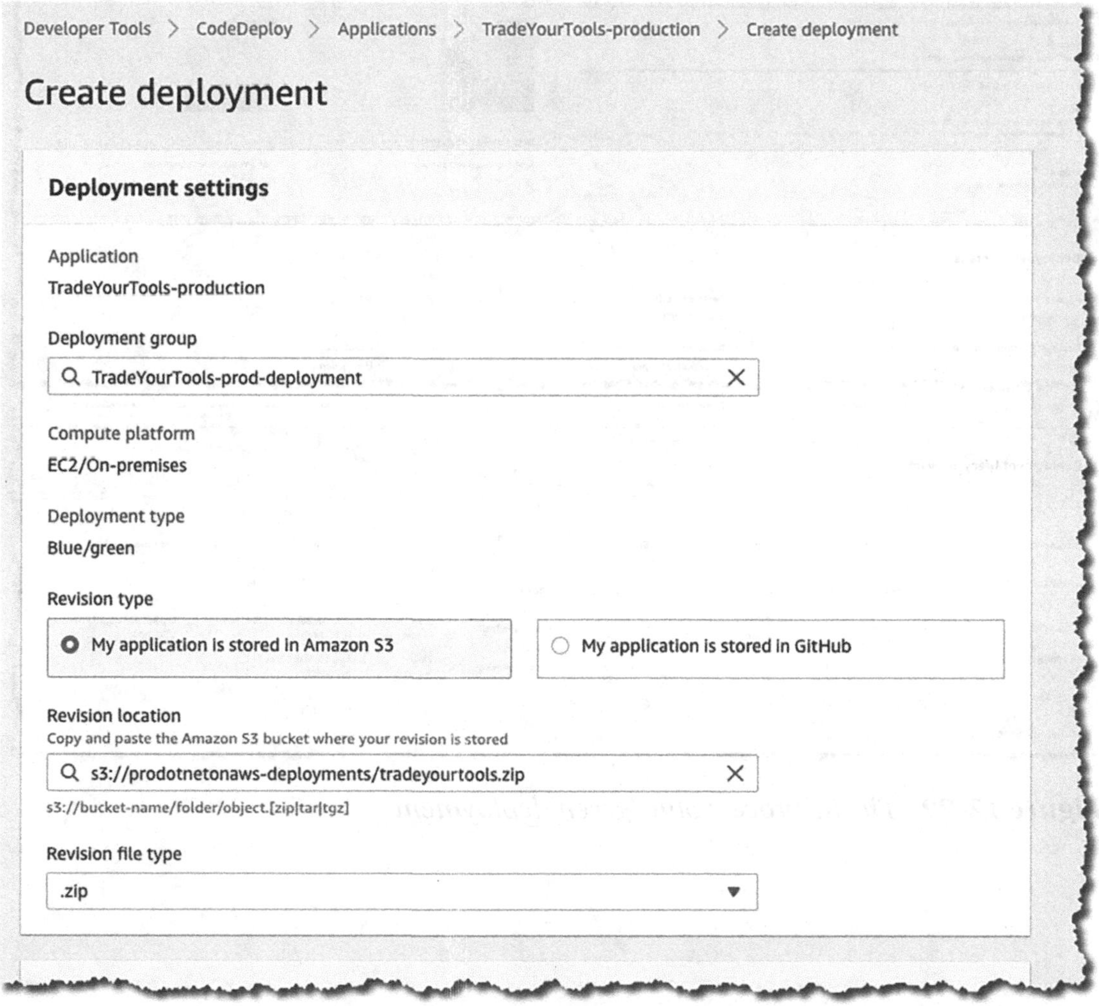

Developer Tools > CodeDeploy > Applications > TradeYourTools-production > Create deployment

Create deployment

Deployment settings

Application
TradeYourTools-production

Deployment group

```
Q   TradeYourTools-prod-deployment                                    ✕
```

Compute platform
EC2/On-premises

Deployment type
Blue/green

Revision type

| ● My application is stored in Amazon S3 | ○ My application is stored in GitHub |

Revision location
Copy and paste the Amazon S3 bucket where your revision is stored

```
Q   s3://prodotnetonaws-deployments/tradeyourtools.zip           ✕
```
s3://bucket-name/folder/object.[zip|tar|tgz]

Revision file type

```
.zip                                                              ▼
```

Figure 12-21. *Starting the deployment of the new application revision*

The first time you run the deployment, it's interesting to watch the process play out, as CodeDeploy provisions new replacement instances, downloads the archive to each, unpacks it, and runs the included scripts, and then traffic shifts the replacement instances into play in the load balancer and retires the old instances – all without stopping the application being served to our customers at any point. You can watch the deployment as a whole or drill into the lifecycle hook events on a per-instance basis. Figure 12-22 shows an interim state as the deployment progresses.

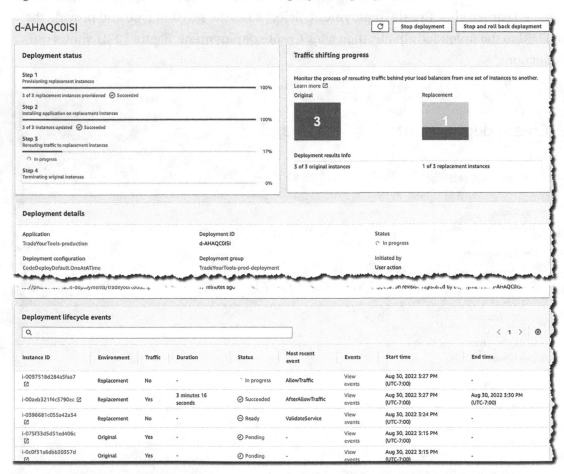

Figure 12-22. *The in-process blue/green deployment*

We've shown a lot of quite detailed console screens for CodeDeploy, so you may be wondering at this point where automation comes in! Rest assured, everything we've shown in the section can be driven by automation, using the SDKs or command-line tools, and CI/CD pipelines. You don't need to go into the CodeDeploy console and work through these screens for every new revision of your application! However, we hope you now have a feel for how CodeDeploy can fit into scenarios where you need to deploy applications (and not just .NET ones too) to virtual machines.

Summary

Virtual machines are a familiar mechanism that some teams may prefer when beginning their move to the cloud, and still have a role to play for many. AWS provides Amazon EC2 and AWS Elastic Beanstalk as options for hosting of .NET and .NET Framework applications in virtual machine environments, together with tooling in Visual Studio, at the command line, and via AWS CodeDeploy to make the process of deployment simple and convenient, whether you're deploying as part of day-to-day development iteration or using a CI/CD pipeline.

Containers, though, are the current "hot property," and in the next chapter, we'll look at deploying applications to AWS container services.

CHAPTER 13

Containerizing

We just went over the processing of taking your applications and moving them to virtual machines in the cloud. In this chapter, we are going to show ways in which you can containerize your applications for deployment into the cloud, the next step in minimizing resource usage and likely saving money. This chapter differs from Chapter 5 in that the previous chapter was a discussion of containers and running them within the AWS infrastructure. This chapter is more practical and based upon getting to that point from an existing noncontainerized application.

There are several different approaches that we will go over. The first is converting your existing .NET Framework 4.*x* web application to run on a Windows container and then going over the ramifications of working with a Windows container in AWS' Linux-centric infrastructure. We will then cover containerizing a .NET Core application and finish with an approach to containerizing a running application making no changes to the code. Let's get started and containerize!

General Requirements

In Chapter 5, we briefly talked about some of the system prerequisites necessary to work locally with code designed to run in containers. Well, that's not completely accurate in that you can work on the code, but without these prerequisites, you cannot really debug and step through your code – and that requires a lot more confidence than either of us has as we really like debugging!

The main prerequisite is **Docker Desktop**. You can download this from `www.docker.com/products/docker-desktop`. There are multiple versions including Mac with Intel Chip, Mac with Apple Chip, and Windows (x86-64 only!), and multiple Linux versions including Fedora, CentOS, AWS, Azure, Ubuntu, and Debian – so you should be able to find and run the appropriate desktop for your local machine. The use of this application is free as long as it is for personal use, education, or noncommercial open source projects so your use, in this case, is perfectly acceptable.

475

Our recommendation for installing Docker Desktop would be to follow the default values for your system. We are not going to be digging deep into the internals of the application; instead, we are going to simply take advantage of its functionality to build container images and provide a platform on which they can run for debugging and code walkthrough. Our examples are going to be captured using Windows 10 Pro and Windows Server 2019, so it is possible that those of you in a different operating system may have slightly different behavior.

Containers and Networking

Before we get too far into the containerization process, let us first spend some time going a little deeper into how networking may affect your ability to work with containers. As you have probably already noticed, AWS generally defaults to the most secure configuration possible, which means that you will need to ensure that your containers are configured correctly to be able to connect to the Internet, receive inbound calls, or even talk to other containers. And, of course, each of the primary container management approaches used by AWS does it differently.

Amazon ECS

The first of these security concerns, *being able to reach out to the Internet*, is necessary in many different cases; perhaps you have third-party systems you are connecting to, or you are using licensed controls that require periodic check-in to a central licensing service, as well as many other reasons. If your containerized application has this requirement, then you have two different options: the first is by using a public subnet and Internet gateway, while the second uses a private subnet and NAT gateway.

The first of these approaches is straightforward. Running your containerized application in a public subnet that has an assigned Internet gateway will ensure that your container can be assigned a public IP address that can be reached from the Internet. This public IP address enables users on the Internet to reach your application as well as allow your application to reach out to the Internet. Because of this bidirectional nature, you will need to ensure that you are managing your security appropriately. You can see what this arrangement looks like in Figure 13-1.

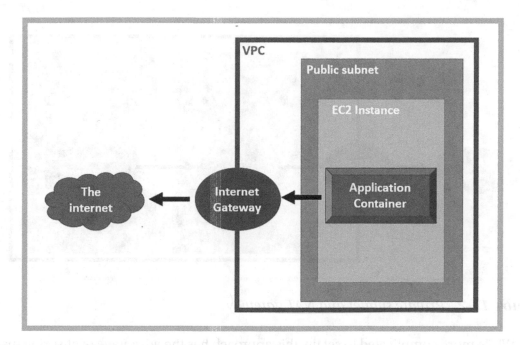

Figure 13-1. *Public subnet with Internet gateway*

The second of these approaches, using a private subnet and NAT gateway, ensures that the host has a private IP address that can be reached within the VPC but is not routable from the Internet. Instead, you use a Network Address Translation (NAT) gateway that is inside a publicly reachable public subnet with an Internet gateway. This arrangement can be seen in Figure 13-2.

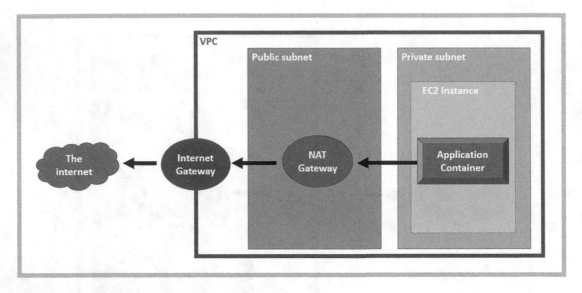

Figure 13-2. *Private subnet and NAT gateway*

While more complicated to set up, this approach has the advantage of ensuring that the VPC in which you are running your applications is not accessible from the Internet without additional networking configuration. However, be aware that NAT gateways can be expensive as you are charged for both hourly usage and data processing. Also, for redundancy purposes, you should have a NAT gateway in each Availability Zone, which will also increase costs while ensuring that a loss of availability in a single zone does not affect your outbound connectivity.

Both networking approaches are supported for ECS regardless of whether you are using ECS on EC2 or when using AWS Fargate. The next security concern is around *receiving inbound connections from the Internet.* The first way is one that we already touched on, running your application in a public subnet with an Internet gateway and an associated public IP address. However, for those looking for a more secure approach, we have three recommendations for routing inbound requests to your containerized application running in a private subnet.

The first approach is by using an Application Load Balancer (ALB) that is running in a public subnet, much like the NAT gateway was earlier. An ALB functions at the application layer, which means that it can handle SSL/TLS termination so that the application itself does not have to. Using an ALB also supports advanced routing, so you can support multiple hostnames as well as the ability to route requests based on request path or other characteristics within the request. An ALB also supports gRPC and websockets, so applications using those features can be safely supported as well.

The second approach is by using a Network Load Balancer (NLB) that is running in a public subnet. An NLB runs at a lower level than an ALB, so it doesn't have the same level of application support that you can find with the ALB. However, it offers other benefits, such as end-to-end encryption, TLS encryption, and the support of non-HTTP workloads and communications protocols other than TCP – mainly because of how the balancer passes the packets on without reading or otherwise concerning itself with the content in the packets.

The last approach for routing inbound requests to a containerized application is by using Amazon API Gateway. As we discussed in earlier chapters, API Gateway is a serverless approach that is heavily suited for HTTP applications. Since API Gateway is serverless, it has a different pricing structure than either ALB or NLB, which each include an hourly price. API Gateway, on the other hand, charges for each request, so if there are no requests, there is no charge.

Plugging in an API Gateway is different than what we have already gone over because there is no public subnet involved as there is with both load balancer approaches. Instead, API Gateway uses a VPC Link that allows the service to reach hosts within the private subnet. This approach is shown in Figure 13-3.

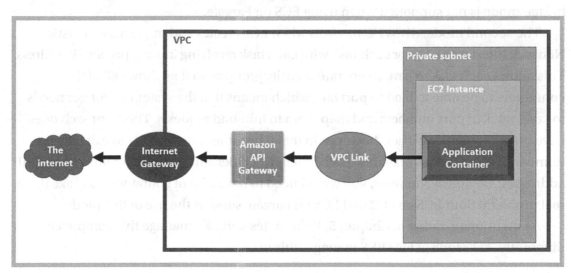

Figure 13-3. *Using Amazon API Gateway to manage inbound traffic*

API Gateway has more features as it not only supports load balancing like the ALB but also has additional API management capabilities. The Gateway also supports additional capabilities such as client authorization and modification of the request and/or response. We will go over the API Gateway in more detail in a future chapter. All three of these approaches equally support ECS hosted on EC2 instances as well as ECS on Fargate.

The last networking concern is around *how containers communicate with one another*. This is a problem unique to containers because it requires an additional level of networking than other workloads, especially if the containers running within a single host need the ability to intercommunicate. AWS recommends two different modes to manage this.

The first of these, *bridge mode*, is when you use a virtual network bridge that acts as an intermediary between the host and the container. This bridge then creates port mappings between a host port and a container port. ECS does most of the work around selecting and updating the various values so that it can ensure traffic delivery; however, because these services could be assigned to any random port, it makes it difficult to create specific rules regarding one service talking to another specific service. Also, the bridge mode is not supported when using ECS on Fargate.

The second mode, *AWSVPC mode*, is when ECS creates and manages an Elastic Network Interface (ENI) for each task with each task receiving its own private IP Address. This allows each task to have a separate security group as well as allows all of the containers to be able to bind to port 80 – which means that the system no longer needs to keep track of port numbers and map them to inbound requests. This approach does have one potential drawback, however, in that it becomes much easier to exhaust the number of IP addresses available in a subnet, which defaults to an upper limit of 4,091 IP addresses. Obviously, however, you would need to have a lot of containers to make this a real problem! Both ECS on EC2 and ECS on Fargate support the use of this mode.

As mentioned earlier in Chapter 5, Kubernetes and EKS manage this completely differently. Let's look at how EKS manages this now.

Amazon EKS

Where ECS concerned itself with the subnets within a VPC, EKS takes a different approach to how the various components interact with a VPC as shown in Figure 13-4.

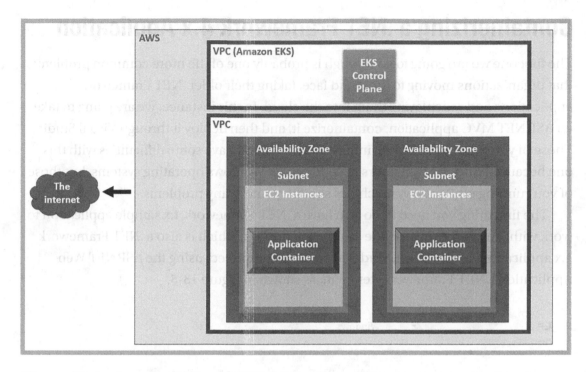

Figure 13-4. *Amazon EKS and VPC interactions*

For EKS, all resources are deployed to one region. Each subnet exists in one Availability Zone and can be either a private or public subnet. When using a private subnet, however, you will need to ensure that the pod (or container) can access other needed services in AWS such as ECR. The Control Plane and the nodes must be able to talk to each other through all ports using security groups.

The EKS control plane is deployed into an EKS-managed VPC and, by default, has a public endpoint exposed so that clients and nodes can communicate with the cluster. Each of the EC2 instances is deployed to a subnet, with each node being assigned a private IP address using the Amazon VPC Container Network Interface (CNI) plugin. These various IP addresses are then managed through the AWS load balancer controller add-in where there is the option to create an Application Load Balancer or a Network Load Balancer – the same types of load balancers that we saw in ECS with the same advantages and features that we saw there. At this time, there is no comparable API Gateway experience to that offered by ECS.

Now that we have gone over some of the networking requirements, the next step is to containerize an application. Let's do that next.

Containerizing a .NET Framework 4.x Application

The first one we are going to go through is probably one of the more common problems that organizations moving to the cloud face, taking their older .NET Framework applications and redeploying them into the cloud. In this instance, we are going to take an ASP.NET MVC application, containerize it, and then deploy it through Visual Studio. Those of you running on non-Windows machines will have some difficulties with this one because Windows containers need to run on Windows operating systems, but those of you running on Windows machines should not have any problems.

The first thing you need to do is to have a .NET Framework 4.x sample application to work with. You can either use the sample application, which is also a .NET Framework 4.x application, or use Visual Studio to create a new project using the ASP.NET Web Application (.NET Framework) template as shown in Figure 13-5.

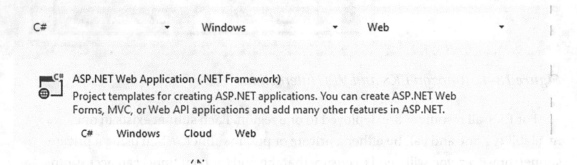

Figure 13-5. *Creating a sample .NET application*

Then ensure that you have an older .NET Framework selected as shown in Figure 13-6.

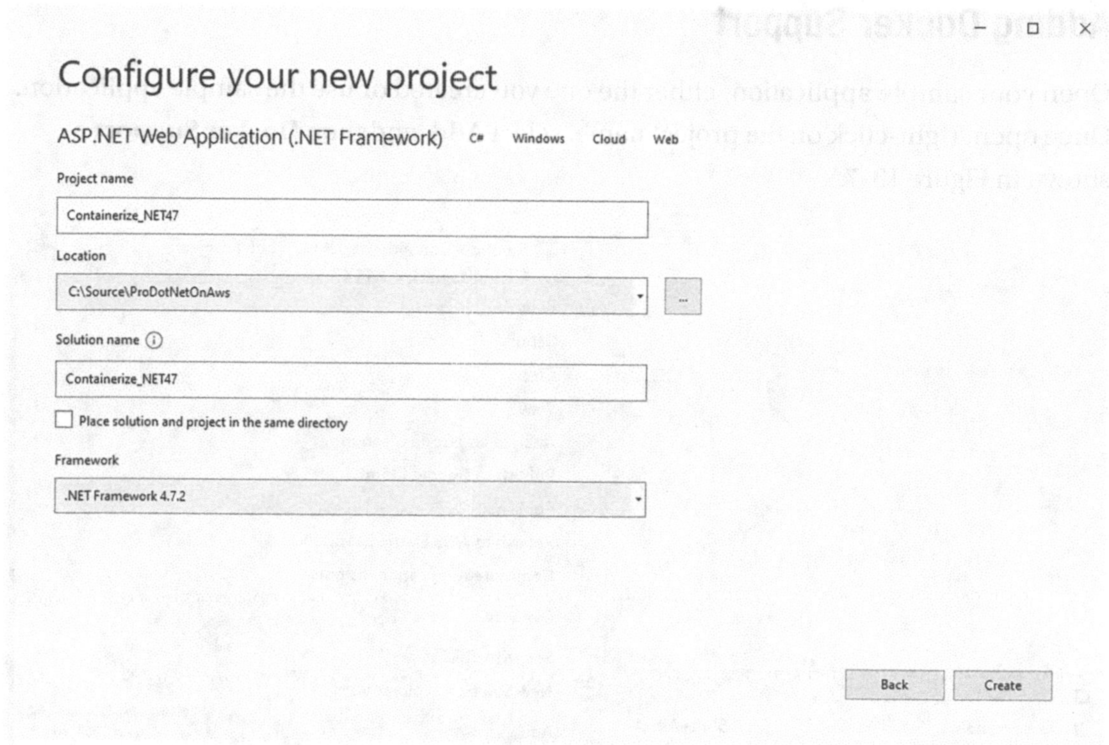

Figure 13-6. *Using an older .NET Framework on project creation*

Once you have your application, you'll notice a few things, such as your default setting is to debug using *IIS Express (Default browser)*. Building and running the application will open your browser to **https://localhost:xxxxx/** because it is running the application under your local IIS Express. Those of you that may have Internet Information Services (IIS) running locally may have different behavior, but the result will be the same as you end up running your application under your local web server.

The next step is to containerize your application. This is a simple process in Visual Studio as there is built-in functionality to support this. Unfortunately, this same support is not available in JetBrains Rider or VS Code. We will, instead, walk through making the changes manually if using one of those environments.

Using Visual Studio

Adding container support using Visual Studio is straightforward.

Adding Docker Support

Open your sample application, either the one you created or use the sample application. Once open, right-click on the project name, select **Add**, and then **Docker Support** as shown in Figure 13-7.

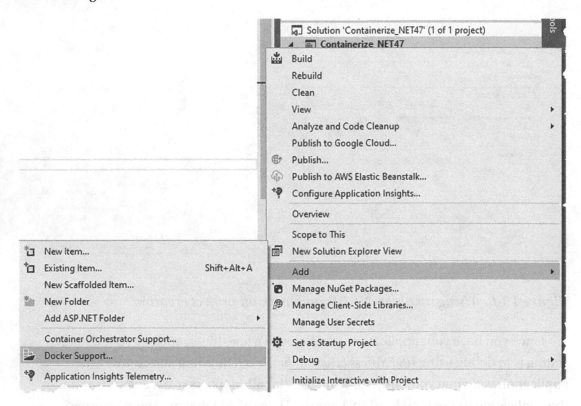

Figure 13-7. *Adding Docker Support to an application*

Your *Output* view, when set to showing output from Container Tools, will show multiple steps being performed, and then it should finish successfully. When completed, you will see two new files added in the Solution Explorer: **Dockerfile** and a subordinate **.dockerignore** file. You will also see that your default Debug setting has changed to Docker. You can see both changes in Figure 13-8.

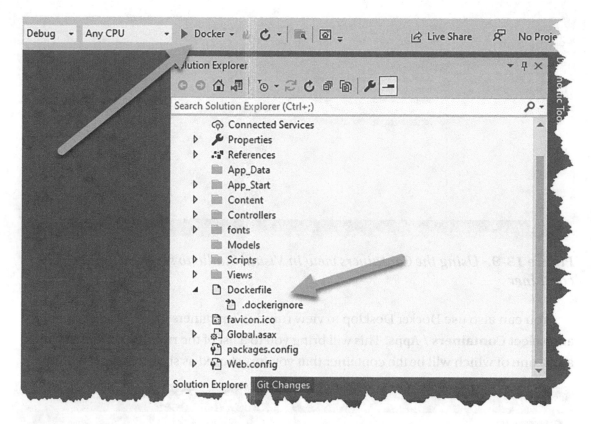

Figure 13-8. *Changes in Visual Studio after adding Docker Support*

You can test the support by clicking the Docker button. This will build the container, run it under your local Docker Desktop, and then open your default browser. This time, rather than going to a localhost URL, you will instead go to an IP address, and if you compare the IP address in the URL to your local IP, you will see that they are not the same. That is because this new IP address points to the container running on your system.

Before closing the browser and stopping the debug process, you will be able to confirm that the container is running by using the Containers view in Visual Studio as shown in Figure 13-9.

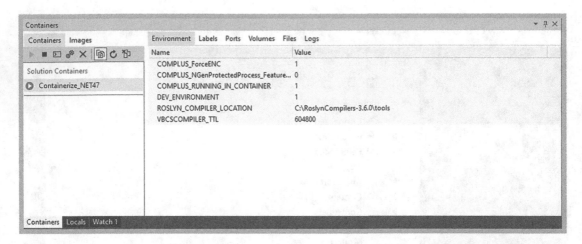

Figure 13-9. *Using the Containers view in Visual Studio to see the running container*

You can also use Docker Desktop to view running containers. Open *Docker Desktop* and select **Containers / Apps**. This will bring you to a list of the running containers and apps, one of which will be the container that you just started as shown in Figure 13-10.

Figure 13-10. *Viewing a running container in Docker Desktop*

Once these steps have been completed, you are ready to deploy your container to ECR.

Deploying Your Windows Container to ECR

There are some complications with this when compared to how we went through the process earlier, as the AWS Toolkit for Visual Studio does not support the container deployment options we saw in Chapter 5 when working with Windows containers. Instead, we are going to use the AWS PowerShell tools to build and publish your image to ECR. At a high level, the steps are as follows:

- **Build your application in Release mode** – This is the only way that Visual Studio puts the appropriate files in the right place, namely, the **obj\Docker\publish** subdirectory of your project directory. You can see this value called out in the last line of your Dockerfile: COPY ${source:-obj/Docker/publish} .

- **Refresh your ECR authentication token** – You need this later in the process so that you can log in to ECR to push the image.

- **Build the Docker image.**

- **Tag the image** – Creates the image tag on the repository.

- **Push the image to the server** – Copy the image into ECR.

Let's walk through them now. The first step is to build your application in Release mode. However, before you can do that, you will need to stop your currently running container. You can do that through either Docker Desktop or the Containers view in Visual Studio. If you do not do this, your build will fail because you will not be able to override the necessary files. Once that is completed, your Release mode build should be able to run without problem.

Next, open PowerShell and navigate to your project directory. This directory needs to be the one that contains the Dockerfile. First thing we will do is to set the authentication context. We do that by first getting the command to execute and then executing that command. That is why this process has two steps:

```
$loginCommand = Get-ECRLoginCommand -Region <repository region>
```

and then

```
Invoke-Expression $loginCommand.Command
```

This refreshed the authentication token into ECR. The remaining commands are based upon an existing ECR repository. You can access this information through the AWS Explorer by clicking on the repository name. This will bring up the details page as shown in Figure 13-11.

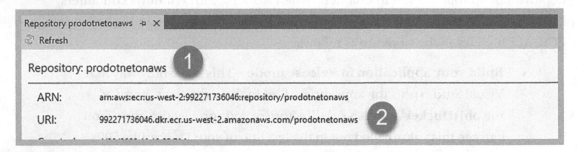

Figure 13-11. *Viewing a running container in Docker Desktop*

The value shown by the 1 is the repository name and by number 2 is the repository URI. You will need both of those values for the remaining steps. Build the image:

```
docker build -t <repository_value-1> .
```

The next step is to tag the image. In this example, we are setting this version as the *latest* version by appending both the repository name and URI with ":latest".

```
docker tag <repository_value-1>:latest <URI_value-2>:latest
```

The last step is to push the image to the server:

```
docker push <URI_value-2>:latest
```

You will see a lot of work going on as everything is pushed to the repository, but eventually, it will finish processing and you will be able to see your new image in the repository.

Note   Not all container services on AWS support Windows containers. Amazon ECS on AWS Fargate is one of the services that does as long as you make the appropriate choices as you configure your tasks. There are detailed directions to doing just that at `https://aws.amazon.com/blogs/containers/running-windows-containers-with-amazon-ecs-on-aws-fargate/`.

While Visual Studio offers a menu-driven approach to containerizing your application, you always have the option to containerize your application manually.

Containerizing Manually

Containerizing an application manually requires several steps. You'll need to create your Dockerfile and then coordinate the build of the application so that it works with the Dockerfile you created. We'll start with those steps first, and we'll do it using JetBrains Rider. The first thing you'll need to do is to add a Dockerfile to your sample application, called **Dockerfile**. This file needs to be in the root of your active project directory. Once you have this added to the project, right-click the file to open the *Properties* window and change the *Build action* to **None** and the *Copy to output directory* to **Do not copy** as shown in Figure 13-12.

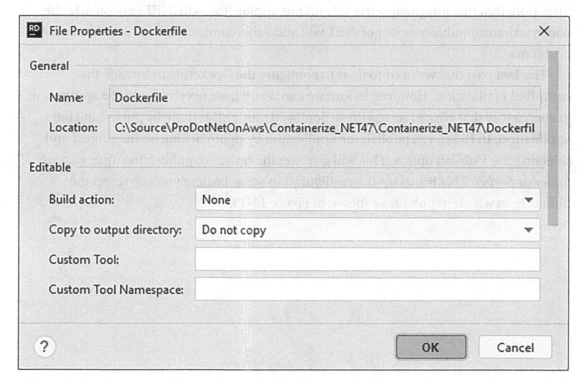

Figure 13-12. *Build properties for the new Dockerfile*

This is important because it makes sure that the Dockerfile itself will not end up deployed into the container.

Now that we have the file, let's start adding the instructions:

```
FROM mcr.microsoft.com/dotnet/framework/aspnet:4.8-
windowsservercore-ltsc2019
ARG source
WORKDIR /inetpub/wwwroot
```

These commands are defining the source image with FROM, defining an argument, and then defining the directory and entry point where the code is going to be running on the container. The source image that we have defined includes support for ASP.NET and .NET version 4.8, `mcr.microsoft.com/dotnet/framework/aspnet:4.8`, and is being deployed onto Windows Server 2019, `windowsservercore-ltsc2019`. There is an image for Windows Server 2022, `windowsservercore-ltsc2022`, but this may not be usable for you if you are not running the most current version of Windows on your machine. Also, note that this image supports 4.8 and our application is in .NET version 4.7. The backward-compatibility aspect of .NET will allow this combination to run without any problems.

The last part that we need to do is to configure the Dockerfile to include the compiled application. However, before we can do that, we need to build the application in such a way that we can access these deployed bits. This is done by publishing the application. In Rider, you publish the application by right-clicking on the project and selecting the **Publish** option. This will give you the option to publish to either a *Local folder* or *Server*. This brings up the configuration screen where you can select the directory in which to publish as shown in Figure 13-13.

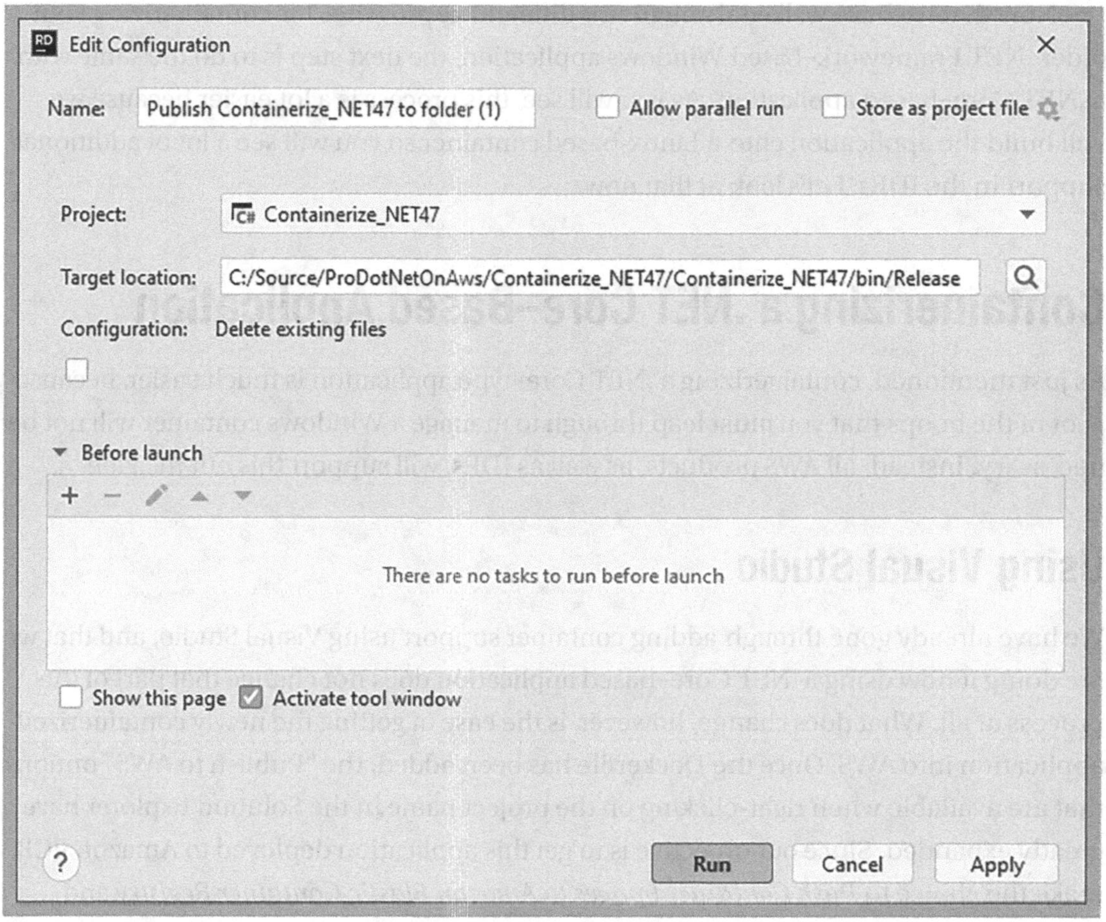

Figure 13-13. *Selecting a publish directory*

It will be easiest if you select a directory underneath the project directory; we recommend within the bin directory so that the IDEs and source code management tools will tend to ignore it. Clicking the **Run** button will publish the app to the directory. The last step is to add one more command to the Dockerfile where you point the source command to the directory in which you published the application. Please note that this Dockerfile is not building the application but is instead pointing to the build directory where the build was performed manually.

```
COPY ${source:-bin/release} .
```

Once you add this last line into the Dockerfile, you are ready to deploy the Windows container to ECR using the steps that we went through in the last section.

Now that we have walked through two different approaches for containerizing your older .NET Framework–based Windows application, the next step is to do the same with a .NET Core–based application. As you will see, this process is a lot easier because we will build the application onto a Linux-based container so you will see a lot of additional support in the IDEs. Let's look at that now.

Containerizing a .NET Core–Based Application

As just mentioned, containerizing a .NET Core–type application is much easier, because a lot of the hoops that you must leap through to manage a Windows container will not be necessary. Instead, all AWS products, as well as IDEs, will support this out the gate.

Using Visual Studio

We have already gone through adding container support using Visual Studio, and that we are doing it now using a .NET Core–based application does not change that part of the process at all. What does change, however, is the ease of getting the newly containerized application into AWS. Once the Dockerfile has been added, the "Publish to AWS" options that are available when right-clicking on the project name in the Solution Explorer have greatly expanded. Since our objective is to get this application deployed to Amazon ECR, make the choice to *Push Container Images to Amazon Elastic Container Registry* and click the **Publish** button. You will see the process walk through a few steps, and it will end with a message stating that the image has been successfully deployed into ECR.

Using JetBrains Rider

The process of adding a container using JetBrains Rider is very similar to the process used in Visual Studio. Open your application in Rider, right-click the project, select **Add,** and then **Docker Support** as shown in Figure 13-14.

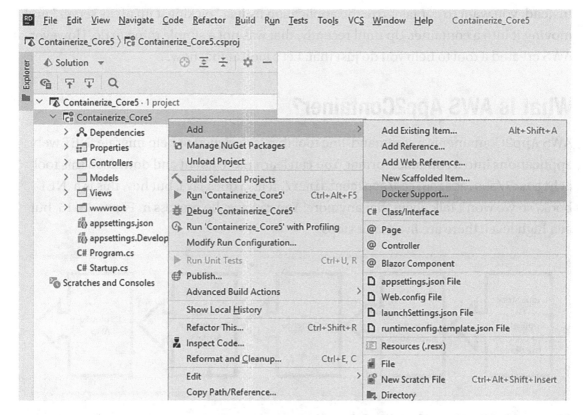

Figure 13-14. *Adding Docker Support in JetBrains Rider*

This will bring up a window where you select the **Target OS**, in this case, Linux. Once you have this finished, you will see a *Dockerfile* show up in your solution. Unfortunately, the AWS Toolkit for Rider does not currently support deploying the new container image to ECR. This means that any deployment to the cloud must be done with the AWS CLI or the AWS Tools for PowerShell and would be the same as the upload process used when storing a Windows container in ECR that we went over earlier.

Containerizing a Running Application

Now that we have gone through containerizing an already existing application where you have access to the source code, let's look at containerizing a .NET application in a different way. This is for those applications you may have that are running and where you may not have access to the source code, or you don't deploy it, or there are other reasons where you don't want to change the source code as we just went over earlier.

Instead, you want to containerize the application by just "picking it up off its server" and moving it into a container. Up until recently, that was not a simple thing to do. However, AWS created a tool to help you do just that. Let's look at that now.

What Is AWS App2Container?

AWS App2Container is a command-line tool that is designed to help migrate .NET web applications into a container format. You can learn more about and download this tool at `https://aws.amazon.com/app2container/`. It also does Java, but hey, this is a .NET book, so we won't talk about that anymore! You can see the process in Figure 13-15, but at a high level, there are five major steps.

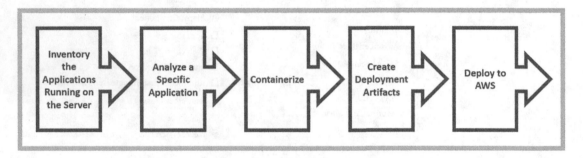

Figure 13-15. *How AWS App2Container works*

These steps are as follows:

1. **Inventory** – This step goes through the applications running on the server looking for running applications. At the time of writing, App2Container supports ASP.NET 3.5, and greater, applications running in IIS 7.5+ on Windows.

2. **Analyze** – A chosen application is analyzed in detail to identify dependencies including known cooperating processes and network port dependencies. You can also manually add any dependencies that App2Container was unable to find.

3. **Containerize** – In this step, all the application artifacts discovered during the "Analyze" phase are "dockerized."

4. **Create** – This step creates the various deployment artifacts (generally as CloudFormation templates) such as ECS task or Kubernetes pod definitions.

5. **Deploy** – Store the image in Amazon ECR and deploy to ECS or EKS as desired.

There are three different modes in which you can use App2Container. The first is a mode where you perform the steps on two different machines. If using this approach, App2Container must be installed on both machines. The first machine, the *Server*, is the machine on which the application(s) that you want to containerize is running. You will run the first two steps on the server. The second machine, the *Worker*, is the machine that will perform the final three steps of the process based on artifacts that you copy from the server. The second mode is when you perform all the steps on the same machine, so it basically fills both the server and worker roles. The third mode is when you run all the commands on your worker machine, connecting to the server machine using the Windows Remote Management (WinRM) protocol. This approach has the benefit of not having to install App2Container on the server, but it also means that you must have WinRM installed and running. We will not be demonstrating this mode.

App2Container is a command-line tool that has some prerequisites that must be installed before the tool will run. These prerequisites are listed as follows:

- **AWS CLI** – Must be installed on both server and worker.

- **PowerShell 5.0+** – Must be installed on both server and worker.

- **Administrator rights** – You must be running as a Windows administrator.

- **Appropriate permissions** – You must have AWS credentials stored on the worker machine as was discussed in the earlier chapters when installing the AWS CLI.

- **Docker tools** – Docker version 17.07 or later must be installed on worker.

- **Windows Server OS** – Your worker system must run on Windows OS versions that support containers, namely, Windows Server 2016 or 2019. If working in server/worker mode, the server system must be Windows 2008+.

- **Free Space** – 20–30 GB of free space should be available on both server and worker.

The currently supported types of applications are as follows:

- Simple ASP.NET applications running on a single server

- A Windows service running on a single server

- Complex ASP.NET applications that depend on WCF, running on a single server or multiple servers

- Complex ASP.NET applications that depend on Windows services or processes outside of IIS, running on a single server or multiple servers

- Complex, multinode IIS or Windows service applications, running on a single server or multiple servers

There are also two types of applications that are not supported:

- ASP.NET applications that use files and registries outside of IIS web application directories

- ASP.NET applications that depend on features of a Windows operating system version prior to Windows Server Core 2016

Now that we have described App2Container as well as the .NET applications on which it will and will not work, the next step is to show how to use the tool.

Using AWS App2Container to Containerize an Application

We will first describe the application that we are going to containerize. We have installed a .NET Framework 4.7.2 application onto a Windows EC2 instance that supports containers; the AMI we used is shown in Figure 13-16. Please note that since EC2 regularly revises its AMIs, you may see a different Id.

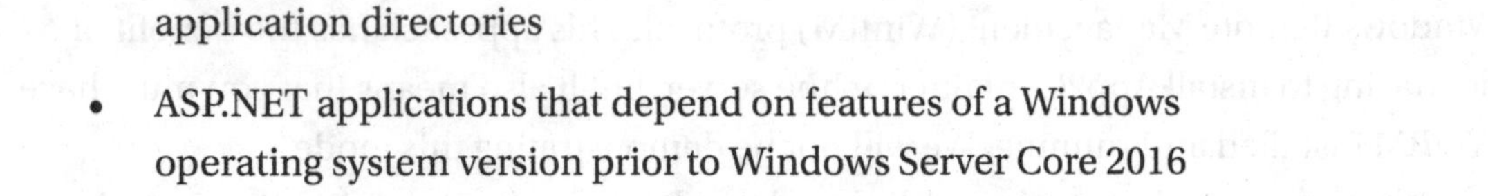

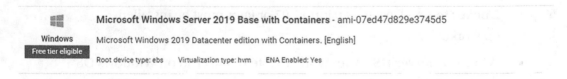

Figure 13-16. *AMI used to host the website to containerize*

The application is connected to an RDS SQL Server instance for database access using Entity Framework, and the connection string is stored in the web.config file.

The next step, now that we have a running application, is to download the AWS App2Container tool. You can access the tool by going to https://aws.amazon.com/app2container/ and clicking the **Download AWS App2Container** button at the top of the page. This will bring you to the *Install App2Container* page in the documentation, which has a link to download a zip file containing the App2Container installation package. Download the file and extract it to a folder on the server. If you are doing the work using the server/worker mode, then download and extract the file on both servers. After you unzip the downloaded file, you should have five files, one of which is another zipped file.

Open PowerShell and navigate to the folder containing App2Container. You must then run the install script.

```
PS C:\App2Container> .\install.ps1
```

You will see the script running through several checks and then present some terms and conditions text that will require you to respond with a y to continue. You will then be able to see the tool complete its installation.

The next step is to initialize and configure App2Container. If using server/worker mode, then you will need to do this on each machine. You start the initializing with the following command:

```
PS C:\App2Container> app2container init
```

It will then prompt you for a *Workspace directory path for artifacts* value. This is where the files from the analysis and any containerization will be stored. Click **enter** to accept the default value or enter a new directory. It will then ask for an *Optional AWS Profile*. You can click enter if you have a default profile setup or you can enter the name of the profile to use if different.

Note   It is likely that a server running the application you want to containerize does not have the appropriate profile available. If not, you can set one up by running the aws configure command to set up your CLI installation that App2Container will use to create and upload the created container.

Next, the initialization will ask you for an *Optional S3 bucket for application artifacts.* Providing a value in this step will result in the tool output also being copied to the provided bucket. You can click **enter** to use the default of "no bucket"; however, at the time of this writing, you must have this value configured so that it can act as storage for moving the container image into ECR. We used an S3 bucket called "prodotnetonaws-app2container". The next initialization step is whether you wish *to Report usage metrics to AWS? (Y/N)*. No personal or confidential information is gathered, so we recommend that you click **enter** to accept the default of "Y". The following initialization prompt asks if you want to *Automatically upload logs and App2Container generated artifacts on crashes and internal errors? (Y/N)*. We want AWS to know as soon as possible if something went wrong so we selected "y". The last initialization prompt is asking whether to *Require images to be signed using Docker Content Trust (DCT)? (Y/N)*. We selected the default value, "n". The initialization will then display the path in which the artifacts will be created and stored. Figure 13-17 shows our installation when completed.

```
Administrator: Windows PowerShell
PS C:\App2Container>
Workspace directory path for artifacts[default: C:\Users\Administrator\AppData\Local\app2container]:
Optional AWS Profile (configured using 'aws configure --profile')[default: default]:
Optional S3 bucket for application artifacts[default: prodotnetonaws-app2container]:
Report usage metrics to AWS? (Y/N)[default: y]:
Automatically upload logs and App2Container generated artifacts on crashes and internal errors? (Y/N)[default: y]:
Require images to be signed using Docker Content Trust (DCT)? (Y/N)[default: n]:
Configuration saved
All application artifacts will be created under C:\Users\Administrator\AppData\Local\app2container. Please ensure that the folder permissions are secure.
PS C:\App2Container>
```

Figure 13-17. *Output from running the App2Container initialization*

For those of you using the server/worker mode approach, take note of the application artifact directory displayed in the last line of the command output as this will contain the artifacts that you will need to move to the worker machine. Now that the application is initialized, the next step is to take the inventory of eligible applications running on the server. You do this by issuing the following command:

```
PS C:\App2Container> app2container inventory
```

The output from this command is a JSON object collection that has one entry for each application. The output on our EC2 server is shown as follows:

```
{
    "iis-demo-site-a7b69c34": {
        "siteName": "Demo Site",
        "bindings": "http/*:8080:",
        "applicationType": "IIS"
```

```
    },
    "iis-tradeyourtools-6bc0a317": {
        "siteName": "TradeYourTools",
        "bindings": "http/*:80:",
        "applicationType": "IIS"
    }
}
```

As you can see, there are two applications on our server: the "Trade Your Tools" app we described earlier as well as another website "Demo Site" that is running under IIS and is bound to port 8080. The initial key is the application ID that you will need moving forward.

Note   You can only containerize one application at a time. If you wish to containerize multiple applications from the same server, you will need to repeat the following steps for each one of those applications.

The next step is to analyze the specific application that you are going to containerize. You do that with the following command, replacing the application ID (APPID) in the command with your own:

```
PS C:\App2Container> app2container analyze --application-id APPID
```

You will see a lot of flashing that shows the progress output as the tool analyzes the application, and when it is complete, you will get output like that shown in Figure 13-18.

```
Administrator: Windows PowerShell
PS C:\App2Container>                     --application-id iis-tradeyourtools-6bc0a317
√ Created artifacts folder C:\Users\Administrator\AppData\Local\app2container\iis-tradeyourtools-6bc0a317
√ Generated analysis data in C:\Users\Administrator\AppData\Local\app2container\iis-tradeyourtools-6bc0a317\analysis.json
Analysis successful for application iis-tradeyourtools-6bc0a317

Next Steps:
1. View the application analysis file at C:\Users\Administrator\AppData\Local\app2container\iis-tradeyourtools-6bc0a317\analysis.json.
2. Edit the application analysis file as needed.
3. Start the containerization process using this command: app2container containerize --application-id iis-tradeyourtools-6bc0a317
PS C:\App2Container> _
```

Figure 13-18. *Output from running the App2Container analyze command*

The primary output from this analysis is the *analysis.json* file that is listed in the command output. Locating and opening that file will allow you to see the information that the tool gathered about the application, much of which is a capture of the IIS configuration for the site running your application. We won't show the contents of the file here as it is several hundred lines long; however, much of the content of this file can be edited as you see necessary.

The next steps branch depending upon whether you are using a single server or using the server/worker mode.

When Containerizing on a Single Server

Once you are done reviewing the artifacts created from the analysis, the next step is to containerize the application. You do this with the following command:

```
PS C:\App2Container> app2container containerize --application-id APPID
```

The processing in this step may take some time to run, especially if, like us, you used a free-tier low-powered machine! Once completed, you will see output like Figure 13-19.

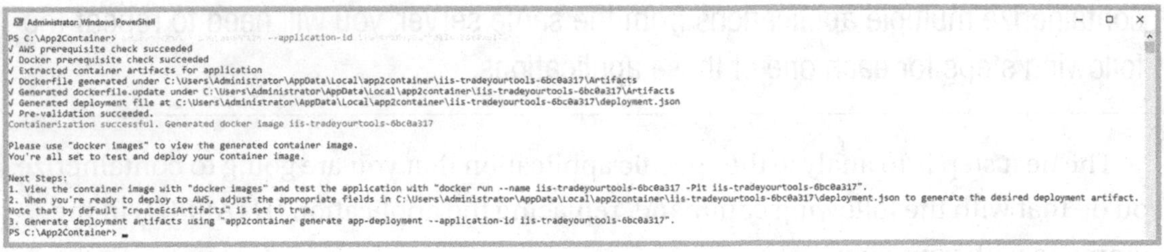

Figure 13-19. Output from containerizing an application in App2Container

At this point, you are ready to deploy your container and can skip to the "Deploying…" section if you don't care about containerizing using server/worker mode.

When Containerizing Using Server/Worker Mode

Once you are done reviewing the artifacts created from the analysis, the next step is to extract the application. This will create the archive that will need to be moved to the worker machine for containerizing. Also, the tool will upload the archive to the S3 bucket provided during initialization. Since we didn't provide a bucket, we must manually copy the file. The command to extract the application is

```
PS C:\App2Container> app2container extract --application-id APPID
```

This command will process, and you should get a simple "Extraction successful" message.

Returning to the artifact directory that was displayed when initializing App2Container, you will see a new zip file named with your Application ID. Copy this file to the worker server.

Once you are on the worker server and App2Container has been initialized, the next step is to containerize the content from the archive. You do that with the following command:

```
PS C:\App2Container> app2container containerize --input-archive PathToZip
```

The output from this step matches the output from running the containerization on a single server and can be seen in Figure 13-19.

Deploying New Container Using AWS App2Container

The last step is to deploy the container. The default approach is to deploy a container image to ECR and then create the CloudFormation templates to run that image in Amazon ECS using Fargate. If you would prefer to deploy to Amazon EKS instead, you will need to go to the *deployment.json* file in the output directory. This editable file contains the default settings for the application: ECR, ECS, and EKS. We will walk through each of the major areas in turn.

The first section is responsible for defining the application and is shown as follows:

```
"a2CTemplateVersion": "1.0",
"applicationId": "iis-tradeyourtools-6bc0a317",
"imageName": "iis-tradeyourtools-6bc0a317",
"exposedPorts": [
        {
                "localPort": 80,
                "protocol": "http"
        }
],
"environment": [],
```

The applicationId and the imageName are values we have seen before when going through App2Containers. The exposedPorts value should contain all of the IIS ports configured for the application. The one used in the example was not configured for HTTPS, but if it was, there would be another entry for that value. The environment value

501

allows you to enter any environment variables as key/value pairs that may be used by the application. Unfortunately, App2Container is not able to determine those because it does its analysis on running code rather than the code base. In our example, there are no environmental variables that are necessary.

Note   If you aren't sure whether there are environment variables that your application may access, you can see which variables are available by going into the *System ➤ Advanced system settings ➤ Environment variables.* This will provide you with a list of available variables, and you can evaluate those as to their relevance to your application.

The next section is quite small and contains the ECR configuration. The ECR repository that will be created is named with the `imageName` from before and then versioned with the value in the `ecrRepoTag` as shown in the following:

```
"ecrParameters": {
        "ecrRepoTag": "latest"
},
```

We are using the value *latest* as our version tag.

There are two remaining sections in the deployment.json file. The first is the ECS setup information with the second being the EKS setup information. We will first look at the ECS section. This entire section is listed as follows:

```
"ecsParameters": {
        "createEcsArtifacts": true,
        "ecsFamily": "iis-tradeyourtools-6bc0a317",
        "cpu": 2,
        "memory": 4096,
        "dockerSecurityOption": "",
        "enableCloudwatchLogging": false,
        "publicApp": true,
        "stackName": "a2c-iis-tradeyourtools-6bc0a317-ECS",
        "resourceTags": [
                {
                        "key": "example-key",
```

```
                "value": "example-value"
            }
        ],
        "reuseResources": {
            "vpcId": "vpc-f4e4d48c",
            "reuseExistingA2cStack": {
                "cfnStackName": "",
                "microserviceUrlPath": ""
            },
            "sshKeyPairName": "",
            "acmCertificateArn": ""
        },
        "gMSAParameters": {
            "domainSecretsArn": "",
            "domainDNSName": "",
            "domainNetBIOSName": "",
            "createGMSA": false,
            "gMSAName": ""
        },
        "deployTarget": "FARGATE",
        "dependentApps": []
},
```

The most important value here is `createEcsArtifacts`, which, if set to `true`, means
that deploying with App2Container will deploy the image into ECS. The next ones to
look at are `cpu` and `memory`. These values are only used for Linux containers. In our case,
these values do not matter because this is a Windows container. The next two values,
`dockerSecurityOption` and `enableCloudwatchLogging`, are only changed in special
cases, so they will generally stay at their default values. The next value, `publicApp`,
determines whether the application will be configured into a public subnet with a public
endpoint. This is set to *true* because this is our hoped-for behavior. The next value,
`stackName,` defines the name of the CloudFormation stack, while the value after that,
`resourceTags`, is the custom tags that should be added to the ECS task definition. There
is a default set of key/values in the file, but those will not be used if kept in; only keys that
are not defined as `example-key` will be added.

The next section, reuseResources, is where you can configure whether you wish to use any preexisting resources, namely, VPC (Virtual Private Cloud) – which is added to the vpcId value. When left blank, as shown in the following, App2Container will create a new VPC.

```
"reuseResources": {
    "vpcId": "",
    "reuseExistingA2cStack": {
        "cfnStackName": "",
        "microserviceUrlPath": ""
    },
    "sshKeyPairName": "",
    "acmCertificateArn": ""
}
```

Running the deployment with these settings will result in a brand-new VPC being created. This means that, by default, you wouldn't be able to connect in or out of the VPC without making changes to the VPC. If, however, you have an already existing VPC that you want to use, update the vpcId key with the ID of the appropriate VPC.

Note   App2Container requires that the included VPC has a routing table that is associated with at least two subnets and an Internet gateway. The CloudFormation template for the ECS service requires this so that there is a route from your service to the Internet from at least two different AZs for availability. Currently, there is no way for you to define these subnets. You will receive a *Resource creation failures: PublicLoadBalancer: At least two subnets in two different Availability Zones must be specified message* if your VPC is not set up properly.

You can also choose to reuse an existing stack created by App2Container. Doing this will ensure that the application is deployed into the already-existing VPC and that the URL for the new application is added to the already-created Application Load Balancer rather than being added to a new ALB.

The next value, sshKeyPairName, is the name of the EC2 key pair used for the instances on which your container runs. Using this rather defeats the point of using containers, so we left it blank as well. The last value, acmCertificateArn, is for the AWS Certificate Manager ARN that you want to use if you are enabling HTTPS on the created ALB. This parameter is required if you use an HTTPS endpoint for your ALB, and remember as we went over earlier, this means that the request being forwarded into the application will be on port 80 and unencrypted because this would have been handled in the ALB.

The next set of configuration values is part of the `gMSAParameters` section. This becomes important to manage if your application relies upon group Managed Service Account (gMSA) Active Directory groups. This can only be used if deploying to EC2 and not Fargate (more on this later). These individual values are as follows:

- **domainSecretsArn** – The AWS Secrets Manager ARN containing the domain credentials required to join the ECS nodes to Active Directory

- **domainDNSName** – The DNS Name of the Active Directory the ECS nodes will join

- **domainNetBIOSName** – The NetBIOS name of the Active Directory to join

- **createGMSA** – A flag determining whether to create the gMSA Active Directory security group and account using the name supplied in the *gMSAName* field

- **gMSAName** – The name of the Active Directory account the container should use for access

There are two fields remaining: `deployTarget` and `dependentApps`. For deployTarget, there are two valid values for .NET applications running on Windows: *fargate* and *ec2*. You can only deploy to Fargate if your container is Windows 2019 or more recent. This would only be possible if your worker machine, the one you used for containerizing, was running Windows 2019+. Also, you cannot deploy to Fargate if you are using gMSA.

The value `dependentApps` is interesting, as it handles those applications that AWS defines as "complex Windows applications." We won't go into it in more detail here, but you can go to `https://docs.aws.amazon.com/app2container/latest/UserGuide/summary-complex-win-apps.html` if you are interested in learning more about these types of applications.

The next section in the *deployment.json* file is eksParameters. You will see that much of these parameters are the same as what we went over when talking about the ECS parameters. The only differences are the createEksArtifacts parameter, which needs to be set to *true* if deploying to EKS, and in the *gMSA* section, the gMSAName parameter has inexplicably been changed to gMSAAccountName.

Once you have the deployment file set as desired, you next deploy the container:

```
PS C:\App2Container> app2container generate app-deployment --application-id
APPID --deploy
```

This process takes several minutes, and you should get an output like Figure 13-20. The gold arrow points to the URL where you can go see your deployed application – go ahead and look at it to confirm that it has been successfully deployed and is running.

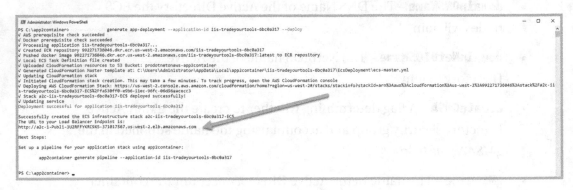

Figure 13-20. *Output from generating an application deployment in App2Container*

Logging into the AWS console and going to Amazon ECR will show you the ECR repository that was created to store your image as shown in Figure 13-21.

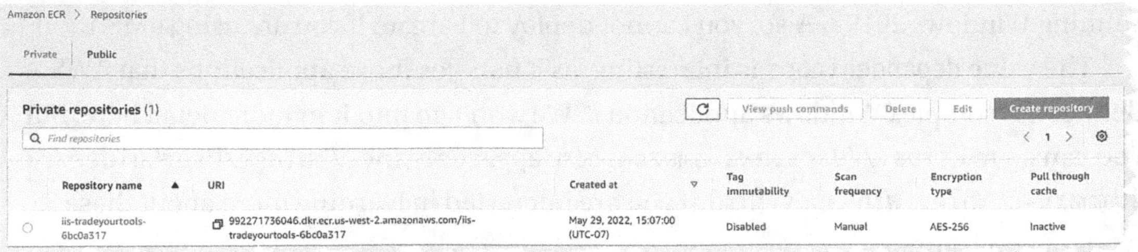

Figure 13-21. *Verifying the new container image is available in ECR*

Once everything has been deployed and verified, you can poke around in ECS to see how it is all put together. Remember though, if you are looking to make modifications, it is highly recommended that you use the CloudFormation templates, make the changes there, and then reupload them as a new version. That way, you will be able to easily redeploy as needed and not worry about losing any changes that you may have added. You can either alter the templates in the CloudFormation section of the console or you can find the templates in your App2Container working directory, update those, and then use those to update the stack.

Summary

In this chapter, we walked through several approaches for containerizing applications and getting those container images into AWS container registry: ECR. We first went over using both Visual Studio and a manual approach to getting older .NET Framework 4.x applications containerized. We then moved to .NET Core–based applications and containerized them using Visual Studio and JetBrains Rider features.

We then walked through using AWS App2Container to containerize a running application and then deploy it into Amazon ECS. We validated the deployment by going to the provided load balancer endpoint that was created in a CloudFormation template. We then expanded a bit more on the various networking approaches when using AWS container management services.

We have now covered moving existing applications into AWS either through using virtual machines (previous chapter) or through containerization. We will next look at bringing data from external sources into AWS.

CHAPTER 14

Migrating Your Data

We have just walked through several different ways to get your application running in the cloud, from running your application on virtual machines to running within containers. In this chapter, we are going to take this a bit further by bringing your application data into the cloud as well. In an earlier chapter, we moved data into RDS SQL Server by using a backup/restore process from another SQL Server instance, but that may not be possible due to many different reasons. Do not despair though, as AWS offers several other approaches to moving your data into a data service within the AWS cloud.

There are several different approaches that we will go over. The first approach is the AWS Database Migration Service, which supports data movement into AWS-hosted databases. The next is the AWS Schema Conversion Tool, which allows you to copy your database schema between different database systems. Lastly, we will walk through a complete migration of SQL Server data into Amazon Aurora to take advantage of the lower costs and serverless capabilities of Aurora.

AWS Database Migration Service

The AWS Database Migration Service (AWS DMS) was designed to help quickly and securely migrate databases into AWS. The premise is that the source database remains available during the migration to help minimize application downtown. AWS DMS supports homogeneous migrations such as SQL Server to SQL Server or Oracle to Oracle as well as some heterogeneous migrations between different platforms. You can also use the service to continuously replicate data from any supported source to any supported target, meaning you can use DMS for both one-time replications and ongoing replications. AWS DMS works with relational databases and NoSQL databases as well as other types of data stores. One thing to note, however, is that at least one end of your migration must be on an AWS service; you cannot use AWS DMS to migrate between two on-premises databases.

© William Penberthy and Steve Roberts 2023
W. Penberthy and S. Roberts, *Pro .NET on Amazon Web Services*,
https://doi.org/10.1007/978-1-4842-8907-5_14

How Does It Work?

You can best think of DMS as replication software running on a server in the cloud. There are literally dozens of these kinds of tools, some cloud based, some that you install locally to move data between on-premises systems. The DMS' claim to fame is that you only pay for the work that you have it perform – there is no licensing fee for the service itself like with most of the other software solutions.

Figure 14-1 shows DMS at a high level. The green box in the figure is the overall service and contains three major subcomponents. Two of these are endpoints used to connect to the source and target databases, and the third is the replication instance.

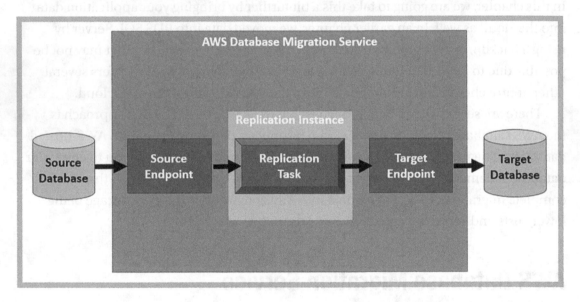

Figure 14-1. *A high-level look at AWS Data Migration Service*

The replication instance is an Amazon EC2 instance that provides the resources necessary to carry out the database migration. Since it is a replication instance, you can get high availability and failover support if you select to use a multiregion-based process.

AWS DMS uses this replication instance to connect to your source database through the source endpoint. The instance then reads the source data and performs any data formatting necessary to make it compatible with the target database. The instance then loads that data into the target database. Much of this processing is done in memory; however, large data sets may need to be buffered onto disk as part of the transfer. Logs and other replication-specific data are also written onto the replication instance.

Creating a Replication Instance

Enough about the way that it is put together, let's jump directly into creating a migration service, and we will go over the various options as they come up in the process.

Note   Not all EC2 instance classes are available for use as a replication instance. As of the time of this writing, only T3 (general purpose), C5 (compute optimized), and R5 (memory optimized) Amazon EC2 instance classes can be used. You can use a *t3.micro* instance under the AWS Free Tier; however, there is a chance that you may be charged if the utilization of the instance over a rolling 24-hour period exceeds the baseline utilization. This will not be a problem in our example, but it may be with other approaches, especially if you use ongoing replication.

You can get to the AWS DMS console by searching in the console for "DMS" or by going into the *Migration & Transfer* service group and selecting it there. Click the **Create replication instance** button once you get to the console landing page. This will take you to the creation page. Remember as you go through this that all we are doing here is creating the EC2 instance that DMS will use for processing, so all the questions will be around that.

The fields that you can enter in the *Replication instance configuration* section are as follows:

- **Name** – Must be unique across all replication instances in the current region.

- **Descriptive Amazon Resource Name (ARN)** – This field is optional, but it allows you to use a friendly name for the ARN rather than the typical set of nonsense that AWS creates by default. This value cannot be changed after creation.

- **Description** – Short description of the instance.

- **Instance class** – This is where you select the instance class on which your migration process will be running.

- **Engine version** – This option allows the targeting of previous versions of DMS, or the software that runs within the instance class – though we have no idea why you would ever target an older version.

511

- **Allocated storage** – The amount of storage space that you want in your instance. This is where items like log files will be stored and will also be used for disk caching if the instance's memory is not sufficient to handle all of the processing.

- **VPC** – Where the instance should be run.

- **Multi-AZ** - You can choose between *Production workload,* which will set up multi-AZ, or *Dev or test workload,* which will create the instance in a single AZ.

- **Publicly accessible** – This is necessary if you are looking to connect to databases outside of your VPC, or even outside of AWS.

There are three additional sections that you can configure. The first of these is *Advanced security and network configuration* where you can define the specific subnet group for your replication instance, the Availability Zone in which your replication instance should run, and VPC security groups that you want to be assigned to your replication instance, and the AWS Key Management Service key that you would like used.

The next section is *Maintenance,* where you can define the weekly maintenance window that AWS will use for maintaining the DMS engine software and operating system. You must have this configured, and AWS will set up a default window for you. The last section that you can configure is, of course, *Tags.*

Once you click the **Create** button, you will see that your replication instance is being created as shown in Figure 14-2. This creation process will take several minutes.

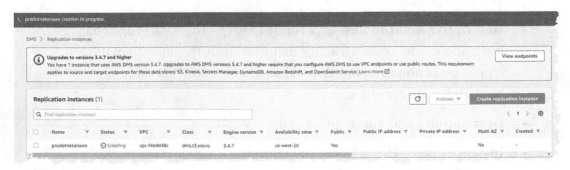

Figure 14-2. *Creating a DMS replication instance*

Now that you have a replication instance, the next step is to create your endpoints.

Creating Your Source and Target Endpoints

As briefly mentioned previously, the endpoints manage the connection to your source and target databases. They are managed independently from the replication instance because there are many cases where there are multiple replications that talk to a single source or target, such as copying one set of data to one target and another set of data from the same source to a second target such as shown in Figure 14-3.

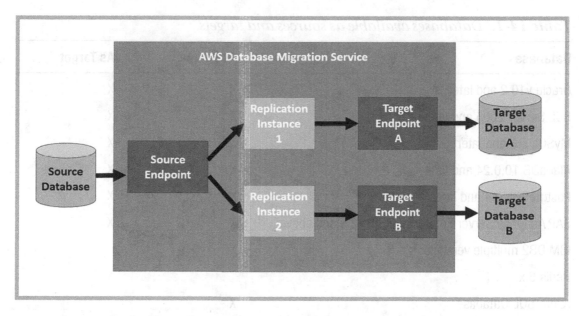

Figure 14-3. *Multiple replications against a single source endpoint*

To create an endpoint, go into *Endpoints* and select **Create endpoint**. This will bring up the *Create endpoint* screen. Your first option is to define the *Endpoint type*, as shown in Figure 14-4.

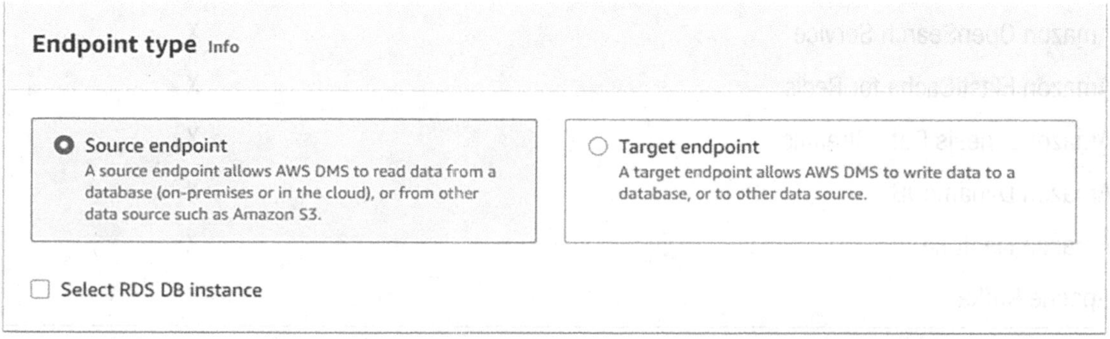

Endpoint type Info

○ **Source endpoint**
   A source endpoint allows AWS DMS to read data from a database (on-premises or in the cloud), or from other data source such as Amazon S3.

○ **Target endpoint**
   A target endpoint allows AWS DMS to write data to a database, or to other data source.

☐ Select RDS DB instance

Figure 14-4. *Endpoint type options when creating a DMS endpoint*

Your first option when creating the endpoint is to determine whether the endpoint is going to be a source or target endpoint. You would think that this wouldn't really matter because a database connection is a database connection whether you are reading or writing, but DMS has made decisions around which databases they will support reading from and which databases you can write to, and as you can likely predict, they are not the same list. Table 14-1 lists the different databases supported for each endpoint type, as of the time of this writing.

Table 14-1. *Databases available as sources and targets*

Database	As Source	As Target
Oracle v10.2 and later	X	X
SQL Server 2005 and later	X	X
MySQL 5.5 and later	X	X
MariaDB 10.0.24 and later	X	X
PostgreSQL 9.4 and later	X	X
SAP Adaptive Server Enterprise (ASE) 12.5 and above	X	X
IBM DB2 multiple versions	X	
Redis 6.x		X
Azure SQL Database	X	
Google Cloud for MySQL	X	
All RDS instance databases	X	
Amazon S3	X	
Amazon DocumentDB	X	
Amazon OpenSearch Service		X
Amazon ElastiCache for Redis		X
Amazon Kinesis Data Streams		X
Amazon DynamoDB		X
Amazon Neptune		X
Apache Kafka		X

The next option in the *Endpoint type* section is a check box to *Select RDS DB instance*. Checking this box will bring up a drop-down containing a list of RDS instances as shown in Figure 14-5.

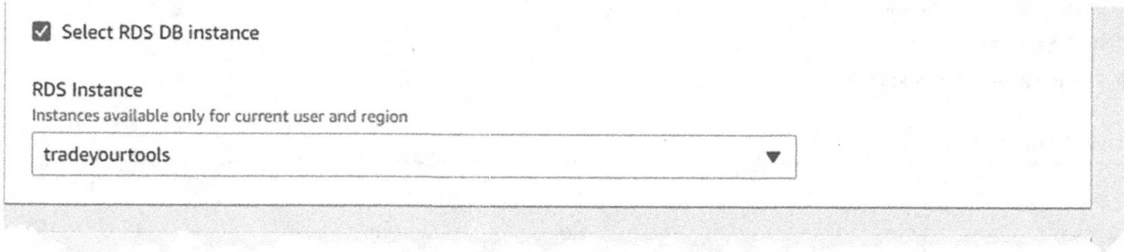

Figure 14-5. *Selecting an RDS database when creating an endpoint*

The next area is the *Endpoint configuration*. There are two primary sections in this area: the first allows you to name the endpoint and select the type of database to which you are connecting, and the second is *Endpoint settings* where you can define those additional settings needed to access a specific database. Selecting the *Source/Target engine* will expand the form, adding some additional fields.

The first of these fields is *Access to endpoint database*. There are two options available, and the choice you make will change the rest of the form. These two options are *AWS Secrets Manager*, where you use stored secrets for the login credentials, and *Provide access information manually* where you manually configure the database connection.

Selecting to use *AWS Secrets Manager* will bring up additional fields as described in the following. These fields are used to fetch and access the appropriate secret.

- **Secret ID** – The actual secret to be used when logging into the database

- **IAM role** – The IAM role that grants Amazon DMS the appropriate permissions to use the necessary secret

- **Secure Socket Layer (SSL) mode** – Whether to use SSL when connecting to the database

Selecting to *Provide access information manually* brings up the various fields necessary to connect to that identified engine. Figure 14-6 shows what this looks like when connecting to a SQL Server, and hopefully, all these values look familiar because we have used them multiple times in earlier chapters.

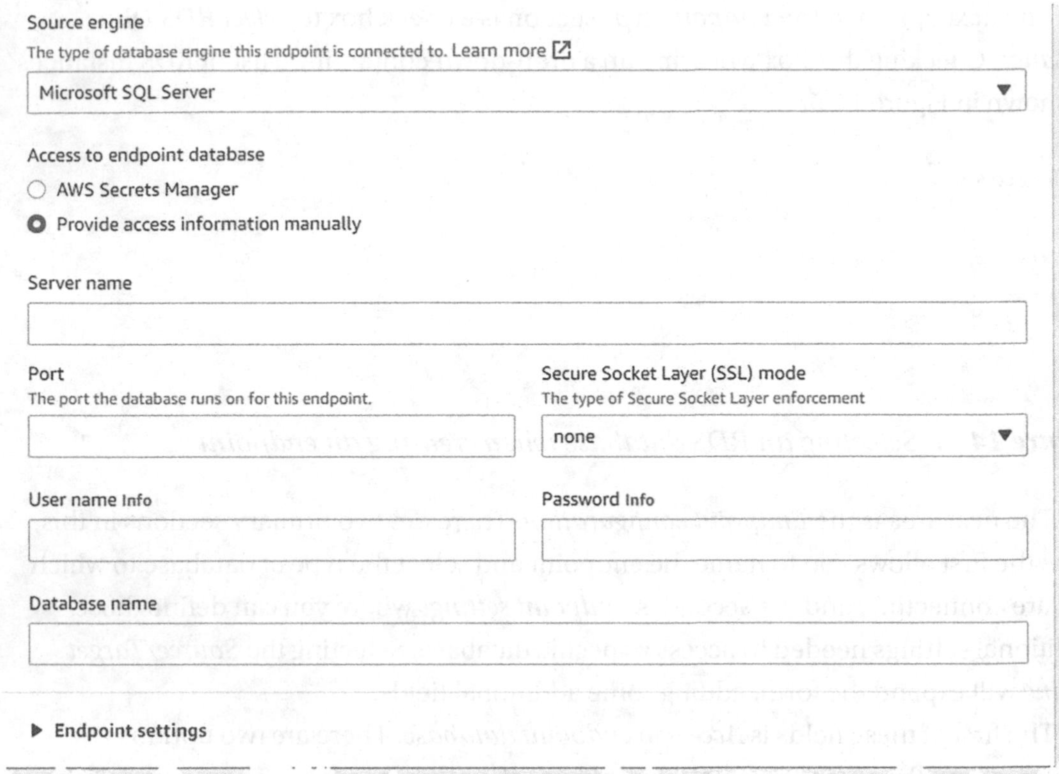

Source engine

The type of database engine this endpoint is connected to. Learn more ↗

Microsoft SQL Server   ▼

Access to endpoint database

○ AWS Secrets Manager

● Provide access information manually

Server name

Port   Secure Socket Layer (SSL) mode

The port the database runs on for this endpoint.   The type of Secure Socket Layer enforcement

                                                   none   ▼

User name Info   Password Info

Database name

▶ Endpoint settings

Figure 14-6. *Providing SQL Server information manually for an endpoint*

The next section is the *Endpoint settings* section. The purpose of this section is to add any additional settings that may be necessary for this particular instance of the database to which it is connecting. There are two ways in which you can provide this information. The first is through a *Wizard*, while the second is through an *Editor*. When using the *Wizard* approach, clicking the **Add new setting** button will bring up a *Setting/Value* row, with the *Setting* being a drop-down list of known settings as shown in Figure 14-7. These values will be different for each engine as well as whether you are using the endpoint as a source or a target.

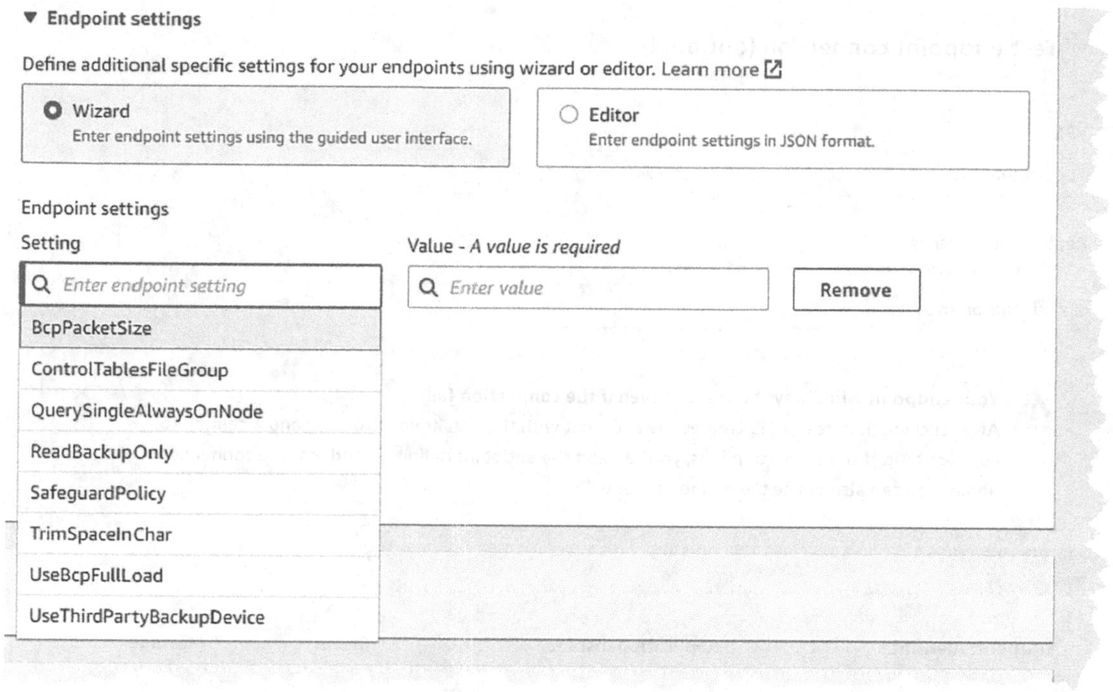

Figure 14-7. *Endpoint settings section when creating a SQL Server endpoint*

Selecting to use the *Editor* approach will bring up a large text box where you can enter the endpoint settings in JSON format. This would likely be the best approach if you need to configure multiple DMS endpoints with the same additional settings.

Once you have *Endpoint* configuration section complete, the next section is *KMS key* where you select the appropriate key to be used when encrypting the data that you have input into the configuration. The next section is *Tags*. The last section entitled *Test endpoint connection (optional)* is shown in Figure 14-8 and is where you can test all the information that you have just filled out.

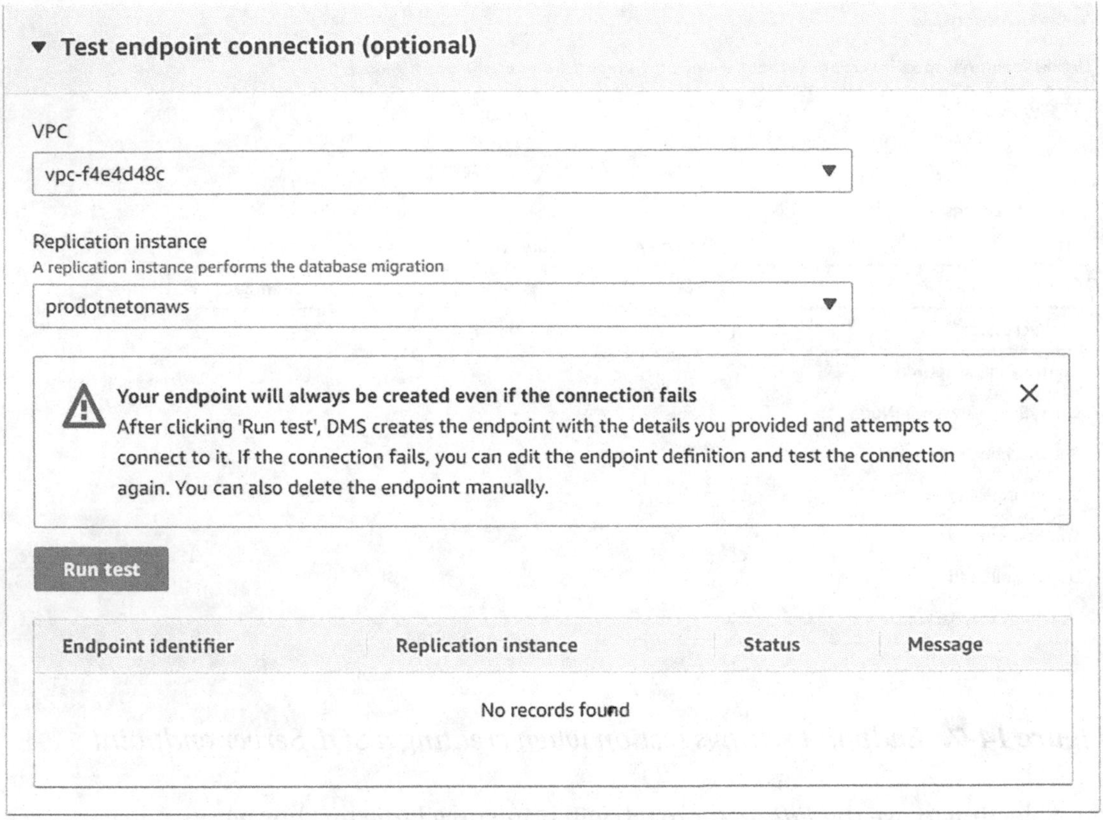

▼ **Test endpoint connection (optional)**

VPC

| vpc-f4e4d48c | ▼ |

Replication instance
A replication instance performs the database migration

| prodotnetonaws | ▼ |

> ⚠ **Your endpoint will always be created even if the connection fails**   ✕
> After clicking 'Run test', DMS creates the endpoint with the details you provided and attempts to
> connect to it. If the connection fails, you can edit the endpoint definition and test the connection
> again. You can also delete the endpoint manually.

Run test

Endpoint identifier	Replication instance	Status	Message
	No records found		

Figure 14-8. *Testing an endpoint configuration*

There are two values that you must identify before you can run the test, and that is
the VPC and replication instance that you want to use, which is why we had you create
the replication instance first! These are necessary because these are the resources that
will be used to perform the work of connecting to the database. Once the values are
selected, click the **Run test** button. After a surprising amount of time where you see
indications that the test is running, you should get confirmation that your test was
successful. This output is shown in Figure 14-9.

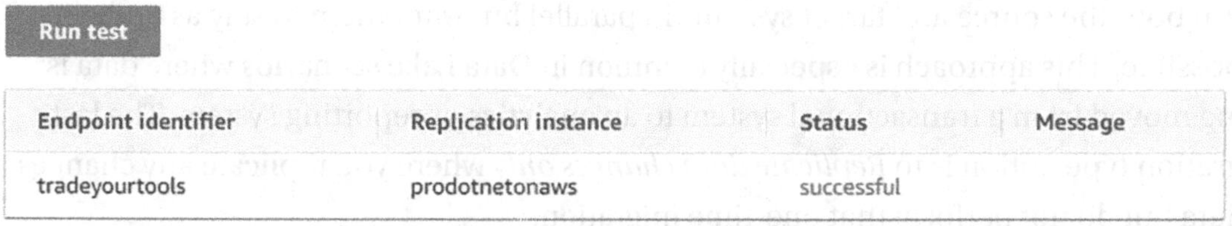

Run test			
Endpoint identifier	Replication instance	Status	Message
tradeyourtools	prodotnetonaws	successful	

Figure 14-9. *Successful test on an endpoint configuration*

Obviously, you will need to configure at least one source endpoint and one target endpoint before you can run DMS end to end. However, you also need to make sure that you have each of them configured before you can configure the database migration task.

Creating Your Database Migration Task

So far, we have defined the resource set that is going to do the work as well as the places where data will be coming from and where it will be going. There is one area that we have not yet defined, and that is the database migration task. This task defines the work that will be done. As part of this task, you can specify which tables to use, define any special processing, configure logging, etc. Let's take a look at creating one of these tasks.

First, go into the *Database migration tasks* screen in the AWS DMS console and then click the **Create task** button. This will bring up the creation screen, with the first section being *Task configuration*. This section allows you to

- Provide a *Task identifier* or name for the task

- Select the *Replication instance* to use

- Select the *Source database* endpoint

- Select the *target database* endpoint

- Select the *Migration type*

The Migration type is where you tell DMS the kind of work that you want this task to perform. There are three different options that you can select. The first is to *Migrate existing data*. Using this as a migration type means that you're looking to do a one-time copy of the data and would be ideal for doing that one-time migration. The next option is to *Migrate existing data and replicate ongoing changes*. The name pretty much describes what is going on with this approach, and it is most appropriate when you need

519

to run both the source and target systems in parallel but want them to stay as updated as possible. This approach is especially common in Data Lake scenarios where data is being moved from a transactional system to an analytics or reporting system. The last migration type option is to *Replicate data changes only* where you replicate any changes in data but do not perform that one-time migration.

The next major section to complete when creating a migration task is the *Task settings*. Task settings control the behavior of your task and can be configured through a *Wizard* or through a *JSON editor*. We will use the wizard mode as shown in Figure 14-10 so that we can more easily talk about the major settings.

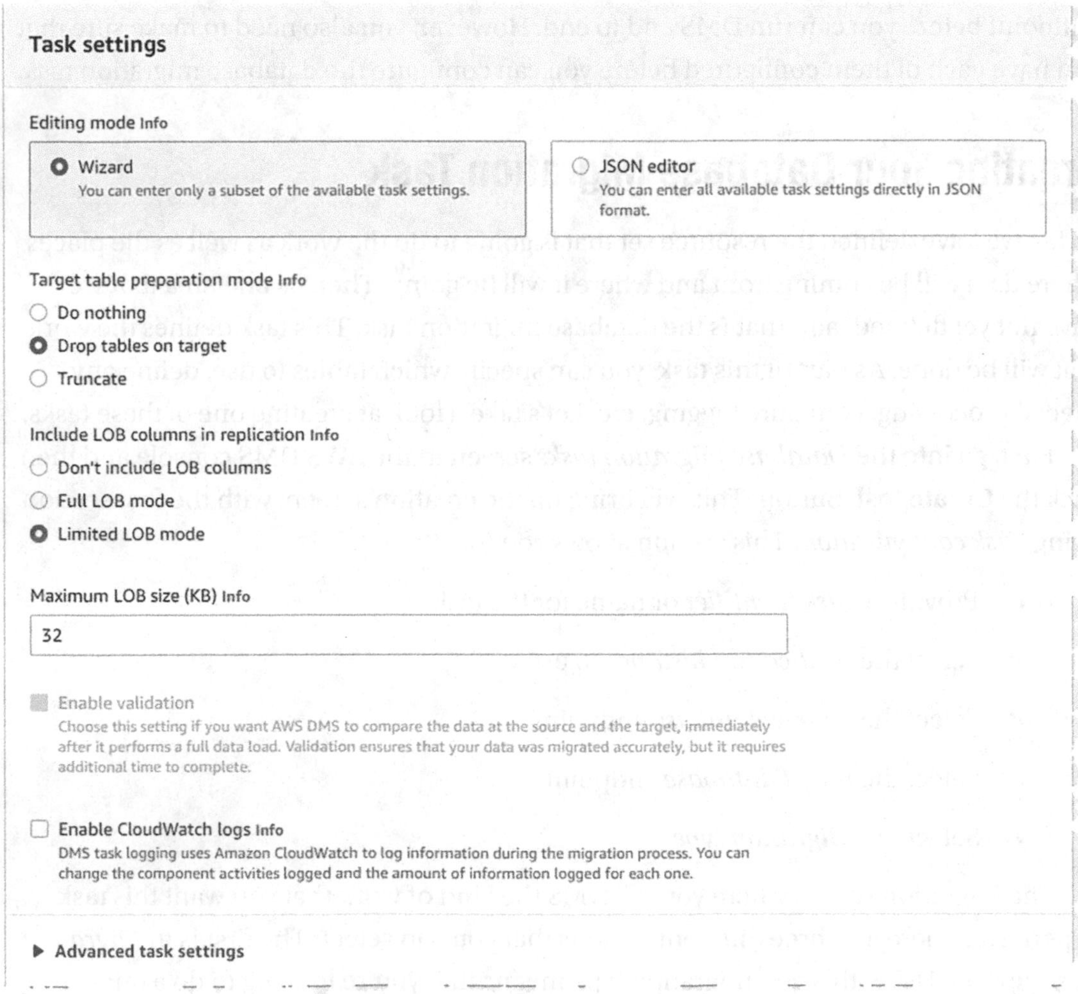

Task settings

Editing mode Info

- ● **Wizard**
  You can enter only a subset of the available task settings.

- ○ **JSON editor**
  You can enter all available task settings directly in JSON format.

Target table preparation mode Info

- ○ Do nothing
- ● Drop tables on target
- ○ Truncate

Include LOB columns in replication Info

- ○ Don't include LOB columns
- ○ Full LOB mode
- ● Limited LOB mode

Maximum LOB size (KB) Info

32

- ☐ Enable validation
  Choose this setting if you want AWS DMS to compare the data at the source and the target, immediately after it performs a full data load. Validation ensures that your data was migrated accurately, but it requires additional time to complete.

- ☐ Enable CloudWatch logs Info
  DMS task logging uses Amazon CloudWatch to log information during the migration process. You can change the component activities logged and the amount of information logged for each one.

▶ Advanced task settings

Figure 14-10. *Wizard for filling out the task settings*

The first item to configure is the *Target table preparation mode*, or how DMS should be preparing the tables at the target endpoint. There are three options: *Do nothing, Drop tables on target*, and *Truncate*. When you select the "do nothing" option, then target tables will not be affected. Any tables that do not exist will be created. When you select to drop the tables, then DMS will drop and recreate all affected tables. Truncating means that all tables and metadata remain, but all of the data is removed.

The next item to configure is *Include LOB columns in replication*. LOB are large objects, and you have the option as to whether or not you want to include those object columns in the target data. You have three options, the first of which is *Don't include LOB columns*, and the second of which is *Full LOB mode*; both of which are rather straightforward. The third option is *Limited LOB mode*. In this mode, DMS will truncate each LOB to a defined size: the *Maximum LOB size (kb)* value.

You then can configure whether you want to *Enable validation*. Checking this box will cause DMS to compare the source and target data immediately after the full load is performed. This ensures your data is migrated correctly, but it takes additional time to perform and thus increases cost. You next can *Enable CloudWatch logs*. There are also some advanced task settings, but we won't go into those as part of this discussion.

The next section is *Table mappings*. This section is where you define the rules about what data is moved and how it is moved. At a high level, you will create a *Selection rule*, which determines the data that you wish to replicate, and then you can create a *Transformation rule* that modifies the selected data before it is provided to the destination endpoint. The table mappings section also gives you the opportunity to use a Wizard approach or a JSON editor to enter all table mappings in JSON. We will walk through using the wizard.

The first step is to select the **Add new selection rule** button. This expands the selection rule section as shown in Figure 14-11.

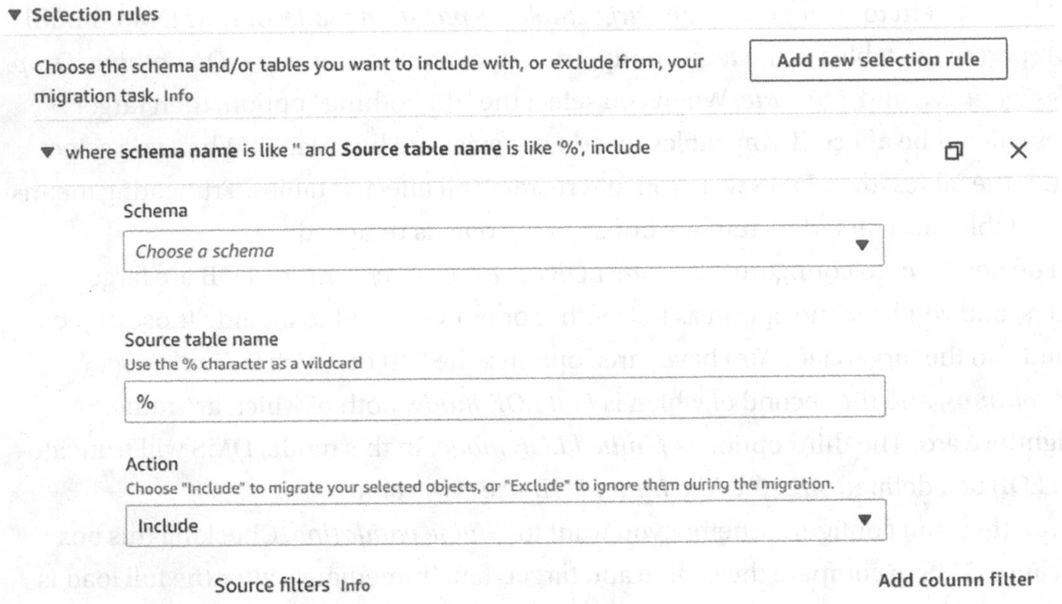

▼ **Selection rules**

Choose the schema and/or tables you want to include with, or exclude from, your migration task. Info

[Add new selection rule]

▼ where **schema name** is like '' and **Source table name** is like '%', include

Schema

| Choose a schema ▼ |

Source table name
Use the % character as a wildcard

| % |

Action
Choose "Include" to migrate your selected objects, or "Exclude" to ignore them during the migration.

| Include ▼ |

Source filters Info   Add column filter

Figure 14-11. *Creating selection rules for a database migration task*

Expanding the *Schema* drop-down will show that there is only one option – to *Enter a schema*. Selecting this option will add another textbox in which you can provide the *Source name*. This allows you to limit, by schema, the data that is being selected. You can enter **%** to select all schemas in the database or enter the schema name. You do the same for the Source table name, entering **%** if you want all the tables replicated. Once you have those defined, you then select the appropriate *Action*, to either *Include* or *Exclude* the items that fit your selection criteria. You can create as many rules as desired; however, you must always have at least one rule with an **include** action.

Once you have the selection rule configured, you can *Add column filter*. This allows you to limit the number and type of records. A column filter requires the *Column name*, one or more *Conditions*, and then one or more comparative values. You have the following options for the conditions:

- Less than or equal to

- Greater than or equal to

- Equal to

- Not equal to

- Equal to or between two values

- Not between two values

- Null

- Not null

You can create any number of column filters per each selection rule.

Once you have completed your selection rule, you can then add one or more *Transformation rules*. These rules allow you to change or transform schema, table, or column names of some or all the items that you have selected. Since we are simply copying the database across, we do not need to add any of these, especially since any changes will likely break our code!

Your next option is to determine whether you want to *Enable premigration assessment run*. This will warn you of any potential migration issues. Checking the box will expand the UI and present you with a set of Assessments to run as shown in Figure 14-12.

☑ Enable premigration assessment run

Premigration assessment run name
Use a friendly name to help you find your assessment run.

```
Assessment-run-2022-08-06-11-28-55
```

The assessment run name can only have valid characters: a-z, A-Z, 0-9, space, and - (hyphen).

Assessments to run

☑ **Large objects (LOBs) are used but target LOB columns are not nullable**
Checks for nullability of a LOB column in the target when full LOB mode or inline LOB mode is used. AWS DMS requires a target LOB column to be nullable when using these LOB modes.

☑ **Source table with LOBs but without primary keys or unique constraints**
Checks for the presence of source tables with LOBs but without a primary key or unique key. For AWS DMS to migrate LOBs, a source table must have a primary key or unique key.

☑ **Unsupported data types**
Checks for data types unsupported by AWS DMS in the source endpoint. Not all data types can be migrated between endpoint types.

▢ Source table without primary key for CDC or full load and CDC tasks only
Checks for the presence of a primary key or a unique key in source tables. The lack of a primary key or a unique key during change data capture (CDC) can cause performance issues during replication.

▢ Target table without primary keys for CDC tasks only
Checks for the presence of a primary key or a unique key in already created target tables for a database migration task performing a change data capture (CDC) replication. Lack of a primary key or unique key in a target table can cause full table scans on the target when AWS DMS applies updates or deletes. This can result in performance issues during replication.

▢ Unsupported source primary key types - composite primary keys
Checks for the presence of composite primary keys in source tables. This option is for migrating to either Amazon DynamoDB (applies to all DMS replication instance versions) or Amazon Elasticsearch Service (applies only to DMS replication instances before 3.3.3). The source table's primary key must be a single column.

Assessment report storage
Amazon S3 bucket or bucket folder path to store the assessment result report.

🔍 s3://bucket-name/bucket-folder/	View 🗗	**Browse S3**

IAM role
IAM role that can access the S3 bucket.

Choose an IAM role ▼

Figure 14-12. *Enabling premigration assessment run on a scheduled task*

Once you have all of your selection and transformation rules created, you can select to *Start migration task* either *Automatically on Create*, the default, or *Manually later*. Lastly, add any tags that you desire and click the **Create task** button.

This will bring you back to the database migration tasks list screen where you will see your task being created. Once created, you can either start the task manually or allow it to run itself if so configured. You will be able to watch the table count move from *Tables queued* to *Tables Loading* to *Tables loaded* as they are processed. Returning to the AWS DMS Dashboard will show that there is 1 Load complete as shown in Figure 14-13.

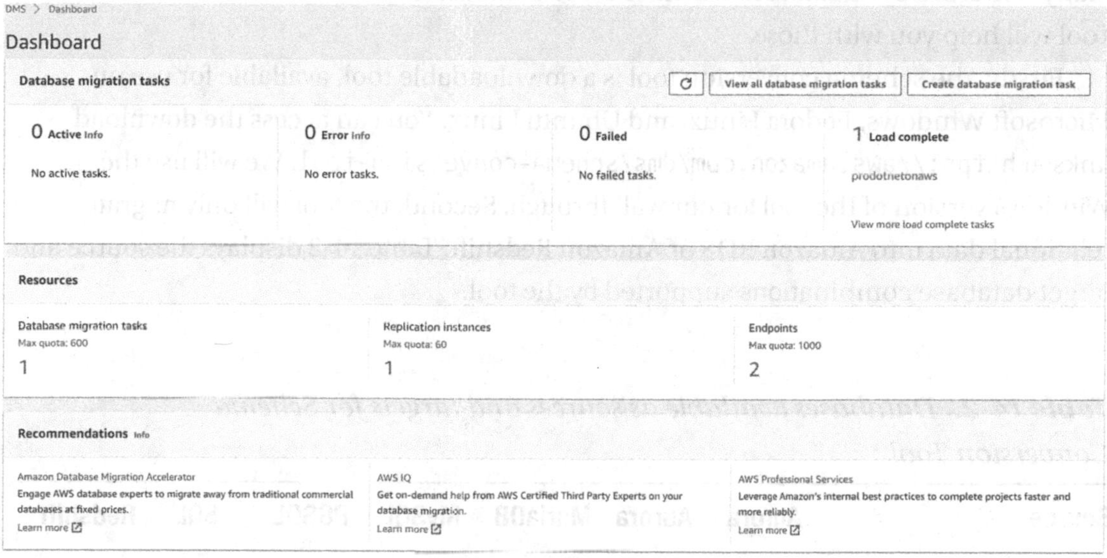

Figure 14-13. Dashboard showing the completed migration task

For those cases where you simply want to migrate data sets with minimal changes other than perhaps renaming some columns, the Database Migration Service works like a dream. Relatively painless to set up and powerful enough to move data between servers, even servers that are of dissimilar types, such as where we just copied data from SQL Server to Amazon Aurora. However, there is a tool that will help you move more disparate data between different database engines. Let's take a look at that tool now.

AWS Schema Conversion Tool

The AWS Schema Conversion Tool is designed to make cross-engine database migrations more predictable. It does this by automatically converting not only the source data but also most of the database objects such as views, stored procedures, and functions. If you think back to the previous section, you may recall that there was no mention of those database objects; the objective was simply to move all of the database tables. And since that is all our sample database had, that was quite sufficient. However, many "enterprisey" databases will have these database objects. The Schema Conversion Tool will help you with those.

Firstly, the schema conversion tool is a downloadable tool, available for use on Microsoft Windows, Fedora Linux, and Ubuntu Linux. You can access the download links at `https://aws.amazon.com/dms/schema-conversion-tool`. We will use the Windows version of the tool for our walkthrough. Second, the tool will only migrate relational data into Amazon RDS or Amazon Redshift. Table 14-2 displays the source and target database combinations supported by the tool.

Table 14-2. Databases available as sources and targets for Schema Conversion Tool

Source	Aurora MySQL	Aurora PGSQL	MariaDB	MySQL	PGSQL	SQL Server	Redshift
Oracle	X	X	X	X	X		
Oracle Data Warehouse							X
Azure SQL Database	X	X		X	X		
Microsoft SQL Server	X	X	X	X	X	X	X
Teradata							X
IBM Netezza							X
Greenplum							X
HPE Vertica							X
MySQL		X			X	X	

(continued)

Table 14-2. (*continued*)

Source	Aurora MySQL	Aurora PGSQL	MariaDB	MySQL	PGSQL	SQL Server	Redshift
PostgreSQL (PGSQL)	X	X		X	X		
IBM DB2 LUW		X	X	X	X	X	
IBM Db2 for z/OS	X	X		X	X		
SAP ASE		X	X	X	X	X	
Amazon Redshift						X	
Azure Synapse Analytics						X	
Snowflake							X

Clicking the download tool link will start the downloading of a zip file. Once the file is downloaded, extract the content to a working directory. There will be a .msi installation file and two folders. Run the installation file and start the application when the installation is completed.

Configuring the Source

Upon your first run of the tool, you will be presented with the terms of use. Accepting these terms will open the application and present the *Create a new database migration project* screen as shown in Figure 14-14.

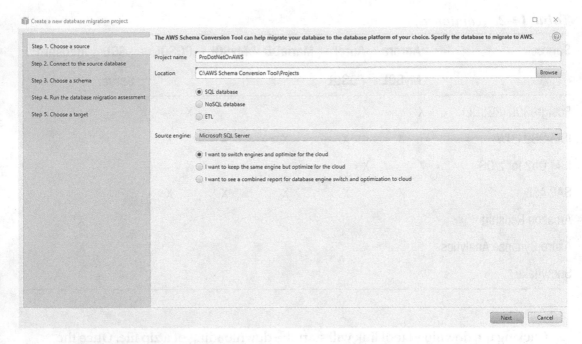

Figure 14-14. *Create a new database migration project screen in SCT*

We selected Microsoft SQL Server as our source engine, and this enabled the three radio buttons that give some direction as to how the conversion process should proceed. The three choices are as follows:

- I want to switch engines and optimize for the cloud (default).

- I want to keep the same engine but optimize for the cloud.

- I want to see a combined report for database engine switch and optimization to cloud.

Each of these selections will alter the logic of the migration project; for example, selecting to keep the same engine will provide you with a different set of destinations than selecting to switch engines.

Completing the fields in Step 1 and clicking the **Next** button will take you to the *Step 2. Connect to the source database* screen as shown in Figure 14-15.

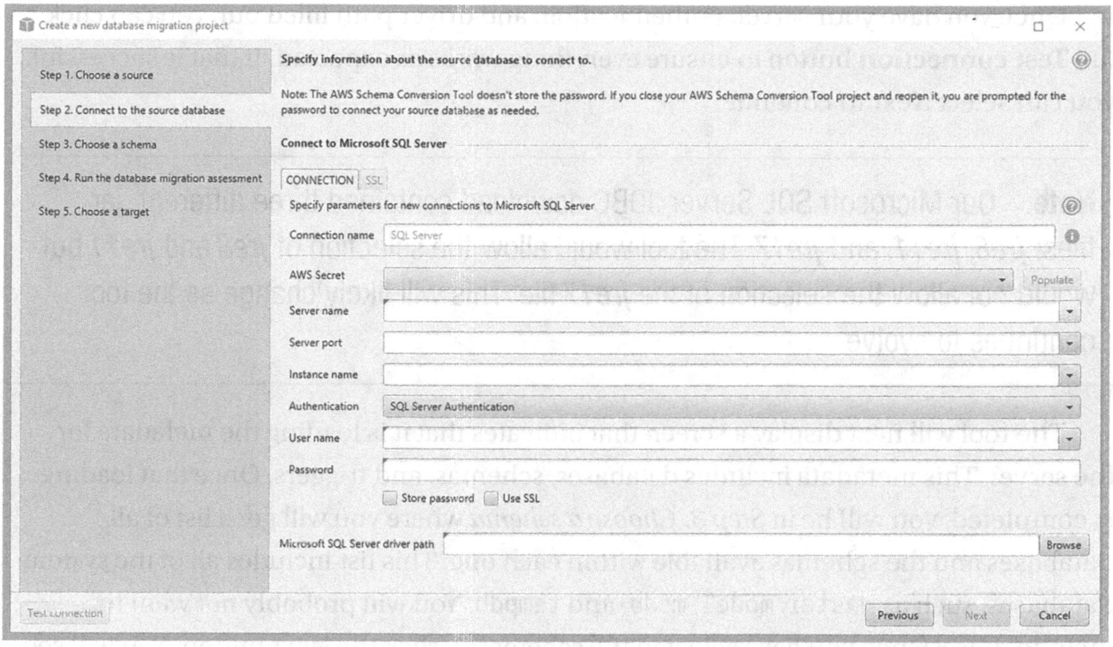

Figure 14-15. *Specifying connection information for the source database*

As shown in Figure 14-15, there are four fields that have the upper-left corner of the field displaying a red tick. Those fields are required for the connection, and three of them are fields that you should be well acquainted with by now: the *Server Name*, *User name*, and *Password* (when accessing the source database using SQL Server Authentication). However, the last field, *Microsoft SQL Server driver path*, is a new one and points to the directory in which the Microsoft SQL Server JDBC driver is located, which we didn't have installed. Fortunately, AWS helpfully provides a page with links to the various database drivers at https://docs.aws.amazon.com/SchemaConversionTool/latest/userguide/CHAP_Installing.html. You will need to install drivers for both your source and target databases. We went through and downloaded the drivers for SQL Server (our source database) and the drivers for Amazon Aurora MySQL (our destination database). Once the appropriate JDBC drivers are installed, you can point to the SQL Server driver path as shown in Figure 14-16.

Microsoft SQL Server driver path C:\AWS Schema Conversion Tool\sqljdbc_10.2\enu\mssql-jdbc-10.2.1.jre11.jar Browse

Figure 14-16. *Specifying SQL Server JDBC path*

Once you have your server, authentication, and driver path filled out, you can click the **Test connection** button to ensure everything works as expected. If that is successful, you can select **Next** to continue.

Note   Our Microsoft SQL Server JDBC download contained three different .jar files: *jre8*, *jre11*, and *jre17*. The tool would allow the selection of *jre8* and *jre11* but would not allow the selection of the *jre17* file. This will likely change as the tool continues to evolve.

The tool will next display a screen that indicates that it is loading the metadata for the server. This metadata includes databases, schemas, and triggers. Once that loading is completed, you will be in *Step 3. Choose a schema* where you will get a list of all databases and the schemas available within each one. This list includes all of the system databases, such as `master`, `model`, `msdb`, and `tempdb`. You will probably not want to include those! Once you have selected the schema(s), click the **Next** button. You will see the "Loading metadata" screen again as the tool gets all the database objects based upon your selected schema(s). This process will take a few minutes.

Database Migration Assessment Screen

Once completed, you will be taken to the *Step 4. Run the Database migration assessment screen*. The first thing that you will see is the assessment report. This report was created by the tool taking all the metadata that it found and analyzing it to see how well it would convert into the various source databases. At the top of the report is the *Executive summary*. This lists all of the potential target platforms and summarizes the types of actions that need to be taken. An example of this report is shown in Figure 14-17.

Executive summary

Target platform	Auto or minimal changes			Complex actions			
	Storage objects	Code objects	Conversion actions	Storage objects		Code objects	
				Objects count	Conversion actions	Objects count	Conversion actions
Amazon RDS for MySQL	1 (100%)	7 (100%)	0	0 (0%)	0	0 (0%)	0
Amazon Aurora (MySQL compatible)	28 (100%)	8 (100%)	0	0 (0%)	0	0 (0%)	0
Amazon RDS for PostgreSQL	27 (100%)	1 (12%)	65	0 (0%)	0	7 (88%)	18
Amazon Aurora (PostgreSQL compatible)	27 (100%)	1 (12%)	65	0 (0%)	0	7 (88%)	18
Amazon RDS for MariaDB	28 (100%)	1 (12%)	71	0 (0%)	0	7 (88%)	19
Amazon Redshift	28 (100%)	0 (0%)	86	0 (0%)	0	8 (100%)	17
Amazon Glue	0 (0%)	7 (100%)	0	0 (0%)	0	0 (0%)	0
Babelfish for Aurora PostgreSQL	26 (93%)	1 (12%)	8	2 (7%)	2	7 (88%)	30

Figure 14-17. *Executive summary of the migration assessment report*

Immediately under the executive summary is a textual analysis of the data in the chart. Each of the line items is described with an estimation of the percentage of database storage objects and database code objects that can be automatically converted. In our case, both Amazon RDS for MySQL and Amazon Aurora (MySQL compatible) can be converted at 100%. None of the other target platforms scored that high.

Additional detail is displayed further down the page as shown in Figure 14-18.

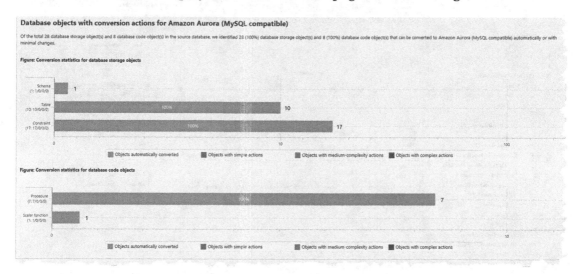

Figure 14-18. *Details on migrating to Amazon Aurora MySQL*

This section demonstrates that 1 schema, 10 tables, 17 constraints, 7 procedures, and 1 scalar function can be successfully converted to Amazon Aurora (MySQL compatible).

Configuring the Destination

Once you have completed your review of the potential destination, click the **Next** button. This will bring you to *Step 5. Choose a target* page where you select the target engine and configure the connection to the target database. When we got to the page, Amazon RDS for MySQL was selected as the target engine, so we went with that and created a new Amazon RDS for MySQL instance in the RDS console, making sure that we enabled external access. Filling out the connection information and clicking the **Test connection** button demonstrated that we had filled the information out appropriately, so we clicked the **Finish** button.

Completing the Migration

This brings you to the project page as shown in Figure 14-19.

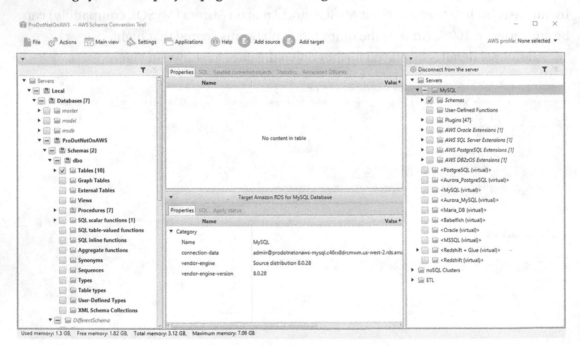

Figure 14-19. *Schema conversion tool conversion project*

Just like with DMS, the conversion tool gives you the ability to add mapping and transformation rules. You do this by clicking on the **Main view** icon in the toolbar and selecting the **Mapping view**. This changes the center section of the screen. In this section, you can add Transformation rules. These transformation rules, just as with

DMS, allow you to alter the name of items that are going to be migrated. You can create a rule where you create the appropriate filters to determine which objects will be affected, and you have the following options on how the names will be changed:

- Add prefix

- Add suffix

- Convert lowercase

- Convert uppercase

- Move to

- Remove prefix

- Remove suffix

- Rename

- Replace prefix

- Replace suffix

These different transformations are useful when working with database schemas that user older design approaches such as using a prefix of "t" before the name to show that the object is a table, or "v" to indicate that it's a view. We will not be using any transformations as part of our conversion.

Since we are converting our *ProDotNetOnAWS* database and its *dbo* schema, you need to go to the left window where the SQL Server content is displayed, right-click on the *dbo* schema, and select **Convert schema** from the pop-up menu. You will get an additional popup that shows the copying of the schema to the source destination. Once completed, the right window will look like Figure 14-20 where it shows that the schema has been copied over along with tables, procedures, views, and functions (if you have all of those).

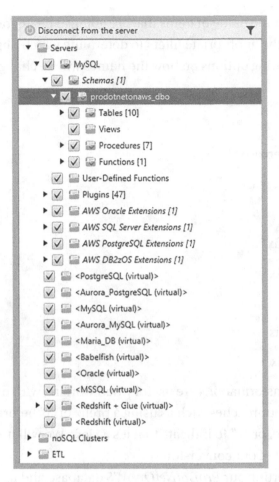

Figure 14-20. *Schema converted to source database*

Note that this design change has not yet been applied to the destination server and is instead a local representation of what it would look like once applied. Your next step is to apply the changes to the destination. You do this by right-clicking on the destination schema and selecting **Apply to database**. This will bring up a pop-up confirmation window after which you will see the schema being processed. The window will close once completed.

At this point, your schema has been transferred to the source database. Figure 14-21 shows the destination database in MySQL Workbench, and you can see that the schema defined in the tool has been successfully migrated.

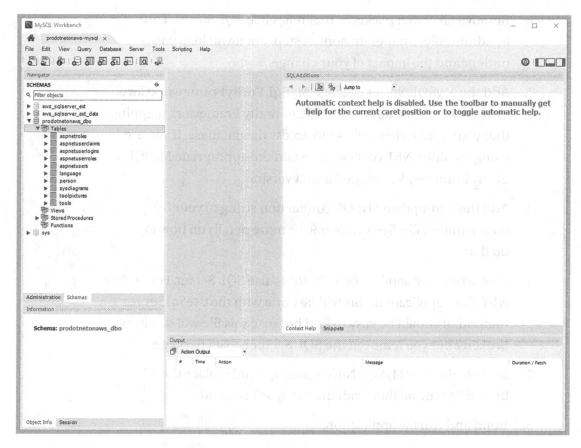

Figure 14-21. *Viewing converted schema in MySQL Workbench*

Once your data has been migrated, the last step is to convert your code so that it can access your new database.

Using the New Database

The last step in this migration is making the appropriate code changes so that your application can access the new database. For a simple application, especially one in .NET Core (.NET 5+), this can be very straightforward as there are only a few changes that you have to make because of how good a job Entity Framework Core does of abstracting the database away from the code.

1. Remove all NuGet packages that reference SQL Server. This is, admittedly, a rather draconian step, but it will help you understand the impact of your change.

2. Add the MySQL NuGet package **MySql.EntityFrameworkCore**. This package provides the MySQL to Entity Framework mapping that your application will use to access the database. If you are using an older .NET version, then add the appropriate MySQL + Entity Framework package for that version.

3. Add the appropriate MySQL connection string to your configuration file. See Chapter 9 for more details on how to do that.

4. Find where the application is "told" to use SQL Server. For an ASP. NET Core application, this will be done with the `UseSqlServer` method. It should be easy to find because this file will surely be broken after you removed the SQL Server NuGet packages.

5. Include the new MySQL NuGet package and replace the `UseSqlServer` method with the `UseMySql` method.

6. Build and run the application.

More complex applications, or older .NET applications, will have more difficulties as the specific database tends to be more tightly bound into the code. Older .NET Framework data context classes, for example, were often built with dependencies on a SQL Server library. Unfortunately, you will have to go through and manually fix those one by one.

Also, if you are taking advantage of the `SqlCommand` method and providing SQL within your application, then you will have to take special care in ensuring that the commands provided conform to the new database. Generally, this shouldn't be a problem, but there is the chance that complicated or nonstandard SQL (such as T-SQL) may need to be reworked.

Summary

Moving the running environments of your applications to the cloud provides long-term savings as you can scale the environments up and down based on your usage. Moving your databases to the cloud provides you the opportunity to manage these costs as well, most commonly by migrating to an open source database that does not have any licensing costs. This can save you thousands of dollars over a commercial database such as Microsoft SQL Server or Oracle. As we saw earlier, all of the open source databases in RDS work well with your .NET applications, so there is likely a cheaper alternative to your current commercial database.

To help you make this move, AWS provides two different tools. The first, Database Migration Service (DMS), is an online service that helps you move database tables between different database engines. You also have the ability to change some of the schemas and tables, filter data, etc. – all things that make DMS an effective tool for migrating databases. The second tool, the AWS Schema Conversion Tool, is a client-side tool that walks you through the same process using a visual tool that you have installed on your own system.

To continue this approach of helping you modernize your applications, the next chapter will help you move your application code base from previous versions of .NET that required you to run on Microsoft Windows to modern .NET that can run in multiple operating systems.

CHAPTER 15

Re-platforming and Refactoring

The .NET Framework, as of version 4.8, is now locked in stasis – security patches aside. All future enhancements and improvements to .NET are being funneled into the .NET Core–based, cross-platform, version of .NET. If you're a developer working on older ASP.NET or .NET Framework applications, you are currently tied to Windows and may therefore want to consider moving to .NET to take advantage of future enhancements.

Note   For the rest of this chapter, we'll use ".NET" to refer collectively to .NET Core or .NET 5 or higher versions and ".NET Framework" to refer to v4.8 and below.

Re-platforming (porting) from the Windows-bound .NET Framework to cross-platform .NET enables you to take advantage of a wider set of choices for hosting your application code on AWS, reduce and simplify your licensing costs by eliminating the need for Windows licenses, and set you up to take advantage of the price-performance improvements touted by Amazon's ARM64-based Graviton processors.

You may also be interested in refactoring your applications to make use of microservice architectures. Obviously, you can re-platform without refactoring, or refactor without re-platforming. Or you can do both. The choice is yours based on your needs for the application(s) in question.

Refactoring and/or re-platforming an existing application isn't without effort, however. In this chapter, we'll look at two further tools that can help in porting and modernizing your .NET Framework–based applications. You'll find these tools, both free to use, in the category of "assistive" tools available from AWS.

© William Penberthy and Steve Roberts 2023
W. Penberthy and S. Roberts, *Pro .NET on Amazon Web Services*,
https://doi.org/10.1007/978-1-4842-8907-5_15

Assistive Tools for Re-platforming and Refactoring

We've already seen one of AWS' assistive tools, App2Container, in Chapter 13. In that chapter, we showed how you can use App2Container to take a .NET Framework–based application, even one for which you no longer have the source code, and containerize it to run on Amazon ECS/EKS. However, that application is still using .NET Framework and is running on a Windows container, so is otherwise unchanged throughout the process.

Within the assistive tooling collection, AWS provides two further tools you can use to refactor and re-platform: the Porting Assistant for .NET and the Microservice Extractor for .NET. Both tools contain automation to handle some of the heavy lift involved in changing your application when re-platforming and refactoring. No automation, to our knowledge, can currently address all the changes you need to make, but hey, some are better than none, right?

Re-platform, Then Refactor? Or Refactor, Then Re-platform?

This is largely a matter of preference, and you may prefer to do only one depending on your future goals for the application in question.

For older, larger, and complex monolithic applications, you may prefer to tease out a piece at a time as a microservice. You could also port those pieces to .NET as you extract them, effectively refactoring and re-platforming as you go. This approach enables you to build a collection of microservices representing the application's core functionality and potentially leaving the remaining UI components running on .NET Framework. Recall, however, that version 4.8 of the .NET Framework is the "end of the line" and will receive only critical security fixes from now on (until such point as even those updates cease).

Or for smaller applications, you could port the whole application to .NET first and then refactor to microservices, or leave the monolith as is but now running on .NET. You'll have gained platform and license freedom and be running on a supported version of .NET (if you choose a Long-Term Support (LTS) version).

Whichever route you take, you can use the Porting Assistant and Microservices Extractor separately, or in combination, to achieve your end goal. Let's start by examining re-platforming using the Porting Assistant.

Re-platforming to .NET

The Porting Assistant for .NET is a tool that helps you assess the complexity of moving your .NET Framework application to .NET by providing an assessment of the use of incompatible NuGet packages and APIs across the projects making up your application. Beyond assessing compatibility, you can also use the assistant to perform some of the "grunge work" involved in porting, such as updating project files, switching to compatible NuGet references, and helping pinpoint and resolve the use of incompatible APIs. As we noted previously, automation can't handle all the changes your application may need, so be prepared to roll up your sleeves and make manual code changes too!

Getting Started with the Porting Assistant for .NET

Two versions of the Porting Assistant are available: a standalone desktop version (obviously for Windows!) and a plug-in for Visual Studio. The desktop version installer is available from the AWS' .NET home site (`https://aws.amazon.com/dotnet`). It installs to the local user account without needing administrative privileges. The plug-in version is installable from the Visual Studio marketplace (`https://marketplace.visualstudio.com/`).

Note   At the time of writing, there are two versions listed in the marketplace: one for Visual Studio 2019 (`https://marketplace.visualstudio.com/items?itemName=AWSPA.AWSPortingAssistant`) and the other for Visual Studio 2022 (`https://marketplace.visualstudio.com/items?itemName=AWSPA.AWSPortingAssistant2022`).

Tip   The client applications are open source on GitHub at `https://github.com/aws/porting-assistant-dotnet-client`, along with other components that make up the tool, such as the Code Translation Assistant, which is used to apply code translations based on rules. You can find details in the README file in the repository. Also note the Porting Assistant is available as a NuGet package for use in your own applications!

Using the assistant in Visual Studio has the advantage that you are immediately "in the right place" to make edits to your application using the tool's guidance. However, the level of information provided by the plug-in version isn't as extensive, or as visual, as the standalone application. For example, the project dependency view that we'll look at shortly isn't available in the IDE. This view is quite useful to determine where to start to get the most "bang per buck" for your porting efforts. Instead, the IDE plug-in simply lists all the incompatibilities in the Error List window, an approach we hope the team will eventually change in favor of an easier-to-use custom view. In this chapter, therefore, we'll focus on the standalone application for the wider range of information it shows.

Once you've installed the assistant (desktop or IDE plug-in), you'll need to provide it with a credential profile and a default .NET target (Core 3.1, 5.0, or 6.0 at the time of writing). You're also asked to opt in to telemetry so the team can make further improvements based on assessment data. The telemetry data contains no personal code, data, or details of private NuGet packages. Figure 15-1 shows the setup page in the desktop application, which will appear the first time you run the tool after installation. Thereafter, you can change the credential profile using the hamburger button in the upper left of the application, which will fly out a panel with a **Settings** entry you can select to access this data.

Note   As this book was going to press, a new version of the Porting Assistant was released that removed the need to select a credential profile. You no longer need an AWS account to use the assistant.

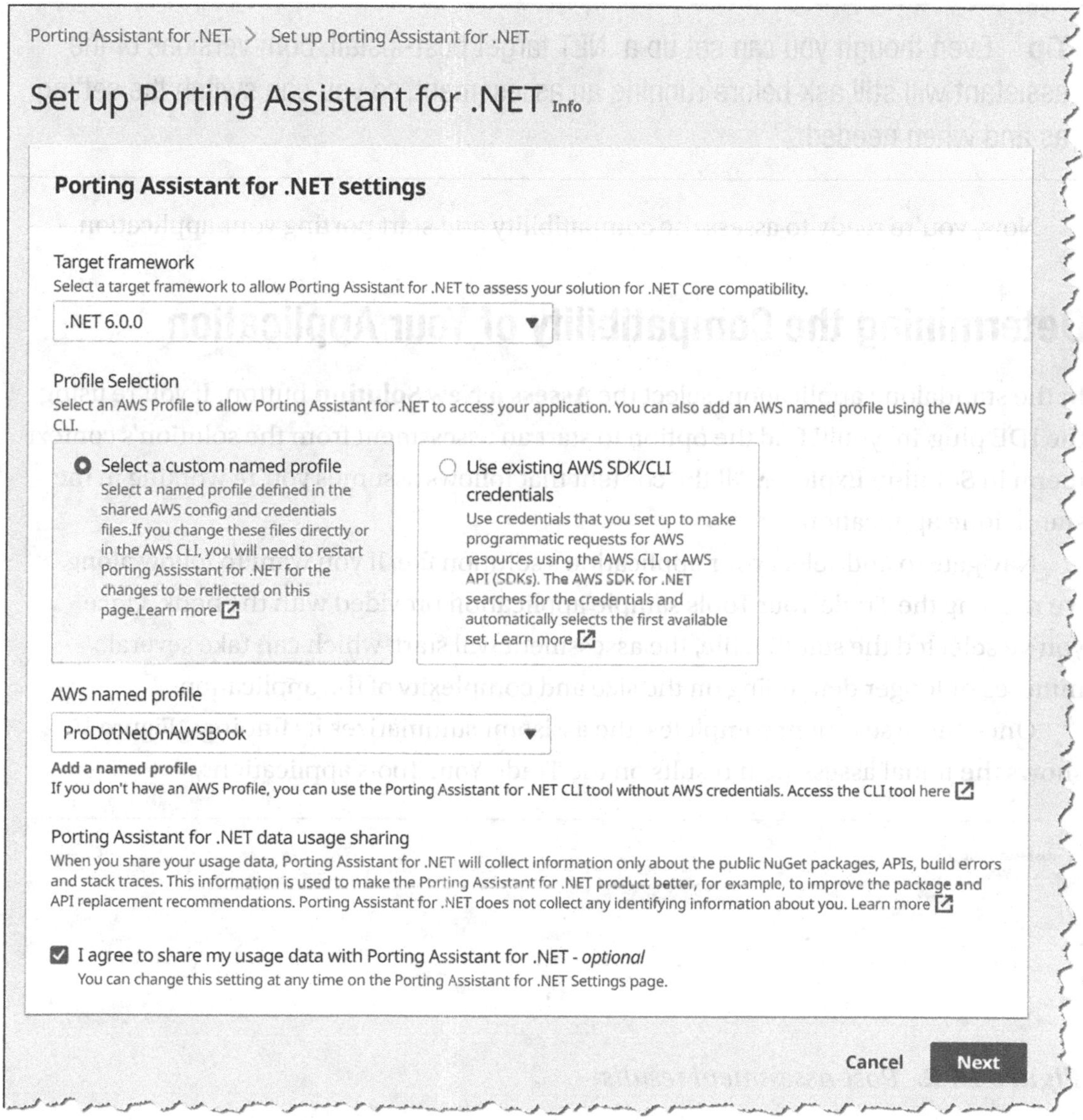

Porting Assistant for .NET > Set up Porting Assistant for .NET

Set up Porting Assistant for .NET Info

Porting Assistant for .NET settings

Target framework
Select a target framework to allow Porting Assistant for .NET to assess your solution for .NET Core compatibility.

.NET 6.0.0 ▼

Profile Selection
Select an AWS Profile to allow Porting Assistant for .NET to access your application. You can also add an AWS named profile using the AWS CLI.

● **Select a custom named profile**
Select a named profile defined in the shared AWS config and credentials files.If you change these files directly or in the AWS CLI, you will need to restart Porting Assistant for .NET for the changes to be reflected on this page.Learn more 🔗

○ **Use existing AWS SDK/CLI credentials**
Use credentials that you set up to make programmatic requests for AWS resources using the AWS CLI or AWS API (SDKs). The AWS SDK for .NET searches for the credentials and automatically selects the first available set. Learn more 🔗

AWS named profile

ProDotNetOnAWSBook ▼

Add a named profile
If you don't have an AWS Profile, you can use the Porting Assistant for .NET CLI tool without AWS credentials. Access the CLI tool here 🔗

Porting Assistant for .NET data usage sharing
When you share your usage data, Porting Assistant for .NET will collect information only about the public NuGet packages, APIs, build errors and stack traces. This information is used to make the Porting Assistant for .NET product better, for example, to improve the package and API replacement recommendations. Porting Assistant for .NET does not collect any identifying information about you. Learn more 🔗

☑ I agree to share my usage data with Porting Assistant for .NET - *optional*
You can change this setting at any time on the Porting Assistant for .NET Settings page.

Cancel   **Next**

Figure 15-1. *Configuring credentials and default .NET target*

In the IDE, go to the **Extensions** menu and select **Porting Assistant for .NET**, followed by **Settings** (or just go into the IDE's **Options** dialog and locate the relevant settings group).

Tip   Even though you can set up a .NET target post-install, both versions of the assistant will still ask before running an assessment, so you can switch the setting as and when needed.

Now, you're ready to assess the compatibility and start porting your application.

Determining the Compatibility of Your Application

In the standalone application, select the **Assess a New Solution** button. If you're using the IDE plug-in, you'll find the option to start an assessment from the solution's context menu in Solution Explorer. All the content that follows assumes you're working in the standalone application.

Navigate to and select your application's solution file. If you want to follow along, we're using the Trade Your Tools sample application provided with the book. Once you've selected the solution file, the assessment will start, which can take several minutes or longer depending on the size and complexity of the application.

Once the assessment completes, the assistant summarizes its findings. Figure 15-2 shows the initial assessment results on the Trade Your Tools application.

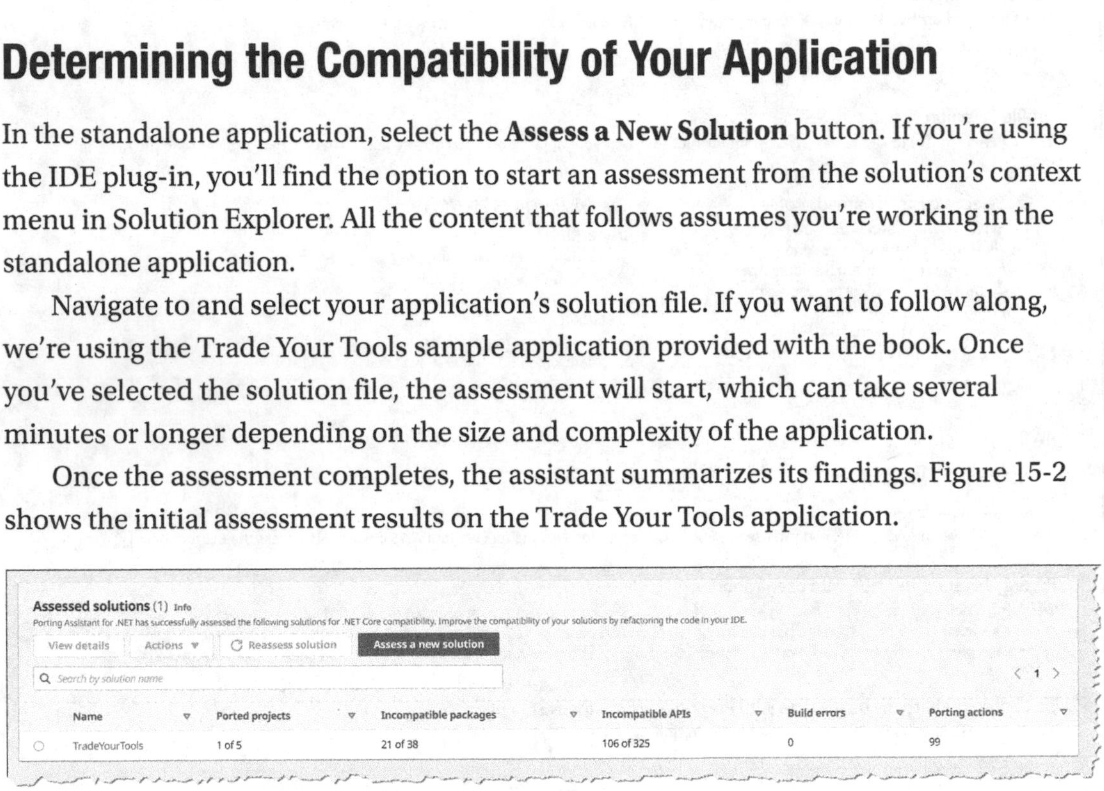

Figure 15-2. Post-assessment results

The assistant summarizes the number of ported (or compatible with .NET) projects, the number of NuGet packages that are being used that are incompatible, the number of .NET APIs (types, methods, etc.) being used that need to be ported, and any build errors (the assistant builds the solution as part of the assessment). Incompatible packages mean the package doesn't target either a specific version of .NET Core (.NET Core 3.1 or .NET 5+) or the netstandard2.0 target (introduced back with .NET Core 2.0).

Porting Actions refers to what you may expect, the number of changes you need to make to bring the incompatible packages and API usages to zero. This value can help you comprehend the scale of changes needed for a project, and the overall application, to make it compatible with .NET. The higher the number, the more changes you need to make! Recall, however, that the assistant can automate some changes, such as updating project file formats, NuGet package versions, and some code changes.

You might be curious about the single ported project noted in Figure 15-2. As we'll see, this project targets netstandard2.0 and, therefore, is already compatible with .NET 6.

Note   If it's not apparent from the use of a list view in Figure 15-2, when using the standalone assistant application, you're able to assess and work on porting multiple solutions in parallel. When using the IDE plug-in, you can only assess projects in the opened solution file.

Let's dig deeper by selecting the application name and head into the heart of the assistant – the assessment details view – shown in Figure 15-3.

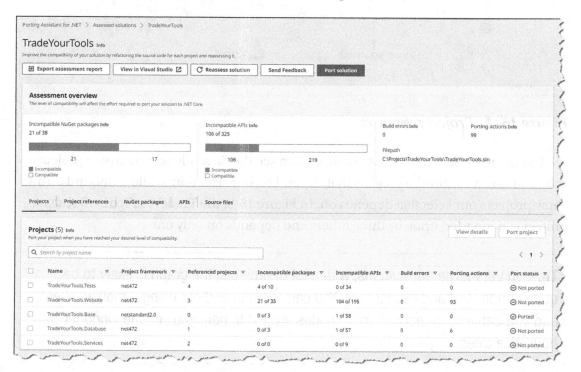

Figure 15-3. Assessment details

From the details view, you're able to get a sense of the best starting point to maximize your initial efforts by highlighting the projects that make up the bulk of where you'll need to make changes. For a larger and more complex application, you may find that the changes are more evenly spread across your projects, leaving no clear "winner." However, it's more than likely one or two will clearly stand out.

In Figure 15-3, one project stands out above the others, TradeYourTools.Website, based on the number of porting actions it needs. There's another view that can help you in selecting your start point – the **Project references** tab, shown in Figure 15-4.

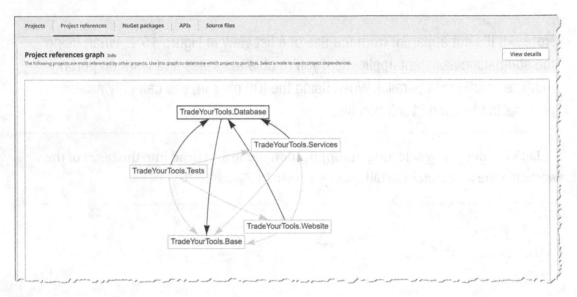

Figure 15-4. *Project references*

Using the Project references graph, we can see the dependencies between projects. Inbound arrows show the projects that depend on our selection, while outbound arrows show projects our selection depends on. In Figure 15-3, the `TradeYourTools.Database` project is depended upon by three others and depends on only one.

Tip   In very large applications, with a lot of projects, the graph is likely to be quite condensed and overlapping. You can zoom in and out using a mouse wheel, and you can also select and move nodes around to help you see the wood for the figurative trees.

To maximize "bang per buck" efforts when porting, it makes sense to select either a project with many porting actions or a project that is more highly depended upon. Sometimes, this may be the same project, but not always, which is why we suggest using the **Projects** and **Project references**' views to fine-tune your decision-making.

The remaining views detail the usage of both public and private NuGet packages, .NET APIs, and source files (telemetry data, if you opted in, does not contain details of private packages). We'll leave you to explore the NuGet and API usage views on your own as they are fairly self-evident. Before moving on to porting, however, we want to highlight one last view, **Source files**, which showcases the exact locations where your application is calling incompatible APIs and shows where the assistant can change these calls without effort from you. Figure 15-5 shows an example from the standalone assistant application. If you're using the IDE plug-in, note that it uses green "squigglies" to highlight this data when you open the file in the editor.

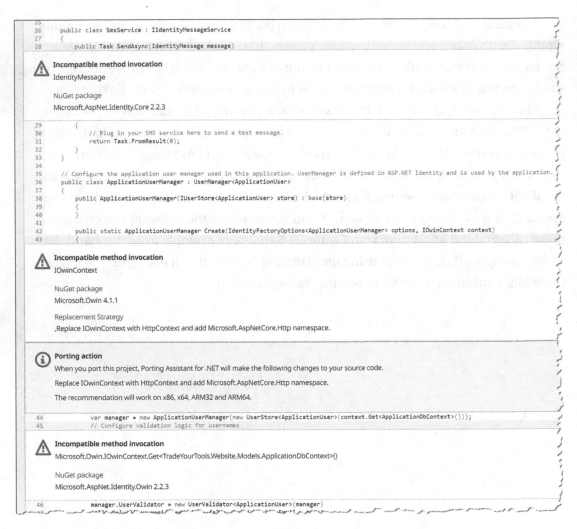

Figure 15-5. *Incompatible API usage highlighted in source files*

Once you've decided where to start your porting efforts, return to the overall **Project assessment** view (Figure 15-2) and click **Port solution** to change your project and, where possible, source files, to make them compatible with .NET.

File Modifications When Porting

When you start the port, the assistant first asks how you'd like to handle changes to your applications project and source files, as shown in Figure 15-6.

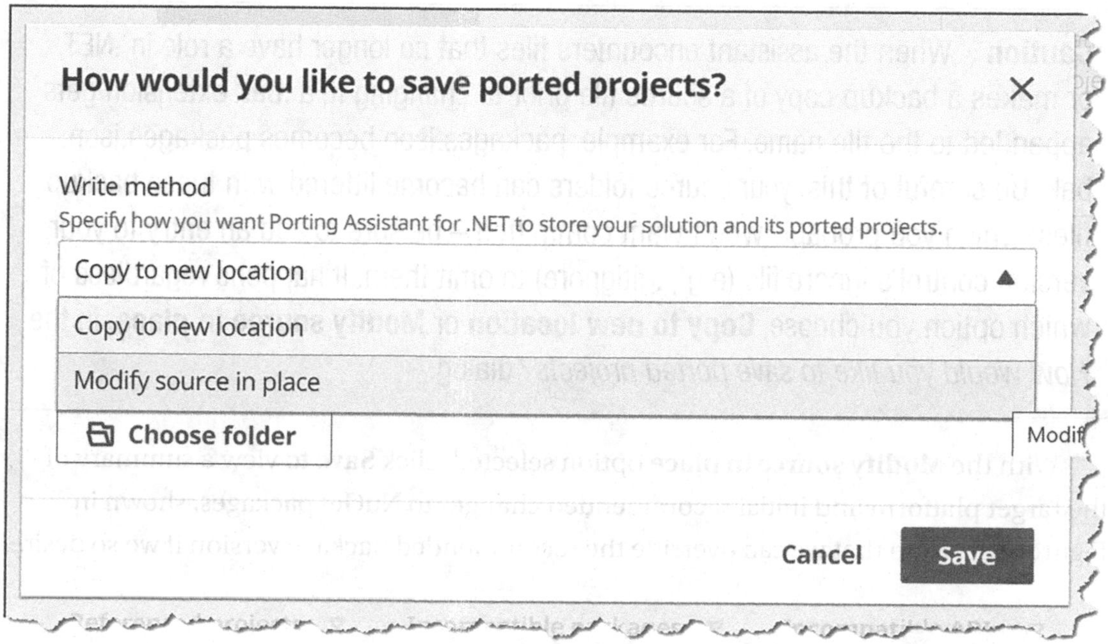

Figure 15-6. *File modification options when porting*

The default option is to copy the solution, project, and source files to a new location. No source control repository information, or history, gets copied along with the projects and source files. It's really a simple folder-by-folder copy of the content to a root folder you choose. Once porting is done, you need to either use an external diff/merge tool to apply those changes back into your source repository version or "blanket copy" the files back, both of which could be tedious!

The other choice, **Modify source in place**, allows the assistant to make in-place changes to your application's source files. If your application is version controlled, and branches in that version control system are cheap to create and use (e.g., Git), then we feel this is a better choice. You can use your existing source control diff procedures to monitor file changes before committing them. For large applications with multiple solution files in one repository, this also avoids having to copy files around, with potential errors, when our source control allows us to revert as needed if things go awry during the port.

Caution   When the assistant encounters files that no longer have a role in .NET, or makes a backup copy of a source file prior to changing it, a .bak extension gets appended to the file name. For example, packages.json becomes packages.json. bak. Be careful of this, your source folders can become littered with these backup files, which you probably won't want committed – be sure to add an entry to your version control's ignore file (e.g., .gitignore) to omit them. It happens regardless of which option you choose, **Copy to new location** or **Modify source in place**, in the *How would you like to save ported projects?* dialog.

With the **Modify source in place** option selected, click **Save** to view a summary of the target platform and initial recommended changes to NuGet packages, shown in Figure 15-7. Note that we can override the recommended package version if we so desire.

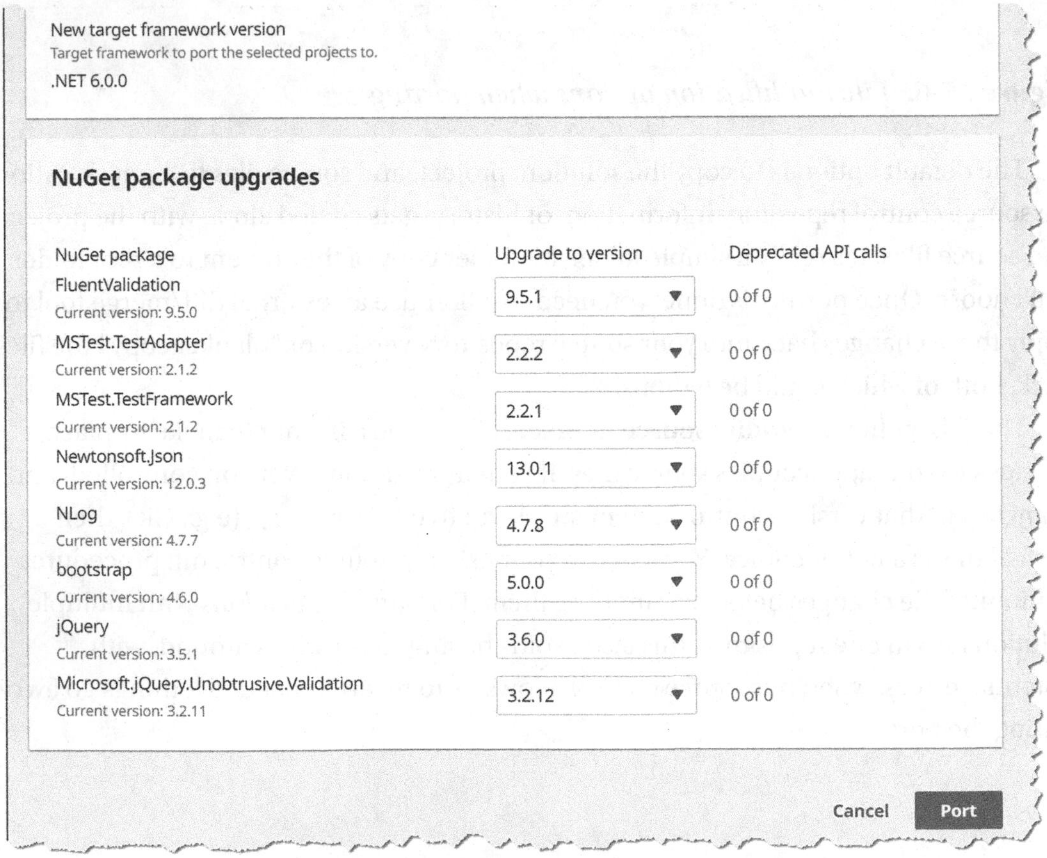

Figure 15-7. Initial NuGet package change recommendations

Click **Port** to upgrade the project file formats and recommended (or overridden) package versions.

Round and Round We Go – Porting the Application

Once updates to the project files and initial code changes that can be automated have been completed, the assistant will then reassess the solution. This action, as before, can take a few minutes to complete. When it does, you'll get an updated summary as shown in Figure 15-8.

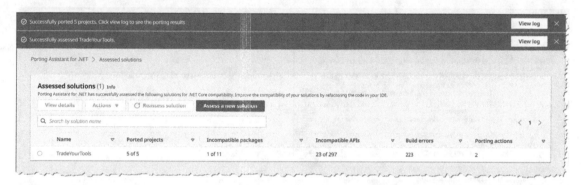

Figure 15-8. *Assessment after the first set of automated changes*

However, Figure 15-8 shows an interesting update – build errors! When we started, we had none, so does this mean we're going backward? Not really, the assistant has done quite a lot of work for us already, but there's further work needed.

Recall from earlier in the chapter we said that no automation we're aware of can take a real-world .NET Framework application and port it to .NET without some manual intervention and code correction. The build errors are those remaining now that the grunge work of changing project file formats, updating NuGet package versions, and some automatable code changes have been done. The rest of the work that's not (yet) automated is up to us, that is, you. Depending on the size and complexity of the application, this might require several iterations before you eliminate all the build errors and the application is completely re-platformed.

What Did the Assistant Do for Us?

To close out this section on the Porting Assistant, let's review aspects of the grunge work the assistant has successfully handled for us. Project files for .NET applications are much simpler than those used with the .NET Framework. Manually having to remove all the unnecessary settings, and items and property groups, from projects spanning a typical real-world application (tens, if not more) would be quite tedious and error prone. Figure 15-9 shows just some changes, from the Git diff view, in Visual Studio to one project we ported – a big time saver.

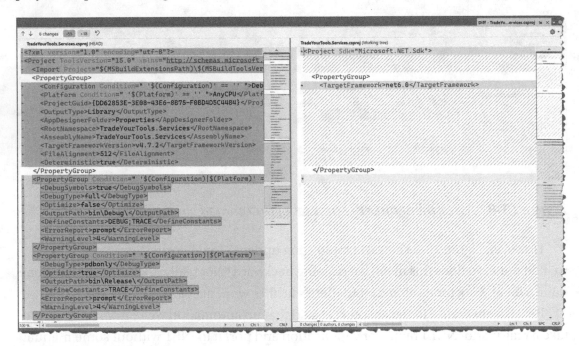

Figure 15-9. *Project file updates handled by the Porting Assistant*

Figure 15-10 shows automated changes to one of the source files. Yes, some of this could be done by global search and replace, but do you know precisely which changes are needed? The assistant does – and takes care of as much of it as possible for you. It even adds comments guiding you on further changes (seen as "Added by CTA…" in the screenshot. CTA stands for Code Translation Assistant, a core part of the Porting Assistant); an example is shown in Figure 15-10.

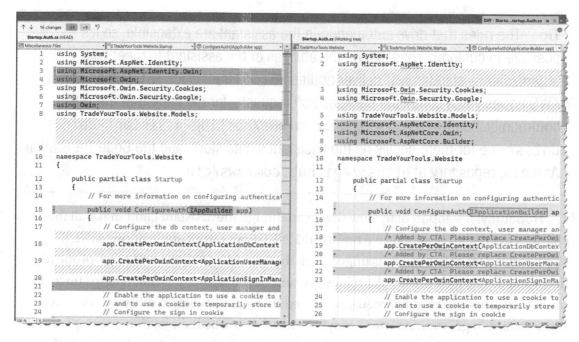

Figure 15-10. *Automated code file changes*

Figure 15-11 shows comments added to the changed file to guide you on further changes you need to make.

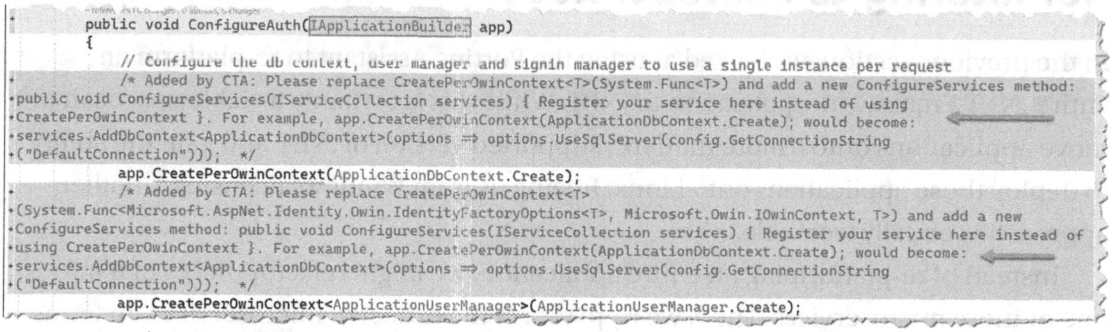

```
    public void ConfigureAuth(IApplicationBuilder app)
    {
        // Configure the db context, user manager and signin manager to use a single instance per request
        /* Added by CTA: Please replace CreatePerOwinContext<T>(System.Func<T>) and add a new ConfigureServices method:
public void ConfigureServices(IServiceCollection services) { Register your service here instead of using
CreatePerOwinContext }. For example, app.CreatePerOwinContext(ApplicationDbContext.Create); would become:
services.AddDbContext<ApplicationDbContext>(options => options.UseSqlServer(config.GetConnectionString
("DefaultConnection"))); */
        app.CreatePerOwinContext(ApplicationDbContext.Create);
        /* Added by CTA: Please replace CreatePerOwinContext<T>
(System.Func<Microsoft.AspNet.Identity.Owin.IdentityFactoryOptions<T>, Microsoft.Owin.IOwinContext, T>) and add a new
ConfigureServices method: public void ConfigureServices(IServiceCollection services) { Register your service here instead of
using CreatePerOwinContext }. For example, app.CreatePerOwinContext(ApplicationDbContext.Create); would become:
services.AddDbContext<ApplicationDbContext>(options => options.UseSqlServer(config.GetConnectionString
("DefaultConnection"))); */
        app.CreatePerOwinContext<ApplicationUserManager>(ApplicationUserManager.Create);
```

Figure 15-11. *Guiding comments added to source files*

Tip   The rules that drive automation in the assistant are extensible, so it's possible to customize and extend the abilities of the assistant to meet your organization's standards or deliver additional code translation automation (which AWS hopes you'll contribute back, as pull requests, for the benefit of the .NET community. See `https://github.com/aws/porting-assistant-dotnet-datastore` for more details on the assistant's data store, and the Code Translation Assistant repository at `https://github.com/aws/cta`.

Hopefully, it's apparent by now that even though the assistant can't make all the changes needed to re-platform a real-world .NET Framework application to .NET, it can handle a lot of heavy-lift "grunge" work that would be tedious and error-prone to do yourself. The idea behind the telemetry sent by the assistant is that it helps uncover more scenarios where automated changes could be applicable. In this way, we expect the assistant to get even smarter – maybe one day it will be the tool that can re-platform that .NET Framework application you have without needing much in the way of effort from you!

Refactoring to Microservices

In the previous section, we looked at using the Porting Assistant to re-platform an entire .NET Framework application to .NET. While this is certainly a viable approach to move applications onto a more modern, supported version of .NET and gain the ability to deploy those applications onto Linux, freeing us from Windows licensing, another approach is equally workable.

Instead of re-platforming an entire application, we might refactor pieces of it into one or more microservices. Then, we re-platform the extracted microservices. In terms of effort to re-platform, this may be less effort than working on the entire application.

To help with refactoring, AWS makes available another free, assistive tool – the Microservice Extractor for .NET. Unlike the Porting Assistant, which only works with .NET Framework applications, the extractor can be used on ASP.NET applications built using either .NET Framework or .NET.

The Microservice Extractor analyzes an application to discover internal dependencies. To do this, it uses static code analysis (your code must build cleanly!), optionally in combination with runtime profile data. Using a dependency visualization, you build groups of logical functionalities (e.g., classes related to a back-end shopping cart experience). Once a group of functionalities has been defined, you use the extractor to extract the code for the classes in the group into a separate project representing the microservice. The extractor also updates the original code to either redirect calls to the extracted service (as a REST API) or to continue using the original internal classes, but with comments added to guide you in future refactoring.

Once extracted, the microservice(s) can then be re-platformed and deployed to Lambda or run within containers in ECS. To make the microservices callable in the cloud, we can place them behind API endpoints, perhaps using API Gateway (we showed an example of this, using Lambda, in Chapter 6).

Getting Started with the Microservice Extractor for .NET

Download the tool from the tools page of the .NET on AWS site (`https://aws.amazon.com/dotnet`) and then install it.

Some setup is required the first time you run the extractor, which you start by clicking **Get Started** on the main page. Similar to the Porting Assistant, the Microservice Extractor will ask you to supply an AWS credential profile. It also asks you to select a region (us-east-1 or us-west-2 currently) and a working directory it will use during code extraction. While we're here, consider opting into sending telemetry data so that the development team can further improve the tool for the community. With these settings in place, click **Update** to save them. We can then proceed to analyzing our application(s).

Tip   AWS provides a helpful workshop for Microservice Extractor, which you can find at `https://bit.ly/3BvYWgL`. The example application we'll use in this section, GadgetsOnline, is from that workshop. The sample application code is available on GitHub at `https://github.com/aws-samples/dotnet-modernization-gadgetsonline`.

Analyzing an Application

Microservice Extractor calls analyzing an application "onboarding," which comprises static inspection of the code. Analysis can also include optional runtime profiling data, providing call counts along with dependency data.

Note   We won't cover runtime profiling here for space reasons. It uses a custom .dll that you download and install into IIS on the system running the application, which you then exercise. Output from the profiler is a CSV-format file you specify during application onboarding. Find more details in the Runtime profiling prerequisites section of the tools' user guide: `https://docs.aws.amazon. com/microservice-extractor/latest/userguide`.

Begin by clicking the **Onboard application** button from the extractor application's home screen. In the form that opens, give the application analysis a name and browse to select your application's solution file. The extractor needs to build your application and will attempt to auto-detect MSBuild to do so. However, you can customize the MSBuild location if it can't be found automatically or you need to use a specific MSBuild version. You're also able to set and necessary build settings for the build.

If you collected runtime profile data, you can add it into the analysis here. Also, if you have the Porting Assistant for .NET installed, you can enable additional analysis on the feasibility and effort required to re-platform the classes you identify to be extracted into a microservice to instead run on Linux. This will help guide you on whether to re-platform after extraction or leave the microservice using .NET Framework.

Figure 15-12 shows the options when beginning to onboard an application.

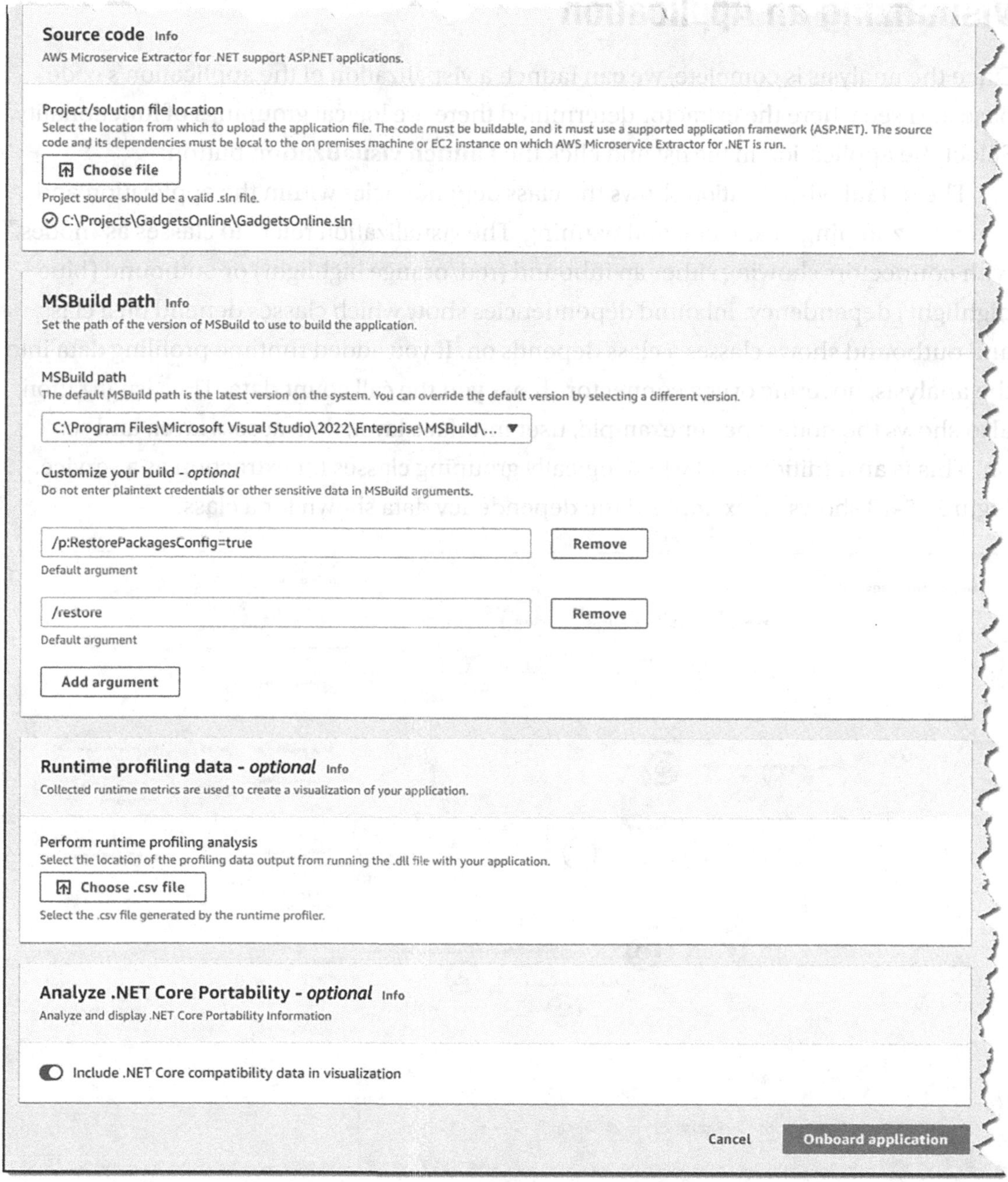

Source code Info

AWS Microservice Extractor for .NET support ASP.NET applications.

Project/solution file location

Select the location from which to upload the application file. The code must be buildable, and it must use a supported application framework (ASP.NET). The source code and its dependencies must be local to the on premises machine or EC2 instance on which AWS Microservice Extractor for .NET is run.

[🔼 **Choose file**]

Project source should be a valid .sln file.

⊘ C:\Projects\GadgetsOnline\GadgetsOnline.sln

MSBuild path Info

Set the path of the version of MSBuild to use to build the application.

MSBuild path

The default MSBuild path is the latest version on the system. You can override the default version by selecting a different version.

[C:\Program Files\Microsoft Visual Studio\2022\Enterprise\MSBuild\... ▼]

Customize your build - *optional*

Do not enter plaintext credentials or other sensitive data in MSBuild arguments.

[/p:RestorePackagesConfig=true]   [Remove]

Default argument

[/restore]   [Remove]

Default argument

[**Add argument**]

Runtime profiling data - *optional* Info

Collected runtime metrics are used to create a visualization of your application.

Perform runtime profiling analysis

Select the location of the profiling data output from running the .dll file with your application.

[🔼 **Choose .csv file**]

Select the .csv file generated by the runtime profiler.

Analyze .NET Core Portability - *optional* Info

Analyze and display .NET Core Portability Information

[⬤] Include .NET Core compatibility data in visualization

Cancel   [**Onboard application**]

Figure 15-12. *Onboarding an application into Microservice Extractor*

Once you've completed the options, click **Onboard application** to start the analysis.

Visualizing an Application

Once the analysis is complete, we can launch a visualization of the application's code base and see where the extractor determined there are logical groupings of functionality. Select the application in the list and click the **Launch visualization** button.

The default visualization shows the class dependencies within the application and supports zooming in and out, and panning. The visualization refers to classes as "nodes," with connectors showing either an inbound (red/orange highlight) or outbound (blue highlight) dependency. Inbound dependencies show which classes depend on a class, and outbound shows classes a class depends on. If you added runtime profiling data into the analysis, hovering over a connector shows you the call count data. The visualization also shows the node type, for example, user interface layer, data access layer, and so on. This is an additional aid when logically grouping classes for extraction as a service. Figure 15-13 shows an example of the dependency data shown for a class.

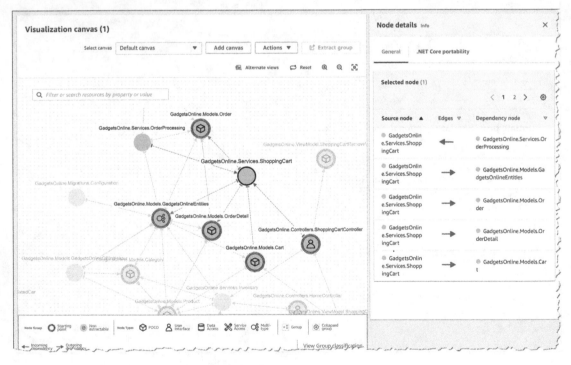

Figure 15-13. *Visualized class dependencies*

Two other visualization modes are available by clicking the **Alternate views** button. Our aim is to find logical groups of functionalities suitable to extract as a standalone service, so it's worth exploring these alternate views to see if they provide a clearer overview. The first alternate visualization, **Namespaces**, shows classes grouped by, well, their namespaces. The second, **Islands**, groups together classes that have dependencies on each other, but not outside their group. Just as with the default visualization, the alternate views identify node types (UI, data, etc.). While in Figure 15-14 you can't read the text at the zoom level, you can see the boxed islands (with dependency connections shown inside each island), to contrast it with the default visualization which just lays down all classes, and their dependencies, from Figure 15-13.

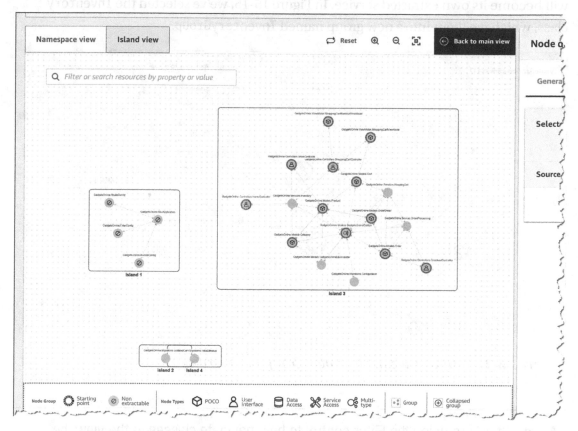

Figure 15-14. *Islands visualization (zoomed out) for comparison*

With the three provided visualizations, you have a basis to understand class relationships within the application and can consider extracting one or more classes to form an independent microservice that's separately maintained, deployed, and scaled from the main application.

Extracting a Microservice

To extract classes into a new microservice, they first need to be collected into a user-defined group, representing a unit of extraction. Do this by right-clicking on a class, in whatever visualization you choose, and selecting **Add to group** from the resulting context menu. You can add the class to a new group or to an existing one. It's possible to define multiple groups, which you can differentiate with different colors, but each group will become its own extracted service. In Figure 15-15, we've selected the Inventory class, which we'll put into a new group named InventoryGroup.

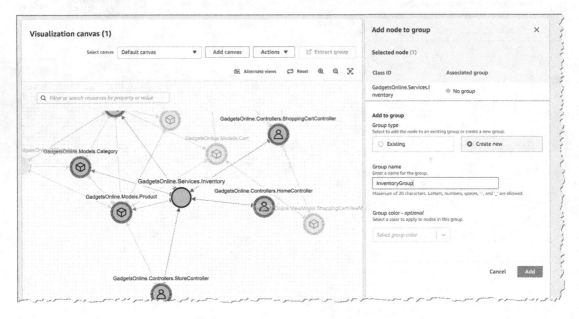

Figure 15-15. *Adding a class to a new group for a service*

Note   If you're using the Filter control to help navigate classes in the view, be aware that right-clicking isn't available while a filter is active. You need to clear the filter and then right-click.

Click the **Add** button in the panel to create the group, which will cause a bounded rectangle, tagged with the group name and containing the selected class, to be added to the visualization, shown in Figure 15-16. You can drag additional classes into the group, or continue to select classes and use the context menu to populate it.

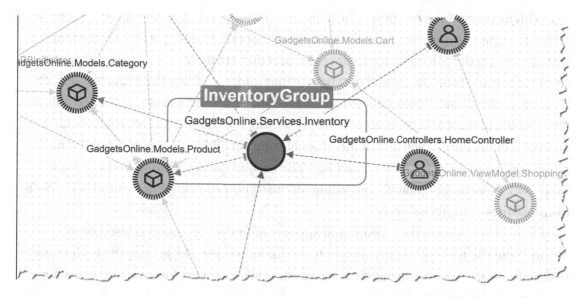

Figure 15-16. *Group indicator with initial selected node (class)*

Once the group contains the classes needed for the service (you don't need to select their dependencies), it's ready for extraction. Start by clicking inside the group rectangle to select the group and then clicking the **Extract group** button in the **General** tab of the **Group details** pane that is displayed. In the dialog that's then shown, choose a name for the new service (InventoryService).

The most important setting is found at the foot of the dialog, in the panel titled **Method invocations from the application to the extracted service**. It relates to how you'd prefer the extractor update the application once it has extracted the selected classes into the new service, shown in Figure 15-17.

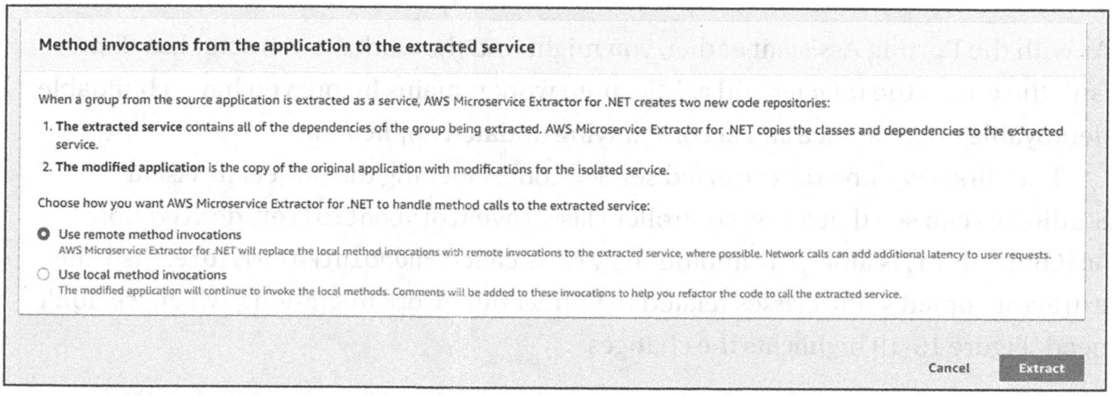

Method invocations from the application to the extracted service

When a group from the source application is extracted as a service, AWS Microservice Extractor for .NET creates two new code repositories:

1. **The extracted service** contains all of the dependencies of the group being extracted. AWS Microservice Extractor for .NET copies the classes and dependencies to the extracted service.
2. **The modified application** is the copy of the original application with modifications for the isolated service.

Choose how you want AWS Microservice Extractor for .NET to handle method calls to the extracted service:

○ Use remote method invocations
    AWS Microservice Extractor for .NET will replace the local method invocations with remote invocations to the extracted service, where possible. Network calls can add additional latency to user requests.

○ Use local method invocations
    The modified application will continue to invoke the local methods. Comments will be added to these invocations to help you refactor the code to call the extracted service.

Cancel   **Extract**

Figure 15-17. *Update options for the application and extracted service*

Whichever option you choose, both the application code and the extracted service code are copied to new locations underneath the working folder you selected when you first set up the Microservice Extractor. Extraction creates a new, randomly named, subfolder, and within that, you'll find two further folders holding the extracted service and the application. In the extracted service folder, you'll find a new project and solution file, and the classes and dependencies representing the extracted service (the solution and project file names will match the original solution and project name, not the name of the service you chose when extracting). The copy of the application in the second folder will have been updated depending on the option you chose in Figure 15-16. We'll examine these changes shortly.

Figure 15-18 shows the prompt that appears after the successful extraction of a group. Note the two copy icons alongside the folder names. These copy the folder names to the clipboard, which you can then paste into a Windows Explorer view to open the location and inspect the files.

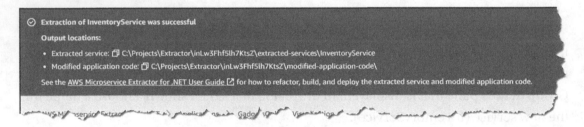

Figure 15-18. *File locations for the extracted service and updated application*

What Did the Extractor Do for Us?

As with the Porting Assistant earlier, you might find the work the extractor has done isn't the end of the refactor and a little more work remains before you have a buildable, deployable microservice and accompanying updated application.

Let's first examine the extracted service code. Opening the project in Visual Studio, we can see that a new controller class, InventoryController, derived from ApiController, is alongside another new class called EndpointParamStore. Also, the extractor copied some classes related to Entity Framework migrations, which we don't need. Figure 15-19 highlights the changes.

```
namespace GadgetsOnline.Controllers
{
    [RoutePrefix ( "api/Inventory" )]

    public class InventoryController : ApiController
    {
        [Route("GetBestSellers_6da88c34")]
        [ResponseType(typeof(List<Product>))]
        [HttpPost]

        public IHttpActionResult GetBestSellers_6da88c34Wrapper(dynamic endpointContainer)
        {
            try
            {
                dynamic ctorContainer = EndpointParamStore.GetConstructorContainer(endpointContainer);
                dynamic methodContainer = EndpointParamStore.GetMethodContainer(endpointContainer);
                Inventory myInstance = null;
                string ctorParamHash = EndpointParamStore.GetConstructorParamHash(ctorContainer);
                // Initialize the right constructor
                if (ctorParamHash.Equals("e3b0c442"))
                {
                    myInstance = new Inventory();
```

Figure 15-19. *Extracted service files*

The new controller shouldn't come as much of a surprise since we'll need something to expose the ASP.NET API endpoints for the service. The EndpointParamStore helper class is used to bind the new controller's methods to the constructor and methods in the original Inventory class, which the extraction did not change.

To complete the refactoring of this service, you'll first remove the unneeded Entity Framework migration files that the extractor copied. Then, as a best practice, update the classes returned from the Inventory class' methods to be "plain old CLR objects," also referred to as Data Transfer Objects (DTOs). Currently, the extracted service code returns Entity Framework entities – this isn't something the extractor changes for you. You may find you also need to update some or all NuGet package references. Once done, and the code compiles, you have a microservice that you can now independently develop and deploy.

Note   Recall we stated earlier in this chapter that no tool automation we know of currently can "get everything right" in terms of re-platforming and refactoring code into external services. You should expect to review the extracted code, and be prepared for a few compile/fix/compile iterations, before the extraction can be considered complete and ready to test.

Turning to the updated application copy, we see the following changes, highlighted in Figure 15-20:

- Updates to the original `HomeController` methods. Instead of directly accessing the `Inventory` class, they now route via methods on a new `InventoryEndpointFactory` class.

- The addition of a new folder, named *EndpointAdapter*. This contains the code that enables the application to call either the original, local, `Inventory` class, or the extracted service.

- The original `Inventory` class is still in the project.

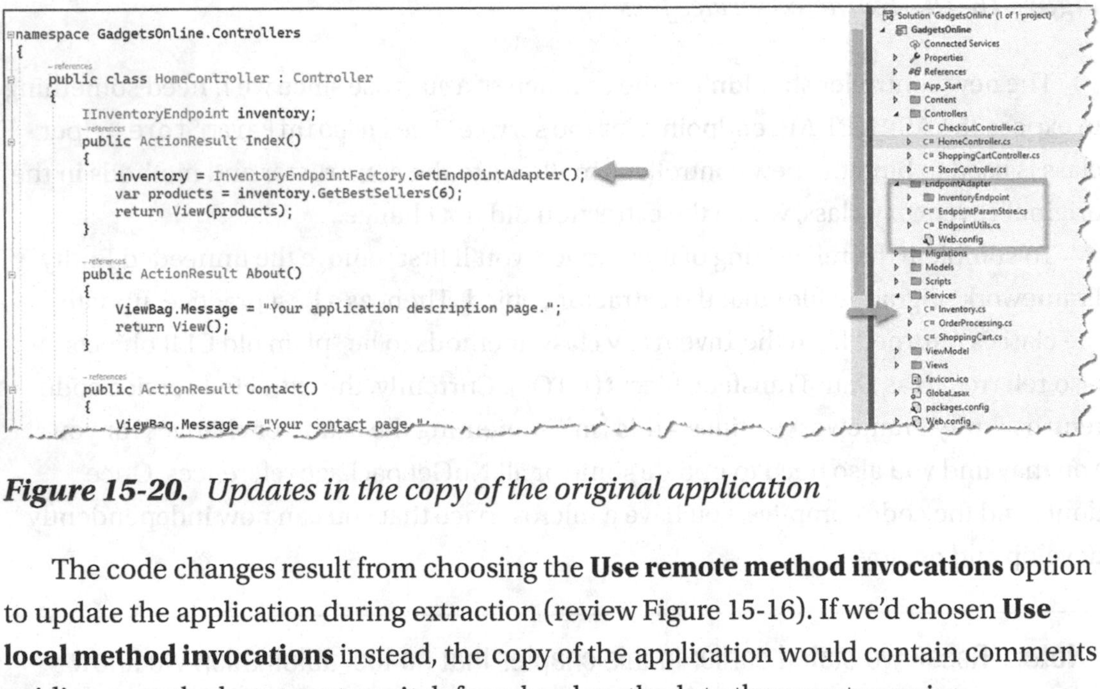

Figure 15-20. *Updates in the copy of the original application*

The code changes result from choosing the **Use remote method invocations** option to update the application during extraction (review Figure 15-16). If we'd chosen **Use local method invocations** instead, the copy of the application would contain comments guiding us to the last steps to switch from local methods to the remote service.

Caution   You extract groups into services one at a time, with the output (extracted service project and updated application copy) placed into a randomly named subfolder beneath the working folder you specified when configuring the extractor. As you continue to extract further groups, a project file and extracted code for the group are placed into a new subfolder using the chosen service name. However, the extractor recreates the copy of the application on each service extraction, containing only the changes applicable to the last-extracted service. Changes applied to the application copy from previous group extractions get deleted. Figure 15-21 shows the application copy after we extracted a second service to represent the shopping cart. Notice that the InventoryEndpoint changes from Figure 15-20 are missing from the application! Therefore, be sure to take a backup of the application copy after each extraction if you plan on extracting several groups. This will enable you to "replay" the individual application changes needed to support each extracted service.

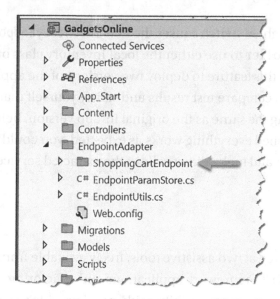

Figure 15-21. *Application copy changes are not cumulative (compare to Figure 15-20)*

Returning to our original extraction to create the InventoryService, a final question remains: How does the application switch between calling the original in-project version of the Inventory class and the newly extracted service version? The answer lies in the Web.config file in the EndpointAdapter folder, shown in Figure 15-22.

```xml
<?xml version="1.0"?>
<configuration>
  <system.web>
  </system.web>
  <appSettings>
    <add key="RemoteRoutingToMicroservice" value="true" />  ⬅
    <!--Set to true on non-prod/test machine to disable HTTPS endpoint cert check-->
    <add key="SkipCertificateValidation" value="false" />
  </appSettings>
  <connectionStrings>
    <add name="EndpointConnectionString" connectionString="" />
  </connectionStrings>
</configuration>
```

Figure 15-22. *Switching between local and extracted versions*

Toggling the highlighted switch causes the new `InventoryEndpointFactory` class used in the `HomeController` to use either the local Inventory class or the extracted service. You might use this feature to deploy two versions of the application, each using a different endpoint, to compare test results and satisfy yourself that the newly extracted microservice is working the same as the original in-app version, before switching over completely. Once satisfied everything works as expected, you could then remove the endpoint adapter code and make direct calls to the extracted service.

Summary

In this chapter, we looked at two assistive tools, freely available from AWS, to help with re-platforming your .NET Framework applications and refactoring .NET Framework and .NET applications to microservices. While neither tool provides a complete solution, and you'll still need to do some additional work, they handle a reasonable amount of the heavy lift involved in these tasks and can get you a fair way down the road toward a more modern, microservices-based application that's using a modern and support version of .NET, and that's deployable to platforms other than Windows. In the next chapter, we'll look at the role events and messaging play in architecting fully decoupled applications in the cloud.

PART V

Building Cloud-Native Applications

CHAPTER 16

Events and Messaging

Everything we have talked about so far is about getting individual applications and systems running in the cloud. In this chapter, we are going to take it one step further and show how to get multiple applications and systems to work together. In the last chapter, we went over using the Microservice Extractor for .NET to break an application into smaller components, but we didn't spend a lot of time talking about why that is important. We will remedy that in this chapter as we go over several modern application design architectures, with the predominant one being event and message-based architecture.

After this mostly theoretical discussion, we will move into practical implementation. We will do this by going over two different AWS services. The first of these services, Amazon Simple Notification Service (SNS), is a managed messaging service that allows you to decouple publishers from subscribers. The second service is Amazon EventBridge, which is a serverless event bus. As we are going over each, we will also review the inclusion of these services into a .NET application so that you can see how it works.

Modern Application Design

The growth in the public cloud and its ability to quickly scale computing resources up and down has made the building of complex systems much easier. Let's start by looking at what the Microservice Extractor for .NET did for us last chapter. Figure 16-1 shows the initial design and then the design after the extractor was run.

© William Penberthy and Steve Roberts 2023
W. Penberthy and S. Roberts, *Pro .NET on Amazon Web Services*,
https://doi.org/10.1007/978-1-4842-8907-5_16

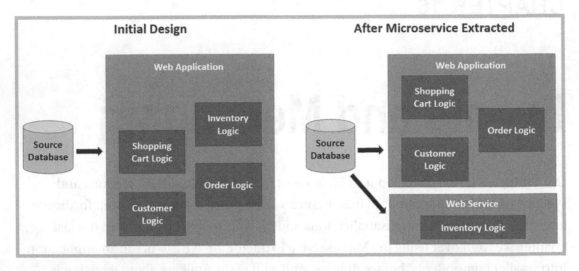

Figure 16-1. *Pre and Post design after running the Microservice Extractor*

Why is this important? Well, consider the likely usage of this system. If you think about a typical e-commerce system, you will see that the inventory logic, the logic that was extracted, is a highly used set of logic. It is needed to work with the catalog pages. It is needed when working with orders, or with the shopping cart. This means that this logic may act as a bottleneck for the entire application. To get around this with the initial design means that you would need to deploy additional web applications to ease the load off and minimize this bottleneck.

Evolving into Microservices

However, the extractor allows us to use a different approach. Instead of horizontally scaling the entire application, scale the set of logic that gets the most use. This allows you to minimize the number of resources necessary to keep the application optimally running. There is another benefit to this approach as you now have an independently managed application, which means that it can have its own development and deployment processes and can be interacted with independently of the rest of the application stack. This means that a fully realized microservices approach could look more like that shown in Figure 16-2.

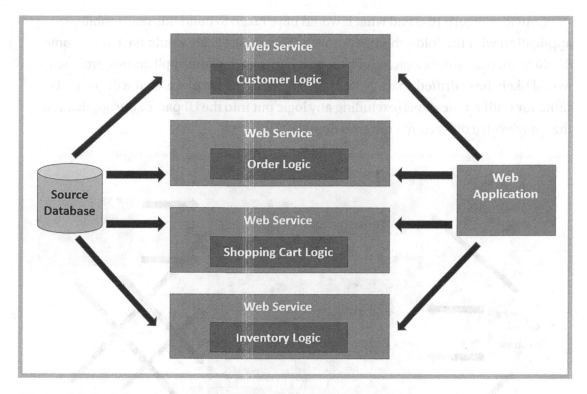

Figure 16-2. *Microservices-based system design*

This approach allows you to scale each web service as needed. You may only need one "Customer" web service running but need multiples of the "Shopping Cart" and "Inventory" running to ensure performance. This approach means you can also do work in one of the services, say, "Shopping Cart," and not have to worry about testing anything within the other services because those won't have been impacted – and you can be positive of that because they are completely different code lines.

This more decoupled approach also allows you to manage business changes more easily.

Note   Tightly coupled systems have dependencies between the systems that affect the flexibility and reusability of the code. Loosely coupled, or decoupled, systems have minimal dependencies between each other and allow for greater code reuse and flexibility.

Consider Figure 16-3 and what it would have taken to build this new mobile application with the "old-school" approach. There most likely would have been some duplication of business logic, which means that as each of the applications evolves, they would likely have drifted apart. Now, that logic is in a single place, so it will always be the same for both applications (excluding any logic put into the UI part of the application that may evolve differently – but who does that?)

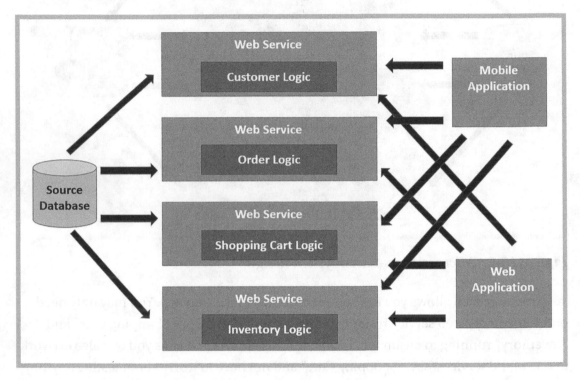

Figure 16-3. *Microservices-based system supporting multiple applications*

One look at Figure 16-3 shows how this system is much more loosely coupled than was the original application. However, there is still a level of coupling within these different subsystems. Let's look at those next and figure out what to do about them.

Deep Dive into Decoupling

Without looking any deeper into the systems than the drawing in Figure 16-3, you should see one aspect of tight coupling that we haven't addressed: the "Source Database." Yes, this shared database indicates that there is still a less than optimal coupling between the different web services. Think about how we used the Extractor to pull out the "Inventory" service so we could scale that independently of the regular application. We did not do the same to the database service that is being accessed by all these web services. So we still have that quandary, only at the database layer rather than at the business logic layer.

The next logical step in decoupling these systems would be to break out the database responsibilities as well, resulting in a design like that shown in Figure 16-4.

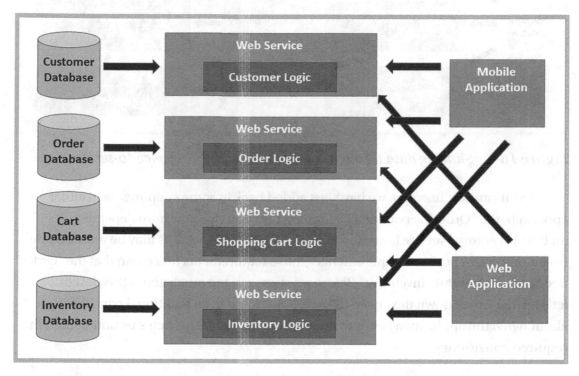

Figure 16-4. *Splitting the database to support decoupled services*

Unfortunately, it is not that easy. Think about what is going on within each of these different services. How useful is a "Shopping Cart" or an "Order" without any knowledge of the "Inventory" being added to the cart, or sold? Sure, those services do not need to know everything about "Inventory," but they need to either interact with the "Inventory" service or go directly into the database to get information. These two options are shown in Figure 16-5.

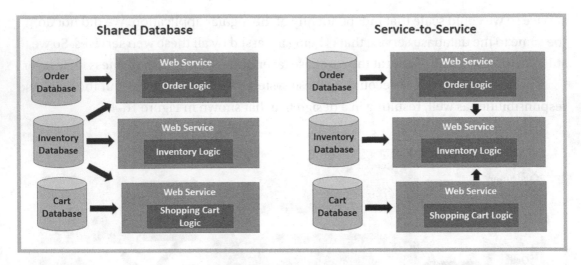

Figure 16-5. *Sharing data through a shared database or service-to-service calls*

As you can see, however, we have just added back in some coupling, as in either approach, the "Order" service and "Shopping Cart" service now have dependencies on the "Inventory" service in some form or another. However, this may be unavoidable based on certain business requirements – those requirements that mean that the "Order" needs to know about "Inventory." Before we stress out too much about this design, let's further break down this "need to know" by adding in an additional consideration about *when* the application needs to know about the data. This helps us understand the required consistency.

Strong Consistency

Strong consistency means that all applications and systems see the same data at the same time. The solutions in Figure 16-5 represent this approach because, regardless of whether you are calling the database directly or through the web service, you are seeing the most current set of the data, and it is available immediately after the data is persisted. There may easily be requirements where that is required. However, there may just as easily be requirements where a slight delay between the "Inventory" service and the "Shopping Cart" service knowing information may be acceptable.

For example, consider how a change in inventory availability (the quantity available for the sale of a product) may affect the shopping cart system differently than the order system. The shopping cart represents items that have been selected as part of an order, so inventory availability is important to it – it needs to know that the items are available before those items can be processed as an order. But when does it need to know that? That's where the business requirements come into play. If the user must know about the change right away, that will likely require some form of strong consistency. If, on the other hand, the inventory availability is only important when the order is placed, then strong consistency is not as necessary. That means there may be a case for eventual consistency.

Eventual Consistency

As the name implies, data will be consistent within the various services eventually – not right away. This difference may be as slight as milliseconds or it can be seconds or even minutes, all depending upon business needs and system design. The smaller the timeframe necessary, the more likely you will need to use strong consistency. However, there are plenty of instances where seconds and even minutes are ok. An order, for example, needs some information about a product so that it has context. This could be as simple as the product name or more complex relationships such as the warehouses and storage locations for the products. But the key factor is that changes in this data are not really required to be available immediately to the order system. Does the order system need to know about a new product added to the inventory list? Probably not – as it is highly unlikely that this new product will be included in an order within milliseconds of becoming active. Being available within seconds should be just fine. Figure 16-6 shows a time-series graph of the differences between strong and eventual consistency.

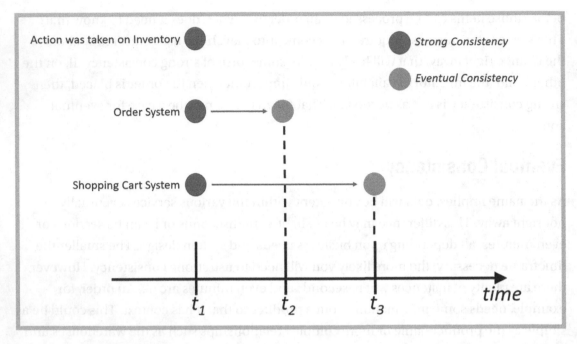

Figure 16-6. *Time series showing the difference between strong and eventual consistency*

What does the concept of eventual consistency mean when we look at Figure 16-5 showing how these three services can have some coupling? It gives us the option for a paradigm shift. Our assumption up to this time is that data is stored in a single source, whether all the data is stored in a big database or whether each service has its own database – such as the Inventory service "owning" the Inventory database that stores all the Inventory information. Thus, any system needing inventory data would have to go through these services/databases in some way.

This means our paradigm understands and accepts the concept of a microservice being responsible for maintaining its own data – that relationship between the inventory service and the inventory database. Our paradigm shift is around the definition of the data that should be persisted in the microservices database. For example, currently, the order system stores only data that describes orders – which is why we need the ability to somehow pull data from the inventory system. However, this other information is obviously critical to the order, so instead of making the call to the inventory system, we instead store that critical inventory-related data in the order system. Think what that would be like.

Oh No! Not Duplicated Data!

Yes, this means some data may be saved in multiple places. And you know what? That's ok. Because it is not going to be all the data, but just those pieces of data that the other systems may care about. That means the databases in a system may look like those shown in Figure 16-7 where there may be overlap in the data being persisted.

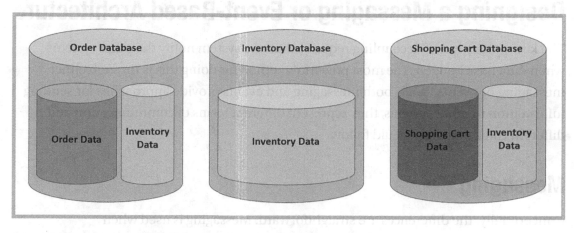

Figure 16-7. *Data duplication between databases*

This data overlap or duplication is important because it eliminates the coupling that we identified when we realized that the inventory data was important to other systems. By including the interesting data in each of the subsystems, we no longer have that coupling, and that means our system will be much more resilient.

If we continued to have that dependency between systems, then an outage in the inventory system means that there would also be an outage in the shopping cart and order systems, because those systems have that dependency upon the inventory system for data. With this data being persisted in multiple places, an outage in the inventory system will NOT cause any outage in those other systems. Instead, those systems will continue to happily plug along without any concern for what is going on over in inventory-land. It can go down, whether intentionally because of a product release or unintentionally, say, by a database failure, and the rest of the systems continue to function. That is the beauty of decoupled systems and why modern system architectural design relies heavily on decoupling business processes.

We have shown the importance of decoupling and how the paradigm shift of allowing some duplication of data can lead to that decoupling. However, we haven't touched on how we would do this. In this next section, we will go into one of the most common ways to drive this level of decoupling and information sharing.

Designing a Messaging or Event-Based Architecture

The key to this level of decoupling requires that one system notify the other systems when data has changed. The most powerful method for doing this is through either messaging or events. While both messaging and events provide approaches for sending information to other systems, they represent different forms of communication and different rules that they should follow.

Messaging

Conceptually, the differences are straightforward. Messaging is used when

- **Transient Data is needed** – This data is only stored until the message consumer has processed the message or it hits a timeout or expiration period.

- **Two-way Communication is desired** – Also known as a request/ reply approach, one system sends a request message, and the receiving system sends a response message in reply to the request.

- **Reliable Targeted Delivery** – Messages are generally targeted to a specific entity. Thus, by design, a message can have one and only one recipient as the message will be removed from the queue once the first system processes it.

Even though messages tend to be targeted, they provide decoupling because there is no requirement that the targeted system is available when the message is sent. If the target system is down, then the message will be stored until the system is back up and accepting messages. Any missed messages will be processed in a first-in, first-out process, and the targeted system will be able to independently catch up on its work without affecting the sending system.

When we look at the decoupling we discussed earlier, it becomes apparent that messaging may not be the best way to support eventual consistency as there is more than one system that could be interested in the data within the message. And by design, messaging isn't a big fan of this happening. So with these limitations, when would messaging make sense?

Note   There are technical design approaches that allow you to send a single message that can be received by multiple targets. This is done through a *recipient list*, where the message sender sends a single message and then there is code around the recipient list that duplicates that message to every target in the list. We won't go into these approaches here.

The key thing to consider about messaging is that it focuses on *assured delivery* and *once and once-only* processing. This provides insight into the types of operations best supported by messaging. An example may be the web application submitting an order. Think of the chaos if this order was received and processed by some services but not the order service. Instead, this submission should be a message targeted at the order service. Sure, in many instances, we are handling this as an HTTP request (note the similarities between a message and the HTTP request), but that may not always be the best approach. Instead, our ordering system sends a message that is assured of delivery to a single target.

Events

Events, on the other hand, are traditionally used to represent "something that happened" – an action performed by the service that some other systems may find interesting. Events are for when you need:

- **Scalable consumption** – Multiple systems may be interested in the content within a single event.

- **History** – The history of the "thing that happened" is useful. Generally, the database will provide the current state of information. The event history provides insight into when and what caused changes to that data. This can be very valuable insight.

- **Immutable data** – Since an event represents "something that already happened," the data contained in an event is immutable – that data cannot be changed. This allows for very accurate tracing of changes, including the ability to recreate database changes.

Events are generally designed to be sent by a system, with that system having no concern about whether other systems receive the event or act upon it. The sender fires the event and then forgets about it.

When you consider the decoupled design that we worked through earlier, it becomes quickly obvious that events are the best approach to provide any changed inventory data to the other systems. Let's jump right into Amazon Simple Notification Service (SNS) and talk more about events within our application using SNS as our guide.

Amazon Simple Notification Service (SNS)

SNS, as you can probably guess from its name, is a straightforward service that uses pub/sub messaging to deliver messages. Pub/Sub, or Publish/Subscribe, messaging is an asynchronous communication method. This model includes the *publisher* who sends the data, a *subscriber* that receives the data, and the *message broker* that handles the coordination between the publisher and subscriber. In this case, Amazon SNS is the message broker because it handles the message transference from publisher to subscriber.

Note   The language used when looking at *events* and *messaging* as we did previously can be confusing. *Messaging* is the pattern we discussed previously. *Messages* are the data being sent and are part of both events and messaging. The term "message" is considered interchangeable with notification or event – even to the point where you will see articles about the messaging pattern that refer to the messages as events.

The main responsibility of the message broker is to determine which subscribers should be sent what messages. It does this using a *topic*. A topic can be thought of as a category that describes the data contained within the message. These topics are defined based on your business. There will be times that a broad approach is best, so perhaps topics for "Order" and "Inventory" where all messages for each topic are sent. Thus, the order topic could include messages for "Order Placed" and "Order Shipped," and the subscribers will get all of those messages. There may be other times where a very narrow focus is more appropriate, in which case you may have an "Order Placed" topic and an "Order Shipped" topic where systems can subscribe to them independently. Both approaches have their strength and weaknesses.

Tip   Typically, we use past tense for event names because the event has already happened.

When you look at the concept of messaging, where one message has one recipient, the advantage that a service like SNS offers is the ability to distribute a single message to multiple recipients as shown in Figure 16-8, which is one of the key requisites of event-based architecture.

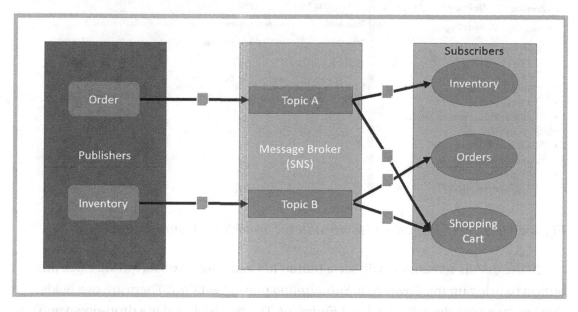

Figure 16-8. *Pub/Sub pattern using Amazon SNS*

Now that we have established that SNS can be effectively used when building in an event-based architecture, let's go do just that!

Using AWS Toolkit for Visual Studio

If you're a Visual Studio user, you can do a lot of the configuration and management through the toolkit. Going into Visual Studio and examining the AWS Explorer will show that one of the options is Amazon SNS. At this point, you will not be able to expand the service in the tree control because you have not yet started to configure it. Right-clicking on the service will bring up a menu with three options: *Create topic*, *View subscriptions*, and *Refresh*. Let's get started by creating our first topic. Click on the **Create topic** link and create a topic. We created a topic named "ProDotNetOnAWS" – it seems to be a trend with us. Once you save the topic, you will see it show up in the AWS Explorer.

Right-click on the newly created topic and select to **View topic**. This will add the topic details screen into the main window as shown in Figure 16-9.

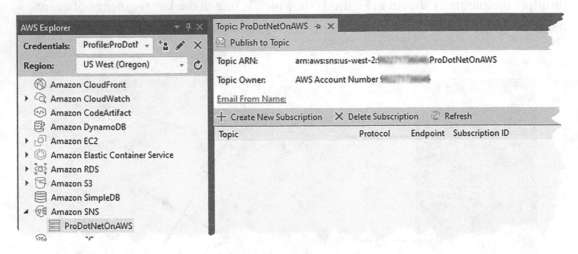

Figure 16-9. *SNS topic details screen in the Toolkit for Visual Studio*

In the details screen, you will see a button to **Create New Subscription**. Click this button to bring up the *Create New Subscription* pop-up window. There are two fields that you can complete: *Protocol* and *Endpoint*. The protocol field is a drop-down and contains various choices.

HTTP or HTTPS Protocol Subscription

The first two of these choices are **HTTP** and **HTTPS**. Choosing one of these protocols will result in SNS making an HTTP (or HTTPS) POST to the configured endpoint. This POST will result in a JSON document with the following name-value pairs:

- **Message** – The content of the message that was published to the topic.

- **MessageId** – A universally unique identifier for each message that was published.

- **Signature** – Base64-encoded signature of the Message, MessageId, Subject, Type, Timestamp, and TopicArn values.

- **SignatureVersion** – Version of the signature used.

- **SigningCertUrl** – The URL of the certificate that was used to sign the message.

- **Subject** – The optional subject parameter used when the notification was published to a topic. In those examples where the topic is broadly based, the subject can be used to narrow down the subscriber audience.

- **Timestamp** – The time (GMT) when the notification was published.

- **TopicARN** – The Amazon Resource Name (ARN) for the topic.

- **Type** – The type of message being sent. For an SNS message, this type is *Notification*.

At a minimum, your subscribing system will care about the message, as this message contains the information that was provided by the publisher. One of the biggest advantages of using an HTTP or HTTPS protocol subscription is that the system that is subscribed does not have to do anything other than accept the message that is submitted. There is no special library to consume, no special interactions that must happen, just an endpoint that accepts requests.

Some considerations as you think about using SNS to manage your event notifications. There are several different ways to manage the receipt of these notifications. The first is to create a single endpoint for each topic to which you subscribe. This makes each endpoint very discrete and only responsible for handling one thing, usually considered a plus in the programming world. However, this means that the subscribing service has some limitations as there are now external dependencies on multiple endpoints. Changing an endpoint URL, for example, will now require coordination across multiple systems.

On the other hand, there is another approach where you create a single endpoint that acts as the recipient of messages across multiple topics. The code within the endpoint identifies the message and then forwards it through the appropriate process. This approach abstracts away any work within the system, as all of those changes happen below this single broadly bound endpoint. We have seen both of those approaches working successfully; it really comes down to your own business needs and how you see your systems evolving as you move forward.

Other Protocol Subscriptions

There are other protocol subscriptions that are available in the toolkit. The next two in the list are *Email and Email (JSON)*. Notifications sent under this protocol are sent to the email address that is entered as the endpoint value. This email is sent in two ways, where the Message field of the notification becomes the body of the email or where the email body is a JSON object very similar to that used when working with the HTTP/HTTPS protocols. There are some business-to-business needs for this, such as sending a confirmation to a third party upon processing an order; but you will generally find any discussion of these two protocols under Application-to-Person (A2P) in the documentation and examples.

The next protocol that is available in the toolkit is *Amazon SQS*. Amazon Simple Queue Service (SQS) is a queue service that follows the messaging pattern that we discussed earlier where one message has one recipient and one recipient only.

The last protocol available in the toolkit is *Lambda*. Choosing this protocol means that a specified Lambda function will be called with the message payload being set as an input parameter. This option makes a great deal of sense if you are building a system based on serverless functions. Of course, you can also use HTTP/HTTPS protocol and make the call to the endpoint that surfaces the Lambda method; but using this direct approach will remove much of that intermediate processing.

Choosing either the SQS or Lambda protocols will activate the *Add permission for SNS topic to send messages to AWS resources* check box as shown in Figure 16-10.

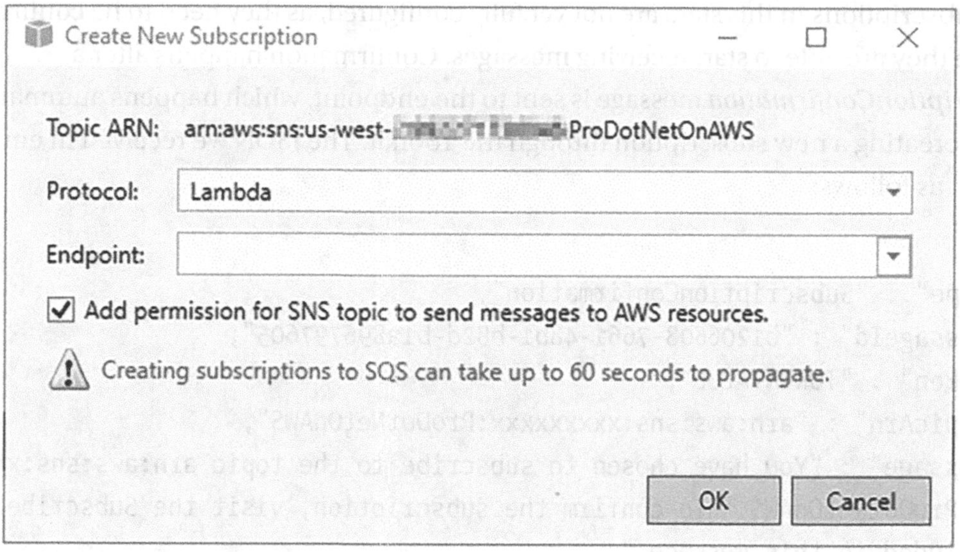

Figure 16-10. *Create New Subscription window in the Toolkit for Visual Studio*

Checking this box will create the necessary permissions allowing the topic to interact with AWS resources. This is not necessary if you are using HTTP/HTTPS or Email.

For the sake of this walkthrough, we used an approach that is ridiculous for enterprise systems; we selected the Email (JSON) protocol. Why? So we could easily show you the next few steps in a way that you could easily duplicate. This is important because all you can do in the Toolkit is to create the topic and the subscription. However, as shown in Figure 16-11, this leaves the subscription in a *PendingConfirmation* state.

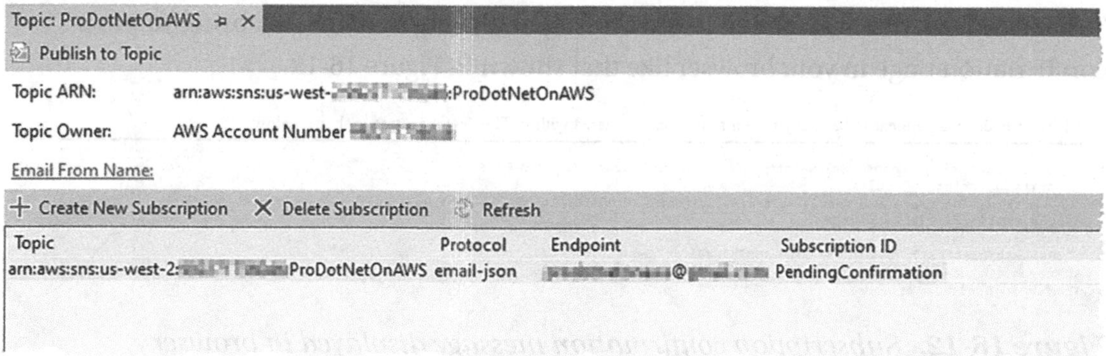

Figure 16-11. *Newly created SNS topic subscription in Toolkit for Visual Studio*

Subscriptions in this state are not yet fully configured, as they need to be confirmed before they are able to start receiving messages. Confirmation happens after a *SubscriptionConfirmation* message is sent to the endpoint, which happens automatically when creating a new subscription through the Toolkit. The JSON we received in email is shown as follows:

```
{
  "Type" : "SubscriptionConfirmation",
  "MessageId" : "b1206608-7661-48b1-b82d-b1a896797605",
  "Token" : "TOKENVALUE",
  "TopicArn" : "arn:aws:sns:xxxxxxxxx:ProDotNetOnAWS",
  "Message" : "You have chosen to subscribe to the topic arn:aws:sns:xxxxx
  xx:ProDotNetOnAWS.\nTo confirm the subscription, visit the SubscribeURL
  included in this message.",
  "SubscribeURL" : "https://sns.us-west-2.amazonaws.com/?Action=Confirm
  Subscription&TopicArn=xxxxxxxx",
  "Timestamp" : "2022-08-20T19:18:27.576Z",
  "SignatureVersion" : "1",
  "Signature" : "xxxxxxxxxxxxx==",
  "SigningCertURL" : "https://sns.us-west-2.amazonaws.com/Simple
  NotificationService-56e67fcb41f6fec09b0196692625d385.pem"
}
```

The *Message* indicates the action that needs to be taken – you need to visit the **SubscribeURL** that is included in the message. Clicking that link will bring you to a confirmation page in your browser like that shown in Figure 16-12.

This XML file does not appear to have any style information associated with it. The document tree is shown below.

```
▼<ConfirmSubscriptionResponse xmlns="http://sns.amazonaws.com/doc/2010-03-31/">
  ▼<ConfirmSubscriptionResult>
      <SubscriptionArn>arn:aws:sns:us-west-2:█████████:ProDotNetOnAWS:2434c4c5-987d-4b37-aa0b-7c1a9e60a456</SubscriptionArn>
  </ConfirmSubscriptionResult>
  ▼<ResponseMetadata>
      <RequestId>e8ff537c-8cad-5fde-9fac-0807b78e0efc</RequestId>
  </ResponseMetadata>
</ConfirmSubscriptionResponse>
```

Figure 16-12. *Subscription confirmation message displayed in browser*

Refreshing the topic in the Toolkit will show you that the PendingConfirmation message is gone and has been replaced with a real *Subscription ID*.

Using the Console

The process for using the console is very similar to the process we just walked through in the Toolkit. You can get to the service by searching in the console for Amazon SNS or by going into the *Application Integration* group under the services menu. Once there, select **Create topic**. At this point, you will start to see some differences in the experiences.

The first is that you have a choice on the topic *Type*, as shown in Figure 16-13. You can select from *FIFO (first-in, first-out)* and *Standard*. FIFO is selected by default. However, selecting FIFO means that the service will follow the messaging architectural approach that we went over earlier where there is exactly once message delivery and message ordering is strictly preserved. The Standard type, on the other hand, supports "at least once message delivery," which means that it supports multiple subscriptions.

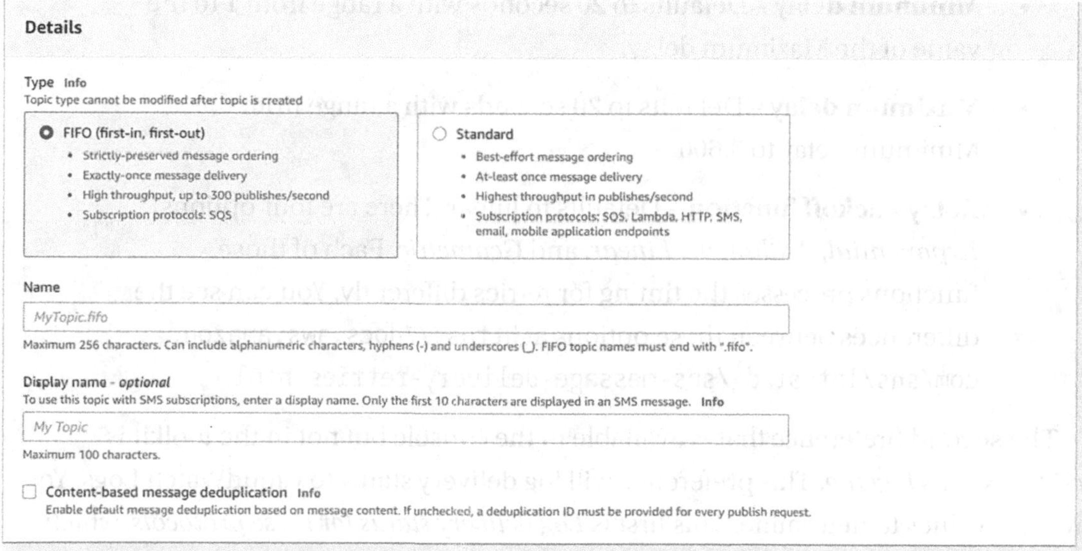

Figure 16-13. Creating an SNS topic in the AWS console

Figure 16-13 also displays a check box labeled *Content-based message deduplication*. This selection is only available when *FIFO* type is selected. When selected, the message being sent is assumed to be unique, and SNS will not provide a unique deduplication value. Otherwise, SNS will add a unique value to each message that it will use to determine whether a particular message has been delivered.

Another difference between creating a topic in the console vs. in the toolkit is that you can optionally set preferences around message encryption, access policy, delivery status logging, delivery retry policy (HTTP/S), and, of course, tags. Let's look in more detail at two of those preferences. The first of these is the *Delivery retry policy*. This allows you to set retry rules for how SNS will retry sending failed deliveries to HTTP/S endpoints. These are the only endpoints that support retry. You can manage the following values:

- **Number of retries** – Defaults to 3 but can be any value between 1 and 100.

- **Retries without delay** – Defaults to 0 and represents how many of those retries should happen before the system waits for a retry.

- **Minimum delay** – Defaults to 20 seconds with a range from 1 to the value of the Maximum delay.

- **Maximum delay** – Defaults to 20 seconds with a range from the Minimum delay to 3,600.

- **Retry backoff function** – Defaults to linear. There are four options: *Exponential*, *Arithmetic*, *Linear*, and *Geometric*. Each of those functions processes the timing for retries differently. You can see the differences between these options at `https://docs.aws.amazon.com/sns/latest/dg/sns-message-delivery-retries.html`.

The second preference that is available in the console but not in the toolkit is *Delivery status logging*. This preference will log delivery status to CloudWatch Logs. You have two values to determine. This first is *Log delivery status for these protocols,* which presents a series of check boxes for *AWS Lambda, Amazon SQS, HTTP/S, Platform application endpoint,* and *Amazon Kinesis Data Firehose.* These last two options are a preview of the next big difference between working through the toolkit or through the console.

Additional Subscriptions in the Console

Once you have finished creating the topic, you can then create a subscription. There are several protocols available for use in the console that are not available in the toolkit. These include the following:

- **Amazon Kinesis Data Firehose** – Configure this subscription to go to Kinesis Data Firehose. From there, you can send notifications to Amazon S3, Amazon Redshift, Amazon OpenSearch Service, and third-party service providers such as Datadog, New Relic, MongoDB, and Splunk.

- **Platform-application endpoint** – This protocol sends the message to an application on a mobile device. Push notification messages sent to a mobile endpoint can appear in the mobile app as message alerts, badge updates, or even sound alerts. Go to `https://docs.aws.amazon.com/sns/latest/dg/sns-mobile-application-as-subscriber.html` for more information on configuring your SNS topic to deliver to a mobile device.

- **SMS** – This protocol delivers text messages, or SMS messages, to SMS-enabled devices. Amazon SNS supports SMS messaging in several regions, and you can send messages to more than 200 countries and regions. An interesting aspect of SMS is that your account starts in an SMS sandbox or nonproduction environment with a set of limits. Once you are convinced that everything is correct, you must create a case with AWS support to move your account out of the sandbox and actually start sending messages to nonlimited numbers.

Now that we have configured our SNS topic and subscription, let's next look at sending a message.

.NET and Amazon SNS

The first step to interacting with SNS from within your .NET application is to install the appropriate NuGet package, **AWSSDK.SimpleNotificationService**. This will also install **AWSSDK.Core**. Once you have the NuGet package, you can access the appropriate APIs by adding several using statements:

```
using Amazon.SimpleNotificationService;
using Amazon.SimpleNotificationService.Model;
```

These namespaces provide access to the `AmazonSimpleNotificationServiceClient` class that manages the interaction with the SNS service as well as the models that are represented in the client methods. There are a lot of different types of interactions that you can support with this client. A list of the more commonly used methods is displayed as follows:

- `PublishAsync` – Send a message to a specific topic for processing by SNS.

- `PublishBatchAsync` – Send multiple messages to a specific topic for processing by SNS.

- `Subscribe` – Subscribe a new endpoint to a topic.

- `Unsubscribe` – Remove an endpoint's subscription to a topic.

These four methods allow you to add and remove subscriptions as well as publish messages. There are dozens of other methods available from that client, including the ability to manage topics and confirm subscriptions.

The following code is a complete console application that sends a message to a specific topic:

```
static void Main(string[] args)
{
    string topicArn = "Arn for the topic to publish";
    string messageText = "Message from ProDotNetOnAWS_SNS";

    var client = new AmazonSimpleNotificationServiceClient();

    var request = new PublishRequest
    {
        TopicArn = topicArn,
        Message = messageText,
        Subject = Guid.NewGuid().ToString()
    };

    var response = client.PublishAsync(request).Result;

    Console.WriteLine(
        $"Published message ID: {response.MessageId}");

    Console.ReadLine();
}
```

As you can see, the topic needs to be described with the *Arn* for the topic rather than simply the topic name. Publishing a message entails the instantiation of the client and then defining a `PublishRequest` object. This object contains all of the fields that we are intending to send to the recipient, which in our case is simply the subject and message. Running the application presents a console as shown in Figure 16-14.

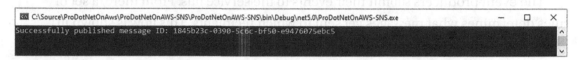

Figure 16-14. *Console application that sent message through SNS*

The message that was processed can be seen in Figure 16-15. Note the *MessageId* values are the same as in Figure 16-14.

AWS Notifications <no-reply@sns.amazonaws.com>   3:35 PM (2 minutes ago)   ☆   ↩   ⋮
to prodotnetonaws ▾

```
{
  "Type" : "Notification",
  "MessageId" : "1845b23c-0390-5c6c-bf50-e9476075ebc5",
  "TopicArn" : "arn:aws:sns:us-west-2:          ProDotNetOnAWS",
  "Subject" : "c84891ea-4e48-4438-8ef9-1bab97969f55",
  "Message" : "Message from ProDotNetOnAWS_SNS",
  "Timestamp" : "2022-08-20T22:35:17.522Z",
  "SignatureVersion" : "1",
  "Signature" : "2X/NIR4RAzzw4YrJZkJh+Tfxpq8/0HrjxLbIxAkRr3tCyRB7bUb1b1xkTKWXNS+OujKXe0xIQoCWIENDiEWrv/OMp
T1cQEU/lRiIe4J0yadVq9y6nLzyNCWcEcEdFU12pY2kaAk+ObXndz/31c7zARhxyWF0FPNuGtwQG/t8BGCa2cpbtbF
vxhYCXpfM4EZKFWhLhAInnO86jIhiDXWnCr8iLZ0r6Qh0aVhEeEnCqhuQKmMV7i7qrD1REiFjyMGuxXKainjdUN9Qy
nTTmCEKsXeIZHMCs9F/wek/Ik7vJZ2CDHsBFJh+1uqNSp8AKf133i4ZxtxOZJdwiKuJc7MdjQ==",
  "SigningCertURL" : "https://sns.us-west-2.amazonaws.com/SimpleNotificationService-56e67fcb41f6fec09b019669262
5d385.pem",
  "UnsubscribeURL" : "https://sns.us-west-2.amazonaws.com/?Action=Unsubscribe&SubscriptionArn=arn:aws:sns:us-west-
2:          ProDotNetOnAWS:2434c4c5-987d-4b37-aa0b-7c1a9e60a456"
}
```

Figure 16-15. *Message sent through console application*

We have only touched on the capabilities of Amazon SNS and its capacity to help implement event-driven architecture. However, there is another AWS service that is even more powerful: Amazon EventBridge. Let's look at that now.

Amazon EventBridge

As briefly mentioned earlier, Amazon EventBridge is a serverless event bus service designed to deliver data from applications and services to a variety of targets. It uses a different methodology than does SNS to distribute events.

The event producers submit their events to the service bus. From there, a set of rules determines what messages get sent to which recipients. This flow is shown in Figure 16-16.

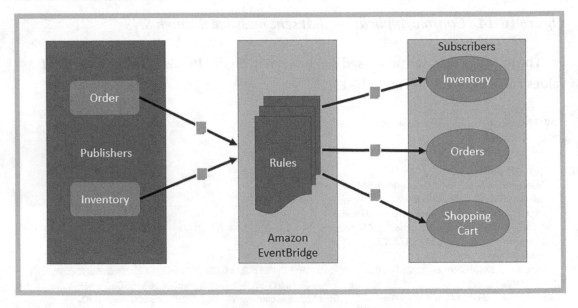

Figure 16-16.   *Message flow through Amazon EventBridge*

The key difference between SNS and EventBridge is that in SNS, you send your message to a topic, so the sender makes some decisions about where the message is going. These topics can be very broadly defined and domain focused so that any application interested in order-related messages subscribes to the order topic, but this still obligates the sender to have some knowledge about the messing system.

In EventBridge, you simply toss messages into the bus, and the rules sort them to the appropriate destination. Thus, unlike SNS where the messages themselves don't really matter as much as the topic, in EventBridge, you can't define rules without an understanding of the message on which you want to apply rules. With that in mind, we'll go in a bit of a different order now and go into using EventBridge within a .NET application; that way, we'll have a definition of the message on which we want to apply rules.

.NET and Amazon EventBridge

The first step to interacting with EventBridge from within your .NET application is to install the appropriate NuGet package: **AWSSDK.EventBridge**. This will also install **AWSSDK.Core**. Once you have the NuGet package, you can access the appropriate APIs by adding several using statements:

```
using Amazon.EventBridge;
using Amazon.EventBridge.Model;
```

You will also need to ensure that you have added:

```
using System.Collections.Generic;
using System.Text.Json;
```

These namespaces provide access to the AmazonEventBridgeClient class that manages the interaction with the EventBridge service as well as the models that are represented in the client methods. As with SNS, you can manage all aspects of creating the various EventBridge parts such as service buses, rules, and endpoints. You can also use the client to push events to the bus, which is what we do now. Let's first look at the complete code, and then we will walk through the various sections.

```
static void Main(string[] args)
{
    var client = new AmazonEventBridgeClient();

    var order = new Order();

    var message = new PutEventsRequestEntry
    {
        Detail = JsonSerializer.Serialize(order),
        DetailType = "CreateOrder",
        EventBusName = "default",
        Source = "ProDotNetOnAWS"
    };

    var putRequest = new PutEventsRequest
    {
        Entries = new List<PutEventsRequestEntry> { message }
    };
```

```
    var response = client.PutEventsAsync(putRequest).Result;
    Console.WriteLine(
        $"Request processed with ID of
                    #{response.ResponseMetadata.RequestId}");
    Console.ReadLine();
}
```

The first thing we are doing in the code is newing up our `AmazonEventBridgeClient` so that we can use the `PutEventsAsync` method, which is the method used to send the event to EventBridge. That method expects a `PutEventsRequest` object that has a field `Entries` that are a list of `PutEventsRequestEntry` objects. There should be a `PutEventsRequestEntry` object for every event that you want to be processed by EventBridge, so a single push to EventBridge can include multiple events.

Tip   One model of event-based architecture is to use multiple small messages that imply different items of interest. Processing an order, for example, may result in a message regarding the order itself as well as messages regarding each of the products included in the order so that the inventory count can be managed correctly. This means the Product domain doesn't listen for order messages; they only pay attention to product messages. Each of these approaches has its own advantages and disadvantages.

The `PutEventsRequestEntry` contains the information to be sent. It has the following properties:

- **Detail** – A valid JSON object that cannot be more than 100 levels deep.

- **DetailType** – A string that provides information about the kind of detail contained within the event.

- **EventBusName** – A string that determines the appropriate event bus to use. If absent, the event will be processed by the default bus.

- **Resources** – A `List<string>` that contains ARNs which the event primarily concerns. May be empty.

- **Source** – A string that defines the source of the event.

- **Time** – A string that sets the timestamp of the event. If not provided, EventBridge will use the timestamp of when the Put call was processed.

In our code, we only set the `Detail`, `DetailType`, `EventBusName`, and `Source`.

This code is set up in a console, so running the application gives results similar to that shown in Figure 16-17.

Figure 16-17. *Console application that sent a message through EventBridge*

We then used Progress Telerik Fiddler to view the request so we can see the message that was sent. The JSON from this message is as follows:

```
{
    "Entries":
    [
        {
            "Detail": "{\"Id\":0,
                        \"OrderDate\":
                                \"0001-01-01T00:00:00\",
                        \"CustomerId\":0,
                        \"OrderDetails\":[]}",
            "DetailType": "CreateOrder",
            "EventBusName": "default",
            "Source": "ProDotNetOnAWS"
        }
    ]
}
```

Now that we have the message that we want to process in EventBridge, the next step is to set up EventBridge. At a high level, configuring EventBridge in the AWS console is simple.

Configuring EventBridge in the Console

You can find Amazon EventBridge by searching in the console or by going into the *Application Integration* group. Your first step is to decide whether you wish to use your account's default event bus or create a new one. Creating a custom event bus is simple as all you need to provide is a name, but we will use the default event bus.

Before going any further, you should translate the event that you sent to the event that EventBridge will be processing. You do this by going into **Event buses** and selecting the **default** event bus. This will bring you to the *Event bus detail* page. On the upper right, you will see a button **Send events**. Clicking this button will bring you to the Send events page where you can configure an event. Using the values from the JSON we looked at earlier, fill out the values as shown in Figure 16-18

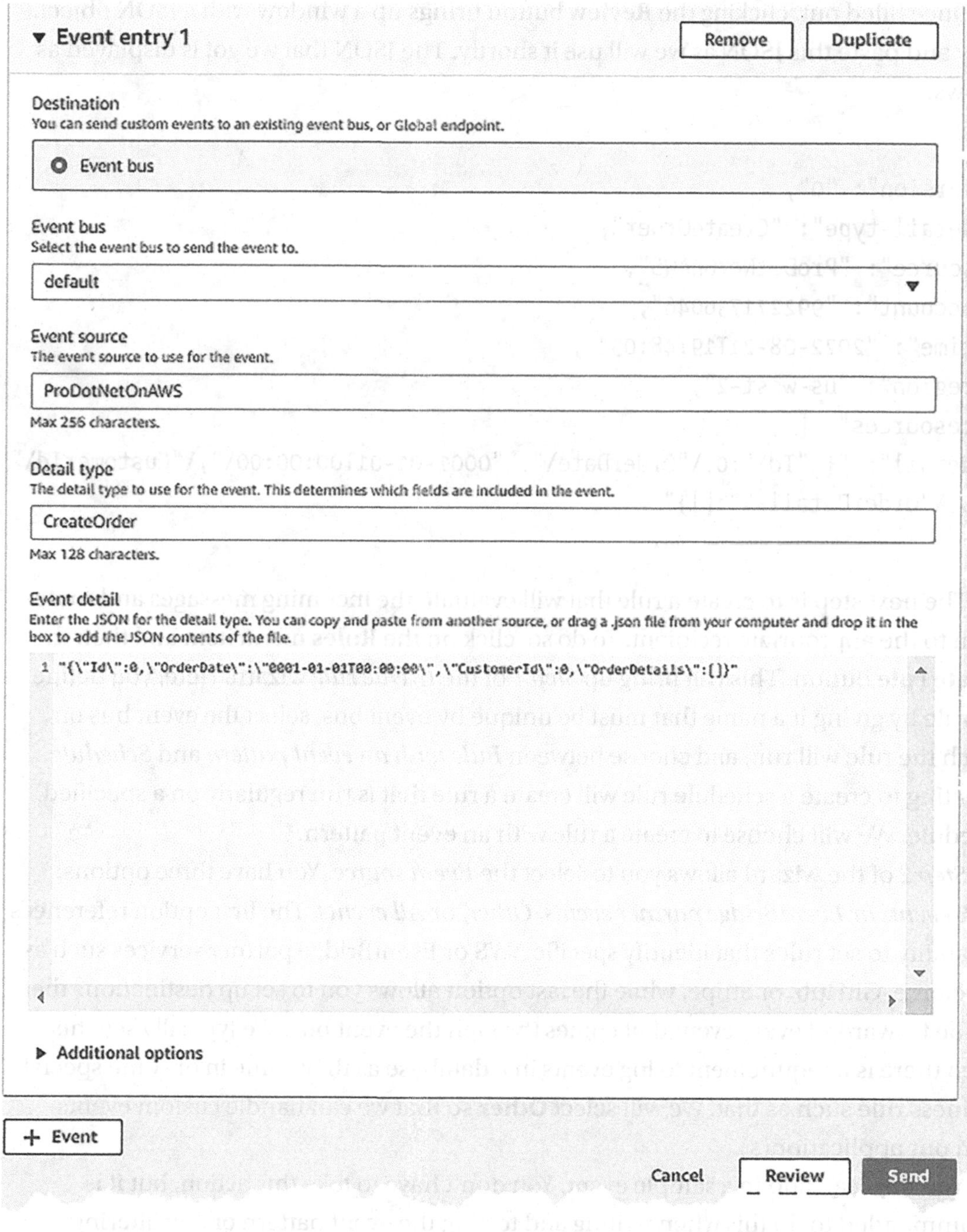

▼ Event entry 1 [Remove] [Duplicate]

Destination
You can send custom events to an existing event bus, or Global endpoint.

⦿ Event bus

Event bus
Select the event bus to send the event to.

default ▼

Event source
The event source to use for the event.

ProDotNetOnAWS

Max 256 characters.

Detail type
The detail type to use for the event. This determines which fields are included in the event.

CreateOrder

Max 128 characters.

Event detail
Enter the JSON for the detail type. You can copy and paste from another source, or drag a .json file from your computer and drop it in the box to add the JSON contents of the file.

```
1  "{\"Id\":0,\"OrderDate\":\"0001-01-01T00:00:00\",\"CustomerId\":0,\"OrderDetails\":[]}"
```

▶ Additional options

[+ Event]

[Cancel]   [Review]   [Send]

Figure 16-18. *Getting the "translated" event for EventBridge*

Once filled out, clicking the **Review** button brings up a window with a JSON object. Copy and paste this JSON as we will use it shortly. The JSON that we got is displayed as follows:

```
{
  "version": "0",
  "detail-type": "CreateOrder",
  "source": "ProDotNetOnAWS",
  "account": "992271736046",
  "time": "2022-08-21T19:48:09Z",
  "region": "us-west-2",
  "resources": [],
  "detail": "{\"Id\":0,\"OrderDate\":\"0001-01-01T00:00:00\",\"CustomerId\"
  :0,\"OrderDetails\":[]}"
}
```

The next step is to create a rule that will evaluate the incoming messages and route them to the appropriate recipient. To do so, click on the **Rules** menu item and then the **Create rule** button. This will bring up *Step 1* of the *Create rule* wizard. Here, you define the rule by giving it a name that must be unique by event bus, select the event bus on which the rule will run, and choose between *Rule with an event pattern* and *Schedule*. Selecting to create a schedule rule will create a rule that is run regularly on a specified schedule. We will choose to create a rule with an event pattern.

Step 2 of the wizard allows you to select the *Event source*. You have three options: *AWS events or EventBridge partner events*, *Other*, or *All events*. The first option references the ability to set rules that identify specific AWS or EventBridge partner services such as Salesforce, GitHub, or Stripe, while the last option allows you to set up destinations that will be forwarded every event that comes through the event bus. We typically see this when there is a requirement to log events in a database as they come in or some special business rule such as that. We will select **Other** so that we can handle custom events from our application(s).

You next can add in a sample event. You don't have to take this action, but it is recommended to do this when writing and testing the event pattern or any filtering criteria. Since we have a sample message, we will select **Enter my own** and paste the sample event into the box as shown in Figure 16-19.

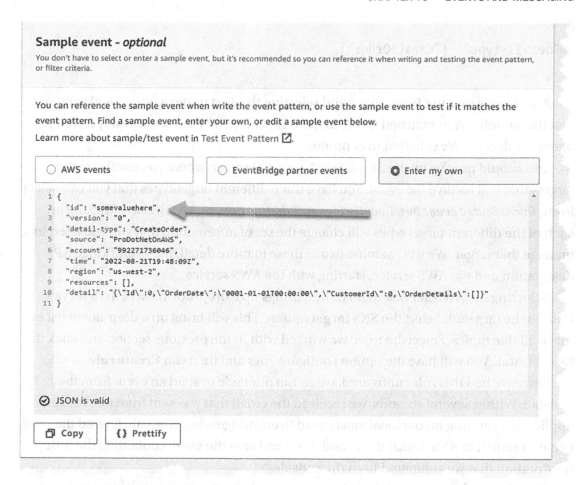

Figure 16-19. *Adding a sample event when configuring EventBridge*

Be warned, however, if you just paste the event directly into the sample event, it will not work as the matching algorithms will reject it as invalid without an id added into the JSON as highlighted by the golden arrow in Figure 16-19.

Once you have your sample event input, the next step is to create the *Event pattern* that will determine where this message should be sent. Since we are using a custom event, select the **Custom patterns (JSON editor)** option. This will bring a JSON editor window in which you enter your rule. There is a drop-down of helper functions that will help you put the proper syntax into the window, but, of course, there is no option for simple matching – you have to know what that syntax is already. Fortunately, it is identical to the rule itself, so adding an event pattern that will select every event that has a detail type of "Create Order" is

```
{
  "detail-type": ["CreateOrder"]
}
```

Adding this into the JSON editor and selecting the **Test pattern** button will validate that the sample event matched the event pattern. Once you have successfully tested your pattern, select the **Next** button to continue.

You should now be on the *Step 3 Select Target(s)* screen where you configure the targets that will receive the event. You have three different target types that you can select from: *EventBridge event bus, EventBridge API destination*, or *AWS service*. Clicking on each of the different target types will change the set of information that you will need to manage that target. We will examine two of these in more detail, the EventBridge API destination and the AWS service, starting with the AWS service.

Selecting the **AWS service** radio button brings up a drop-down list of AWS services that can be targeted. Select the **SNS target** option. This will bring up a drop-down list of the available topics. Select the topic we worked with in the previous section and click the **Next** button. You will have the option configure *Tags* and then can **Create rule**.

Once we had this rule configured, we re-ran our code to send an event from the console. Within several seconds, we received the email that was sent from our console application running on our local machine to EventBridge where the rule filtered the event to send it to SNS, which then configured and sent the email containing the order information that we submitted from the console.

Now that we have verified the rule the fun way, let's go back into it and make it more realistic. You can edit the targets for a rule by going into *Rules* from the Amazon EventBridge console and selecting the rule that you want to edit. This will bring up the details page. Click on the **Targets** tab and then click the **Edit** button. This will bring you back to the *Step 3 Select Target(s)* screen. From here, you can choose to add an additional target (you can have up to five targets for each rule) or replace the target that pointed to the SNS service. We chose to replace our existing target.

Since we are looking at using EventBridge to communicate between various microservices in our application, we will configure the target to go to a custom endpoint. To do so requires that we choose a *Target type* of **EventBridge API destination**. We will then choose to **Create a new API destination**, which will provide all of the destination fields that we need to configure. These fields are listed as follows:

- **Name** – The name of the API destination. Destinations can be reused in different rules, so make sure the name is clear.

- **Description** – Optional value describing the destination.

- **API destination endpoint** – The URL to the endpoint that will receive the event.

- **HTTP *method*** – The HTTP method used to send the event, can be any of the HTTP methods.

- **Invocation rate limit per second** – An optional value, defaulted to 300, of the number of invocations per second. Smaller values mean that events may not be delivered.

The next section to configure is the Connection. The connection contains information about authorization as every API request must have some kind of security method enabled. Connections can be reused as well, and there are three different Authorization types supported. These types are as follows:

- **Basic (Username/Password)** – Where a username and password combination is entered into the connection definition

- **OAuth Client Credentials** – Where you enter the OAuth configuration information such as Authorization endpoint, Client ID, and Client secret

- **API Key** – Which adds up to five key/value pairs in the header

Once you have configured your authorization protocol, you can select the **Next** button to once again complete moving through the EventBridge rules creation UI.

There are two approaches that are commonly used when creating the rule to target API endpoint mapping. The first is a single endpoint per type of expected message. This means that, for example, if you were expecting "OrderCreated" and "OrderUpdated" messages, then you would have created two separate endpoints, one to handle each message. The second approach is to create a generic endpoint for your service to which all inbound EventBridge messages are sent and then the code within the service evaluates each message and manages it from there.

Modern Event Infrastructure Creation

So far, we have managed all the event management through the console, creating topics and subscriptions in SNS and rules, connections, and targets in EventBridge. However, taking this approach in the real world will be extremely painful. Instead, modern applications are best served by modern methods of creating services, methods that can be run on their own without any human intervention. There are two approaches that we want to touch on now: Infrastructure as Code (IaC) and in-application code.

Infrastructure as Code

Using AWS CloudFormation or AWS Cloud Development Kit within the build and release process allows developers to manage the growth of their event infrastructure as their usage of events grows. Typically, you would see the work breakdown as being the teams building the systems sending events are responsible for creating the infrastructure required for sending and the teams for the systems listening for events need to manage the creation of that infrastructure. Thus, if you are planning on using SNS, then the sending system would have the responsibility for adding the applicable topic(s) while the receiving system would be responsible for adding the appropriate subscription(s) to the topics in which they are interested.

Using IaC to build out your event infrastructure allows you to scale your use of events easily and quickly. It also makes it easier to manage any changes that you may feel are necessary, as it is very common for the messaging approach to be adjusted several times as you determine the level of messaging that is appropriate for the interactions needed within your overall system.

In-Application Code

In-application code is a completely different approach from IaC as the code to create the infrastructure resides within your application. This approach is commonly used in "configuration-oriented design," where configuration is used to define the relationship(s) that each application plays. An example of a configuration that could be used when an organization is using SNS is as follows:

```
{
     "sendrules":[{"name":"Order", "key":"OrdersTopic"}],
     "receiverules": [{"name":" ProductUpdates",
                    "key":" Products",
                    "endpoint":"$URL/events/product"}],
}
```

The code in the application would then ensure that every entry in the `sendrules` property has the appropriate topic created, so using the preceding example, the `name` value represents the topic name, and the key value represents the value that will be used within the application to map to the "Order" topic in SNS. The code in the application would then evaluate the `receiverules` value and create subscriptions for each entry.

This seems like a lot of extra work, but for environments that do not support IaC, then this may be the easiest way to allow developers to manage the building of the event's infrastructure. We have seen this approach built as a framework library included in every application that used events, and every application provided a configuration file that represented the messages they were sending and receiving. This framework library would evaluate the service(s) to see if there was anything that needed to be added and if so, then add them.

Summary

Regardless of the way in which you decide to manage your event infrastructure, you will find the addition of messages and events critical to being able to build decoupled applications that are still able to share information between themselves without really knowing anything about where the information is coming from and where it is being sent.

There are two services that we went over. The first was Amazon Simple Notification Service (SNS), which uses a pub/sub model where publishers send information to a specific topic and subscribers sign up to receive information from that topic. The second service we went over is Amazon EventBridge, a serverless event bus. Here, publishers send events to the service, which then distributes these events based on rules. They each offer their own approach for adding events to your system; it simply comes down to which model works best for you as there is no single best approach.

Modern applications are based on communications between different services and systems. We walked through some very simple approaches here, but imagine a world where you have a lot of services exchanging messages back and forth. How do you figure out what is going on within your entire system? Luckily, the next chapter will give you some insight on how monitoring and observability can help you better understand what is going on within your overall system.

CHAPTER 17

Monitoring and Observability

Up to now in this book, we've been focused on familiarizing you with the tools and services available to take your new or existing .NET applications and their supporting data and host them on AWS. However, deployment to the cloud is rarely the end of the story. Once the application is in the cloud, how do you know it's working efficiently (or even at all)? It may be available but perhaps is operating in a degraded state leading to frustration among your end users as they struggle with a slow site or continual errors.

Hopefully, everything is working well. If you're like us, however, you'd like an early heads-up if something goes awry and certainly before users begin to notice. Or you want to continue to iterate on the application and as you do so, gather insights on its behavior so you can make changes, without resorting to guesswork, to continue to improve the end-user experience.

We thought it appropriate to end the book with a "jumping off" chapter to provide information on some of those next steps. With the exception of a couple of extension libraries, the services we're going to discuss here – Amazon CloudWatch and AWS X-Ray – are not .NET-specific. But as a .NET developer, you do need to be aware of them, as they can help significantly in your monitoring and observability efforts.

© William Penberthy and Steve Roberts 2023
W. Penberthy and S. Roberts, *Pro .NET on Amazon Web Services*,
https://doi.org/10.1007/978-1-4842-8907-5_17

Why Do We Want to Monitor and Observe?

While our applications are running, there are some obvious items we might monitor because they indicate the application is continuing to work well, or, more importantly, because they're a potential warning that trouble lies ahead. For example:

- **Performance metrics** – Are we seeing unexpected spikes in requests, or increased latency in request processing time? Sudden drops in request metrics might also indicate requests are being discarded by, or not even making it through to, to an overloaded set of servers.

- **Logs** – Is there a sudden (or even steady) increase in error logs?

- **Startup** – During deployment, and for a period after deployment, is there a spike in "bad" behavior (performance or availability metrics worsen, etc.)?

- **Application evolution** – As we continue to develop the applications, are the changes we're making negatively affecting the overall latency of a request in the affected area? Or worse, an area we thought was unrelated to where we're making changes?

We're sure there are other items you can think of for your own applications that might indicate continued good health. Or a prior warning of doom and maybe the likelihood of support pagers ringing in the near future. When (not if, when!) events occur that impact users, it may be worth taking a leaf out of Amazon's Correction of Errors (COEs) process and its "5 Whys" working backward process to determine what was missed, or could have been improved on, to have provided earlier warning. This COE process is part of the AWS Well-Architected Framework, which you can find at `https://aws.amazon.com/architecture/well-architected/`.

One of us (mentioning no names, SR) has been through his share of COEs and "5 Whys" over the years. In pretty much every case, the team identified a gap in monitoring, along with associated automated alarms, that would have avoided the pain for both end users and the development team. There's more about the process in a blog post at `https://aws.amazon.com/blogs/mt/why-you-should-develop-a-correction-of-error-coe/`.

In the "old days," we were able to monitor and observe applications running on a server, or a small collection of servers, usually under someone's desk or in a dedicated server room co-located with the development team. When a problem arose, we didn't think twice about remoting into a server to inspect logs, events, and performance traces to figure out what had gone wrong. In the cloud world, however, this shouldn't be possible.

First, no one should be accessing production servers unless it's an absolute "break glass" last resort (and if you get to this point, you're probably in real trouble). Second, at cloud scale, there are quite likely too many servers to inspect, especially if the issue happens during scale-out under application load, as might occur if there's a spike in requests. All of this pre-supposes we're using traditional virtual machines too. If we've adopted serverless architectures, there are no servers to access remotely – we don't have access to them.

Knowing, at a minimum, what to monitor and observe is half the battle. It's also critical to have a plan, before deployment, on how to use the data you're gathering to diagnose faults efficiently without needing to "touch" the servers. To get started on that plan and develop a monitoring and observability strategy, let's introduce the services we'll be working with most often to address those needs, and how we can use them from .NET applications, to understand what our code is doing (or is not doing).

Instrumenting Code

You might remember (or still use, in some cases) instrumenting code using `Console.WriteLine` statements, liberally scattered throughout the code base in the hope you'd have half a chance of figuring out which code paths were taken, and why, when servicing a request. This might work with Lambda functions, where the output of these statements is forwarded to CloudWatch Logs on your behalf (we'll be discussing CloudWatch Logs later in the chapter). However, the problem is that these statements rarely capture all the context needed to fully understand what's happened (or is happening).

We've lost track of the number of times we've had to dive into this kind of output, fully expecting an "ah-ah!" moment of revelation on seeing a certain data item in the output only to be let down because we forgot to track something and have needed to tweak what we were logging and then redeploy to try and re-capture that tantalizing bit of data that will help us understand what went wrong. Or, on the other hand, the data we have captured has led us down an irrelevant rabbit hole for several pointless hours. If we're attempting to diagnose latency increases, the overhead of sprinkling these statements to capture start/end times compounds the misery. While moving away from manual `Console.WriteLine` instrumentation doesn't necessarily save us from these issues, it does relieve us of one more potentially error-prone path.

AWS X-Ray (`https://aws.amazon.com/xray`) is a service that provides an end-to-end trace of user requests as they travel through the various tiers of your application, including reporting on calls made to AWS services without the need to add tracing statements to your code. A sampling of the requests that arrive at your application is collated into *traces*, which can then be visualized in a *service map*. Individual request traces are composed of *segments* that can be further divided into *subsegments* to provide more granular information. It's also possible to define your own segments in your code so as to more easily identify particular sections of the code in a trace.

Note   X-Ray does not capture every single request that's made to your application. The default sampling captures the initial request, then 5% of all subsequent requests, to keep your costs to use the service down. It is, however, possible to ramp up (or down) the sampling rate if needed, which might be done for different sections of the application or application code.

Using the data captured in a trace, it's possible to analyze performance bottlenecks that may occur in distributed applications or places where, based on some input data, an unexpected "wrong turn" was taken. The map enables us to observe average request latency, including within subsegments. The nodes in the service map reflect traffic (larger node = more traffic), and errors (4xx, 5xx) are shown as orange or red borders, respectively, on the node. The angular extent of the color border surrounding the ring is relative to the percentage of failures being experienced there. In addition, each node shows the latency experienced at that point in the flow. The connecting vertices show the request counts/per minute. You can click nodes, or vertices, to drill deeper into the request traces.

Figure 17-1 shows a very simple service map for a web application that makes calls to Amazon DynamoDB.

Note   Service maps and traces can be viewed in both the original X-Ray console and the Amazon CloudWatch console. We're using the CloudWatch console as it's, well, more attractive! More importantly, the CloudWatch dashboard offers a "single pane of glass" approach to other monitoring and observability data and operations, saving clicks.

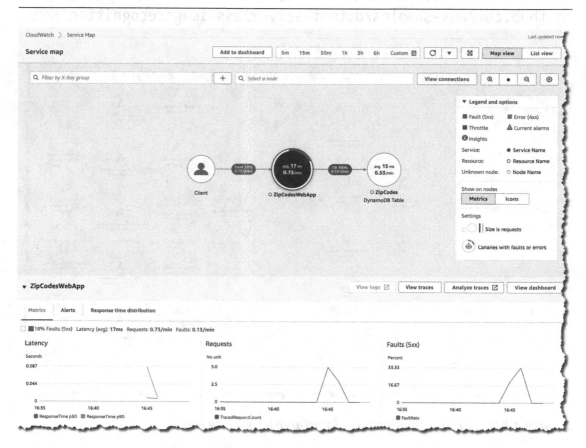

Figure 17-1. *Service map showing application calls to AWS services*

In the real world, service maps are almost never this simple! Figure 17-2 shows a more realistic map, this time from a fully serverless "photo gallery" sample application written in .NET that uses a containerized web front end in Amazon ECS, Amazon S3 for storage, and several Lambda functions making up an image tagging and processing workflow orchestrated by AWS Step Functions (https://aws.amazon.com/step-functions). At the captured scale, you can't read the labels, but it serves to show how a service map can provide a contextual overview of the way requests and data flow through an application.

Tip   The sample application captured in Figure 17-2 is available at https://github.com/aws-samples/dotnet-serverless-imagerecognition.

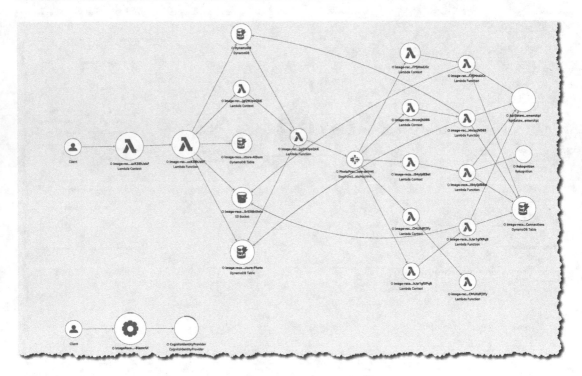

Figure 17-2. *A more involved, and real-world, service map*

While a service map provides some context, more benefits become apparent as we start to drill down into a request trace which we do by clicking on nodes in the map.

In Figure 17-1, a red segment in the border of the **ZipCodeWebApp** node shows that 5xx errors are being triggered during processing of some requests. We can drill down into the traces to try and understand the "where" and, hopefully, "why" (sometimes, however, additional data may be needed to completely understand the "why"). Still, drilling into the traces is a start.

Figure 17-3 shows the metrics available, to date, on the *ZipCodesWebApp* node in the map. We can clearly see a spike in 5xx errors being triggered in this component.

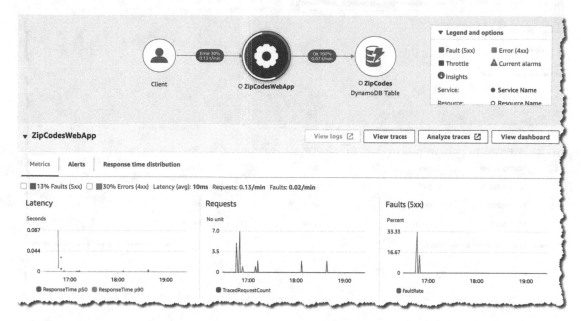

Figure 17-3. *Errors on the front-end application component*

Clicking the Client node, then View traces, we can start to trace a sampling of requests to try and determine what may be going wrong. The top of the page, shown in Figure 17-4, allows us to run queries to narrow traces based on a set of refinements including HTTP method, URL, Client IP, User, and more. Because we started from the client node in the map, Client IP is automatically selected, and we can view the IP addresses that requests came from.

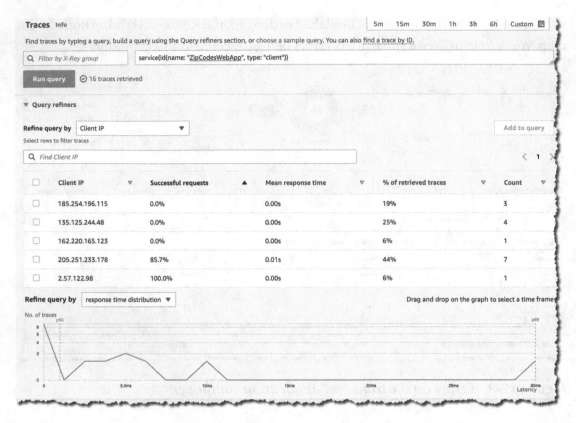

Figure 17-4. *Tracing requests that came into the application*

You'll need to scroll down to see the retrieved traces, shown in Figure 17-5, where it's apparent we have a mix of successful requests, 4xx, and 5xx errors over time.

Traces (16)

This table shows the most recent traces with an average response time of 0.00s. It shows as many as 1000 traces.

Add to dashboard

Q Start typing to filter trace list   ‹ 1 2 › ⚙

ID	Trace status	Timestamp	Response code	Response Time	Duration	HTTP Method
...cd867a01397d60068740b8ae	⚠ Error (4xx)	3.5min (2022-09-05 19:43:21)	404	0s	0s	POST
...394a085ad0bc65d3b8f4c8d5	⚠ Error (4xx)	1.1h (2022-09-05 18:37:50)	400	0.003s	0.003s	POST
...93801f5d5f95874e52c7fad3	⚠ Error (4xx)	1.1h (2022-09-05 18:37:49)	404	0s	0s	GET
...2904e14decad3779441d5bf3	⚠ Error (4xx)	1.7h (2022-09-05 18:07:10)	404	0s	0s	GET
...9f14ad3b3af77f92795a9bd8	⚠ Error (4xx)	1.7h (2022-09-05 18:07:09)	400	0.001s	0.001s	POST
...9237b89a5f8c3282fa5be337	⚠ Error (4xx)	2.6h (2022-09-05 17:12:35)	404	0s	0s	GET
...9e183497060c5af3096c2ef6	⚠ Error (4xx)	2.6h (2022-09-05 17:12:34)	400	0.001s	0.001s	POST
...6242f89b95d8e3d41458792f	⚠ Error (4xx)	2.6h (2022-09-05 17:09:04)	404	0s	0s	GET
...93accb22bbcef28fc1e2e57b	⊘ OK	2.9h (2022-09-05 16:52:48)	200	0s	0s	GET
...98b56a74ec4667fbfb9ed394	⊘ OK	3.0h (2022-09-05 16:49:34)	200	0.005s	0.005s	GET
...fb5ba7f7c2061d839770a2d2	⊘ OK	3.0h (2022-09-05 16:49:26)	200	0.004s	0.004s	GET
...d627c433dd03496256a39595	⊘ OK	3.0h (2022-09-05 16:49:19)	200	0.005s	0.005s	GET
...a45e9f01197f2ff4aa5ca47f	⊗ Fault (5xx)	3.0h (2022-09-05 16:49:12)	500	0.011s	0.011s	GET
...16374a8b378ade1f6a5ae	⊘ OK	3.0h (2022-09-05 16:49:07)	200	0.007s	0.007s	GET

Figure 17-5. *Traces corresponding to the query filter*

Clicking a trace with a 5xx error and scrolling down, we see a segment timeline, shown in Figure 17-6. From this, we can infer the problems lie not with the DynamoDB query but something in the code that made the query, which is looking for zip code data (in this sample) belonging to the state of Idaho.

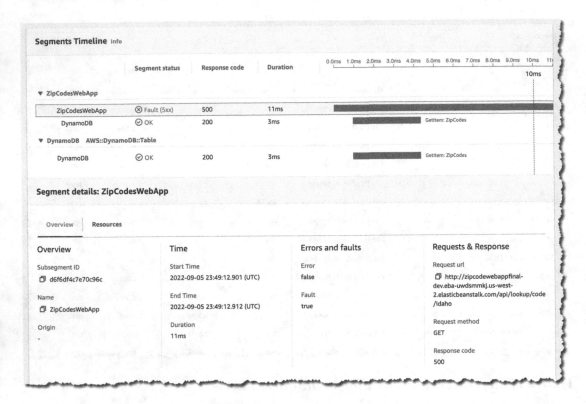

Figure 17-6. *Segments in the faulting trace*

At this point, for the sake of space and brevity, we're going to cheat and confess to prior knowledge! We've spiked the table so that it doesn't contain data for Idaho and, further, the code that processes query results does not protect against an empty data set being returned, and so causes a fault from trying to process an empty item, shown in Figure 17-7.

```
93
94
                3 references
95       IDictionary<string, object> ConvertItemToDTO(IDictionary<string, AttributeValue>
             item)
96       {
97           return new Dictionary<string, object>
98           {
99               { "Code", item["Code"].S },
100              { "Latitude", item["Latitude"].N },
101              { "Longitude", item["Longitude"].N },
102              { "City", item["City"].S },
103              { "State", item["State"].S }
104          };
105      }
106  }
107 }
```

Figure 17-7. *The faulting code (easy when you know where it is!)*

Ok, we admit this was cheating…a bit. However, we hope you can see the potential, and had this been a real-world and more complex system, the ability to drill down a request trace obtained from X-Ray instrumentation, inspect the individual subsegments to zero in on the faulting location, and zoom in on the "why" could save you considerable time.

Tip   AWS provides a free workshop on observability, a part of which covers drilling into X-Ray traces to determine the root cause. You can find the workshop at `https://catalog.workshops.aws/observability/en-US/xray/explore-xray`.

The X-Ray Agent

To capture trace data, X-Ray uses a daemon that needs to be installed on the compute resource hosting your application, for example, an EC2 instance or a container in Amazon ECS. As the instrumentation in your application gathers data, it's forwarded to the daemon, which in turn sends it onto the service where it's made available for analysis in just a few minutes. Some services, like AWS Elastic Beanstalk, include the daemon in the images they provide, and it's activated using a simple configuration switch at deployment time (or you can enable it subsequently). Figure 17-8 shows a page in the Publish to AWS Elastic Beanstalk wizard, from the AWS Toolkit for Visual Studio, when publishing .NET Framework applications, with the option to enable the daemon.

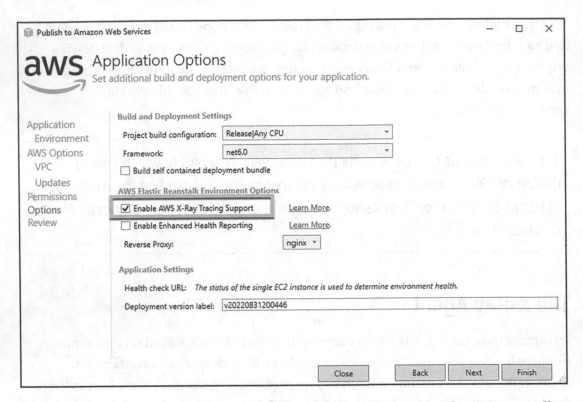

Figure 17-8. *Activating the X-Ray daemon when publishing to Elastic Beanstalk*

As you should expect by now, the daemon needs permissions to be able to forward trace data on your application's behalf. To do this, you attach a policy to the role assigned to the compute host. AWS provides a managed policy, *AWSXRayDaemonWriteAccess*, that makes this convenient. Listing 17-1 shows the statements in this policy as of the time of this writing.

Listing 17-1. The AWSXRayDaemonWriteAccess managed policy

```
{
    "Version": "2012-10-17",
    "Statement": [
        {
            "Effect": "Allow",
            "Action": [
                "xray:PutTraceSegments",
                "xray:PutTelemetryRecords",
```

```
        "xray:GetSamplingRules",
        "xray:GetSamplingTargets",
        "xray:GetSamplingStatisticSummaries"
      ],
      "Resource": [
        "*"
      ]
    }
  ]
}
```

Enabling the daemon, however, isn't enough. Your code still needs to be instrumented to send data to the daemon, and this is where the AWS X-Ray SDK comes into play.

AWS X-Ray and .NET

.NET and .NET Framework applications can make use of X-Ray with several packages available on NuGet. These packages enable the instrumentation of code using a few simple calls, usually made during application startup. The default instrumentation provided by these calls may be sufficient, but it's also possible to add further code and configuration settings to your application to fine-tune traces based on your particular needs. Using the NuGet packages for X-Ray, you can generate traces containing calls to AWS services, downstream HTTP web APIs, and SQL databases to provide an overall picture of how your application is performing in the cloud.

Tip   The AWS SDK for X-Ray is maintained as an open source project on GitHub. You can find it at `https://github.com/aws/aws-xray-sdk-dotnet`.

AWS X-Ray NuGet Packages

There are actually two freely available SDKs for instrumenting and tracing .NET code with AWS X-Ray: first, the original *AWS X-Ray SDK for .NET,* and second, the *AWS Distro for OpenTelemetry* (ADOT) SDK (in which X-Ray is just one of many possible tracing solutions). In this chapter, we'll focus on using the AWS SDK for X-Ray SDK. To learn more about the Distro for OpenTelemetry SDK, and when you might want to choose it, see https://docs.aws.amazon.com/xray/latest/devguide/xray-instrumenting-your-app.html#xray-instrumenting-choosing in the AWS X-Ray Developer Guide.

The following is the list of packages available on NuGet, and where you'd use them, in the AWS SDK for X-Ray:

- **AWSXRayRecorder** – Umbrella package causes all X-Ray packages to be added to your application. Choose this one if you're not sure of the specific package(s) the application will need or just want to experiment.

- **AWSXRayRecorder.Core** – Core support dependency consumed by all X-Ray packages. It in turn depends on the **AWSSDK.Core** package from the AWS SDK for .NET.

- **AWSXRayRecorder.Handlers.AspNet** – Traces requests arriving at ASP.NET application endpoints.

- **AWSXRayRecorder.Handlers.AspNetCore** – Traces requests arriving at ASP.NET Core application endpoints.

- **AWSXRayRecorder.Handlers.AwsSdk** – Include this package to trace requests made to AWS services using the AWS SDK for .NET. You can instrument all service calls, or specific services.

- **AWSXRayRecorder.Handlers.EntityFramework** – Traces SQL queries made using Entity Framework (version 6.2.0 or higher) and Entity Framework Core (version 3 or higher).

- **AWSXRay.Handlers.SqlServer** – Supports tracing SQL queries dispatched using the System.Data.SqlClient.SqlCommand class to a SQL Server database instance. The database can be running in Amazon RDS, or on an EC2 instance.

- **AWSXRay.Handlers.System.Net** – Traces downstream HTTP requests. Use this to trace calls made to microservices that you've extracted from the application, services shared across applications via a URL endpoint, or even services external to your organization.

Instrumenting .NET Code with X-Ray

Instrumenting .NET and .NET Framework applications to emit trace data to X-Ray needs only a handful of lines of code. The GitHub repository for the SDK (`https://github.com/aws/aws-xray-sdk-dotnet`) provides clear instructions on how to configure the SDK for the different use cases represented by the NuGet packages we just listed, so we won't repeat them all here.

However, to show how easy it is, let's briefly walk through the steps to show how we could configure an ASP.NET e-commerce application that uses a SQL Server database instance to provide inventory data and an Amazon DynamoDB table to provide a shopping cart. We want to capture incoming requests to the web front end, SQL queries to the inventory (from Entity Framework), and queries to the DynamoDB table. To do this, we'll use the AWS X-Ray SDK for .NET (it's a similar process if you use the AWS Distro for OpenTelemetry SDK).

To capture incoming requests to the ASP.NET application front end, we start by adding either of the **AWSXRayRecorder** or **AWSXRayRecorder.Handlers.AspNet** NuGet packages. We have an ASP.NET application using the .NET Framework, so we override the Init() method of the application class (derived from System.Web.HttpApplication), supplying the application instance and a name for the segment, shown in Listing 17-2.

Note   The code shown in Listing 17-2 is for ASP.NET applications built with the .NET Framework. If you're using ASP.NET Core, you need to use the **AWSXRayRecorder.Handlers.AspNetCore** package and slightly different initialization code. You can find an example for ASP.NET Core applications in the GitHub repository documentation.

Listing 17-2. Initializing X-Ray to capture requests to the application

```
// in global.asax
using Amazon.XRay.Recorder.Handlers.AspNet;

public TradeYourToolsApplication : System.Web.HttpApplication
{
   ...
```

```
public override void Init()
{
    base.Init();
    AWSXRayASPNET.RegisterXRay(this,
                              "TradeYourTools.Website");
}
```
...

Next, we want to add instrumentation for calls made using the AWS SDK for .NET to Amazon DynamoDB. These calls will be added to the trace as subsegments. We have two options here; we can enable instrumentation for all SDK service clients or just specific services. The former is useful if we know we're going to expand our SDK usage to other, as yet unknown, services in the future. Here, we'll instrument specifically for DynamoDB.

We add the NuGet package **AWSXRay.Handlers.AwsSdk** to our application (unless we used **AWSXRayRecorder** shown previously, in which case we already have the AWS SDK handler package). Then, before we instantiate any SDK service client, we call X-Ray to register that we want the specific service client to be instrumented, shown in Listing 17-3.

Listing 17-3. Adding instrumentation for calls to DynamoDB

```
using Amazon.XRay.Recorder.Handlers.AwsSdk;
using Amazon.DynamoDB;

...

// inside a method called at startup
AWSSDKHandler.RegisterForXRay<IAmazonDynamoDB>();

...
```

Note   Registering SDK service clients for instrumentation must be done before a service client is instantiated. If you're using dependency injection, perhaps in an ASP.NET Core application, make sure to perform the registration before you add service clients to the dependency injection service. If you don't do this, the SDK service client will not be instrumented. This can lead to a few moments of puzzlement as to why trace data isn't being recorded!

Our final requirement was to trace SQL queries. If we're using Entity Framework, we add the NuGet package **AWSXRayRecorder.Handlers.EntityFramework** (unless we added the umbrella **AWSXRayRecorder** package earlier). If we're not using Entity Framework, or we're using System.Data.SqlClient.SqlCommand directly, we add the package **AWSXRayRecorder.Handlers.SqlServer**.

Tracing of queries run using Entity Framework can be enabled during application startup, or on construction of a DbConfiguration instance. Both options are shown in Listing 17-4. You should choose one only to avoid duplicated tracing. It is confusing, but while the code seems like it is only for Entity Framework 6 (AWSXRayEntityFramework6), it works for v.6.2 and Entity Framework Core.

Listing 17-4. Instrumenting Entity Framework queries

```
using Amazon.XRay.Recorder.Handlers.EntityFramework;

// Initialize during app startup
protected void Application_Start()
{
    AWSXRayEntityFramework6.AddXRayInterceptor();
}

// ...or initialize in your derived DbConfiguration class
public class MyAppDbConfiguration: DbConfiguration
{
    public MyAppDbConfiguration()
    {
        AWSXRayEntityFramework6.AddXRayInterceptor();
    }
}
```

Tracing of SQL queries made using SqlCommand is handled with the TraceableSqlCommand wrapper class, which can be used from both synchronous and asynchronous call patterns, shown in Listing 17-5.

Listing 17-5. Tracing SQL queries through SqlCommand

```
using Amazon.XRay.Recorder.Handlers.SqlServer;
// synchronous pattern
using (var conn = new SqlConnection("connection-string"))
{
    var sql = "SELECT ...";
    using (var cmd = new TraceableSqlCommand(sql, conn))
    {
        cmd.Connection.Open();
        cmd.ExecuteNonQuery();
    }
}

// asynchronous pattern
using (var conn = new SqlConnection("connection-string"))
{
    var sql = "SELECT ...";
    using (var cmd = new TraceableSqlCommand(sql, conn))
    {
        await cmd.ExecuteXmlReaderAsync();
    }
}
```

It's also possible to collect the actual query text in the trace. To specify collection
of SQL command text at the application configuration level in .NET Framework
applications (app.config/web.config), use <add key="CollectSqlQueries"
value="true" /> in the appSettings group. For .NET applications (in appsettings.json),
use "XRay": { "CollectSqlQueries": "true" }.

Alternatively, set the property when you instantiate a TraceableSqlCommand object:
var cmd = new TraceableSqlCommand(cmd, conn, collectSqlQueries:true).

Caution   Do not enable collection of SQL query text if your queries include
sensitive information in plain text. That information will be visible in the
request trace!

There's a lot more capability built into the AWS X-Ray SDK for .NET, including adding further metadata into the request traces, specifying custom subsegments, and annotations. Check the X-Ray Developer Guide (`https://docs.aws.amazon.com/xray/latest/devguide`) and GitHub repository for more ideas on how you can extend code instrumentation for your particular needs.

Instrumenting code, while certainly useful, isn't the end of the monitoring and observability story. While it provides the ability to see what our code has done and dive into request traces to see where latency has increased or an unexpected exception be thrown, it doesn't give us prior warning of problems ahead. For that, we turn to a suite of functionality available in the aptly named *Amazon CloudWatch* service.

Amazon CloudWatch

Amazon CloudWatch (`https://aws.amazon.com/cloudwatch/`) is the central AWS monitoring and observability service. It surfaces monitoring and operational data for your applications such as logs, metrics, and events in a console dashboard and is capable of showing data for resources in different regions, as well as owned by different accounts. It also, as we noted earlier, surfaces X-Ray service maps and traces, with handy query mechanisms to enable you to quickly and efficiently drill down into trace and log data to isolate elements of interest.

The surfacing of operational and monitoring data into dashboards isn't the only capability. CloudWatch also enables the detection of anomalies in your application's behavior and uses alarms to give you an early alert that something is out of the ordinary. Anomaly detection uses machine learning that, based on continuous analysis of metric data from your applications, identifies out-of-the-ordinary behavior, against which alarms can be configured. In general, investing time in setting up the right alarms (which admittedly may take time and some COEs to develop), it should be possible for you to get alerted to developing issues before they start to impact customers, at least to a significant degree.

CloudWatch can be considered as a portfolio of related monitoring and observability services, with the aim of providing comprehensive visibility and insight into your running applications. The primary components, but by no means all, are listed as follows:

- **Dashboards** – Customizable home pages, within the CloudWatch console, where you can monitor your resources (including those in other regions and accounts). Dashboards contain metrics and alarms, allowing for "at a glance" oversight of how things are working (or not!).

- **Alarms** – Notifications that a metric for a resource is in a non-normal or unanticipated state. Besides alerting us that something isn't "right," alarms can be used to trigger automated processing, for example, automatic scale-up or down of instances in an Auto Scaling group.

- **Logs** – Near real-time, centralized collection of logs from your applications, and the resources and AWS services involved in hosting those applications.

- **Metrics** – Data points on infrastructure and application usage over time. Metrics can be configured with thresholds, which, when breached, trigger alarms.

- **Events** – Near real-time delivery of a stream of events that denote changes in resources. Using rules, you can match events and deliver them to further downstream functions or streams to process. An example of an event would be when an EC2 instance changes state, say, from *pending* to *running*, that you could then process using further automation.

- **Insights** – This is available for container and serverless (Lambda) applications. Insights collects, aggregates, and summarizes metrics and logs from said applications with the aim of further helping faster diagnosis and resolution time. For containers, additional data such as container restart failures is tracked. For Lambda, you can see data on cold starts for Lambda functions. Using this, you can experiment with different memory and CPU settings to "fine-tune" the Lambda function's environment. There's also *Contributor Insights*, which you can use to determine "top-N" contributions to performance issues using captured time-series data.

Space constraints mean we're going to have to focus briefly on just three components: logging, metrics, and alarms. These three, however, will give you a good head start on developing a monitoring strategy. The rest can be investigated and adopted once you have the basics in place (and could easily fill their own book!).

Logging

CloudWatch Logs is the AWS solution to collecting logging information, at scale, from applications running on the variety of compute infrastructure – EC2 instances, Lambda, and containers. It can also be used by other AWS services to surface operational data on resources provisioned and managed on your behalf. For example, databases in Amazon RDS can be configured such that error logs are forwarded automatically to CloudWatch Logs.

After using `Console.WriteLine` statements to trace application activity, as we discussed earlier when we looked at X-Ray, logging is probably the next step developers take to track and understand application behavior – at least to the extent of tracking why an application took a particular action. The switch to using something like CloudWatch may be a big change for some .NET developers, especially those used to working with log files written onto the running server. In those cases, the developer is familiar with logging into the server to be able to view the logs.

In our new cloud-based world, this is not as easy. Sure, you can probably take this approach if you are using EC2 (recalling our warning, however, asking are you *really* sure you want people remoting into your production servers?). However, for those of you using containers or serverless, then that is no longer really an option. And even if it were, a switch to more distributed architecture would mean that you may have a lot of itty-bitty services running, not to mention more compute hosts (servers, etc.) running the code, so finding the appropriate log entry becomes problematic when running at scale.

To help solve the issue of logs being dispersed across multiple computer hosts or resources, CloudWatch arranges log data into *log groups*, each of which contains zero or more *log streams*. Log streams are what you'd expect, a sequence of log events that originate from the same source, for example, an instance of your application on a compute host, or a particular resource. Each event in stream carries a timestamp and the raw event data. We recommend using JSON strings to convey the raw event data, as it makes searching using queries easier compared to hunting through unstructured text.

To illustrate log groups and streams, Figure 17-9 shows the two log streams within the **TradeYourTools.Website** log group for the sample application, being viewed from within JetBrains Rider. We're running the sample application on two EC2 instances, behind a load balancer – therefore, there are two log streams, one per instance. In the figure, you can also see a mix of other log groups for another (serverless) application we're running, which contain a mix of service-generated build time logs (from CodeBuild) and custom logs emitted from the Lambda-based components of that application.

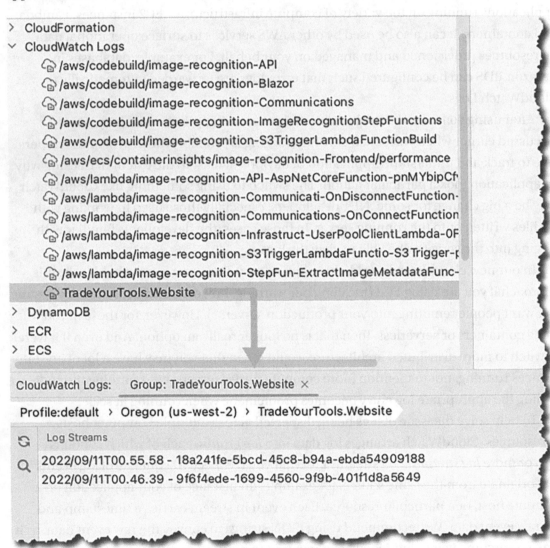

Figure 17-9. *Log streams for the sample application's instances*

Still inside the Rider IDE, we can drill further into the events contained within a log stream, shown in Figure 17-10. You can similarly view and work with log groups and their streams in the toolkits for Visual Studio and Visual Studio Code.

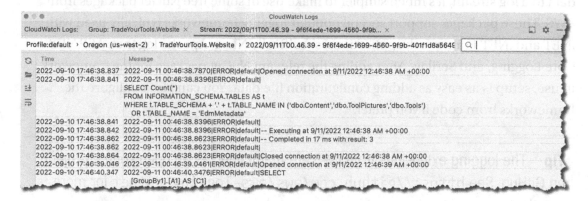

Figure 17-10. *Viewing output in a log stream in JetBrains Rider*

Logging data but not using it is, well, not much use. That being said, applications can generate huge quantities of log data over time, so we often need help to efficiently maximize the signal-to-noise ratio. CloudWatch Logs Insights is your friend here. It provides a simple, purpose-built query language enabling efficient drill down into reams of log data, which is especially helpful when you're attempting to respond quickly to an operational issue and are faced with a mass of log streams and associated data.

Another feature you should consider taking advantage of is the automated monitoring of log data. Consider a scenario where you've deployed an update to an application, either straight to the production fleet (if you're brave) or through some staging environments, where the application "bakes" before finally reaching production. Wouldn't it be useful to have something monitoring incoming logs, checking for increases in error data, and sending you a notification when the error rate exceeds some threshold? This is possible in CloudWatch Logs without needing changes to your application. The service can monitor log data for specific text, for example, the name of an exception, or count error status codes that appear at certain positions in the data. Once found, they're reported against a metric you specify, which you can then attach an alarm to.

There's much more to CloudWatch Logs than we have space for here, and we strongly recommend being familiar with all the capabilities. However, let's move on to looking at how easy it is to get logs from our applications into the service in the first instance.

CloudWatch Logs and .NET

While you could call CloudWatch Log's APIs from the AWS SDK for .NET to emit log data to a log stream, it's much simpler to make use of some free NuGet packages from AWS. These packages support several popular logging frameworks typically used with .NET and .NET Framework applications, specifically NLog, Apache log4net, ASP.NET Core Logging, and Serilog. After adding the relevant NuGet package for the framework in use, setup is as easy as adding configuration file data. You can also configure the frameworks from code if you prefer.

Tip   The logging extensions from AWS are maintained as an open source project on GitHub. See `https://github.com/aws/aws-logging-dotnet` for more details.

For an example, let's say we have an application that uses the NLog logging framework. To set up this application so that log data is forwarded to a log stream in CloudWatch logs, we first add a dependency on the NuGet package **AWS.Logger.Nlog**.

Next, we add a configuration file appropriate to the logging framework. By default, NLog looks for a file named *NLog.config* to obtain the settings it should use. In there, we add a reference to the AWS library and a log target that configures logging output to be sent to a log group in CloudWatch Logs. An example is shown in Listing 17-6.

Listing 17-6. Configuring NLog to route to CloudWatch

```xml
<?xml version="1.0" encoding="utf-8" ?>
<nlog xmlns="http://www.nlog-project.org/schemas/NLog.xsd"
      xmlns:xsi="http://www.w3.org/2001/XMLSchema-instance">
  <extensions>
    <add assembly="NLog.AWS.Logger" />
  </extensions>
  <targets>
    <target name="aws"
            type="AWSTarget"
            logGroup="TradeYourTools.Website"/>
    <target name="logfile"
```

```
        xsi:type="File"
        fileName="log.txt" layout="${longdate}|${level:uppercase=true}|
        ${logger}|${message}
  />
</targets>
<rules>
  <logger name="*" minlevel="Debug" writeTo="logfile" />
  <logger name="*" minlevel="Info" writeTo="aws" />
</rules>
</nlog>
```

To work with CloudWatch Logs, the extension requires credentials and region information, and you may be wondering about where those are specified. Credentials are obtained automatically using the standard search path that's also used by the AWS SDK for .NET, if your application makes calls to services using it. First, the extension will look for a local credential profile named *default*. While this is fine for code running on your own machine, we advise **very strongly** against this approach for any code deployed to the cloud! Instead, use the standard practice of specifying a trust relationship to the compute service (`ec2.amazonaws.com`, `ecs-tasks.amazonaws.com`, or `lambda.amazonaws.com`) in the application's IAM role to provide temporary credentials as we showed earlier in the book. Just like the SDKs, the extension will obtain and rotate the necessary credentials when needed.

The region containing the log group can be specified using a `region` property on the `target` element (the property value is the system name of the region, e.g., `us-west-2`). You only need to specify this if the application is running in a different region to where logs are being collected; like credentials, the extension is able to automatically infer the region if it's available on the host environment, just as the AWS SDKs are able to.

As you might expect, you do need to ensure permissions to call the necessary CloudWatch Logs APIs are provided in the role. Listing 17-7 lists the actions you must permit (they are the same regardless of logging framework, and extension package, being used). Add these to the application role using a custom policy that you can also scope to the specific log groups; AWD does not provide a suitable managed policy for this.

Listing 17-7. CloudWatch Logs actions required by the logging extensions

```
logs:CreateLogGroup
logs:CreateLogStream
logs:PutLogEvents
logs:DescribeLogGroups
```

After deploying the TradeYourTools application containing this log configuration file (we deployed it to Elastic Beanstalk), log output from the application begins to surface in the specified log group. The log group and its streams are created for you automatically if they don't already exist. Figure 17-11 shows the group with some log data related to the Entity Framework queries made by the app, viewed this time in Visual Studio.

Tip   You can also work with log groups and streams at the command line, including running queries against them, using the AWS CLI or AWS Tools for PowerShell.

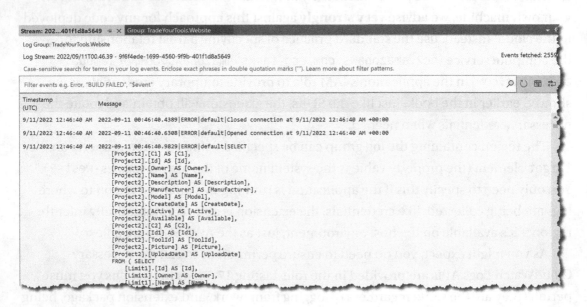

Figure 17-11. *Entity Framework queries in the logs*

Now that we know how to trace what our applications are doing once deployed, using X-Ray and traditional logging, let's turn our attention briefly to monitoring running applications and how CloudWatch can help us get those early "heads-up" notifications that something is amiss.

Metrics and Alarms

Unlike for tracing and logging, there are no .NET extension libraries from AWS for working with metrics and alarms in CloudWatch, at least at the time of this writing. However, there's nothing in these areas that's really .NET specific.

Helpfully, the CloudWatch User Guide (`https://docs.aws.amazon.com/AmazonCloudWatch/latest/monitoring/`) is clear and sufficiently detailed in how to set up metrics and alarms, with plenty of scenarios and examples, that we don't actually need to go into much detail ourselves here. Instead, we'll point out some features that you should go and learn more about to ensure you make the most of the service's many features for monitoring and alarming.

CloudWatch describes itself, at its most basic level, as a metrics repository. *Metrics*, which are time-series data points arranged in namespaces, flow into the repository from multiple sources. Some are provided automatically by AWS services without needing any setup from you, for example, EC2 posts compute resource metrics such as CPU usage, EBS posts storage metrics, and so on. These are arranged in namespaces using the naming convention AWS/*service*, for example, AWS/EC2 and AWS/EBS.

The default metrics posted by many AWS services are provided free of charge. However, some services also provided more frequent or detailed metrics, at a cost. An example is the "enhanced health monitoring" provided as an option for Elastic Beanstalk, which can be enabled in the Publish to Elastic Beanstalk wizard we covered in Chapter 12. Unfortunately, not every service identifies these more detailed metrics using the same name or terminology, so it's not immediately obvious there's an associated cost.

We might use the freely available metrics for dev/test use, or for monitoring deployment rollouts that we allow to "bake" for a time before releasing the update fully into production. More detailed, or more frequently provided, metrics could then be reserved for our most critical production applications to save cost. That choice is yours to make!

Besides the metrics provided automatically by AWS services, you can also post your own custom metrics, in namespaces you define, direct from your applications, by calling CloudWatch's `PutMetricData` API using an AWS SDK. You don't have to use an SDK either; metrics can be written, and read back, using the AWS CLI and AWS Tools for PowerShell if so desired.

Tip   The `PutMetricData` API documentation for .NET Framework applications can be found at `https://docs.aws.amazon.com/sdkfornet/v3/apidocs/items/CloudWatch/MCloudWatchPutMetricDataPutMetricDataRequest.html`. For .NET applications, only an async version is supported, which you'll find at `https://docs.aws.amazon.com/sdkfornet/v3/apidocs/items/CloudWatch/MCloudWatchPutMetricDataAsyncPutMetricDataRequest CancellationToken.html`.

Metrics ingested into the repository are retained for 15 months. As new metrics come in, older metrics age out and are discarded without any input needed from you. Note, however, that any metric that's had no update for 15 months also expires.

As with log data, metrics held in a repository are of little use unless we're able to make use of them. Built atop the metrics repository are features to support analytic queries, automated anomaly detection, and dashboards. Figure 17-12 shows part of the *Resource Health* metrics dashboard for the EC2 instances hosting our sample application. We're using a simple PowerShell script to send continuous requests to the site, similar to how we might test during a deployment rollout looking for issues that might indicate we should roll the deployment back.

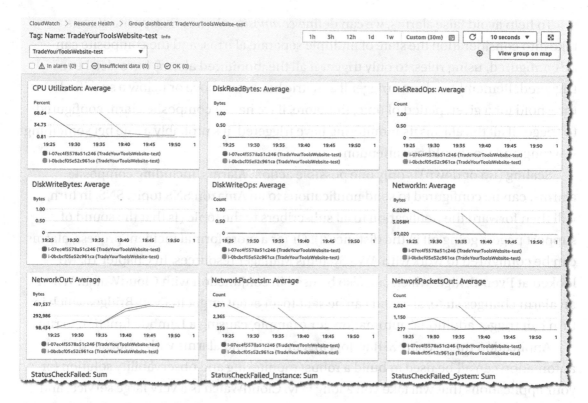

Figure 17-12. *Out-of-the-box metrics dashboard*

Surfacing metrics onto dashboards is great for operator oversight, but not everyone wants to sit and watch graphs all day. Other computers, and automation, are ideal "watchers"; we only need to know when something is amiss – and even then, automation may be able to take care of it for us.

Alarms trigger when the single metric they are monitoring has gone above, or below, a specified threshold for a period of time, and can be surfaced on dashboards. Putting them on dashboards, while being informative and interesting, is only really useful if someone is actually watching! It's therefore good that alarms can also be configured to trigger automated actions. In some cases, these actions can be configured to affect resources. For example, a rise in CPU usage for an EC2 instance, or request counts to a load balancer, might indicate we need to scale a compute fleet for a time. In that scenario, the alarm could cause an Auto Scaling group to begin scaling the fleet. We probably only want to do this if the triggered alarm has been steady in that triggered state for a while so that suddenly start scaling for a one-off alarm that returns to normal very quickly. In other words, we probably want to avoid false alarms.

To help avoid false alarms, we can define *composite alarms*. Composite alarms take into consideration the state of multiple separate alarms, and the composite can be configured, using rules, to only trigger if all the monitored alarms have also been triggered. Remember, alarms trigger if a metric has been above or below a specified threshold for a given period of time; therefore, if we have a composite alarm configured to trigger if all the alarms its monitoring have triggered, it's probably a safe bet something is wrong and we should pay attention.

Scaling (up or down) is only one possible action. Alarms, including composite alarms, can be configured to send notifications to an Amazon SNS topic. SNS, in turn, will then forward the notification to all subscribers to the topic (Is that the sound of support pagers going off in the distance?!). Or for a more formal incident process, alarms can be configured to work with AWS Systems Manager resources. In Chapter 16, we looked at EventBridge, which can also be used in conjunction with CloudWatch. When an alarm changes state, an event can be sent to an event target in EventBridge, which in turn can trigger additional automation, for example, causing a Lambda function to run.

Application traces using X-Ray, logging, metrics, and alarms with associated automation can all be used to build a robust monitoring and observability solution for your applications that will take you a long way. CloudWatch is a very large service, and we don't have space in this book to really dive into all the features – it would almost be a separate book! For once, time spent reading the various CloudWatch guides is time well spent, and we can't recommend it enough.

Amazon and AWS use fully automated, totally human-free, deployments at a scale that's quite mind boggling. This automation is made possible, in part, based on metrics and alarms. If you're interested in reading how they do it, and how deployments roll out safely in ever-increasing waves across regions around the globe, we recommend you take a look at the Amazon Builders Library article *"Automating safe, hands-off deployments"* (`https://aws.amazon.com/builders-library/automating-safe-hands-off-deployments`). While you may never need to deploy updates at the same frequency and scale, we think you'll find the "how to do so" fascinating, and it may well give you some ideas of how you can further put CloudWatch metrics and alarms to good use in your own organization. There's also an article *"Building dashboards for operational visibility"* (`https://aws.amazon.com/builders-library/building-dashboards-for-operational-visibility`) based on best practices worked out at Amazon over the years.

Summary

You may be a developer for whom code never goes wrong in production. If so, congratulations are in order! For the rest of us, however, having additional monitoring and observability services that we can lean on to watch over our code in production, alert us to impending doom, and help us diagnose faults faster is a necessity for modern, distributed, and scaled applications. It also helps us sleep better at night! Learning to put AWS X-Ray and Amazon CloudWatch to work with your .NET and .NET Framework applications is time well used and something we completely recommend.

A Final Word

This book has been quite a journey. When we started out, we obviously had a rough plan of topics we wanted to cover, but as we turned out chapters, we kept discovering more and more about the depth of .NET support on AWS. While these discoveries weren't completely unsurprising to us, it does turn upside down the notion we've heard from some quarters that there isn't much for .NET developers on AWS.

As a result, we had to cut back on some topics to help meet time and space deadlines! What didn't we cover? Continuous integration and deployment (CI/CD) was a notable casualty. However, it turns out there's not much, if anything, that's .NET-specific in there. CodeBuild takes your application code (from GitHub, CodeCommit, or other source control repositories) and builds it using a container image you specify, emitting the artifacts. CodePipeline orchestrates the whole process, with CodeDeploy (which we covered in Chapter 12) one option to place the application onto the chosen compute infrastructure.

User authentication was another casualty of space. Here, there is at least Amazon Cognito with extension libraries available on NuGet to integrate with your .NET applications and simplify the process (they're also open source at `https://github.com/aws/aws-sdk-net-extensions-cognito`).

Another area that we were not able to cover to the depth that we would have liked is a much deeper dive into modern .NET application architecture and how you can implement that architecture on AWS. Sure, we talked some about event-driven architecture, but there are a lot of other architectural designs and approaches that take advantage of the AWS' cloud-native capabilities. Easily another book's worth of them!

We also didn't even touch on the ways in which a .NET-based system can be connected in a hybrid fashion across multiple cloud providers, or between your on-premises systems and the cloud. That approach is becoming more and more viable as each of the providers grows in slightly different ways, meaning that a "best-of-breed" architecture and implementation could easily span multiple providers.

That there is this frighteningly long list of areas that we did not cover should tell you one thing, and that is that there is a lot of support for .NET on AWS. Sure, it may be inconsistent or seemingly incomplete in places, but the depth and breadth of coverage and support for .NET development is growing every week. During the writing of this book, we have gone through the initial release of several of the tools that we talked about as well as an upgrade in the AWS Toolkit for Visual Studio. Who knows what will have been released or improved by the time you are reading this?

Index

A

M

R

S

Printed in the United States
by Baker & Taylor Publisher Services